The Golden Age of American Philosophy

E

The
GOLDEN AGE
of AMERICAN
PHILOSOPHY

Selected and edited

with an introduction and notes by

CHARLES FRANKEL

GEORGE BRAZILLER, INC.

NEW YORK   1960

Acknowledgments

The editor and publisher have made every effort to determine and credit the holders of copyright of the selections in this book. Any errors or omissions may be rectified in future volumes. For permission to use these selections, the editor and publisher make grateful acknowledgment to the following authors and publishers who reserve all rights to the matter reprinted:

From LAW AND THE SOCIAL ORDER by Morris R. Cohen. Copyright 1933. Used by permission of Harry N. Rosenfield, Administrator, Estate of Morris R. Cohen.

From MIND AND THE WORLD ORDER by C. I. Lewis. Reprinted by permission of Dover Publications, Inc., New York 14, N. Y. ($1.95)

From REASON AND NATURE by Morris R. Cohen. Copyright 1953. Used by permission of The Free Press, Glencoe, Illinois.

From THE COLLECTED PAPERS OF CHARLES SANDERS PEIRCE, edited by Charles Hartshorne and Paul Weiss. Copyright 1931 (1959), 1932 (1960), 1933, 1935 by The President and Fellows of Harvard College. Used by permission of Harvard University Press.

From THE THOUGHT AND CHARACTER OF WILLIAM JAMES by Ralph Barton Perry. Used by permission of Harvard University Press.

From RECONSTRUCTION IN PHILOSOPHY by John Dewey. Copyright 1920 by Henry Holt and Company; copyright 1948 by John Dewey. By permission of the publisher.

From THE PHILOSOPHY OF LOYALTY by Josiah Royce. Copyright 1908. Published by The Macmillan Company; used by permission of the estate of Josiah Royce. From THE CONTEMPORARY AMERICAN PHILOSOPHY by G. P. Adams and W. P. Montague, reprinted by permission of The Macmillan Company; and from DEMOCRACY AND EDUCATION by John Dewey, copyright 1917 by The Macmillan Company. Used with the permission of the publisher.

From FREEDOM AND CULTURE by John Dewey. Copyright 1939, and from
THE QUEST FOR CERTAINTY by John Dewey. Copyright 1929. Used by permission of G. P. Putnam's Sons.

From PRAGMATISM by William James. Copyright 1907 by William James. Reprinted by permission of Paul R. Reynolds & Son, 599 Fifth Avenue, New York 17,
N. Y.

From THE WORKS OF GEORGE SANTAYANA, Triton Edition, copyright 1936,
1937 By Charles Scribner's Sons. And from THE LIFE OF REASON by George
Santayana: *Reason in Common Sense,* copyright 1905, 1922 by Charles Scribner's
Sons, renewal copyright 1933, 1950 by George Santayana; *Reason in Religion,*
copyright 1905, by Charles Scribner's Sons, renewal copyright 1933 by George
Santayana; *Reason in Art,* copyright 1905 by Charles Scribner's Sons, renewal
copyright 1933 by George Santayana; *Reason in Science,* copyright 1906 by
Charles Scribner's Sons, renewal copyright, 1934 by George Santayana. And from
THE LETTERS OF SANTAYANA, edited by Daniel Cory, copyright © 1955
by Daniel M. Cory. And from SKEPTICISM AND ANIMAL FAITH by George
Santayana, published by Charles Scribner's Sons; and from DIALOGUES IN
LIMBO by George Santayana, published by Charles Scribner's Sons. Reprinted
by permission of the publisher.

Contents

Introduction

by Charles Frankel

IN THIS BOOK THE READER WILL FIND A PROFILE OF AMERICAN PHILOSOPHY during the period in which it came to maturity. Between two great turning points in American history—the Civil War and the Great Depression—the men whose ideas are set forth in these pages, and others who were only a little less important, built a legacy of sophisticated philosophic discussion in the United States, and helped Western thought turn a corner in its history. In the ambitions they brought to philosophy, and in the freshness and energy of their ideas, they created what may be justly called a "golden age of American Philosophy."

It was an important episode in American history because it marked the appearance of American philosophers not as Americans but as philosophers, as full partners in an ancient enterprise of a larger civilization. It did not occur to these men that they were dealing with peculiarly American problems, or had a duty to speak as Americans in giving answers to the questions that interested them. The significant influences on them, the intimate intellectual company they kept, were not Puritan divines—not even Jonathan Edwards or Emerson—but Kant and John Stuart Mill, Darwin and Hegel, Bergson and Bertrand Russell. They responded to philosophers elsewhere as their compatriots, and philosophers elsewhere responded to them as equals. For they were concerned with the perennial issues of philosophy and with winds of doctrine that were blowing through the entire Western world.

And yet there was an air about them, a posture toward ideas, a view of themselves and of what they were doing, that was—or that seemed—new. They were philosophers living in a place, a time, and a moral climate not quite like that in which any philosophers had lived before, and underlying their arguments there were attitudes that were not argued and idioms they could not help but use. They spoke, not in the high official tones of so much nineteenth-century philosophy, but with the simplicity and directness of American manners at their best. Although they approached their sub-

1

ject as professionals, they took philosophy personally—took it to heart—
and were not afraid to let their feelings and idiosyncrasies show through
their philosophic beards. Even their easy hospitality to ideas from all traditions, and their relative independence from a precisely defined philosophic
tradition of their own, was itself a departure from the philosophic norm.
Though the fact is not important in judging their contributions to philosophy,
they seemed quite clearly to be American philosophers. And before we
consider the intrinsic merits of their ideas, it would be well to try to fix
the peculiar accent they brought to philosophy, an accent that sounded
American in foreign ears, and that has helped many Americans themselves
to define what they regard as an American outlook.

To fix this accent is not easy. The United States is a continental nation
that faces East and West, and that contains the children of old New
Englanders, new immigrants and former slaves. To suggest that any group
of philosophers speak with a common voice comes close to a contradiction in terms; to suggest that they are the authentic voice of a society as
diversified as the United States is almost as absurd. The philosophers whose
ideas appear here had different interests and sometimes radically different
angles of vision on the world. Chauncey Wright and Charles Peirce were
interested mainly in science. William James, who disliked neat systems,
and Josiah Royce, who devoted his life to building one, were troubled,
attracted, and preoccupied by religion. John Dewey, who wrote so badly
that his merits as a philosopher have been denied, was a social reformer.
George Santayana, who wrote so well that his right to be called a philosopher
has been questioned, was a conservative so deeply alienated from the main
currents of life in his time that he grew to think his philosophy could be
nothing but a personal soliloquy.

And yet it is difficult to escape the impression that certain themes and
counter-themes move through the philosophies that were produced in
America between 1870 and 1930, and that these themes are in some way
American themes. There are dominant motifs, attitudes and interests that
gave American philosophy in this period its animation and its appeal to
a wide public. To some philosophers of the period these themes were
native and congenial—so much so that they were hardly aware of how
much in their philosophies lay below the level of argument. To other
philosophers these themes seemed foolish or perverse—so much so that
they could not get them out of their minds. But philosophers are held together not only by the things on which they agree; they are held together
by the things on which they think it important to disagree. And underneath even the most technical controversies between Wright and Peirce,
James and Royce, or Dewey and Santayana, one can glimpse certain common and unspoken topics of discourse to which everyone's attention is
turned and around which attitudes that are pre-philosophic in character

swing and swing away. This is why the debates continued, passionately, insistently, and sometimes irritably, long after everybody had made the logic of his position clear. Royce, James, Santayana and the others all danced differently to the tunes they heard; but they were dancing to the same tunes.

What, then, were these underlying themes? There was, first, an excitement about a new and frankly humanistic conception of philosophy. Peirce, James, Santayana, Dewey, and even Royce in his own way, all had something in common. They all looked at philosophy from the outside, trying to understand it and to reformulate its problems in the light of psychology, sociology, the methods of science, or the insights of literature. They were opposed to insularity in philosophy, to a failure to see its problems in a larger human and social context, to a lack of philosophy about philosophy itself. "In a subject like philosophy," William James wrote, "it is really fatal to lose connection with the open air of human nature, and to think in terms of shop-tradition only." Few of his contemporaries in American philosophy would have disagreed with him.

Philosophy, as most of the philosophers of the "golden age" viewed it, was not simply a self-enclosed discipline with its own specialized problems. It was an instrument of living creatures struggling with personal problems or social discontents, and trying to be clear about their standards and aims amidst the shocks of their daily experience. At the beginning of the "golden age" Chauncey Wright wrote: "The questions of philosophy proper are human desires and fears and aspirations—human emotions—taking an intellectual form." Wright meant by these words to distinguish philosophy from the cooler, more impersonal methods of science. But even those who believed that philosophy would do well to emulate the methods of the sciences also thought that philosophy was a disciplined revelation of one's human commitments. "Philosophy is the study of the *a priori*," wrote C. I. Lewis towards the close of the "golden age," "and therefore of the mind's own active attitudes." Sixty years separate Lewis' remark from Wright's, but the connection between them indicates a main path which American philosophy followed during that period.

Such a view of philosophy was not, of course, altogether new. Many traditional thinkers had taken such an approach to philosophy implicitly or explicitly. Plato employed myths, and placed his dialogues in dramatic settings, to express his conviction that philosophy begins in the dilemmas of ordinary life, and that it is nourished by human passions, including erotic fancies, the impulse to self-justification, and the desire for another world to live in. Thomas Hobbes, Spinoza, Bishop Berkeley and John Stuart Mill were all clearly aware that there is a connection between the lives men lead and the philosophies they profess. What was new in American philosophy after the Civil War was only that it took this position

deliberately, systematically, and eagerly. When most traditional philosophers had pointed to the influence of human nature on philosophy they
had meant to point to the reason why philosophy did not achieve the
divine impartiality at which it aimed. When most American philosophers
pointed to the influence of human nature on philosophy they meant to
point to philosophy's proper function as an expression and instrument of
human needs. They were humble about philosophy, but they were also
extraordinarily ambitious for it. For in placing philosophy on the same
plane with all other human arts and disciplines, they hoped to release it
not only from its sectarian arrogance but from its sectarian interests. They
hoped to set it free to range over the whole spectrum of human activities.

There is, accordingly, an element of disagreement with traditional
thought in the American philosophy that developed after the Civil War and
also an element of profound affinity. One major tradition in Western
philosophy has made the subject a vehicle for attaining a special sort of
truth all its own, and has assigned to philosophers a special wisdom which
others do not have. This view, which was Plato's, has not been the prevailing view among influential American philosophers since "pragmatism"
and "the new realism" put Josiah Royce's philosophical idealism on the
defensive. And yet the men whose ideas can be found in this book helped
renew the Platonic conception of philosophy's social tasks. They attacked
Plato's belief in a detached, immaculate philosophic truth, but they did so
because they wished philosophy to serve in the clarification and appraisal
of actual human ideas and institutions and in the practical organization
of human affairs. For all the skepticism about the classic ideals of philosophy that one can find in John Dewey, for example, and for all his efforts
to take a realistic and worldly view of the relation of ideas to events, he is
ironically like Plato in his belief that the world would be very different
if only philosophers did their proper jobs.

This view of the nature and mission of philosophy was reflected in the
subjects to which the thinkers of this period turned their attention. One
of the diseases that recurrently weakens philosophy is its tendency to feed
on itself, to deal exclusively with problems that have grown up only in
the intra-mural debates of philosophers. Between 1870 and 1930, however, fresh winds from biology and psychology, and from sociology, economics and law, blew across American philosophy and blew away a great
deal of accumulated academic dust. From Chauncey Wright to Morris
Cohen philosophers looked outside philosophy for subjects and for illumination. To be sure, they continued to debate the classic technical issues—
no serious philosopher can avoid them. But they also thought about science,
religion and art, and about politics and education, and what they learned
in these fields affected what they had to say about the classic issues.

And their view of philosophy also affected their principles of workman-
ship. There is a drive and personal immediacy in the philosophy of the

"golden age," and a desire on the part of almost all its principal figures to communicate not only to professional philosophers but to the educated public at large. If the philosophers who appear in this book were not all men of the world, they were at least not men who had turned their backs on the world. And there is in their work as a consequence an absence of artificiality and paradox. Santayana once said of himself: "I stand in philosophy exactly where I stand in daily life; I should not be honest otherwise." Of all those who wrote or taught philosophy in America during this period, Santayana was surely the least interested in using philosophy as an instrument of practical action. But like his colleagues, he thought that philosophy had an obligation to respect the facts of daily life and to refuse to make a mystery out of the ordinary substance of human experience. In taking a humanistic view of philosophy, the thinkers who brought philosophy to maturity in America meant to tie it down to the common knowledge and shared experience of ordinary human beings.

This attitude towards philosophy brings us, however, to another master theme that moved through this era in American thought. It is the sheer confidence in the normal workings of the responsible mind, confidence in its ability to make out the true and the good, and confidence in something more—in the power of the mind to make the world over. William James once remarked that when a man's work is done and he is dead, everything he did can be reduced to a single cry. In James and John Dewey, and even in Josiah Royce, this single cry was that the universe was unfinished and plastic, and that the human intellect had the power to make its ideals come true. And when Santayana said that he was "not an American, except by long association," he probably had this strain in American thought most in mind.

For there is a reiterated note in the philosophy of the "golden age." It is the belief, in words Ralph Barton Perry used to describe James' doctrine, that "the mind of man is the principal agent in its own formation." The emphasis on the power of the human mind to make itself and the world over is strongest, indeed, in precisely that variety of American philosophy —pragmatism—which is commonly held to be most typically American, and which is said by its critics to show contempt for ideas. The pragmatists —Peirce, James, Dewey—thought that ideas could really lead the way in human life: this ideal stands behind their insistence that the truth of ideas lies in their power to carry us through experience in a desirable way. And all this, as Josiah Royce was fond of pointing out, was what modern philosophic idealism had also been saying. He too was a pragmatist, he proclaimed, in his readiness to test ideas by their fruitfulness in producing the sort of experience at which we aim.

This confidence in the powers of the mind is all the more remarkable when we recall the intellectual backgrounds of these men and their affinities with movements of thought elsewhere in the world. Their approach to philosophy grew out of a combination of the philosophies of Kant or Hegel with evolutionary theories, and belongs to the same large stream of thought that also produced Marx, Nietzsche, and contemporary existentialism. Kant had emphasized the fact that human experience is not a purely passive affair and that men bring certain ready-made forms of thought with them when they enter into commerce with the world. Hegel had traced the growth of the mind through time, and had treated all philosophies as the expressions of particular stages and perspectives in history. Peirce, James, Santayana and Dewey interpreted these ideas in biological rather than metaphysical terms. They reacted in different ways to evolutionary theory itself, but, like evolutionary philosophers elsewhere, they all assumed that human thinking is always moved by some specific, vital purpose, and that religion, science, philosophy, and even the principles of logic, must be understood as instruments of animal adaptation.

But they turned this stream of thought in a direction of their own. Marx used these ideas to show that philosophy might discover—in fact, had already discovered—the laws of social evolution which determine the course of human affairs and fix the values men ought to choose. Contemporary existentialists use these ideas to stress the limits of reason and science, the speciousness of common sense, and the absurdity of human ideals. In contrast, the philosophers of the American "golden age" never seriously thought that a philosopher could look at the world with a divine eye; but neither did they doubt that there was such a thing as objectivity, nor assert that the deliverances of practical wisdom, science and the enlightened moral conscience were mere subjective delusions.

There is an absence of *Weltschmerz* in the classic figures of American philosophy. It is singular when we remember that they all grew up in the nineteenth century. In their time the doctrine was asserted, as it seems to be reasserted today, that all thinking exists merely to defend material interests or unconscious wishes which thinking cannot change. Few American philosophers were touched by this doctrine. When William James was at the height of his career, sympathetically exploring mysticism and defending its authority, at least for mystics, Henri Bergson in France was developing the view, not unlike that of James, that all ordinary thinking takes place to secure or to fortify some selected human interest. But Bergson used this doctrine to justify the conclusion that philosophy must employ a form of higher intuition to accomplish its tasks. For all his admiration of the intuitive in thinking, James did not go so far. He was sorely tempted to do so; but when he argued that we must have the courage of our hopes, and that we must be willing to leap in the dark where our deepest values are concerned, he had the grace to say explicitly that it was a leap in the dark, an act of personal faith and individual resolution, and not an impersonal revelation of the universe's deeper truth. Nor did he or most of his contemporaries believe that human ideals had been compromised in any way because they had been shown to have material and practical origins. They believed, on the contrary, that human ideals had been shown to have a natural home in the world, and that new ways of thinking had been found by which these ideals could be more effectively realized.

Indeed, they seemed to believe that the world was a peculiarly friendly place to those who were willing to put their minds and spirits to improving it. With the possible exception of George Santayana, the leading American philosophers who accepted a naturalistic view of man accepted it with moral enthusiasm and with something approaching religious delight. They did not say, as Bertrand Russell did, that men enlightened in the outlook of modern science must henceforth build a habitation for their ideals on the rock of "unyielding despair." Instead they dwelt almost more on nature's cooperation with man than on nature's indifference to human concerns. Their imaginations were dominated, not by the stars and the vast empty spaces of the universe, and not by the Darwinian view of nature "red in tooth and claw," but by the possible connection of everything with human ideals. Whether this was the accent of a New World it is hard to say. But it was the accent that one would expect to find among philosophical idealists or Unitarian ministers. It was not the accent of classic naturalists like Lucretius or Diderot. American philosophy between 1870 and 1930 was distinctive for its combination of naturalism and undismayed rationalism. It was even more distinctive for its combination of naturalism with attitudes towards nature that had belonged to quite different traditions.

We come here to another of the key motifs in American philosophy during the period of its high ambition. "Damn the Absolute!" James once said to Royce, and he meant to damn any belief that set limits to what the human mind and will could accomplish. "Pragmatism looks to the future," he wrote repeatedly. And this future was open. Its character depended almost exclusively on what human beings did; and what human beings did depended in large part on their capacity to throw off their inherited beliefs in eternal truths and their inherited yearning for absolutes.

If there is a criticism to be made of pragmatism, it is not that it denies the importance of ideas, and certainly not that it sees their importance only in the utilitarian fields of engineering, industry, and the practical arts. It is that Royce was more right than he knew, and that pragmatism, like philosophic idealism, seems to erase the distinction between the structure of the mind and the structure of the universe, between the knowledge of facts and facts that exist whether or not they are known. The power of ideas to give an order to an open unlimited world is so strongly emphasized in pragmatism that there seems to be no antecedent order in the world, no organization of things that is what it is, quite independently of what we think or desire. This is the issue around which so much technical controversy turned, both in America and abroad.

There is less reason to raise this question in the case of Peirce than there is in the case of James or Dewey. James' essay, "The Will to Believe," suggests that we can make our most heartfelt beliefs come true if only we believe in them strongly enough. Dewey's writings are full of attacks upon the classic belief in an "antecedent reality"—a reality with fixed properties that cannot be changed by the inquiring mind. Neither philosopher, we may be fairly certain, meant to deny that there is a world which exists independently of the presence of human beings. But there is room to doubt that they were entirely clear as to what they did mean. And what is plain is that Dewey and James—and Peirce too—found it extremely difficult to accept the notion that anything in the world was finally settled or finished.

It cannot be doubted that most of the leading philosophers of the "golden age" rejected an old posture toward the world—what Bertrand Russell has called "the emotional realization of human impotence in face of natural forces." The rejection was spontaneous in Dewey; in James it was consciously willed. But even in Royce the rejection is there. And yet "the emotional realization of human impotence in face of natural forces" is often an emotional reaction to human impotence in face of human forces. It was natural that American philosophers at the turn of the century should be insensitive or hostile to the acceptance of human impotence. They were opposed to industrial barbarities justified on the ground that they rested on untouchable natural rights that would endure forever. They were critical of programs of education which consisted simply in drilling into children an inherited, and presumably unchangeable, body of lore. America did not seem to these men to be the kind of country in which such things had to be accepted.

For the America these men knew had also been made by generations of immigrants who had broken with their pasts. Most of its citizens had not been brought up to take fixed social distinctions, or any other kind of fixed distinction, seriously. America had just finished settling a continent, and it was proud of its inventiveness, its ingenuity, its freedom from precedent. It had no memory of an ancient, heavy, ineradicable past; it had no ruins that it wished to restore. The Civil War was still too recent for anyone to foresee that America, like other nations, could also inherit an ancestral evil. "American disorder is sweet beside European order: it is so full of promise," William James' father once wrote. Philosophers in America at the turn of the century spoke as one would expect men of good will in such a place and time to speak. They spoke like men who had credit at the moral bank and who thought there was room in the world for their plans and projects.

And so we come to a final motif in the philosophies that are represented in this book. Like Emerson, James, Santayana, Dewey and Royce were all primarily moralists in their approach to philosophy. They were interested, that is to say, in human ideas about the world even more than in that world itself, and they were interested most of all in the uses to which human beings put their ideas. But while, in Santayana, this moral interest was contemplative and detached, the interest of an observer and not an actor, the moral interest of most of his colleagues was active and passionate. It was, as Santayana saw it, "moralism"—an insistence on framing issues in terms of action and a disposition to see the world always in terms of struggle, improvement, and achievement.

"Moralism," surely, is a disagreeable word. To apply it to men like James, Royce or Dewey is to slur over their good nature, their aesthetic sensibilities, and their sense of the complexities of human life. But while the word is the wrong one, it points to something that these men inherited from the American past. For James or for Dewey what men receive from their societies, what they find in their physical environments, what they find in themselves, is always raw material: it exists to be used—to be changed, modified and made better, to be turned into an exhibit of the power of the human mind and will. In their indifference or antipathy to "the emotional realization of human impotence," the philosophers of the "golden age" rejected one main strand of Calvinist and Puritan theology. But Calvinism and Puritanism contain another strand—the stress on the morally athletic life, the view of the world as primarily a scene for strenuous moral endeavor. It is an emphasis that remained when Calvinism gave way to Unitarianism among New England intellectuals, and it remained as well in the philosophy that developed in America after the Civil War.

When James disagreed with Royce, he emphasized that it was ultimately because Royce's belief in the Absolute entitled men to take a moral holiday. And when Royce defended his system, it was ultimately on the ground that it made moral holidays impossible. Again and again the philosophers of this period turn an intellectual issue into a matter of the moral position that one ought to take. Whether Santayana and Cohen found this note in American philosophy repugnant because they were immigrants who had closer ties to Old World cultures it is hard to say. But it is plain that for men like James, Dewey or Royce an espousal of detachment would have been an artifice, a kind of posturing they would have thought as inappropriate in a philosopher as in any other human being. The philosophy of the "golden age" is predominantly the philosophy of men who thought that the world was good but that it needed to be changed—who thought that the world was good, indeed, because it needed to be changed.

What were the issues, and the movements of opinion and feeling, with which these men felt that they had to come to terms? At bottom there were three sets of ideas to which their philosophies were responses—the theory of evolution, the deterministic ideals of nineteenth-century science, and the social outlook represented by the name of Herbert Spencer. The first and largest of these was the theory of evolution.

"This is what the world has been most thinking of for the last forty years," wrote Peirce in 1897. And it had a great deal to think about. For before the advent of Darwin's theory it was still possible for educated men, long after they had rejected a literal interpretation of the Bible, to believe that things were in their proper places, or, at any rate, that there was a fixed plan of development in the world. But Darwin's theory challenged some of Western man's most deep-seated moral and intellectual habits. It did not explain events by referring to the ends that they might serve. It asserted that evolution took place by *chance* variation, and that the occasional usefulness of a new trait explained its survival but not its first appearance. If there was a Designer in this universe in which so much was wasted and lost, in which every instance of happy adaptation was bought at the price of innumerable failures, he did not seem to know what his purposes were until after the event. Indeed, in the evolutionary scheme of things there could be nothing final, no fixed ends or ultimate goals, not even any human ideals that were not subject to change. Darwin's theory seemed to make it impossible even to define the idea of Design.

The worst suspicions that had been set loose by the tradition of Lucretius, Thomas Hobbes and the French materialists of the eighteenth century seemed thus to have been confirmed by a sober Englishman who claimed that his main talent lay simply in the industrious collecting of facts. Did "science" show that human ideals were mere oddities in the universe, and that charity and compassion were wistful and hopeless gestures? Did the theory of evolution indicate that human reason, since it was the product of an animal past, was only the voice of instinct and the helpless servant of natural forces it could not control? The question bothered Darwin himself, who wrote to Chauncey Wright, "As your mind is so clear, and as you consider so carefully the meaning of words, I wish you would take some incidental occasion to consider when a thing may properly be said to be affected by the mind of man."

Wright took the occasion, as did most of the leading figures who came after him in American philosophy. Their great effort was to show how the mind of man, though it might have an animal base, could still be said to achieve genuine knowledge and truth and to make an independent difference in the world. For evolution required philosophers to ask themselves all over again the old aching questions about the reality of free will. And it required them to ask as well whether "truth" could be regarded as an unchanging standard, whether the moral life could be built on absolutes, whether, amidst the universal flux and the clash of animal drives struggling for satisfaction, any independent and impersonal principles could be discerned by which men could make out what they meant when they spoke of "true belief" or "right conduct." It is a measure of the achievement of American philosophers that most of them managed to reaffirm their belief in human freedom and in the existence of objective standards while facing the full force of Darwin's theories and remaining wholly faithful to them.

Moreover, the shock of Darwin was reinforced by still another idea. This was the idea of "mechanistic determinism"—a notion that expressed the dominant ideal of nineteenth-century science. "Mechanistic determinism" was not a scientific theory but a notion about the structure that the universe would be seen to have if all the goals of science had been achieved. Imagine an omiscient observer, the French mathematician and astronomer Laplace had suggested, who already knew everything that men were still struggling through their scientific activities to find out. Such an observer, by specifying the position and velocity of each body in the universe, and by calculating their motions in accordance with the appropriate physical laws, could predict the entire future course of events in the universe. At one moment, here and now, the entire history of everything would be present to his mind. In short, "mechanistic determinism" suggested that it is only human ignorance that prevents us from seeing that the future is already determined and set, and that the struggles, hopes and decisions of human beings are merely incidents in a play that has already been written.

When American philosophy was stirred to such remarkable life after the Civil War, the conception of a "block universe" in which all possibilities had already been foreclosed was, accordingly, one of the first notions to which it had to address itself. Although "determinism," in some sense of that ambiguous word, is by no means a dead letter in contemporary science and philosophy, it is now plain that nineteenth-century "mechanistic determinism" at best expressed an ideal which applies to only a small area of natural science, and which cannot be extended to other sciences that do not fit the form of classical mechanics. Partly through the work of Peirce, indeed, it is now not unusual to argue that "chance" stands for something more than an event whose causes human beings do not know, and that it designates an objective property of nature. But in every generation it is necessary for men to try to be clear about the meaning of the science of their time in order to determine the place it should take in the structure of their beliefs and ideals. American philosophers had to face the challenge of nineteenth-century determinism just as contemporary philosophers have to make sense of quantum physics or the theory of probability. And the challenge it posed was all the more difficult because most of the leaders of American philosophy after the Civil War were men with a great sympathy for science and a conviction that its findings must be respected.

The challenge was also the more poignant because it seemed to involve more than an abstract puzzle about the nature of free will. In the decades between 1870 and 1930 there were quite practical problems about freedom in the concrete. During these years, as we do not need to be reminded, the United States was making extraordinary industrial progress, largely by permitting the relatively unchecked growth of corporate economic power. But these were also the years of industrial slums and company towns, the years during which Mr. Justice Holmes was forced to remind his colleagues on the Supreme Court that the Fourteenth Amendment was not intended to enact the philosophy of Herbert Spencer. Mr. Justice Holmes expressed this view in a dissenting opinion, and most philosophical opinion about social affairs during these years was also dissenting opinion.

For the prevailing doctrine of the time was that of Spencer and the "social Darwinists." The impact of Darwin's theories cannot be understood unless we recall that they were used to give specious support to a social outlook that had existed long before the appearance of *The Origin of Speces*. In essence this doctrine asserted that unbridled competition between individuals was nature's sole way of improving the condition of the race. Poverty and suffering were nature's instruments for eliminating the unfit; charity and compassion, unless carefully controlled, were dangers; and a sense of responsibility, though it might be a good thing in politics or personal relations, was out of place in the management of a business.

The doctrine was a strange amalgam of incompatible notions. It combined a belief in universal change with a belief in an eternally right and unalterable order of society. It confused natural facts or pseudo-facts with moral laws. It applied generalizations about biological individuals to legal constructs like corporations. It assumed that the State was the only agency in society that could place barriers in the path of individual initiative. Yet this doctrine was no stranger than many similar combinations of scientific misinformation and special pleading that existed before and exist today, and it exerted an enormous practical influence. It provided a main theme to which a great deal of philosophical discussion during the "golden age" moved in counterpoint. Underneath the most abstract philosophical discussions—discussions about the reality of the Absolute, the meaning of truth, the logic of value-judgments—one can hear the echoes of a clamorous social scene and one can sense the impatience of sensitive men with ideas that had become the cloaks of callousness and complacency. In their attempts to redefine the meaning of individualism, in their re-examination of conceptions like "freedom" and "property," in their refusal to make their peace with the notion that men must live in passive conformity to antecedent natural laws, the philosophers who taught and wrote during the period of America's great industrial expansion were trying to fashion the instruments for moral criticism of their age.

For a great many of those who taught or wrote philosophy in America before World War I—indeed, probably for the majority—the answer to evolution, mechanistic determinism, and Spencerian individualism lay in the tradition for which Josiah Royce was the most eloquent spokesman— "that post-Kantian idealistic philosophy," in Ralph Barton Perry's words, "which, invigorated by its transplantation from Germany to a foreign soil, had become the bulwark of English-speaking Protestant piety." Idealism met the challenge of nineteeth-century science by a flanking movement. It asserted that all scientific theories were limited and relative, that they dealt only with a world of appearance, and that philosophy revealed the nature of reality. And it argued that this reality was a single, harmonious moral order, and that the passionate hopes of the moral idealist and the enlightened religious believer, despite all appearances to the contrary, were therefore essentially correct. Fifty years ago, it has been remarked, professors of philosophy were the unofficial chaplains of most American universities. The pre-eminence of idealism may explain why this was so, for in the late nineteenth century idealism provided the main academic support for the inherited religious outlook and the main intellectual platform for the moral criticism of the status quo.

But idealism left a great many questions unanswered. It took refuge in unhelpful formulas like "loyalty to loyalty" when men were confronted by practical conflicts between their loyalties. It cheerfully implied that all clashes of social interest were cases of misunderstanding, and that a "higher synthesis" could always be found within which these clashes could be resolved to the satisfaction of all parties. Most of all, it attempted to demonstrate by pure dialectic alone what the nature of the universe must necessarily be. Such a philosophy could not satisfy men who had come to respect the piecemeal and empirical methods of the sciences, and who were being instructed by the logicians in the relativity of all first principles. For such men it was not idealism but something more radical that was needed—a thorough re-examination, in the light of evolutionary science, of the methods appropriate to human thinking and of the ideals that should guide inquiry and moral choice. To provide this re-examination was the task which two groups of philosophers, the "pragmatists" and the "new realists," set themselves.

If we do not measure the importance of a philosophy by the number of its adherents, but rather by its success in stoking the flames of philosophic discussion, pragmatism was the most important philosophy of the "golden age." It seemed radical, whether it really was or not. It chose the themes that were debated. And it gave to the most adventurous minds of two generations, in politics, law, history and economics as well as in philosophy, the sense that old delusions had been cut open and discarded, and that the human mind could now address itself to what really mattered.

Royce had written that his age needed a philosophy that would "give form to the spiritual interests of humanity." Pragmatism was the attempt to perform this task while remaining true to the spirit of science. It denied that sharp lines can be drawn between "matter" and "mind," "science" and "morals," "experience" and "reason." It asserted, on the contrary, that human ideas and ideals must be studied from a biological and social point of view, and they must be judged as instruments by which human beings bring some order into the buzzing confusion of their experience.

Human inquiry or human moral choice only arise, the pragmatists argued, when habitual patterns of thought and action are blocked. They end, for the time being, when habits have been reformed and the specific problem which provoked the inquiry has been settled. This idea placed most philosophical issues in a new light. For if we take such a view of human thought and action, the most ancient of philosophic dreams has been rejected. There are no ultimate principles, no self-evident ideas or irreducible sense-data, on which everything can be said to rest. The desire for absolute certainty has no place, and neither has the notion that men can solve their moral dilemmas by turning to some ready-made hierarchy of abstract values. From the pragmatic point of view, an idea or ideal must be judged in terms of the specific context in which it arises, and its worth must be measured by its capacity to solve the particular problems that call it forth.

The heart of pragmatism lay in the so-called "pragmatic method," which proposed that we find out what our ideas mean by tracing their consequences in our actual experience. The method was a technique for criticizing abstractions, for pinning thinking down and making it responsible by testing it in the face of observed facts. On one side, its use was that it unmasked ideas. Pragmatists in the law compared abstractions about "natural freedom" with the social facts like sweat shops to which these abstractions led when they were put into practice. Pragmatists in political theory compared abstractions like "the general welfare" with the actual competition among pressure groups by which policy in a democracy is determined. But, on the other side, the pragmatic method was also a technique for bringing ideas to life, an instrument by which men hoped to combine realism with moral idealism. For it proposed, not simply that men re-examine their behavior in the light of their ideals, but that they rethink their ideals in the light of scientific information and the changing character of their actual experience.

Pragmatism, however, was anything but a monolithic system of thought. When Peirce dwelt on the "consequences" of ideas, he meant their logical implications not their psychological effects. He meant, still more, the scientific function of ideas, their role in advancing the work of an historical community of investigators seeking reasoned agreement. He was a pragmatist who was more interested in theory than in action, and he valued ideas most of all for their power to lead to still further generalization, to still more orderliness and "concrete reasonableness" in human thought and action.

James, in contrast, was not primarily interested in the logic of ideas. He was a physiologist and a psychologist, interested in ideas as events in personal experience and as instruments of will and desire. Religion was one of the great interests of his life, and when he spoke of "sick souls," "conversion," or "the will to believe," he spoke from his own experience. Pragmatism, accordingly, was for James a means of personal therapy, a way of lifting his spirits by their philosophical bootstraps.

And for John Dewey pragmatism was something still different. In his views of the nature of pragmatism, he was closer to Peirce than to James. But he was neither a specialized student of logic and science nor a thinker concerned to use philosophy to appease personal anxieties. He was interested in social criticism, and he used the pragmatic method to reinterpret the function in human civilization of education, logic, the arts, and philosophic inquiry itself.

Few philosophies have been more thoroughly criticized than pragmatism, and there is little doubt but that many of these criticisms are justified. It has been pointed out again and again that Dewey's pragmatic logic, though it teems with fresh and liberating ideas, is dispiritingly vague and inexact, and that James' argument in "The Will to Believe" seems suspiciously like the suggestion that when we do not know the answer to a question, we are free to believe what we wish to believe. And yet, despite such merited criticisms, there can be found in Dewey, in James, and most of all, perhaps, in Peirce, many of the insights which philosophers today are greeting with the joy of first discovery when they find them in the pages of Ludwig Wittgenstein. An idea, said the pragmatists, is not to be judged as a transcript of a reality that already exists. The meaning of an idea depends upon its use in a particular context, and its value lies in its fruitfulness in leading to observations that human beings would not otherwise make and in giving an order to human experience that it would not otherwise have. So we cannot and do not find out whether an idea is true by employing some general, abstract definition of truth; and we cannot and do not settle our moral problems by invoking some general definition of "the good." All such judgments are made in some particular context, and before we can make them we have to find out first what the concrete problems are, what definitions and assumptions have been made, what goals and values are taken for granted, and what procedures are available. Even our doubts have to be defined in terms of what, at the moment, we do not doubt. Such arguments left very few issues in philosophy where they had been when pragmatism entered the scene.

In the end, the difficulty with pragmatism was a defect of its virtues. The pragmatists saw more clearly than had most of their predecessors that a system of ideas does not serve simply as a summary of experience, but that its central function is to provide a set of rules or habits of inference by which the mind can move from premise to conclusion in a satisfactory way. But they stated their fundamental insight, as have many other thinkers who know they have something new and important to say, in an exaggerated and overly-generalized way. To come to any conclusions about the nature of the world we need not only rules for drawing inferences but premises from which these inferences can be drawn; and some of these premises must refer to facts in the world and not just to human habits of inference. Pragmatism laid such great stress on the active role of ideas in giving a pattern to human experience that it seemed to leave a large question unanswered. Is the only order in the world what the inquiring mind puts there?

In the last analysis, this is why "the new realists," who are represented in this book by Perry, found almost as much to criticize in pragmatism as they did in idealism. It is the source of Morris Cohen's attacks on pragmatism, and it is the central problem with which C. I. Lewis' sophisticated restatement of pragmatism tries to deal. And it is why Santayana preferred to call himself a "materialist" in natural philosophy, and why as he grew older he placed steadily greater stress on the merely lyric character of ideas and on their essential insignificance in the natural order. For he wished to state the simple orthodox belief of inarticulate men that ideas are not things, and that the world has its own order and regularity whatever men may say about it.

But Santayana's early work, *The Life of Reason*—the book that the older Santayana did not like—is a symbol of the achievement of American philosophy in its "golden age." It broke upon a world nagged by Victorian doubts and worried that evolution, geology and physics had proved that human ideals were mere evanescent accidents without purpose or power in the universe. It showed that these ideals were as legitimate as ever, and that they could be made more responsible, and have a better chance to be realized, when their dependence on natural conditions was taken into account. Most of all, it explored the ideals that Americans held at a given moment of their history, placed these ideals in a wider frame of human purposes, and helped make Americans more aware of what they were choosing and what they were rejecting in their scheme of human excellence.

"Philosophic study," William James once wrote, "means the habit of always seeing an alternative, of not taking the usual for granted, of making conventionalities fluid again, of imagining foreign states of mind." This is what American philosophers between the Civil War and the Great Depression did for their contemporaries. They brought the American imagination into closer touch with the classic themes of secular European thought, and through what they were as individuals as well as through what they taught, they showed that philosophy can help men to take a fresh look at the world and an independent position towards its problems. They did not succeed more than have other philosophers in arriving at beliefs with which all reasonable men will agree. But there is a value in philosophy which depends on the earnestness with which it seeks this goal and not on its success in attaining it. It is an instrument by which men, through learning to examine the alternatives to their own beliefs and values, learn to know what they believe and what they value, and why. If civilization means growth in self-awareness, the American philosophers of the "golden age" helped make America a more civilized society.

Philosophers today believe that they have methods more subtle and powerful than any available to the philosophers of a generation ago. To an extent this is true; but these methods are not a substitute for what the philosophers of the "golden age" possessed—courage, enterprise, and an eye for the main issues. They left us questions they did not answer and problems they helped create. But they faced the questions that needed to be faced in their own day. They stood up to the shock of new scientific ideas and kept their balance; they tried to fit this science into the humane concerns of men; and they provided the social ideas that their society used as it moved from brawling industrial disorder into the world of the New Freedom and the New Deal. They did not retreat from the dangerous in philosophy, nor did they make philosophy a retreat from the urgent problems felt by other men. They rejected only obscurantism, arrogance, and the view that the mind of man must bow down before mysteries it can never understand.

This is the source of the excitement these men still convey. We live in a different world from the one they inhabited, and we cannot use all their ideas—nor, it is likely, would they have wished us to do so—in the form in which they transmitted them to us. But without their ideas it is unlikely that we could move on the contemporary scene even as well as we do. And over and above their ideas the philosophers of the "golden age" left us something else—the contagion of open imaginations, and of unflagging devotion to the ideals of reasoned argument and the examined life. In them philosophy comes alive as a form of responsible discourse in which men speak humbly but candidly to one another, declaring themselves on the issues that count.

CHAUNCEY WRIGHT

(1830-1875)

In the early eighteen-seventies a group of men, including Charles Peirce, William James and Oliver Wendell Holmes, Jr., met in Cambridge to discuss philosophical questions. They called themselves "The Metaphysical Club," and the acknowledged leader of the Club was Chauncey Wright— "our boxing-master," Peirce wrote, whom the members of the Club faced to be "severely pummelled." Wright was born in 1830 and died in 1875, after serving for some years as Secretary of the American Academy of Arts and Sciences. His early death is an almost melodramatic symbol of the impression of great but unfulfilled powers which he made on those who knew him. Henry James speaks of him as "the most wasted and doomed, the biggest at once and the gentlest, of the great intending and unproducing . . . bachelors of philosophy, bachelors of attitude and of life."

Yet while Wright developed most of his ideas in the counter-thrusts of his conversation, and his literary remains consist mainly of reviews and occasional essays, the impact of his ideas on the first generation of philosophers of the "golden age" is unmistakable. He was an uncompromising disciple of Darwin's, and his long essay, "The Evolution of Self-Consciousness," in which he attempted to satisfy Darwin's request to show "when a thing may properly be said to be affected by the mind of man," contains many of the ideas which later appear in James' account of "the stream of consciousness" and in his "philosophy of pure experience." Fundamental ideas that characterized pragmatism—the emphasis on the importance of language and symbols, the criticism of traditional philosophy's emphasis on contemplation rather than experiment and manipulation, the suggestion that metaphysics is a poetic rather than a strictly scientific discipline—can be found in Wright's essays and reviews. Not least, Wright's emphasis on the role of general principles in science as instruments for finding and not merely summarizing the facts is perhaps the major element in Peirce's and Dewey's interpretations of science.

But Wright was not quite a pragmatist. He reacted to the problems raised by the science of his time essentially by drawing a sharp line between science on one side and philosophy, morals and religion on the other. He took it that the business of science was simply to describe the regular relations between phenomena, and that any order which it found in events did not need a deeper explanation. The order that science revealed to exist here and there among phenomena was merely "the cosmical weather," and as much a brute fatality as a cold day in May. So science in and by itself could not be used to support any moral or religious view—these, ultimately, were matters of feeling and faith. The most that science could do was to communicate to other departments of human life the spirit that animated its own inquiries—its caution, its respect for facts, its disrespect for wishful thinking, its sense of the imperfection of what is known.

To the more speculative Peirce and the more impulsive James, accordingly, Wright seemed to be what is sometimes known as a "merely negative" thinker. Peirce, who placed Wright's abilities on the same level with those of John Stuart Mill, was also capable of calling him "an acute but shallow fellow." And James, who wrote once that men had a "duty to believe," reacted to Wright's careful and parsimonious mind by saying that there was a defect in "the active or impulsive part" of Wright's mental nature. He thought Wright anti-religious, and in one of his earliest essays he described Wright's position as "nihilism." To this charge Wright's own words, written on the margin of James' manuscript, are a more than adequate response: "But after all, nihilism is rather a discipline than a positive doctrine; an exorcism of the vague; a criticism of questions which by habit have passed beyond the real practical grounds or causes of question. Common sense is opposed only so far as common sense is not critical." Like the so-called "negativism" of David Hume, Wright's "nihilism" left a quite positive deposit in the doctrines of the men who set out to refute him. He made it inescapable that they would face towards science rather than away from it in dealing with philosophical issues; he sketched ideas that foreshadow themes that can be found in Santayana, Dewey, C. I. Lewis or Morris Cohen; and at the outset of the "golden age" he set an example of disciplined analytic thinking that helped give American philosophy an intellectual spine.

The first of the selections that follow is taken from a general examination of Herbert Spencer's philosophy which Wright published in the North American Review in 1865. The second essay from which selections have been made is a review of a book, Contributions to the Theory of Natural Selection, by Darwin's co-discoverer of this theory, the Australian naturalist, A. R. Wallace. Wright published this review in the North American Review in 1870. Both essays are reprinted in a collection of Wright's works, Philosophical Discussions, edited by Charles Eliot Norton (1877).

The Philosophy of Herbert Spencer

WHY THE INDUCTIVE AND MATHEMATICAL SCIENCES, AFTER THEIR FIRST rapid development at the culmination of Greek civilization, advanced so slowly for two thousand years,—and why in the following two hundred years a knowledge of natural and mathematical science has accumulated, which so vastly exceeds all that was previously known that these sciences may be justly regarded as the products of our own times,—are questions which have interested the modern philosopher not less than the objects with which these sciences are more immediately conversant. Was it in the employment of a new method of research, or in the exercise of greater virtue in the use of old methods, that this singular modern phenomenon had its origin? Was the long period one of arrested development, and is the modern era one of a normal growth? or should we ascribe the characteristics of both periods to so-called historical accidents,—to the influence of conjunctions in circumstances of which no explanation is possible, save in the omnipotence and wisdom of a guiding Providence?

The explanation which has become commonplace, that the ancients employed deduction chiefly in their scientific inquiries, while the moderns employ induction, proves to be too narrow, and fails upon close examination to point with sufficient distinctness the contrast that is evident between ancient and modern scientific doctrines and inquiries. For all knowledge is founded on observation, and proceeds from this by analysis and synthesis, by synthesis and analysis, by induction and deduction, and if possible by verification, or by new appeals to observation under the guidance of deduction,—by steps which are indeed correlative parts of one method; and the ancient sciences afford examples of every one of these methods, or parts of the one complete method, which have been generalized from the examples of science.

A failure to employ or to employ adequately any one of these partial methods, an imperfection in the arts and resources of observation and experiment, carelessness in observation, neglect of relevant facts, vagueness and carelessness in reasoning, and the failure to draw the consequences of theory and test them by appeal to experiment and observation,—these are the faults which cause all failures to ascertain truth, whether among the ancients or the moderns; but this statement does not explain why the mod-

22

ern is possessed of a greater virtue, and by what means he attained to his superiority. Much less does it explain the sudden growth of science in recent times.

The attempt to discover the explanation of this phenomenon in the antithesis of "facts" and "theories" or "facts" and "ideas,"—in the neglect among the ancients of the former, and their too exclusive attention to the latter,—proves also to be too narrow, as well as open to the charge of vagueness. For, in the first place, the antithesis is not complete. Facts and theories are not co-ordinate species. Theories, if true, are facts,—a particular class of facts indeed, generally complex ones, but still facts. Facts, on the other hand, even in the narrowest signification of the word, if they be at all complex, and if a logical connection subsists between their constituents, have all the positive attributes of theories.

Nevertheless, this distinction, however inadequate it may be to explain the source of true method in science, is well founded, and connotes an important character in true method. A fact is a proposition of which the verification by an appeal to the primary sources of our knowledge or to experience is direct and simple. A theory, on the other hand, if true, has all the characteristics of a fact, except that its verification is possible only by indirect, remote, and difficult means. To convert theories into facts is to add *simple verification,* and the theory thus acquires the full characteristics of a fact. When Pascal caused the Torricellian tube to be carried up the Puy de Dôme, and thus showed that the mercurial column was sustained by the weight of the atmosphere, he brought the theory of atmospheric pressure nearly down to the level of a fact of observation. But even in this most remarkable instance of scientific discovery theory was not wholly reduced to fact, since the verification, though easy, was not entirely simple, and was incomplete until further observations showed that the quantity of the fall in the Torricellian tube agreed with deductions from the combined theories of atmospherical pressure and elasticity. In the same way the theory of universal gravitation fails to become a fact in the proper sense of this word, however complete its verification, because this verification is not simple and direct, or through the immediate activity of our perceptive powers.

Modern science deals then no less with theories than with facts, but always as much as possible with the verification of theories,—if not to make them facts by simple verification through experiment and observation, at least to prove their truth by indirect verification.

The distinction of fact and theory thus yields an important principle, of which M. Comte and his followers have made much account. It is in the employment of verification, they say, and in the possibility of it, that the superiority of modern inductive research consists; and it is because the ancients did not, or could not, verify their theories, that they made such insignificant progress in science. It is indisputable that verification is essential to the completeness of scientific method; but there is still room for debate as to what constitutes verification in the various departments of philosophical inquiry. So long as the philosophy of method fails to give a complete inventory of our primary sources of knowledge, and cannot decide authoritatively what are the origins of first truths, or the truths of observation, so long will it remain uncertain what is a legitimate appeal to observation, or what is a real verification. The Platonists or the rationalists may equally with the empiricists claim verification for their theories; for do they not appeal to the reason for confirmation of deductions from their theories, which they regard as founded on observation of what the reason reveals to them?

The positivists' principle of verification comes, then, only to this,—that, inasmuch as mankind are nearly unanimous about the testimony and trustworthiness of their senses, but are divided about the validity of all other kinds of authority, which they in a word call the reason, or internal sense, therefore verification by the senses produces absolute conviction, while verification by the reason settles nothing, but is liable to the same uncertainty which attends the primary appeals to this authority for the data of speculative knowledge.

But not only does the so-called metaphysical philosophy employ a species of verification by appealing to the testimony of reason, consciousness, or internal sense; but the ancient physical sciences afford examples of the confirmation of theory by observation proper. The Ptolemaic system of astronomy was an instance of the employment of every one of the partial steps of true method; and the theory of epicycles not only sought to represent the facts of observation, but also by the prediction of astronomical phenomena to verify the truth of its representation. Modern astronomy does not proceed otherwise, except that its theories represent a much greater number of facts of observation, and are confirmed by much more efficient experimental tests.

The difference, then, between ancient and modern science is not truly characterized by any of the several explanations which have been proposed. The explanation, however, which, in our opinion, comes nearest to the true solution, and yet fails to designate the real point of difference, is that which the positivists find in the distinction between "objective method" and "subjective method." The objective method is verification by sensuous tests, tests of sensible experience,—a deduction from theory of consequences, of which we may have sensible experiences if they be true. The subjective method, on the other hand, appeals to the tests of internal evidence, tests of reason, and the data of self-consciousness. But whatever be the origin of the theories of science, whether from a systematic examination of empirical facts by conscious induction, or from the natural biases of the mind, the so-called intuitions of reason, in other words what seems probable without a distinct survey of our experiences,—whatever the origin, real or ideal, the *value* of these theories can only be tested, say the positivists, by an appeal to sensible experience, by deductions from them of consequences which we can confirm by the undoubted testimony of the senses. Thus, while ideal or transcendental elements are admitted into scientific researches, though in themselves insusceptible of simple verification, they must still show credentials from the senses, either by affording from themselves consequences capable of sensuous verification, or by yielding such consequences in conjunction with ideas which by themselves are verifiable.

It is undoubtedly true, that one of the leading traits of modern scientific research is this reduction of ideas to the tests of experience. The systematic development of ideas through induction from the first and simplest facts of observation, is by no means so obvious a characteristic. Inductions are still performed for the most part unconsciously and unsystematically. Ideas are developed by the sagacity of the expert, rather than by the systematic procedures of the philosopher. But when and however ideas are developed science cares nothing, for it is only by subsequent tests of sensible experience that ideas are admitted into the pandects of science.

It is of no consequence to scientific astronomy whence the theory of gravitation arose; whether as an induction from the theories of attractions and the law of radiations, or from the rational simplicity of this law itself, as the most natural supposition which could be made. Science asks no questions about the ontological pedigree or *a priori* character of a theory, but is content to judge it by its performance; and it is thus that a knowledge of nature, having all the certainty which the senses are competent to inspire, has been attained,—a knowledge which maintains a strict neutrality toward all philosophical systems, and concerns itself not at all with the genesis or *a priori* grounds of ideas.

This mode of philosophizing is not, however, exclusively found in modern scientific research. Ptolemy claimed for his epicycles only that "they saved the appearances;" and he might have said, with as much propriety as Newton, *"Hypotheses non fingo,"* for it was the aim of his research to represent abstractly, and by the most general formulas, the characteristics of the movements of the planets,—an aim which modern astronomy, with a much simpler hypothesis, and with immensely increased facilities, still pursues.

We find, therefore, that while moderns follow a true method of investigation with greater facilities and greater fidelity than the ancients, and with a clearer apprehension of its elements and conditions, yet that no new discoveries in method have been made, and no general sources of truth have been pointed out, which were not patent and known to the ancients; and we have so far failed to discover any solution to the problem with which we began. We have seen that it was not by the employment of a new method of research, but in the exercise of greater virtue in the use of old methods, that modern scientific researches have succeeded. But whence this greater virtue? What vivifying, energizing influence awakened the sixteenth century to the movement, which has continued down to the present day to engross, and even to create, the energies of philosophic thought in the study of natural phenomena? Obviously some interest was awakened, which had before been powerless, or had influenced only men of rare and extraordinary genius, or else some opposing interest had ceased to exercise a preponderating influence.

We have now arrived at a new order of inquiries. We ask no longer what are the differences of *method* between ancient and modern scientific researches, but we seek the difference in the *motives* which actuated the philosophic inquiries of the two periods. We seek for the interests which in modern times have so powerfully drawn men of all orders of intelligence to the pursuit of science, and to an observance of the conditions requisite for its successful prosecution. We do not inquire what course has led to successful answers in science, but what motives have prompted the pertinent questions.

In place of the positivists' phraseology, that the ancients followed "the subjective method," or appealed for the verification of their theories to natural beliefs, while the moderns follow "the objective method," or appeal to new and independent experimental evidence,—if we substitute the word "motive" for "method," we have the terms of one of the conclusions on which we wish to insist. But these require explanation.

By a subjective motive we mean one having its origin in natural universal human interests and emotions, which existed before philosophy was born, which continue to exist in the maturity of philosophy, and determine the character of an important and by no means defunct order of human speculations. By an objective motive we mean one having an empirical origin, arising in the course of an inquiry; springing from interests which are defined by what we already know, and not by what we have always felt,—interests which depend on acquired knowledge, and not on natural desires and emotions. Among the latter we must include the natural desire for knowledge, or the primitive, undisciplined sentiment of curiosity. This becomes an objective motive when it ceases to be associated with our fears, our respects, our aspirations,—our emotional nature; when it ceases to prompt questions as to what relates to our personal destiny, our ambitions, our moral worth; when it ceases to have man, his personal and social nature, as its central and controlling objects. A curiosity which is determined chiefly or solely by the felt imperfections of knowledge as such, and without reference to the uses this knowledge may subserve, is prompted by what we call an objective motive.

A spirit of inquiry which is freed from the influence of our active powers, and the interests that gave birth to theological and metaphysical philosophies,—which yields passively and easily to the direction of objective motives, to the felt imperfections of knowledge as such,—is necessarily, at all times, a weak feeling; and before a body of systematic, well-digested, and well-ascertained scientific truth had been generated, could hardly have had any persistent influence on the direction of inquiry.

The motives to theological and metaphysical speculation exist from the beginning of civilized human life in the active emotional nature of man. Curiosity as a love of the marvelous, or as a love of facts,—new facts, prized because they are new and stimulating,—also dates back of civilized life. These motives find play in human nature, as it emerges from a semi-animal state; but they also persist and determine the growth of the human mind in its most advanced development.

The questions of philosophy proper are human desires and fears and aspirations—human emotions—taking an intellectual form. Science follows, but does not supersede, this philosophy. The three phases which the positivists assign to the development of the human mind—the Theological, the Metaphysical, and the Positive or Scientific—are not in reality successive, except in their beginnings. They co-exist in all the highest developments of civilization and mental activity. They co-existed in the golden age of Greek civilization, in the intense mental activity of the Middle Ages. They move on together in this marvelous modern era. But until this latest epoch positive science was always the inferior philosophy,—hardly a distinct philosophy at all,—not yet born. But at the beginning of the modern era its gestation was completed. A body of knowledge existed, sufficiently extensive, coherent, and varied, to bear within it a life of its own,—an independent life,—which was able to collect to itself, by its own determinations, the materials of a continued, new, and ever-increasing mental activity,—an activity determined solely by an objective curiosity, or by curiosity in its purest, fullest, and highest energy.

We are probably indebted to the few men of scientific genius who lived during the slow advancement of modern civilization for the foundation of this culture,—for the accumulation of the knowledge requisite for this subsequent growth. These men were doubtless, for the most part, the products of their own time and civilization, as indeed all great men have been, but still originators, by concentrating and making productive the energies, tendencies, and knowledges which, but for them, would have remained inert and unfruitful. It is to such men, born at long intervals in the slow progress of civilization, each carrying forward a little the work of his predecessor, that we probably owe our modern science, rather than to the influence of any single mind, like Bacon, who was, like his predecessors, but the lens which collected the light of his times,—who prophesied rather than inaugurated the new era. And we owe science to the combined energies of individual men of genius, rather than to any tendency to progress inherent in civilization.

We find, then, the explanation of the modern development of science in the accumulation of a body of certified knowledge, sufficiently extensive to engage and discipline a rational scientific curiosity, and stimulate it to act independently of other motives. It is doubtless true that other motives have influenced this development, and especially that motives of material utility have had a powerful effect in stimulating inquiry. Ancient schools of philosophy despised narrow material utilities, the servile arts, and sought no instruction in what moderns dignify by the name of useful arts; but modern science finds in the requirements of the material arts the safest guide to exact knowledge. A theory which is utilized receives the highest possible certificate of truth. Navigation by the aid of astronomical tables, the magnetic telegraph, the innumerable utilities of mechanical and chemical science, are constant and perfect tests of scientific theories, and afford the standard of certitude, which science has been able to apply so extensively in its interpretations of natural phenomena.

But the motives proper to science, though purified by their dissociation from the subjective determinations and tendencies, which gave an anthropomorphic and teleological character to ancient views of nature, are not the only legitimate motives to philosophical inquiry. There is another curiosity purified by its association with the nobler sentiments,—with wonder, admiration, veneration,—and with the interests of our moral and æsthetical natures. This curiosity is the motive to philosophy proper. "Wonder is a highly philosophical affection," says Plato's Socrates; "indeed, there is no other principle of philosophy but this."

Curiosity determined by natural sentiments and emotions—subjective curiosity—is the cause of a culture co-extensive with civilization, long preceding the growth of science, and constituting all that is peculiar to civilized life except the material arts. However meanly the conclusions of theological and metaphysical speculations may appear, when tried by the objective standard of science, they too have their superiorities, by the test of which science becomes in turn insignificant. Unverified conclusions, vague ideas, crude fancies, they may be, but they certainly are the products of activities which constitute more of human happiness and human worth than the narrow material standards of science have been able to measure.

Philosophy proper should be classed with the Religions and with the Fine Arts, and estimated rather by the dignity of its motives, and the value it directs us to, than by the value of its own attainments. To condemn this pursuit because it fails to accomplish what science does, would be to condemn that which has formed in human nature habits, ideas, and associations on which all that is best in us depends,—would warrant the condemnation of science itself, since science scarcely existed at all for two thousand years of civilization, and represented as a distinct department during this period only the interests of the servile arts. The objects of Philosophy were those which the religious ideas and emotions of man presented to his speculative curiosity. These motives, though proper to Philosophy, also gave direction to inquiries in Physics and Astronomy. The Fine Arts sprang from the same interests, and persisted through the conservative power of religious interests in a development to which the modern world offers no parallel. We have no styles in Art, no persistently pursued efforts for perfection in beauty, because we are not held to the conditions of this perfection by the religious motives which directed ancient Art. The growth of Theology and Metaphysics is less vigorous now for the same reason. Theology was Philosophy developed in the interests of Religion or of religious feeling, and Metaphysics was cultivated in the interests of Theology. Both aimed at truth; both were determined by the same love of simplicity and unity in knowledge, which determines all search after truth; but neither cared for simple truth alone. When pursued for the truth of fact alone, they both degenerate into affectation and emptiness. We do not omit the sceptical philosophies of antiquity from this description, because they were not held independently of the religious interests of the orthodox philosophy, but in opposition to them or in criticism of them.

Theology and Metaphysics failed to apply a correct method and to arrive at certain results, not because philosophers were ignorant of method, but because the object-matters of their research were not questions of sensible experience,—were not mere questions of facts of which the mind is the passive recipient through the senses. Their aim was to *prove* truth, not to discover it,—to reduce opinions and ideas which had the warrant of religious associations to the simplicity and consistency of truth; and when ideas and opinions have this warrant, it does not require the verification of the senses to make the conclusions of Philosophy acceptable and true to the religious instincts. To educe conclusions acceptable to these instincts and in opposition to no known truth,—in other words, to free religious beliefs from contradictions and to give them consistency,—was the aspiration and the devoted service of Philosophy.

Philosophy has in fact three phases instead of two. For as Theology was a speculation prosecuted in the interest of religious feeling, and Metaphysics a speculation in defense or criticism of the doctrines of Theology, so Criticism or Critical Philosophy is an examination of metaphysical conclusions. But the latter is properly, in its motives, a scientific speculation. Such is the true logical order of Philosophy proper, though all these phases may and do co-exist in history.

It is the opinion of many modern thinkers, besides the so-called Positivists, or avowed followers of M. Comte, that science, as we have defined it, or truth pursued simply in the interests of a rational curiosity, and for the mental discipline and the material utilities of its processes and conclusions, will hereafter occupy more and more the attention of mankind, to the exclusion of the older philosophy. It is also the opinion of these thinkers, that this is not to be regretted, but rather welcomed as a step forward in the advancement of human welfare and civilization; that the pursuit of science and its utilities is capable of inspiring as great and earnest a devotion as those which religious interests have inspired, and which have hitherto determined the destinies of mankind and given form to human thought, and one vastly more beneficent.

Whatever foundations there are for these opinions, it is certain that the claims of science, as a new power in the world, to the regard of thoughtful and earnest men, are receiving a renewed and more candid attention. Through its recent progress, many of the questions which have hitherto remained in the arena of metaphysical disputation are brought forward in new forms and under new auspices. Scientific investigations promise to throw a flood of light on subjects which have interested mankind since the beginning of speculation,—subjects related to universal human interests. History, society, laws, and morality,—all are claimed as topics with which scientific methods are competent to deal. Scientific solutions are proposed to all the questions of philosophy which scientific illumination may not show to have their origin in metaphysical hallucination.

Prominent in the ranks of the new school stands Mr. Herbert Spencer, whose versatility has already given to the world many ingenious and original essays in this new philosophy, and whose aspiring genius projects many more, which, if his strength does not fail, are to develop the capacities of a scientific method in dealing with all the problems that ought legitimately to interest the human mind.

The programme of his future labors which his publishers have advertised might dispose a prejudiced critic to look with suspicion on what he has already accomplished; but the favorable impression which his works have made, and the plaudits of an admiring public, demand a suspension of judgment; and the extravagance of his pretensions should for the present be credited to the strength of his enthusiasm.

It is through the past labors of an author that we must judge of his qualifications for future work, and the completeness of his preparation. Mr. Spencer's writings evince an extensive knowledge of facts political and scientific, but extensive rather than profound, and mainly at second hand. It is not, of course, to be expected that a philosopher will be an original investigator in all the departments of knowledge with which he is obliged to have dealings. He must take much at second hand. But original investigations in some department of empirical science are a discipline which best tests and develops even a philosopher's powers. He has in this at least an experience of what is requisite to an adequate comprehension of facts. He learns how to make knowledge profitable to the ascertainment of new truths,—an art in which the modern natural philosopher excels. By new truths must be understood such as are not implied in what we already know, or educible from what is patent to common observation.

However skillfully the philosopher may apply his analytical processes to the abstraction of the truths involved in patent facts, the utility of his results will depend not so much on their value and extent as mere abstractions, as on their capacity to enlarge our experience by bringing to notice residual phenomena, and making us observe what we have entirely overlooked, or search out what has eluded our observation. Such is the character of the principles of modern natural philosophy, both mathematical and physical. They are rather the eyes with which nature is seen, than the elements and constituents of the objects discovered. It was in a clear apprehension of this value in the principles of mathematical and experimental science, that the excellence of Newton's genius consisted; and it is this value which the Positive Philosophy most prizes. But this is not the value which we find in Mr. Spencer's speculations.

Mr. Spencer is not a positivist, though that was not a very culpable mistake which confounded his speculations with the writings of this school. For however much he differs from the positivists in his methods and opinions, he is actuated by the same confidence in the capacities of a scientific method, and by the same disrespect for the older philosophies. Mr. Spencer applies a method for the ascertainment of ultimate truths, which a positivist would regard as correct only on the supposition that the materials of truth have all been collected, and that the research of science is no longer for the enlargement of our experience or for the informing of the mind. Until these conditions be realized, the positivist regards such attempts as Mr. Spencer's as not only faulty, but positively pernicious and misleading. Nothing justifies the development of abstract principles in science but their utility in enlarging our concrete knowledge of nature. The ideas on which mathematical Mechanics and the Calculus are founded, the morphological ideas of Natural History, and the theories of Chemistry are such working ideas,—finders, not merely summaries of truth. . . .

The idea which has exercised the profoundest influence on the course of Mr. Spencer's thought, as well as on all thought in modern times, and one which appears more or less distinctly in nearly all of Mr. Spencer's writings, is the idea which he elaborates in his "First Principles" as the "Law of Evolution." But what is the origin and value of this idea? Ostensibly it was derived from the investigations of the physiologists in embryology, from Harvey down to the present time. The formula of Von Baer was the first adequate statement of it. This formula Mr. Spencer has elaborated and completed, so as to apply, he thinks, not only to the phenomena of embryology, but to the phenomena of nature generally, and especially, as it appears, to those which we know least about, and to those which we only guess at.

But while this is the ostensible origin and scientific value of this idea, its real origin is a very curious and instructive fact in human nature. Progress is a grand idea,—Universal Progress is a still grander idea. It strikes the key-note of modern civilization. Moral idealism is the religion of our times. What the ideas God, the One and the All, the Infinite First Cause, were to an earlier civilization, such are Progress and Universal Progress to the modern world,—a reflex of its moral ideas and feelings, and not a tradition. Men ever worship the Best, and the consciousness that the Best is attainable is the highest moral consciousness, the most inspiring of truths. And when indications of that attainment are visible not merely to the eye of faith, but in sensible progress, scientifically measurable, civilization is inspired with a new devotion. Faith that moral perfectibility is possible, not in remote times and places, not in the millennium, not in heaven, but in the furtherance of a present progress, is a faith which to possess in modern times does not make a man suspected of folly or fanaticism. He may forget the past, cease to be religious in the conventional sense of the word, but he is the modern prophet.

When Plato forsook the scientific studies of his youth, and found the truest interpretations of nature by asking his own mind what was the best, according to which, he felt sure, the order and framework of nature must be determined, he did but illustrate the influence which strongly impressed moral ideas have on speculative thought at all times; but he did it consciously and avowedly. Modern thinkers may be less conscious of this influence, may endeavor to suppress what consciousness they have of it, warned by the history of philosophy that teleological speculations are exploded follies; nevertheless, the influence surrounds and penetrates them like an atmosphere, unless they be moral phlegmatics and mere lookers-on.

It was Mr. Spencer's aim to free the law of evolution from all teleological implications, and to add such elements and limitations to its definition as should make it universally applicable to the movement of nature. Having done this, as he thinks, he arrives at the following definition: "Evolution is a change from an indefinite incoherent homogeneity to a definite coherent heterogeneity through continuous differentiations and integrations." But teleology is a subtle poison, and lurks where least suspected. The facts of the sciences which Dr. Whewell calls palætiological, like the various branches of geology, and every actual concrete series of events which together form an object of interest to us, are apt, unless we are fully acquainted with the actual details through observation or by actual particular deductions from well-known particular facts and general laws, to fall into a dramatic procession in our imaginations. The mythic instinct slips into the place of the chronicles at every opportunity. All history is written on dramatic principles. All cosmological speculations are strictly teleological. We never can comprehend the whole of a concrete series of events. What arrests our attention in it is what constitutes the parts of an *order* either real or imaginary, and all merely imaginary orders are dramatic, or are determined by interests which are spontaneous in human life. Our speculations about what we have not really observed, to which we supply the order and most of the facts, are necessarily determined by some principle of order in our minds. Now the most general principle which we can have is this: that the concrete series shall be an intelligible series in its entirety; thus alone can it interest and attract our thoughts and arouse a rational curiosity.

But to suppose that such series exist anywhere but where observation and legitimate particular inferences from observation warrant the supposition, is to commit the same mistake which has given rise to teleological theories of nature. The "law of causation," the postulate of positive science, does not go to this extent. It does not suppose that there are throughout nature unbroken series in causation, forming in their entirety intelligible wholes, determinable in their beginnings, their progressions, and their ends, with a birth, a growth, a maturation, and a decay. It only presumes that the perhaps unintelligible wholes, both in the sequences and the co-existences of natural phenomena, are composed of intelligible elements; that chaos does not subsist at the heart of things; that the order in nature which is discernible vaguely even to the unobservant implies at least a precise *elementary* order, or fixed relations of antecedents and consequents in its ultimate parts and constituents; that the apparently irregular heterogeneous masses, the concrete series of events, are crystalline in their substance.

To discover these elementary fixed relations of antecedents and consequents, is the work of scientific induction; and the only postulate of science is, that these relations are everywhere to be found. To account, as far as possible, for any concrete order, intelligible as a whole, or regular, like that of life, is the work of scientific explanation, by deductions from the elementary fixed relations which induction may have discovered. But to explain any such order by simply defining it externally in vague, abstract terms, and to postulate such orders as the components of nature and parts of one complete and intelligible order, is to take a step in advance of legitimate speculation, and a step backward in scientific method,—is to commit the mistake of the ancient philosophies of nature.

But Mr. Spencer thinks he has established his "Law of Evolution" by induction. The examples from which he has analyzed his law, the examples of progress in the development of the several elements of civilization, such as languages, laws, fashions, and ideas,—the hypothetical examples of the Nebular Hypothesis and the Development Hypothesis, and the example of embryological development (the only one our conceptions of which are not liable to be tainted by teleological biases),—are examples which, according to Mr. Spencer's philosophy, afford both the definition and its justification. In other words, his definitions are only carefully elaborated general descriptions in abstract terms; or statements of facts which are observed in numerous instances or classes of instances, in terms detached from all objects, in abstract terms, of which the intension is fully known, but of which the extension is unknown except through the descriptions they embody. This, though a useful, is a precarious kind of induction, and is apt to lead to premature and false generalizations, or extensions of descriptions to what is hypothetical or unknown. Such inductions are liable to be mistaken for another sort, and to be regarded as not merely general, but universal descriptions, and as applicable to what they do not really apply to. This liability is strong just in proportion as prominence is given to such definitions in a philosophical system. No convert to Mr. Spencer's philosophy doubts the substantial correctness of the Nebular and Development Hypotheses, though these are only hypothetical examples of Mr. Spencer's law.

The other sort of inductions to which we have referred are peculiar to the exact inductive sciences. Facts which are not merely general, but, from their elementary character and their immediate relations to the orderliness of nature, are presumed to be universal facts, are the sort which the positive philosophy most prizes, and of which the law of gravitation is the typical example. The honor must be conceded to Mr. Spencer of having elaborated a precise and very abstract description of certain phenomena, the number, the other characters, and the extent of which are, however, unknown, but are all the more imposing from this circumstance.

The law of gravity was a key which deciphered a vast body of otherwise obscure phenomena, and (what is more to the purpose) was successfully applied to the solution of all the problems these phenomena presented. It is common to ascribe to Newton the merit of having discovered the law of gravity, in the same sense in which Mr. Spencer may be said to have discovered his law. The justness of this praise may well be doubted; for others had speculated and defined the law of gravity before Newton. What he really discovered was the *universality* of this law, or so nearly discovered it that the astronomers who completed the investigation did not hesitate to concede to him the full honor. He established for it such a degree of probability that his successors pursued the verification with unhesitating confidence, and still pursue it in the fullness of faith.

Mr. Spencer's law is founded on examples, of which only one class, the facts of embryology, are properly scientific. The others are still debated as to their real characters. Theories of society and of the character and origin of social progress, theories on the origins and the changes of organic forms, and theories on the origins and the causes of cosmical bodies and their arrangements, are all liable to the taint of teleological and cosmological conceptions,—to spring from the order which the mind imposes upon what it imperfectly observes, rather than from that which the objects, were they better known, would supply to the mind.

To us Mr. Spencer's speculation seems but the abstract statement of the cosmological conceptions, and that kind of orderliness which the hu-

man mind spontaneously supplies in the absence of facts sufficiently numerous and precise to justify sound scientific conclusions. Progress and
development, when they mean more than a continuous proceeding, have
a meaning suspiciously like what the moral and mythic instincts are inclined to,—something having a beginning, a middle, and an end,—an epic
poem, a dramatic representation, a story, a cosmogony. It is not sufficient
for the purposes of science that the idea of progress be freed from any
reference to human happiness as an end. Teleology does not consist entirely of speculations having happy *dénouements,* save that the perfection
or the end to which the progress tends is a happiness to the intellect that
contemplates it in its evolution and beauty of orderliness. Plato's astronomical speculations were teleological in this artistic sense.

It is not sufficient for the purposes of science, that the idea of progress
be thus purified; and it would be better if science itself were purified of
this idea, at least until proof of its extent and reality be borne in upon the
mind by the irresistible force of a truly scientific induction. Aristotle exhibited the characteristics of scientific genius in no way more distinctly
than in the rejection of this idea, and of all cosmological speculations.

But there is a truth implied in this idea, and an important one,—the
truth, namely, that the proper objects of scientific research are all of them
processes and the results of processes; not the immutable natures which
Plato sought for above a world of confusion and unreality, in the world
of his own intelligence, but the immutable elements in the orders of all
changes, the permanent relations of co-existences and sequences, which
are hidden in the confusions of complex phenomena. Thought itself is a
process and the mind a complex series of processes, the immutable elements of which must be discovered, not merely by introspection or by
self consciousness, but by the aid of physiological researches and by indirect observation. Everything out of the mind is a product, the result of
some process. Nothing is exempt from change. Worlds are formed and
dissipated. Races of organic beings grow up like their constituent individual members, and disappear like these. Nothing shows a trace of an
original, immutable nature, except the unchangeable laws of change. These
point to no beginning and to no end in time, nor to any bounds in space.
All indications to the contrary in the results of physical research are
clearly traceable to imperfections in our present knowledge of all the laws
of change, and to that disposition to cosmological speculations which still
prevails even in science.

We propound these doctrines not as established ones, but as having a
warrant from the general results of physical research similar to that which
the postulate of science, the law of causation, has in the vaguely discerned
order in nature, which forces itself on the attention even of the unobservant. But as a mind unfamiliar with science is easily persuaded that
there are phenomena in nature to which the law of causation does not

apply, phenomena intrinsically arbitrary and capricious, so even to those most familiar with our present knowledge of physical laws, but who have not attended to the implication of their general characters and relations, the supposition is not incredible that there is a tendency in the forces of nature to a permanent or persistently progressive change in the theatre of their operations, and to an ultimate cessation of all the particular conditions on which their manifestations depend. . . .

Limits of Natural Selection

FEW SCIENTIFIC THEORIES HAVE MET WITH SUCH A CORDIAL RECEPTION by the world of scientific investigators, or created in so short a time so complete a revolution in general philosophy, as the doctrine of the derivation of organic species by Natural Selection; perhaps in this respect no other can compare with it when we consider the incompleteness of the proofs on which it still relies, or the previous prejudice against the main thesis implied in it, the theory of the development or transmutation of species. The Newtonian theory of gravity, or Harvey's theory of the circulation of the blood, in spite of the complete and overwhelming proofs by which these were soon substantiated, were much longer in overcoming to the same degree the deeply-rooted prejudices and preconceptions opposed to them. In less than a decade the doctrine of Natural Selection had conquered the opposition of the great majority of the students of natural history, as well as of the students of general philosophy; and it seems likely that we shall witness the unparalleled spectacle of an all but universal reception by the scientific world of a revolutionary doctrine in the lifetime of its author; though by the rigorous tests of scientific induction it will yet hardly be entitled to more than the rank of a very probable hypothesis. How is this singular phenomenon to be explained? Doubtless in great part by the extraordinary skill which Mr. Darwin has brought to the proof and promulgation of his views.

But the skillful combination of inductive and deductive proofs with hypothesis, though a powerful engine of scientific discovery, must yet work upon the basis of a preceding and simpler induction. Pythagoras would never have demonstrated the "forty-seventh," if he had not had some ground of believing in it beforehand. The force and value of the preceding and simpler induction have been obscured in this case by subsequent investigations. And yet that more fundamental evidence accounts for the fact that two such skillful observers and reasoners as Mr. Wallace and Mr. Darwin arrived at the same convictions in regard to the derivation of species, in entire independence of each other, and were constrained to accept the much-abused and almost discarded "transmutation hypothesis." And both moreover reached, independently, the same explanation of the process of derivation. This was obviously from their similar experiences as naturalists; from the force of the same obscure and puzzling facts which their studies of the geographical distributions of animals and plants had brought to their notice, though the Malthusian doctrine of population was, doubtless, the original source of their common theory. Mr. Darwin, in the Introduction to his later work on "The Variation of Animals and Plants under Domestication," attributes the beginnings of his speculations to the phenomena of the distributions of life over large continental areas, and in the islands of large archipelagoes, and especially refers to the curious phenomena of life in the Galapagos Islands in the Pacific Ocean. Mr. Wallace, in his first essay, originally published in 1855, four years earlier than "The Origin of Species," refers to the same class of facts, and the same special facts in regard to the Galapagos Islands, as facts which demand the transmutation hypothesis for their sufficient explanation.

While then much is to be credited to the sagacity and candor of these most accomplished travelers and observers in appreciating the force of obscure and previously little studied facts, yet their theoretical discussions of the hypothesis brought forward to explain them have been of still more importance in arousing an ever-increasing activity in the same field, and in creating a new and most stimulating interest in the external economy of life,—in the relations of living beings to the special conditions of their existence. And so the discussion is no longer closet work. It is no web woven from self-consuming brains, but a vast accumulation of related facts of observation, bound together by the bond of what must still be regarded as an hypothesis,—an hypothesis, however, which has no rival with any student of nature in whose mind reverence does not, in some measure, neutralize the aversion of the intellect to what is arbitrary.

In anticipating the general acceptance of the doctrine which Mr. Darwin and Mr. Wallace have done so much to illustrate, we ought to except those philosophers who, from a severe, ascetic, and self-restraining temper, or from preoccupation with other researches, are disposed to regard such speculations as beyond the proper province of scientific inquiry. But to stop short in a research of "secondary causes," so long as experience or reason can suggest any derivation of laws and relations in nature which must otherwise be accepted as ultimate facts, is not agreeable to that Aristotelian type of mind which scientific culture so powerfully tends to produce. Whatever the theological tendencies of such a mind, whether ultimate facts are regarded by it as literally arbitrary, the decrees of an absolute will, or are summarily explained by what Professor De Morgan calls "that exquisite atheism, 'the nature of things,'" it still cannot look upon the intricate system of adaptations, peculiar to the organic world (which illustrates what Cuvier calls "the principle of *the conditions of existence,* vulgarly called the principle of *final causes*"),—it cannot look upon this as an arbitrary system, or as composed of facts independent of all ulterior facts (like the axioms of mechanics or arithmetic or geometry), so long as any explanation, not tantamount to arbitrariness itself, has any probability in the order of nature. This scientific instinct stops far short of an irreverent attitude of mind, though it does not permit things that claim its reverence to impede its progress. And so a class of facts, of which the organical sciences had previously made some use as instruments of scientific discovery, but which was appropriated especially to the reasonings of Natural Theology, has fallen to the province of the discussions of Natural Selection, and has been wonderfully enlarged in consequence. It cannot be denied that this change has weakened the force of the *arguments* of Natural Theology; but it is simply by way of subtraction or by default, and not as offering any arguments opposed to the main conclusions of theology. "Natural Selection is not inconsistent with Natural Theology," in the sense of refuting the main conclusions of that science; it only reduces to the condition of an arbitrary assumption one important point in the interpretation of special adaptations in organic life, namely, the assumption that in such adaptations foresight and special provision is shown, analogous to the designing, anticipatory imaginings and volitions in the mental actions of the higher animals, and especially in the mind of man.

Upon this point the doctrine of Natural Selection assumes only such general anticipation of the wants or advantages of an animal or plant as is implied in the laws of inheritance. That is, an animal or plant is produced adapted to the *general* conditions of its existence, with only such anticipations of a change or of varieties in these conditions as is implied in its *general* tendency to vary from the inherited type. Particular uses have no special causal relations to the variations that occur and become of use. In other words, Natural Selection, as an hypothesis, does not assume, and, so far as it is based on observation, it affords no evidence, that any adaptation is specially anticipated in the order of nature. From this point of view, the wonderfully intricate system of special adaptations in the organic world is, at any epoch of its history, altogether retrospective. Only so far as the past affords a type of the future, both in the organism itself and in its external conditions, can the conditions of existence be said to determine the adaptations of life. As thus interpreted, the doctrine of Final Causes is deprived of the feature most obnoxious to its opponents, that abuse of the doctrine "which makes the cause to be engendered by the effect." But it is still competent to the devout mind to take a broader view of the organic world, to regard, not its single phases only, but the whole system from its first beginnings as presupposing all that it exhibits, or has exhibited, or could exhibit, of the contrivances and adaptations which may thus in one sense be said to be foreordained. In this view, however, the organical sciences lose their traditional and peculiar value to the arguments of Natural Theology, and become only a part of the universal order of nature, like the physical sciences generally, in the principles of which philosophers have professed to find no sign of a divinity. But may they not, while professing to exclude the *idea* of God from their systems, have really included him unwittingly, as immanent in the very thought that denies, in the very systems that ignore him?

So far as Natural Theology aims to prove that the principles of utility and adaptation are all-pervasive laws in the organic world, Natural Selection is not only not inconsistent, but is identical with it. But here Natural Selection pauses. It does not go on to what has been really the peculiar province of Natural Theology, to discover, or trace the analogies of organic adaptations to proper designs, or to the anticipations of wants and advantages in the mental actions of man and the higher animals. In themselves these mental actions bear a striking resemblance to those aspects of organic life in general, which Natural Selection regards; and according to the views of the experiential psychologist, this resemblance is not a mere analogy. In themselves, and without reference to the external uses of these mental actions, they are the same generalized reproductions of a past experience as those which the organic world exhibits in its laws of inheritance, and are modified by the same tentative powers and processes of variation, but to a much greater degree. But here the resemblance ceases. The relations of such mental actions to the external life of an organism, in which they are truly prophetic and providential agencies, though founded themselves on the observation of a past order in experience, are entirely unique and unparalleled, so far as any assumption in the doctrine of Natural Selection, or any proofs which it adduces are concerned. Nevertheless a greater though vaguer analogy remains. *Some* of the wants and adaptations of men and animals are anticipated by their designing mental actions. Does not a like foreseeing power, ordaining and governing the whole of nature, anticipate and specially provide for *some* of its adaptations? This appears to be the distinctive position in which Natural Theology now stands.

We have dwelt somewhat at length on this aspect of our author's subject, with reference to its bearing on his philosophical views, set forth in his concluding essay on "The Limits of Natural Selection as applied to Man," in which his theological position appears to be that which we have just defined. . . . Mr. Wallace thinks, and argues in his concluding essay, that this marvelous being, the human mind, cannot be a product of Natural Selection; that some, at least, of the mental and moral qualities of man are beyond the jurisdiction and measure of utility; that Natural Selection has its limits, and that among the most conspicuous examples of its failure to explain the order of nature are the more prominent and characteristic distinctions of the human race. . . .

In his obvious anxiety to establish for the worth of human nature the additional dignity of metaphysical isolation, Mr. Wallace maintains the extraordinary thesis that "the brain of the savage is larger than he needs it to be"; from which he would conclude that there is in the size of the savage's brain a special anticipation or prophecy of the civilized man, or even of the philosopher, though the inference would be far more natural, and entirely consistent with Natural Selection, that the savage has degenerated from a more advanced condition. The proofs of our author's position consist in showing that there is a very slight difference between the average size of the savage's brain and that of the European, and that even in prehistoric man the capacity of the skull approaches very near to that of the modern man, as compared to the largest capacity of anthropoid skulls. Again, the size of the brain is a measure of intellectual power, as proved by the small size of idiotic brains, and the more than average size of the brains of great men, or "those who combine acute perception with great reflective powers, strong passions, and general energy of character." By these considerations "the idea is suggested of a surplusage of power, of an instrument beyond the needs of its possessor." From a rather artificial and arbitrary measure of intellectual power, the scale of marks in university examinations, as compared to the range of sizes in brains, Mr. Wallace concludes it to be fairly inferred, "that the savage possesses a brain capable, if cultivated and developed, of performing work of a kind and degree far beyond what he ever requires it to do." But how far removed is this conclusion from the idea that the savage has more brains than he needs! Why may it not be that all that he can do with his brains beyond his needs is only incidental to the powers which are directly serviceable? Of what significance is it that his brain is twice as great as that of the man-ape, while the philosopher only surpasses him one sixth, so long as we have no real measure of the brain power implied in the one universal characteristic of humanity, the power of language,—that is, the power to invent and use arbitrary signs?

Mr. Wallace most unaccountably overlooks the significance of what has always been regarded as the most important distinction of the human race, —its rationality as shown in language. He even says that "the mental requirements of savages, and the faculties actually exercised by them, are very little above those of animals." We would not call in question the accuracy of Mr. Wallace's observations of savages; but we can hardly accord equal credit to his accuracy in estimating the mental rank of their faculties. No doubt the savage mind seems very dull as compared with the sagacity shown by many animals; but a psychological analysis of the faculty of language shows that even the smallest proficiency in it might require more brain power than the greatest in any other direction. For this faculty implies a complete inversion of the ordinary and natural orders of association in the mind, or such an inversion as in mere parroting would be implied by the repetition of the words of a sentence in an inverse order,—a most difficult feat even for a philosopher. "The power of abstract reasoning and ideal conception," which Mr. Wallace esteems as a very great advance on the savage's proficiency, is but another step in the same direction, and here, too, *ce n'est que le premier pas qui coûte.* It seems probable enough that brain power proper, or its spontaneous and internal determinations of the perceptive faculties, should afford directly that *use* or *command* of a *sign* which is implied in language, and essentially consists in the power of turning back the attention from a suggested fact or idea to the suggesting ones, with reference to their use, in place of the naturally passive following and subserviency of the mind to the orders of first impressions and associations. By inverting the proportions which the latter bear to the forces of internal impressions, or to the powers of imagination in animals, we should have a fundamentally new order of mental actions; which, with the requisite motives to them, such as the social nature of man would afford, might go far towards defining the relations, both mental and physical, of human races to the higher brute animals. Among these the most sagacious and social, though they may understand language, or follow its significations, and even by indirection acquire some of its uses, yet have no direct *power of using,* and no power of *inventing* it. . . .

The theories of associational psychology are so admirably adapted to the solution of problems, for which Mr. Wallace seems obliged to call in the aid of miracles, that we are surprised he was not led by his studies to a more careful consideration of them. Thus in regard to the nature of the moral sense, which Mr. Wallace defines in accordance with the intuitional theory as "a feeling,—a sense of right and wrong,—in our nature, antecedent to, and independent of, experiences of utility,"—this sense is capable of an analysis which meets and answers very simply the difficulties he finds in it on the theory of Natural Selection. The existence of feelings of approval and disapproval, or of likings and aversions to certain classes of actions, and a sense of obligation, are eminently useful in the government of human society, even among savages. These feelings may be associated with the really useful and the really harmful classes of actions, or they may not be. Such associations are not determined simply by utility, any oftener than beliefs are by proper evidence. But utility tends to produce the proper associations; and in this, along with the increase of these feelings themselves, consists the moral progress of the race. Why should not a fine sense of honor and an uncompromising veracity be found, then, among savage tribes, as in certain instances cited by Mr. Wallace; since moral feelings, or the motives to the observance of rules of conduct, lie at the foundation of even the simplest human society, and rest directly on the utility of man's political nature; and since veracity and honor are not merely useful, but indispensable in many relations, even in savage lives? Besides, veracity being one of the earliest developed instincts of childhood, can hardly with propriety be regarded as an original moral instinct, since it matures much earlier than the sense of obligation, or any feeling of the sanctity of truth. It belongs rather to that social and intellectual part of human nature from which language itself arises. The desire of communication, and the desire of communicating the truth, are originally identical in the ingenuous social nature. Is not this the source of the "mystical sense of wrong," attached to untruthfulness, which is, after all, regarded by mankind at large as so venial a fault? It needs but little early moral discipline to convert into a strong moral sentiment so natural an instinct. Deceitfulness is rather the acquired quality, so far as utility acts directly on the development of the individual, and for his advantage; but the native instinct of veracity is founded on the more primitive utilities of society and human intercourse. Instead, then, of regarding veracity as an original moral instinct, "antecedent to, and independent of, experiences of utility," it appears to us more natural to regard it as originally an intellectual and social instinct, founded in the broadest and most fundamental utilities of human nature.

The extension of the moral nature beyond the bounds of the necessities and utilities of society does not require a miracle to account for it; since, according to the principles of the associational psychology, it follows necessarily from the elementary laws of the mind. The individual experiences of utility which attach the moral feelings to rules of conduct are more commonly those of rewards and punishments, than of the direct or natural consequences of the conduct itself; and associations thus formed come to supersede all conscious reference to rational ends, and act upon the will in the manner of an instinct. The uncalculating, uncompromising moral imperative is not, it is true, derived from the individual's direct experiences of its utility; but neither does the instinct of the bee, which sacrifices its life in stinging, bear any relation to its individual advantage. Are we warranted, then, in inferring that the sting is useless to the bee? Suppose that whole communities of bees should occasionally be sacrificed to their instinct of self-defense, would this prove their instinct to be independent of a past or present utility, or to be prophetic of some future development of the race? Yet such a conclusion would be exactly parallel to that which Mr. Wallace draws from the fact that savages some times deal honorably with their enemies to their own apparent disadvantage. It is a universal law of the organic world, and a necessary consequence of Natural Selection, that the individual comprises in its nature chiefly what is useful to the race, and only incidentally what is useful to itself; since it is the race, and not the individual, that endures or is preserved. This contrast is the more marked in proportion as a race exhibits a complicated polity or social form of life; and man, even in his savage state, "is more political than any bee or ant." The doctrine of Natural Selection awakens a new interest in the problems of psychology. Its inquiries are not limited to the origin of species. "In the distant future," says Mr. Darwin, "I see open fields for far more important researches. Psychology will be based on a new foundation,—that of the necessary acquirements of each mental power and capacity by gradation. Light will be thrown on the origin of man and his history." More light we are sure can be expected from such researches than has been discovered by Mr. Wallace, in the principles and analysis of a mystical and metaphysical psychology.

The "origin of consciousness," or of sensation and thought, is relegated similarly by Mr. Wallace to the immediate agency or interposition of a metaphysical cause, as being beyond the province of secondary causes, which could act to produce it under the principle of Natural Selection. And it is doubtless true, nay, unquestionable, that sensation as a simple nature, with the most elementary laws of its activity, does really belong to the primordial facts in that constitution of nature, which is presupposed by the principle of utility as the ground or condition of the fitnesses through which the principle acts. In like manner the elements of organization, or the capacities of living matter in general, must be posited as antecedent to the mode of action which has produced in it, and through its elementary laws, such marvelous results. But if we mean by "consciousness" what the word is often and more properly used to express,—that total and complex structure of sensibilities, thoughts, and emotions in an animal mind, which is so closely related to the animal's complex physical organization,—so far is this from being beyond the province of Natural Selection, that it affords one of the most promising fields for its future investigations. . . .*

A much simpler conception than our author's theory, and one that seems to us far more probable is that the phenomena of conscious volition involve in themselves no proper efficiencies or forces coming under the law of the conservation of force, but are rather natural types of causes, purely and absolutely *regulative,* which add nothing to, and subtract nothing from, the quantities of natural forces. No doubt there is in the actions

* . . . The present superiority of the most civilized races, so far as it is independent of any external inheritance of arts, knowledges, and institutions, would appear to depend chiefly upon the *quality* of their brains, and upon characteristics belonging to their moral and emotional natures rather than the intellectual, since the intellectual acquisitions of civilization are more easily communicated by education to the savage than the refinements of its moral and emotional characteristics. Though all records and traces of this development are gone, and a wide gulf separates the lowest man from the highest brute animal, yet elements exist by which we may trace the succession of utilities and advantages that have determined the transition. The most essential are those of the social nature of man, involving mutual assistance in the struggle for existence. Instrumental to these are his mental powers, developed by his social nature, and by the reflective character of his brain's action into a general and common intelligence, instead of the specialized instincts and sagacities characteristic of other animals; and from these came language, and thence all the arts, knowledges, governments, traditions, all the external inheritances, which, reacting on his social nature, have induced the sentiments of morality, worship, and refinement; at which gazing as in a mirror he sees his past, and thinks it his future.

of the nervous system a much closer resemblance than this to a machine. No doubt it is automatically regulated, as well as moved, by physical forces; but this is probably just in proportion as its agency—as in our habits and instincts—is removed from our conscious control. All this machinery is below, beyond, external, or foreign to our consciousness. The profoundest, most attentive introspection gains not a glimpse of its activity, nor do we ever dream of its existence; but both by the laws of its operations, and by the means through which we become aware of its existence, it stands in the broadest, most fundamental contrast to our mental natures; and these, so far from furnishing a type of physical efficiency in our conscious volitions, seem to us rather, in accordance with their general contrast with material phenomena, to afford a type of purely regulative causes, or of an absolutely forceless and unresisted control and regulation of those forces of nature which are comprised in the powers of organic life. Perhaps a still higher type of such regulation is to be found in those "laws of nature," which, without adding to, or subtracting from, the real forces of nature, determine the order of their conversions by *"fixed, stated,* or *settled"* rules of succession; and these may govern also, and probably do govern, the successions of our mental or self-conscious states, both in themselves and in their relations to material conditions. . . .

But it may be said, and it often is said, "that this theory of the Will's agency is directly contradicted in both its features by consciousness; that we are immediately conscious both of energy and freedom in willing." There is much in our volitional consciousness to give countenance to this contradiction; but it is only such as dreams give to contradictions of rational experience. The words "force," "energy," "effort," "resistance," "conflict," all point to states of feeling in our volitional consciousness which seem to a superficial observation to be true intuitions of spontaneous self-originated causes; and it is only when these states of feeling are tested by the scientific definitions and the objective measure of forces, and by the orders of the conversions of force, that they are found to be only vague, subjective accompaniments, instead of distinct objective apprehensions or perceptions of what "force" signifies in science. Such tests prove them to be like the complementary or subjective colors of vision. In one sense they are intuitions of force, our only intuitions of it (as the aspects of nature are our only intuitions of the system of the world); but they are not true perceptions, since they do not afford, each feeling in itself, definite and invariable indications of force as an objective existence, or as affecting all minds alike. Even the sense of weight is no proper measure of weight as an element of force; and the muscular effort of lifting is only a vague and variable perception of this conversion of force, and does not afford even a hint of the great law of the conservation and convertibility of forces, but, on the contrary, seems to contradict it. The muscular feeling of resistance to motion or to a change of motion is an equally vague measure of *inertia*. Indeed, the feelings of weight and resistance, which are often regarded as intuitions of gravity and inertia, are insusceptible of precise measurement or numerical comparison; and though capable of being trained to some degree of precision in estimating what is properly measured by other means, they could never have revealed through their unaided indications the law of the fixed and universal proportionality of these two forces. The feeling of effort itself (more or less intense, and more or less painful, according to circumstances, which are quite irrelevant to its apparent effect) appears by the testimony of consciousness to be the immediate cause of the work which is done,—work really done by forces in the vital organism, which only the most recondite researches of science have disclosed. But if this much-vaunted authority of immediate consciousness so blunders in even the simplest cases, how can our author or any judicious thinker trust its unconfirmed, unsupported testimony in regard to the agency of the Will? Is it not like trusting the testimony of the senses as to the immobility of the earth?

With hardly a point, therefore, of Mr. Wallace's concluding essay are we able to agree; and this impresses us the more, since we find nothing in the rest of his book which appears to us to call for serious criticism, but many things, on the contrary, which command our most cordial admiration. We account for it by the supposition that his metaphysical views, carefully excluded from his scientific work, are the results of an earlier and less severe training than that which has secured to us his valuable positive contributions to the theory of Natural Selection. Mr. Wallace himself is fully aware of this contrast, and anticipates a scornful rejection of his theory by many who in other respects agree with him.

The doctrines of the special and prophetic providences and decrees of God, and of the metaphysical isolation of human nature, are based, after all, on barbaric conceptions of dignity, which are restricted in their application by every step forward in the progress of science. And the sense of security they give us of the most sacred things is more than replaced by the ever-growing sense of the universality of inviolable laws,—laws that underlie our sentiments and desires, as well as all that these can rationally regard in the outer world. It is unfortunate that the prepossessions of religious sentiment in favor of metaphysical theories should make the progress of science always seem like an indignity to religion, or a detraction from what is held as most sacred; yet the responsibility for this belongs neither to the progress of science nor to true religious sentiment, but to a false conservatism, an irrational respect for the ideas and motives of a philosophy which finds it more and more difficult with every advance of knowledge to reconcile its assumptions with facts of observation.

CHARLES PEIRCE

(1839-1914)

Charles Peirce was the son of the distinguished Harvard mathematician, Benjamin Peirce. Born at Cambridge in 1839, he died in 1914 after a career of unusual achievement in logic, geodesy, meteorology, philosophy and other subjects. His originality and brilliance were recognized during his lifetime by Bertrand Russell, James, Royce and Dewey, all of whom acknowledge his great influence upon them. But though he was a close friend of Chauncey Wright, and of William and Henry James and others, Peirce's work was known to only a relatively small circle while he lived. He never received a regular university appointment—in part, probably, because his private life left something to be desired from the point of view of the conventions. And as he grew older, the failure of his path-breaking work in the logic of relations to stir much interest as well as the popular success of cruder and softer versions of pragmatism than his own seem to have discouraged him, and to have led to an increasing crotchetiness and involution in his writing. At any rate, despite the fact that Peirce was immensely learned, and that he had both imagination and a gift for the telling phrase, he did not succeed in having any of his philosophical work published in book form.

Peirce's reputation today, however, is immeasurably improved. He is now generally regarded as the most logically acute of all the pragmatists and as the originator of most of the central ideas in this philosophy. His argument that general ideas are habits of inference not only placed ideas in a biological setting but represented a cogent answer to the belief that general ideas have no existence of their own and are merely shorthand summaries of our observations of individual things. In his insistence that inquiry is a social affair, the activity of a community of men joined together by common procedures and goals, he gave a sociological and naturalistic account of traditional intellectual ideals like "objectivity" and "rational proof." Further, he made it plain that the fundamental value of an idea lies neither in its psychological effects on those who hold it nor even in its capacity to solve a particular problem, but in its role in further-ing the unending process of inquiry itself. Peirce's pragmatism was a theory of the way human ideas hang together and of the sort of evidence *that supports them. It challenged traditional ideals of reason, proposed an alternative to both dogmatism and wholesale skepticism, and suggested a method by which philosophical problems could be treated more firmly and clearly than they had in the past. In its fundamental intentions and logic, it should be added, it was radically different from the pragmatism of James, and Peirce eventually came to call his own philosophy "pragmaticism" to underline the difference.*

Peirce, however, also influenced a great many thinkers outside pragmatic circles. Reading Peirce's essays constitutes, indeed, something close to a short introduction to contemporary philosophy. He is one of those responsible for restoring mathematics to an important place in philosophy, and Bertrand Russell's contributions to mathematical logic were based originally on a combination of Peirce's work and that of the Italian logician, Peano. But Peirce also had a strong influence on less scientifically minded philosophers. His essay, "The Law of Mind," greatly affected the later development of Royce's philosophy, and Royce's theory of the universe as a "Universal Community" is a metaphysical extension of Peirce's doctrine that ideas acquire their meaning from their place in the cooperative inquiries of the scientific community. Indeed, though Peirce is the inventor of the term "pragmatism" and the unmistakable author of that philosophy's central ideas, his work as a whole cannot be characterized as "pragmatic" or "empirical." He brought the spirit of laboratory science to philosophy, but he also brought the tradition of romantic idealists like Schelling.

Peirce's works have now been gathered together in his Collected Papers, *edited by Charles Hartshorne and Paul Weiss, and published by the Harvard University Press. "Concerning the Author," the first of the following selections, was written about 1897. "The Fixation of Belief" and "How to Make Our Ideas Clear," the two essays in which Peirce developed the basic ideas of pragmatism, appeared in* Popular Science Monthly *in November, 1877, and January, 1878. "Evolutionary Love," in which Peirce stated his moral and speculative reactions to the ideas of Darwin and Spencer, appeared in* The Monist *in 1893. "What Pragmatism Is" appeared in the same periodical in 1905, and offers Peirce's retrospective and reconsidered account of pragmatism.*

Concerning the Author

THE READER HAS A RIGHT TO KNOW HOW THE AUTHOR'S OPINIONS WERE formed. Not, of course, that he is expected to accept any conclusions which are not borne out by argument. But in discussions of extreme difficulty, like these, when good judgment is a factor, and pure ratiocination is not everything, it is prudent to take every element into consideration. From the moment when I could think at all, until now, about forty years, I have been diligently and incessantly occupied with the study of methods [of] inquiry, both those which have been and are pursued and those which ought to be pursued. For ten years before this study began, I had been in training in the chemical laboratory. I was thoroughly grounded not only in all that was then known of physics and chemistry, but also in the way in which those who were successfully advancing knowledge proceeded. I have paid the most attention to the methods of the most exact sciences, have intimately communed with some of the greatest minds of our times in physical science, and have myself made positive contributions —none of them of any very great importance, perhaps—in mathematics, gravitation, optics, chemistry, astronomy, etc. I am saturated, through and through, with the spirit of the physical sciences. I have been a great student of logic, having read everything of any importance on the subject, devoting a great deal of time to medieval thought, without neglecting the works of the Greeks, the English, the Germans, the French, etc., and have produced systems of my own both in deductive and in inductive logic. In metaphysics my training has been less systematic; yet I have read and deeply pondered upon all the main systems, never being satisfied until I was able to think about them as their own advocates thought.

The first strictly philosophical books that I read were of the classical German schools; and I became so deeply imbued with many of their ways of thinking that I have never been able to disabuse myself of them. Yet my attitude was always that of a dweller in a laboratory, eager only to learn what I did not yet know, and not that of philosophers bred in theological seminaries, whose ruling impulse is to teach what they hold to be infallibly true. I devoted two hours a day to the study of Kant's *Critic of the Pure Reason* for more than three years, until I almost knew the whole book by heart, and had critically examined every section of it. For about two years, I had long and almost daily discussions with Chauncey Wright, one of the most acute of the followers of J. S. Mill.

The effect of these studies was that I came to hold the classical German philosophy to be, upon its argumentative side, of little weight; although I esteem it, perhaps am too partial to it, as a rich mine of philosophical suggestions. The English philosophy, meagre and crude, as it is, in its conceptions, proceeds by surer methods and more accurate logic. The doctrine of the association of ideas is, to my thinking, the finest piece of philosophical work of the prescientific ages. Yet I can but pronounce English sensationalism to be entirely destitute of any solid bottom. From the evolutionary philosophers, I have learned little; although I admit that, however hurriedly their theories have been knocked together, and however antiquated and ignorant Spencer's *First Principles* and general doctrines, yet they are under the guidance of a great and true idea, and are developing it by methods that are in their main features sound and scientific.

The works of Duns Scotus have strongly influenced me. If his logic and metaphysics, not slavishly worshipped, but torn away from its medievalism, be adapted to modern culture, under continual wholesome reminders of nominalistic criticisms, I am convinced that it will go far toward supplying the philosophy which is best to harmonize with physical science. But other conceptions have to be drawn from the history of science and from mathematics.

Thus, in brief, my philosophy may be described as the attempt of a physicist to make such conjecture as to the constitution of the universe as the methods of science may permit, with the aid of all that has been done by previous philosophers. I shall support my propositions by such arguments as I can. Demonstrative proof is not to be thought of. The demonstrations of the metaphysicians are all moonshine. The best that can be done is to supply a hypothesis, not devoid of all likelihood, in the general line of growth of scientific ideas, and capable of being verified or refuted by future observers.

Religious infallibilism, caught in the current of the times, shows symptoms of declaring itself to be only practically speaking infallible; and when it has thus once confessed itself subject to gradations, there will remain over no relic of the good old tenth-century infallibilism, except that of the infallible scientists, under which head I include, not merely the kind of characters that manufacture scientific catechisms and homilies, churches and creeds, and who are indeed "born missionaries," but all those respectable and cultivated persons who, having acquired their notions of science from reading, and not from research, have the idea that "science" means knowledge, while the truth is, it is a misnomer applied to the pursuit of those who are devoured by a desire to find things out. . . .

Though infallibility in scientific matters seems to me irresistibly comical, I should be in a sad way if I could not retain a high respect for those who lay claim to it, for they comprise the greater part of the people who have any conversation at all. When I say they lay claim to it, I mean they assume the functions of it quite naturally and unconsciously. The full meaning of the adage *Humanum est errare,* they have never waked up to. In those sciences of measurement which are the least subject to error— metrology, geodesy, and metrical astronomy—no man of self-respect ever now states his result, without affixing to it its *probable error;* and if this practice is not followed in other sciences it is because in those the probable errors are too vast to be estimated.

I am a man of whom critics have never found anything good to say. When they could see no opportunity to injure me, they have held their peace. The little laudation I have had has come from such sources, that the only satisfaction I have derived from it, has been from such slices of bread and butter as it might waft my way. Only once, as far as I remember, in all my lifetime have I experienced the pleasure of praise—not for what it might bring but in itself. That pleasure was beatific; and the praise that conferred it was meant for blame. It was that a critic said of me that I did not seem to be *absolutely sure of my own conclusions.* Never, if I can help it, shall that critic's eye ever rest on what I am now writing; for I owe a great pleasure to him; and, such was his evident animus, that should he find that out, I fear the fires of hell would be fed with new fuel in his breast.

My book will have no instruction to impart to anybody. Like a mathematical treatise, it will suggest certain ideas and certain reasons for holding them true; but then, if you accept them, it must be because you like my reasons, and the responsibility lies with you. Man is essentially a social animal: but to be social is one thing, to be gregarious is another: I decline to serve as bellwether. My book is meant for people who *want to find out;* and people who want philosophy ladled out to them can go elsewhere. There are philosophical soup shops at every corner, thank God!

The development of my ideas has been the industry of thirty years. I did not know as I ever should get to publish them, their ripening seemed so slow. But the harvest time has come, at last, and to me that harvest seems a wild one, but of course it is not I who have to pass judgment. It is not quite you, either, individual reader; it is experience and history.

For years in the course of this ripening process, I used for myself to collect my ideas under the designation *fallibilism;* and indeed the first step toward *finding out* is to acknowledge you do not satisfactorily know already; so that no blight can so surely arrest all intellectual growth as the blight of cocksureness; and ninety-nine out of every hundred good heads are reduced to impotence by that malady—of whose inroads they are most strangely unaware!

Indeed, out of a contrite fallibilism, combined with a high faith in the reality of knowledge, and an intense desire to find things out, all my philosophy has always seemed to me to grow. . . .

The Fixation of Belief

FEW PERSONS CARE TO STUDY LOGIC, BECAUSE EVERYBODY CONCEIVES himself to be proficient enough in the art of reasoning already. But I observe that this satisfaction is limited to one's own ratiocination, and does not extend to that of other men.

We come to the full possession of our power of drawing inferences, the last of all our faculties; for it is not so much a natural gift as a long and difficult art. The history of its practice would make a grand subject for a book. The medieval schoolmen, following the Romans, made logic the earliest of a boy's studies after grammar, as being very easy. So it was as they understood it. Its fundamental principle, according to them, was, that all knowledge rests either on authority or reason; but that whatever is deduced by reason depends ultimately on a premiss derived from authority. Accordingly, as soon as a boy was perfect in the syllogistic procedure, his intellectual kit of tools was held to be complete.

To Roger Bacon, that remarkable mind who in the middle of the thirteenth century was almost a scientific man, the schoolmen's conception of reasoning appeared only an obstacle to truth. He saw that experience alone teaches anything—a proposition which to us seems easy to understand, because a distinct conception of experience has been handed down to us from former generations; which to him likewise seemed perfectly clear, because its difficulties had not yet unfolded themselves. Of all kinds of experience, the best, he thought, was interior illumination, which teaches many things about Nature which the external senses could never discover, such as the transubstantiation of bread.

Four centuries later, the more celebrated Bacon, in the first book of his *Novum Organum,* gave his clear account of experience as something which must be open to verification and reëxamination. But, superior as Lord Bacon's conception is to earlier notions, a modern reader who is not in awe of his grandiloquence is chiefly struck by the inadequacy of his view of scientific procedure. That we have only to make some crude experiments, to draw up briefs of the results in certain blank forms, to go through these by rule, checking off everything disproved and setting down the alternatives, and that thus in a few years physical science would be finished up—what an idea! "He wrote on science like a Lord Chancellor," indeed, as Harvey, a genuine man of science said.

53

The early scientists, Copernicus, Tycho Brahe, Kepler, Galileo, Harvey, and Gilbert, had methods more like those of their modern brethren. Kepler undertook to draw a curve through the places of Mars, and to state the times occupied by the planet in describing the different parts of that curve; but perhaps his greatest service to science was in impressing on men's minds that this was the thing to be done if they wished to improve astronomy; that they were not to content themselves with inquiring whether one system of epicycles was better than another, but that they were to sit down to the figures and find out what the curve, in truth, was. He accomplished this by his incomparable energy and courage, blundering along in the most inconceivable way (to us), from one irrational hypothesis to another, until, after trying twenty-two of these, he fell, by the mere exhaustion of his invention, upon the orbit which a mind well furnished with the weapons of modern logic would have tried almost at the outset.*

In the same way, every work of science great enough to be well remembered for a few generations affords some exemplification of the defective state of the art of reasoning of the time when it was written; and each chief step in science has been a lesson in logic. It was so when Lavoisier and his contemporaries took up the study of Chemistry. The old chemist's maxim had been "Lege, lege, lege, labora, ora, et relege." Lavoisier's method was not to read and pray, but to dream that some long and complicated chemical process would have a certain effect, to put it into practice with dull patience, after its inevitable failure, to dream that with some modification it would have another result, and to end by publishing the last dream as a fact: his way was to carry his mind into his laboratory, and literally to make of his alembics and cucurbits instruments of thought, giving a new conception of reasoning as something which was to be done with one's eyes open, in manipulating real things instead of words and fancies.

The Darwinian controversy is, in large part, a question of logic. Mr. Darwin proposed to apply the statistical method to biology. The same thing has been done in a widely different branch of science, the theory of gases. Though unable to say what the movements of any particular molecule of gas would be on a certain hypothesis regarding the constitution of this class of bodies, Clausius and Maxwell were yet able, eight years before the publication of Darwin's immortal work, by the application of the doctrine of probabilities, to predict that in the long run such and such a proportion of the molecules would, under given circumstances,

* I am ashamed at being obliged to confess that this volume contains a very false and foolish remark about Kepler. When I wrote it, I had never studied the original book as I have since. It is now my deliberate opinion that it is the most marvellous piece of inductive reasoning I have been able to find.—[This footnote represents Peirce's afterthought, written in 1893.]

acquire such and such velocities; that there would take place, every second, such and such a relative number of collisions, etc.; and from these propositions were able to deduce certain properties of gases, especially in regard to their heat-relations. In like manner, Darwin, while unable to say what the operation of variation and natural selection in any individual case will be, demonstrates that in the long run they will, or would, adapt animals to their circumstances. Whether or not existing animal forms are due to such action, or what position the theory ought to take, forms the subject of a discussion in which questions of fact and questions of logic are curiously interlaced.

The object of reasoning is to find out, from the consideration of what we already know, something else which we do not know. Consequently, reasoning is good if it be such as to give a true conclusion from true premises, and not otherwise. Thus, the question of validity is purely one of fact and not of thinking. A being the facts stated in the premises and B being that concluded, the question is, whether these facts are really so related that if A were B would generally be. If so, the inference is valid; if not, not. It is not in the least the question whether, when the premises are accepted by the mind, we feel an impulse to accept the conclusion also. It is true that we do generally reason correctly by nature. But that is an accident; the true conclusion would remain true if we had no impulse to accept it; and the false one would remain false, though we could not resist the tendency to believe in it.

We are, doubtless, in the main, logical animals, but we are not perfectly so. Most of us, for example, are naturally more sanguine and hopeful than logic would justify. We seem to be so constituted that in the absence of any facts to go upon we are happy and self-satisfied; so that the effect of experience is continually to contract our hopes and aspirations. Yet a lifetime of the application of this corrective does not usually eradicate our sanguine disposition. Where hope is unchecked by any experience, it is likely that our optimism is extravagant. Logicality in regard to practical matters (if this be understood, not in the old sense, but as consisting in a wise union of security with fruitfulness of reasoning) is the most useful quality an animal can possess, and might, therefore, result from the action of natural selection; but outside of these it is probably of more advantage to the animal to have his mind filled with pleasing and encouraging visions, independently of their truth; and thus, upon unpractical subjects, natural selection might occasion a fallacious tendency of thought.

That which determines us, from given premises, to draw one inference rather than another, is some habit of mind, whether it be constitutional or acquired. The habit is good or otherwise, according as it produces true conclusions from true premises or not; and an inference is regarded as valid or not, without reference to the truth or falsity of its conclusion specially, but according as the habit which determines it is such as to produce true conclusions in general or not. The particular habit of mind which governs this or that inference may be formulated in a proposition whose truth depends on the validity of the inferences which the habit determines; and such a formula is called a *guiding principle* of inference. Suppose, for example, that we observe that a rotating disk of copper quickly comes to rest when placed between the poles of a magnet, and we infer that this will happen with every disk of copper. The guiding principle is, that what is true of one piece of copper is true of another. Such a guiding principle with regard to copper would be much safer than with regard to many other substances—brass, for example.

A book might be written to signalize all the most important of these guiding principles of reasoning. It would probably be, we must confess, of no service to a person whose thought is directed wholly to practical subjects, and whose activity moves along thoroughly-beaten paths. The problems that present themselves to such a mind are matters of routine which he has learned once for all to handle in learning his business. But let a man venture into an unfamiliar field, or where his results are not continually checked by experience, and all history shows that the most masculine intellect will ofttimes lose his orientation and waste his efforts in directions which bring him no nearer to his goal, or even carry him entirely astray. He is like a ship in the open sea, with no one on board who understands the rules of navigation. And in such a case some general study of the guiding principles of reasoning would be sure to be found useful.

The subject could hardly be treated, however, without being first limited; since almost any fact may serve as a guiding principle. But it so happens that there exists a division among facts, such that in one class are all those which are absolutely essential as guiding principles, while in the others are all which have any other interest as objects of research. This division is between those which are necessarily taken for granted in asking why a certain conclusion is thought to follow from certain premisses, and those which are not implied in such a question. A moment's thought will show that a variety of facts are already assumed when the logical question is first asked. It is implied, for instance, that there are such states of mind as doubt and belief—that a passage from one to the other is possible, the object of thought remaining the same, and that this transition is subject to some rules by which all minds are alike bound. As these are facts which we must already know before we can have any clear conception of reasoning at all, it cannot be supposed to be any longer of much interest to inquire into their truth or falsity. On the other hand, it is easy to believe that those rules of reasoning which are deduced from the very idea of the process are the ones which are the most essential; and, indeed, that so long as it conforms to these it will, at least, not lead to false conclusions from true premisses. In point of fact, the importance of what may be deduced from the assumptions involved in the logical question turns out to be greater than might be supposed, and this for reasons which it is difficult to exhibit at the outset. The only one which I shall here mention is, that conceptions which are really products of logical reflection, without being readily seen to be so, mingle with our ordinary thoughts, and are frequently the causes of great confusion. This is the case, for example, with the conception of quality. A quality, as such, is never an object of observation. We can see that a thing is blue or green, but the quality of being blue and the quality of being green are not things which we see; they are products of logical reflections. The truth is, that common-sense, or thought as it first emerges above the level of the narrowly practical, is deeply imbued with that bad logical quality to which the epithet *metaphysical* is commonly applied; and nothing can clear it up but a severe course of logic.

We generally know when we wish to ask a question and when we wish to pronounce a judgment, for there is a dissimilarity between the sensation of doubting and that of believing.

But this is not all which distinguishes doubt from belief. There is a practical difference. Our beliefs guide our desires and shape our actions. The Assassins, or followers of the Old Man of the Mountain, used to rush into death at his least command, because they believed that obedience to him would insure everlasting felicity. Had they doubted this, they would not have acted as they did. So it is with every belief, according to its degree. The feeling of believing is a more or less sure indication of there being established in our nature some habit which will determine our actions. Doubt never has such an effect.

Nor must we overlook a third point of difference. Doubt is an uneasy and dissatisfied state from which we struggle to free ourselves and pass into the state of belief; while the latter is a calm and satisfactory state which we do not wish to avoid, or to change to a belief in anything else. On the contrary, we cling tenaciously, not merely to believing, but to believing just what we do believe.

Thus, both doubt and belief have positive effects upon us, though very different ones. Belief does not make us act at once, but puts us into such a condition that we shall behave in some certain way, when the occasion arises. Doubt has not the least such active effect, but stimulates us to inquiry until it is destroyed. This reminds us of the irritation of a nerve and the reflex action produced thereby; while for the analogue of belief, in the nervous system, we must look to what are called nervous associations—for example, to that habit of the nerves in consequence of which the smell of a peach will make the mouth water.

The irritation of doubt causes a struggle to attain a state of belief. I shall term this struggle *Inquiry,* though it must be admitted that this is sometimes not a very apt designation.

The irritation of doubt is the only immediate motive for the struggle to attain belief. It is certainly best for us that our beliefs should be such as may truly guide our actions so as to satisfy our desires; and this reflection will make us reject every belief which does not seem to have been so formed as to insure this result. But it will only do so by creating a doubt in the place of that belief. With the doubt, therefore, the struggle begins, and with the cessation of doubt it ends. Hence, the sole object of inquiry is the settlement of opinion. We may fancy that this is not enough for us, and that we seek, not merely an opinion, but a true opinion. But put this fancy to the test, and it proves groundless; for as soon as a firm belief is reached we are entirely satisfied, whether the belief be true or false. And it is clear that nothing out of the sphere of our knowledge can be our object, for nothing which does not affect the mind can be the motive for mental effort. The most that can be maintained is, that we seek for a belief that we shall *think* to be true. But we think each one of our beliefs to be true, and, indeed, it is mere tautology to say so.

That the settlement of opinion is the sole end of inquiry is a very important proposition. It sweeps away, at once, various vague and erroneous conceptions of proof. A few of these may be noticed here.

1. Some philosophers have imagined that to start an inquiry it was only necessary to utter a question whether orally or by setting it down upon paper, and have even recommended us to begin our studies with questioning everything! But the mere putting of a proposition into the interrogative form does not stimulate the mind to any struggle after belief. There must be a real and living doubt, and without this all discussion is idle.

2. It is a very common idea that a demonstration must rest on some ultimate and absolutely indubitable propositions. These, according to one school, are first principles of a general nature; according to another, are first sensations. But, in point of fact, an inquiry, to have that completely satisfactory result called demonstration, has only to start with propositions perfectly free from all actual doubt. If the premises are not in fact doubted at all, they cannot be more satisfactory than they are.

3. Some people seem to love to argue a point after all the world is fully convinced of it. But no further advance can be made. When doubt ceases, mental action on the subject comes to an end; and, if it did go on, it would be without a purpose.

If the settlement of opinion is the sole object of inquiry, and if belief is of the nature of a habit, why should we not attain the desired end, by taking as answer to a question any we may fancy, and constantly reiterating it to ourselves, dwelling on all which may conduce to that belief, and learning to turn with contempt and hatred from anything that might disturb it? This simple and direct method is really pursued by many men. I remember once being entreated not to read a certain newspaper lest it might change my opinion upon free-trade. "Lest I might be entrapped by its fallacies and misstatements," was the form of expression. "You are not," my friend said, "a special student of political economy. You might, therefore, easily be deceived by fallacious arguments upon the subject. You might, then, if you read this paper, be led to believe in protection. But you admit that free-trade is the true doctrine; and you do not wish to believe what is not true." I have often known this system to be deliberately adopted. Still oftener, the instinctive dislike of an undecided state of mind, exaggerated into a vague dread of doubt, makes men cling spasmodically to the views they already take. The man feels that, if he only holds to his belief without wavering, it will be entirely satisfactory. Nor can it be denied that a steady and immovable faith yields great peace of mind. It may, indeed, give rise to inconveniences, as if a man should resolutely continue to believe that fire would not burn him, or that he would be eternally damned if he received his *ingesta* otherwise than through a stomach-pump. But then the man who adopts this method will not allow that its inconveniences are greater than its advantages. He will say, "I hold steadfastly to the truth, and the truth is always wholesome." And in many cases it may very well be that the pleasure he derives from his calm faith overbalances any inconveniences resulting from its deceptive character. Thus, if it be true that death is annihilation, then the man who believes that he will certainly go straight to heaven when he dies, provided he have fulfilled certain simple observances in this life, has a cheap pleasure which will not be followed by the least disappointment. A similar consideration seems to have weight with many persons in religious topics, for we frequently hear it said, "Oh, I could not believe so-and-so, because I should be wretched if I did." When an ostrich buries its head in the sand as danger approaches, it very likely takes the happiest course. It hides the danger, and then calmly says there is no danger; and, if it feels perfectly sure there is none, why should it raise its head to see? A man may go through life, systematically keeping out of view all that might cause a change in his opinions, and if he only succeeds—basing his method, as he does, on two fundamental psychological laws—I do not see what can be said against his doing so. It would be an egotistical impertinence to object that his procedure is irrational, for that only amounts to saying that his method of settling belief is not ours. He does not propose to himself to be rational, and, indeed, will often talk with scorn of man's weak and illusive reason. So let him think as he pleases.

But this method of fixing belief, which may be called the method of tenacity, will be unable to hold its ground in practice. The social impulse is against it. The man who adopts it will find that other men think differently from him, and it will be apt to occur to him, in some saner moment, that their opinions are quite as good as his own, and this will shake his confidence in his belief. This conception, that another man's thought or sentiment may be equivalent to one's own, is a distinctly new step, and a highly important one. It arises from an impulse too strong in man to be suppressed, without danger of destroying the human species. Unless we make ourselves hermits, we shall necessarily influence each other's opinions; so that the problem becomes how to fix belief, not in the individual merely, but in the community.

Let the will of the state act, then, instead of that of the individual. Let an institution be created which shall have for its object to keep correct doctrines before the attention of the people, to reiterate them perpetually, and to teach them to the young; having at the same time power to prevent contrary doctrines from being taught, advocated, or expressed. Let all possible causes of a change of mind be removed from men's apprehensions. Let them be kept ignorant, lest they should learn of some reason to think otherwise than they do. Let their passions be enlisted, so that they may regard private and unusual opinions with hatred and horror. Then, let all men who reject the established belief be terrified into silence. Let the people turn out and tar-and-feather such men, or let inquisitions be made into the manner of thinking of suspected persons, and when they are found guilty of forbidden beliefs, let them be subjected to some signal punishment. When complete agreement could not otherwise be reached, a general massacre of all who have not thought in a certain way has proved a very effective means of settling opinion in a country. If the power to do this be wanting, let a list of opinions be drawn up, to which no man of the least independence of thought can assent, and let the faithful be required to accept all these propositions, in order to segregate them as radically as possible from the influence of the rest of the world.

This method has, from the earliest times, been one of the chief means of upholding correct theological and political doctrines, and of preserving their universal or catholic character. In Rome, especially, it has been practised from the days of Numa Pompilius to those of Pius Nonus. This is the most perfect example in history; but wherever there is a priesthood —and no religion has been without one—this method has been more or less made use of. Wherever there is an aristocracy, or a guild, or any association of a class of men whose interests depend, or are supposed to depend, on certain propositions, there will be inevitably found some traces of this natural product of social feeling. Cruelties always accompany this system; and when it is consistently carried out, they become atrocities of the most horrible kind in the eyes of any rational man. Nor should this occasion surprise, for the officer of a society does not feel justified in surrendering the interests of that society for the sake of mercy, as he might his own private interests. It is natural, therefore, that sympathy and fellowship should thus produce a most ruthless power.

In judging this method of fixing belief, which may be called the method of authority, we must, in the first place, allow its immeasurable mental and moral superiority to the method of tenacity. Its success is proportionately greater; and, in fact, it has over and over again worked the most majestic results. The mere structures of stone which it has caused to be put together—in Siam, for example, in Egypt, and in Europe—have many of them a sublimity hardly more than rivalled by the greatest works of Nature. And, except the geological epochs, there are no periods of time so vast as those which are measured by some of these organized faiths. If we scrutinize the matter closely, we shall find that there has not been one of their creeds which has remained always the same; yet the change is so slow as to be imperceptible during one person's life, so that individual belief remains sensibly fixed. For the mass of mankind, then, there is perhaps no better method than this. If it is their highest impulse to be intellectual slaves, then slaves they ought to remain.

But no institution can undertake to regulate opinions upon every subject. Only the most important ones can be attended to, and on the rest men's minds must be left to the action of natural causes. This imperfection will be no source of weakness so long as men are in such a state of culture that one opinion does not influence another—that is, so long as they cannot put two and two together. But in the most priest-ridden states some individuals will be found who are raised above that condition. These men possess a wider sort of social feeling; they see that men in other countries and in other ages have held to very different doctrines from those which they themselves have been brought up to believe; and they cannot help seeing that it is the mere accident of their having been taught as they have, and of their having been surrounded with the manners and associations they have, that has caused them to believe as they do and not far differently. Nor can their candour resist the reflection that there is no reason to rate their own views at a higher value than those of other nations and other centuries; thus giving rise to doubts in their minds.

They will further perceive that such doubts as these must exist in their minds with reference to every belief which seems to be determined by the caprice either of themselves or of those who originated the popular opinions. The willful adherence to a belief, and the arbitrary forcing of it upon others, must, therefore, both be given up. A different new method of settling opinions must be adopted, that shall not only produce an impulse to believe, but shall also decide what proposition it is which is to be believed. Let the action of natural preferences be unimpeded, then, and under their influence let men, conversing together and regarding matters in different lights, gradually develop beliefs in harmony with natural causes. This method resembles that by which conceptions of art have been brought to maturity. The most perfect example of it is to be found in the history of metaphysical philosophy. Systems of this sort have not usually rested upon any observed facts, at least not in any great degree. They have been chiefly adopted because their fundamental propositions seemed "agreeable to reason." This is an apt expression; it does not mean

that which agrees with experience, but that which we find ourselves inclined to believe. Plato, for example, finds it agreeable to reason that the
distances of the celestial spheres from one another should be proportional to the different lengths of strings which produce harmonious chords.
Many philosophers have been led to their main conclusions by considerations like this*; but this is the lowest and least developed form which the
method takes, for it is clear that another man might find Kepler's theory,
that the celestial spheres are proportional to the inscribed and circum-
scribed spheres of the different regular solids, more agreeable to *his*
reason. But the shock of opinions will soon lead men to rest on preferences of a far more universal nature. Take, for example, the doctrine that
man only acts selfishly—that is, from the consideration that acting in one
way will afford him more pleasure than acting in another. This rests on
no fact in the world, but it has had a wide acceptance as being the only
reasonable theory.

This method is far more intellectual and respectable from the point of
view of reason than either of the others which we have noticed. Indeed, as
long as no better method can be applied, it ought to be followed, since it
is then the expression of instinct which must be the ultimate cause of be-

* Let us see in what manner a few of the greatest philosophers have undertaken to
settle opinion, and what their success has been. Descartes, who would have a man
begin by doubting everything, remarks that there is one thing he will find himself
unable to doubt, and that is, that he does doubt; and when he reflects that he doubts,
he can no longer doubt that he exists. Then, because he is all the while doubting
whether there are any such things as shape and motion, Descartes thinks he must be
persuaded that shape and motion do not belong to his nature, or anything else but
consciousness. This is taking it for granted that nothing in his nature lies hidden beneath the surface. Next, Descartes asks the doubter to remark that he has the idea of
a Being, in the highest degree intelligent, powerful, and perfect. Now a Being would
not have these qualities unless he existed necessarily and eternally. By existing necessarily he means existing by virtue of the existence of the idea. Consequently, all doubt
as to the existence of this Being must cease. This plainly supposes that belief is to be
fixed by what men find in their minds. He is reasoning like this: I find it written in
the volume of my mind that there is something X, which is such a sort of thing that
the moment it is written down it exists. Plainly, he is aiming at a kind of truth which
saying so can make to be so. He gives two further proofs of God's existence. Descartes makes God easier to know than anything else; for whatever we think He is,
He is. He fails to remark that this is precisely the definition of a *figment*. In particular, God cannot be a deceiver; whence it follows, that whatever we quite clearly
and distinctly think to be true about any subject, must *be* true. Accordingly, if people
will thoroughly discuss a subject, and quite clearly and distinctly make up their
minds what they think about it, the desired settlement of the question will be reached.
I may remark that the world has pretty thoroughly deliberated upon that theory
and has quite distinctly come to the conclusion that it is utter nonsense; whence
that judgment is indisputably right.

Many critics have told me that I misrepresent the *a priori* philosophers, when I
represent them as adopting whatever opinion there seems to be a natural inclination
to adopt. But nobody can say the above does not accurately define the position of
Descartes, and upon what does he repose except natural ways of thinking? Perhaps
I shall be told, however, that since Kant, that vice has been cured. Kant's great boast

lief in all cases. But its failure has been the most manifest. It makes of inquiry something similar to the development of taste; but taste, unfortunately, is always more or less a matter of fashion, and accordingly metaphysicians have never come to any fixed agreement, but the pendulum has swung backward and forward between a more material and a more spiritual philosophy, from the earliest times to the latest. And so from this, which has been called the *a priori* method, we are driven, in Lord Bacon's phrase, to a true induction. We have examined into this *a priori* method as something which promised to deliver our opinions from their accidental and capricious element. But development, while it is a process which eliminates the effect of some casual circumstances, only magnifies that of others. This method, therefore, does not differ in a very essential way from that of authority. The government may not have lifted its finger to influence my convictions; I may have been left outwardly quite free to choose, we will say, between monogamy and polygamy, and, appealing to my conscience only, I may have concluded that the latter practice is in itself licentious. But when I come to see that the chief obstacle to the spread of Christianity among a people of as high culture as the Hindoos

---

is that he critically examines into our natural inclinations toward certain opinions. An opinion that something is *universally* true clearly goes further than experience can warrant. An opinion that something is *necessarily* true (that is, not merely is true in the existing state of things, but would be true in every state of things) equally goes further than experience will warrant. Those remarks had been made by Leibniz and admitted by Hume; and Kant reiterates them. Though they are propositions of a nominalistic cast, they can hardly be denied. I may add that whatever is held to be precisely true goes further than experience can possibly warrant. Accepting those criteria of the origin of ideas, Kant proceeds to reason as follows: Geometrical propositions are held to be universally true. Hence, they are not given by experience. Consequently, it must be owing to an inward necessity of man's nature that he sees everything in space. Ergo, the sum of the angles of a triangle will be equal to two right angles for all the objects of our vision. Just that, and nothing more, is Kant's line of thought. But the dry-rot of reason in the seminaries has gone to the point where such stuff is held to be admirable argumentation. I might go through the *Critic of the Pure Reason,* section by section, and show that the thought throughout is precisely of this character. He everywhere shows that ordinary objects, such as trees and gold-pieces, involve elements not contained in the first presentations of sense. But we cannot persuade ourselves to give up the reality of trees and gold-pieces. There is a general inward insistence upon them, and that is the warrant for swallowing the entire bolus of general belief about them. This is merely accepting without question a belief as soon as it is shown to please a great many people very much. When he comes to the ideas of God, Freedom, and Immortality, he hesitates; because people who think only of bread and butter, pleasure and power, are indifferent to those ideas. He subjects these ideas to a different kind of examination, and finally admits them upon grounds which appear to the seminarists more or less suspicious, but which in the eyes of laboratorists are infinitely stronger than the grounds upon which he has accepted space, time, and causality. Those last grounds amount to nothing but this, that what there is a very decided and general inclination to believe must be true. Had Kant merely said, I shall adopt for the present the belief that the three angles of a triangle are equal to two right angles because nobody but brother Lambert and some Italian has ever called it in question, his attitude would be well enough. But on the contrary, he and those who today represent his

has been a conviction of the immorality of our way of treating women, I cannot help seeing that, though governments do not interfere, sentiments in their development will be very greatly determined by accidental causes. Now, there are some people, among whom I must suppose that my reader is to be found, who, when they see that any belief of theirs is determined by any circumstance extraneous to the facts, will from that moment not merely admit in words that that belief is doubtful, but will experience a real doubt of it, so that it ceases in some degree at least to be a belief.

To satisfy our doubts, therefore, it is necessary that a method should be found by which our beliefs may be determined by nothing human, but by some external permanency—by something upon which our thinking has no effect. Some mystics imagine that they have such a method in a private inspiration from on high. But that is only a form of the method of tenacity, in which the conception of truth as something public is not yet developed. Our external permanency would not be external, in our sense, if it was restricted in its influence to one individual. It must be something which affects, or might affect, every man. And, though these affections are necessarily as various as are individual conditions, yet the method must be such that the ultimate conclusion of every man shall be the same. Such is the method of science. Its fundamental hypothesis, restated in more familiar language, is this: There are Real things, whose

---

school distinctly maintain the proposition is *proved,* and the Lambertists *refuted,* by what comes merely to general disinclination to think with them.

As for Hegel, who led Germany for a generation, he recognizes clearly what he is about. He simply launches his boat into the current of thought and allows himself to be carried wherever the current leads. He himself calls his method *dialectic,* meaning that a frank discussion of the difficulties to which any opinion spontaneously gives rise will lead to modification after modification until a tenable position is attained. This is a distinct profession of faith in the method of inclinations.

Other philosophers appeal to "the test of inconceivability of the opposite," to "presuppositions" (by which they mean *Voraussetzungen,* properly translated, *postulates*), and other devices; but all these are but so many systems of rummaging the garret of the skull to find an enduring opinion about the Universe.

When we pass from the perusal of works upholding the method of authority to those of the philosophers, we not only find ourselves in a vastly higher intellectual atmosphere, but also in a clearer, freer, brighter, and more refreshing moral atmosphere. All this, however, is beside the one significant question of whether the method succeeds in fixing men's opinions. The projects of these authors are most persuasive. One dare swear they should succeed. But in point of fact, up to date they decidedly do not; and the outlook in this direction is most discouraging. The difficulty is that the opinions which today seem most unshakable are found tomorrow to be out of fashion. They are really far more changeable than they appear to a hasty reader to be; since the phrases made to dress out defunct opinions are worn at second hand by their successors.

We still talk of "cause and effect" although, in the mechanical world, the opinion that phrase was meant to express has been shelved long ago. We now know that the acceleration of a particle at any instant depends upon its position relative to other particles at that same instant; while the old idea was that the past affects the future, while the future does not affect the past. So the "law of demand and supply" has utterly different meanings with different economists. [Added in 1893.]

characters are entirely independent of our opinions about them; those Reals affect our senses according to regular laws, and, though our sensations are as different as are our relations to the objects, yet, by taking advantage of the laws of perception, we can ascertain by reasoning how things really and truly are; and any man, if he have sufficient experience and he reason enough about it, will be led to the one True conclusion. The new conception here involved is that of Reality. It may be asked how I know that there are any Reals. If this hypothesis is the sole support of my method of inquiry, my method of inquiry must not be used to support my hypothesis. The reply is this: 1. If investigation cannot be regarded as proving that there are Real things, it at least does not lead to a contrary conclusion; but the method and the conception on which it is based remain ever in harmony. No doubts of the method, therefore, necessarily arise from its practice, as is the case with all the others. 2. The feeling which gives rise to any method of fixing belief is a dissatisfaction at two repugnant propositions. But here already is a vague concession that there is some *one* thing which a proposition should represent. Nobody, therefore, can really doubt that there are Reals, for, if he did, doubt would not be a source of dissatisfaction. The hypothesis, therefore, is one which every mind admits. So that the social impulse does not cause men to doubt it. 3. Everybody uses the scientific method about a great many things, and only ceases to use it when he does not know how to apply it. 4. Experience of the method has not led us to doubt it, but, on the contrary, scientific investigation has had the most wonderful triumphs in the way of settling opinion. These afford the explanation of my not doubting the method or the hypothesis which it supposes; and not having any doubt, nor believing that anybody else whom I could influence has, it would be the merest babble for me to say more about it. If there be anybody with a living doubt upon the subject, let him consider it.

To describe the method of scientific investigation is the object of this series of papers. At present I have only room to notice some points of contrast between it and other methods of fixing belief.

This is the only one of the four methods which presents any distinction of a right and a wrong way. If I adopt the method of tenacity, and shut myself out from all influences, whatever I think necessary to doing this, is necessary according to that method. So with the method of authority: the state may try to put down heresy by means which, from a scientific point of view, seem very ill-calculated to accomplish its purposes; but the only test *on that method* is what the state thinks, so that it cannot pursue the method wrongly. So with the *a priori* method. The very essence of it is to think as one is inclined to think. All metaphysicians will be sure to do that, however they may be inclined to judge each other to be perversely wrong. The Hegelian system recognizes every natural tendency of thought as logical, although it be certain to be abolished by counter-tendencies. Hegel thinks there is a regular system in the succession of these tendencies, in consequence of which, after drifting one way and the other for a long time, opinion will at last go right. And it is true that metaphysicians do get the right ideas at last; Hegel's system of Nature represents tolerably the science of his day; and one may be sure that whatever scientific investigation shall have put out of doubt will presently receive *a priori* demonstration on the part of the metaphysicians. But with the scientific method the case is different. I may start with known and observed facts to proceed to the unknown; and yet the rules which I follow in doing so may not be such as investigation would approve. The test of whether I am truly following the method is not an immediate appeal to my feelings and purposes, but, on the contrary, itself involves the application of the method. Hence it is that bad reasoning as well as good reasoning is possible; and this fact is the foundation of the practical side of logic.

It is not to be supposed that the first three methods of settling opinion present no advantage whatever over the scientific method. On the contrary, each has some peculiar convenience of its own. The *a priori* method is distinguished for its comfortable conclusions. It is the nature of the process to adopt whatever belief we are inclined to, and there are certain flatteries to the vanity of man which we all believe by nature, until we are awakened from our pleasing dream by rough facts. The method of authority will always govern the mass of mankind; and those who wield the various forms of organized force in the state will never be convinced that dangerous reasoning ought not to be suppressed in some way. If liberty of speech is to be untrammelled from the grosser forms of constraint, then uniformity of opinion will be secured by a moral terrorism to which the respectability of society will give its thorough approval. Following the method of authority is the path of peace. Certain non-conformities are permitted; certain others (considered unsafe) are forbidden. These are different in different countries and in different ages; but, wherever you are, let it be known that you seriously hold a tabooed belief, and you may be perfectly sure of being treated with a cruelty less brutal but more refined than hunting you like a wolf. Thus, the greatest intellectual benefactors of mankind have never dared, and dare not now, to utter the whole of their thought; and thus a shade of *prima facie* doubt is cast upon every proposition which is considered essential to the security of society. Singularly enough, the persecution does not all come from without; but a man torments himself and is oftentimes most distressed at finding himself believing propositions which he has been brought up to regard with aversion. The peaceful and sympathetic man will, therefore, find it hard to resist the temptation to submit his opinions to authority. But most of all I admire the method of tenacity for its strength, simplicity, and directness. Men who pursue it are distinguished for their decision of character, which becomes very easy with such a mental rule. They do not waste time in trying to make up their minds what they want, but, fastening like lightning upon whatever alternative comes first, they hold it to the end, whatever happens, without an instant's irresolution. This is one of the splendid qualities which generally accompany brilliant, unlasting success. It is impossible not to envy the man who can dismiss reason, although we know how it must turn out at last.

Such are the advantages which the other methods of settling opinion have over scientific investigation. A man should consider well of them; and then he should consider that, after all, he wishes his opinions to coincide with the fact, and that there is no reason why the results of those three first methods should do so. To bring about this effect is the prerogative of the method of science. Upon such considerations he has to make his choice—a choice which is far more than the adoption of any intellectual opinion, which is one of the ruling decisions of his life, to which, when once made, he is bound to adhere. The force of habit will sometimes cause a man to hold on to old beliefs, after he is in a condition to see that they have no sound basis. But reflection upon the state of the case will overcome these habits, and he ought to allow reflection its full weight. People sometimes shrink from doing this, having an idea that beliefs are wholesome which they cannot help feeling rest on nothing. But let such persons suppose an analogous though different case from their own. Let them ask themselves what they would say to a reformed Mussulman who should hesitate to give up his old notions in regard to the relations of the sexes; or to a reformed Catholic who should still shrink from reading the Bible. Would they not say that these persons ought to consider the matter fully, and clearly understand the new doctrine, and then ought to embrace it, in its entirety? But, above all, let it be considered that what is more wholesome than any particular belief is integrity of belief, and that to avoid looking into the support of any belief from a fear that it may turn out rotten is quite as immoral as it is disadvantageous. The person who confesses that there is such a thing as truth, which is distinguished from falsehood simply by this, that if acted on it should, on full consideration, carry us to the point we aim at and not astray, and then, though convinced of this, dares not know the truth and seeks to avoid it, is in a sorry state of mind indeed.

Yes, the other methods do have their merits: a clear logical conscience does cost something—just as any virtue, just as all that we cherish, costs us dear. But we should not desire it to be otherwise. The genius of a man's logical method should be loved and reverenced as his bride, whom he has chosen from all the world. He need not contemn the others; on the contrary, he may honour them deeply, and in doing so he only honours her the more. But she is the one that he has chosen, and he knows that he was right in making that choice. And having made it, he will work and fight for her, and will not complain that there are blows to take, hoping that there may be as many and as hard to give, and will strive to be the worthy knight and champion of her from the blaze of whose splendours he draws his inspiration and his courage.

How to Make Our Ideas Clear

WHOEVER HAS LOOKED INTO A MODERN TREATISE ON LOGIC OF THE common sort, will doubtless remember the two distinctions between *clear* and *obscure* conceptions, and between *distinct* and *confused* conceptions. They have lain in the books now for nigh two centuries, unimproved and unmodified, and are generally reckoned by logicians as among the gems of their doctrine.

A clear idea is defined as one which is so apprehended that it will be recognized wherever it is met with, and so that no other will be mistaken for it. If it fails of this clearness, it is said to be obscure.

This is rather a neat bit of philosophical terminology; yet, since it is clearness that they were defining, I wish the logicians had made their definition a little more plain. Never to fail to recognize an idea, and under no circumstances to mistake another for it, let it come in how recondite a form it may, would indeed imply such prodigious force and clearness of intellect as is seldom met with in this world. On the other hand, merely to have such an acquaintance with the idea as to have become familiar with it, and to have lost all hesitancy in recognizing it in ordinary cases, hardly seems to deserve the name of clearness of apprehension, since after all it only amounts to a subjective feeling of mastery which may be entirely mistaken. I take it, however, that when the logicians speak of "clearness," they mean nothing more than such a familiarity with an idea, since they regard the quality as but a small merit, which needs to be supplemented by another, which they call *distinctness*.

A distinct idea is defined as one which contains nothing which is not clear. This is technical language; by the *contents* of an idea logicians understand whatever is contained in its definition. So that an idea is *distinctly* apprehended, according to them, when we can give a precise definition of it, in abstract terms. Here the professional logicians leave the subject; and I would not have troubled the reader with what they have to say, if it were not such a striking example of how they have been slumbering through ages of intellectual activity, listlessly disregarding the enginery of modern thought, and never dreaming of applying its lessons to the improvement of logic. It is easy to show that the doctrine that familiar use and abstract distinctness make the perfection of apprehension has its only true place in philosophies which have long been extinct; and it is now time to formulate the method of attaining to a more perfect clearness of thought, such as we see and admire in the thinkers of our own time.

When Descartes set about the reconstruction of philosophy, his first step was to (theoretically) permit scepticism and to discard the practice of the schoolmen of looking to authority as the ulimate source of truth. That done, he sought a more natural fountain of true principles, and thought he found it in the human mind; thus passing, in the directest way, from the method of authority to that of apriority, as described in my first paper. Self-consciousness was to furnish us with our fundamental truths, and to decide what was agreeable to reason. But since, evidently, not all ideas are true, he was led to note, as the first condition of infallibility, that they must be clear. The distinction between an idea *seeming* clear and really being so, never occurred to him. Trusting to introspection, as he did, even for a knowledge of external things, why should he question its testimony in respect to the contents of our own minds? But then, I suppose, seeing men, who seemed to be quite clear and positive, holding opposite opinions upon fundamental principles, he was further led to say that clearness of ideas is not sufficient, but that they need also to be distinct, *i.e.,* to have nothing unclear about them. What he probably meant by this (for he did not explain himself with precision) was, that they must sustain the test of dialectical examination; that they must not only seem clear at the outset, but that discussion must never be able to bring to light points of obscurity connected with them.

Such was the distinction of Descartes, and one sees that it was precisely on the level of his philosophy. It was somewhat developed by Leibniz. This great and singular genius was as remarkable for what he failed to see as for what he saw. That a piece of mechanism could not do work perpetually without being fed with power in some form, was a thing perfectly apparent to him; yet he did not understand that the machinery of the mind can only transform knowledge, but never originate it, unless it be fed with facts of observation. He thus missed the most essential point of the Cartesian philosophy, which is, that to accept propositions which seem perfectly evident to us is a thing which, whether it be logical or illogical, we cannot help doing. Instead of regarding the matter in this way, he sought to reduce the first principles of science to two classes, those which cannot be denied without self-contradiction, and those which result from the principle of sufficient reason (of which more anon), and was apparently unaware of the great difference between his position and that of Descartes. So he reverted to the old trivialities of logic; and, above all, abstract definitions played a great part in his philosophy. It was quite natural, therefore, that on observing that the method of Descartes laboured under the difficulty that we may seem to ourselves to have clear apprehensions of ideas which in truth are very hazy, no better remedy occurred to him than to require an abstract definition of every important term. Accordingly, in adopting the distinction of *clear* and *distinct* notions, he described the latter quality as the clear apprehensions of everything contained in definition; and the books have ever since copied his words. There is no danger that his chimerical scheme will ever again be over-valued. Nothing new can ever be learned by analyzing definitions. Nevertheless, our existing beliefs can be set in order by this process, and order is an essential element of intellectual economy, as of every other. It may be acknowledged, therefore, that the books are right in making familiarity with a notion the first step toward clearness of apprehension, and the defining of it the second. But in omitting all mention of any higher perspicuity of thought, they simply mirror a philosophy which was exploded a hundred years ago. That much-admired "ornament of logic"—the doctrine of clearness and distinctness—may be pretty enough, but it is high time to relegate to our cabinet of curiosities the antique *bijou,* and to wear about us something better adapted to modern uses.

The very first lesson that we have a right to demand that logic shall teach us is, how to make our ideas clear; and a most important one it is, depreciated only by minds who stand in need of it. To know what we think, to be masters of our own meaning, will make a solid foundation for great and weighty thought. It is most easily learned by those whose ideas are meagre and restricted; and far happier they than such as wallow helplessly in a rich mud of conceptions. A nation, it is true, may, in the course of generations, overcome the disadvantage of an excessive wealth of language and its natural concomitant, a vast, unfathomable deep of ideas. We may see it in history, slowly perfecting its literary forms, sloughing at length its metaphysics, and, by virtue of the untirable patience which is often a compensation, attaining great excellence in every branch of mental acquirement. The page of history is not yet unrolled that is to tell us whether such a people will or will not in the long run prevail over one whose ideas (like the words of their language) are few, but which possesses a wonderful mastery over those which it has. For an individual, however, there can be no question that a few clear ideas are worth more than many confused ones. A young man would hardly be persuaded to sacrifice the greater part of his thoughts to save the rest; and the muddled head is the least apt to see the necessity of such a sacrifice. Him we can usually only commiserate, as a person with a congenital defect. Time will help him, but intellectual maturity with regard to clearness is apt to come rather late. This seems an unfortunate arrangement of Nature, inasmuch as clearness is of less use to a man settled in life, whose errors have in great measure had their effect, than it would be to one whose path lay before him. It is terrible to see how a single unclear idea, a single formula without meaning, lurking in a young man's head, will sometimes act like an obstruction of inert matter in an artery, hindering the nutrition of the brain, and condemning its victim to pine away in the fullness of his intellectual vigour and in the midst of intellectual plenty. Many a man has cherished for years as his hobby some vague shadow of an idea, too meaningless to be positively false; he has, nevertheless, passionately loved it, has made it his companion by day and by night, and has given to it his strength and his life, leaving all other occupations for its sake, and in short has lived with it and for it, until it has become, as it were, flesh of his flesh and bone of his bone; and then he has waked up some bright morning to find it gone, clean vanished away like the beautiful Melusina of the fable, and the essence of his life gone with it. I have myself known such a man; and who can tell how many histories of circle-squarers; metaphysicians, astrologers, and what not, may not be told in the old German [French!] story?

The principles set forth in the first part* of this essay lead, at once, to a method of reaching a clearness of thought of higher grade than the "distinctness" of the logicians. It was there noticed that the action of thought is excited by the irritation of doubt, and ceases when belief is attained; so that the production of belief is the sole function of thought. All these words, however, are too strong for my purpose. It is as if I had described the phenomena as they appear under a mental miscroscope. Doubt and Belief, as the words are commonly employed, relate to religious or other grave discussions. But here I use them to designate the starting of any question, no matter how small or how great, and the resolution of it. If, for instance, in a horse-car, I pull out my purse and find a five-cent nickel and five coppers, I decide, while my hand is going to the purse, in which way I will pay my fare. To call such a question Doubt, and my decision Belief, is certainly to use words very disproportionate to the occasion. To speak of such a doubt as causing an irritation which needs to be appeased, suggests a temper which is uncomfortable to the verge of insanity. Yet, looking at the matter minutely, it must be admitted that, if there is the least hesitation as to whether I shall pay the five coppers or the nickel (as there will be sure to be, unless I act from some previously contracted habit in the matter), though irritation is too strong a word, yet I am excited to such small mental activity as may be necessary to deciding how I shall act. Most frequently doubts arise from some indecision, however momentary, in our action. Sometimes it is not so. I have, for example, to wait in a railway-station, and to pass the time I read the advertisements on the walls. I compare the advantages of different trains and different routes which I never expect to take, merely fancying myself to be in a state of hesitancy, because I am bored with having nothing to trouble me. Feigned hesitancy, whether feigned for mere amusement or with a lofty purpose, plays a great part in the production of scientific inquiry. However

* ["The Fixation of Belief."]

the doubt may originate, it stimulates the mind to an activity which may be slight or energetic, calm or turbulent. Images pass rapidly through consciousness, one incessantly melting into another, until at last, when all is over—it may be in a fraction of a second, in an hour, or after long years— we find ourselves decided as to how we should act under such circumstances as those which occasioned our hesitation. In other words, we have attained belief.

In this process we observe two sorts of elements of consciousness, the distinction between which may best be made clear by means of an illustration. In a piece of music there are the separate notes, and there is the air. A single tone may be prolonged for an hour or a day, and it exists as perfectly in each second of that time as in the whole taken together; so that, as long as it is sounding, it might be present to a sense from which everything in the past was as completely absent as the future itself. But it is different with the air, the performance of which occupies a certain time, during the portions of which only portions of it are played. It consists in an orderliness in the succession of sounds which strike the ear at different times; and to perceive it there must be some continuity of consciousness which makes the events of a lapse of time present to us. We certainly only perceive the air by hearing the separate notes; yet we cannot be said to directly hear it, for we hear only what is present at the instant, and an orderliness of succession cannot exist in an instant. These two sorts of objects, what we are *immediately* conscious of and what we are *mediately* conscious of, are found in all consciousness. Some elements (the sensations) are completely present at every instant so long as they last, while others (like thought) are actions having beginning, middle, and end, and consist in a congruence in the succession of sensations which flow through the mind. They cannot be immediately present to us, but must cover some portion of the past or future. Thought is a thread of melody running through the succession of our sensations.

We may add that just as a piece of music may be written in parts, each part having its own air, so various systems of relationship of succession subsist together between the same sensations. These different systems are distinguished by having different motives, ideas, or functions. Thought is only one such system, for its sole motive, idea, and function is to produce belief, and whatever does not concern that purpose belongs to some other system of relations. The action of thinking may incidentally have other results; it may serve to amuse us, for example, and among *dilettanti* it is not rare to find those who have so perverted thought to the purposes of pleasure that it seems to vex them to think that the questions upon which they delight to exercise it may ever get finally settled; and a positive discovery which takes a favourite subject out of the arena of literary debate is met with ill-concealed dislike. This disposition is the very debauchery of thought. But the soul and meaning of thought, abstracted from the other elements which accompany it, though it may be voluntarily thwarted, can never be made to direct itself toward anything but the production of belief. Thought in action has for its only possible motive the attainment of thought at rest; and whatever does not refer to belief is no part of the thought itself.

And what, then, is belief? It is the demi-cadence which closes a musical phrase in the symphony of our intellectual life. We have seen that it has just three properties: First, it is something that we are aware of; second, it appeases the irritation of doubt; and, third, it involves the establishment in our nature of a rule of action, or, say for short, a *habit*. As it appeases the irritation of doubt, which is the motive for thinking, thought relaxes, and comes to rest for a moment when belief is reached. But, since belief is a rule for action, the application of which involves further doubt and further thought, at the same time that it is a stopping-place, it is also a new starting-place for thought. That is why I have permitted myself to call it thought at rest, although thought is essentially an action. The *final* upshot of thinking is the exercise of volition, and of this thought no longer forms a part; but belief is only a stadium of mental action, an effect upon our nature due to thought, which will influence future thinking.

The essence of belief is the establishment of a habit; and different beliefs are distinguished by the different modes of action to which they give rise. If beliefs do not differ in this respect, if they appease the same doubt by producing the same rule of action, then no mere differences in the manner of consciousness of them can make them different beliefs, any more than playing a tune in different keys is playing different tunes. Imaginary distinctions are often drawn between beliefs which differ only in their mode of expression;—the wrangling which ensues is real enough, however. . . . Such false distinctions do as much harm as the confusion of beliefs really different, and are among the pitfalls of which we ought constantly to beware, especially when we are upon metaphysical ground. One singular deception of this sort, which often occurs, is to mistake the sensation produced by our own unclearness of thought for a character of the object we are thinking. Instead of perceiving that the obscurity is purely subjective, we fancy that we contemplate a quality of the object which is essentially mysterious; and if our conception be afterward presented to us in a clear form we do not recognize it as the same, owing to the absence of the feeling of unintelligibility. So long as this deception lasts, it obviously puts an impassable barrier in the way of perspicuous thinking; so that it equally interests the opponents of rational thought to perpetuate it, and its adherents to guard against it.

Another such deception is to mistake a mere difference in the grammatical construction of two words for a distinction between the ideas they express. In this pedantic age, when the general mob of writers attend so much more to words than to things, this error is common enough. When

I just said that thought is an *action,* and that it consists in a *relation,* although a person performs an action but not a relation, which can only be the result of an action, yet there was no inconsistency in what I said, but only a grammatical vagueness.

From all these sophisms we shall be perfectly safe so long as we reflect that the whole function of thought is to produce habits of action; and that whatever there is connected with a thought, but irrelevant to its purpose, is an accretion to it, but no part of it. If there be a unity among our sensations which has no reference to how we shall act on a given occasion, as when we listen to a piece of music, why we do not call that thinking. To develop its meaning, we have, therefore, simply to determine what habits it produces, for what a thing means is simply what habits it involves. Now, the identity of a habit depends on how it might lead us to act, not merely under such circumstances as are likely to arise, but under such as might possibly occur, no matter how improbable they may be. What the habit is depends on *when* and *how* it causes us to act. As for the *when,* every stimulus to action is derived from perception; as for the *how,* every purpose of action is to produce some sensible result. Thus, we come down to what is tangible and conceivably practical, as the root of every real distinction of thought, no matter how subtle it may be; and there is no distinction of meaning so fine as to consist in anything but a possible difference of practice.

To see what this principle leads to, consider in the light of it such a doctrine as that of transubstantiation. The Protestant churches generally hold that the elements of the sacrament are flesh and blood only in a tropical sense; they nourish our souls as meat and the juice of it would our bodies. But the Catholics maintain that they are literally just meat and blood; although they possess all the sensible qualities of wafer-cakes and diluted wine. But we can have no conception of wine except what may enter into a belief, either—

1. That this, that, or the other, is wine; or,
2. That wine possesses certain properties.

Such beliefs are nothing but self-notifications that we should, upon occasion, act in regard to such things as we believe to be wine according to the qualities which we believe wine to possess. The occasion of such action would be some sensible perception, the motive of it to produce some sensible result. Thus our action has exclusive reference to what affects the senses, our habit has the same bearing as our action, our belief the same as our habit, our conception the same as our belief; and we can consequently mean nothing by wine but what has certain effects, direct or indirect, upon our senses; and to talk of something as having all the sensible characters of wine, yet being in reality blood, is senseless jargon. Now, it is not my object to pursue the theological question; and having used it as a logical example I drop it, without caring to anticipate the theologian's reply. I only desire to point out how impossible it is that we should have an idea in our minds which relates to anything but conceived sensible effects of things. Our idea of anything *is* our idea of its sensible effects; and if we fancy that we have any other we deceive ourselves, and mistake a mere sensation accompanying the thought for a part of the thought itself. It is absurd to say that thought has any meaning unrelated to its only function. It is foolish for Catholics and Protestants to fancy themselves in disagreement about the elements of the sacrament, if they agree in regard to all their sensible effects, here and hereafter.

It appears, then, that the rule for attaining the third grade of clearness of apprehension is as follows: Consider what effects, that might conceivably have practical bearings, we conceive the object of our conception to have. Then, our conception of these effects is the whole of our conception of the object.

Let us illustrate this rule by some examples; and, to begin with the simplest one possible, let us ask what we mean by calling a thing *hard*. Evidently that it will not be scratched by many other substances. The whole conception of this quality, as of every other, lies in its conceived effects. There is absolutely no difference between a hard thing and a soft thing so long as they are not brought to the test. Suppose, then, that a diamond could be crystallized in the midst of a cushion of soft cotton, and should remain there until it was finally burned up. Would it be false to say that that diamond was soft? This seems a foolish question, and would be so, in fact, except in the realm of logic. There such questions are often of the greatest utility as serving to bring logical principles into sharper relief than real discussions ever could. In studying logic we must not put them aside with hasty answers, but must consider them with attentive care, in order to make out the principles involved. We may, in the present case, modify our question, and ask what prevents us from saying that all hard bodies remain perfectly soft until they are touched, when their hardness increases with the pressure until they are scratched. Reflection will show that the reply is this: there would be no *falsity* in such modes of speech. They would involve a modification of our present usage of speech with regard to the words hard and soft, but not of their meanings. For they represent no fact to be different from what it is; only they involve arrangements of facts which would be exceedingly maladroit.[2] This leads us to remark that the question of what would occur under circumstances which do not actually arise is not a question of fact, but only of the most perspicuous arrangement of them. For example, the question of free-will and fate in its simplest form, stripped of verbiage, is something like this: I have done something of which I am ashamed; could I, by an effort of the will, have resisted the temptation, and done otherwise? The philosophical reply is, that this is not a question of fact, but only of the arrangement of facts. Arranging them so as to exhibit what is particularly pertinent to my question—namely, that I ought to blame myself for having done wrong— it is perfectly true to say that, if I had willed to do otherwise than I did, I should have done otherwise. On the other hand, arranging the facts so as to exhibit another important consideration, it is equally true that, when a temptation has once been allowed to work, it will, if it has a certain force, produce its effect, let me struggle how I may. There is no objection to a contradiction in what would result from a false supposition. The *reductio ad absurdum* consists in showing that contradictory results would follow from a hypothesis which is consequently judged to be false. Many questions are involved in the free-will discussion, and I am far from desiring to say that both sides are equally right. On the contrary, I am of opinion that one side denies important facts, and that the other does not. But what I do say is, that the above single question was the origin of the whole doubt; that, had it not been for this question, the controversy would never have arisen; and that this question is perfectly solved in the manner which I have indicated. . . .

Let us now approach the subject of logic, and consider a conception which particularly concerns it, that of *reality*. Taking clearness in the sense of familiarity, no idea could be clearer than this. Every child uses it with perfect confidence, never dreaming that he does not understand it. As for clearness in its second grade, however, it would probably puzzle most men, even among those of a reflective turn of mind, to give an abstract definition of the real. Yet such a definition may perhaps be reached by considering the points of difference between reality and its opposite, fiction. A figment is a product of somebody's imagination; it has such characters as his thought impresses upon it. That those characters are independent of how you or I think is an external reality. There are, however, phenomena within our own minds, dependent upon our thought, which are at the same time real in the sense that we really think them. But though their characters depend on how we think, they do not depend on what we think those characters to be. Thus, a dream has a real existence as a mental phenomenon, if somebody has really dreamt it; that he dreamt so and so, does not depend on what anybody thinks was dreamt, but is completely independent of all opinion on the subject. On the other hand, considering, not the fact of dreaming, but the thing dreamt, it retains its peculiarities by virtue of no other fact than that it was dreamt to possess them. Thus we may define the real as that whose characters are independent of what anybody may think them to be.

But, however satisfactory such a definition may be found, it would be a great mistake to suppose that it makes the idea of reality perfectly clear. Here, then, let us apply our rules. According to them, reality, like every other quality, consists in the peculiar sensible effects which things partaking of it produce. The only effect which real things have is to cause belief, for all the sensations which they excite emerge into consciousness in the form of beliefs. The question therefore is, how is true belief (or belief in the real) distinguished from false belief (or belief in fiction). Now, as we have seen in the former paper, the ideas of truth and falsehood, in their full development, appertain exclusively to the experiential method of settling opinion. A person who arbitrarily chooses the propositions which he will adopt can use the word truth only to emphasize the expression of his determination to hold on to his choice. Of course, the method of tenacity never prevailed exclusively; reason is too natural to men for that. But in the literature of the dark ages we find some fine examples of it. When Scotus Erigena is commenting upon a poetical passage in which hellebore is spoken of as having caused the death of Socrates, he does not hesitate to inform the inquiring reader that Helleborus and Socrates were two eminent Greek philosophers, and that the latter, having been overcome in argument by the former, took the matter to heart and died of it! What sort of an idea of truth could a man have who could adopt and teach, without the qualification of a perhaps, an opinion taken so entirely at random? The real spirit of Socrates, who I hope would have been delighted to have been "overcome in argument," because he would have learned something by it, is in curious contrast with the naïve idea of the glossist, for whom (as for "the born missionary" of today) discussion would seem to have been simply a struggle. When philosophy began to awake from its long slumber, and before theology completely dominated it, the practice seems to have been for each professor to seize upon any philosophical position he found unoccupied and which seemed a strong one, to intrench himself in it, and to sally forth from time to time to give battle to the others. Thus, even the scanty records we possess of those disputes enable us to make out a dozen or more opinions held by different teachers at one time concerning the question of nominalism and realism. Read the opening part of the *Historia Calamitatum* of Abélard, who was certainly as philosophical as any of his contemporaries, and see the spirit of combat which it breathes. For him, the truth is simply his particular stronghold. When the method of authority prevailed, the truth meant little more than the Catholic faith. All the efforts of the scholastic doctors are directed toward harmonizing their faith in Aristotle and their faith in the Church, and one may search their ponderous folios through without finding an argument which goes any further. It is noticeable that where different faiths flourish side by side, renegades are looked upon with contempt even by the party whose belief they adopt; so completely has the idea of loyalty replaced that of truth-seeking. Since the time of Descartes, the defect in the conception of truth has been less apparent. Still, it will sometimes strike a scientific man that the philosophers have been less intent on finding out what the facts are, than on inquiring what belief is most in harmony with their system. It is hard to convince a follower of the *a priori* method by adducing facts; but show him that an opinion he is defending is inconsistent with what he has laid down elsewhere, and he will be very apt to retract it. These minds do not seem to believe that disputation is ever to cease; they seem to think that the opinion which is natural for one man is not so for another, and that belief will, consequently, never be settled. In contenting themselves with fixing their own opinions by a method which would lead another man to a different result, they betray their feeble hold of the conception of what truth is.

On the other hand, all the followers of science are animated by a cheerful hope that the processes of investigation, if only pushed far enough, will give one certain solution to each question to which they apply it. One man may investigate the velocity of light by studying the transits of Venus and the aberration of the stars; another by the oppositions of Mars and the eclipses of Jupiter's satellites; a third by the method of Fizeau; a fourth by that of Foucault; a fifth by the motions of the curves of Lissajoux; a sixth, a seventh, an eighth, and a ninth, may follow the different methods of comparing the measures of statical and dynamical electricity. They may at first obtain different results, but, as each perfects his method and his processes, the results are found to move steadily together toward a destined centre. So with all scientific research. Different minds may set out with the most antagonistic views, but the progress of investigation carries them by a force outside of themselves to one and the same conclusion. This activity of thought by which we are carried, not where we wish, but to a fore-ordained goal, is like the operation of destiny. No modification of the point of view taken, no selection of other facts for study, no natural bent of mind even, can enable a man to escape the predestinate opinion. This great hope is embodied in the conception of truth and reality. The opinion which is fated to be ultimately agreed to by all who investigate, is what we mean by the truth, and the object represented in this opinion is the real. That is the way I would explain reality.

But it may be said that this view is directly opposed to the abstract definition which we have given of reality, inasmuch as it makes the characters of the real depend on what is ultimately thought about them. But the answer to this is that, on the one hand, reality is independent, not necessarily of thought in general, but only of what you or I or any finite number of men may think about it; and that, on the other hand, though the object of the final opinion depends on what that opinion is, yet what that opinion is does not depend on what you or I or any man thinks. Our perversity and that of others may indefinitely postpone the settlement of opinion; it might even conceivably cause an arbitrary proposition to be universally accepted as long as the human race should last. Yet even that would not change the nature of the belief, which alone could be the result of investigation carried sufficiently far; and if, after the extinction of our race, another should arise with faculties and disposition for investigation, that true opinion must be the one which they would ultimately come to. "Truth crushed to earth shall rise again," and the opinion which would finally result from investigation does not depend on how anybody may actually think. But the reality of that which is real does depend on the real fact that investigation is destined to lead, at last, if continued long enough, to a belief in it.

But I may be asked what I have to say to all the minute facts of history, forgotten never to be recovered, to the lost books of the ancients, to the buried secrets.

> Full many a gem of purest ray serene
>   The dark, unfathomed caves of ocean bear;
> Full many a flower is born to blush unseen,
>   And waste its sweetness on the desert air.

Do these things not really exist because they are hopelessly beyond the reach of our knowledge? And then, after the universe is dead (according to the prediction of some scientists), and all life has ceased forever, will not the shock of atoms continue though there will be no mind to know it? To this I reply that, though in no possible state of knowledge can any number be great enough to express the relation between the amount of what rests unknown to the amount of the known, yet it is unphilosophical to suppose that, with regard to any given question (which has any clear meaning), investigation would not bring forth a solution of it, if it were carried far enough. Who would have said, a few years ago, that we could ever know of what substances stars are made whose light may have been longer in reaching us than the human race has existed? Who can be sure of what we shall not know in a few hundred years? Who can guess what would be the result of continuing the pursuit of science for ten thousand years, with the activity of the last hundred? And if it were to go on for a million, or a billion, or any number of years you please, how is it possible to say that there is any question which might not ultimately be solved?

But it may be objected, "Why make so much of these remote considerations, especially when it is your principle that only practical distinctions have a meaning?" Well, I must confess that it makes very little difference whether we say that a stone on the bottom of the ocean, in complete darkness, is brilliant or not—that is to say, that it *probably* makes no difference, remembering always that that stone *may* be fished up tomorrow. But that there are gems at the bottom of the sea, flowers in the untravelled desert, etc., are propositions which, like that about a diamond being hard when it is not pressed, concern much more the arrangement of our language than they do the meaning of our ideas.

It seems to me, however, that we have, by the application of our rule, reached so clear an apprehension of what we mean by reality, and of the fact which the idea rests on, that we should not, perhaps, be making a pretension so presumptuous as it would be singular, if we were to offer a metaphysical theory of existence for universal acceptance among those who employ the scientific method of fixing belief. However, as metaphysics is a subject much more curious than useful, the knowledge of which, like that of a sunken reef, serves chiefly to enable us to keep clear of it, I will not trouble the reader with any more Ontology at this moment. I have already been led much further into that path than I should have desired; and I have given the reader such a dose of mathematics, psychology, and all that is most abstruse, that I fear he may already have left me, and that what I am now writing is for the compositor and proof-reader exclusively. I trusted to the importance of the subject. There is no royal road to logic, and really valuable ideas can only be had at the price of close attention. But I know that in the matter of ideas the public prefer the cheap and nasty; and in my next paper[3] I am going to return to the easily intelligible, and not wander from it again. The reader who has been at the pains of wading through this paper, shall be rewarded in the next one by seeing how beautifully what has been developed in this tedious way can be applied to the ascertainment of the rules of scientific reasoning.

We have, hitherto, not crossed the threshold of scientific logic. It is certainly important to know how to make our ideas clear, but they may be ever so clear without being true. How to make them so, we have next to study. How to give birth to those vital and procreative ideas which multiply into a thousand forms and diffuse themselves everywhere, advancing civilization and making the dignity of man, is an art not yet reduced to rules, but of the secret of which the history of science affords some hints.

Evolutionary Love

AT FIRST BLUSH. COUNTER-GOSPELS

PHILOSOPHY, WHEN JUST ESCAPING FROM ITS GOLDEN PUPA-SKIN, MYTH-ology, proclaimed the great evolutionary agency of the universe to be Love. Or, since this pirate-lingo, English, is poor in such-like words, let us say Eros, the exuberance-love. Afterwards, Empedocles set up passionate-love and hate as the two co-ordinate powers of the universe. In some passages, kindness is the word. But certainly, in any sense in which it has an opposite, to be senior partner of that opposite, is the highest position that love can attain. Nevertheless, the ontological gospeller, in whose days those views were familiar topics, made the One Supreme Being, by whom all things have been made out of nothing, to be cherishing-love. What, then, can he say to hate? Never mind, at this time, what the scribe of the apocalypse, if he were John, stung at length by persecution into a rage unable to dis-tinguish suggestions of evil from visions of heaven, and so become the Slanderer of God to men, may have dreamed. The question is rather what the sane John thought, or ought to have thought, in order to carry out his idea consistently. His statement that God is love seems aimed at that say-ing of Ecclesiastes that we cannot tell whether God bears us love or hatred. "Nay," says John, "we can tell, and very simply! We know and have trusted the love which God hath in us. God is love." There is no logic in this, unless it means that God loves all men. In the preceding paragraph, he had said, "God is light and in him is no darkness at all." We are to understand, then, that as darkness is merely the defect of light, so hatred and evil are mere imperfect stages of ἀγάπη and ἀγαθόν, love and loveliness. This concords with that utterance reported in John's Gospel: "God sent not the Son into the world to judge the world; but that the world should through him be saved. He that believeth on him is not judged: he that believeth not hath been judged already. . . . And this is the judgment, that the light is come into the world, and that men loved darkness rather than the light." That is to say, God visits no punishment on them; they punish themselves, by their natural affinity for the defective. Thus, the love that God is, is not a love of which hatred is the contrary; otherwise Satan would be a co-ordinate power; but it is a love which embraces hatred as an im-

81

perfect stage of it, an Anteros—yea, even needs hatred and hatefulness as its object. For self-love is no love; so if God's self is love, that which he loves must be defect of love; just as a luminary can light up only that which otherwise would be dark. Henry James,* the Swedenborgian, says: "It is no doubt very tolerable finite or creaturely love to love one's own in another, to love another for his conformity to one's self: but nothing can be in more flagrant contrast with the creative Love, all whose tenderness *ex vi termini* must be reserved only for what intrinsically is most bitterly hostile and negative to itself." This is from *Substance and Shadow:* an *Essay on the Physics of Creation.* It is a pity he had not filled his pages with things like this, as he was able easily to do, instead of scolding at his reader and at people generally, until the physics of creation was well-nigh forgot. I must deduct, however, from what I just wrote: obviously no genius could make his every sentence as sublime as one which discloses for the problem of evil its everlasting solution.

The movement of love is circular, at one and the same impulse projecting creations into independency and drawing them into harmony. This seems complicated when stated so; but it is fully summed up in the simple formula we call the Golden Rule. This does not, of course, say, Do everything possible to gratify the egoistic impulses of others, but it says, Sacrifice your own perfection to the perfectionment of your neighbor. Nor must it for a moment be confounded with the Benthamite, or Helvetian, or Beccarian motto, Act for the greatest good of the greatest number. Love is not directed to abstractions but to persons; not to persons we do not know, nor to numbers of people, but to our own dear ones, our family and neighbors. "Our neighbor," we remember, is one whom we live near, not locally perhaps, but in life and feeling.

Everybody can see that the statement of St. John is the formula of an evolutionary philosophy, which teaches that growth comes only from love, from—I will not say self-*sacrifice,* but from the ardent impulse to fulfil another's highest impulse. Suppose, for example, that I have an idea that interests me. It is my creation. It is my creature; for as shown in last July's *Monist,* it is a little person. I love it; and I will sink myself in perfecting it. It is not by dealing out cold justice to the circle of my ideas that I can make them grow, but by cherishing and tending them as I would the flowers in my garden. The philosophy we draw from John's gospel is that this is the way mind develops; and as for the cosmos, only so far as it yet is mind, and so has life, is it capable of further evolution. Love, recognizing germs of loveliness in the hateful, gradually warms it into life, and makes it lovely. That is the sort of evolution which every careful student of my essay *The Law of Mind,* must see that *synechism* calls for.

The nineteenth century is now fast sinking into the grave, and we all

---

* The father of William and Henry James.

begin to review its doings and to think what character it is destined to bear as compared with other centuries in the minds of future historians. It will be called, I guess, the Economical Century; for political economy has more direct relations with all the branches of its activity than has any other science. Well, political economy has its formula of redemption, too. It is this: Intelligence in the service of greed ensures the justest prices, the fairest contracts, the most enlightened conduct of all the dealings between men, and leads to the *summum bonum,* food in plenty and perfect comfort. Food for whom? Why, for the greedy master of intelligence. I do not mean to say that this is one of the legitimate conclusions of political economy, the scientific character of which I fully acknowledge. But the study of doctrines, themselves true, will often temporarily encourage generalizations extremely false, as the study of physics has encouraged necessitarianism. What I say, then, is that the great attention paid to economical questions during our century has induced an exaggeration of the beneficial effects of greed and of the unfortunate results of sentiment, until there has resulted a philosophy which comes unwittingly to this, that greed is the great agent in the elevation of the human race and in the evolution of the universe.

I open a handbook of political economy,—the most typical and middling one I have at hand,—and there find some remarks of which I will here make a brief analysis. I omit qualifications, sops thrown to Cerberus, phrases to placate Christian prejudice, trappings which serve to hide from author and reader alike the ugly nakedness of the greed-god. But I have surveyed my position. The author enumerates "three motives to human action:

The love of self;

The love of a limited class having common interests and feelings with one's self;

The love of mankind at large."

Remark, at the outset, what obsequious title is bestowed on greed,— "the love of self." Love! The second motive *is* love. In place of "a limited class" put "certain persons," and you have a fair description. Taking "class" in the old-fashioned sense, a weak kind of love is described. In the sequel, there seems to be some haziness as to the delimitation of this motive. By the love of mankind at large, the author does not mean that deep, subconscious passion that is properly so called; but merely public-spirit, perhaps little more than a fidget about pushing ideas. The author proceeds to a comparative estimate of the worth of these motives. Greed, says he, but using, of course, another word, "is not so great an evil as is commonly supposed. . . . Every man can promote his own interests a great deal more effectively than he can promote any one else's, or than any one else can promote his." Besides, as he remarks on another page, the more miserly a man is, the more good he does. The second motive "is the most dangerous one to which society is exposed." Love is all very pretty: "no higher or purer source of human happiness exists." (Ahem!) But it is a "source of enduring injury," and, in short, should be overruled by something wiser. What is this wiser motive? We shall see.

As for public spirit, it is rendered nugatory by the "difficulties in the way of its effective operation." For example, it might suggest putting checks upon the fecundity of the poor and the vicious; and "no measure of repression would be too severe," in the case of criminals. The hint is broad. But unfortunately, you cannot induce legislatures to take such measures, owing to the pestiferous "tender sentiments of man towards man." It thus appears, that public-spirit, or Benthamism, is not strong enough to be the effective tutor of love, (I am skipping to another page), which must, therefore, be handed over to "the motives which animate men in the pursuit of wealth," in which alone we can confide, and which "are in the highest degree beneficent." Yes, in the "highest degree" without exception are they beneficent to the being upon whom all their blessings are poured out, namely, the Self, whose "sole object," says the writer in accumulating wealth is his individual "sustenance and enjoyment." Plainly, the author holds the notion that some other motive might be in a higher degree beneficent even for the man's self to be a paradox wanting in good sense. He seeks to gloze and modify his doctrine; but he lets the perspicacious reader see what his animating principle is; and when, holding the opinions I have repeated, he at the same time acknowledges that society could not exist upon a basis of intelligent greed alone, he simply pigeon-holes himself as one of the eclectics of inharmonious opinions. He wants his mammon flavored with a *soupçon* of god.

The economists accuse those to whom the enunciation of their atrocious villainies communicates a thrill of horror of being *sentimentalists*. It may be so: I willingly confess to having some tincture of sentimentalism in me, God be thanked! Ever since the French Revolution brought this leaning of thought into ill-repute,—and not altogether undeservedly, I must admit, true, beautiful, and good as that great movement was,—it has been the tradition to picture sentimentalists as persons incapable of logical thought and unwilling to look facts in the eyes. This tradition may be classed with the French tradition that an Englishman says *godam* at every second sentence, the English tradition that an American talks about "Britishers," and the American tradition that a Frenchman carries forms of etiquette to an inconvenient extreme, in short with all those traditions which survive simply because the men who use their eyes and ears are few and far between. Doubtless some excuse there was for all those opinions in days gone by; and sentimentalism, when it was the fashionable amusement to spend one's evenings in a flood of tears over a woeful performance on a candle-litten stage, sometimes made itself a little ridiculous. But what after all is sentimentalism? It is an *ism,* a doctrine, namely, the doctrine that great respect should be paid to the natural judgments of the sensible heart. This is what sentimentalism precisely is; and I entreat the reader to consider whether to contemn it is not of all blasphemies the most degrading. Yet the nineteenth century has steadily contemned it, because it brought about the Reign of Terror. That it did so is true. Still, the whole question is one of *how much*. The Reign of Terror was very bad; but now the Gradgrind banner has been this century long flaunting in the face of heaven, with an insolence to provoke the very skies to scowl and rumble. Soon a flash and quick peal will shake economists quite out of their complacency, too late. The twentieth century, in its latter half, shall surely see the deluge-tempest burst upon the social order,—to clear upon a world as deep in ruin as that greed-philosophy has long plunged it into guilt. No post-thermidorian high jinks then!

So a miser is a beneficent power in a community, is he? With the same reason precisely, only in a much higher degree, you might pronounce the Wall Street sharp to be a good angel, who takes money from heedless persons not likely to guard it properly, who wrecks feeble enterprises better stopped, and who administers wholesome lessons to unwary scientific men, by passing worthless checks upon them,—as you did, the other day, to me, my millionaire Master in glomery, when you thought you saw your way to using my process without paying for it, and of so bequeathing to your children something to boast of their father about,—and who by a thousand wiles puts money at the service of intelligent greed, in his own person. Bernard Mandeville, in his *Fable of the Bees,* maintains that private vices of all descriptions are public benefits, and proves it, too, quite as cogently as the economist proves his point concerning the miser. He even argues, with no slight force, that but for vice civilization would never have existed. In the same spirit, it has been strongly maintained and is to-day widely believed that all acts of charity and benevolence, private and public, go seriously to degrade the human race.

The *Origin of Species* of Darwin merely extends politico-economical views of progress to the entire realm of animal and vegetable life. The vast majority of our contemporary naturalists hold the opinion that the true cause of those exquisite and marvellous adaptations of nature for which, when I was a boy, men used to extol the divine wisdom is that creatures are so crowded together that those of them that happen to have the slightest advantage force those less pushing into situations unfavorable to multiplication or even kill them before they reach the age of reproduction. Among animals, the mere mechanical individualism is vastly reënforced as a power making for good by the animal's ruthless greed. As Darwin puts it on his title-page, it is the struggle for existence; and he should have added for his motto: Every individual for himself, and the Devil take the hindmost! Jesus, in his sermon on the Mount, expressed a different opinion.

Here, then, is the issue. The gospel of Christ says that progress comes from every individual merging his individuality in sympathy with his neighbors. On the other side, the conviction of the nineteenth century is that progress takes place by virtue of every individual's striving for himself with all his might and trampling his neighbor under foot whenever he gets a chance to do so. This may accurately be called the Gospel of Greed.

Much is to be said on both sides. I have not concealed, I could not conceal, my own passionate predilection. Such a confession will probably shock my scientific brethren. Yet the strong feeling is in itself, I think, an argument of some weight in favor of the agapastic theory of evolution,— so far as it may be presumed to bespeak the normal judgment of the Sensible Heart. Certainly, if it were possible to believe in agapasm without believing it warmly, that fact would be an argument against the truth of the doctrine. At any rate, since the warmth of feeling exists, it should on every account be candidly confessed; especially since it creates a liability to onesidedness on my part against which it behooves my readers and me to be severally on our guard.

SECOND THOUGHTS. IRENICA.

Let us try to define the logical affinities of the different theories of evolution. Natural selection, as conceived by Darwin, is a mode of evolution in which the only positive agent of change in the whole passage from moner to man is fortuitous variation. To secure advance in a definite direction chance has to be seconded by some action that shall hinder the propagation of some varieties or stimulate that of others. In natural selection, strictly so called, it is the crowding out of the weak. In sexual selection, it is the attraction of beauty, mainly.

The *Origin of Species* was published toward the end of the year 1859. The preceding years since 1846 had been one of the most productive seasons,—or if extended so as to cover the great book we are considering, *the* most productive period of equal length in the entire history of science from its beginnings until now. The idea that chance begets order, which is one of the corner-stones of modern physics (although Dr. Carus considers it "the weakest point in Mr. Peirce's system,") was at that time put into its clearest light. Quetelet had opened the discussion by his *Letters on the Application of Probabilities to the Moral and Political Sciences,* a work which deeply impressed the best minds of that day, and to which Sir John Herschel had drawn general attention in Great Britain. In 1857, the first volume of Buckle's *History of Civilisation* had created a tremendous sensation, owing to the use he made of this same idea. Meantime, the "statistical method" had, under that very name, been applied with brilliant success to molecular physics. Dr. John Herapath, an English chemist, had in 1847 outlined the kinetical theory of gases in his *Mathematical Physics;* and the interest the theory excited had been refreshed in 1856 by notable memoirs by Clausius and Krönig. In the very summer preceding Darwin's publication, Maxwell had read before the British Association the first and most important of his researches on this subject. The consequence was that the idea that fortuitous events may result in a physical law, and further that this is the way in which those laws which appear to conflict with the principle of the conservation of energy are to be explained, had taken a strong hold upon the minds of all who were abreast of the leaders of thought. By such minds, it was inevitable that the *Origin of Species,* whose teaching was simply the application of the same principle to the explanation of another "non-conservative" action, that of organic development, should be hailed and welcomed. The sublime discovery of the conservation of energy by Helmholtz in 1847, and that of the mechanical theory of heat by Clausius and by Rankine, independently, in 1850, had decidedly overawed all those who might have been inclined to sneer at physical science. Thereafter a belated poet still harping upon "science peddling with the names of things" would fail of his effect. Mechanism was now known to be all, or very nearly so. All this time, utilitarianism,—that improved substitute for the Gospel,—was in its fullest feather; and was a natural ally of an individualistic theory. Dean Mansell's injudicious advocacy had led to mutiny among the bondsmen of Sir William Hamilton, and the nominalism of Mill had profited accordingly; and although the real science that Darwin was leading men to was sure some day to give a death-blow to the sham-science of Mill, yet there were several elements of the Darwinian theory which were sure to charm the followers of Mill. Another thing: anæsthetics had been in use for thirteen years. Already, people's acquaintance with suffering had dropped off very much; and as a consequence, that unlovely hardness by which our times are so contrasted with those that immediately preceded them, had already set in, and inclined people to relish a ruthless theory. The reader would quite mistake the drift of what I am saying if he were to understand me as wishing to suggest that any of those things (except perhaps Malthus) influenced Darwin himself. What I mean is that his hypothesis, while without dispute one of the most ingenious and pretty ever devised, and while argued with a wealth of knowledge, a strength of logic, a charm of rhetoric, and above all with a certain magnetic genuineness that was almost irresistible, did not appear, at first, at all near to being proved; and to a sober mind its case looks less hopeful now than it did twenty years ago; but the extraordinarily favorable reception it met with was plainly owing, in large measure, to its ideas being those toward which the age was favorably disposed, especially, because of the encouragement it gave to the greed-philosophy.

Diametrically opposed to evolution by chance, are those theories which attribute all progress to an inward necessary principle, or other form of necessity. Many naturalists have thought that if an egg is destined to go through a certain series of embryological transformations, from which it is perfectly certain not to deviate, and if in geological time almost exactly the same forms appear successively, one replacing another in the same

order, the strong presumption is that this latter succession was as prede-
terminate and certain to take place as the former. So, Nägeli, for instance,
conceives that it somehow follows from the first law of motion and the
peculiar, but unknown, molecular constitution of protoplasm, that forms
must complicate themselves more and more. Kölliker makes one form generate another after a certain maturation has been accomplished. Weismann,
too, though he calls himself a Darwinian, holds that nothing is due to
chance, but that all forms are simple mechanical resultants of the heredity
from two parents. It is very noticeable that all these different sectaries seek
to import into their science a mechanical necessity to which the facts that
come under their observation do not point. Those geologists who think
that the variation of species is due to cataclysmic alterations of climate or
of the chemical constitution of the air and water are also making mechanical necessity chief factor of evolution.

Evolution by sporting and evolution by mechanical necessity are conceptions warring against one another. A third method, which supersedes
their strife, lies enwrapped in the theory of Lamarck. According to his
view, all that distinguishes the highest organic forms from the most rudimentary has been brought about by little hypertrophies or atrophies which
have affected individuals early in their lives, and have been transmitted to
their offspring. Such a transmission of acquired characters is of the general
nature of habit-taking, and this is the representative and derivative within
the physiological domain of the law of mind. Its action is essentially dissimilar to that of a physical force; and that is the secret of the repugnance
of such necessitarians as Weismann to admitting its existence. The
Lamarckians further suppose that although some of the modifications of
form so transmitted were originally due to mechanical causes, yet the
chief factors of their first production were the straining of endeavor and
the overgrowth superinduced by exercise, together with the opposite actions. Now, endeavor, since it is directed toward an end, is essentially
psychical, even though it be sometimes unconscious; and the growth due to
exercise, as I argued in my last paper, follows a law of a character quite
contrary to that of mechanics.

Lamarckian evolution is thus evolution by the force of habit.—That
sentence slipped off my pen while one of those neighbors whose function
in the social cosmos seems to be that of an Interrupter, was asking me a
question. Of course, it is nonsense. Habit is mere inertia, a resting on one's
oars, not a propulsion. Now it is energetic projaculation (lucky there is
such a word, or this untried hand might have been put to inventing one) by
which in the typical instances of Lamarckian evolution the new elements
of form are first created. Habit, however, forces them to take practical
shapes, compatible with the structures they affect, and in the form of
heredity and otherwise, gradually replaces the spontaneous energy that sustains them. Thus, habit plays a double part; it serves to establish the new

features, and also to bring them into harmony with the general morphology and function of the animals and plants to which they belong. But if the reader will now kindly give himself the trouble of turning back a page or two, he will see that this account of Lamarckian evolution coincides with the general description of the action of love, to which, I suppose, he yielded his assent.

Remembering that all matter is really mind, remembering, too, the continuity of mind, let us ask what aspect Lamarckian evolution takes on within the domain of consciousness. Direct endeavor can achieve almost nothing. It is as easy by taking thought to add a cubit to one's stature, as it is to produce an idea acceptable to any of the Muses by merely straining for it, before it is ready to come. We haunt in vain the sacred well and throne of Mnemosyne; the deeper workings of the spirit take place in their own slow way, without our connivance. Let but their bugle sound, and we may then make our effort, sure of an oblation for the altar of whatsoever divinity its savor gratifies. Besides this inward process, there is the operation of the environment, which goes to break up habits destined to be broken up and so to render the mind lively. Everybody knows that the long continuance of a routine of habit make us lethargic, while a succession of surprises wonderfully brightens the ideas. Where there is a motion, where history is a-making, there is the focus of mental activity, and it has been said that the arts and sciences reside within the temple of Janus, waking when that is open, but slumbering when it is closed. Few psychologists have perceived how fundamental a fact this is. A portion of mind abundantly commissured to other portions works almost mechanically. It sinks to a condition of a railway junction. But a portion of mind almost isolated, a spiritual peninsula, or *cul-de-sac,* is like a railway terminus. Now mental commissures are habits. Where they abound, originality is not needed and is not found; but where they are in defect, spontaneity is set free. Thus, the first step in the Lamarckian evolution of mind is the putting of sundry thoughts into situations in which they are free to play. As to growth by exercise, I have already shown, in discussing *Man's Glassy Essence,* in last October's *Monist,* what its *modus operandi* must be conceived to be, at least, until a second equally definite hypothesis shall have been offered. Namely, it consists of the flying asunder of molecules, and the reparation of the parts by new matter. It is, thus, a sort of reproduction. It takes place only during exercise, because the activity of protoplasm consists in the molecular disturbance which is its necessary condition. Growth by exercise takes place also in the mind. Indeed, that is what it is to *learn*. But the most perfect illustration is the development of a philosophical idea by being put into practice. The conception which appeared, at first, as unitary, splits up into special cases; and into each of these new thought must enter to make a practicable idea. This new thought, however, follows pretty closely the model of the parent conception; and thus a homogeneous development takes place. The parallel between this and the course of molecular occurrences is apparent. Patient attention will be able to trace all these elements in the transaction called learning.

Three modes of evolution have thus been brought before us; evolution by fortuitous variation, evolution by mechanical necessity, and evolution by creative love. We may term them *tychastic* evolution, or *tychasm, anancastic* evolution, or *anancasm,* and *agapastic* evolution, or *agapasm.* The doctrines which represent these as severally of principal importance, we may term *tychasticism, anancasticism,* and *agapasticism.* On the other hand the mere propositions that absolute chance, mechanical necessity, and the law of love, are severally operative in the cosmos, may receive the names of *tychism, anancism,* and *agapism.*

All three modes of evolution are composed of the same general elements. Agapasm exhibits them the most clearly. The good result is here brought to pass, first, by the bestowal of spontaneous energy by the parent upon the offspring, and, second, by the disposition of the latter to catch the general idea of those about it and thus to subserve the general purpose. In order to express the relation that tychasm and anancasm bear to agapasm, let me borrow a word from geometry. An ellipse crossed by a straight line is a sort of cubic curve; for a cubic is a curve which is cut thrice by a straight line; now a straight line might cut the ellipse twice and its associated straight line a third time. Still the ellipse with the straight line across it would not have the characteristics of a cubic. It would have, for instance, no contrary flexure, which no true cubic wants; and it would have two nodes, which no true cubic has. The geometers say that it is a *degenerate* cubic. Just so, tychasm and anancasm are degenerate forms of agapasm.

Men who seek to reconcile the Darwinian idea with Christianity will remark that tychastic evolution, like the agapastic, depends upon a reproductive creation, the forms preserved being those that use the spontaneity conferred upon them in such wise as to be drawn into harmony with their original, quite after the Christian scheme. Very good! This only shows that just as love cannot have a contrary, but must embrace what is most opposed to it, as a degenerate case of it, so tychasm is a kind of agapasm. Only, in the tychastic evolution progress is solely owing to the distribution of the napkin-hidden talent of the rejected servant among those not rejected, just as ruined gamesters leave their money on the table to make those not yet ruined so much the richer. It makes the felicity of the lambs just the damnation of the goats, transposed to the other side of the equation. In genuine agapasm, on the other hand, advance takes place by virtue of a positive sympathy among the created springing from continuity of mind. This is the idea which tychasticism knows not how to manage.

The anancasticist might here interpose, claiming that the mode of evolution for which he contends agrees with agapasm at the point at which tychasm departs from it. For it makes development go through certain phases, having its inevitable ebbs and flows, yet tending on the whole to a foreordained perfection. Bare existence by this its destiny betrays an intrinsic affinity for the good. Herein, it must be admitted, anancasm shows itself to be in a broad acception a species of agapasm. Some forms of it might easily be mistaken for the genuine agapasm. The Hegelian philosophy is such an anancasticism. With its revelatory religion, with its synechism (however imperfectly set forth), with its "reflection," the whole idea of the theory is superb, almost sublime. Yet, after all, living freedom is practically omitted from its method. The whole movement is that of a vast engine, impelled by a *vis a tergo,* with a blind and mysterious fate of arriving at a lofty goal. I mean that such an engine it *would be,* if it really worked; but in point of fact, it is a Keely motor. Grant that it really acts as it professes to act, and there is nothing to do but accept the philosophy. But never was there seen such an example of a long chain of reasoning,—shall I say with a flaw in every link?—no, with every link a handful of sand, squeezed into shape in a dream. Or say, it is a pasteboard model of a philosophy that in reality does not exist. If we use the one precious thing it contains, the idea of it, introducing the tychism which the arbitrariness of its every step suggests, and make that the support of a vital freedom which is the breath of the spirit of love, we may be able to produce that genuine agapasticism, at which Hegel was aiming.

A THIRD ASPECT. DISCRIMINATION

In the very nature of things, the line of demarcation between the three modes of evolution is not perfectly sharp. That does not prevent its being quite real; perhaps it is rather a mark of its reality. There is in the nature of things no sharp line of demarcation between the three fundamental colors, red, green, and violet. But for all that they are really different. The main question is whether three radically different evolutionary elements have been operative; and the second question is what are the most striking characteristics of whatever elements have been operative.

I propose to devote a few pages to a very slight examination of these questions in their relation to the historical development of human thought. I first formulate for the reader's convenience the briefest possible definitions of the three conceivable modes of development of thought, distinguishing also two varieties of anancasm and three of agapasm. The tychastic development of thought, then, will consist in slight departures from habitual ideas in different directions indifferently, quite purposeless and quite unconstrained whether by outward circumstances or by force of logic, these new departures being followed by unforeseen results which tend to fix some of them as habits more than others. The anancastic development of thought will consist of new ideas adopted without foreseeing whither they tend, but having a character determined by causes either external to the mind, such as changed circumstances of life, or internal to the mind as logical developments of ideas already accepted, such as generalizations. The agapastic development of thought is the adoption of certain mental tendencies, not altogether heedlessly, as in tychasm, nor quite blindly by the mere force of circumstances or of logic, as in anancasm, but by an immediate attraction for the idea itself, whose nature is divined before the mind possesses it, by the power of sympathy, that is, by virtue of the continuity of mind; and this mental tendency may be of three varieties, as follows: First, it may affect a whole people or community in its collective personality, and be thence communicated to such individuals as are in powerfully sympathetic connection with the collective people, although they may be intellectually incapable of attaining the idea by their private understandings or even perhaps of consciously apprehending it. Second, it may affect a private person directly, yet so that he is only enabled to apprehend the idea, or to appreciate its attractiveness, by virtue of his sympathy with his neighbors, under the influence of a striking experience or development of thought. The conversion of St. Paul may be taken as an example of what is meant. Third, it may affect an individual, independently of his human affections, by virtue of an attraction it exercises upon his mind, even before he has comprehended it. This is the phenomenon which has been well called the *divination* of genius; for it is due to the continuity between the man's mind and the Most High.

Let us next consider by means of what tests we can discriminate between these different categories of evolution. No absolute criterion is possible in the nature of things, since in the nature of things there is no sharp line of demarcation between the different classes. Nevertheless, quantitative symptoms may be found by which a sagacious and sympathetic judge of human nature may be able to estimate the approximate proportions in which the different kinds of influence are commingled.

So far as the historical evolution of human thought has been tychastic, it should have proceeded by insensible or minute steps; for such is the nature of chances when so multiplied as to show phenomena of regularity. For example, assume that of the native-born white adult males of the United States in 1880, one-fourth part were below 5 feet 4 inches in stature and one-fourth part above 5 feet 8 inches. Then by the principles of probability, among the whole population, we should expect

	216 under	4 feet	6	inches,		216 above	6 feet	6	inches
	48	" 4	" 5	"		48	" 6	" 7	"
	9	" 4	" 4	"		9	" 6	" 8	"
less than	2	" 4	" 3	"	less than	2	" 6	" 9	"

I set down these figures to show how insignificantly few are the cases in which anything very far out of the common run presents itself by chance. Though the stature of only every second man is included within the four inches between 5 feet 4 inches and 5 feet 8 inches, yet if this interval be extended by thrice four inches above and below, it will embrace all our 8 millions odd of native-born adult white males (of 1880), except only 9 taller and 9 shorter.

The test of minute variation, if *not* satisfied, absolutely negatives tychasm. If it *is* satisfied, we shall find that it negatives anancasm but not agapasm. We want a positive test, satisfied by tychasm, only. Now wherever we find men's thought taking by imperceptible degrees a turn contrary to the purposes which animate them, in spite of their highest impulses, there, we may safely conclude, there has been a tychastic action.

Students of the history of mind there be of an erudition to fill an imperfect scholar like me with envy edulcorated by joyous admiration, who maintain that ideas when just started are and can be little more than freaks, since they cannot yet have been critically examined, and futher that everywhere and at all times progress has been so gradual that it is difficult to make out distinctly what original step any given man has taken. It would follow that tychasm has been the sole method of intellectual development. I have to confess I cannot read history so; I cannot help thinking that while tychasm has sometimes been operative, at others great steps covering nearly the same ground and made by different men independently, have been mistaken for a succession of small steps, and further that students have been reluctant to admit a real entitative "spirit" of an age or of a people, under the mistaken and unscrutinized impression that they should thus be opening the door to wild and unnatural hypotheses. I find, on the contrary, that, however it may be with the education of individual minds, the historical development of thought has seldom been of a tychastic nature, and exclusively in backward and barbarizing movements. I desire to speak with the extreme modesty which befits a student of logic who is required to survey so very wide a field of human thought that he can cover it only by a reconnaissance, to which only the greatest skill and most adroit methods can impart any value at all; but, after all, I can only express my own opinions and not those of anybody else; and in my humble judgment, the largest example of tychasm is afforded by the history of Christianity, from about its establishment by Constantine, to, say, the time of the Irish monasteries, an era or eon of about 500 years. Undoubtedly the external circumstance which more than all others at first inclined men to accept Christianity in its loveliness and tenderness, was the fearful extent to which society was broken up into units by the unmitigated greed and hard-heartedness into which the Romans had seduced the world. And yet it was that very same fact, more than any other external circumstance, that fostered that bitterness against the wicked world of which the primitive gospel of Mark contains not a single trace. At least, I do not detect it in the remark about the blasphemy against the Holy Ghost, where nothing is said about vengeance, nor even in that speech where the closing lines of Isaiah are quoted, about the worm and the fire that feed upon the "carcasses of the men that have transgressed against me." But little by little the bitterness increases until in the last book of the New Testament, its poor distracted author represents that all the time Christ was talking about having come to save the world, the secret design was to catch the entire human race, with the exception of a paltry 144,000, and souse them all in a brimstone lake, and as the smoke of their torment went up forever and ever, to turn and remark, "There is no curse any more." Would it be an insensible smirk or a fiendish grin that should accompany such an utterance? I wish I could believe St. John did not write it; but it is his gospel which tells about the "resurrection unto condemnation,"—that is of men's being resuscitated just for the sake of torturing them;—and, at any rate, the Revelation is a very ancient composition. One can understand that the early Christians were like men trying with all their might to climb a steep declivity of smooth wet clay; the deepest and truest element of their life, animating both heart and head, was universal love; but they were continually, and against their wills, slipping into a party spirit, every slip serving as a precedent, in a fashion but too familiar to every man. This party feeling insensibly grew until by about A.D. 330 the luster of the pristine integrity that in St. Mark reflects the white spirit of light was so far tarnished that Eusebius, (the Jared Sparks of that day), in the preface to his History, could announce his intention of exaggerating everything that tended to the glory of the church and of suppressing whatever might disgrace it. His Latin contemporary Lactantius is worse, still; and so the darkling went on increasing until before the end of the century the great library of Alexandria was destroyed by Theophilus, until Gregory the Great, two centuries later, burnt the great library of Rome, proclaiming that "Ignorance is the mother of devotion," (which is true, just as oppression and injustice is the mother of spirituality), until a sober description of the state of the church would be a thing our not too nice newspapers would treat as "unfit for publication." All this movement is shown by the application of the test given above to have been tychastic. Another very much like it on a small scale, only a hundred times swifter, for the study of which there are documents by the library-full, is to be found in the history of the French Revolution.

Anancastic evolution advances by successive strides with pauses between. The reason is that in this process a habit of thought having been overthrown is supplanted by the next strongest. Now this next strongest is sure to be widely disparate from the first, and as often as not is its direct contrary. It reminds one of our old rule of making the second candidate vice-president. This character, therefore, clearly distinguishes anancasm from tychasm. The character which distinguishes it from agapasm is its purposelessness. But external and internal anancasm have to be examined separately. Development under the pressure of external circumstances, or cataclysmine evolution, is in most cases unmistakable enough. It has numberless degrees of intensity, from the brute force, the plain war, which has more than once turned the current of the world's thought, down to the hard fact of evidence, or what has been taken for it, which has been known to convince men by hordes. The only hesitation that can subsist in the presence of such a history is a quantitative one. Never are external influences the only ones which affect the mind, and therefore it must be a matter of judgment for which it would scarcely be worth while to attempt to set rules, whether a given movement is to be regarded as principally governed from without or not. In the rise of medieval thought, I mean scholasticism and the synchronistic art developments, undoubtedly the crusades and the discovery of the writings of Aristotle were powerful influences. The development of scholasticism from Roscellin to Albertus Magnus closely follows the successive steps in the knowledge of Aristotle. Prantl thinks that that is the whole story, and few men have thumbed more books than Carl Prantl. He has done good solid work, notwithstanding his slap-dash judgments. But we shall never make so much as a good beginning of comprehending scholasticism until the whole has been systematically explored and digested by a company of students regularly organized and held under rule for that purpose. But as for the period we are now specially considering, that which synchronised the Romanesque architecture, the literature is easily mastered. It does not quite justify Prantl's dicta as to the slavish dependence of these authors upon their authorities. Moreover, they kept a definite purpose steadily before their minds, throughout all their studies. I am, therefore, unable to offer this period of scholasticism as an example of pure external anancasm, which seems to be the fluorine of the intellectual elements. Perhaps the recent Japanese reception of western ideas is the purest instance of it in history. Yet in combination with other elements, nothing is commoner. If the development of ideas under the influence of the study of external facts be considered as external anancasm,—it is on the border between the external and the internal forms,—it is, of course, the principal thing in modern learning. But Whewell, whose masterly comprehension of the history of science critics have been too ignorant properly to appreciate, clearly shows that it is far from being the overwhelmingly preponderant influence, even there.

Internal anancasm, or logical groping, which advances upon a pre-destined line without being able to foresee whither it is to be carried nor to steer its course, this is the rule of development of philosophy. Hegel first made the world understand this; and he seeks to make logic not merely

the subjective guide and monitor of thought, which was all it had been
ambitioning before, but to be the very mainspring of thinking, and not
merely of individual thinking but of discussion, of the history of the
development of thought, of all history, of all development. This involves
a positive, clearly demonstrable error. Let the logic in question be of
whatever kind it may, a logic of necessary inference or a logic of probable
inference (the theory might perhaps be shaped to fit either), in any case
it supposes that logic is sufficient of itself to determine what conclusion
follows from given premises; for unless it will do so much, it will not suffice
to explain why an individual train of reasoning should take just the course
it does take, to say nothing of other kinds of development. It thus supposes
that from given premises, only one conclusion can logically be drawn,
and that there is no scope at all for free choice. That from given premises
only one conclusion can be logically be drawn, is one of the false notions
which have come from logicians' confining their attention to that Nan-
tucket of thought, the logic of non-relative terms. In the logic of relatives,
it does not hold good.

One remark occurs to me. If the evolution of history is in considerable
part of the nature of internal anancasm, it resembles the development of
individual men; and just as 33 years is a rough but natural unit of time
for individuals, being the average age at which man has issue, so there
should be an approximate period at the end of which one great historical
movement ought to be likely to be supplanted by another. Let us see if we
can make out anything of the kind. Take the governmental development
of Rome as being sufficiently long and set down the principal dates.

B.C.   753, Foundation of Rome.
B.C.   510, Expulsion of the Tarquins.
B.C.   27, Octavius assumes title Augustus.
A.D.   476, End of Western Empire.
A.D.   962, Holy Roman Empire.
A.D. 1453, Fall of Constantinople.

The last event was one of the most significant in history, especially for
Italy. The intervals are 243, 483, 502, 486, 491 years. All are rather
curiously near equal, except the first which is half the others. Successive
reigns of kings would not commonly be so near equal. Let us set down a
few dates in the history of thought.

B.C.   585, Eclipse of Thales. Beginning of Greek philosophy.
A.D.   30, The crucifixion.
A.D.   529, Closing of Athenian schools. End of Greek philosophy.
A.D. 1125, (Approximate) Rise of the Universities of Bologna and Paris.
A.D. 1543, Publication of the "De Revolutionibus" of Copernicus. Be-
            ginning of Modern Science.

The intervals are 615, 499, 596, 418, years. In the history of metaphysics, we may take the following:

B.C. 322, Death of Aristotle.
A.D. 1274, Death of Aquinas.
A.D. 1804, Death of Kant.

The intervals are 1595 and 530 years. The former is about thrice the latter.

From these figures, no conclusion can fairly be drawn. At the same time, they suggest that perhaps there may be a rough natural era of about 500 years. Should there be any independent evidence of this, the intervals noticed may gain some significance.

The agapastic development of thought should, if it exists, be distinguished by its purposive character, this purpose being the development of an idea. We should have a direct agapic or sympathetic comprehension and recognition of it, by virtue of the continuity of thought. I here take it for granted that such continuity of thought has been sufficiently proved by the arguments used in my paper on the "Law of Mind" in *The Monist* of last July. Even if those arguments are not quite convincing in themselves, yet if they are reënforced by an apparent agapasm in the history of thought, the two propositions will lend one another mutual aid. The reader will, I trust, be too well grounded in logic to mistake such mutual support for a vicious circle in reasoning. If it could be shown directly that there is such an entity as the "spirit of an age" or of a people, and that mere individual intelligence will not account for all the phenomena, this would be proof enough at once of agapasticism and of synechism. I must acknowledge that I am unable to produce a cogent demonstration of this; but I am, I believe, able to adduce such arguments as will serve to confirm those which have been drawn from other facts. I believe that all the greatest achievements of mind have been beyond the powers of unaided individuals; and I find, apart from the support this opinion receives from synechistic considerations, and from the purposive character of many great movements, direct reason for so thinking in the sublimity of the ideas and in their occurring simultaneously and independently to a number of individuals of no extraordinary general powers. The pointed Gothic architecture in several of its developements appears to me to be of such a character. All attempts to imitate it by modern architects of the greatest learning and genius appear flat and tame, and are felt by their authors to be so. Yet at the time the style was living, there was quite an abundance of men capable of producing works of this kind of gigantic sublimity and power. In more than one case, extant documents show that the cathedral chapters, in the selection of architects, treated high artistic genius as a secondary consideration, as if there were no lack of persons able to supply that; and the results justify their confidence. Were individuals in general, then, in those ages possessed of such lofty natures and high intellect? Such an opinion would break down under the first examination.

How many times have men now in middle life seen great discoveries made independently and almost simultaneously! The first instance I remember was the prediction of a planet exterior to Uranus by Leverrier and Adams. One hardly knows to whom the principle of the conservation of energy ought to be attributed, although it may reasonably be considered as the greatest discovery science has ever made. The mechanical theory of heat was set forth by Rankine and by Clausius during the same month of February, 1850; and there are eminent men who attribute this great step to Thomson. The kinetical theory of gases, after being started by John Bernoulli and long buried in oblivion, was reinvented and applied to the explanation not merely of the laws of Boyle, Charles, and Avogadro, but also of diffusion and viscosity, by at least three modern physicists separately. It is well known that the doctrine of natural selection was presented by Wallace and by Darwin at the same meeting of the British Association; and Darwin in his "Historical Sketch" prefixed to the later editions of his book shows that both were anticipated by obscure forerunners. The method of spectrum analysis was claimed for Swan as well as for Kirchhoff, and there were others who perhaps had still better claims. The authorship of the Periodical Law of the Chemical Elements is disputed between a Russian, a German, and an Englishman; although there is no room for doubt that the principal merit belongs to the first. These are nearly all the greatest discoveries of our times. It is the same with the inventions. It may not be surprising that the telegraph should have been independently made by several inventors, because it was an easy corollary from scientific facts well made out before. But it was not so with the telephone and other inventions. Ether, the first anæsthetic, was introduced independently by three different New England physicians. Now ether had been a common article for a century. It had been in one of the pharmacopœias three centuries before. It is quite incredible that its anæsthetic property should not have been known; it was known. It had probably passed from mouth to ear as a secret from the days of Basil Valentine; but for long it had been a secret of the Punchinello kind. In New England, for many years, boys had used it for amusement. Why then had it not been put to its serious use? No reason can be given, except that the motive to do so was not strong enough. The motives to doing so could only have been desire for gain and philanthropy. About 1846, the date of the introduction, philanthropy was undoubtedly in an unusually active condition. That sensibility, or sentimentalism, which had been introduced in the previous century, had undergone a ripening process, in consequence of which, though now less intense than it had previously been, it was more likely to influence unreflecting people than it had ever been. All three of the ether-claimants had probably been influenced by the desire for gain; but nevertheless they were certainly not insensible to the agapic influences.

I doubt if any of the great discoveries ought, properly, to be considered as altogether individual achievements; and I think many will share this doubt. Yet, if not, what an argument for the continuity of mind, and for agapasticism is here! I do not wish to be very strenuous. If thinkers will only be persuaded to lay aside their predjudicies and apply themselves to studying the evidences of this doctrine, I shall be fully content to await the final decision.

What Pragmatism Means

THE WRITER OF THIS ARTICLE HAS BEEN LED BY MUCH EXPERIENCE TO BE-
lieve that every physicist, and every chemist, and, in short, every master
in any department of experimental science, has had his mind moulded by
his life in the laboratory to a degree that is little suspected. The experimentalist himself can hardly be fully aware of it, for the reason that the men
whose intellects he really knows about are much like himself in this respect.
With intellects of widely different training from his own, whose education
has largely been a thing learned out of books, he will never become inwardly intimate, be he on ever so familiar terms with them; for he and they
are as oil and water, and though they be shaken up together, it is remarkable how quickly they will go their several mental ways, without having
gained more than a faint flavour from the association. Were those other men
only to take skillful soundings of the experimentalist's mind—which is just
what they are unqualified to do, for the most part—they would soon discover that, excepting perhaps upon topics where his mind is trammelled by
personal feeling or by his bringing up, his disposition is to think of everything just as everything is thought of in the laboratory, that is, as a question
of experimentation. Of course, no living man possesses in their fullness all the attributes characteristic of his type: it is not the typical doctor
whom you will see every day driven in buggy or coupé, nor is it the typical
pedagogue that will be met with in the first schoolroom you enter. But
when you have found, or ideally constructed upon a basis of observation,
the typical experimentalist, you will find that whatever assertion you may
make to him, he will either understand as meaning that if a given prescrip-
tion for an experiment ever can be and ever is carried out in act, an experience of a given description will result, or else he will see no sense at all
in what you say. If you talk to him as Mr. Balfour talked not long ago
to the British Association saying that "the physicist . . . seeks for something deeper than the laws connecting possible objects of experience," that
"his object is physical reality" unrevealed in experiments, and that the
existence of such non-experiential reality "is the unalterable faith of science," to all such ontological meaning you will find the experimentalist
mind to be colour-blind. What adds to that confidence in this, which the
writer owes to his conversations with experimentalists, is that he himself

may almost be said to have inhabited a laboratory from the age of six until long past maturity; and having all his life associated mostly with experimentalists, it has always been with a confident sense of understanding them and of being understood by them.

That laboratory life did not prevent the writer (who here and in what follows simply exemplifies the experimentalist type) from becoming interested in methods of thinking; and when he came to read metaphysics, although much of it seemed to him loosely reasoned and determined by accidental prepossessions, yet in the writings of some philosophers, especially Kant, Berkeley, and Spinoza, he sometimes came upon strains of thought that recalled the ways of thinking of the laboratory, so that he felt he might trust to them; all of which has been true of other laboratory-men.

Endeavouring, as a man of that type naturally would, to formulate what he so approved, he framed the theory that a *conception,* that is, the rational purport of a word or other expression, lies exclusively in its conceivable bearing upon the conduct of life; so that, since obviously nothing that might not result from experiment can have any direct bearing upon conduct, if one can define accurately all the conceivable experimental phenomena which the affirmation or denial of a concept could imply, one will have therein a complete definition of the concept, and *there is absolutely nothing more in it.* For this doctrine he invented the name *pragmatism.* Some of his friends wished him to call it *practicism* or *practicalism* (perhaps on the ground that πρακτικός is better Greek than πραγματικός). But for one who had learned philosophy out of Kant, as the writer, along with nineteen out of every twenty experimentalists who have turned to philosophy, had done, and who still thought in Kantian terms most readily, *praktisch* and *pragmatisch* were as far apart as the two poles, the former belonging in a region of thought where no mind of the experimentalist type can ever make sure of solid ground under his feet, the latter expressing relation to some definite human purpose. Now quite the most striking feature of the new theory was its recognition of an inseparable connection between rational cognition and rational purpose; and that consideration it was which determined the preference for the name *pragmatism.*

Concerning the matter of philosophical nomenclature, there are a few plain considerations, which the writer has for many years longed to submit to the deliberate judgment of those few fellow-students of philosophy, who deplore the present state of that study, and who are intent upon rescuing it therefrom and bringing it to a condition like that of the natural sciences, where investigators, instead of contemning each the work of most of the others as misdirected from beginning to end, coöperate, stand upon one another's shoulders, and multiply incontestable results; where every observation is repeated, and isolated observations go for little; where every hypothesis that merits attention is subjected to severe but fair examination, and only after the predictions to which it leads have been remarkably borne out by experience is trusted at all, and even then only provisionally; where a radically false step is rarely taken, even the most faulty of those theories which gain wide credence being true in their main experiential predictions. To those students, it is submitted that no study can become scientific in the sense described, until it provides itself with a suitable technical nomenclature, whose every term has a single definite meaning universally accepted among students of the subject, and whose vocables have no such sweetness or charms as might tempt loose writers to abuse them—which is a virtue of scientific nomenclature too little appreciated. It is submitted that the experience of those sciences which have conquered the greatest difficulties of terminology, which are unquestionably the taxonomic sciences, chemistry, mineralogy, botany, zoölogy, has conclusively shown that the one only way in which the requisite unanimity and requisite ruptures with individual habits and preferences can be brought about is so to shape the canons of terminology that they shall gain the support of *moral principle* and of every man's sense of decency; and that, in particular (under defined restrictions), the general feeling shall be that he who introduces a new conception into philosophy is under an obligation to invent acceptable terms to express it, and that when he has done so, the duty of his fellow-students is to accept those terms, and to resent any wresting of them from their original meanings, as not only a gross discourtesy to him to whom philosophy was indebted for each conception, but also as an injury to philosophy itself; and furthermore, that once a conception has been supplied with suitable and sufficient words for its expression, no other *technical* terms denoting the same things, considered in the same relations, should be countenanced. Should this suggestion find favour, it might be deemed needful that the philosophians in congress assembled should adopt, after due deliberation, convenient canons to limit the application of the principle. Thus, just as is done in chemistry, it might be wise to assign fixed meanings to certain prefixes and suffixes. For example, it might be agreed, perhaps, that the prefix *prope-* should mark a broad and rather indefinite extension of the meaning of the term to which it was prefixed; the name of a doctrine would naturally end in *-ism*, while *-icism* might mark a more strictly defined acception of that doctrine, etc. Then again, just as in biology no account is taken of terms antedating Linnaeus, so in philosophy it might be found best not to go back of the scholastic terminology. To illustrate another sort of limitation, it has probably never happened that any philosopher has attempted to give a general name to his own doctrine without that name's soon acquiring in common philosophical usage, a signification much broader than was originally intended. Thus, special systems go by the names Kantianism, Benthamism, Comteanism, Spencerianism, etc., while transcendentalism, utilitarianism, positivism, evolutionism, synthetic philosophy, etc., have irrevocably and very conveniently been elevated to broader governments.

After awaiting in vain, for a good many years, some particularly opportune conjuncture of circumstances that might serve to recommend his notions of the ethics of terminology, the writer has now, at last, dragged them in over head and shoulders, on an occasion when he has no specific proposal to offer nor any feeling but satisfaction at the course usage has run without any canons or resolutions of a congress. His word "pragmatism" has gained general recognition in a generalized sense that seems to argue power of growth and vitality. The famed psychologist, James, first took it up, seeing that his "radical empiricism" substantially answered to the writer's definition of pragmatism, albeit with a certain difference in the point of view. Next, the admirably clear and brilliant thinker, Mr. Ferdinand C. S. Schiller, casting about for a more attractive name for the "anthropomorphism" of his *Riddle of the Sphinx,* lit, in that most remarkable paper of his on *Axioms as Postulates,* upon the same designation "pragmatism," which in its original sense was in generic agreement with his own doctrine, for which he has since found the more appropriate specification "humanism," while he still retains "pragmatism" in a somewhat wider sense. So far all went happily. But at present, the word begins to be met with occasionally in the literary journals, where it gets abused in the merciless way that words have to expect when they fall into literary clutches. Sometimes the manners of the British have effloresced in scolding at the word as ill-chosen—ill-chosen, that is, to express some meaning that it was rather designed to exclude. So then, the writer, finding his bantling "pragmatism" so promoted, feels that it is time to kiss his child good-by and relinquish it to its higher destiny; while to serve the precise purpose of expressing the original definition, he begs to announce the birth of the word "pragmaticism," which is ugly enough to be safe from kidnappers.

Much as the writer has gained from the perusal of what other pragmatists have written, he still thinks there is a decisive advantage in his original conception of the doctrine. From this original form every truth that follows from any of the other forms can be deduced, while some errors can be avoided into which other pragmatists have fallen. The original view appears, too, to be a more compact and unitary conception than the others. But its capital merit, in the writer's eyes, is that it more readily connects itself with a critical proof of its truth. Quite in accord with the logical order of investigation, it usually happens that one first forms an hypothesis that seems more and more reasonable the further one examines into it, but that only a good deal later gets crowned with an adequate proof. The present writer having had the pragmatist theory under consideration for many years longer than most of its adherents, would naturally have given more attention to the proof of it. At any rate, in endeavouring to explain pragmatism, he may be excused for confining himself to that form of it that he knows best. In the present article there will be space only to explain just what this doctrine (which, in such hands as it has now fallen into, may probably play a pretty prominent part in the philosophical discussions of the next coming years), really consists in. Should the exposition be found to interest readers of *The Monist,* they would certainly be much more interested in a second article which would give some samples of the manifold applications of pragmaticism (assuming it to be true) to the solution of problems of different kinds. After that, readers might be prepared to take an interest in a proof that the doctrine is true—a proof which seems to the writer to leave no reasonable doubt on the subject, and to be the one contribution of value that he has to make to philosophy. For it would essentially involve the establishment of the truth of synechism.

The bare definition of pragmaticism could convey no satisfactory comprehension of it to the most apprehensive of minds, but requires the commentary to be given below. Moreover, this definition takes no notice of one or two other doctrines without the previous acceptance (or virtual acceptance) of which pragmaticism itself would be a nullity. They are included as a part of the pragmatism of Schiller, but the present writer prefers not to mingle different propositions. The preliminary propositions had better be stated forthwith.

The difficulty in doing this is that no formal list of them has ever been made. They might all be included under the vague maxim, "Dismiss make-believes." Philosophers of very diverse stripes propose that philosophy shall take its start from one or another state of mind in which no man, least of all a beginner in philosophy, actually is. One proposes that you shall begin by doubting everything, and says that there is only one thing that you cannot doubt, as if doubting were "as easy as lying." Another proposes that we should begin by observing "the first impressions of sense," forgetting that our very percepts are the results of cognitive elaboration. But in truth, there is but one state of mind from which you can "set out," namely, the very state of mind in which you actually find yourself at the time you do "set out"—a state in which you are laden with an immense mass of cognition already formed, of which you cannot divest yourself if you would; and who knows whether, if you could, you would not have made all knowledge impossible to yourself? Do you call it *doubting* to write down on a piece of paper that you doubt? If so, doubt has nothing to do with any serious business. But do not make believe; if pedantry has not eaten all the reality out of you, recognize, as you must, that there is much that you do not doubt, in the least. Now that which you do not at all doubt, you must and do regard as infallible, absolute truth. Here breaks in Mr. Make Believe: "What! Do you mean to say that one is to believe what is not true, or that what a man does not doubt is *ipso facto* true?" No, but unless he can make a thing white and black at once, *he* has to regard what he does not doubt as absolutely true. Now you, *per hypothesiu,* are that man. "But you tell me there are scores of things I do not doubt. I really cannot persuade myself that there is not some one of them about which I am mistaken." You are adducing one of your make-believe facts, which, even if it were established, would only go to show that doubt has a *limen*, that is, is only called into being by a certain finite stimulus. You only puzzle yourself by talking of this metaphysical "truth" and metaphysical "falsity," that you know nothing about. All you have any dealings with are your doubts and beliefs, with the course of life that forces new beliefs upon you and gives you power to doubt old beliefs. If your terms "truth" and "falsity" are taken in such senses as to be definable in terms of doubt and belief and the course of experience (as for example they would be, if you were to define the "truth" as that to a belief in which belief would tend if it were to tend indefinitely toward absolute fixity), well and good: in that case, you are only talking about doubt and belief. But if by truth and falsity you mean something not definable in terms of doubt and belief in any way, then you are talking of entities of whose existence you can know nothing, and which Ockham's razor would clean shave off. Your problems would be greatly simplified, if, instead of saying that you want to know the "Truth," you were simply to say that you want to attain a state of belief unassailable by doubt.

Belief is not a momentary mode of consciousness; it is a habit of mind essentially enduring for some time, and mostly (at least) unconscious; and like other habits, it is (until it meets with some surprise that begins its dissolution) perfectly self-satisfied. Doubt is of an altogether contrary genus. It is not a habit, but the privation of a habit. Now a privation of a habit, in order to be anything at all, must be a condition of erratic activity that in some way must get superseded by a habit.

Among the things which the reader, as a rational person, does not doubt, is that he not merely has habits, but also can exert a measure of self-control over his future actions; which means, however, *not* that he can impart to them any arbitrarily assignable character, but, on the contrary, that a process of self-preparation will tend to impart to action (when the occasion for it shall arise), one fixed character, which is indicated and perhaps roughly measured by the absence (or slightness) of the feeling of self-reproach, which subsequent reflection will induce. Now, this subsequent reflection is part of the self-preparation for action on the next occasion. Consequently, there is a tendency, as action is repeated again and again, for the action to approximate indefinitely toward the perfection of that fixed character, which would be marked by entire absence of self-reproach. The more closely this is approached, the less room for self-control there will be; and where no self-control is possible there will be no self-reproach.

These phenomena seem to be the fundamental characteristics which distinguish a rational being. Blame, in every case, appears to be a modification, often accomplished by a transference, or "projection," of the primary feeling of self-reproach. Accordingly, we never blame anybody for what had been beyond his power of previous self-control. Now, thinking is a species of conduct which is largely subject to self-control. In all their features (which there is no room to describe here), logical self-control is a perfect mirror of ethical self-control—unless it be rather a species under that genus. In accordance with this, what you cannot in the least help believing is not, justly speaking, wrong belief. In other words, for you it is the absolute truth. True, it is conceivable that what you cannot help believing today, you might find you thoroughly disbelieve tomorrow. But then there is a certain distinction between things you "cannot" do, merely in the sense that nothing stimulates you to the great effort and endeavours that would be required, and things you cannot do because in their own nature they are insusceptible of being put into practice. In every stage of your excogitations, there is something of which you can only say, "I cannot think otherwise," and your experientially based hypothesis is that the impossibility is of the second kind.

There is no reason why "thought," in what has just been said, should be taken in that narrow sense in which silence and darkness are favourable to thought. It should rather be understood as covering all rational life, so that an experiment shall be an operation of thought. Of course, that ultimate state of habit to which the action of self-control ultimately tends, where no room is left for further self-control, is, in the case of thought, the state of fixed belief, or perfect knowledge.

Two things here are all-important to assure oneself of and to remember. The first is that a person is not absolutely an individual. His thoughts are what he is "saying to himself," that is, is saying to that other self that is just coming into life in the flow of time. When one reasons, it is that critical self that one is trying to persuade; and all thought whatsoever is a sign, and is mostly of the nature of language. The second thing to remember is that the man's circle of society (however widely or narrowly this phrase may be understood), is a sort of loosely compacted person, in some respects of higher rank than the person of an individual organism. It is these two things alone that render it possible for you—but only in the abstract, and in a Pickwickian sense—to distinguish between absolute truth and what you do not doubt.

Let us now hasten to the exposition of pragmaticism itself. Here it will be convenient to imagine that somebody to whom the doctrine is new, but of rather preternatural perspicacity, asks questions of a pragmaticist. Everything that might give a dramatic illusion must be stripped off, so that the result will be a sort of cross between a dialogue and a catechism, but a good deal liker the latter—something rather painfully reminiscent of Mangnall's *Historical Questions*.

Questioner: I am astounded at your definition of your pragmatism, because only last year I was assured by a person above all suspicion of warping the truth—himself a pragmatist—that your doctrine precisely was "that a conception is to be tested by its practical effects." You must surely, then, have entirely changed your definition very recently.

Pragmaticist: If you will turn to Vols. VI and VII of the *Revue Philoso-phique,* or to the *Popular Science Monthly* for November 1877 and January 1878,[15] you will be able to judge for yourself whether the interpretation you mention was not then clearly excluded. The exact wording of the English enunciation (changing only the first person into the second) was: "Consider what effects that might conceivably have practical bearing you conceive the object of your conception to have. Then your conception of those effects is the WHOLE of your conception of the object."

Questioner: Well, what reason have you for asserting that this is so?

Pragmaticist: That is what I specially desire to tell you. But the question had better be postponed until you clearly understand what those reasons profess to prove.

Questioner: What, then, is the *raison d'être* of the doctrine? What advantage is expected from it?

Pragmaticist: It will serve to show that almost every proposition of ontological metaphysics is either meaningless gibberish—one word being defined by other words, and they by still others, without any real conception ever being reached—or else is downright absurd; so that all such rubbish being swept away, what will remain of philosophy will be a series of problems capable of investigation by the observational methods of the true sciences—the truth about which can be reached without those interminable misunderstandings and disputes which have made the highest of the positive sciences a mere amusement for idle intellects, a sort of chess—idle pleasure its purpose, and reading out of a book its method. In this regard, pragmaticism is a species of prope-positivism. But what distinguishes it from other species is, first, its retention of a purified philosophy; secondly, its full acceptance of the main body of our instinctive beliefs; and thirdly, its strenuous insistence upon the truth of scholastic realism (or a close approximation to that, well-stated by the late Dr. Francis Ellingwood Abbot in the Introduction to his *Scientific Theism).* So, instead of merely jeering at metaphysics, like other prope-positivists, whether by long-drawn-out parodies or otherwise, the pragmaticist extracts from it a precious essence, which will serve to give life and light to cosmology and physics. At the same time, the moral applications of the doctrine are positive and potent; and there are many other uses of it not easily classed. On another occasion, instances may be given to show that it really has these effects.

Questioner: I hardly need to be convinced that your doctrine would wipe out metaphysics. Is it not as obvious that it must wipe out every proposition of science and everything that bears on the conduct of life? For you say that the only meaning that, for you, any assertion bears is that a certain experiment has resulted in a certain way: Nothing else but an experiment enters into the meaning. Tell me, then, how can an experiment, in itself, reveal anything more than that something once happened to an individual object and that subsequently some other individual event occurred?

Pragmaticist: That question is, indeed, to the purpose—the purpose being to correct any misapprehensions of pragmaticism. You speak of an experiment in itself, emphasizing *"in itself."* You evidently think of each experiment as isolated from every other. It has not, for example, occurred to you, one might venture to surmise, that every connected series of experiments constitutes a single collective experiment. What are the essential ingredients of an experiment? First, of course, an experimenter of flesh and blood. Secondly, a verifiable hypothesis. This is a proposition relating to the universe environing the experimenter, or to some well-known part of it and affirming or denying of this only some experimental possibility or impossibility. The third indispensable ingredient is a sincere doubt in the experimenter's mind as to the truth of that hypothesis.

Passing over several ingredients on which we need not dwell, the purpose, the plan, and the resolve, we come to the act of choice by which the experimenter singles out certain identifiable objects to be operated upon. The next is the external (or quasi-external) ACT by which he modifies those objects. Next, comes the subsequent *reaction* of the world upon the experimenter in a perception; and finally, his recognition of the teaching of the experiment. While the two chief parts of the event itself are the action and the reaction, yet the unity of essence of the experiment lies in its purpose and plan, the ingredients passed over in the enumeration.

Another thing: in representing the pragmaticist as making rational meaning to consist in an experiment (which you speak of as an event in the past), you strikingly fail to catch his attitude of mind. Indeed, it is not in an experiment, but in *experimental phenomena,* that rational meaning is said to consist. When an experimentalist speaks of a *phenomenon,* such as "Hall's phenomenon," "Zeemann's phenomenon" and its modification, "Michelson's phenomenon," or "the chessboard phenomenon," he does not mean any particular event that did happen to somebody in the dead past, but what *surely will* happen to everybody in the living future who shall fulfill certain conditions. The phenomenon consists in the fact that when an experimentalist shall come to *act* according to a certain scheme that he has in mind, then will something else happen, and shatter the doubts of sceptics, like the celestial fire upon the altar of Elijah.

And do not overlook the fact that the pragmaticist maxim says nothing of single experiments or of single experimental phenomena (for what is conditionally true *in futuro* can hardly be singular), but only speaks of *general kinds* of experimental phenomena. Its adherent does not shrink from speaking of general objects as real, since whatever is true represents a real. Now the laws of nature are true.

The rational meaning of every proposition lies in the future. How so? The meaning of a proposition is itself a proposition. Indeed, it is no other than the very proposition of which it is the meaning: it is a translation of it. But of the myriads of forms into which a proposition may be translated, what is that one which is to be called its very meaning? It is, according to the pragmaticist, that form in which the proposition becomes applicable to human conduct, not in these or those special circumstances, nor when one entertains this or that special design, but that form which is most directly applicable to self-control under every situation, and to every purpose. This is why he locates the meaning in future time; for future conduct is the only conduct that is subject to self-control. But in order that that form of the proposition which is to be taken as its meaning should be applicable to every situation and to every purpose upon which the proposition has any bearing, it must be simply the general description of all the experimental phenomena which the assertion of the proposition virtually predicts. For an experimental phenomenon is the fact asserted by the proposition that action of a certain description will have a certain kind of experimental result; and experimental results are the only results that can affect human conduct. No doubt, some unchanging idea may come to influence a man more than it had done; but only because some experience equivalent to an experiment has brought its truth home to him more intimately than before. Whenever a man acts purposively, he acts under a belief in some experimental phenomenon. Consequently, the sum of the experimental phenomena that a proposition implies makes up its entire bearing upon human conduct. Your question, then, of how a pragmaticist can attribute any meaning to any assertion other than that of a single occurrence is substantially answered.

Questioner: I see that pragmaticism is a thorough-going phenomenalism. Only why should you limit yourself to the phenomena of experimental science rather than embrace all observational science? Experiment, after all, is an uncommunicative informant. It never expatiates: it only answers "yes" or "no"; or rather it usually snaps out "No!", or at best only utters an inarticulate grunt for the negation of its "no." The typical experimentalist is not much of an observer. It is the student of natural history to whom nature opens the treasury of her confidence, while she treats the cross-examining experimentalist with the reserve he merits. Why should your phenomenalism sound the meagre jew's-harp of experiment rather than the glorious organ of observation?

Pragmaticist: Because pragmaticism is not definable as "thorough-going phenomenalism," although the latter doctrine may be a kind of pragmatism. The *richness* of phenomena lies in their sensuous quality. Pragmaticism does not intend to define the phenomenal equivalents of words and general ideas, but, on the contrary, eliminates their sential element, and endeavours to define the rational purport, and this it finds in the purposive bearing of the word or proposition in question.

Questioner: Well, if you choose so to make Doing the Be-all and the End-all of human life, why do you not make meaning to consist simply in doing? Doing has to be done at a certain time upon a certain object. Individual objects and single events cover all reality, as everybody knows, and as a practicalist ought to be the first to insist. Yet, your meaning, as you have described it, is *general*. Thus, it is of the nature of a mere word and not a reality. You say yourself that your meaning of a proposition is only the same proposition in another dress. But a practical man's meaning is the very thing he means. What do you make to be the meaning of "George Washington"?

Pragmaticist: Forcibly put! A good half dozen of your points must certainly be admitted. It must be admited, in the first place, that if pragmaticism really made Doing to be the Be-all and the End-all of life, that would be its death. For to say that we live for the mere sake of action, as action, regardless of the thought it carries out, would be to say that there is no such thing as rational purport. Secondly, it must be admitted that every proposition professes to be true of a certain real individual object, often the environing universe. Thirdly, it must be admitted that pragmaticism fails to furnish any translation or meaning of a proper name, or other designation of an individual object. Fourthly, the pragmaticistic meaning is undoubtedly general; and it is equally indisputable that the general is of the nature of a word or sign. Fifthly, it must be admitted that individuals alone exist; and sixthly, it may be admitted that the very meaning of a word or significant object ought to be the very essence of reality of what it signifies. But when those admissions have been unreservedly made, you find the pragmaticist still constrained most earnestly to deny the force of your objection, you ought to infer that there is some consideration that has escaped you. Putting the admissions together, you will perceive that the pragmaticist grants that a proper name (although it is not customary to say that it has a *meaning)* has a certain denotative function peculiar, in each case, to that name and its equivalents; and that he grants that every assertion contains such a denotative or pointing-out function. In its peculiar individuality, the pragmaticist excludes this from the rational purport of the assertion, although *the like* of it, being common to all assertions, and so, being general and not individual, may enter into the pragmaticistic purport. Whatever exists, *ex-sists,* that is, really acts upon other existents, so obtains a self-identity, and is definitely individual. As to the general, it will be a help to thought to notice that there are two ways of being general. A statue of a soldier on some village monument, in his overcoat and with his musket, is for each of a hundred families the image of its uncle, its sacrifice to the Union. That statue, then, though it is itself single, represents any one man of whom a certain predicate may be true. It is *objectively* general. The word "soldier," whether spoken or written, is general in the same way; while the name, "George Washington," is not so. But each of these two terms remains one and the same noun, whether it be spoken or written, and whenever and wherever it be spoken or written. This noun is not an existent thing: it is a *type,* or *form,* to which objects, both those that are externally existent and those which are imagined, may *conform,* but which none of them can exactly be. This is subjective generality. The pragmaticistic purport is general in both ways.

As to reality, one finds it defined in various ways; but if that principle of terminological ethics that was proposed be accepted, the equivocal language will soon disappear. For *realis* and *realitas* are not ancient words. They were invented to be terms of philosophy in the thirteenth century, and the meaning they were intended to express is perfectly clear. That is *real* which has such and such characters, whether anybody thinks it to have those characters or not. At any rate, that is the sense in which the pragmaticist uses the word. Now, just as conduct controlled by ethical reason tends toward fixing certain habits of conduct, the nature of which (as to illustrate the meaning, peaceable habits and not quarrelsome habits) does not depend upon any accidental circumstances, and *in that sense* may be said to be *destined;* so, thought, controlled by a rational experimental logic, tends to the fixation of certain opinions, equally destined, the nature of which will be the same in the end, however the perversity of thought of whole generations may cause the postponement of the ultimate fixation. If this be so, as every man of us virtually assumes that it is, in regard to each matter the truth of which he seriously discusses, then, according to the adopted definition of "real," the state of things which will be believed in that ultimate opinion is real. But, for the most part, such opinions will be general. Consequently, *some* general objects are real. (Of course, nobody ever thought that *all* generals were real; but the scholastics used to assume that generals were real when they had hardly any, or quite no, experiential evidence to support their assumption; and their fault lay just there, and not in holding that generals could be real.) One is struck with the inexactitude of thought even of analysts of power, when they touch upon modes of being. One will meet, for example, the virtual assumption that what is relative to thought cannot be real. But why not, exactly? *Red* is relative to sight, but the fact that this or that is in that relation to vision that we call being red is not *itself* relative to sight; it is a real fact.

Not only may generals be real, but they may also be *physically efficient,* not in every metaphysical sense, but in the common-sense acception in which human purposes are physically efficient. Aside from metaphysical nonsense, no sane man doubts that if I feel the air in my study to be stuffy, that thought may cause the window to be opened. My thought, be it granted, was an individual event. But what determined it to take the particular determination it did, was in part the general fact that stuffy air is unwholesome, and in part other *Forms,* concerning which Dr. Carus has caused so many men to reflect to advantage—or rather, *by* which, and the general truth concerning which Dr. Carus's mind was determined to the forcible enunciation of so much truth. For truths, on the average, have a greater tendency to get believed than falsities have. Were it otherwise, considering that there are myriads of false hypotheses to account for any given phenomenon, against one sole true one (or if you will have it so, against every true one), the first step toward genuine knowledge must have been next door to a miracle. So, then, when my window was opened, because of the truth that stuffy air is *malsain,* a physical effort was brought into existence by the efficiency of a general and non-existent truth. This has a droll sound because it is unfamiliar; but exact analysis is with it and not against it; and it has besides, the immense advantage of not blinding us to great facts—such as that the ideas "justice" and "truth" are, notwithstanding the iniquity of the world, the mightiest of the forces that move it. Generality is, indeed, an indispensable ingredient of reality; for mere individual existence or actuality without any regularity whatever is a nullity. Chaos is pure nothing.

That which any true proposition asserts is *real,* in the sense of being as it is regardless of what you or I may think about it. Let this proposition be a general conditional proposition as to the future, and it is a real general such as is calculated really to influence human conduct; and such the pragmaticist holds to be the rational purport of every concept.

Accordingly, the pragmaticist does not make the *summum bonum* to consist in action, but makes it to consist in that process of evolution whereby the existent comes more and more to embody those generals which were just now said to be *destined,* which is what we strive to express in calling them *reasonable*. In its higher stages, evolution takes place more and more largely through self-control, and this gives the pragmaticist a sort of justification for making the rational purport to be general.

There is much more in elucidation of pragmaticism that might be said to advantage, were it not for the dread of fatiguing the reader. It might, for example, have been well to show clearly that the pragmaticist does not attribute any different essential mode of being to an event in the future from that which he would attribute to a similar event in the past, but only that the practical attitude of the thinker toward the two is different. It would also have been well to show that the pragmaticist does not make Forms to be the *only* realities in the world, any more than he makes the reasonable purport of a word to be the only kind of meaning there is. These things are, however, implicitly involved in what has been said. . . .

WILLIAM JAMES

(1842-1910)

If Peirce was the logician of pragmatism, William James was its poet. Looking back on his teachers at Harvard, C. I. Lewis has remarked: "James . . . had a swift way of being right, but how he reached his conclusions was his own secret." James' talent lay in a quick sympathy of mind and feeling, in the evocation of philosophic moods and the intuitive piercing of abstractions to the human attitudes beneath them. He was a well-informed scholar, but the distinction of his work comes from his incapacity for pedantry and his impatience with cold intellectual formulas. He was a pragmatist by temperament as much as by conviction and he treated ideas as incidents, not in an academic tradition, but in the struggles of individual men for understanding and security.

James was not, however, a merely impulsive thinker. Exactness and precision were not as natural to him as the imaginative guess or the suggestive metaphor, but he could nevertheless produce subtle and novel arguments—for example, that "consciousness" is "the name of a nonentity"—that impressed even so astringent a critic as Bertrand Russell. James had been solidly trained in the sciences, furthermore, and he maintained, particularly in his early years, a stout interest in pursuing empirical inquiry as far as it would go before abandoning it for other methods. His Principles of Psychology, *which is probably his most substantial intellectual achievement, is one of the pioneer codifications of biological or "functional" psychology. In its attempt to introduce the conceptions and methods of the physiologist's laboratory into the study of the mind it defined an epoch in the history of psychology. Even here, however, James' sober experimental approach was supplemented by his power of fresh imagination, his ability to break through encrusted "intellectualist" traditions in psychology, to look at things with his own eyes, and to speak about the formation of habits or the stream of consciousness with a poet's directness and simplicity.*

James was born in New York in 1842. The son of a free-wheeling and oddly interesting intellectual, Henry James, Sr., and the older brother of Henry James the novelist, he was brought up in a home in which it was habitual, as he said, "to have a say about the deepest reasons of the universe." He had an unorganized but cosmopolitan education in Europe and America, and at the age of eighteen thought of becoming a painter. But he gave up this plan, entered the Lawrence scientific school at Harvard, and eventually, after a number of interruptions, received his degree as a doctor of medicine in 1869.

James, however, never practiced medicine. Like John Stuart Mill earlier in the century, James went through a period of acute mental depression during the years between 1867 and 1872. He was helped to overcome his melancholia, according to his report, by reading, in 1870, the discussion of free will by the French philosopher Renouvier. James decided, so he wrote, that "my first act of free will would be to believe in free will." This assertion that the will has a right to have its demands honored is a main theme in James' version of pragmatism, and his life-long objection to determinism of any sort, as well as his interest in the psychology of religion, reflect the influence which this period of his life steadily exercized on his thought.

James began his work at Harvard as a teacher of physiology, but moved in a few years to psychology and then to philosophy. Although he did not find his vocation and powers until he was in his thirties, James developed into an accomplished and prolific writer and became perhaps the first American to have a worldwide reputation as a philosopher. The warmth and liveliness of his writing was matched, furthermore, by the warmth and generosity he showed in his teaching and personal life. Peirce, who had his intellectual disagreements with James, described James after his death as "about as perfect a lover of truth as it is possible for a man to be," and "even greater in practice than in theory of psychology." Troubled by bad health in his last years, James nevertheless continued to write, lecture, and give his energies to students and others who turned to him. He died in 1910.

The first of the essays that follow, "The Sentiment of Rationality," is the classic expression of one of James' earliest and most persisting interests —the motives for philosophizing. It is based in part on an article published in Mind *in 1879, and in part on an address delivered in 1880 to the Harvard Philosophical Club and subsequently published in the* Princeton Review. *James' best-known essay, "The Will to Believe," was first delivered to The Yale and Brown Philosophical Clubs and subsequently published in 1896 in the* New World. *"The Dilemma of Determinism," an address to the Harvard Divinity Students, was published in 1884 in the* Unitarian Review. *The chapter on habit, from* The Principles of Psychology, *was first published separately in the* Popular Science Monthly *in 1887. James' lectures on pragmatism, from which the fifth of the following selections has been taken, were delivered during the winter of 1906-7 at the Lowell Institute in Boston and at Columbia University in New York. They were published in 1907 under the title* Pragmatism: A New Name for Some Old Ways of Thinking. *The final selection is from the concluding chapter of* Varieties of Religious Experience, *which James delivered as the Gifford Lectures in Scotland in 1901-2.*

The Sentiment of Rationality

WHAT IS THE TASK WHICH PHILOSOPHERS SET THEMSELVES TO PERFORM; and why do they philosophize at all? Almost every one will immediately reply: They desire to attain a conception of the frame of things which shall on the whole be more rational than that somewhat chaotic view which every one by nature carries about with him under his hat. But suppose this rational conception attained, how is the philosopher to recognize it for what it is, and not let it slip through ignorance? The only answer can be that he will recognize its rationality as he recognizes everything else, by certain subjective marks with which it affects him. When he gets the marks, he may know that he has got the rationality.

What, then, are the marks? A strong feeling of ease, peace, rest, is one of them. The transition from a state of puzzle and perplexity to rational comprehension is full of lively relief and pleasure.

But this relief seems to be a negative rather than a positive character. Shall we then say that the feeling of rationality is constituted merely by the absence of any feeling of irrationality? I think there are very good grounds for upholding such a view. All feeling whatever, in the light of certain recent psychological speculations, seems to depend for its physical condition not on simple discharge of nerve-currents, but on their discharge under arrest, impediment, or resistance. Just as we feel no particular pleasure when we breathe freely, but a very intense feeling of distress when the respiratory motions are prevented,—so any unobstructed tendency to action discharges itself without the production of much cogitative accompaniment, and any perfectly fluent course of thought awakens but little feeling; but when the movement is inhibited, or when the thought meets with difficulties, we experience distress. It is only when the distress is upon us that we can be said to strive, to crave, or to aspire. When enjoying plenary freedom either in the way of motion or of thought, we are in a sort of anæsthetic state in which we might say with Walt Whitman, if we cared to say anything about ourselves at such times, "I am sufficient as I am." This feeling of the sufficiency of the present moment, of its absoluteness,— this absence of all need to explain it, account for it, or justify it,—is what I call the Sentiment of Rationality. As soon, in short, as we are enabled from any cause whatever to think with perfect fluency, the thing we think of seems to us *pro tanto* rational.

116

Whatever modes of conceiving the cosmos facilitate this fluency, produce the sentiment of rationality. Conceived in such modes, being vouches for itself and needs no further philosophic formulation. But this fluency may be obtained in various ways; and first I will take up the theoretic way.

The facts of the world in their sensible diversity are always before us, but our theoretic need is that they should be conceived in a way that reduces their manifoldness to simplicity. Our pleasure at finding that a chaos of facts is the expression of a single underlying fact is like the relief of the musician at resolving a confused mass of sound into melodic or harmonic order. The simplified result is handled with far less mental effort than the original data; and a philosophic conception of nature is thus in no metaphorical sense a labor-saving contrivance. The passion for parsimony, for economy of means in thought, is the philosophic passion *par excellence;* and any character or aspect of the world's phenomena which gathers up their diversity into monotony will gratify that passion, and in the philosopher's mind stand for that essence of things compared with which all their other determinations may by him be overlooked.

More universality or extensiveness is, then, one mark which the philosopher's conceptions must possess. Unless they apply to an enormous number of cases they will not bring him relief. The knowledge of things by their causes, which is often given as a definition of rational knowledge, is useless to him unless the causes converge to a minimum number, while still producing the maximum number of effects. The more multiple then are the instances, the more flowingly does his mind rove from fact to fact. The phenomenal transitions are no real transitions; each item is the same old friend with a slightly altered dress.

Who does not feel the charm of thinking that the moon and the apple are, as far as their relation to the earth goes, identical; of knowing respiration and combustion to be one; of understanding that the balloon rises by the same law whereby the stone sinks; of feeling that the warmth in one's palm when one rubs one's sleeve is identical with the motion which the friction checks; of recognizing the difference between beast and fish to be only a higher degree of that between human father and son; of believing our strength when we climb the mountain or fell the tree to be no other than the strength of the sun's rays which made the corn grow out of which we got our morning meal?

But alongside of this passion for simplification there exists a sister passion, which in some minds—though they perhaps form the minority—is its rival. This is the passion for distinguishing; it is the impulse to be *acquainted* with the parts rather than to comprehend the whole. Loyalty to clearness and integrity of perception, dislike of blurred outlines, of vague identifications, are its characteristics. It loves to recognize particulars in their full completeness, and the more of these it can carry the happier it is.

It prefers any amount of incoherence, abruptness, and fragmentariness (so long as the literal details of the separate facts are saved) to an abstract way of conceiving things that, while it simplifies them, dissolves away at the same time their concrete fulness. Clearness and simplicity thus set up rival claims, and make a real dilemma for the thinker.

A man's philosophic attitude is determined by the balance in him of these two cravings. No system of philosophy can hope to be universally accepted among men which grossly violates either need, or entirely subordinates the one to the other. The fate of Spinoza, with his barren union of all things in one substance, on the one hand; that of Hume, with his equally barren 'looseness and separateness' of everything, on the other,—neither philosopher owning any strict and systematic disciples to-day, each being to posterity a warning as well as a stimulus,—show us that the only possible philosophy must be a compromise between an abstract monotony and a concrete heterogeneity. But the only way to mediate between diversity and unity is to class the diverse items as cases of a common essence which you discover in them. Classification of things into extensive 'kinds' is thus the first step; and classification of their relations and conduct into extensive 'laws' is the last step, in their philosophic unification. A completed theorctic philosophy can thus never be anything more than a completed classification of the world's ingredients; and its results must always be abstract, since the basis of every classification is the abstract essence embedded in the living fact,—the rest of the living fact being for the time ignored by the classifier. This means that none of our explanations are complete. They subsume things under heads wider or more familiar; but the last heads, whether of things or of their connections, are mere abstract genera, data which we just find in things and write down.

When, for example, we think that we have rationally explained the connection of the facts A and B by classing both under their common attribute x, it is obvious that we have really explained only so much of these items as is x. To explain the connection of choke-damp and suffocation by the lack of oxygen is to leave untouched all the other peculiarities both of choke-damp and of suffocation,—such as convulsions and agony on the one hand, density and explosibility on the other. In a word, so far as A and B contain l, m, n, and o, p, q, respectively, in addition to x, they are not explained by x. Each additional particularity makes its distinct appeal. A single explanation of a fact only explains it from a single point of view. The entire fact is not accounted for until each and all of its characters have been classed with their likes elsewhere. To apply this now to the case of the universe, we see that the explanation of the world by molecular movements explains it only so far as it actually is such movements. To invoke the 'Unknowable' explains only so much as is unknowable, 'Thought' only so much as is thought, 'God' only so much as is God. $Which$ thought? $Which$ God?—are questions that have to be answered by bringing in again the residual data from which the general term was abstracted. All those data that cannot be analytically identified with the attribute invoked as universal principle, remain as independent kinds or natures, associated empirically with the said attribute but devoid of rational kinship with it.

Hence the unsatisfactoriness of all our speculations. On the one hand, so far as they retain any multiplicity in their terms, they fail to get us out of the empirical sand-heap world; on the other, so far as they eliminate multiplicity the practical man despises their empty barrenness. The most they can say is that the elements of the world are such and such, and that each is identical with itself wherever found; but the question Where is it found? the practical man is left to answer by his own wit. Which, of all the essences, shall here and now be held the essence of this concrete thing, the fundamental philosophy never attempts to decide. We are thus led to the conclusion that the simple classification of things is, on the one hand, the best possible theoretic philosophy, but is, on the other, a most miserable and inadequate substitute for the fulness of the truth. It is a monstrous abridgment of life, which, like all abridgments is got by the absolute loss and casting out of real matter. This is why so few human beings truly care for philosophy. The particular determinations which she ignores are the real matter exciting needs, quite as potent and authoritative as hers. What does the moral enthusiast care for philosophical ethics? Why does the *Æsthetik* of every German philosopher appear to the artist an abomination of desolation?

> Grau, theurer Freund, ist alle Theorie
> Und grün des Lebens goldner Baum.

The entire man, who feels all needs by turns, will take nothing as an equivalent for life but the fulness of living itself. Since the essences of things are as a matter of fact disseminated through the whole extent of time and space, it is in their spread-outness and alternation that he will enjoy them. When weary of the concrete clash and dust and pettiness, he will refresh himself by a bath in the eternal springs, or fortify himself by a look at the immutable natures. But he will only be a visitor, not a dweller in the region; he will never carry the philosophic yoke upon his shoulders, and when tired of the gray monotony of her problems and insipid spaciousness of her results, will always escape gleefully into the teeming and dramatic richness of the concrete world.

So our study turns back here to its beginning. Every way of classifying a thing is but a way of handling it for some particular purpose. Conceptions, 'kinds,' are teleological instruments. No abstract concept can be a valid substitute for a concrete reality except with reference to a particular interest in the conceiver. The interest of theoretic rationality, the relief of identification, is but one of a thousand human purposes. When others rear their heads, it must pack up its little bundle and retire till its turn recurs.

The exaggerated dignity and value that philosophers have claimed for their solutions is thus greatly reduced. The only virtue their theoretic conception need have is simplicity, and a simple conception is an equivalent for the world only so far as the world is simple,—the world meanwhile, whatever simplicity it may harbor, being also a mightily complex affair. Enough simplicity remains, however, and enough urgency in our craving to reach it, to make the theoretic function one of the most invincible of human impulses. The quest of the fewest elements of things is an ideal that some will follow, as long as there are men to think at all.

But suppose the goal attained. Suppose that at last we have a system unified in the sense that has been explained. Our world can now be conceived simply, and our mind enjoys the relief. Our universal concept has made the concrete chaos rational. But now I ask, Can that which is the ground of rationality in all else be itself properly called rational? It would seem at first sight that it might. One is tempted at any rate to say that, since the craving for rationality is appeased by the identification of one thing with another, a datum which left nothing else outstanding might quench that craving definitively, or be rational *in se*. No otherness being left to annoy us, we should sit down at peace. In other words, as the theoretic tranquillity of the boor results from his spinning no further considerations about his chaotic universe, so any datum whatever (provided it were simple, clear, and ultimate) ought to banish puzzle from the universe of the philosopher and confer peace, inasmuch as there would then be for him absolutely no further considerations to spin.

This in fact is what some persons think. Professor Bain says,—

"A difficulty is solved, a mystery unriddled, when it can be shown to resemble something else; to be an example of a fact already known. Mystery is isolation, exception, or it may be apparent contradiction: the resolution of the mystery is found in assimilation, identity, fraternity. When all things are assimilated, so far as assimilation can go, so far as likeness holds, there is an end to explanation; there is an end to what the mind can do, or can intelligently desire. . . . The path of science as exhibited in modern ages is toward generality, wider and wider, until we reach the highest, the widest laws of every department of things; there explanation is finished, mystery ends, perfect vision is gained."

But, unfortunately, this first answer will not hold. Our mind is so wedded to the process of seeing an *other* beside every item of its experience, that when the notion of an absolute datum is presented to it, it goes through its usual procedure and remains pointing at the void beyond, as if in that lay further matter for contemplation. In short, it spins for itself the further positive consideration of a nonentity enveloping the being of its datum; and as that leads nowhere, back recoils the thought toward its datum again. But there is no natural bridge between nonentity and this particular datum, and the thought stands oscillating to and fro, wondering "Why was there anything but nonentity; why just this universal datum and not another?" and finds no end, in wandering mazes lost. Indeed, Bain's words are so untrue that in reflecting men it is just when the attempt to fuse the manifold into a single totality has been most successful, when the conception of the universe as a unique fact is nearest its perfection, that the craving for further explanation, the ontological wonder-sickness, arises in its extremest form. As Schopenhauer says, "The uneasiness which keeps the never-resting clock of metaphysics in motion, is the consciousness that the non-existence of this world is just as possible as its existence."

The notion of nonentity may thus be called the parent of the philosophic craving in its subtilest and profoundest sense. Absolute existence is absolute mystery, for its relations with the nothing remain unmediated to our understanding. One philosopher only has pretended to throw a logical bridge over this chasm. Hegel, by trying to show that nonentity and concrete being are linked together by a series of identities of a synthetic kind, binds everything conceivable into a unity, with no outlying notion to disturb the free rotary circulation of the mind within its bounds. Since such unchecked movement gives the feeling of rationality, he must be held, if he has succeeded, to have eternally and absolutely quenched all rational demands.

But for those who deem Hegel's heroic effort to have failed, nought remains but to confess that when all things have been unified to the supreme degree, the notion of a possible other than the actual may still haunt our imagination and prey upon our system. The bottom of being is left logically opaque to us, as something which we simply come upon and find, and about which (if we wish to act) we should pause and wonder as little as possible. The philosopher's logical tranquillity is thus in essence no other than the boor's. They differ only as to the point at which each refuses to let further considerations upset the absoluteness of the data he assumes. The boor does so immediately, and is liable at any moment to the ravages of many kinds of doubt. The philosopher does not do so till unity has been reached, and is warranted against the inroads of those considerations, but only practically, not essentially, secure from the blighting breath of the ultimate Why? If he cannot exorcise this question, he must ignore or blink it, and, assuming the data of his system as something given, and the gift as ultimate, simply proceed to a life of contemplation or of action based on it. There is no doubt that this acting on an opaque necessity is accompanied by a certain pleasure. See the reverence of Carlyle for brute fact: "There is an infinite significance in fact." "Necessity," says Dühring, and he means not rational but given necessity, "is the last and highest point that we can reach. . . . It is not only the interest of ultimate and definitive knowledge, but also that of the feelings, to find a last repose and an ideal equilibrium in an uttermost datum which can simply not be other than it is."

Such is the attitude of ordinary men in their theism, God's fiat being in physics and morals such an uttermost datum. Such also is the attitude of all hard-minded analysts and *Verstandesmenschen*. Lotze, Renouvier, and Hodgson promptly say that of experience as a whole no account can be given, but neither seek to soften the abruptness of the confession nor to reconcile us with our impotence.

But mediating attempts may be made by more mystical minds. The peace of rationality may be sought through ecstasy when logic fails. To religious persons of every shade of doctrine moments come when the world, as it is, seems so divinely orderly, and the acceptance of it by the heart so rapturously complete, that intellectual questions vanish; nay, the intellect itself is hushed to sleep,—as Wordsworth says, "thought is not; in enjoyment it expires." Ontological emotion so fills the soul that ontological speculation can no longer overlap it and put her girdle of interrogation-marks round existence. Even the least religious of men must have felt with Walt Whitman, when loafing on the grass on some transparent summer morning, that "swiftly arose and spread round him the peace and knowledge that pass all the argument of the earth." At such moments of energetic living we feel as if there were something diseased and contemptible, yea vile, in theoretic grubbing and brooding. In the eye of healthy sense the philosopher is at best a learned fool.

Since the heart can thus wall out the ultimate irrationality which the head ascertains, the erection of its procedure into a systematized method would be a philosophic achievement of first-rate importance. But as used by mystics hitherto it has lacked universality, being available for few persons and at few times, and even in these being apt to be followed by fits of reaction and dryness; and if men should agree that the mystical method is a subterfuge without logical pertinency, a plaster but no cure, and that the idea of nonentity can never be exorcised, empiricism will be the ultimate philosophy. Existence then will be a brute fact to which as a whole the emotion of ontologic wonder shall rightfully cleave, but remain eternally unsatisfied. Then wonderfulness or mysteriousness will be an essential attribute of the nature of things, and the exhibition and emphasizing of it will continue to be an ingredient in the philosophic industry of the race. Every generation will produce its Job, its Hamlet, its Faust, or its Sartor Resartus.

With this we seem to have considered the possibilities of purely theoretic rationality. But we saw at the outset that rationality meant only unimpeded mental function. Impediments that arise in the theoretic sphere might perhaps be avoided if the stream of mental action should leave that sphere betimes and pass into the practical. Let us therefore inquire what constitutes the feeling of rationality in its *practical* aspect. If thought is not to stand forever pointing at the universe in wonder, if its movement is to be diverted from the issueless channel of purely theoretic contemplation, let us ask what conception of the universe will awaken active impulses capable of effecting this diversion. A definition of the world which will give back to the mind the free motion which has been blocked in the purely contemplative path may so far make the world seem rational again.

Well, of two conceptions equally fit to satisfy the logical demand, that one which awakens the active impulses, or satisfies other æsthetic demands better than the other, will be accounted the more rational conception, and will deservedly prevail.

There is nothing improbable in the supposition that an analysis of the world may yield a number of formulæ, all consistent with the facts. In physical science different formulæ may explain the phenomena equally well,—the one-fluid and the two-fluid theories of electricity, for example. Why may it not be so with the world? Why may there not be different points of view for surveying it, within each of which all data harmonize, and which the observer may therefore either choose between, or simply cumulate one upon another? A Beethoven string-quartet is truly, as some one has said, a scraping of horses' tails on cats' bowels, and may be exhaustively described in such terms; but the application of this description in no way precludes the simultaneous applicability of an entirely different description. Just so a thorough-going interpretation of the world in terms of mechanical sequence is compatible with its being interpreted teleologically, for the mechanism itself may be designed.

If, then, there were several systems excogitated, equally satisfying to our purely logical needs, they would still have to be passed in review, and approved or rejected by our æsthetic and practical nature. Can we define the tests of rationality which these parts of our nature would use?

Philosophers long ago observed the remarkable fact that mere familiarity with things is able to produce a feeling of their rationality. The empiricist school has been so much struck by this circumstance as to have laid it down that the feeling of rationality and the feeling of familiarity are one and the same thing, and that no other kind of rationality than this exists. The daily contemplation of phenomena juxtaposed in a certain order begets an acceptance of their connection, as absolute as the repose engendered by theoretic insight into their coherence. To explain a thing is to pass easily back to its antecedents; to know it is easily to foresee its consequents. Custom, which lets us do both, is thus the source of whatever rationality tho thing may gain in our thought.

In the broad sense in which rationality was defined at the outset of this essay, it is perfectly apparent that custom must be one of its factors. We said that any perfectly fluent and easy thought was devoid of the sentiment of irrationality. Inasmuch then as custom acquaints us with all the relations of a thing, it teaches us to pass fluently from that thing to others, and *pro tanto* tinges it with the rational character.

Now, there is one particular relation of greater practical importance than all the rest,—I mean the relation of a thing to its future consequences. So long as an object is unusual, our expectations are baffled; they are fully determined as soon as it becomes familiar. I therefore propose this as the first practical requisite which a philosophic conception must satisfy: *It must, in a general way at least, banish uncertainty from the future.* The permanent presence of the sense of futurity in the mind has been strangely ignored by most writers, but the fact is that our consciousness at a given moment is never free from the ingredient of expectancy. Every one knows how when a painful thing has to be undergone in the near future, the vague feeling that it is impending penetrates all our thought with uneasiness and subtly vitiates our mood even when it does not control our attention; it keeps us from being at rest, at home in the given present. The same is true when a great happiness awaits us. But when the future is neutral and perfectly certain, 'we do not mind it,' as we say, but give an undisturbed attention to the actual. Let now this haunting sense of futurity be thrown off its bearings or left without an object, and immediately uneasiness takes possession of the mind. But in every novel or unclassified experience this is just what occurs; we do not know what will come next; and novelty *per se* becomes a mental irritant, while custom *per se,* is a mental sedative, merely because the one baffles while the other settles our expectations.

Every reader must feel the truth of this. What is meant by coming 'to feel at home' in a new place, or with new people? It is simply that, at first, when we take up our quarters in a new room, we do not know what draughts may blow in upon our back, what doors may open, what forms may enter, what interesting objects may be found in cupboards and corners. When after a few days we have learned the range of all these possibilities, the feeling of strangeness disappears. And so it does with people, when we have got past the point of expecting any essentially new manifestations from their character.

The utility of this emotional effect of expectation is perfectly obvious; 'natural selection,' in fact, was bound to bring it about sooner or later. It is of the utmost practical importance to an animal that he should have prevision of the qualities of the objects that surround him, and especially that he should not come to rest in presence of circumstances that might be fraught either with peril or advantage,—go to sleep, for example, on the brink of precipices, in the dens of enemies, or view with indifference some new-appearing object that might, if chased, prove an important addition to the larder. Novelty *ought* to irritate him. All curiosity has thus a practical genesis. We need only look at the physiognomy of a dog or a horse when a new object comes into his view, his mingled fascination and fear, to see that the element of conscious insecurity or perplexed expectation lies at the root of his emotion. A dog's curiosity about the movements of his master or a strange object only extends as far as the point of deciding what is going to happen next. That settled, curiosity is quenched. The dog quoted by Darwin, whose behavior in presence of a newspaper moved by the wind seemed to testify to a sense 'of the supernatural,' was merely exhibiting the irritation of an uncertain future. A newspaper which could move spontaneously was in itself so unexpected that the poor brute could not tell what new wonders the next moment might bring forth.

To turn back now to philosophy. An ultimate datum, even though it be logically unrationalized, will, if its quality is such as to define expectancy, be peacefully accepted by the mind; while if it leave the least opportunity for ambiguity in the future, it will to that extent cause mental uneasiness if not distress. Now, in the ultimate explanations of the universe which the craving for rationality has elicited from the human mind, the demands of expectancy to be satisfied have always played a fundamental part. The term set up by philosophers as primordial has been one which banishes the incalculable. 'Substance,' for example, means, as Kant says, *das Beharr-liche,* which will be as it has been, because its being is essential and eternal. And although we may not be able to prophesy in detail the future phenomena to which the substance shall give rise, we may set our minds at rest in a general way, when we have called the substance God, Perfection, Love, or Reason, by the reflection that whatever is in store for us can never at bottom be inconsistent with the character of this term; so that our attitude even toward the unexpected is in a general sense defined. Take again the notion of immortality, which for common people seems to be the touchstone of every philosophic or religious creed: what is this but a way of saying that the determination of expectancy is the essential factor of rationality? The wrath of science against miracles, of certain philosophers against the doctrine of free-will, has precisely the same root, —dislike to admit any ultimate factor in things which may rout our prevision or upset the stability of our outlook.

Anti-substantialist writers strangely overlook this function in the doctrine of substance: "If there be such a *substratum,*" says Mill, "suppose it at this instant miraculously annihilated, and let the sensations continue to occur in the same order, and how would the *substratum* be missed? By what signs should we be able to discover that its existence had terminated? Should we not have as much reason to believe that it still existed as we now have? And if we should not then be warranted in believing it, how can we be so now?" Truly enough, if we have already securely bagged our facts in a certain order, we can dispense with any further warrant for that order. But with regard to the facts yet to come the case is far different. It does not follow that if substance may be dropped from our conception of the irrecoverably past, it need be an equally empty complication to our notions of the future. Even if it were true that, for aught we know to the contrary, the substance might develop at any moment a wholly new set of attributes, the mere logical form of referring things to a substance would still (whether rightly or wrongly) remain accompanied by a feeling of rest and future confidence. In spite of the acutest nihilistic criticism, men will therefore always have a liking for any philosophy which explains things *per substantiam*.

A very natural reaction against the theosophizing conceit and hide-bound confidence in the upshot of things, which vulgarly optimistic minds display, has formed one factor of the scepticism of empiricists, who never cease to remind us of the reservoir of possibilities alien to our habitual experience which the cosmos may contain, and which, for any warrant we have to the contrary, may turn it inside out to-morrow. Agnostic substantialism like that of Mr. Spencer, whose Unknowable is not merely the unfathomable but the absolute-irrational, on which, if consistently represented in thought, it is of course impossible to count, performs the same function of rebuking a certain stagnancy and smugness in the manner in which the ordinary philistine feels his security. But considered as anything else than as reactions against an opposite excess, these philosophies of uncertainty cannot be acceptable; the general mind will fail to come to rest in their presence, and will seek for solutions of a more reassuring kind.

We may then, I think, with perfect confidence lay down as a first point gained in our inquiry, that a prime factor in the philosophic craving is the desire to have expectancy defined; and that no philosophy will definitively triumph which in an emphatic manner denies the possibility of gratifying this need.

We pass with this to the next great division of our topic. It is not sufficient for our satisfaction merely to know the future as determined, for it may be determined in either of many ways, agreeable or disagreeable. For a philosophy to succeed on a universal scale it must define the future *congruously with our spontaneous powers*. A philosophy may be unimpeachable in other respects, but either of two defects will be fatal to its universal acceptance. First, its ultimate principle must not be one that essentially baffles and disappoints our dearest desires and most cherished powers. A pessimistic principle like Schopenhauer's incurably vicious Will-substance, or Hartmann's wicked jack-of-all-trades the Unconscious, will perpetually call forth essays at other philosophies. Incompatibility of the future with their desires and active tendencies is, in fact, to most men a source of more fixed disquietude than uncertainty itself. Witness the attempts to overcome the 'problem of evil,' the 'mystery of pain.' There is no 'problem of good.'

But a second and worse defect in a philosophy than that of contradicting our active propensities is to give them no object whatever to press against. A philosophy whose principle is so incommensurate with our most intimate powers as to deny them all relevancy in universal affairs, as to annihilate their motives at one blow, will be even more unpopular

than pessimism. Better face the enemy than the eternal Void! This is
why materialism will always fail of universal adoption, however well it
may fuse things into an atomistic unity, however clearly it may prophesy
the future eternity. For materialism denies reality to the objects of almost
all the impulses which we most cherish. The real *meaning* of the impulses,
it says, is something which has no emotional interest for us whatever.
Now, what is called 'extradition' is quite as characteristic of our emotions as of our senses: both point to an object as the cause of the present
feeling. What an intensely objective reference lies in fear! In like manner an enraptured man and a dreary-feeling man are not simply aware
of their subjective states; if they were, the force of their feelings would all
evaporate. Both believe there is outward cause why they should feel as
they do: either, "It is a glad world! how good life is!" or, "What a
loathsome tedium is existence!" Any philosophy which annihilates the
validity of the reference by explaining away its objects or translating
them into terms of no emotional pertinency, leaves the mind with little to
care or act for. This is the opposite condition from that of nightmare,
but when acutely brought home to consciousness it produces a kindred
horror. In nightmare we have motives to act, but no power; here we have
powers, but no motives. A nameless *unheimlichkeit* comes over us at the
thought of there being nothing eternal in our final purposes, in the objects
of those loves and aspirations which are our deepest energies. The mon-
strously lopsided equation of the universe and its knower, which we
postulate as the ideal of cognition, is perfectly paralleled by the no less
lopsided equation of the universe and the *doer*. We demand in it a character for which our emotions and active propensities shall be a match.
Small as we are, minute as is the point by which the cosmos impinges
upon each one of us, each one desires to feel that his reaction at that
point is congruous with the demands of the vast whole,—that he balances
the latter, so to speak, and is able to do what it expects of him. But as his
abilities to do lie wholly in the line of his natural propensities; as he
enjoys reacting with such emotions as fortitude, hope, rapture, admiration, earnestness, and the like; and as he very unwillingly reacts with fear,
disgust, despair, or doubt,—a philosophy which should only legitimate
emotions of the latter sort would be sure to leave the mind a prey to
discontent and craving.

It is far too little recognized how entirely the intellect is built up of
practical interests. The theory of evolution is beginning to do very good
service by its reduction of all mentality to the type of reflex action. Cognition, in this view, is but a fleeting moment, a cross-section at a certain
point, of what in its totality is a motor phenomenon. In the lower forms
of life no one will pretend that cognition is anything more than a guide
to appropriate action. The germinal question concerning things brought
for the first time before consciousness is not the theoretic 'What is that?'

but the practical 'Who goes there?' or rather, as Horwicz has admirably put it, 'What is to be done?'—'Was fang' ich an?' In all our discussions about the intelligence of lower animals, the only test we use is that of their *acting* as if for a purpose. Cognition, in short, is incomplete until discharged in act; and although it is true that the later mental development, which attains its maximum through the hypertrophied cerebrum of man, gives birth to a vast amount of theoretic activity over and above that which is immediately ministerial to practice, yet the earlier claim is only postponed, not effaced, and the active nature asserts its rights to the end.

When the cosmos in its totality is the object offered to consciousness, the relation is in no whit altered. React on it we must in some congenial way. It was a deep instinct in Schopenhauer which led him to reinforce his pessimistic argumentation by a running volley of invective against the practical man and his requirements. No hope for pessimism unless he is slain!

Helmholtz's immortal works on the eye and ear are to a great extent little more than a commentary on the law that practical utility wholly determines which parts of our sensations we shall be aware of, and which parts we shall ignore. We notice or discriminate an ingredient of sense only so far as we depend upon it to modify our actions. We *comprehend* a thing when we synthetize it by identity with another thing. But the other great department of our understanding, *acquaintance* (the two departments being recognized in all languages by the antithesis of such words as *wissen* and *kennen; scire* and *noscere,* etc.), what is that also but a synthesis,—a synthesis of a passive perception with a certain tendency to reaction? We are acquainted with a thing as soon as we have learned how to behave towards it, or how to meet the behavior which we expect from it. Up to that point it is still 'strange' to us.

If there be anything at all in this view, it follows that however vaguely a philosopher may define the ultimate universal datum, he cannot be said to leave it unknown to us so long as he in the slightest degree pretends that our emotional or active attitude toward it should be of one sort rather than another. He who says "life is real, life is earnest," however much he may speak of the fundamental mysteriousness of things, gives a distinct definition to that mysteriousness by ascribing to it the right to claim from us the particular mood called seriousness,—which means the willingness to live with energy, though energy bring pain. The same is true of him who says that all is vanity. For indefinable as the predicate 'vanity' may be *in se,* it is clearly something that permits anæsthesia, mere escape from suffering, to be our rule of life. There can be no greater incongruity than for a disciple of Spencer to proclaim with one breath that the substance of things is unknowable, and with the next that the thought of it should inspire us with awe, reverence, and a willingness to add our co-operative push in the direction toward which its manifestations seem to be drifting. The unknowable may be unfathomed, but if it make such distinct demands upon our activity we surely are not ignorant of its essential quality.

If we survey the field of history and ask what feature all great periods of revival, of expansion of the human mind, display in common, we shall find, I think, simply this: that each and all of them have said to the human being, "The inmost nature of the reality is congenial to *powers* which you possess." In what did the emancipating message of primitive Christianity consist but in the announcement that God recognizes those weak and tender impulses which paganism had so rudely overlooked? Take repentance: the man who can do nothing rightly can at least repent of his failures. But for paganism this faculty of repentance was a pure supernumerary, a straggler too late for the fair. Christianity took it, and made it the one power within us which appealed straight to the heart of God. And after the night of the middle ages had so long branded with obloquy even the generous impulses of the flesh, and defined the reality to be such that only slavish natures could commune with it, in what did the *sursum corda* of the platonizing renaissance lie but in the proclamation that the archetype of verity in things laid claim on the widest activity of our whole æsthetic being? What were Luther's mission and Wesley's but appeals to powers which even the meanest of men might carry with them,—faith and self-despair,—but which were personal, requiring no priestly intermediation, and which brought their owner face to face with God? What caused the wildfire influence of Rousseau but the assurance he gave that man's nature was in harmony with the nature of things, if only the paralyzing corruptions of custom would stand from between? How did Kant and Fichte, Goethe and Schiller, inspire their time with cheer, except by saying, "Use all your powers; that is the only obedience the universe exacts"? And Carlyle with his gospel of work, of fact, of veracity, how does he move us except by saying that the universe imposes no tasks upon us but such as the most humble can perform? Emerson's creed that everything that ever was or will be is here in the enveloping now; that man has but to obey himself,—"He who will rest in what he *is,* is a part of destiny,"—is in like manner nothing but an exorcism of all scepticism as to the pertinency of one's natural faculties.

In a word, "Son of Man, *stand upon thy feet* and I will speak unto thee!" is the only revelation of truth to which the solving epochs have helped the disciple. But that has been enough to satisfy the greater part of his rational need. *In se* and *per* se the universal essence has hardly been more defined by any of these formulas than by the agnostic *x;* but the mere assurance that my powers, such as they are, are not irrelevant to it, but pertinent; that it speaks to them and will in some way recognize their

reply; that I can be a match for it if I will, and not a footless waif,—
suffices to make it rational to my feeling in the sense given above. Nothing
could be more absurd than to hope for the definitive triumph of any
philosophy which should refuse to legitimate, and to legitimate in an
emphatic manner, the more powerful of our emotional and practical tendencies. Fatalism, whose solving word in all crises of behavior is "all
striving is vain," will never reign supreme, for the impulse to take life
strivingly is indestructible in the race. Moral creeds which speak to that
impulse will be widely successful in spite of inconsistency, vagueness, and
shadowy determination of expectancy. Man needs a rule for his will, and
will invent one if one be not given him.

But now observe a most important consequence. Men's active impulses
are so differently mixed that a philosophy fit in this respect for Bismarck
will almost certainly be unfit for a valetudinarian poet. In other words,
although one can lay down in advance the rule that a philosophy which
utterly denies all fundamental ground for seriousness, for effort, for hope,
which says the nature of things is radically alien to human nature, can
never succeed,—one cannot in advance say what particular dose of hope,
or of gnosticism of the nature of things, the definitely successful philosophy shall contain. In short, it is almost certain that personal temperament will here make itself felt, and that although all men will insist on
being spoken to by the universe in some way, few will insist on being
spoken to in just the same way. We have here, in short, the sphere of
what Matthew Arnold likes to call *Aberglaube,* legitimate, inexpugnable,
yet doomed to eternal variations and disputes.

Take idealism and materialism as examples of what I mean, and suppose
for a moment that both give a conception of equal theoretic clearness and
consistency, and that both determine our expectations equally well. Idealism will be chosen by a man of one emotional constitution, materialism by
another. At this very day all sentimental natures, fond of conciliation and
intimacy, tend to an idealistic faith. Why? Because idealism gives to the
nature of things such kinship with our personal selves. Our own thoughts
are what we are most at home with, what we are least afraid of. To say
then that the universe essentially is thought, is to say that I myself, potentially at least, am all. There is no radically alien corner, but an all-
pervading *intimacy*. Now, in certain sensitively egotistic minds this
conception of reality is sure to put on a narrow, close, sick-room air.
Everything sentimental and priggish will be consecrated by it. That element
in reality which every strong man of common-sense willingly feels there
because it calls forth powers that he owns—the rough, harsh, sea-wave,
north-wind element, the denier of persons, the democratizer—is banished
because it jars too much on the desire for communion. Now, it is the
very enjoyment of this element that throws many men upon the material-

istic or agnostic hypothesis, as a polemic reaction against the contrary extreme. They sicken at a life wholly constituted of intimacy. There is an overpowering desire at moments to escape personality, to revel in the action of forces that have no respect for our ego, to let the tides flow, even though they flow over us. The strife of these two kinds of mental temper will, I think, always be seen in philosophy. Some men will keep insisting on the reason, the atonement, that lies in the heart of things, and that we can act *with;* others, on the opacity of brute fact that we must react *against*.

Now, there is one element of our active nature which the Christian religion has emphatically recognized, but which philosophers as a rule have with great insincerity tried to huddle out of sight in their pretension to found systems of absolute certainty. I mean the element of faith. Faith means belief in something concerning which doubt is still theoretically possible; and as the test of belief is willingness to act, one may say that faith is the readiness to act in a cause the prosperous issue of which is not certified to us in advance. It is in fact the same moral quality which we call courage in practical affairs; and there will be a very widespread tendency in men of vigorous nature to enjoy a certain amount of uncertainty in their philosophic creed, just as risk lends a zest to worldly activity. Absolutely certified philosophies seeking the *inconcussum* are fruits of mental natures in which the passion for identity (which we saw to be but one factor of the rational appetite) plays an abnormally exclusive part. In the average man, on the contrary, the power to trust, to risk a little beyond the literal evidence, is an essential function. Any mode of conceiving the universe which makes an appeal to this generous power, and makes the man seem as if he were individually helping to create the actuality of the truth whose metaphysical reality he is willing to assume, will be sure to be responded to by large numbers.

The necessity of faith as an ingredient in our mental attitudes is strongly insisted on by the scientific philosophers of the present day; but by a singularly arbitrary caprice they say that it is only legitimate when used in the interests of one particular proposition,—the proposition, namely, that the course of nature is uniform. That nature will follow to-morrow the same laws that she follows to-day is, they all admit, a truth which no man can *know;* but in the interests of cognition as well as of action we must postulate or assume it. As Helmholtz says: "Hier gilt nur der eine Rath: vertraue und handle!" And Professor Bain urges: "Our only error is in proposing to give any reason or justification of the postulate, or to treat it as otherwise than begged at the very outset."

With regard to all other possible truths, however, a number of our most influential contemporaries think that an attiude of faith is not only illogical but shameful. Faith in a religious dogma for which there is no outward proof, but which we are tempted to postulate for our emotional interests, just as we postulate the uniformity of nature for our intellectual interests, is branded by Professor Huxley as "the lowest depth of immorality." Citations of this kind from leaders of the modern *Aufklärung* might be multiplied almost indefinitely. Take Professor Clifford's article on the 'Ethics of Belief.' He calls it 'guilt' and 'sin' to believe even the truth without 'scientific evidence.' But what is the use of being a genius, unless *with the same scientific evidence* as other men, one can reach more truth than they? Why does Clifford fearlessly proclaim his belief in the conscious-automation theory, although the 'proofs' before him are the same which make Mr. Lewes reject it? Why does he believe in primordial units of 'mind-stuff' on evidence which would seem quite worthless to Professor Bain? Simply because, like every human being of the slightest mental originality, he is peculiarly sensitive to evidence that bears in some one direction. It is utterly hopeless to try to exorcise such sensitiveness by calling it the disturbing subjective factor, and branding it as the root of all evil. 'Subjective' be it called! and 'disturbing' to those whom it foils! But if it helps those who, as Cicero says, "vim naturæ magis sentiunt," it is good and not evil. Pretend what we may, the whole man within us is at work when we form our philosophical opinions. Intellect, will, taste, and passion co-operate just as they do in practical affairs; and lucky it is if the passion be not something as petty as a love of personal conquest over the philosopher across the way. The absurd abstraction of an intellect verbally formulating all its evidence and carefully estimating the probability thereof by a vulgar fraction by the size of whose denominator and numerator alone it is swayed, is ideally as inept as it is actually impossible. It is almost incredible that men who are themselves working philosophers should pretend that any philosophy can be, or ever has been, constructed without the help of personal preference, belief, or divination. How have they succeeded in so stultifying their sense for the living facts of human nature as not to perceive that every philosopher, or man of science either, whose initiative counts for anything in the evolution of thought, has taken his stand on a sort of dumb conviction that the truth must lie in one direction rather than another, and a sort of preliminary assurance that his notion can be made to work; and has borne his best fruit in trying to make it work? These mental instincts in different men are the spontaneous variations upon which the intellectual struggle for existence is based. The fittest conceptions survive, and with them the names of their champions shining to all futurity.

The coil is about us, struggle as we may. The only escape from faith is mental nullity. What we enjoy most in a Huxley or a Clifford is not the professor with his learning, but the human personality ready to go in for what it feels to be right, in spite of all appearances. The concrete man has but one interest,—to be right. That for him is the art of all arts, and all means are fair which help him to it. Naked he is flung into the world, and between him and nature there are no rules of civilized warfare. The rules of the scientific game, burdens of proof, presumptions, *experimenta crucis,* complete inductions, and the like, are only binding on those who enter that game. As a matter of fact we all more or less do enter it, because it helps us to our end. But if the means presume to frustrate the end and call us cheats for being right in advance of their slow aid, by guess-work or by hook or crook, what shall we say of them? Were all of Clifford's works, except the Ethics of Belief, forgotten, he might well figure in future treatises on psychology in place of the somewhat threadbare instance of the miser who has been led by the association of ideas to prefer his gold to all the goods he might buy therewith.

In short, if I am born with such a superior general reaction to evidence that I can guess right and act accordingly, and gain all that comes of right action, while my less gifted neighbor (paralyzed by his scruples and waiting for more evidence which he dares not anticipate, much as he longs to) still stands shivering on the brink, by what law shall I be forbidden to reap the advantages of my superior native sensitiveness? Of course I yield to my belief in such a case as this or distrust it, alike at my peril, just as I do in any of the great practical decisions of life. If my inborn faculties are good, I am a prophet; if poor, I am a failure: nature spews me out of her mouth, and there is an end of me. In the total game of life we stake our persons all the while; and if in its theoretic part our persons will help us to a conclusion, surely we should also stake them there, however inarticulate they may be.*

But in being myself so very articulate in proving what to all readers with a sense of reality will seem a platitude, am I not wasting words? We cannot live or think at all without some degree of faith. Faith is synonymous with working hypothesis. The only difference is that while some hypotheses can be refuted in five minutes, others may defy ages. A chemist who conjectures that a certain wall-paper contains arsenic, and has faith enough to lead him to take the trouble to put some of it into a hydrogen bottle, finds out by the results of his action whether he was right

---

* At most, the command laid upon us by science to believe nothing not yet verified by the senses is a prudential rule intended to maximize our right thinking and minimize our errors *in the long run.* In the particular instance we must frequently lose truth by obeying it; but on the whole we are safer if we follow it consistently, for we are sure to cover our losses with our gains. It is like those gambling and insurance rules based on probability, in which we secure ourselves against losses in detail by hedging on the total run. But this hedging philosophy requires that long run should be there; and this makes it inapplicable to the question of religious faith as the latter comes home to the individual man. He plays the game of life not to escape losses, for he brings nothing with him to lose; he plays it for gains; and it is now or never with him, for the long run which exists indeed for humanity, is not there for him. Let him doubt, believe, or deny, he runs his risk, and has the natural right to choose which one it shall be.

or wrong. But theories like that of Darwin, or that of the kinetic constitution of matter, may exhaust the labors of generations in their corroboration, each tester of their truth proceeding in this simple way,—that he acts as if it were true, and expects the result to disappoint him if his assumption is false. The longer disappointment is delayed, the stronger grows his faith in his theory.

Now, in such questions as God, immortality, absolute morality, and free-will, no non-papal believer at the present day pretends his faith to be of an essentially different complexion; he can always doubt his creed. But his intimate persuasion is that the odds in its favor are strong enough to warrant him in acting all along on the assumption of its truth. His corroboration or repudiation by the nature of things may be deferred until the day of judgment. The uttermost he now means is something like this: "I *expect* them to triumph with tenfold glory; but if it should turn out, as indeed it may, that I have spent my days in a fool's paradise, why, better have been the dupe of *such* a dreamland than the cunning reader of a world like that which then beyond all doubt unmasks itself to view." In short, we *go in* against materialism very much as we should *go in,* had we a chance, against the second French empire or the Church of Rome, or any other system of things toward which our repugnance is vast enough to determine energetic action, but too vague to issue in distinct argumentation. Our reasons are ludicrously incommensurate with the volume of our feeling, yet on the latter we unhesitatingly act.

Now, I wish to show what to my knowledge has never been clearly pointed out, that belief (as measured by action) not only does and must continually outstrip scientific evidence, but that there is a certain class of truths of whose reality belief is a factor as well as a confessor; and that as regards this class of truths faith is not only licit and pertinent, but essential and indispensable. The truths cannot become true till our faith has made them so.

Suppose, for example, that I am climbing in the Alps, and have had the ill-luck to work myself into a position from which the only escape is by a terrible leap. Being without similar experience, I have no evidence of my ability to perform it successfully; but hope and confidence in myself make me sure I shall not miss my aim, and nerve my feet to execute what without those subjective emotions would perhaps have been impossible. But suppose that, on the contrary, the emotions of fear and mistrust preponderate; or suppose that, having just read the Ethics of Belief, I feel it would be sinful to act upon an assumption unverified by previous experience,—why, then I shall hesitate so long that at last, exhausted and trembling, and launching myself in a moment of despair, I miss my foothold and roll into the abyss. In this case (and it is one of an immense class) the part of wisdom clearly is to believe what one desires; for the belief is one of the indispensable preliminary conditions of the realization of its object. *There are then cases where faith creates its own verification.* Believe, and you shall be right, for you shall save yourself; doubt, and you shall again be right, for you shall perish. The only difference is that to believe is greatly to your advantage.

The future movements of the stars or the facts of past history are determined now once for all, whether I like them or not. They are given irrespective of my wishes, and in all that concerns truths like these subjective preference should have no part; it can only obscure the judgment. But in every fact into which there enters an element of personal contribution on my part, as soon as this personal contribution demands a certain degree of subjective energy which, in its turn, calls for a certain amount of faith in the result,—so that, after all, the future fact is conditioned by my present faith in it,—how trebly asinine would it be for me to deny myself the use of the subjective method, the method of belief based on desire.

In every proposition whose bearing is universal (and such are all the propositions of philosophy), the acts of the subject and their consequences throughout eternity should be included in the formula. If M represent the entire world *minus* the reaction of the thinker upon it, and if $M+x$ represent the absolutely total matter of philosophic propositions (x standing for the thinker's reaction and its results),—what would be a universal truth if the term x were of one complexion, might become egregious error if x altered its character. Let it not be said that x is too infinitesimal a component to change the character of the immense whole in which it lies imbedded. Everything depends on the point of view of the philosophic proposition in question. If we have to define the universe from the point of view of sensibility, the critical material for our judgment lies in the animal kingdom, insignificant as that is, quantitatively considered. The moral definition of the world may depend on phenomena more restricted still in range. In short, many a long phrase may have its sense reversed by the addition of three letters, n-o-t; many a monstrous mass have its unstable equilibrium discharged one way or the other by a feather weight that falls.

Let us make this clear by a few examples. The philosophy of evolution offers us to-day a new criterion to serve as an ethical test between right and wrong. Previous criteria, it says, being subjective, have left us still floundering in variations of opinion and the *status belli.* Here is a criterion which is objective and fixed: *That is to be called good which is destined to prevail or survive.* But we immediately see that this standard can only remain objective by leaving myself and my conduct out. If what prevails and survives does so by my help, and cannot do so without that help; if something else will prevail in case I alter my conduct,—how can I possibly now, conscious of alternative courses of action open before me, either of which I may suppose capable of altering the path of events, decide which course to take by asking what path events will follow? If they follow my direction, evidently my direction cannot wait on them. The only possible manner in which an evolutionist can use his standard is the obsequious method of forecasting the course society would take *but for him,* and then putting an extinguisher on all personal idiosyncrasies of desire and interest, and with bated breath and tiptoe tread following as straight as may be at the tail, and bringing up the rear of everything. Some pious creatures may find a pleasure in this; but not only does it violate our general wish to lead and not to follow (a wish which is surely not immoral if we but lead aright), but if it be treated as every ethical principle must be treated,—namely, as a rule good for all men alike,—its general observance would lead to its practical refutation by bringing about a general deadlock. Each good man hanging back and waiting for orders from the rest, absolute stagnation would ensue. Happy, then, if a few unrighteous ones contribute an initiative which sets things moving again!

All this is no caricature. That the course of destiny may be altered by individuals no wise evolutionist ought to doubt. Everything for him has small beginnings, has a bud which may be 'nipped,' and nipped by a feeble force. Human races and tendencies follow the law, and have also small beginnings. The best, according to evolution, is that which has the biggest endings. Now, if a present race of men, enlightened in the evolutionary philosophy, and able to forecast the future, were able to discern in a tribe arising near them the potentiality of future supremacy; were able to see that their own race would eventually be wiped out of existence by the new-comers if the expansion of these were left unmolested,—these present sages would have two courses open to them, either perfectly in harmony with the evolutionary test: Strangle the new race *now,* and ours survives; help the new race, and *it* survives. In both cases the action is right as measured by the evolutionary standard,—it is action for the winning side.

Thus the evolutionist foundation of ethics is purely objective only to the herd of nullities whose votes count for zero in the march of events. But for others, leaders of opinion or potentates, and in general those to whose actions position or genius gives a far-reaching import, and to the rest of us, each in his measure,—whenever we espouse a cause we contribute to the determination of the evolutionary standard of right. The truly wise disciple of this school will then admit faith as an ultimate ethical factor. Any philosophy which makes such questions as, What is the ideal type of humanity? What shall be reckoned virtues? What conduct is good? depend on the question, What is going to succeed?—must needs fall back on personal belief as one of the ultimate conditions of the truth. For again and again success depends on energy of act; energy again depends on faith that we shall not fail; and that faith in turn on the faith that we are right,—which faith thus verifies itself.

Take as an example the question of optimism or pessimism, which makes so much noise just now in Germany. Every human being must sometime decide for himself whether life is worth living. Suppose that in looking at the world and seeing how full it is of misery, of old age, of wickedness and pain, and how unsafe is his own future, he yields to the pessimistic conclusion, cultivates disgust and dread, ceases striving, and finally commits suicide. He thus adds to the mass M of mundane phenomena, independent of his subjectivity, the subjective complement x, which makes of the whole an utterly black picture illumined by no gleam of good. Pessimism completed, verified by his moral reaction and the deed in which this ends, is true beyond a doubt. $M+x$ expresses a state of things totally bad. The man's belief supplied all that was lacking to make it so, and now that it is made so the belief was right.

But now suppose that with the same evil facts M, the man's reaction x is exactly reversed; suppose that instead of giving way to the evil he braves it, and finds a sterner, more wonderful joy than any passive pleasure can yield in triumphing over pain and defying fear; suppose he does this successfully, and however thickly evils crowd upon him proves his dauntless subjectivity to be more than their match,—will not every one confess that the bad character of the M is here the *conditio sine qua non* of the good character of the x? Will not every one instantly declare a world fitted only for fair-weather human beings susceptible of every passive enjoyment, but without independence, courage, or fortitude, to be from a moral point of view incommensurably inferior to a world framed to elicit from the man every form of triumphant endurance and conquering moral energy? As James Hinton says,—

"Little inconveniences, exertions, pains,—these are the only things in which we rightly feel our life at all. If these be not there, existence becomes worthless, or worse; success in putting them all away is fatal. So it is men engage in athletic sports, spend their holidays in climbing up mountains, find nothing so enjoyable as that which taxes their endurance and their energy. This is the way we are made, I say. It may or may not be a mystery or a paradox; it is a fact. Now, this enjoyment in endurance is just according to the intensity of life: the more physical vigor and balance, the more endurance can be made an element of satisfaction. A sick man cannot stand it. The line of enjoyable suffering is not a fixed one; it fluctuates with the perfectness of the life. That our pains are, as they are, unendurable, awful, overwhelming, crushing, not to be borne save in misery and dumb impatience, which utter exhaustion alone makes patient,— that our pains are thus unendurable, means not that they are too great, but that *we are sick*. We have not got our proper life. So you perceive pain is no more necessarily an evil, but an essential element of the highest good."*

But the highest good can be achieved only by our getting our proper life; and that can come about only by help of a moral energy born of the faith that in some way or other we shall succeed in getting it if we try

* *Life of James Hinton*, pp. 172, 173. See also the excellent chapter on Faith and Sight in the *Mystery of Matter*, by J. Allanson Picton. Hinton's *Mystery of Pain* will undoubtedly always remain the classical utterance on this subject.

pertinaciously enough. This world *is* good, we must say, since it is what we make it,—and we shall make it good. How can we exclude from the cognition of a truth a faith which is involved in the creation of the truth? *M* has its character indeterminate, susceptible of forming part of thorough-going pessimism on the one hand, or of a meliorism, a moral (as distinguished from a sensual) optimism on the other. All depends on the character of the personal contribution *x*. Wherever the facts to be formulated contain such a contribution, we may logically, legitimately, and inexpugnably believe what we desire. The belief creates its verification. The thought becomes literally father to the fact, as the wish was father to the thought.*

Let us now turn to the radical question of life,—the question whether this be at bottom a moral or an unmoral universe,—and see whether the method of faith may legitimately have a place there. It is really the question of materialism. Is the world a simple brute actuality, an existence *de facto* about which the deepest thing that can be said is that it happens so to be; or is the judgment of *better* or *worse,* of *ought,* as intimately pertinent to phenomena as the simple judgment *is* or *is not?* The materialistic theorists say that judgments of worth are themselves mere matters of fact; that the words 'good' and 'bad' have no sense apart from subjective passions and interests which we may, if we please, play fast and loose with at will, so far as any duty of ours to the non-human universe is concerned. Thus, when a materialist says it is better for him to suffer great inconvenience than to break a promise, he only means that his social interests have become so knit up with keeping faith that, those interests once being granted, it *is* better for him to keep the promise in spite of everything. But the interests themselves are neither right nor wrong, except possibly with reference to some ulterior order of interests which themselves again are mere subjective data without character, either good or bad.

For the absolute moralists, on the contrary, the interests are not there merely to be felt,—they are to be believed in and obeyed. Not only is it best for my social interests to keep my promise, but best for me to have those interests, and best for the cosmos to have this me. Like the old woman in the story who described the world as resting on a rock, and then explained that rock to be supported by another rock, and finally when pushed with questions said it was rocks all the way down,—he who

---

* Observe that in all this not a word has been said of free-will. It all applies as well to a predetermined as to an indeterminate universe. If $M+x$ is fixed in advance, the belief which leads to x and the desire which prompts the belief are also fixed. But fixed or not, these subjective states form a phenomenal condition necessarily preceding the facts; necessarily constitutive, therefore, of the truth $M+x$ which we seek. If, however, free acts be possible, a faith in their possibility, by augmenting the moral energy which gives them birth, will increase their frequency in a given individual.

believes this to be a radically moral universe must hold the moral order
to rest either on an absolute and ultimate *should,* or on a series of *shoulds*
all the way down.*

The practical difference between this objective sort of moralist and the
other one is enormous. The subjectivist in morals, when his moral feelings
are at war with the facts about him, is always free to seek harmony by
toning down the sensitiveness of the feelings. Being mere data, neither
good nor evil in themselves, he may pervert them or lull them to sleep by
any means at his command. Truckling, compromise, time-serving, capitula-
tions of conscience, are conventionally opprobrious names for what, if
successfully carried out, would be on his principles by far the easiest and
most praiseworthy mode of bringing about that harmony between inner
and outer relations which is all that he means by good. The absolute
moralist, on the other hand, when his interests clash with the world, is
not free to gain harmony by sacrificing the ideal interests. According to
him, these latter should be as they are and not otherwise. Resistance then,
poverty, martyrdom if need be, tragedy in a word,—such are the solemn
feasts of his inward faith. Not that the contradiction between the two men
occurs every day; in commonplace matters all moral schools agree. It is
only in the lonely emergencies of life that our creed is tested: then routine
maxims fail, and we fall back on our gods. It cannot then be said that the
question, Is this a moral world? is a meaningless and unverifiable question because it deals with something non-phenomenal. Any question is
full of meaning to which, as here, contrary answers lead to contrary behavior. And it seems as if in answering such a question as this we
might proceed exactly as does the physical philosopher in testing an
hypothesis. He deduces from the hypothesis an experimental action, $x;$
this he adds to the facts M already existing. It fits them if the hypothesis
be true; if not, there is discord. The results of the action corroborate or
refute the idea from which it flowed. So here: the verification of the theory
which you may hold as to the objectively moral character of the world
can consist only in this,—that if you proceed to act upon your theory it will
be reversed by nothing that later turns up as your action's fruit; it
will harmonize so well with the entire drift of experience that the latter
will, as it were, adopt it, or at most give it an ampler interpretation, without obliging you in any way to change the essence of its formulation. If
this be an objectively moral universe, all acts that I make on that assumption, all expectations that I ground on it, will tend more and more completely to interdigitate with the phenomena already existing. $M+x$ will
be in accord; and the more I live, and the more the fruits of my activity
come to light, the more satisfactory the consensus will grow. While if it

* In either case, as a later essay explains, the *should* which the moralist regards as
binding upon *him* must be rooted in the feeling of some other thinker, or collection
of thinkers, to whose demands he individually bows.

be not such a moral universe, and I mistakenly assume that it is, the course of experience will throw ever new impediments in the way of my belief, and become more and more difficult to express in its language. Epicycle upon epicycle of subsidiary hypothesis will have to be invoked to give to the discrepant terms a temporary appearance of squaring with each other; but at last even this resource will fail.

If, on the other hand, I rightly assume the universe to be not moral, in what does my verification consist? It is that by letting moral interests sit lightly, by disbelieving that there is any duty about *them* (since duty obtains only as *between* them and other phenomena), and so throwing them over if I find it hard to get them satisfied,—it is that by refusing to take up a tragic attitude, I deal in the long-run most satisfactorily with the facts of life. "All is vanity" is here the last word of wisdom. Even though in certain limited series there may be a great appearance of seriousness, he who in the main treats things with a degree of good-natured scepticism and radical levity will find that the practical fruits of his epicurean hypothesis verify it more and more, and not only save him from pain but do honor to his sagacity. While, on the other hand, he who contrary to reality stiffens himself in the notion that certain things absolutely should be, and rejects the truth that at bottom it makes no difference what is, will find himself evermore thwarted and perplexed and bemuddled by the facts of the world, and his tragic disappointment will, as experience accumulates, seem to drift farther and farther away from that final atonement or reconciliation which certain partial tragedies often get.

Anæsthesia is the watchword of the moral sceptic brought to bay and put to his trumps. *Energy* is that of the moralist. Act on my creed, cries the latter, and the results of your action will prove the creed true, and that the nature of things is earnest infinitely. Act on mine, says the epicurean, and the results will prove that seriousness is but a superficial glaze upon a world of fundamentally trivial import. You and your acts and the nature of things will be alike enveloped in a single formula, a universal *vanitas vanitatum*.

For the sake of simplicity I have written as if the verification might occur in the life of a single philosopher,—which is manifestly untrue, since the theories still face each other, and the facts of the world give countenance to both. Rather should we expect, that, in a question of this scope, the experience of the entire human race must make the verification, and that all the evidence will not be 'in' till the final integration of things, when the last man has had his say and contributed his share to the still unfinished x. Then the proof will be complete; then it will appear without doubt whether the moralistic x has filled up the gap which alone kept the M of the world from forming an even and harmonious unity, or whether the non-moralistic x has given the finishing touches which were alone needed to make the M appear outwardly as vain as it inwardly was.

But if this be so, is it not clear that the facts M, taken *per se,* are inadequate to justify a conclusion either way in advance of my action? My action is the complement which, by proving congruous or not, reveals the latent nature of the mass to which it is applied. The world may in fact be likened unto a lock, whose inward nature, moral or unmoral, will never reveal itself to our simply expectant gaze. The positivists, forbidding us to make any assumptions regarding it, condemn us to eternal ignorance, for the 'evidence' which they wait for can never come so long as we are passive. But nature has put into our hands two keys, by which we may test the lock. If we try the moral key *and it fits,* it is a moral lock. If we try the unmoral key and *it* fits, it is an unmoral lock. I cannot possibly conceive of any other sort of 'evidence' or 'proof' than this. It is quite true that the co-operation of generations is needed to educe it. But in these matters the solidarity (so called) of the human race is a patent fact. The essential thing to notice is that our active preference is a legitimate part of the game,—that it is our plain business as men to try one of the keys, and the one in which we most confide. If then the proof exist not till I have acted, and I must needs in acting run the risk of being wrong, how can the popular science professors be right in objurgating in me as infamous a 'credulity' which the strict logic of the situation requires? If this really be a moral universe; if by my acts I be a factor of its destinies; if to believe where I may doubt be itself a moral act analogous to voting for a side not yet sure to win,—by what right shall they close in upon me and steadily negate the deepest conceivable function of my being by their preposterous command that I shall stir neither hand nor foot, but remain balancing myself in eternal and insoluble doubt? Why, doubt itself is a decision of the widest practical reach, if only because we may miss by doubting what goods we might be gaining by espousing the winning side. But more than that! it is often practically impossible to distinguish doubt from dogmatic negation. If I refuse to stop a murder because I am in doubt whether it be not justifiable homicide, I am virtually abetting the crime. If I refuse to bale out a boat because I am in doubt whether my efforts will keep her afloat, I am really helping to sink her. If in the mountain precipice I doubt my right to risk a leap, I actively connive at my destruction. He who commands himself not to be credulous of God, of duty, of freedom, of immortality, may again and again be indistinguishable from him who dogmatically denies them. Scepticism in moral matters is an active ally of immorality. Who is not for is against. The universe will have no neutrals in these questions. In theory as in practice, dodge or hedge, or talk as we like about a wise scepticism, we are really doing volunteer military service for one side or the other.

Yet obvious as this necessity practically is, thousands of innocent magazine readers lie paralyzed and terrified in the network of shallow negations which the leaders of opinion have thrown over their souls. All they need to be free and hearty again in the exercise of their birthright is that these fastidious vetoes should be swept away. All that the human heart wants is its chance. It will willingly forego certainty in universal matters if only it can be allowed to feel that in them it has that same inalienable right to run risks, which no one dreams of refusing to it in the pettiest practical affairs. And if I, in these last pages, like the mouse in the fable, have gnawed a few of the strings of the sophistical net that has been binding down its lion-strength, I shall be more than rewarded for my pains.

To sum up: No philosophy will permanently be deemed rational by all men which (in addition to meeting logical demands) does not to some degree pretend to determine expectancy, and in a still greater degree make a direct appeal to all those powers of our nature which we hold in highest esteem. Faith, being one of these powers, will always remain a factor not to be banished from philosophic constructions, the more so since in many ways it brings forth its own verification. In these points, then, it is hopeless to look for literal agreement among mankind.

The ultimate philosophy, we may therefore conclude, must not be too strait-laced in form, must not in all its parts divide heresy from orthodoxy by too sharp a line. There must be left over and above the propositions to be subscribed, *ubique, semper, et ab omnibus,* another realm into which the stifled soul may escape from pedantic scruples and indulge its own faith at its own risks; and all that can here be done will be to mark out distinctly the questions which fall within faith's sphere.

The Dilemma of Determinism

A COMMON OPINION PREVAILS THAT THE JUICE HAS AGES AGO BEEN pressed out of the free-will controversy, and that no new champion can do more than warm up stale arguments which every one has heard. This is a radical mistake. I know of no subject less worn out, or in which inventive genius has a better chance of breaking open new ground,—not, perhaps, of forcing a conclusion or of coercing assent, but of deepening our sense of what the issue between the two parties really is, of what the ideas of fate and of free-will imply. At our very side almost, in the past few years, we have seen falling in rapid succession from the press works that present the alternative in entirely novel lights. Not to speak of the English disciples of Hegel, such as Green and Bradley; not to speak of Hinton and Hodgson, nor of Hazard here,—we see in the writings of Renouvier, Fouillée, and Delboeuf* how completely changed and refreshed is the form of all the old disputes. I cannot pretend to vie in originality with any of the masters I have named, and my ambition limits itself to just one little point. If I can make two of the necessarily implied corollaries of determinism clearer to you than they have been made before, I shall have made it possible for you to decide for or against that doctrine with a better understanding of what you are about. And if you prefer not to decide at all, but to remain doubters, you will at least see more plainly what the subject of your hesitation is. I thus disclaim openly on the threshold all pretension to prove to you that the freedom of the will is true. The most I hope is to induce some of you to follow my own example in assuming it true, and acting as if it were true. If it be true, it seems to me that this is involved in the strict logic of the case. Its truth ought not to be forced willy-nilly down our indifferent throats. It ought to be freely espoused by men who can equally well turn their backs upon it. In other words, our first act of freedom, if we are free, ought in all inward propriety to be to affirm that we are free. This should exclude, it seems to me, from the free-will side of the question all hope of a coercive demonstration,—a demonstration which I, for one, am perfectly contented to go without.

With thus much understood at the outset, we can advance. But not without one more point understood as well. The arguments I am about

* And I may now say Charles S. Peirce,—see the *Monist,* for 1892-93.

to urge all proceed on two suppositions: first, when we make theories about the world and discuss them with one another, we do so in order to attain a conception of things which shall give us subjective satisfaction; and, second, if there be two conceptions, and the one seems to us, on the whole, more rational than the other, we are entitled to suppose that the more rational one is the truer of the two. I hope that you are all willing to make these suppositions with me; for I am afraid that if there be any of you here who are not, they will find little edification in the rest of what I have to say. I cannot stop to argue the point; but I myself believe that all the magnificent achievements of mathematical and physical science— our doctrines of evolution, of uniformity of law, and the rest—proceed from our indomitable desire to cast the world into a more rational shape in our minds than the shape into which it is thrown there by the crude order of our experience. The world has shown itself, to a great extent, plastic to this demand of ours for rationality. How much farther it will show itself plastic no one can say. Our only means of finding out is to try; and I, for one, feel as free to try conceptions of moral as of mechanical or of logical rationality. If a certain formula for expressing the nature of the world violates my moral demand, I shall feel as free to throw it over- board, or at least to doubt it, as if it disappointed my demand for uni- formity of sequence, for example; the one demand being, so far as I can see, quite as subjective and emotional as the other is. The principle of causality, for example,—what is it but a postulate, an empty name cover- ing simply a demand that the sequence of events shall some day manifest a deeper kind of belonging of one thing with another than the mere arbi- trary juxtaposition which now phenomenally appears? It is as much an altar to an unknown god as the one that Saint Paul found at Athens. All our scientific and philosophic ideals are altars to unknown gods. Uni- formity is as much so as is free-will. If this be admitted, we can debate on even terms. But if any one pretends that while freedom and variety are, in the first instance, subjective demands, necessity and uniformity are something altogether different, I do not see how we can debate at all.*

* "The whole history of popular beliefs about Nature refutes the notion that the thought of a universal physical order can possibly have arisen from the purely pas- sive reception and association of particular perceptions. Indubitable as it is that men infer from known cases to unknown, it is equally certain that this procedure, if restricted to the phenomenal materials that spontaneously offer themselves, would never have led to the belief in a general uniformity, but only to the belief that law and lawlessness rule the world in motley alternation. From the point of view of strict experience, nothing exists but the sum of particular perceptions, with their coincidences on the one hand, their contradictions on the other.

"That there is more order in the world than appears at first sight is not discovered *till the order is looked for*. The first impulse to look for it proceeds from practical needs: where ends must be attained, we must know trustworthy means which in- fallibly possess a property, or produce a result. But the practical need is only the first occasion for our reflection on the conditions of true knowledge; and even were there no such need, motives would still be present for carrying us beyond the stage

To begin, then, I must suppose you acquainted with all the usual arguments on the subject. I cannot stop to take up the old proofs from causation, from statistics, from the certainty with which we can foretell one another's conduct, from the fixity of character, and all the rest. But there are two *words* which usually encumber these classical arguments, and which we must immediately dispose of if we are to make any progress. One is the eulogistic word *freedom,* and the other is the opprobrious word *chance.* The word 'chance' I wish to keep, but I wish to get rid of the word 'freedom.' Its eulogistic associations have so far overshadowed all the rest of its meaning that both parties claim the sole right to use it, and determinists to-day insist that they alone are freedom's champions. Old-fashioned determinism was what we may call *hard* determinism. It did not shrink from such words as fatality, bondage of the will, necessitation, and the like. Nowadays, we have a *soft* determinism which abhors harsh words, and, repudiating fatality, necessity, and even predetermination, says that its real name is freedom; for freedom is only necessity understood, and bondage to the highest is identical with true freedom. Even a writer as little used to making capital out of soft words as Mr. Hodgson hesitates not to call himself a 'free-will determinist.'

Now, all this is a quagmire of evasion under which the real issue of fact has been entirely smothered. Freedom in all these senses presents simply no problem at all. No matter what the soft determinist mean by it,—whether he mean the acting without external constraint; whether he mean the acting rightly, or whether he mean the acquiescing in the law of the whole,—who cannot answer him that sometimes we are free and sometimes we are not? But there *is* a problem, an issue of fact and not of words, an issue of the most momentous importance, which is often decided without discussion in one sentence,—nay, in one clause of a sentence,—by those very writers who spin out whole chapters in their efforts to show what 'true' freedom is; and that is the question of determinism, about which we are to talk to-night.

Fortunately, no ambiguities hang about this word or about its opposite, indeterminism. Both designate an outward way in which things may happen, and their cold and mathematical sound has no sentimental associations that can bribe our partiality either way in advance. Now, evidence

---

of mere association. For not with an equal interest, or rather with an equal lack of interest, does man contemplate those natural processes in which a thing is linked with its former mate, and those in which it is linked to something else. *The former processes harmonize with the conditions of his own thinking:* the latter do not. In the former, his *concepts, general judgments,* and *inferences* apply to reality: in the latter, they have no such application. And thus the intellectual satisfaction which at first comes to him without reflection, at last excites in him the conscious wish to find realized throughout the entire phenomenal world those rational continuities, uniformities, and necessities which are the fundamental element and guiding principle of his own thought." (Swigart, *Logik,* bd. 2, s. 382.)

of an external kind to decide between determinism and indeterminism is, as I intimated a while back, strictly impossible to find. Let us look at the difference between them and see for ourselves. What does determinism profess?

It professes that those parts of the universe already laid down absolutely appoint and decree what the other parts shall be. The future has no ambiguous possibilities hidden in its womb: the part we call the present is compatible with only one totality. Any other future complement than the one fixed from eternity is impossible. The whole is in each and every part, and welds it with the rest into an absolute unity, an iron block, in which there can be no equivocation or shadow of turning.

> "With earth's first clay they did the last man knead,
> And there of the last harvest sowed the seed.
> And the first morning of creation wrote
> What the last dawn of reckoning shall read."

Indeterminism, on the contrary, says that the parts have a certain amount of loose play on one another, so that the laying down of one of them does not necessarily determine what the others shall be. It admits that possibilities may be in excess of actualities, and that things not yet revealed to our knowledge may really in themselves be ambiguous. Of two alternative futures which we conceive, both may now be really possible; and the one become impossible only at the very moment when the other excludes it by becoming real itself. Indeterminism thus denies the world to be one unbending unit of fact. It says there is a certain ultimate pluralism in it; and, so saying, it corroborates our ordinary unsophisticated view of things. To that view, actualities seem to float in a wider sea of possibilities from out of which they are chosen; and, *somewhere,* indeterminism says, such possibilities exist, and form a part of truth.

Determinism, on the contrary, says they exist *nowhere,* and that necessity on the one hand and impossibility on the other are the sole categories of the real. Possibilities that fail to get realized are, for determinism, pure illusions: they never were possibilities at all. There is nothing inchoate, it says, about this universe of ours, all that was or is or shall be actual in it having been from eternity virtually there. The cloud of alternatives our minds escort this mass of actuality withal is a cloud of sheer deceptions, to which 'impossibilities' is the only name that rightfully belongs.

The issue, it will be seen, is a perfectly sharp one, which no eulogistic terminology can smear over or wipe out. The truth *must* lie with one side or the other, and its lying with one side makes the other false.

The question relates solely to the existence of possibilities, in the strict sense of the term, as things that may, but need not, be. Both sides admit that a volition, for instance, has occurred. The indeterminists say another volition might have occurred in its place: the determinists swear that nothing could possibly have occurred in its place. Now, can science be called in to tell us which of these two point-blank contradicters of each other is right? Science professes to draw no conclusions but such as are based on matters of fact, things that have actually happened; but how can any amount of assurance that something actually happened give us the least grain of information as to whether another thing might or might not have happened in its place? Only facts can be proved by other facts. With things that are possibilities and not facts, facts have no concern. If we have no other evidence than the evidence of existing facts, the possibility-question must remain a mystery never to be cleared up.

And the truth is that facts practically have hardly anything to do with making us either determinists or indeterminists. Sure enough, we make a flourish of quoting facts this way or that; and if we are determinists, we talk about the infallibility with which we can predict one another's conduct; while if we are indeterminists, we lay great stress on the fact that it is just because we cannot foretell one another's conduct, either in war or statecraft or in any of the great and small intrigues and businesses of men, that life is so intensely anxious and hazardous a game. But who does not see the wretched insufficiency of this so-called objective testimony on both sides? What fills up the gaps in our minds is something not objective, not external. What divides us into possibility men and anti-possibility men is different faiths or postulates,—postulates of rationality. To this man the world seems more rational with possibilities in it,—to that man more rational with possibilities excluded; and talk as we will about having to yield to evidence, what makes us monists or pluralists, determinists or indeterminists, is at bottom always some sentiment like this.

The stronghold of the deterministic sentiment is the antipathy to the idea of chance. As soon as we begin to talk indeterminism to our friends, we find a number of them shaking their heads. This notion of alternative possibility, they say, this admission that any one of several things may come to pass, is, after all, only a roundabout name for chance; and chance is something the notion of which no sane mind can for an instant tolerate in the world. What is it, they ask, but barefaced crazy unreason, the negation of intelligibility and law? And if the slightest particle of it exist anywhere, what is to prevent the whole fabric from falling together, the stars from going out, and chaos from recommencing her topsy-turvy reign?

Remarks of this sort about chance will put an end to discussion as quickly as anything one can find. I have already told you that 'chance' was a word I wished to keep and use. Let us then examine exactly what it means, and see whether it ought to be such a terrible bugbear to us. I fancy that squeezing the thistle boldly will rob it of its sting.

The sting of the word 'chance' seems to lie in the assumption that it means something positive, and that if anything happens by chance, it must needs be something of an intrinsically irrational and preposterous sort. Now, chance means nothing of the kind. It is a purely negative and relative term,* giving us no information about that of which it is predicated, except that it happens to be disconnected with something else,—not controlled, secured, or necessitated by other things in advance of its own actual presence. As this point is the most subtile one of the whole lecture, and at the same time the point on which all the rest hinges, I beg you to pay particular attention to it. What I say is that it tells us nothing about what a thing may be in itself to call it 'chance.' It may be a bad thing, it may be a good thing. It may be lucidity, transparency, fitness incarnate, matching the whole system of other things, when it has once befallen, in an unimaginably perfect way. All you mean by calling it 'chance' is that this is not guaranteed, that it may also fall out otherwise. For the system of other things has no positive hold on the chance-thing. Its origin is in a certain fashion negative: it escapes, and says, Hands off! coming, when it comes, as a free gift, or not at all.

This negativeness, however, and this opacity of the chance-thing when thus considered *ab extra,* or from the point of view of previous things or distant things, do not preclude its having any amount of positiveness and luminosity from within, and at its own place and moment. All that its chance-character asserts about it is that there is something in it really of its own, something that is not the unconditional property of the whole. If the whole wants this property, the whole must wait till it can get it, if it be a matter of chance. That the universe may actually be a sort of joint-stock society of this sort, in which the sharers have both limited liabilities and limited powers, is of course a simple and conceivable notion.

Nevertheless, many persons talk as if the minutest dose of disconnectedness of one part with another, the smallest modicum of independence, the faintest tremor of ambiguity about the future, for example, would ruin everything, and turn this goodly universe into a sort of insane sandheap or nulliverse, no universe at all. Since future human volitions are as a matter of fact the only ambiguous things we are tempted to believe in, let us stop for a moment to make ourselves sure whether their independent and accidental character need be fraught with such direful consequences to the universe as these.

What is meant by saying that my choice of which way to walk home after the lecture is ambiguous and matter of chance as far as the present moment is concerned? It means that both Divinity Avenue and Oxford Street are called; but that only one, and that one *either* one, shall be chosen. Now, I ask you seriously to suppose that this ambiguity of my choice is

---

* Speaking technically, it is a word with a positive denotation, but a connotation that is negative. Other things must be silent about *what* it is: it alone can decide that point at the moment in which it reveals itself.

real; and then to make the impossible hypothesis that the choice is made twice over, and each time falls on a different street. In other words, imagine that I first walk through Divinity Avenue, and then imagine that the powers governing the universe annihilate ten minutes of time with all that it contained, and set me back at the door of this hall just as I was before the choice was made. Imagine then that, everything else being the same, I now make a different choice and traverse Oxford Street. You, as passive spectators, look on and see the two alternative universes,—one of them with me walking through Divinity Avenue in it, the other with the same me walking through Oxford Street. Now, if you are determinists you believe one of these universes to have been from eternity impossible: you believe it to have been impossible because of the intrinsic irrationality or accidentality somewhere involved in it. But looking outwardly at these universes, can you say which is the impossible and accidental one, and which the rational and necessary one? I doubt if the most ironclad determinist among you could have the slightest glimmer of light on this point. In other words, either universe *after the fact* and once there would, to our means of observation and understanding, appear just as rational as the other. There would be absolutely no criterion by which we might judge one necessary and the other matter of chance. Suppose now we relieve the gods of their hypothetical task and assume my choice, once made, to be made forever. I go through Divinity Avenue for good and all. If, as good determinists, you now begin to affirm, what all good determinists punctually do affirm, that in the nature of things I *couldn't* have gone through Oxford Street,—had I done so it would have been chance, irrationality, insanity, a horrid gap in nature,—I simply call your attention to this, that your affirmation is what the Germans call a *Machtspruch,* a mere conception fulminated as a dogma and based on no insight into details. Before my choice, either street seemed as natural to you as to me. Had I happened to take Oxford Street, Divinity Avenue would have figured in your philosophy as the gap in nature; and you would have so proclaimed it with the best deterministic conscience in the world.

But what a hollow outcry, then, is this against a chance which, if it were present to us, we could by no character whatever distinguish from a rational necessity! I have taken the most trivial of examples, but no possible example could lead to any different result. For what are the alternatives which, in point of fact, offer themselves to human volition? What are those futures that now seem matters of chance? Are they not one and all like the Divinity Avenue and Oxford Street of our example? Are they not all of them *kinds* of things already here and based in the existing frame of nature? Is any one ever tempted to produce an *absolute* accident, something utterly irrelevant to the rest of the world? Do not all the motives that assail us, all the futures that offer themselves to our choice, spring equally from the soil of the past; and would not either one of them, whether realized through chance or through necessity, the moment it was realized, seem to us to fit that past, and in the completest and most continuous manner to interdigitate with the phenomena already there?*

The more one thinks of the matter, the more one wonders that so empty and gratuitous a hubbub as this outcry against chance should have found so great an echo in the hearts of men. It is a word which tells us absolutely nothing about what chances, or about the *modus operandi* of the chancing; and the use of it as a war-cry shows only a temper of intellectual absolutism, a demand that the world shall be a solid block, subject to one control,—which temper, which demand, the world may not be bound to gratify at all. In every outwardly verifiable and practical respect, a world in which the alternatives that now actually distract *your* choice were decided by pure chance would be by *me* absolutely undistinguished from the world in which I now live. I am, therefore, entirely willing to call it, so far as your choices go, a world of chance for me. To *yourselves,* it is true, those very acts of choice, which to me are so blind, opaque, and external, are the opposites of this, for you are within them and effect them. To you they appear as decisions; and decisions, for him who makes them, are altogether peculiar psychic facts. Self-luminous and self-justifying at the living moment at which they occur, they appeal to no outside moment to put its stamp upon them or make them continuous with the rest of nature. Themselves it is rather who seem to make nature continuous; and in their strange and intense function of granting consent to one possibility and withholding it from another, to transform an equivocal and double future into an inalterable and simple past.

But with the psychology of the matter we have no concern this evening. The quarrel which determinism has with chance fortunately has nothing to do with this or that psychological detail. It is a quarrel altogether metaphysical. Determinism denies the ambiguity of future volitions, because it affirms that nothing future can be ambiguous. But we have said enough to meet the issue. Indeterminate future volitions *do* mean chance. Let us not fear to shout it from the house-tops if need be; for we now know that the idea of chance is, at bottom, exactly the same thing as the idea of gift, —the one simply being a disparaging, and the other a eulogistic, name for

---

* A favorite argument against free-will is that if it be true, a man's murderer may as probably be his best friend as his worst enemy, a mother be as likely to strangle as to suckle her first-born, and all of us be as ready to jump from fourth-story windows as to go out of front doors, etc. Users of this argument should properly be excluded from debate till they learn what the real question is. 'Free-will' does not say that everything that is physically conceivable is also morally possible. It merely says that of alternatives that really *tempt* our will more than one is really possible. Of course, the alternatives that do thus tempt our will are vastly fewer than the physical possibilities we can coldly fancy. Persons really tempted often do murder their best friends, mothers do strangle their first-born, people do jump out of fourth-story windows, etc.

anything on which we have no effective *claim*. And whether the world be the better or the worse for having either chances or gifts in it will depend altogether on *what* these uncertain and unclaimable things turn out to be.

And this at last brings us within sight of our subject. We have seen what determinism means: we have seen that indeterminism is rightly described as meaning chance; and we have seen that chance, the very name of which we are urged to shrink from as from a metaphysical pestilence, means only the negative fact that no part of the world, however big, can claim to control absolutely the destinies of the whole. But although, in discussing the word 'chance,' I may at moments have seemed to be arguing for its real existence, I have not meant to do so yet. We have not yet ascertained whether this be a world of chance or no; at most, we have agreed that it seems so. And I now repeat what I said at the outset, that, from any strict theoretical point of view, the question is insoluble. To deepen our theoretic sense of the *difference* between a world with chances in it and a deterministic world is the most I can hope to do; and this I may now at last begin upon, after all our tedious clearing of the way.

I wish first of all to show you just what the notion that this is a deterministic world implies. The implications I call your attention to are all bound up with the fact that it is a world in which we constantly have to make what I shall, with your permission, call judgments of regret. Hardly an hour passes in which we do not wish that something might be otherwise; and happy indeed are those of us whose hearts have never echoed the wish of Omar Khayam—

> "That we might clasp, ere closed, the book of fate,
>   And make the writer on a fairer leaf
> Inscribe our names, or quite obliterate.

> "Ah! Love, could you and I with fate conspire
> To mend this sorry scheme of things entire,
>   Would we not shatter it to bits, and then
> Remould it nearer to the heart's desire?"

Now, it is undeniable that most of these regrets are foolish, and quite on a par in point of philosophic value with the criticisms on the universe of that friend of our infancy, the hero of the fable The Atheist and the Acorn,—

> "Fool! had that bough a pumpkin bore,
> Thy whimsies would have worked no more," etc.

Even from the point of view of our own ends, we should probably make a botch of remodelling the universe. How much more then from the point of view of ends we cannot see! Wise men therefore regret as little as they can. But still some regrets are pretty obstinate and hard to stifle,—regrets for acts of wanton cruelty or treachery, for example, whether performed by others or by ourselves. Hardly any one can remain *entirely* optimistic after reading the confession of the murderer at Brockton the other day: how, to get rid of the wife whose continued existence bored him, he inveigled her into a desert spot, shot her four times, and then, as she lay on the ground and said to him, "You didn't do it on purpose, did you, dear?" replied, "No, I didn't do it on purpose," as he raised a rock and smashed her skull. Such an occurrence, with the mild sentence and self-satisfaction of the prisoner, is a field for a crop of regrets, which one need not take up in detail. We feel that, although a perfect mechanical fit to the rest of the universe, it is a bad moral fit, and that something else would really have been better in its place.

But for the deterministic philosophy the murder, the sentence, and the prisoner's optimism were all necessary from eternity; and nothing else for a moment had a ghost of a chance of being put into their place. To admit such a chance, the determinists tell us, would be to make a suicide of reason; so we must steel our hearts against the thought. And here our plot thickens, for we see the first of those difficult implications of determinism and monism which it is my purpose to make you feel. If this Brockton murder was called for by the rest of the universe, if it had to come at its preappointed hour, and if nothing else would have been consistent with the sense of the whole, what are we to think of the universe? Are we stubbornly to stick to our judgment of regret, and say, though it *couldn't* be, yet it *would* have been a better universe with something different from this Brockton murder in it? That, of course, seems the natural and spontaneous thing for us to do; and yet it is nothing short of deliberately espousing a kind of pessimism. The judgment of regret calls the murder bad. Calling a thing bad means, if it mean anything at all, that the thing ought not to be, that something else ought to be in its stead. Determinism, in denying that anything else can be in its stead, virtually defines the universe as a place in which what ought to be is impossible,—in other words, as an organism whose constitution is afflicted with an incurable taint, an irremediable flaw. The pessimism of a Schopenhauer says no more than this,—that the murder is a symptom; and that it is a vicious symptom because it belongs to a vicious whole, which can express its nature no otherwise than by bringing forth just such a symptom as that at this particular spot. Regret for the murder must transform itself, if we are determinists and wise, into a larger regret. It is absurd to regret the murder alone. Other things being what they are, *it* could not be different. What we should regret is that whole frame of things of which the murder is one member. I see no escape whatever from this pessimistic conclusion, if, being determinists, our judgment of regret is to be allowed to stand at all.

The only deterministic escape from pessimism is everywhere to abandon the judgment of regret. That this can be done, history shows to be not impossible. The devil, *quoad existentiam,* may be good. That is, although he be a *principle* of evil, yet the universe, with such a principle in it, may practically be a better universe than it could have been without. On every hand, in a small way, we find that a certain amount of evil is a condition by which a higher form of good is bought. There is nothing to prevent anybody from generalizing this view, and trusting that if we could but see things in the largest of all ways, even such matters as this Brockton murder would appear to be paid for by the uses that follow in their train. An optimism *quand même,* a systematic and infatuated optimism like that ridiculed by Voltaire in his Candide, is one of the possible ideal ways in which a man may train himself to look on life. Bereft of dogmatic hardness and lit up with the expression of a tender and pathetic hope, such an optimism has been the grace of some of the most religious characters that ever lived.

> "Throb thine with Nature's throbbing breast,
> And all is clear from east to west."

Even cruelty and treachery may be among the absolutely blessed fruits of time, and to quarrel with any of their details may be blasphemy. The only real blasphemy, in short, may be that pessimistic temper of the soul which lets it give way to such things as regrets, remorse, and grief.

Thus, our deterministic pessimism may become a deterministic optimism at the price of extinguishing our judgments of regret.

But does not this immediately bring us into a curious logical predicament? Our determinism leads us to call our judgments of regret wrong, because they are pessimistic in implying that what is impossible yet ought to be. But how then about the judgments of regret themselves? If they are wrong, other judgments, judgments of approval presumably, ought to be in their place. But as they are necessitated, nothing else *can* be in their place; and the universe is just what it was before,—namely, a place in which what ought to be appears impossible. We have got one foot out of the pessimistic bog, but the other one sinks all the deeper. We have rescued our actions from the bonds of evil, but our judgments are now held fast. When murders and treacheries cease to be sins, regrets are theoretic absurdities and errors. The theoretic and the active life thus play a kind of see-saw with each other on the ground of evil. The rise of either sends the other down. Murder and treachery cannot be good without regret being bad: regret cannot be good without treachery and murder being bad. Both, however, are supposed to have been foredoomed; so something must be fatally unreasonable, absurd, and wrong in the world. It must be a place of which either sin or error forms a necessary part. From this dilemma there seems at first sight no escape. Are we then so soon to fall back into the pessimism from which we thought we had emerged? And is there no possible way by which we may, with good intellectual consciences, call the cruelties and the treacheries, the reluctances and the regrets, *all* good together?

Certainly there is such a way, and you are probably most of you ready to formulate it yourselves. But, before doing so, remark how inevitably the question of determinism and indeterminism slides us into the question of optimism and pessimism, or, as our fathers called it, 'the question of evil.' The theological form of all these disputes is the simplest and the deepest, the form from which there is the least escape,—not because, as some have sarcastically said, remorse and regret are clung to with a morbid fondness by the theologians as spiritual luxuries, but because they are existing facts of the world, and as such must be taken into account in the deterministic interpretation of all that is fated to be. If they are fated to be error, does not the bat's wing of irrationality still cast its shadow over the world?

The refuge from the quandary lies, as I said, not far off. The necessary acts we erroneously regret may be good, and yet our error in so regretting them may be also good, on one simple condition; and that condition is this: The world must not be regarded as a machine whose final purpose is the making real of any outward good, but rather as a contrivance for deepening the theoretic consciousness of what goodness and evil in their intrinsic natures are. Not the doing either of good or of evil is what nature cares for, but the knowing of them. Life is one long eating of the fruit of the tree of *knowledge*. I am in the habit, in thinking to myself, of calling this point of view the *gnostical* point of view. According to it, the world is neither an optimism nor a pessimism, but a *gnosticism*. But as this term may perhaps lead to some misunderstandings, I will use it as little as possible here, and speak rather of *subjectivism,* and the *subjectivistic* point of view.

Subjectivism has three great branches,—we may call them scientificism, sentimentalism, and sensualism, respectively. They all agree essentially about the universe, in deeming that what happens there is subsidiary to what we think or feel about it. Crime justifies its criminality by awakening our intelligence of that criminality, and eventually our remorses and regrets; and the error included in remorses and regrets, the error of supposing that the past could have been different, justifies itself by its use. Its use is to quicken our sense of *what* the irretrievably lost is. When we think of it as that which might have been ('the saddest words of tongue or pen'), the quality of its worth speaks to us with a wilder sweetness; and, conversely, the dissatisfaction wherewith we think of what seems to have driven it from its natural place gives us the severer pang. Admirable artifice of nature! we might be tempted to exclaim,—deceiving us in order the better to enlighten us, and leaving nothing undone to accentuate to our consciousness the yawning distance of those opposite poles of good and evil between which creation swings.

We have thus clearly revealed to our view what may be called the dilemma of determinism, so far as determinism pretends to think things out at all. A merely mechanical determinism, it is true, rather rejoices in not thinking them out. It is very sure that the universe must satisfy its postulate of a physical continuity and coherence, but it smiles at any one who comes forward with a postulate of moral coherence as well. I may suppose, however, that the number of purely mechanical or hard determinists among you this evening is small. The determinism to whose seductions you are most exposed is what I have called soft determinism,—the determinism which allows considerations of good and bad to mingle with those of cause and effect in deciding what sort of universe this may rationally be held to be. The dilemma of this determinism is one whose left horn is pessimism and whose right horn is subjectivism. In other words, if determinism is to escape pessimism, it must leave off looking at the good and ills of life in a simple objective way, and regard them as materials, indifferent in themselves, for the production of consciousness, scientific and ethical, in us.

To escape pessimism is, as we all know, no easy task. Your own studies have sufficiently shown you the almost desperate difficulty of making the notion that there is a single principle of things, and that principle absolute perfection, rhyme together with our daily vision of the facts of life. If perfection be the principle, how comes there any imperfection here? If God be good, how came he to create—or, if he did not create, how comes he to permit—the devil? The evil facts must be explained as seeming: the devil must be whitewashed, the universe must be disinfected, if neither God's goodness nor his unity and power are to remain impugned. And of all the various ways of operating the disinfection, and making bad seem less bad, the way of subjectivism appears by far the best.*

For, after all, is there not something rather absurd in our ordinary notion of external things being good or bad in themselves? Can murders and treacheries, considered as mere outward happenings, or motions of matter, be bad without any one to feel their badness? And could paradise properly be good in the absence of a sentient principle by which the goodness was perceived? Outward goods and evils seem practically indistinguishable except in so far as they result in getting moral judgments made about them. But then the moral judgments seem the main thing, and the outward facts mere perishing instruments for their production. This is subjectivism. Every one must at some time have wondered at that strange paradox of our moral

* To a reader who says he is satisfied with a pessimism, and has no objection to thinking the whole bad, I have no more to say: he makes fewer demands on the world than I, who, making them, wish to look a little further before I give up all hope of having them satisfied. If, however, all he means is that the badness of some parts does not prevent his acceptance of a universe whose *other* parts give him satisfaction, I welcome him as an ally. He has abandoned the notion of the *Whole*, which is the essence of deterministic monism, and views things as a pluralism, just as I do in this paper.

nature, that, though the pursuit of outward good is the breath of its nostrils, the attainment of outward good would seem to be its suffocation and death. Why does the painting of any paradise or utopia, in heaven or on earth, awaken such yawnings for nirvana and escape? The white-robed harp-playing heaven of our sabbath-schools, and the ladylike tea-table elysium represented in Mr. Spencer's Data of Ethics, as the final consummation of progress, are exactly on a par in this respect,—lubberlands, pure and simple, one and all.* We look upon them from this delicious mess of insanities and realities, strivings and deadnesses, hopes and fears, agonies and exultations, which forms our present state, and *tedium vitæ* is the only sentiment they awaken in our breasts. To our crepuscular natures, born for the conflict, the Rembrandtesque moral chiaroscuro, the shifting struggle of the sunbeam in the gloom, such pictures of light upon light are vacuous and expressionless, and neither to be enjoyed nor understood. If *this* be the whole fruit of the victory, we say; if the generations of mankind suffered and laid down their lives; if prophets confessed and martyrs sang in the fire, and all the sacred tears were shed for no other end than that a race of creatures of such unexampled insipidity should succeed, and protract *in saecula saeculorum* their contented and inoffensive lives,—why, at such a rate, better lose than win the battle, or at all events better ring down the curtain before the last act of the play, so that a business that began so importantly may be saved from so singularly flat a winding-up.

All this is what I should instantly say, were I called on to plead for gnosticism; and its real friends, of whom you will presently perceive I am not one, would say without difficulty a great deal more. Regarded as a stable finality, every outward good becomes a mere weariness to the flesh. It must be menaced, be occasionally lost, for its goodness to be fully felt as such. Nay, more than occasionally lost. No one knows the worth of innocence till he knows it is gone forever, and that money cannot buy it back. Not the saint, but the sinner that repenteth, is he to whom the full length and breadth, and height and depth, of life's meaning is revealed. Not the absence of vice, but vice there, and virtue holding her by the throat, seems the ideal human state. And there seems no reason to suppose it not a permanent human state. There is a deep truth in what the school of Schopenhauer insists on,—the illusoriness of the notion of moral progress. The more brutal forms of evil that go are replaced by others more subtle and more poisonous. Our moral horizon moves with us as we move, and never do we draw nearer to the far-off line where the black waves and the azure meet. The final purpose of our creation seems most plausibly to be the greatest possible enrichment of our ethical consciousness, through the intensest play of contrasts and the widest diversity of characters. This of course obliges some of us to be vessels of wrath, while it calls others to

* Compare Sir James Stephen's *Essays by a Barrister,* London, 1862, pp. 138, 318.

be vessels of honor. But the subjectivist point of view reduces all these outward distinctions to a common denominator. The wretch languishing in
the felon's cell may be drinking draughts of the wine of truth that will
never pass the lips of the so-called favorite of fortune. And the peculiar
consciousness of each of them is an indispensable note in the great ethical
concert which the centuries as they roll are grinding out of the living heart
of man.

So much for subjectivism! If the dilemma of determinism be to choose
between it and pessimism, I see little room for hesitation from the strictly
theoretical point of view. Subjectivism seems the more rational scheme.
And the world may, possibly, for aught I know, be nothing else. When the
healthy love of life is on one, and all its forms and its appetites seem so
unutterably real; when the most brutal and the most spiritual things are lit
by the same sun, and each is an integral part of the total richness,—why,
then it seems a grudging and sickly way of meeting so robust a universe to
shrink from any of its facts and wish them not to be. Rather take the
strictly dramatic point of view, and treat the whole thing as a great unending romance which the spirit of the universe, striving to realize its own
content, is eternally thinking out and representing to itself.*

No one, I hope, will accuse me, after I have said all this, of underrating
the reasons in favor of subjectivism. And now that I proceed to say why
those reasons, strong as they are, fail to convince my own mind, I trust
the presumption may be that my objections are stronger still.

I frankly confess that they are of a practical order. If we practically take
up subjectivism in a sincere and radical manner and follow its consequences, we meet with some that make us pause. Let a subjectivism begin
in never so severe and intellectual a way, it is forced by the law of its nature
to develop another side of itself and end with the corruptest curiosity. Once
dismiss the notion that certain duties are good in themselves, and that we
are here to do them, no matter how we feel about them; once consecrate
the opposite notion that our performances and our violations of duty are
for a common purpose, the attainment of subjective knowledge and feeling, and that the deepening of these is the chief end of our lives,—and at
what point on the downward slope are we to stop? In theology, subjectivism develops as its 'left wing' antinomianism. In literature, its left wing
is romanticism. And in practical life it is either a nerveless sentimentality
or a sensualism without bounds.

Everywhere it fosters the fatalistic mood of mind. It makes those who
are already too inert more passive still; it renders wholly reckless those
whose energy is already in excess. All through history we find how sub-

* Cet universe est un spectacle que Dieu se donne à lui-même. Servons les intentions
du grand chorège en contribuant à rendre le spectacle aussi brillant, aussi varié que
possible.—RENAN.

jectivism, as soon as it has a free career, exhausts itself in every sort of
spiritual, moral, and practical license. Its optimism turns to an ethical
indifference, which infallibly brings dissolution in its train. It is perfectly
safe to say now that if the Hegelian gnosticism, which has begun to show
itself here and in Great Britain, were to become a popular philosophy, as
it once was in Germany, it would certainly develop its left wing here as
there, and produce a reaction of disgust. Already I have heard a graduate
of this very school express in the pulpit his willingness to sin like David,
if only he might repent like David. You may tell me he was only sowing his
wild, or rather his tame, oats; and perhaps he was. But the point is that
in the subjectivistic or gnostical philosophy oat-sowing, wild or tame, becomes a systematic necessity and the chief function of life. After the pure
and classic truths, the exciting and rancid ones must be experienced; and
if the stupid virtues of the philistine herd do not then come in and save
society from the influence of the children of light, a sort of inward putre-
faction becomes its inevitable doom.

Look at the last runnings of the romantic school, as we see them in that
strange contemporary Parisian literature, with which we of the less clever
countries are so often driven to rinse out our minds after they have become
clogged with the dulness and heaviness of our native pursuits. The romantic
school began with the worship of subjective sensibility and the revolt
against legality of which Rousseau was the first great prophet: and through
various fluxes and refluxes, right wings and left wings, it stands to-day
with two men of genius, M. Renan and M. Zola, as its principal exponents,
—one speaking with its masculine, and the other with what might be
called its feminine, voice. I prefer not to think now of less noble members of the school, and the Renan I have in mind is of course the Renan
of latest dates. As I have used the term gnostic, both he and Zola are
gnostics of the most pronounced sort. Both are athirst for the facts of
life, and both think the facts of human sensibility to be of all facts the most
worthy of attention. Both agree, moreover, that sensibility seems to be
there for no higher purpose,—certainly not, as the Philistines say, for
the sake of bringing mere outward rights to pass and frustrating outward
wrongs. One dwells on the sensibilities for their energy, the other for their
sweetness; one speaks with a voice of bronze, the other with that of an
Æolian harp; one ruggedly ignores the distinction of good and evil, the
other plays the coquette between the craven unmanliness of his Philosophic
Dialogues and the butterfly optimism of his Souvenirs de Jeunesse. But
under the pages of both there sounds incessantly the hoarse bass of *vanitas
vanitatum, omnia vanitas,* which the reader may hear, whenever he will,
between the lines. No writer of this French romantic school has a word of
rescue from the hour of satiety with the things of life,—the hour in which
we say, "I take no pleasure in them,"—or from the hour of terror at the
world's vast meaningless grinding, if perchance such hours should come.

For terror and satiety are facts of sensibility like any others; and at their own hour they reign in their own right. The heart of the romantic utterances, whether poetical, critical, or historical, is this inward remedilessness, what Carlyle calls this far-off whimpering of wail and woe. And from this romantic state of mind there is absolutely no possible *theoretic* escape. Whether, like Renan, we look upon life in a more refined way, as a romance of the spirit; or whether, like the friends of M. Zola, we pique ourselves on our 'scientific' and 'analytic' character, and prefer to be cynical, and call the world a 'roman expérimental' on an infinite scale,—in either case the world appears to us potentially as what the same Carlyle once called it, a vast, gloomy, solitary Golgotha and mill of death.

The only escape is by the practical way. And since I have mentioned the nowadays much-reviled name of Carlyle, let me mention it once more, and say it is the way of his teaching. No matter for Carlye's life, no matter for a great deal of his writing. What was the most important thing he said to us? He said: "Hang your sensibilities! Stop your snivelling complaints, and your equally snivelling raptures! Leave off your general emotional tomfoolery, and get to WORK like men!" But this means a complete rupture with the subjectivist philosophy of things. It says conduct, and not sensibility, is the ultimate fact for our recognition. With the vision of certain works to be done, of certain outward changes to be wrought or resisted, it says our intellectual horizon terminates. No matter how we succeed in doing these outward duties, whether gladly and spontaneously, or heavily and unwillingly, do them we somehow must; for the leaving of them undone is perdition. No matter how we feel; if we are only faithful in the outward act and refuse to do wrong, the world will in so far be safe, and we quit of our debt toward it. Take, then, the yoke upon our shoulders; bend our neck beneath the heavy legality of its weight; regard something else than our feeling as our limit, our master, and our law; be willing to live and die in its service,—and, at a stroke, we have passed from the subjective into the objective philosophy of things, much as one awakens from some feverish dream, full of bad lights and noises, to find one's self bathed in the sacred coolness and quiet of the air of the night.

But what is the essence of this philosophy of objective conduct, so old-fashioned and finite, but so chaste and sane and strong, when compared with its romantic rival? It is the recognition of limits, foreign and opaque to our understanding. It is the willingness, after bringing about some external good, to feel at peace; for our responsibility ends with the performance of that duty, and the burden of the rest we may lay on higher powers.*
we may say in that philosophy, the moment we have done our stroke of

"Look to thyself, O Universe,
Thou art better and not worse,"

* The burden, for example, of seeing to it that the *end* of all our righteousness be some positive universal gain.

conduct, however small. For in the view of that philosophy the universe belongs to a plurality of semi-independent forces, each one of which may help
or hinder, and be helped or hindered by, the operations of the rest.

But this brings us right back, after such a long détour, to the question
of indeterminism and to the conclusion of all I came here to say to-night.
For the only consistent way of representing a pluralism and a world whose
parts may affect one another through their conduct being either good or
bad is the indeterministic way. What interest, zest, or excitement can
there be in achieving the right way, unless we are enabled to feel that the
wrong way is also a possible and a natural way,—nay, more, a menacing
and an imminent way? And what sense can there be in condemning ourselves for taking the wrong way, unless we need have done nothing of the
sort, unless the right way was open to us as well? I cannot understand the
willingness to act, no matter how we feel, without the belief that acts are
really good and bad. I cannot understand the belief that an act is bad,
without regret at its happening. I cannot understand regret without the
admission of real, genuine possibilities in the world. Only *then* is it other
than a mockery to feel, after we have failed to do our best, that an irreparable opportunity is gone from the universe, the loss of which it must forever after mourn.

If you insist that this is all superstition, that possibility is in the eye of
science and reason impossibility, and that if I act badly 'tis that the universe was foredoomed to suffer this defect, you fall right back into the
dilemma, the labyrinth, of pessimism and subjectivism, from out of whose
toils we have just wound our way.

Now, we are of course, free to fall back, if we please. For my own part,
though, whatever difficulties may beset the philosophy of objective right
and wrong, and the indeterminism it seems to imply, determinism, with its
alternative of pessimism or romanticism, contains difficulties that are
greater still. But you will remember that I expressly repudiated awhile
ago the pretension to offer any arguments which could be coercive in a
so-called scientific fashion in this matter. And I consequently find myself,
at the end of this long talk, obliged to state my conclusions in an altogether
personal way. This personal method of appeal seems to be among the very
conditions of the problem; and the most any one can do is to confess as
candidly as he can the grounds for the faith that is in him, and leave his
example to work on others as it may.

Let me, then, without circumlocution say just this. The world is enigmati-
cal enough in all conscience, whatever theory we may take up toward it.
The indeterminism I defend, the free-will theory of popular sense based
on the judgment of regret, represents that world as vulnerable, and liable
to be injured by certain of its parts if they act wrong. And it represents

their acting wrong as a matter of possibility or accident, neither inevitable nor yet to be infallibly warded off. In all this, it is a theory devoid either of transparency or of stability. It gives us a pluralistic, restless universe, in which no single point of view can ever take in the whole scene; and to a mind possessed of the love of unity at any cost, it will, no doubt, remain forever inacceptable. A friend with such a mind once told me that the thought of my universe made him sick, like the sight of the horrible motion of a mass of maggots in their carrion bed.

But while I freely admit that the pluralism and the restlessness are re-pugnant and irrational in a certain way, I find that every alternative to them is irrational in a deeper way. The indeterminism with its maggots, if you please to speak so about it, offends only the native absolutism of my intellect,—an absolutism which, after all, perhaps, deserves to be snubbed and kept in check. But the determinism with its necessary carrion, to con-tinue the figure of speech, and with no possible maggots to eat the latter up, violates my sense of moral reality through and through. When, for example, I imagine such carrion as the Brockton murder, I cannot con-ceive it as an act by which the universe, as a whole, logically and neces-sarily expresses its nature without shrinking from complicity with such a whole. And I deliberately refuse to keep on terms of loyalty with the uni-verse by saying blankly that the murder, since it does flow from the nature of the whole, is not carrion. There are *some* instinctive reactions which I, for one, will not tamper with. The only remaining alternative, the attitude of gnostical romanticism, wrenches my personal instincts in quite as violent a way. It falsifies the simple objectivity of their deliverance. It makes the goose-flesh the murder excites in me a sufficient reason for the perpetra-tion of the crime. It transforms life from a tragic reality into an insincere melodramatic exhibition, as foul or as tawdry as any one's diseased curiosity pleases to carry it out. And with its consecration of the 'roman naturaliste' state of mind, and its enthronement of the baser crew of Parisian *littérateurs* among the eternally indispensable organs by which the infinite spirit of things attains to that subjective illumination which is the task of its life, it leaves me in presence of a sort of subjective carrion considerably more noisome than the objective carrion I called it in to take away.

No! better a thousand times, than such systematic corruption of our moral sanity, the plainest pessimism, so that it be straightforward; but bet-ter far than that the world of chance. Make as great an uproar about chance as you please, I know that chance means pluralism and nothing more. If some of the members of the pluralism are bad, the philosophy of plural-ism, whatever broad views it may deny me, permits me, at least, to turn to the other members with a clean breast of affection and an unsophisticated moral sense. And if I still wish to think of the world as a totality, it lets me feel that a world with a *chance* in it of being altogether good, even if the chance never come to pass, is better than a world with no such chance at all. That 'chance' whose very notion I am exhorted and conjured to banish from my view of the future as the suicide of reason concerning it, that 'chance' is—what? Just this,—the chance that in moral respects the future may be other and better than the past has been. This is the only chance we have any motive for supposing to exist. Shame, rather, on its repudiation and its denial! For its presence is the vital air which lets the world live, the salt which keeps it sweet.

And here I might legitimately stop, having expressed all I care to see admitted by others to-night. But I know that if I do stop here, misapprehensions will remain in the minds of some of you, and keep all I have said from having its effect; so I judge it best to add a few more words.

In the first place, in spite of all my explanations, the word 'chance' will still be giving trouble. Though you may yourselves be adverse to the deterministic doctrine, you wish a pleasanter word than 'chance' to name the opposite doctrine by; and you very likely consider my preference for such a word a perverse sort of a partiality on my part. It certainly *is* a bad word to make converts with; and you wish I had not thrust it so butt-foremost at you,—you wish to use a milder term.

Well, I admit there may be just a dash of perversity in its choice. The spectacle of the mere word-grabbing game played by the soft determinists has perhaps driven me too violently the other way; and, rather than be found wrangling with them for the good words, I am willing to take the first bad one which comes along, provided it be unequivocal. The question is of things, not of eulogistic names for them; and the best word is the one that enables men to know the quickest whether they disagree or not about the things. But the word 'chance,' with its singular negativity, is just the word for this purpose. Whoever uses it instead of 'freedom,' squarely and resolutely gives up all pretence to control the things he says are free. For *him,* he confesses that they are no better than mere chance would be. It is a word of *impotence,* and is therefore the only sincere word we can use, if, in granting freedom to certain things, we grant it honestly, and really risk the game. "Who chooses me must give and forfeit all he hath." Any other word permits of quibbling, and lets us, after the fashion of the soft determinists, make a pretence of restoring the caged bird to liberty with one hand, while with the other we anxiously tie a string to its leg to make sure it does not get beyond our sight.

But now you will bring up your final doubt. Does not the admission of such an unguaranteed chance or freedom preclude utterly the notion of a Providence governing the world? Does it not leave the fate of the universe at the mercy of the chance-possibilities, and so far insecure? Does it not, in short, deny the craving of our nature for an ultimate peace behind all tempests, for a blue zenith above all clouds?

To this my answer must be very brief. The belief in free-will is not in the least incompatible with the belief in Providence, provided you do not restrict the Providence to fulminating nothing but *fatal* decrees. If you allow him to provide possibilities as well as actualities to the universe, and to carry on his own thinking in those two categories just as we do ours, chances may be there, uncontrolled even by him, and the course of the universe be really ambiguous; and yet the end of all things may be just what he intended it to be from all eternity.

An analogy will make the meaning of this clear. Suppose two men before a chessboard,—the one a novice, the other an expert player of the game. The expert intends to beat. But he cannot foresee exactly what any one actual move of his adversary may be. He knows, however, all the *possible* moves of the latter; and he knows in advance how to meet each of them by a move of his own which leads in the direction of victory. And the victory infallibly arrives, after no matter how devious a course, in the one predestined form of check-mate to the novice's king.

Let now the novice stand for us finite free agents, and the expert for the infinite mind in which the universe lies. Suppose the latter to be thinking out his universe before he actually creates it. Suppose him to say, I will lead things to a certain end, but I will not *now** decide on all the steps thereto. At various points, ambiguous possibilities shall be left open, *either* of which, at a given instant, may become actual. But whichever branch of these bifurcations become real, I know what I shall do at the *next* bifurcation to keep things from drifting away from the final result I intend.*

---

* This of course leaves the creative mind subject to the law of time. And to any one who insists on the timelessness of that mind I have no reply to make. A mind to whom all time is simultaneously present must see all things under the form of actuality, or under some form to us unknown. If he thinks certain moments as ambiguous in their content while future, he must simultaneously know how the ambiguity will have been decided when they are past. So that none of his mental judgments can possibly be called hypothetical, and his world is one from which chance is excluded. Is not, however, the timeless mind rather a gratuitous fiction? And is not the notion of eternity being given at a stroke to omniscience only just another way of whacking upon us the block-universe, and of denying that possibilities exist?— just the point to be proved. To say that time is an illusory appearance is only a roundabout manner of saying there is no real plurality, and that the frame of things is an absolute unit. Admit plurality, and time may be its form.

* And this of course means 'miraculous' interposition, but not necessarily of the gross sort our fathers took such delight in representing, and which has so lost its magic for us. Emerson quotes some Eastern sage as saying that if evil were really done under the sun, the sky would incontinently shrivel to a snakeskin and cast it out in spasms. But, says Emerson, the spasms of Nature are years and centuries; and it will tax man's patience to wait so long. We may think of the reserved possibilities God keeps in his own hand, under as invisible and molecular and slowly self-summating a form as we please. We may think of them as counteracting human agencies which he inspires *ad hoc*. In short, signs and wonders and convulsions of the earth and sky are not the only neutralizers of obstruction to a god's plans of which it is possible to think.

The creator's plan of the universe would thus be left blank as to many of its actual details, but all possibilities would be marked down. The realization of some of these would be left absolutely to chance; that is, would only be determined when the moment of realization came. Other possibilities would be *contingently* determined; that is, their decision would have to wait till it was seen how the matters of absolute chance fell out. But the rest of the plan, including its final upshot, would be rigorously determined once for all. So the creator himself would not need to know *all* the details of actuality until they came; and at any time his own view of the world would be a view partly of facts and partly of possibilities, exactly as ours is now. Of one thing, however, he might be certain; and that is that his world was safe, and that no matter how much it might zigzag he could surely bring it home at last.

Now, it is entirely immaterial, in this scheme, whether the creator leave the absolute chance-possibilities to be decided by himself, each when its proper moment arrives, or whether, on the contrary, he alienate this power from himself, and leave the decision out and out to finite creatures such as we men are. The great point is that the possibilities are really *here*. Whether it be we who solve them, or he working through us, at those soul-trying moments when fate's scales seem to quiver, and good snatches the victory from evil or shrinks nerveless from the fight, is of small account, so long as we admit that the issue is decided nowhere else than *here* and *now*. *That* is what gives the palpitating reality to our moral life and makes it tingle, as Mr. Mallock says, with so strange and elaborate an excitement. This reality, this excitement, are what the determinisms, hard and soft alike, suppress by their denial that *anything* is decided here and now, and their dogma that all things were foredoomed and settled long ago. If it be so, may you and I then have been foredoomed to the error of continuing to believe in liberty.* It is fortunate for the winding up of controversy that in every discussion with determinism this *argumentum ad hominem* can be its adversary's last word.

* As long as languages contain a future perfect tense, determinists, following the bent of laziness or passion, the lines of least resistance, can reply in that tense, saying, "It will have been fated," to the still small voice which urges an opposite course; and thus excuse themselves from effort in a quite unanswerable way.

The Principles of Psychology

HABIT

WHEN WE LOOK AT LIVING CREATURES FROM AN OUTWARD POINT OF VIEW, one of the first things that strike us is that they are bundles of habits. In wild animals, the usual round of daily behavior seems a necessity implanted at birth; in animals domesticated, and especially in man, it seems, to a great extent, to be the result of education. The habits to which there is an innate tendency are called instincts; some of those due to education would by most persons be called acts of reason. It thus appears that habit covers a very large part of life, and that one engaged in studying the objective manifestations of mind is bound at the very outset to define clearly just what its limits are.

The moment one tries to define what habit is, one is led to the fundamental properties of matter. The laws of Nature are nothing but the immutable habits which the different elementary sorts of matter follow in their actions and reactions upon each other. In the organic world, however, the habits are more variable than this. Even instincts vary from one individual to another of a kind; and are modified in the same individual, as we shall later see, to suit the exigencies of the case. The habits of an elementary particle of matter cannot change (on the principles of the atomistic philosophy), because the particle is itself an unchangeable thing; but those of a compound mass of matter can change, because they are in the last instance due to the structure of the compound, and either outward forces or inward tensions can, from one hour to another, turn that structure into something different from what it was. That is, they can do so if the body be plastic enough to maintain its integrity, and be not disrupted when its structure yields. The change of structure here spoken of need not involve the outward shape; it may be invisible and molecular, as when a bar of iron becomes magnetic or crystalline through the action of certain outward causes, or India-rubber becomes friable, or plaster 'sets.' All these changes are rather slow; the material in question opposes a certain resistance to the modifying cause, which it takes time to overcome, but the gradual yielding whereof often saves the material from being disintegrated altogether. When the structure has yielded, the same inertia becomes a condition of its comparative permanence in the new form, and of the new habits the body then manifests. *Plasticity,* then, in the wide sense of the word, means the possession of a structure weak enough to yield to an influence, but strong enough not to yield all at once. Each relatively stable phase of equilibrium in such a structure is marked by what we may call a new set of habits. Organic matter, especially nervous tissue, seems endowed with a very extraordinary degree of plasticity of this sort; so that we may without hesitation lay down as our first proposition the following, that *the phenomena of habit in living beings are due to the plasticity* of the organic materials of which their bodies are composed.* . . .

If habits are due to the plasticity of materials to outward agents, we can immediately see to what outward influences, if to any, the brain-matter is plastic. Not to mechanical pressures, not to thermal changes, not to any of the forces to which all the other organs of our body are exposed; for nature has carefully shut up our brain and spinal cord in bony boxes, where no influences of this sort can get at them. She has floated them in fluid so that only the severest shocks can give them a concussion, and blanketed and wrapped them about in an altogether exceptional way. The only impressions that can be made upon them are through the blood, on the one hand, and through the sensory nerve-roots, on the other; and it is to the infinitely attenuated currents that pour in through these latter channels that the hemispherical cortex shows itself to be so peculiarly susceptible. The currents, once in, must find a way out. In getting out they leave their traces in the paths which they take. The only thing they *can* do, in short, is to deepen old paths or to make new ones; and the whole plasticity of the brain sums itself up in two words when we call it an organ in which currents pouring in from the sense-organs make with extreme facility paths which do not easily disappear. For, of course, a simple habit, like every other nervous event—the habit of snuffling, for example, or of putting one's hands into one's pockets, or of biting one's nails—is, mechanically, nothing but a reflex discharge; and its anatomical substratum must be a path in the system. The most complex habits, as we shall presently see more fully, are, from the same point of view, nothing but *concatenated* discharges in the nerve-centres, due to the presence there of systems of reflex paths, so organized as to wake each other up successively—the impression produced by one muscular contraction serving as a stimulus to provoke the next, until a final impression inhibits the process and closes the chain. The only difficult mechanical problem is to explain the formation *de novo* of a simple reflex or path in a pre-existing nervous system. Here, as in so many other cases, it is only the *premier pas qui coûte.* For the entire nervous system *is* nothing but a system of paths between a sensory *terminus a quo* and a muscular, glandular, or other *terminus ad quem.* A path once traversed by a nerve-current might be expected to follow the law of most of the paths we know, and to be scooped out and made more permeable

---

* In the sense above explained, which applies to inner structure as well as to outer form.

than before;* and this ought to be repeated with each new passage of the current. Whatever obstructions may have kept it at first from being a path should then, little by little, and more and more, be swept out of the way, until at last it might become a natural drainage-channel. This is what happens where either solids or liquids pass over a path; there seems no reason why it should not happen where the thing that passes is a mere wave of rearrangement in matter that does not displace itself, but merely changes chemically or turns itself round in place, or vibrates across the line. The most plausible views of the nerve-current make it out to be the passage of some such wave of rearrangement as this. If only a part of the matter of the path were to 'rearrange' itself, the neighboring parts remaining inert, it is easy to see how their inertness might oppose a friction which it would take many waves of rearrangement to break down and overcome. If we call the path itself the 'organ,' and the wave of rearrangement the 'function,' then it is obviously a case for repeating the celebrated French formula of *'La fonction fait l'organe.'*

So nothing is easier than to imagine how, when a current once has traversed a path, it should traverse it more readily still a second time. But what made it ever traverse it the first time?* In answering this question we can only fall back our general conception of a nervous system as a mass of matter whose parts, constantly kept in states of different tension, are as constantly tending to equalize their states. The equalization between any two points occurs through whatever path may at the moment be most pervious. But, as a given point of the system may belong, actually or potentially, to many different paths, and, as the play of nutrition is subject to accidental changes, *blocks* may from time to time occur, and make currents shoot through unwonted lines. Such an unwonted line would be a new-created path, which if traversed repeatedly, would become the beginning of a new reflex arc. All this is vague to the last degree, and amounts to little more than saying that a new path may beformed by the sort of *chances* that in nervous material are likely to occur. But, vague as it is, it is really the last word of our wisdom in the matter.†

* Some paths, to be sure, are banked up by bodies moving through them under too great pressure, and made impervious. These special cases we disregard.

* We cannot say *the will,* for, though many, perhaps most, human habits were once voluntary actions, no action, as we shall see in a later chapter, can be *primarily* such. While an habitual action may once have been voluntary, the voluntary action must before that, at least once, have been impulsive or reflex. It is this very first occurrence of all that we consider in the text.

† Those who desire a more definite formulation may consult J. Fiske's *Cosmic Philosophy*, Vol. II. pp. 142-146 and Spencer's *Principles of Biology*, sections 302 and 303, and the part entitled Physical Synthesis of his *'Principles of Psychology.'* Mr. Spencer there tries, not only to show how new actions may arise in nervous systems and form new reflex arcs therein, but even how nervous tissue may actually be born by the passage of new waves of isometric transformation through an originally indifferent mass. I cannot help thinking that Mr. Spencer's data, under a great show of precision, conceal vagueness and improbability, and even self-contradiction.

It must be noticed that the growth of structural modification in living matter may be more rapid than in any lifeless mass, because the incessant nutritive renovation of which the living matter is the seat tends often to corroborate and fix the impressed modification, rather than to counteract it by renewing the original constitution of the tissue that has been impressed. Thus, we notice after exercising our muscles or our brain in a new way, that we can do so no longer at that time; but after a day or two of rest, when we resume the discipline, our increase in skill not seldom surprises us. I have often noticed this in learning a tune; and it has led a German author to say that we learn to swim during the winter and to skate during the summer. . . .

Dr. Carpenter's phrase that *our nervous system grows to the modes in which it has been exercised* expresses the philosophy of habit in a nutshell. We may now trace some of the practical applications of the principle to human life.

The first result of it is that *habit simplifies the movements required to achieve a given result, makes them more accurate and diminishes fatigue.* . . .

The next result is that *habit diminishes the conscious attention with which our acts are performed.*

One may state this abstractly thus: If an act require for its execution a chain, *A, B, C, D, E, F, G*, etc., of successive nervous events, then in the first performances of the action the conscious will must choose each of these events from a number of wrong alternatives that tend to present themselves; but habit soon brings it about that each event calls up its own appropriate successor without any alternative offering itself, and without any reference to the conscious will, until at last the whole chain, *A, B, C, D, E, F, G.,* rattles itself off as soon as *A* occurs, just as if *A* and the rest of the chain were fused into a continuous stream. When we are learning to walk, to ride, to swim, skate, fence, write, play, or sing, we interrupt ourselves at every step by unnecessary movements and false notes. When we are proficients, on the contrary, the results not only follow with the very minimum of muscular action requisite to bring them forth, they also follow from a single instantaneous 'cue.' The marksman sees the bird, and, before he knows it, he has aimed and shot. A gleam in his adversary's eye, a momentary pressure from his rapier, and the fencer finds that he has instantly made the right parry and return. A glance at the musical hieroglyphics, and the pianist's fingers have rippled through a cataract of notes. And not only is it the right thing at the right time that we thus involuntarily do, but the wrong thing also, if it be an habitual thing. Who is there that has never wound up his watch on taking off his waistcoat in the daytime, or taken his latchkey out on arriving at the door-step of a friend? Very absent-minded persons in going to their bedroom to dress for dinner have been known to take off one garment after another and finally to get into bed, merely because that was the habitual issue of the first few movements when performed at a later hour. The writer well remembers how, on revisiting Paris after ten years' absence, and, finding himself in the street in which for one winter he had attended school, he lost himself in a brown study, from which he was awakened by finding himself upon the stairs which led to the apartment in a house many streets away in which he had lived during that earlier time, and to which his steps from the school had then habitually led. We all of us have a definite routine manner of performing certain daily offices connected with the toilet, with the opening and shutting of familiar cupboards, and the like. Our lower centres know the order of these movements, and show their knowledge by their 'surprise' if the objects are altered so as to oblige the movement to be made in a different way. But our higher thought-centres know hardly anything about the matter. Few men can tell off-hand which sock, shoe, or trousers-leg they put on first. They must first mentally rehearse the act; and even that is often insufficient—the act must be *performed*. So of the questions, Which valve of my double door opens first? Which way does my door swing? etc. I cannot *tell* the answer; yet my *hand* never makes a mistake. No one can *describe* the order in which he brushes his hair or teeth; yet it is likely that the order is a pretty fixed one in all of us. . . .

This brings us by a very natural transition to the *ethical implications of the law of habit*. They are numerous and momentous. Dr. Carpenter, from whose 'Mental Physiology' we have quoted, has so prominently enforced the principle that our organs grow to the way in which they have been exercised, and dwelt upon its consequences, that his book almost deserves to be called a work of edification, on this account alone. We need make no apology, then, for tracing a few of these consequences ourselves:

"Habit a second nature! Habit is ten times nature," the Duke of Wellington is said to have exclaimed; and the degree to which this is true no one can probably appreciate as well as one who is a veteran soldier himself. The daily drill and the years of discipline end by fashioning a man completely over again, as to most of the possibilities of his conduct.

"There is a story, which is credible enough, though it may not be true, of a practical joker, who, seeing a discharged veteran carrying home his dinner, suddenly called out, 'Attention!' Whereupon the man instantly brought his hands down, and lost his mutton and potatoes in the gutter. The drill had been thorough, and its effects had become embodied in the man's nervous structure."*

Riderless cavalry-horses, at many a battle, have been seen to come together and go through their customary evolutions at the sound of the bugle-call. Most trained domestic animals, dogs and oxen, and omnibus- and car-horses, seem to be machines almost pure and simple, undoubtingly, unhesitatingly doing from minute to minute the duties they have

* Huxley's *Elementary Lessons in Physiology,* lesson XII.

been taught, and giving no sign that the possibility of an alternative ever suggests itself to their mind. Men grown old in prison have asked to be readmitted after being once set free. In a railroad accident to a travelling menagerie in the United States some time in 1884, a tiger, whose cage had broken open, is said to have emerged, but presently crept back again, as if too much bewildered by his new responsibilities, so that he was without difficulty secured.

Habit is thus the enormous fly-wheel of society, its most precious conservative agent. It alone is what keeps us all within the bounds of ordinance, and saves the children of fortune from the envious uprisings of the poor. It alone prevents the hardest and most repulsive walks of life from being deserted by those brought up to tread therein. It keeps the fisherman and the deck-hand at sea through the winter; it holds the miner in his darkness, and nails the countryman to his log-cabin and his lonely farm through all the months of snow; it protects us from invasion by the natives of the desert and the frozen zone. It dooms us all to fight out the battle of life upon the lines of our nurture or our early choice, and to make the best of a pursuit that disagrees, because there is no other for which we are fitted, and it is too late to begin again. It keeps different social strata from mixing. Already at the age of twenty-five you see the professional mannerism settling down on the young commercial traveller, on the young doctor, on the young minister, on the young counsellor-at-law. You see the little lines of cleavage running through the character, the tricks of thought, the prejudices, the ways of the 'shop,' in a word, from which the man can by-and-by no more escape than his coat-sleeve can suddenly fall into a new set of folds. On the whole, it is best he should not escape. It is well for the world that in most of us, by the age of thirty, the character has set like plaster, and will never soften again.

If the period between twenty and thirty is the critical one in the formation of intellectual and professional habits, the period below twenty is more important still for the fixing of *personal* habits, properly so called, such as vocalization and pronunciation, gesture, motion, and address. Hardly ever is a language learned after twenty spoken without a foreign accent; hardly ever can a youth transferred to the society of his betters unlearn the nasality and other vices of speech bred in him by the associations of his growing years. Hardly ever, indeed, no matter how much money there be in his pocket, can he even learn to *dress* like a gentleman-born. The merchants offer their wares as eagerly to him as to the veriest 'swell,' but he simply *cannot* buy the right things. An invisible law, as strong as gravitation, keeps him within his orbit, arrayed this year as he was the last; and how his better-bred acquaintances contrive to get the things they wear will be for him a mystery till his dying day.

The great thing, then, in all education, is to *make our nervous system our ally instead of our enemy*. It is to fund and capitalize our acquisitions, and live at ease upon the interest of the fund. *For this we must make auto-*

matic and habitual, as early as possible, as many useful actions as we can, and guard against the growing into ways that are likely to be disadvantageous to us, as we should guard against the plague. The more of the details of our daily life we can hand over to the effortless custody of automatism, the more our higher powers of mind will be set free for their own proper work. There is no more miserable human being than one in whom nothing is habitual but indecision, and for whom the lighting of every cigar, the drinking of every cup, the time of rising and going to bed every day, and the beginning of every bit of work, are subjects of express volitional deliberation. Full half the time of such a man goes to the deciding, or regretting, of matters which ought to be so ingrained in him as practically not to exist for his consciousness at all. If there be such daily duties not yet ingrained in any one of my readers, let him begin this very hour to set the matter right.

In Professor Bain's chapter on 'The Moral Habits' there are some admirable practical remarks laid down. Two great maxims emerge from his treatment. The first is that in the acquisition of a new habit, or the leaving off of an old one, we must take care to *launch ourselves with as strong and decided an initiative as possible.* Accumulate all the possible circumstances which shall re-enforce the right motives; put yourself assiduously in conditions that encourage the new way; make engagements incompatible with the old; take a public pledge, if the case allows; in short, envelop your resolution with every aid you know. This will give your new beginning such a momentum that the temptation to break down will not occur as soon as it otherwise might; and every day during which a breakdown is postponed adds to the chances of its not occurring at all.

The second maxim is: *Never suffer an exception to occur till the new habit is securely rooted in your life.* Each lapse is like the letting fall of a ball of string which one is carefully winding up; a single slip undoes more than a great many turns will wind again. *Continuity* of training is the great means of making the nervous system act infallibly right. As Professor Bain says:

"The peculiarity of the moral habits, contradistinguishing them from the intellectual acquisitions, is the presence of two hostile powers, one to be gradually raised into the ascendant over the other. It is necessary, above all things, in such a situation, never to lose a battle. Every gain on the wrong side undoes the effect of many conquests on the right. The essential precaution, therefore, is so to regulate the two opposing powers that the one may have a series of uninterrupted successes, until repetition has fortified it to such a degree as to enable it to cope with the opposition, under any circumstances. This is the theoretically best career of mental progress."

The need of securing success at the *outset* is imperative. Failure at first is apt to dampen the energy of all future attempts, whereas past experience of success nerves one to future vigor. Goethe says to a man who consulted him about an enterprise but mistrusted his own powers: "Ach! you need only blow on your hands!" And the remark illustrates the effect on Goethe's spirits of his own habitually successful career. Prof. Baumann, from whom I borrow the anecdote,* says that the collapse of barbarian nations when Europeans come among them is due to their despair of ever succeeding as the new-comers do in the larger tasks of life. Old ways are broken and new ones not formed.

The question of 'tapering-off,' in abandoning such habits as drink and opium-indulgence, comes in here, and is a question about which experts differ within certain limits, and in regard to what may be best for an individual case. In the main, however, all expert opinion would agree that abrupt acquisition of the new habit is the best way, *if there be a real possibility of carrying it out.* We must be careful not to give the will so stiff a task as to insure its defeat at the very outset; but, *provided one can stand it,* a sharp period of suffering, and then a free time, is the best thing to aim at, whether in giving up a habit like that of opium, or in simply changing one's hours of rising or of work. It is surprising how soon a desire will die of inanition if it be *never* fed.

"One must first learn, unmoved, looking neither to the right nor left, to walk firmly on the straight and narrow path, before one can begin 'to make one's self over again.' He who every day makes a fresh resolve is like one who, arriving at the edge of the ditch he is to leap, forever stops and returns for a fresh run. Without *unbroken* advance there is no such thing as *accumulation* of the ethical forces possible, and to make this possible, and to exercise us and habituate us in it, is the sovereign blessing of regular *work*."*

A third maxim may be added to the preceding pair: *Seize the very first possible opportunity to act on every resolution you make, and on every emotional prompting you may experience in the direction of the habits you aspire to gain.* It is not in the moment of their forming, but in the moment of their producing *motor effects,* that resolves and aspirations communicate the new 'set' to the brain. As the author last quoted remarks:

"The actual presence of the practical opportunity alone furnishes the fulcrum upon which the lever can rest, by means of which the moral will may multiply its strength, and raise itself aloft. He who has no solid ground to press against will never get beyond the stage of empty gesture-making."

No matter how full a reservoir of *maxims* one may possess, and no matter how good one's *sentiments* may be, if one have not taken advantage of every concrete opportunity to *act,* one's character may remain entirely unaffected for the better. With mere good intentions, hell is proverbially paved. And this is an obvious consequence of the principles we have laid down. A 'character,' as J. S. Mill says, 'is a completely fashioned will'; and a will, in the sense in which he means it, is an aggregate of tendencies

* See the admirable passage about success at the outset, in his *Handbuch der Moral* (1878), pp. 38-43.
* J. Bahnsen: *Beiträge zu Charakterologie* (1867), vol. 1. p. 209.

to act in a firm and prompt and definite way upon all the principal emergencies of life. A tendency to act only becomes effectively ingrained in us in proportion to the uninterrupted frequency with which the actions actually occur, and the brain 'grows' to their use. Every time a resolve or a fine glow of feeling evaporates without bearing practical fruit is worse than a chance lost; it works so as positively to hinder future resolutions and emotions from taking the normal path of discharge. There is no more contemptible type of human character than that of the nerveless sentimentalist and dreamer, who spends his life in a weltering sea of sensibility and emotion, but who never does a manly concrete deed. Rousseau, inflaming all the mothers of France, by his eloquence, to follow Nature and nurse their babies themselves, while he sends his own children to the foundling hospital, is the classical example of what I mean. But every one of us in his measure, whenever, after glowing for an abstractly formulated Good, he practically ignores some actual case, among the squalid 'other particulars' of which that same Good lurks disguised, treads straight on Rousseau's path. All Goods are disguised by the vulgarity of their concomitants, in this work-a-day world; but woe to him who can only recognize them when he thinks them in their pure and abstract form! The habit of excessive novel-reading and theatre-going will produce true monsters in this line. The weeping of a Russian lady over the fictitious personages in the play, while her coachman is freezing to death on his seat outside, is the sort of thing that everywhere happens on a less glaring scale. Even the habit of excessive indulgence in music, for those who are neither performers themselves nor musically gifted enough to take it in a purely intellectual way, has probably a relaxing effect upon the character. One becomes filled with emotions which habitually pass without prompting to any deed, and so the inertly sentimental condition is kept up. The remedy would be, never to suffer one's self to have an emotion at a concert, without expressing it afterward in *some* active way.* Let the expression be the least thing in the world—speaking genially to one's aunt, or giving up one's seat in a horse-car, if nothing more heroic offers—but let it not fail to take place.

These latter cases make us aware that it is not simply *particular lines* of discharge, but also *general forms* of discharge, that seem to be grooved out by habit in the brain. Just as, if we let our emotions evaporate, they get into a way of evaporating; so there is reason to suppose that if we often flinch from making an effort, before we know it the effort-making capacity will be gone; and that, if we suffer the wandering of our attention, presently it will wander all the time. Attention and effort are, as we shall see later, but two names for the same psychic fact. To what brain-processes they correspond we do not know. The strongest reason for believing that they do depend on brain-processes at all, and are not pure acts of the spirit, is just this fact, that they seem in some degree subject to the law of

---

* See for remarks on this subject a readable article by Miss V. Scudder on 'Musical Devotees and Morals,' in the *Andover Review* for January, 1887.

habit, which is a material law. As a final practical maxim, relative to these habits of the will, we may, then, offer something like this: *Keep the faculty of effort alive in you by a little gratuitous exercise every day*. That is, be systematically ascetic or heroic in little unnecessary points, do every day or two something for no other reason than that you would rather not do it, so that when the hour of dire need draws nigh, it may find you not unnerved and untrained to stand the test. Asceticism of this sort is like the insurance which a man pays on his house and goods. The tax does him no good at the time, and possibly may never bring him a return. But if the fire *does* come, his having paid it will be his salvation from ruin. So with the man who has daily inured himself to habits of concentrated attention, energetic volition, and self-denial in unnecessary things. He will stand like a tower when everything rocks around him, and when his softer fellow-mortals are winnowed like chaff in the blast.

The physiological study of mental conditions is thus the most powerful ally of hortatory ethics. The hell to be endured hereafter, of which theology tells, is no worse than the hell we make for ourselves in this world by habitually fashioning our characters in the wrong way. Could the young but realize how soon they will become mere walking bundles of habits, they would give more heed to their conduct while in the plastic state. We are spinning our own fates, good or evil, and never to be undone. Every smallest stroke of virtue or of vice leaves its never so little scar. The drunken Rip Van Winkle, in Jefferson's play, excuses himself for every fresh dereliction by saying, 'I won't count this time!' Well! he may not count it, and a kind Heaven may not count it; but it is being counted none the less. Down among his nerve-cells and fibres the molecules are counting it, registering and storing it up to be used against him when the next temptation comes. Nothing we ever do is, in strict scientific literalness, wiped out. Of course, this has its good side as well as its bad one. As we become permanent drunkards by so many separate drinks, so we become saints in the moral, and authorities and experts in the practical and scientific spheres, by so many separate acts and hours of work. Let no youth have any anxiety about the upshot of his education, whatever the line of it may be. If he keep faithfully busy each hour of the working-day, he may safely leave the final result to itself. He can with perfect certainty count on waking up some fine morning, to find himself one of the competent ones of his generation, in whatever pursuit he may have singled out. Silently, between all the details of his business, the *power of judging* in all that class of matter will have built itself up within him as a possession that will never pass away. Young people should know this truth in advance. The ignorance of it has probably engendered more discouragement and faint-heartedness in youths embarking on arduous careers than all other causes put together.

The Will to Believe

IN THE RECENTLY PUBLISHED LIFE BY LESLIE STEPHEN OF HIS BROTHER, Fitz-James, there is an account of a school to which the latter went when he was a boy. The teacher, a certain Mr. Guest, used to converse with his pupils in this wise: "Gurney, what is the difference between justification and sanctification?—Stephen, prove the omnipotence of God!" etc. In the midst of our Harvard freethinking and indifference we are prone to imagine that here at your good old orthodox College conversation continues to be somewhat upon this order; and to show you that we at Harvard have not lost all interest in these vital subjects, I have brought with me to-night something like a sermon on justification by faith to read to you,—I mean an essay in justification *of* faith, a defence of our right to adopt a believing attitude in religious matters, in spite of the fact that our merely logical intellect may not have been coerced. 'The Will to Believe,' accordingly, is the title of my paper.

I have long defended to my own students the lawfulness of voluntarily adopted faith; but as soon as they have got well imbued with the logical spirit, they have as a rule refused to admit my contention to be lawful philosophically, even though in point of fact they were personally all the time chock-full of some faith or other themselves. I am all the while, however, so profoundly convinced that my own position is correct, that your invitation has seemed to me a good occasion to make my statements more clear. Perhaps your minds will be more open than those with which I have hitherto had to deal. I will be as little technical as I can, though I must begin by setting up some technical distinctions that will help us in the end.

I.

Let us give the name of *hypothesis* to anything that may be proposed to our belief; and just as the electricians speak of live and dead wires, let us speak of any hypothesis as either *live* or *dead*. A live hypothesis is one which appeals as a real possibility to him to whom it is proposed. If I ask you to believe in the Mahdi, the notion makes no electric connection with your nature,—it refuses to scintillate with any credibility at all. As an hypothesis it is completely dead. To an Arab, however (even if he be not one of the Mahdi's followers), the hypothesis is among the mind's

175

possibilities: it is alive. This shows that deadness and liveness in an hypothesis are not intrinsic properties, but relations to the individual thinker. They are measured by his willingness to act. The maximum of liveness in an hypothesis means willingness to act irrevocably. Practically, that means belief; but there is some believing tendency wherever there is willingness to act at all.

Next, let us call the decision between two hypotheses an *option*. Options may be of several kinds. They may be—1, *living* or *dead;* 2, *forced* or *avoidable;* 3, *momentous* or *trivial;* and for our purposes we may call an option a *genuine* option when it is of the forced, living, and momentous kind.

1. A living option is one in which both hypotheses are live ones. If I say to you: "Be a theosophist or be a Mohammedan," it is probably a dead option, because for you neither hyopthesis is likely to be alive. But if I say: "Be an agnostic or be a Christian," it is otherwise: trained as you are, each hypothesis makes some appeal, however small, to your belief.

2. Next, if I say to you: "Choose between going out with your umbrella or without it," I do not offer you a genuine option, for it is not forced. You can easily avoid it by not going out at all. Similarly, if I say, "Either love me or hate me," "Either call my theory true or call it false," your option is avoidable. You may remain indifferent to me, neither loving nor hating, and you may decline to offer any judgment as to my theory. But if I say, "Either accept this truth or go without it," I put on you a forced option, for there is no standing place outside of the alternative. Every dilemma based on a complete logical disjunction, with no possibility of not choosing, is an option of this forced kind.

3. Finally, if I were Dr. Nansen and proposed to you to join my North Pole expedition, your option would be momentous; for this would probably be your only similar opportunity, and your choice now would either exclude you from the North Pole sort of immortality altogether or put at least the chance of it into your hands. He who refuses to embrace a unique opportunity loses the prize as surely as if he tried and failed. *Per contra,* the option is trivial when the opportunity is not unique, when the stake is insignificant, or when the decision is reversible if it later prove unwise. Such trivial options abound in the scientific life. A chemist finds an hypothesis live enough to spend a year in its verification: he believes in it to that extent. But if his experiments prove inconclusive either way, he is quit for his loss of time, no vital harm being done.

It will facilitate our discussion if we keep all these distinctions well in mind.

II.

The next matter to consider is the actual psychology of human opinion. When we look at certain facts, it seems as if our passional and volitional nature lay at the root of all our convictions. When we look at others, it seems as if they could do nothing when the intellect had once said its say. Let us take the latter facts up first.

Does it not seem preposterous on the very face of it to talk of our opinions being modifiable at will? Can our will either help or hinder our intellect in its perceptions of truth? Can we, by just willing it, believe that Abraham Lincoln's existence is a myth, and that the portraits of him in McClure's Magazine are all of some one else? Can we, by any effort of our will, or by any strength of wish that it were true, believe ourselves well and about when we are roaring with rheumatism in bed, or feel certain that the sum of the two one-dollar bills in our pocket must be a hundred dollars? We can *say* any of these things, but we are absolutely impotent to believe them; and of just such things is the whole fabric of the truths that we do believe in made up,—matters of fact, immediate or remote, as Hume said, and relations between ideas, which are either there or not there for us if we see them so, and which if not there cannot be put there by any action of our own.

In Pascal's Thoughts there is a celebrated passage known in literature as Pascal's wager. In it he tries to force us into Christianity by reasoning as if our concern with truth resembled our concern with the stakes in a game of chance. Translated freely his words are these: You must either believe or not believe that God is—which will you do? Your human reason cannot say. A game is going on between you and the nature of things which at the day of judgment will bring out either heads or tails. Weigh what your gains and your losses would be if you should stake all you have on heads, or God's existence: if you win in such case, you gain eternal beatitude; if you lose, you lose nothing at all. If there were an infinity of chances, and only one for God in this wager, still you ought to stake your all on God; for though you surely risk a finite loss by this procedure, any finite loss is reasonable, even a certain one is reasonable, if there is but the possibility of infinite gain. Go, then, and take holy water, and have masses said; belief will come and stupefy your scruples,—*Cela vous fera croire et vous abêtira.* Why should you not? At bottom, what have you to lose?

You probably feel that when religious faith expresses itself thus, in the language of the gaming-table, it is put to its last trumps. Surely Pascal's own personal belief in masses and holy water had far other springs; and this celebrated page of his is but an argument for others, a last desperate snatch at a weapon against the hardness of the unbelieving heart. We feel that a faith in masses and holy water adopted wilfully after such a mechanical calculation would lack the inner soul of faith's reality; and if we were ourselves in the place of the Deity, we should probably take particular pleasure in cutting off believers of this pattern from their infinite reward. It is evident that unless there be some pre-existing tendency to believe in masses and holy water, the option offered to the will by Pascal is not a living option. Certainly no Turk ever took to masses and holy water on its account; and even to us Protestants these means of salvation seem such foregone impossibilities that Pascal's logic, invoked for them specifically, leaves us unmoved. As well might the Mahdi write to us, saying, "I am the Expected One whom God has created in his effulgence. You shall be infinitely happy if you confess me; otherwise you shall be cut off from the light of the sun. Weigh, then, your infinite gain if I am genuine against your finite sacrifice if I am not!" His logic would be that of Pascal; but he would vainly use it on us, for the hypothesis he offers us is dead. No tendency to act on it exists in us to any degree.

The talk of believing by our volition seems, then, from one point of view, simply silly. From another point of view it is worse than silly, it is vile. When one turns to the magnificent edifice of the physical sciences, and sees how it was reared; what thousands of disinterested moral lives of men lie buried in its mere foundations; what patience and postponement, what choking down of preference, what submission to the icy laws of outer fact are wrought into its very stones and mortar; how absolutely impersonal it stands in its vast augustness,—then how besotted and contemptible seems every little sentimentalist who comes blowing his voluntary smoke-wreaths, and pretending to decide things from out of his private dream! Can we wonder if those bred in the rugged and manly school of science should feel like spewing such subjectivism out of their mouths? The whole system of loyalties which grow up in the schools of science go dead against its toleration; so that it is only natural that those who have caught the scientific fever should pass over to the opposite extreme, and write sometimes as if the incorruptibly truthful intellect ought positively to prefer bitterness and unacceptableness to the heart in its cup.

> It fortifies my soul to know
> That, though I perish, Truth is so—

sings Clough, while Huxley exclaims: "My only consolation lies in the reflection that, however bad our posterity may become, so far as they hold by the plain rule of not pretending to believe what they have no reason to believe, because it may be to their advantage so to pretend [the word 'pretend' is surely here redundant], they will not have reached the lowest depth of immorality." And that delicious *enfant terrible* Clifford writes: "Belief is desecrated when given to unproved and unquestioned statements for the solace and private pleasure of the believer. . . . Whoso would deserve well of his fellows in this matter will guard the purity of his belief with a very fanaticism of jealous care, lest at any time it should rest on an unworthy object, and catch a stain which can never be wiped away. . . . If [a] belief has been accepted on insufficient evidence [even though the belief be true, as Clifford on the same page explains] the pleasure is a stolen one. . . . It is sinful because it is stolen in defiance of our duty to mankind. That duty is to guard ourselves from such beliefs as from a pestilence which may shortly master our own body and then spread to the rest of the town. . . . It is wrong always, everywhere, and for every one, to believe anything upon insufficient evidence."

III.

All this strikes one as healthy, even when expressed, as by Clifford, with somewhat too much of robustious pathos in the voice. Free-will and simple wishing do seem, in the matter of our credences, to be only fifth wheels to the coach. Yet if any one should thereupon assume that intellectual insight is what remains after wish and will and sentimental preference have taken wing, or that pure reason is what then settles our opinions, he would fly quite as directly in the teeth of the facts.

It is only our already dead hypotheses that our willing nature is unable to bring to life again. But what has made them dead for us is for the most part a previous action of our willing nature of an antagonistic kind. When I say 'willing nature,' I do not mean only such deliberate volitions as may have set up habits of belief that we cannot now escape from,—I mean all such factors of belief as fear and hope, prejudice and passion, imitation and partisanship, the circumpressure of our caste and set. As a matter of fact we find ourselves believing, we hardly know how or why. Mr. Balfour gives the name of 'authority' to all those influences, born of the intellectual climate, that make hypotheses possible or impossible for us, alive or dead. Here in this room, we all of us believe in molecules and the conservation of energy, in democracy and necessary progress, in Protestant Christianity and the duty of fighting for 'the doctrine of the immortal Monroe,' all for no reasons worthy of the name. We see into these matters with no more inner clearness, and probably with much less, than any disbeliever in them might possess. His unconventionality would probably have some grounds to show for its conclusions; but for us, not insight, but the *prestige* of the opinions, is what makes the spark shoot from them and light up our sleeping magazines of faith. Our reason is quite satisfied, in nine hundred and ninety-nine cases out of every thousand of us, if it can find a few arguments that will do to recite in case our credulity is criticised by some one else. Our faith is faith in some one else's faith, and in the greatest matters this is most the case. Our belief in truth itself, for instance, that there is a truth, and that our minds and it are made for each other,—what is it but a passionate affirmation of desire, in which our social system backs us up? We want to have a truth; we want to believe that our experiments and studies and discussions must put us in a continually better and better position towards it; and on this line we agree to fight out our thinking lives. But if a pyrrhonistic sceptic asks us *how we know* all this, can our logic find a reply? No! certainly it cannot. It is just one volition against another,

—we willing to go in for life upon a trust or assumption which he, for his part, does not care to make.*

As a rule we disbelieve all facts and theories for which we have no use. Clifford's cosmic emotions find no use for Christian feelings. Huxley belabors the bishops because there is no use for sacerdotalism in his scheme of life. Newman, on the contrary, goes over to Romanism, and finds all sorts of reasons good for staying there, because a priestly system is for him an organic need and delight. Why do so few 'scientists' even look at the evidence for telepathy, so called? Because they think, as a leading biologist, now dead, once said to me, that even if such a thing were true, scientists ought to band together to keep it suppressed and concealed. It would undo the uniformity of Nature and all sorts of other things without which scientists cannot carry on their pursuits. But if this very man had been shown something which as a scientist he might *do* with telepathy, he might not only have examined the evidence, but even have found it good enough. This very law which the logicians would impose upon us— if I may give the name of logicians to those who would rule out our willing nature here—is based on nothing but their own natural wish to exclude all elements for which they, in their professional quality of logicians, can find no use.

Evidently, then, our non-intellectual nature does influence our convictions. There are passional tendencies and volitions which run before and others which come after belief, and it is only the latter that are too late for the fair; and they are not too late when the previous passional work has been already in their own direction. Pascal's argument, instead of being powerless, then seems a regular clincher, and is the last stroke needed to make our faith in masses and holy water complete. The state of things is evidently far from simple; and pure insight and logic, whatever they might do ideally, are not the only things that really do produce our creeds.

IV.

Our next duty, having recognized this mixed-up state of affairs, is to ask whether it be simply reprehensible and pathological, or whether, on the contrary, we must treat it as a normal element in making up our minds. The thesis I defend is, briefly stated, this: *Our passional nature not only lawfully may, but must, decide an option between propositions, whenever it is a genuine option that cannot by its nature be decided on intellectual grounds; for to say, under such circumstances, "Do not decide, but leave the question open," is itself a passional decision,—just like deciding yes or nor,—and is attended with the same risk of losing the truth.* The thesis thus abstractly expressed will, I trust, soon become quite clear. But I must first indulge in a bit more of preliminary work.

* Compare the admirable page 310 in S. H. Hodgson's *Time and Space*, London, 1865.

V.

It will be observed that for the purposes of this discussion we are on 'dogmatic' ground,—ground, I mean, which leaves systematic philosophical scepticism altogether out of account. The postulate that there is truth, and that it is the destiny of our minds to attain it, we are deliberately resolving to make, though the sceptic will not make it. We part company with him, therefore, absolutely, at this point. But the faith that truth exists, and that our minds can find it, may be held in two ways. We may talk of the *empiricist* way and of the *absolutist* way of believing in truth. The absolutists in this matter say that we not only can attain to knowing truth, but we can *know when* we have attained to knowing it; while the empiricists think that although we may attain it, we cannot infallibly know when. To *know* is one thing, and to know for certain *that* we know is another. One may hold to the first being possible without the second; hence the empiricists and the absolutists, although neither of them is a sceptic in the usual philosophic sense of the term, show very different degrees of dogmatism in their lives.

If we look at the history of opinions, we see that the empiricist tendency has largely prevailed in science, while in philosophy the absolutist tendency has had everything its own way. The characteristic sort of happiness, indeed, which philosophies yield has mainly consisted in the conviction felt by each successive school or system that by it bottom-certitude had been attained. "Other philosophies are collections of opinions, mostly false; *my* philosophy gives standing-ground forever,"—who does not recognize in this the key-note of every system worthy of the name? A system, to be a system at all, must come as a *closed* system, reversible in this or that detail, perchance, but in its essential features never!

Scholastic orthodoxy, to which one must always go when one wishes to find perfectly clear statement, has beautifully elaborated this absolutist conviction in a doctrine which it calls that of 'objective evidence.' If, for example, I am unable to doubt that I now exist before you, that two is less than three, or that if all men are mortal then I am mortal too, it is because these things illumine my intellect irresistibly. The final ground of this objective evidence possessed by certain propositions is the *adæquatio intellectûs nostri cum rê.* The certitude it brings involves an *aptitudinem ad extorquendum certum assensum* on the part of the truth envisaged, and on the side of the subject a *quietem in cognitione,* when once the object is mentally received, that leaves no possibility of doubt behind; and in the whole transaction nothing operates but the *entitas ipsa* of the object and the *entitas ipsa* of the mind. We slouchy modern thinkers dislike to talk in Latin,—indeed, we dislike to talk in set terms at all; but at bottom our own state of mind is very much like this whenever we uncritically abandon ourselves: You believe in objective evidence, and I do. Of some things we feel that we are certain: we know, and we know that we do know. There is something that gives a click inside of us, a bell that strikes twelve, when the hands of our mental clock have swept the dial and meet over the meridian hour. The greatest empiricists among us are only empiricists on reflection: when left to their instincts, they dogmatize like infallible popes. When the Cliffords tell us how sinful it is to be Christians on such 'insufficient evidence,' insufficiency is really the last thing they have in mind. For them the evidence is absolutely sufficient, only it makes the other way. They believe so completely in an antichristian order of the universe that there is no living option: Christianity is a dead hypothesis from the start.

VI.

But now, since we are all such absolutists by instinct, what in our quality of students of philosophy ought we to do about the fact? Shall we espouse and indorse it? Or shall we treat it as a weakness of our nature from which we must free ourselves, if we can?

I sincerely believe that the latter course is the only one we can follow as reflective men. Objective evidence and certitude are doubtless very fine ideals to play with, but where on this moonlit and dream-visited planet are they found? I am, therefore, myself a complete empiricist so far as my theory of human knowledge goes. I live, to be sure, by the practical faith that we must go on experiencing and thinking over our experience, for only thus can our opinions grow more true; but to hold any one of them—I absolutely do not care which—as if it never could be reinterpretable or corrigible, I believe to be a tremendously mistaken attitude, and I think that the whole history of philosophy will bear me out. There is but one indefectibly certain truth, and that is the truth that pyrrhonistic scepticism itself leaves standing,—the truth that the present phenomenon of consciousness exists. That, however, is the bare starting-point of knowledge, the mere admission of a stuff to be philosophized about. The various philosophies are but so many attempts at expressing what this stuff really is. And if we repair to our libraries what disagreement do we discover! Where is a certainly true answer found? Apart from abstract propositions of comparison (such as two and two are the same as four), propositions which tell us nothing by themselves about concrete reality, we find no proposition ever regarded by any one as evidently certain that has not either been called a falsehood, or at least had its truth sincerely questioned by some one else. The transcending of the axioms of geometry, not in play but in earnest, by certain of our contemporaries (as Zöllner and Charles H. Hinton) and the rejection of the whole Aristotelian logic by the Hegelians, are striking instances in point.

No concrete test of what is really true has ever been agreed upon.

Some make the criterion external to the moment of perception, putting it either in revelation, the *consensus gentium,* the instincts of the heart, or the systematized experience of the race. Others make the perceptive moment its own test,—Descartes, for instance, with his clear and distinct ideas guaranteed by the veracity of God; Reid with his 'common-sense;' and Kant with his forms of synthetic judgment *a priori.* The inconceivability of the opposite; the capacity to be verified by sense; the possession of complete organic unity or self-relation, realized when a thing is its own other,—are standards which, in turn, have been used. The much lauded objective evidence is never triumphantly there; it is a mere aspiration or *Grenzbegriff,* marking the infinitely remote ideal of our thinking life. To claim that certain truths now possess it, is simply to say that when you think them true and they *are* true, then their evidence is objective, otherwise it is not. But practically one's conviction that the evidence one goes by is of the real objective brand, is only one more subjective opinion added to the lot. For what a contradictory array of opinions have objective evidence and absolute certitude been claimed! The world is rational through and through,—its existence is an ultimate brute fact; there is a personal God,—a personal God is inconceivable; there is an extra-mental physical world immediately known,—the mind can only know its own ideas; a moral imperative exists,—obligation is only the resultant of desires; a permanent spiritual principle is in every one,—there are only shifting states of mind; there is an endless chain of causes,—there is an absolute first cause; an eternal necessity,—a freedom; a purpose,—no purpose; a primal One,—a primal Many; a universal continuity,—an essential discontinuity in things; an infinity,—no infinity. There is this,—there is that; there is indeed nothing which some one has not thought absolutely true, while his neighbor deemed it absolutely false; and not an absolutist among them seems ever to have considered that the trouble may all the time be essential, and that the intellect, even with truth directly in its grasp, may have no infallible signal for knowing whether it be truth or no. When, indeed, one remembers that the most striking practical application to life of the doctrine of objective certitude has been the conscientious labors of the Holy Office of the Inquisition, one feels less tempted than ever to lend the doctrine a respectful ear.

But please observe, now, that when as empiricists we give up the doctrine of objective certitude, we do not thereby give up the quest or hope of truth itself. We still pin our faith on its existence, and still believe that we gain an even better position towards it by systematically continuing to roll up experiences and think. Our great difference from the scholastic lies in the way we face. The strength of his system lies in the principles, the origin, the *terminus a quo* of his thought; for us the strength is in the outcome, the upshot, the *terminus ad quem.* Not where it comes from but what it leads to is to decide. It matters not to an empiricist from what quarter an hypothesis may come to him: he may have acquired it by fair means or by foul; passion may have whispered or accident suggested it; but if the total drift of thinking continues to confirm it, that is what he means by its being true.

VII.

One more point, small but important, and our preliminaries are done. There are two ways of looking at our duty in the matter of opinion,—ways entirely different, and yet ways about whose difference the theory of knowledge seems hitherto to have shown very little concern. *We must know the truth;* and *we must avoid error,*—these are our first and great commandments as would-be knowers; but they are not two ways of stating an identical commandment, they are two separable laws. Although it may indeed happen that when we believe the truth *A,* we escape as an incidental consequence from believing the falsehood *B,* it hardly ever happens that by merely disbelieving *B* we necessarily believe *A.* We may in escaping *B* fall into believing other falsehoods, *C* or *D,* just as bad as *B;* or we may escape *B* by not believing anything at all, not even *A.*

Believe truth! Shun error!—these, we see, are two materially different laws; and by choosing between them we may end by coloring differently our whole intellectual life. We may regard the chase for truth as paramount, and the avoidance of error as secondary; or we may, on the other hand, treat the avoidance of error as more imperative, and let truth take its chance. Clifford, in the instructive passage which I have quoted, exhorts us to the latter course. Believe nothing, he tells us, keep your mind in suspense forever, rather than by closing it on insufficient evidence incur the awful risk of believing lies. You, on the other hand, may think that the risk of being in error is a very small matter when compared with the blessings of real knowledge, and be ready to be duped many times in your investigation rather than postpone indefinitely the chance of guessing true. I myself find it impossible to go with Clifford. We must remember that these feelings of our duty about either truth or error are in any case only expressions of our passional life. Biologically considered, our minds are as ready to grind out falsehood as veracity, and he who says, "Better go without belief forever than believe a lie!" merely shows his own preponderant private horror of becoming a dupe. He may be critical of many of his desires and fears, but this fear he slavishly obeys. He cannot imagine any one questioning its binding force. For my own part, I have also a horror of being duped; but I can believe that worse things than being duped may happen to a man in this world: so Clifford's exhortation has to my ears a thoroughly fantastic sound. It is like a general informing his soldiers that it is better to keep out of battle forever than to risk a single wound. Not so are victories either over enemies or over nature gained. Our errors are surely not such awfully solemn things.

In a world where we are so certain to incur them in spite of all our caution, a certain lightness of heart seems healthier than this excessive nervousness on their behalf. At any rate, it seems the fittest thing for the empiricist philosopher.

VIII.

And now, after all this introduction, let us go straight at our question. I have said, and now repeat it, that not only as a matter of fact do we find our passional nature influencing us in our opinions, but that there are some options between opinions in which this influence must be regarded both as an inevitable and as a lawful determinant of our choice.

I fear here that some of you my hearers will begin to scent danger, and lend an inhospitable ear. Two first steps of passion you have indeed had to admit as necessary,—we must think so as to avoid dupery, and we must think so as to gain truth; but the surest path to those ideal consummations, you will probably consider, is from now onwards to take no futher passional step.

Well, of course, I agree as far as the facts will allow. Wherever the option between losing truth and gaining it is not momentous, we can throw the chance of *gaining truth* away, and at any rate save ourselves from any chance of *believing falsehood,* by not making up our minds at all till objective evidence has come. In scientific questions, this is almost always the case; and even in human affairs in general, the need of acting is seldom so urgent that a false belief to act on is better than no belief at all. Law courts, indeed, have to decide on the best evidence attainable for the moment, because a judge's duty is to make law as well as to ascertain it, and (as a learned judge once said to me) few cases are worth spending much time over: the great thing is to have them decided on *any* acceptable principle, and got out of the way. But in our dealings with objective nature we obviously are recorders, not makers, of the truth; and decisions for the mere sake of deciding promptly and getting on to the next business would be wholly out of place. Throughout the breadth of physical nature facts are what they are quite independently of us, and seldom is there any such hurry about them that the risks of being duped by believing a premature theory need be faced. The questions here are always trivial options, the hypotheses are hardly living (at any rate not living for us spectators), the choice between believing truth or falsehood is seldom forced. The attitude of sceptical balance is therefore the absolutely wise one if we would escape mistakes. What difference, indeed, does it make to most of us whether we have or have not a theory of the Röntgen rays, whether we believe or not in mind-stuff, or have a conviction about the causality of conscious states? It makes no difference. Such options are not forced on us. On every account it is better not to make them, but still keep weighing reasons *pro et contra* with an indifferent hand.

I speak, of course, here of the purely judging mind. For purposes of discovery such indifference is to be less highly recommended, and science would be far less advanced than she is if the passionate desires of individuals to get their own faiths confirmed had been kept out of the game. See for example the sagacity which Spencer and Weismann now display. On the other hand, if you want an absolute duffer in an investigation, you must, after all, take the man who has no interest whatever in its results: he is the warranted incapable, the positive fool. The most useful investigator, because the most sensitive observer, is always he whose eager interest in one side of the question is balanced by an equally keen nervousness lest he become deceived.* Science has organized this nervousness into a regular *technique,* her so-called method of verification; and she has fallen so deeply in love with the method that one may even say she has ceased to care for truth by itself at all. It is only truth as technically verified that interests her. The truth of truths might come in merely affirmative form, and she would decline to touch it. Such truth as that, she might repeat with Clifford, would be stolen in defiance of her duty to mankind. Human passions, however, are stronger than technical rules. "Le coeur a ses raisons," as Pascal says, "que la raison ne connait pas;" and however indifferent to all but the bare rules of the game the umpire, the abstract intellect, may be, the concrete players who furnish him the materials to judge of are usually, each one of them, in love with some pet 'live hypothesis' of his own. Let us agree, however, that wherever there is no forced option, the dispassionately judicial intellect with no pet hypothesis, saving us, as it does, from dupery at any rate, ought to be our ideal.

The question next arises: Are there not somewhere forced options in our speculative questions, and can we (as men who may be interested at least as much in positively gaining truth as in merely escaping dupery) always wait with impunity till the coercive evidence shall have arrived? It seems *a priori* improbable that the truth should be so nicely adjusted to our needs and powers as that. In the great boarding-house of nature, the cakes and the butter and the syrup seldom come out so even and leave the plates so clean. Indeed, we should view them with scientific suspicion if they did.

IX.

Moral questions immediately present themselves as questions whose solution cannot wait for sensible proof. A moral question is a question not of what sensibly exists, but of what is good, or would be good if it did exist. Science can tell us what exists; but to compare the *worths,* both of what exists and of what does not exist, we must consult not science, but what Pascal calls our heart. Science herself consults her heart when she lays it down that the infinite ascertainment of fact and correction of false belief are the supreme goods for man. Challenge the statement,

* Compare Wilfrid Ward's essay, "The Wish to Believe," in his *Witnesses to the Unseen,* Macmillan & Co., 1893.

and science can only repeat it oracularly, or else prove it by showing that such ascertainment and correction bring man all sorts of other goods which man's heart in turn declares. The question of having moral beliefs at all or not having them is decided by our will. Are our moral preferences true or false, or are they only odd biological phenomena, making things good or bad for *us,* but in themselves indifferent? How can your pure intellect decide? If your heart does not *want* a world of moral reality, your head will assuredly never make you believe in one. Mephistophelian scepticism, indeed, will satisfy the head's play-instincts much better than any rigorous idealism can. Some men (even at the student age) are so naturally cool-hearted that the moralistic hypothesis never has for them any pungent life, and in their supercilious presence the hot young moralist always feels strangely ill at ease. The appearance of knowingness is on their side, of *naïveté* and gullibility on his. Yet, in the inarticulate heart of him, he clings to it that he is not a dupe, and that there is a realm in which (as Emerson says) all their wit and intellectual superiority is no better than the cunning of a fox. Moral scepticism can no more be refuted or proved by logic than intellectual scepticism can. When we stick to it that there *is* truth (be it of either kind), we do so with our whole nature, and resolve to stand or fall by the results. The sceptic with his whole nature adopts the doubting attitude; but which of us is the wiser, Omniscience only knows.

Turn now from these wide questions of good to a certain class of questions of fact, questions concerning personal relations, states of mind between one man and another. *Do you like me or not?*—for example. Whether you do or not depends, in countless instances, on whether I meet you half-way, am willing to assume that you must like me, and show you trust and expectation. The previous faith on my part in your liking's existence is in such cases what makes your liking come. But if I stand aloof, and refuse to budge an inch until I have objective evidence, until you shall have done something apt, as the absolutists say, *ad extorquendum assensum meum,* ten to one your liking never comes. How many women's hearts are vanquished by the mere sanguine insistence of some man that they *must* love him! he will not consent to the hypothesis that they cannot. The desire for a certain kind of truth here brings about that special truth's existence; and so it is in innumerable cases of other sorts. Who gains promotions, boons, appointments, but the man in whose life they are seen to play the part of live hypotheses, who discounts them, sacrifices other things for their sake before they have come, and takes risks for them in advance? His faith acts on the powers above him as a claim, and creates its own verification.

A social organism of any sort whatever, large or small, is what it is because each member proceeds to his own duty with a trust that the other members will simultaneously do theirs. Wherever a desired result is achieved by the co-operation of many independent persons, its existence as a fact is a pure consequence of the precursive faith in one another of those immediately concerned. A government, an army, a commercial system, a ship, a college, an athletic team, all exist on this condition, without which not only is nothing achieved, but nothing is even attempted. A whole train of passengers (individually brave enough) will be looted by a few highwaymen, simply because the latter can count on one another, while each passenger fears that if he makes a movement of resistance, he will be shot before any one else backs him up. If we believed that the whole carfull would rise at once with us, we should each severally rise, and train-robbing would never even be attempted. There are, then, cases where a fact cannot come at all unless a preliminary faith exists in its coming. *And where faith in a fact can help create the fact,* that would be an insane logic which should say that faith running ahead of scientific evidence is the 'lowest kind of immorality' into which a thinking being can fall. Yet such is the logic by which our scientific absolutists pretend to regulate our lives!

X.

In truths dependent on our personal action, then, faith based on desire is certainly a lawful and possibly an indispensable thing.

But now, it will be said, these are all childish human cases, and have nothing to do with great cosmical matters, like the question of religious faith. Let us then pass on to that. Religions differ so much in their accidents that in discussing the religious question we must make it very generic and broad. What then do we now mean by the religious hypothesis? Science says things are; morality says some things are better than other things; and religion says essentially two things.

First, she says that the best things are the more eternal things, the overlapping things, the things in the universe that throw the last stone, so to speak, and say the final word. "Perfection is eternal,"—this phrase of Charles Secrétan seems a good way of putting this first affirmation of religion, an affirmation which obviously cannot yet be verified scientifically at all.

The second affirmation of religion is that we are better off even now if we believe her first affirmation to be true.

Now, let us consider what the logical elements of this situation are *in case the religious hypothesis in both its branches be really true.* (Of course, we must admit that possibility at the outset. If we are to discuss the question at all, it must involve a living option. If for any of you religion be a hypothesis that cannot, by any living possibility, be true, then you need go no farther. I speak to the 'saving remnant' alone.) So proceeding, we see, first, that religion offers itself as a *momentous* option. We are supposed to gain, even now, by our belief, and to lose by our non-belief, a certain vital good. Secondly, religion is a *forced* option, so far as that good goes. We cannot escape the issue by remaining sceptical and waiting for more light, because, although we do avoid error in that way *if religion be untrue,* we lose the good, *if it be true,* just as certainly as if we positively chose to disbelieve. It is as if a man should hesitate indefinitely to ask a certain woman to marry him because he was not perfectly sure that she would prove an angel after he brought her home. Would he not cut himself off from that particular angel-possibility as decisively as if he went and married some one else? Scepticism, then, is not avoidance of option; it is option of a certain particular kind of risk. *Better risk loss of truth than chance of error,*—that is your faith-vetoer's exact position. He is actively playing his stake as much as the believer is; he is backing the field against the religious hypothesis, just as the believer is backing the religious hypothesis against the field. To preach scepticism to us as a duty until 'sufficient evidence' for religion be found, is tantamount therefore to telling us, when in presence of the religious hypothesis, that to yield to our fear of its being error is wiser and better than to yield to our hope that it may be true. It is not intellect against all passions, then; it is only intellect with one passion laying down its law. And by what, forsooth, is the supreme wisdom of this passion warranted? Dupery for dupery, what proof is there that dupery through hope is so much worse than dupery through fear? I, for one, can see no proof; and I simply refuse obedience to the scientist's command to imitate his kind of option, in a case where my own stake is important enough to give me the right to choose my own form of risk. If religion be true and the evidence for it be still insufficient, I do not wish, by putting your extinguisher upon my nature (which feels to me as if it had after all some business in this matter), to forfeit my sole chance in life of getting upon the winning side,—that chance depending, of course, on my willingness to run the risk of acting as if my passional need of taking the world religiously might be prophetic and right.

All this is on the supposition that it really may be prophetic and right, and that, even to us who are discussing the matter, religion is a live hypothesis which may be true. Now, to most of us religion comes in a still further way that makes a veto on our active faith even more illogical. The more perfect and more eternal aspect of the universe is represented in our religions as having personal form. The universe is no longer a mere *It* to us, but a *Thou,* if we are religious; and any relation that may be possible from person to person might be possible here. For instance, although in one sense we are passive portions of the universe, in another we show a curious autonomy, as if we were small active centres on our own account. We feel, too, as if the appeal of religion to us were made to our own active good-will, as if evidence might be forever withheld from us unless we met the hypothesis half-way. To take a trivial illustration: just as a man who in a company of gentlemen made no advances, asked a warrant for every concession, and believed no one's word without proof, would cut himself off by such churlishness from all the social rewards that a more trusting spirit would earn,—so here, one who should shut himself up in snarling logicality and try to make the gods extort his recognition willy-nilly, or not get it at all, might cut himself off forever from his only opportunity of making the gods' acquaintance. This feeling, forced on us we know not whence, that by obstinately believing that there are gods (although not to do so would be so easy both for our logic and our life) we are doing the universe the deepest service we can, seems part of the living essence of the religious hypothesis. If the hypothesis *were* true in all its parts, including this one, then pure intellectualism, with its veto on our making willing advances, would be an absurdity; and some participation of our sympathetic nature would be logically required. I, therefore, for one, cannot see my way to accepting the agnostic rules for truth-seeking, or wilfully agree to keep my willing nature out of the game. I cannot do so for this plain reason, that *a rule of thinking which would absolutely prevent me from acknowledging certain kinds of truth if those kinds of truth were really there, would be an irrational rule.* That for me is the long and short of the formal logic of the situation, no matter what the kinds of truth might materially be.

I confess I do not see how this logic can be escaped. But sad experience makes me fear that some of you may still shrink from radically saying with me, *in abstracto,* that we have the right to believe at our own risk any hypothesis that is live enough to tempt our will. I suspect, however, that if this is so, it is because you have got away from the abstract logical point of view altogether, and are thinking (perhaps without realizing it) of some particular religious hypothesis which for you is dead. The freedom to 'believe what we will' you apply to the case of some patent superstition; and the faith you think of is the faith defined by the schoolboy when he said, "Faith is when you believe something that you know ain't true." I can only repeat that this is misapprehension. *In concreto,* the freedom to believe can only cover living options which the intellect of the individual cannot by itself resolve; and living options never seem absurdities to him who has them to consider. When I look at the religious question as it really puts itself to concrete men, and when I think of all the possibilities which both practically and theoretically it involves, then this command that we shall put a stopper on our heart, instincts, and courage, and *wait*— acting of course meanwhile more or less as if religion were *not* true*—till doomsday, or till such time as our intellect and senses working together

* Since belief is measured by action, he who forbids us to believe religion to be true, necessarily also forbids us to act as we should if we did believe it to be true. The whole defence of religious faith hinges upon action. If the action required or inspired by the religious hypothesis is in no way different from that dictated by the naturalistic hypothesis, then religious faith is a pure superfluity, better pruned away, and controversy about its legitimacy is a piece of idle trifling, unworthy of serious minds. I myself believe, of course, that the religious hypothesis gives to the world an expression which specifically determines our reactions, and makes them in a large part unlike what they might be on a purely naturalistic scheme of belief.

may have raked in evidence enough,—this command, I say, seems to me the queerest idol ever manufactured in the philosophic cave. Were we scholastic absolutists, there might be more excuse. If we had an infallible intellect with its objective certitudes, we might feel ourselves disloyal to such a perfect organ of knowledge in not trusting to it exclusively, in not waiting for its releasing word. But if we are empiricists, if we believe that no bell in us tolls to let us know for certain when truth is in our grasp, then it seems a piece of idle fantasticality to preach so solemnly our duty of waiting for the bell. Indeed we *may* wait if we will,—I hope you do not think that I am denying that,—but if we do so, we do so at our peril as much as if we believed. In either case we *act,* taking our life in our hands. No one of us ought to issue vetoes to the other, nor should we bandy words of abuse. We ought, on the contrary, delicately and profoundly to respect one another's mental freedom: then only shall we bring about the intellectual republic; then only shall we have that spirit of inner tolerance without which all our outer tolerance is soulless, and which is empiricism's glory; then only shall we live and let live, in speculative as well as in practical things.

I began by a reference to Fitz James Stephen; let me end by a quotation from him. "What do you think of yourself? What do you think of the world? . . . These are questions with which all must deal as it seems good to them. They are riddles of the Sphinx, and in some way or other we must deal with them. . . . In all important transactions of life we have to take a leap in the dark. . . . If we decide to leave the riddles unanswered, that is a choice; if we waver in our answer, that, too, is a choice: but whatever choice we make, we make it at our peril. If a man chooses to turn his back altogether on God and the future, no one can prevent him; no one can show beyond reasonable doubt that he is mistaken. If a man thinks otherwise and acts as he thinks, I do not see that any one can prove that *he* is mistaken. Each must act as he thinks best; and if he is wrong, so much the worse for him. We stand on a mountain pass in the midst of whirling snow and blinding mist, through which we get glimpses now and then of paths which may be deceptive. If we stand still we shall be frozen to death. If we take the wrong road we shall be dashed to pieces. We do not certainly know whether there is any right one. What must we do? 'Be strong and of good courage.' Act for the best, hope for the best, and take what comes. . . . If death ends all, we cannot meet death better."*

* *Liberty, Equality, Fraternity,* p. 353, 2d edition. London, 1874.

Pragmatism

WHAT PRAGMATISM MEANS

SOME YEARS AGO, BEING WITH A CAMPING PARTY IN THE MOUNTAINS, I RE-turned from a solitary ramble to find every one engaged in a ferocious metaphysical dispute. The *corpus* of the dispute was a squirrel—a live squirrel supposed to be clinging to one side of a tree-trunk; while over against the tree's opposite side a human being was imagined to stand. This human witness tries to get sight of the squirrel by moving rapidly round the tree, but no matter how fast he goes, the squirrel moves as fast in the opposite direction, and always keeps the tree between himself and the man, so that never a glimpse of him is caught. The resultant metaphysical problem now is this: *Does the man go round the squirrel or not?* He goes round the tree, sure enough, and the squirrel is on the tree; but does he go round the squirrel? In the unlimited leisure of the wilderness, discussion had been worn threadbare. Everyone had taken sides, and was obstinate; and the numbers on both sides were even. Each side, when I appeared therefore appealed to me to make it a majority. Mindful of the scholastic adage that whenever you meet a contradiction you must make a distinction, I immediately sought and found one, as follows: "Which party is right," I said, "depends on what you *practically mean* by 'going round' the squirrel. If you mean passing from the north of him to the east, then to the south, then to the west, and then to the north of him again, obviously the man does go round him, for he occupies these successive positions. But if on the contrary you mean being first in front of him, then on the right of him, then behind him, then on his left, and finally in front again, it is quite as obvious that the man fails to go round him, for by the compensating movements the squirrel makes, he keeps his belly turned towards the man all the time, and his back turned away. Make the distinction, and there is no occasion for any farther dispute. You are both right and both wrong according as you conceive the verb 'to go round' in one practical fashion or the other."

Although one or two of the hotter disputants called my speech a shuffling evasion, saying they wanted no quibbling or scholastic hair-splitting, but meant just plain honest English 'round,' the majority seemed to think that the distinction had assuaged the dispute.

I tell this trivial anecdote because it is a peculiarly simple example of what I wish now to speak of as *the pragmatic method*. The pragmatic method is primarily a method of settling metaphysical disputes that otherwise might be interminable. Is the world one or many?—fated or free?—material or spiritual?—here are notions either of which may or may not hold good of the world; and disputes over such notions are unending. The pragmatic method in such cases is to try to interpret each notion by tracing its respective practical consequences. What difference would it practically make to any one if this notion rather than that notion were true? If no practical difference whatever can be traced, then the alternatives mean practically the same thing, and all dispute is idle. Whenever a dispute is serious, we ought to be able to show some practical difference that must follow from one side or the other's being right.

A glance at the history of the idea will show you still better what pragmatism means. The term is derived from the same Greek word πράγμα, meaning action, from which our words 'practice' and 'practical' come. It was first introduced into philosophy by Mr. Charles Peirce in 1878. In an article entitled 'How to Make Our Ideas Clear,' in the 'Popular Science Monthly' for January of that year* Mr. Peirce, after pointing out that our beliefs are really rules for action, said that, to develop a thought's meaning, we need only determine what conduct it is fitted to produce: that conduct is for us its sole significance. And the tangible fact at the root of all our thought-distinctions, however subtle, is that there is no one of them so fine as to consist in anything but a possible difference of practice. To attain perfect clearness in our thoughts of an object, then, we need only consider what conceivable effects of a practical kind the object may involve—what sensations we are to expect from it, and what reactions we must prepare. Our conception of these effects, whether immediate or remote, is then for us the whole of our conception of the object, so far as that conception has positive significance at all.

This is the principle of Peirce, the principle of pragmatism. It lay entirely unnoticed by any one for twenty years, until I, in an address before Professor Howison's philosophical union at the university of California, brought it forward again and made a special application of it to religion. By that date (1898) the times seemed ripe for its reception. The word 'pragmatism' spread, and at present it fairly spots the pages of the philosophic journals. On all hands we find the 'pragmatic movement' spoken of, sometimes with respect, sometimes with contumely, seldom with clear understanding. It is evident that the term applies itself conveniently to a number of tendencies that hitherto have lacked a collective name, and that it has 'come to stay.'

To take in the importance of Peirce's principle, one must get accus-

* Translated in the *Revue Philosophique* for January, 1879 (vol. vii).

tomed to applying it to concrete cases. I found a few years ago that Ostwald, the illustrious Leipzig chemist, had been making perfectly distinct
use of the principle of pragmatism in his lectures on the philosophy of science, though he had not called it by that name.

"All realities influence our practice," he wrote me, "and that influence is
their meaning for us. I am accustomed to put questions to my classes in
this way: In what respects would the world be different if this alternative
or that were true? If I can find nothing that would become different, then
the alternative has no sense."

That is, the rival views mean practically the same thing, and meaning,
other than practical, there is for us none. Ostwald in a published lecture
gives this example of what he means. Chemists have long wrangled over
the inner constitution of certain bodies called 'tautomerous.' Their properties seemed equally consistent with the notion that an instable hydrogen
atom oscillates inside of them, or that they are instable mixtures of two
bodies. Controversy raged, but never was decided. "It would never have
begun," says Ostwald, "if the combatants had asked themselves what particular experimental fact could have been made different by one or the
other view being correct. For it would then have appeared that no difference of fact could possibly ensue; and the quarrel was as unreal as if,
theorizing in primitive times about the raising of dough by yeast, one party
should have invoked a 'brownie,' while another insisted on an 'elf' as the
true cause of the phenomenon."*

It is astonishing to see how many philosophical disputes collapse into
insignificance the moment you subject them to this simple test of tracing
a concrete consequence. There can *be* no difference anywhere that doesn't
make a difference elsewhere—no difference in abstract truth that doesn't
express itself in a difference in concrete fact and in conduct consequent
upon that fact, imposed on somebody, somehow, somewhere, and some-
when. The whole function of philosophy ought to be to find out what definite difference it will make to you and me, at definite instants of our life,
if this world-formula or that world-formula be the true one.

There is absolutely nothing new in the pragmatic method. Socrates was
an adept at it. Aristotle used it methodically. Locke, Berkeley, and Hume
made momentous contributions to truth by its means. Shadworth Hodgson
keeps insisting that realities are only what they are 'known as.' But these
forerunners of pragmatism used it in fragments: they were preluders only.
Not until in our time has it generalized itself, become conscious of a uni-

* 'Theorie und Praxis,' *Zeitsch. des Oesterreichischen Ingenieur u. Architecten-
Vereines*, 1905, Nr. 4 u. 6. I find a still more radical pragmatism than Ostwald's in
an address by Professor W. S. Franklin: "I think that the sickliest notion of physics,
even if a student gets it, is that it is 'the science of masses, molecules, and the ether.'
And I think that the healthiest notion, even if a student does not wholly get it, is
that physics is the science of the ways of taking hold of bodies and pushing them!"
(*Science*, January 2, 1903.)

versal mission, pretended to a conquering destiny. I believe in that destiny, and I hope I may end by inspiring you with my belief.

Pragmatism represents a perfectly familiar attitude in philosophy, the empiricist attitude, but it represents it, as it seems to me, both in a more radical and in a less objectionable form than it has ever yet assumed. A pragmatist turns his back resolutely and once for all upon a lot of inveterate habits dear to professional philosophers. He turns away from abstraction and insufficiency, from verbal solutions, from bad *a priori* reasons, from fixed principles, closed systems, and pretended absolutes and origins. He turns towards concreteness and adequacy, towards facts, towards action and towards power. That means the empiricist temper regnant and the rationalist temper sincerely given up. It means the open air and possibilities of nature, as against dogma, artificiality, and the pretence of finality in truth.

At the same time it does not stand for any special results. It is a method only. But the general triumph of that method would mean an enormous change in what I called in my last lecture the 'temperament' of philosophy. Teachers of the ultra-rationalistic type would be frozen out, much as the courtier type is frozen out in republics, as the ultramontane type of priest is frozen out in protestant lands. Science and metaphysics would come much nearer together, would in fact work absolutely hand in hand.

Metaphysics has usually followed a very primitive kind of quest. You know how men have always hankered after unlawful magic, and you know what a great part in magic *words* have always played. If you have his name, or the formula of incantation that binds him, you can control the spirit, genie, afrite, or whatever the power may be. Solomon knew the names of all the spirits, and having their names, he held them subject to his will. So the universe has always appeared to the natural mind as a kind of enigma, of which the key must be sought in the shape of some illuminating or power-bringing word or name. That word names the universe's *principle,* and to possess it is after a fashion to possess the universe itself. 'God,' 'Matter,' 'Reason,' 'the Absolute,' 'Energy,' are so many solving names. You can rest when you have them. You are at the end of your metaphysical quest.

But if you follow the pragmatic method, you cannot look on any such word as closing your quest. You must bring out of each word its practical cash-value, set it at work within the stream of your experience. It appears less as a solution, then, than as a program for more work, and more particularly as an indication of the ways in which existing realities may be *changed.*

Theories thus become instruments, not answers to enigmas, in which we can rest. We don't lie back upon them, we move forward, and, on occasion, make nature over again by their aid. Pragmatism unstiffens all our theories, limbers them up and sets each one at work. Being nothing essentially new, it harmonizes with many ancient philosophic tendencies. It agrees with nominalism for instance, in always appealing to particulars; with utilitarianism in emphasizing practical aspects; with positivism in its disdain for verbal solutions, useless questions and metaphysical abstractions.

All these, you see, are *anti-intellectualist* tendencies. Against rationalism as a pretension and a method pragmatism is fully armed and militant. But, at the outset, at least, it stands for no particular results. It has no dogmas, and no doctrines save its method. As the young Italian pragmatist Papini has well said, it lies in the midst of our theories, like a corridor in a hotel. Innumerable chambers open out of it. In one you may find a man writing an atheistic volume; in the next some one on his knees praying for faith and strength; in a third a chemist investigating a body's properties. In a fourth a system of idealistic metaphysics is being excogitated; in a fifth the impossibility of metaphysics is being shown. But they all own the corridor, and all must pass through it if they want a practicable way of getting into or out of their respective rooms.

No particular results then, so far, but only an attitude of orientation, is what the pragmatic method means. *The attitude of looking away from first things, principles, 'categories,' supposed necessities; and of looking towards last things, fruits, consequences, facts. . . .*

See the exquisite contrast of the types of mind! The pragmatist clings to facts and concreteness, observes truth at its work in particular cases, and generalizes. Truth, for him, becomes a class-name for all sorts of definite working-values in experience. For the rationalist it remains a pure abstraction, to the bare name of which we must defer. When the pragmatist undertakes to show in detail just *why* we must defer, the rationalist is unable to recognize the concretes from which his own abstraction is taken. He accuses us of *denying* truth; whereas we have only sought to trace exactly why people follow it and always ought to follow it. Your typical ultra-abstractionist fairly shudders at concreteness: other things equal, he positively prefers the pale and spectral. If the two universes were offered, he would always choose the skinny outline rather than the rich thicket of reality. It is so much purer, clearer, nobler.

I hope that as these lectures go on, the concreteness and closeness to facts of the pragmatism which they advocate may be what approves itself to you as its most satisfactory peculiarity. It only follows here the example of the sister-sciences, interpreting the unobserved by the observed. It brings old and new harmoniously together. It converts the absolutely empty notion of a static relation of 'correspondence' (what that may mean we must ask later) between our minds and reality, into that of a rich and active commerce (that any one may follow in detail and understand) between particular thoughts of ours, and the great universe of other experiences in which they play their parts and have their uses.

But enough of this at present? The justification of what I say must be postponed. I wish now to add a word in further explanation of the claim I made at our last meeting, that pragmatism may be a happy harmonizer of empiricist ways of thinking with the more religious demands of human beings.

Men who are strongly of the fact-loving temperament, you may remember me to have said, are liable to be kept at a distance by the small sympathy with facts which that philosophy from the present-day fashion of idealism offers them. It is far too intellectualistic. Old fashioned theism was bad enough, with its notion of God as an exalted monarch, made up of a lot of unintelligible or preposterous 'attributes'; but, so long as it held strongly by the argument from design, it kept some touch with concrete realities. Since, however, darwinism has once for all displaced design from the minds of the 'scientific,' theism has lost that foothold; and some kind of an immanent or pantheistic deity working *in* things rather than above them is, if any, the kind recommended to our contemporary imagination. Aspirants to a philosophic religion turn, as a rule, more hopefully nowadays towards idealistic pantheism than towards the older dualistic theism, in spite of the fact that the latter still counts able defenders.

But, as I said in my first lecture, the brand of pantheism offered is hard for them to assimilate if they are lovers of facts, or empirically minded. It it the absolutistic brand, spurning the dust and reared upon pure logic. It keeps no connexion whatever with concreteness. Affirming the Absolute Mind, which is its substitute for God, to be the rational presupposition of all particulars of fact, whatever they may be, it remains supremely indifferent to what the particular facts in our world actually are. Be they what they may, the Absolute will father them. Like the sick lion in Esop's fable, all footprints lead into his den, but *nulla vestigia retrorsum.* You cannot redescend into the world of particulars by the Absolute's aid, or deduce any necessary consequences of detail important for your life from your idea of his nature. He gives you indeed the assurance that all is well with *Him,* and for his eternal way of thinking; but thereupon he leaves you to be finitely saved by your own temporal devices.

Far be it from me to deny the majesty of this conception, or its capacity to yield religious comfort to a most respectable class of minds. But from the human point of view, no one can pretend that it doesn't suffer from the faults of remoteness and abstractness. It is eminently a product of what I have ventured to call the rationalistic temper. It disdains empiricism's needs. It substitutes a pallid outline for the real world's richness. It is dapper, it is noble in the bad sense, in the sense in which to be noble is to be inapt for humble service. In this real world of sweat and dirt, it seems to me that when a view of things is 'noble,' that ought to count as a presumption against its truth, and as a philosophic disqualification. The prince of darkness may be a gentleman, as we are told he is, but whatever the God of earth and heaven is, he can surely be no gentleman. His menial services are needed in the dust of our human trials, even more than his dignity is needed in the empyrean.

Now pragmatism, devoted though she be to facts, has no such materialistic bias as ordinary empiricism labors under. Moreover, she has no objection whatever to the realizing of abstractions, so long as you get about among particulars with their aid and they actually carry you somewhere. Interested in no conclusions but those which our minds and our experiences work out together, she has no *a priori* prejudices against theology. *If theological ideas prove to have a value for concrete life, they will be true, for pragmatism, in the sense of being good for so much. For how much more they are true, will depend entirely on their relations to the other truths that also have to be acknowledged.*

What I said just now about the Absolute, of transcendental idealism, is a case in point. First, I called it majestic and said it yielded religious comfort to a class of minds, and then I accused it of remoteness and sterility. But so far as it affords such comfort, it surely is not sterile; it has that amount of value; it performs a concrete function. As a good pragmatist, I myself ought to call the Absolute true 'in so far forth,' then; and I unhesitatingly now do so.

But what does *true in so far forth* mean in this case? To answer, we need only apply the pragmatic method. What do believers in the Absolute mean by saying that their belief affords them comfort? They mean that since, in the Absolute finite evil is 'overruled' already, we may, therefore, whenever we wish, treat the temporal as if it were potentially the eternal, be sure that we can trust its outcome, and, without sin, dismiss our fear and drop the worry of our finite responsibility. In short, they mean that we have a right ever and anon to take a moral holiday, to let the world wag in its own way, feeling that its issues are in better hands than ours and are none of our business.

The universe is a system of which the individual members may relax their anxieties occasionally, in which the don't-care mood is also right for men, and moral holidays in order,—that, if I mistake not, is part, at least, of what the Absolute is 'known-as,' that is the great difference in our particular experiences which his being true makes, for us, that is his cash-value when he is pragmatically interpreted. Farther than that the ordinary lay-reader in philosophy who thinks favorably of absolute idealism does not venture to sharpen his conceptions. He can use the Absolute for so much, and so much is very precious. He is pained at hearing you speak incredulously of the Absolute, therefore, and disregards your criticisms because they deal with aspects of the conception that he fails to follow.

If the Absolute means this, and means no more than this, who can possibly deny the truth of it? To deny it would be to insist that men should never relax, and that holidays are never in order.

I am well aware how odd it must seem to some of you to hear me say that an idea is 'true' so long as to believe it is profitable to our lives. That it is *good,* for as much as it profits, you will gladly admit. If what we do by its aid is good, you will allow the idea itself to be good in so far forth, for we are the better for possessing it. But is it not a strange misuse of the word 'truth,' you will say, to call ideas also 'true' for this reason?

To answer this difficulty fully is impossible at this stage of my account. You touch here upon the very central point of Messrs. Schiller's, Dewey's and my own doctrine of truth, which I can not discuss with detail until my sixth lecture. Let me now say only this, that truth is *one species of good,* and not, as is usually supposed, a category distinct from good, and co-ordinate with it. *The true is the name of whatever proves itself to be good in the way of belief, and good, too, for definite, assignable reasons.* Surely you must admit this, that if there were *no* good for life in true ideas, or if the knowledge of them were positively disadvantageous and false ideas the only useful ones, then the current notion that truth is divine and precious, and its pursuit a duty, could never have grown up or become a dogma. In a world like that, our duty would be to *shun* truth, rather. But in this world, just as certain foods are not only agreeable to our taste, but good for our teeth, our stomach, and our tissues; so certain ideas are not only agreeable to think about, or agreeable as supporting other ideas that we are fond of, but they are also helpful in life's practical struggles. If there be any life that it is really better we should lead, and if there be any idea which, if believed in, would help us to lead that life, then it would be really *better for us* to believe in that idea, *unless, indeed, belief in it incidentally clashed with other greater vital benefits.*

'What would be better for us to believe'! This sounds very like a defini- tion of truth. It comes very near to saying 'what we *ought to believe':* and in *that* definition none of you would find any oddity. Ought we ever not to believe what it is *better for us* to believe? And can we then keep the notion of what is better for us, and what is true for us, permanently apart?

Pragmatism says no, and I fully agree with her. Probably you also agree, so far as the abstract statement goes, but with a suspicion that if we prac- tically did believe everything that made for good in our own personal lives, we should be found indulging all kinds of fancies about this world's affairs, and all kinds of sentimental superstitions about a world hereafter. Your suspicion here is undoubtedly well founded, and it is evident that something happens when you pass from the abstract to the concrete that complicates the situation.

I said just now that what is better for us to believe is true *unless the be- lief incidentally clashes with some other vital benefit.* Now in real life what vital benefits is any particular belief of ours most liable to clash with?

What indeed except the vital benefits yielded by *other beliefs* when these prove incompatible with the first ones? In other words, the greatest enemy of any one of our truths may be the rest of our truths. Truths have once for all this desperate instinct of self-preservation and of desire to extinguish whatever contradicts them. My belief in the Absolute, based on the good it does me, must run the gauntlet of all my other beliefs. Grant that it may be true in giving me a moral holiday. Nevertheless, as I conceive it,—and let me speak now confidentially, as it were, and merely in my own private person,—it clashes with other truths of mine whose benefits I hate to give up on its account. It happens to be associated with a kind of logic of which I am the enemy, I find that it entangles me in metaphysical paradoxes that are inacceptable, etc., etc. But as I have enough trouble in life already without adding the trouble of carrying these intellectual inconsistencies, I personally just give up the Absolute. I just *take* my moral holidays; or else as a professional philosopher, I try to justify them by some other principle.

If I could restrict my notion of the Absolute to its bare holiday-giving value, it wouldn't clash with my other truths. But we can not easily thus restrict our hypotheses. They carry supernumerary features, and these it is that clash so. My disbelief in the Absolute means then disbelief in those other supernumerary features, for I fully believe in the legitimacy of taking moral holidays.

You see by this what I meant when I called pragmatism a mediator and reconciler and said, borrowing the word from Papini, that she 'unstiffens' our theories. She has in fact no prejudices whatever, no obstructive dogmas, no rigid canons of what shall count as proof. She is completely genial. She will entertain any hypothesis, she will consider any evidence. It follows that in the religious field she is at a great advantage both over positivistic empiricism, with its anti-theological bias, and over religious rationalism, with its exclusive interest in the remote, the noble, the simple, and the abstract in the way of conception.

In short, she widens the field of search for God. Rationalism sticks to logic and the empyrean. Empiricism sticks to the external senses. Pragmatism is willing to take anything, to follow either logic or the senses and to count the humblest and most personal experiences. She will count mystical experiences if they have practical consequences. She will take a God who lives in the very dirt of private fact—if that should seem a likely place to find him.

Her only test of probable truth is what works best in the way of leading us, what fits every part of life best and combines with the collectivity of experience's demands, nothing being omitted. If theological ideas should do this, if the notion of God, in particular, should prove to do it, how could pragmatism possibly deny God's existence? She could see no meaning in treating as 'not true' a notion that was pragmatically so successful. What other kind of truth could there be, for her, than all this agreement with concrete reality?

In my last lecture I shall return again to the relations of pragmatism with religion. But you see already how democratic she is. Her manners are as various and flexible, her resources as rich and endless, and her conclusions as friendly as those of mother nature.

PRAGMATISM'S CONCEPTION OF TRUTH

When Clerk-Maxwell was a child it is written that he had a mania for having everything explained to him, and that when people put him off with vague verbal accounts of any phenomenon he would interrupt them impatiently by saying, 'Yes; but I want you to tell me the *particular go* of it!' Had his question been about truth, only a pragmatist could have told him the particular go of it. I believe that our contemporary pragmatists, especially Messrs. Schiller and Dewey, have given the only tenable account of this subject. It is a very ticklish subject, sending subtle rootlets into all kinds of crannies, and hard to treat in the sketchy way that alone befits a public lecture. But the Schiller-Dewey view of truth has been so ferociously attacked by rationalistic philosophers, and so abominably misunderstood, that here, if anywhere, is the point where a clear and simple statement should be made.

I fully expect to see the pragmatist view of truth run through the classic stages of a theory's career. First, you know, a new theory is attacked as absurd; then it is admitted to be true, but obvious and insignificant; finally it is seen to be so important that its adversaries claim that they themselves discovered it. Our doctrine of truth is at present in the first of these three stages, with symptoms of the second stage having begun in certain quarters. I wish that this lecture might help it beyond the first stage in the eyes of many of you.

Truth, as any dictionary will tell you, is a property of certain of our ideas. It means their 'agreement,' as falsity means their disagreement, with 'reality.' Pragmatists and intellectualists both accept this definition as a matter of course. They begin to quarrel only after the question is raised as to what may precisely be meant by the term 'agreement,' and what by the term 'reality,' when reality is taken as something for our ideas to agree with.

In answering these questions the pragmatists are more analytic and painstaking, the intellectualists more offhand and irreflective. The popular notion is that a true idea must copy its reality. Like other popular views, this one follows the analogy of the most usual experience. Our true ideas of sensible things do indeed copy them. Shut your eyes and think of yonder clock on the wall, and you get just such a true picture or copy of its dial. But your idea of its 'works' (unless you are a clockmaker) is much less of a copy, yet it passes muster, for it in no way clashes with the reality. Even though it should shrink to the mere word 'works,' that word still serves you truly; and when you speak of the 'time-keeping function' of the clock, or of its spring's 'elasticity,' it is hard to see exactly what your ideas can copy.

You perceive that there is a problem here. Where our ideas cannot copy definitely their object, what does agreement with that object mean? Some idealists seem to say that they are true whenever they are what God means that we ought to think about that object. Others hold the copy-view all through, and speak as if our ideas possessed truth just in proportion as they approach to being copies of the Absolute's eternal way of thinking.

These views, you see, invite pragmatistic discussion. But the great assumption of the intellectualists is that truth means essentially an inert static relation. When you've got your true idea of anything, there's an end of the matter. You're in possession; you *know;* you have fulfilled your thinking destiny. You are where you ought to be mentally; you have obeyed your categorical imperative; and nothing more need follow on that climax of your rational destiny. Epistemologically you are in stable equilibrium.

Pragmatism, on the other hand, asks its usual question. "Grant an idea or belief to be true," it says, "what concrete difference will its being true make in any one's actual life? How will the truth be realized? What experiences will be different from those which would obtain if the belief were false? What, in short, is the truth's cash-value in experiential terms?"

The moment pragmatism asks this question, it sees the answer: *True ideas are those that we can assimilate, validate, corroborate and verify. False ideas are those that we can not.* That is the practical difference it makes to us to have true ideas; that, therefore, is the meaning of truth, for it is all that truth is known-as.

This thesis is what I have to defend. The truth of an idea is not a stagnant property inherent in it. Truth *happens* to an idea. It *becomes* true, is *made* true by events. Its verity *is* in fact an event, a process: the process namely of its verifying itself, its veri-*fication*. Its validity is the process of its valid-*ation*.

But what do the words verification and validation themselves pragmatically mean? They again signify certain practical consequences of the verified and validated idea. It is hard to find any one phrase that characterizes these consequences better than the ordinary agreement-formula—just such consequences being what we have in mind whenever we say that our ideas 'agree' with reality. They lead us, namely, through the acts and other ideas which they instigate, into or up to, or towards, other parts of experience with which we feel all the while—such feeling being among our potentialities—that the original ideas remain in agreement. The connexions and transitions come to us from point to point as being progressive, harmonious, satisfactory. This function of agreeable leading is what we mean by an idea's verification. Such an account is vague and it sounds at first quite trivial, but it has results which it will take the rest of my hour to explain.

Let me begin by reminding you of the fact that the possession of true thoughts means everywhere the possession of invaluable instruments of action; and that our duty to gain truth, so far from being a blank command from out of the blue, or a 'stunt' self-imposed by our intellect, can account for itself by excellent practical reasons.

The importance to human life of having true beliefs about matters of fact is a thing too notorious. We live in a world of realities that can be infinitely useful or infinitely harmful. Ideas that tell us which of them to expect count as the true ideas in all this primary sphere of verification, and the pursuit of such ideas is a primary human duty. The possession of truth, so far from being here an end in itself, is only a preliminary means towards other vital satisfactions. If I am lost in the woods and starved, and find what looks like a cow-path, it is of the utmost importance that I should think of a human habitation at the end of it, for if I do so and follow it, I save myself. The true thought is useful here because the house which is its object is useful. The practical value of true ideas is thus primarily derived from the practical importance of their objects to us. Their objects are, indeed, not important at all times. I may on another occasion have no use for the house; and then my idea of it, however verifiable, will be practically irrelevant, and had better remain latent. Yet since almost any object may some day become temporarily important, the advantage of having a general stock of *extra* truths, of ideas that shall be true of merely possible situations, is obvious. We store such extra truths away in our memories, and with the overflow we fill our books of reference. Whenever such an extra truth becomes practically relevant to one of our emergencies, it passes from cold-storage to do work in the world and our belief in it grows active. You can say of it then either that 'it is useful because it is true' or that 'it is true because it is useful.' Both these phrases mean exactly the same thing, namely that here is an idea that gets fulfilled and can be verified. True is the name for whatever idea starts the verification-process, useful is the name for its completed function in experience. True ideas would never have been singled out as such, would never have acquired a class-name, least of all a name suggesting value, unless they had been useful from the outset in this way.

From this simple cue pragmatism gets her general notion of truth as something essentially bound up with the way in which one moment in our · experience may lead us towards other moments which it will be worth while to have been led to. Primarily, and on the common-sense level, the truth of a state of mind means this function of *a leading that is worth while*. When a moment in our experience, of any kind whatever, inspires us with a thought that is true, that means that sooner or later we dip by that thought's guidance into the particulars of experience again and make advantageous connexion with them. This is a vague enough statement, but I beg you to retain it, for it is essential.

Our experience meanwhile is all shot through with regularities. One bit of it can warn us to get ready for another bit, can 'intend' or be 'significant of' that remoter object. The object's advent is the significance's verification. Truth, in these cases, meaning nothing but eventual verification, is manifestly incompatible with waywardness on our part. Woe to him whose beliefs play fast and loose with the order which realities follow in his experience; they will lead him nowhere or else make false connexions.

By 'realities' or 'objects' here, we mean either things of common sense, sensibly present, or else common-sense relations, such as dates, places, distances, kinds, activities. Following our mental image of a house along the cow-path, we actually come to see the house; we get the image's full verification. *Such simply and fully verified leadings are certainly the originals and prototypes of the truth-process.* Experience offers indeed other forms of truth-process, but they are all conceivable as being primary verifications arrested, multiplied or substituted one for another.

Take, for instance, yonder object on the wall. You and I consider it to be a 'clock,' altho no one of us has seen the hidden works that make it one. We let our notion pass for true without attempting to verify. If truths mean verification-process essentially, ought we then to call such unverified truths as this abortive? No, for they form the overwhelmingly large number of the truths we live by. Indirect as well as direct verifications pass muster. Where circumstantial evidence is sufficient, we can go without eye-witnessing. Just as we here assume Japan to exist without ever having been there, because it *works* to do so, everything we know conspiring with the belief, and nothing interfering, so we assume that thing to be a clock. We *use* it as a clock, regulating the length of our lecture by it. The verification of the assumption here means its leading to no frustration or contradiction. Verifi*ability* of wheels and weights and pendulum is as good as verification. For one truth-process completed there are a million in our lives that function in this state of nascency. They turn us *towards* direct verification; lead us into the *surroundings* of the objects they envisage, and then, if everything runs on harmoniously, we are so sure that verification is possible that we omit it, and are usually justified by all that happens.

Truth lives, in fact, for the most part on a credit system. Our thoughts and beliefs 'pass,' so long as nothing challenges them, just as bank-notes pass so long as nobody refuses them. But this all points to direct face-to-face verifications somewhere, without which the fabric of truth collapses like a financial system with no cash-basis whatever. You accept my verification of one thing, I yours of another. We trade on each other's truth. But beliefs verified concretely by *somebody* are the posts of the whole super-structure.

Another great reason—beside economy of time—for waiving complete verification in the usual business of life is that all things exist in kinds and not singly. Our world is found once for all to have that peculiarity. So that when we have once directly verified our ideas about one specimen of a kind, we consider ourselves free to apply them to other specimens without verification. A mind that habitually discerns the kind of thing before it, and acts by the law of the kind immediately, without pausing to verify, will be a 'true' mind in ninety-nine out of a hundred emergencies, proved so by its conduct fitting everything it meets, and getting no refutation.

Indirectly or only potentially verifying processes may thus be true as well as full verification-processes. They work as true processes would work, give us the same advantages, and claim our recognition for the same reasons. All this on the common-sense level of matters of fact, which we are alone considering.

But matters of fact are not our only stock in trade. *Relations among purely mental ideas* form another sphere where true and false beliefs obtain, and here the beliefs are absolute, or unconditional. When they are true they bear the name either of definitions or of principles. It is either a principle or a definition that 1 and 1 make 2, that 2 and 1 make 3, and so on; that white differs less from gray than it does from black; that when the cause begins to act the effect also commences. Such propositions hold of all possible 'ones,' of all conceivable 'whites' and 'grays' and 'causes.' The objects here are mental objects. Their relations are perceptually obvious at a glance, and no sense-verification is necessary. Moreover, once true, always true, of those same mental objects. Truth here has an 'eternal' character. If you can find a concrete thing anywhere that is 'one' or 'white' or 'gray' or an 'effect,' then your principles will everlastingly apply to it. It is but a case of ascertaining the kind, and then applying the law of its kind to the particular object. You are sure to get truth if you can but name the kind rightly, for your mental relations hold good of everything of that kind without exception. If you then, nevertheless, failed to get truth concretely, you would say that you had classed your real objects wrongly.

In this realm of mental relations, truth again is an affair of leading. We relate one abstract idea with another, framing in the end great systems of logical and mathematical truth, under the respective terms of which the sensible facts of experience eventually arrange themselves, so that our eternal truths hold good of realities also. This marriage of fact and theory is endlessly fertile. What we say is here already true in advance of special verification, *if we have subsumed our objects rightly.* Our ready-made ideal framework for all sorts of possible objects follows from the very structure of our thinking. We can no more play fast and loose with these abstract relations that we can do so with our sense-experiences. They coerce us; we must treat them consistently, whether or not we like the results. The rules of addition apply to our debts as rigorously as to our assets. The hundredth decimal of π, the ratio of the circumference to its diameter, is predetermined ideally now, tho no one may have computed it. If we should ever need the figure in our dealings with an actual circle we should need to have it given rightly, calculated by the usual rules; for it is the same kind of truth that those rules elsewhere calculate.

Between the coercions of the sensible order and those of the ideal order, our mind is thus wedged tightly. Our ideas must agree with realities, be such realities concrete or abstract, be they facts or be they principles, under penalty of endless inconsistency and frustration.

So far, intellectualists can raise no protest. They can only say that we have barely touched the skin of the matter.

Realities mean, then, either concrete facts, or abstract kinds of things and relations perceived intuitively between them. They furthermore and thirdly mean, as things that new ideas of ours must no less take account of, the whole body of other truths already in our possession. But what now does 'agreement' with such threefold realities mean?—to use again the definition that is current.

Here it is that pragmatism and intellectualism begin to part company. Primarily, no doubt, to agree means to copy, but we saw that the mere word 'clock' would do instead of a mental picture of its works, and that of many realities our ideas can only be symbols and not copies. 'Past time,' 'power,' 'spontaneity,'—how can our mind copy such realities?

To 'agree' in the widest sense with a reality *can only mean to be guided either straight up to it or into its surroundings, or to be put into such working touch with it as to handle either it or something connected with it better than if we disagreed*. Better either intellectually or practically! And often agreement will only mean the negative fact that nothing contradictory from the quarter of that reality comes to interfere with the way in which our ideas guide us elsewhere. To copy a reality is, indeed, one very important way of agreeing with it, but it is far from being essential. The essential thing is the process of being guided. Any idea that helps us to *deal,* whether practically or intellectually, with either the reality or its belongings, that doesn't entangle our progress in frustrations, that *fits,* in fact, and adapts our life to the reality's whole setting, will agree sufficiently to meet the requirement. It will hold true of that reality.

Thus, *names* are just as 'true' or 'false' as definite mental pictures are. They set up similar verification-processes, and lead to fully equivalent practical results.

All human thinking gets discursified; we exchange ideas; we lend and borrow verifications, get them from one another by means of social intercourse. All truth thus gets verbally built out, stored up, and made available for every one. Hence, we must *talk* consistently just as we must *think* consistently: for both in talk and thought we deal with kinds. Names are arbitrary, but once understood they must be kept to. We mustn't now call Abel 'Cain' or Cain 'Abel.' If we do, we ungear ourselves from the whole book of Genesis, and from all its connexions with the universe of speech and fact down to the present time. We throw ourselves out of whatever truth that entire system of speech and fact may embody.

The overwhelming majority of our true ideas admit of no direct or face-to-face verification—those of past history, for example, as of Cain and Abel. The stream of time can be remounted only verbally, or verified indirectly by the present prolongations or effects of what the past harbored. Yet if they agree with these verbalities and effects, we can know that our ideas of the past are true. *As true as past time itself was,* so true was Julius Cæsar, so true were antediluvian monsters, all in their proper dates and settings. That past time itself was, is guaranteed by its coherence with everything that's present. True as the present *is,* the past *was* also.

Agreement thus turns out to be essentially an affair of leading—leading that is useful because it is into quarters that contain objects that are important. True ideas lead us into useful verbal and conceptual quarters as well as directly up to useful sensible termini. They lead to consistency, stability and flowing human intercourse. They lead away from excentricity and isolation, from foiled and barren thinking. The untrammelled flowing of the leading-process, its general freedom from clash and contradiction, passes for its indirect verification; but all roads lead to Rome, and in the end and eventually, all true processes must lead to the face of directly verifying sensible experiences *somewhere,* which somebody's ideas have copied.

Such is the large loose way in which the pragmatist interprets the word agreement. He treats it altogether practically. He lets it cover any process of conduction from a present idea to a future terminus, provided only it run prosperously. It is only thus that 'scientific' ideas, flying as they do beyond common sense, can be said to agree with their realities. It is, as I have already said, *as if* reality were made of ether, atoms or electrons, but we mustn't think so literally. The term 'energy' doesn't even pretend to stand for anything 'objective.' It is only a way of measuring the surface of phenomena so as to string their changes on a simple formula.

Yet in the choice of these man-made formulas we can not be capricious with impunity any more than we can be capricious on the common-sense practical level. We must find a theory that will *work;* and that means something extremely difficult; for our theory must mediate between all previous truths and certain new experiences. It must derange common sense and previous belief as little as possible, and it must lead to some sensible terminus or other that can be verified exactly. To 'work' means both these things; and the squeeze is so tight that there is little loose play for any hypothesis. Our theories are wedged and controlled as nothing else is. Yet sometimes alternative theoretic formulas are equally compatible with all the truths we know, and then we choose between them for subjective reasons. We choose the kind of theory to which we are already partial; we follow 'elegance' or 'economy.' Clerk-Maxwell somewhere says it would be 'poor scientific taste' to choose the more complicated of two equally well-evidenced conceptions; and you will all agree with him. Truth in science is what gives us the maximum possible sum of satisfactions, taste included, but consistency both with previous truth and with novel fact is always the most imperious claimant.

I have led you through a very sandy desert. But now, if I may be allowed so vulgar an expression, we begin to taste the milk in the cocoanut. Our rationalist critics here discharge their batteries upon us, and to reply to them will take us out from all this dryness into full sight of a momentous philosophical alternative.

Our account of truth is an account of truths in the plural, of processes of leading, realized *in rebus,* and having only this quality in common, that they *pay.* They pay by guiding us into or toward some part of a system that dips at numerous points into sense-percepts, which we may copy mentally or not, but with which at any rate we are now in the kind of commerce vaguely designated as verification. Truth for us is simply a collective name for verification-processes, just as health, wealth, strength, etc., are names for other processes connected with life, and also pursued because it pays to pursue them. Truth is *made,* just as health, wealth and strength are made, in the course of experience.

Here rationalism is instantaneously up in arms against us. I can imagine a rationalist to talk as follows:

"Truth is not made," he will say; "it absolutely obtains, being a unique relation that does not wait upon any process, but shoots straight over the head of experience, and hits its reality every time. Our belief that yon thing on the wall is a clock is true already, altho no one in the whole history of the world should verify it. The bare quality of standing in that transcendent relation is what makes any thought true that possesses it, whether or not there be verification. You pragmatists put the cart before the horse in making truth's being reside in verification-processes. These are merely signs of its being, merely our lame ways of ascertaining after the fact, which of our ideas already has possessed the wondrous quality. The quality itself is timeless, like all essences and natures. Thoughts partake of it directly, as they partake of falsity or of irrelevancy. It can't be analyzed away into pragmatic consequences."

The whole plausibility of this rationalist tirade is due to the fact to which we have already paid so much attention. In our world, namely, abounding as it does in things of similar kinds and similarly associated, one verification serves for others of its kind, and one great use of knowing things is to be led not so much to them as to their associates, especially to human talk about them. The quality of truth, obtaining *ante rem,* pragmatically means, then, the fact that in such a world innumerable ideas work better by their indirect or possible than by their direct and actual verification. Truth *ante rem* means only verifiability, then; or else it is a case of the stock rationalist trick of treating the *name* of a concrete phenomenal reality as an independent prior entity, and placing it behind the reality as its explanation. Professor Mach quotes somewhere an epigram of Lessing's:

> Sagt Hänschen Schlau zu Vetter Fritz,
> "Wie kommt es, Vetter Fritzen,
> Dass grad' die Reichsten in der Welt,
> Das meiste Geld besitzen?"

Hänschen Schlau here treats the principle 'wealth' as something distinct from the facts denoted by the man's being rich. It antedates them; the facts become only a sort of secondary coincidence with the rich man's essential nature.

In the case of 'wealth' we all see the fallacy. We know that wealth is but a name for concrete processes that certain men's lives play a part in, and not a natural excellence found in Messrs. Rockefeller and Carnegie, but not in the rest of us.

Like wealth, health also lives *in rebus.* It is a name for processes, as digestion, circulation, sleep, etc., that go on happily, tho in this instance we are more inclined to think of it as a principle and to say the man digests and sleeps so well *because* he is so healthy.

With 'strength' we are, I think, more rationalistic still, and decidedly inclined to treat it as an excellence pre-existing in the man and explanatory of the herculean performances of his muscles.

With 'truth' most people go over the border entirely, and treat the rationalistic account as self-evident. But really all these words in *th* are exactly similar. Truth exists *ante rem* just as much and as little as the other things do.

The scholastics, following Aristotle, made much of the distinction between habit and act. Health *in actu* means, among other things, good sleeping and digesting. But a healthy man need not always be sleeping, or always digesting, any more than a wealthy man need be always handling money, or a strong man always lifting weights. All such qualities sink to the status of 'habits' between their times of exercise; and similarly truth becomes a habit of certain of our ideas and beliefs in their intervals of rest from their verifying activities. But those activities are the root of the whole matter, and the condition of there being any habit to exist in the intervals.

'The true,' to put it very briefly, is only the expedient in the way of our thinking, just as 'the right' is only the expedient in the way of our behaving.

Expedient in almost any fashion; and expedient in the long run and on the whole of course; for what meets expediently all the experience in sight won't necessarily meet all farther experiences equally satisfactorily. Experience, as we know, has ways of *boiling over,* and making us correct our present formulas.

The 'absolutely' true, meaning what no farther experience will ever alter, is that ideal vanishing-point towards which we imagine that all our temporary truths will some day converge. It runs on all fours with the perfectly wise man, and with the absolutely complete experience; and, if these ideals are ever realized, they will all be realized together. Meanwhile we have to live to-day by what truth we can get to-day, and be ready to-morrow to call it falsehood. Ptolemaic astronomy, euclidean space, aristotelian logic, scholastic metaphysics, were expedient for centuries, but human experience has boiled over those limits, and we now call these things only relatively true, or true within those borders of experience. 'Absolutely' they are false; for we know that those limits were casual, and might have been transcended by past theorists just as they are by present thinkers.

When new experiences lead to retrospective judgments, using the past tense, what these judgments utter *was* true, even tho no past thinker had been led there. We live forwards, a Danish thinker has said, but we understand backwards. The present sheds a backward light on the world's previous processes. They may have been truth-processes for the actors in them. They are not so for one who knows the later revelations of the story.

This regulative notion of a potential better truth to be established later, possibly to be established some day absolutely, and having powers of retroactive legislation, turns its face, like all pragmatist notions, towards concreteness of fact, and towards the future. Like the half-truths, the absolute truth will have to be *made,* made as a relation incidental to the growth of a mass of verification-experience, to which the half-true ideas are all along contributing their quota.

I have already insisted on the fact that truth is made largely out of previous truths. Men's beliefs at any time are so much experience *funded.* But the beliefs are themselves parts of the sum total of the world's experience, and become matter, therefore, for the next day's funding operations. So far as reality means experienceable reality, both it and the truths men gain about it are everlastingly in process of mutation—mutation towards a definite goal, it may be—but still mutation.

Mathematicians can solve problems with two variables. On the Newtonian theory, for instance, acceleration varies with distance, but distance also varies with acceleration. In the realm of truth-processes facts come independently and determine our beliefs provisionally. But these beliefs make us act, and as fast as they do so, they bring into sight or into existence new facts which re-determine the beliefs accordingly. So the whole coil and ball of truth, as it rolls up, is the product of a double influence. Truths emerge from facts; but they dip forward into facts again and add to them; which facts again create or reveal new truth (the word is indifferent) and so on indefinitely. The 'facts' themselves meanwhile are not *true.* They simply *are.* Truth is the function of the beliefs that start and terminate among them.

The case is like a snowball's growth, due as it is to the distribution of the snow on the one hand, and to the successive pushes of the boys on the other, with these factors co-determining each other incessantly.

The most fateful point of difference between being a rationalist and being a pragmatist is now fully in sight. Experience is in mutation, and our psychological ascertainments of truth are in mutation—so much rationalism will allow; but never that either reality itself or truth itself is mutable. Reality stands complete and ready-made from all eternity, rationalism insists, and the agreement of our ideas with it is that unique unanalyzable virtue in them of which she has already told us. As that intrinsic excellence, their truth has nothing to do with our experiences. It adds nothing to the content of experience. It makes no difference to reality itself; it is supervenient, inert, static, a reflexion merely. It doesn't *exist,* it *holds* or *obtains,* it belongs to another dimension from that of either facts or fact-relations, belongs, in short, to the epistemological dimension—and with that big word rationalism closes the discussion.

Thus, just as pragmatism faces forward to the future, so does rationalism here again face backward to a past eternity. True to her inveterate habit, rationalism reverts to 'principles,' and thinks that when an abstraction once is named, we own an oracular solution.

The tremendous pregnancy in the way of consequences for life of this radical difference of outlook will only become apparent in my later lectures. I wish meanwhile to close this lecture by showing that rationalism's sublimity does not save it from inanity.

When, namely, you ask rationalists, instead of accusing pragmatism of desecrating the notion of truth, to define it themselves by saying exactly what *they* understand by it, the only positive attempts I can think of are these two:

1. "Truth is the system of propositions which have an unconditional claim to be recognized as valid."[1]

2. Truth is a name for all those judgments which we find ourselves under obligation to make by a kind of imperative duty.*

The first thing that strikes one in such definitions is their unutterable triviality. They are absolutely true, of course, but absolutely insignificant

---

[1] A. E. Taylor, *Philosophical Review,* vol. xiv, p. 288.

* H. Rickert, *Der Gegenstand der Erkenntniss,* chapter on 'Die Urtheilsnoth-wendigkeit.'

until you handle them pragmatically. What do you mean by 'claim' here, and what do you mean by 'duty'? As summary names for the concrete reasons why thinking in true ways is overwhelmingly expedient and good for mortal men, it is all right to talk of claims on reality's part to be agreed with, and of obligations on our part to agree. We feel both the claims and the obligations, and we feel them for just those reasons.

But the rationalists who talk of claim and obligation *expressly say that they have nothing to do with our practical interests or personal reasons.* Our reasons for agreeing are psychological facts, they say, relative to each thinker, and to the accidents of his life. They are his evidence merely, they are no part of the life of truth itself. That life transacts itself in a purely logical or epistemological, as distinguished from a psychological, dimension, and its claims antedate and exceed all personal motivations whatsoever. Tho neither man nor God should ever ascertain truth, the word would still have to be defined as that which *ought* to be ascertained and recognized.

There never was a more exquisite example of an idea abstracted from the concretes of experience and then used to oppose and negate what it was abstracted from.

Philosophy and common life abound in similar instances. The 'sentimentalist fallacy' is to shed tears over abstract justice and generosity, beauty, etc., and never to know these qualities when you meet them in the street, because the circumstances make them vulgar. Thus I read in the privately printed biography of an eminently rationalistic mind: "It was strange that with such admiration for beauty in the abstract, my brother had no enthusiasm for fine architecture, for beautiful painting, or for flowers." And in almost the last philosophic work I have read, I find such passages as the following: "Justice is ideal, solely ideal. Reason conceives that it ought to exist, but experience shows that it can not. . . . Truth, which ought to be, can not be. . . . Reason is deformed by experience. As soon as reason enters experience it becomes contrary to reason."

The rationalist's fallacy here is exactly like the sentimentalist's. Both extract a quality from the muddy particulars of experience, and find it so pure when extracted that they contrast it with each and all its muddy instances as an opposite and higher nature. All the while it is *their* nature. It is the nature of truths to be validated, verified. It pays for our ideas to be validated. Our obligation to seek truth is part of our general obligation to do what pays. The payments true ideas bring are the sole why of our duty to follow them. Identical whys exist in the case of wealth and health.

Truth makes no other kind of claim and imposes no other kind of ought than health and wealth do. All these claims are conditional; the concrete benefits we gain are what we mean by calling the pursuit a duty. In the case of truth, untrue beliefs work as perniciously in the long run as true beliefs work beneficially. Talking abstractly, the quality 'true' may thus be said to grow absolutely precious and the quality 'untrue' absolutely damnable: the one may be called good, the other bad, unconditionally. We ought to think the true, we ought to shun the false, imperatively.

But if we treat all this abstraction literally and oppose it to its mother soil in experience, see what a preposterous position we work ourselves into.

We can not then take a step forward in our actual thinking. When shall I acknowledge this truth and when that? Shall the acknowledgment be loud?—or silent? If sometimes loud, sometimes silent, which *now?* When may a truth go into cold-storage in the encyclopedia? and when shall it come out for battle? Must I constantly be repeating the truth 'twice two are four' because of its eternal claim on recognition? or is it sometimes irrelevant? Must my thoughts dwell night and day on my personal sins and blemishes, because I truly have them?—or may I sink and ignore them in order to be a decent social unit, and not a mass of morbid melancholy and apology?

It is quite evident that our obligation to acknowledge truth, so far from being unconditional, is tremendously conditioned. Truth with a big T, and in the singular, claims abstractly to be recognized, of course; but concrete truths in the plural need be recognized only when their recognition is expedient. A truth must always be preferred to a falsehood when both relate to the situation; but when neither does, truth is as little of a duty as falsehood. If you ask me what o'clock it is and I tell you that I live at 95 Irving Street, my answer may indeed be true, but you don't see why it is my duty to give it. A false address would be as much to the purpose.

With this admission that there are conditions that limit the application of the abstract imperative, *the pragmatistic treatment of truth sweeps back upon us in its fulness*. Our duty to agree with reality is seen to be grounded in a perfect jungle of concrete expediencies.

When Berkeley had explained what people meant by matter, people thought that he denied matter's existence. When Messrs. Schiller and Dewey now explain what people mean by truth, they are accused of denying *its* existence. These pragmatists destroy all objective standards, critics say, and put foolishness and wisdom on one level. A favorite formula for describing Mr. Schiller's doctrines and mine is that we are persons who think that by saying whatever you find it pleasant to say and calling it truth you fulfil every pragmatistic requirement.

I leave it to you to judge whether this be not an impudent slander. Pent in, as the pragmatist more than any one else sees himself to be, between the whole body of funded truths squeezed from the past and the coercions of the world of sense about him, who so well as he feels the immense pressure of objective control under which our minds perform their operations? If any one imagines that this law is lax, let him keep its commandment one day, says Emerson. We have heard much of late of the uses of the imagination in science. It is high time to urge the use of a little imagination in philosophy. The unwillingness of some of our critics to read any but the silliest of possible meanings into our statements is as discreditable to their imaginations as anything I know in recent philosophic history. Schiller says the true is that which 'works.' Thereupon he is treated as one who limits verification to the lowest material utilities. Dewey says truth is what gives 'satisfaction.' He is treated as one who believes in calling everything true which, if it were true, would be pleasant.

Our critics certainly need more imagination of realities. I have honestly tried to stretch my own imagination and to read the best possible meaning into the rationalist conception, but I have to confess that it still completely baffles me. The notion of a reality calling on us to 'agree' with it, and that for no reasons, but simply because its claim is 'unconditional' or 'transcendent,' is one that I can make neither head nor tail of. I try to imagine myself as the sole reality in the world, and then to imagine what more I would 'claim' if I were allowed to. If you suggest the possibility of my claiming that a mind should come into being from out of the void inane and stand and *copy* me, I can indeed imagine what the copying might mean, but I can conjure up no motive. What good it would do me to be copied, or what good it would do that mind to copy me, if further consequences are expressly and in principle ruled out as motives for the claim (as they are by our rationalist authorities) I can not fathom. When the Irishman's admirers ran him along to the place of banquet in a sedan chair with no bottom, he said, "Faith, if it wasn't for the honor of the thing, I might as well have come on foot." So here: but for the honor of the thing, I might as well have remained uncopied. Copying is one genuine mode of knowing (which for some strange reason our contemporary transcendentalists seem to be tumbling over each other to repudiate); but when we get beyond copying, and fall back on unnamed forms of agreeing that are expressly denied to be either copyings or leadings or fittings, or any other processes pragmatically definable, the *what* of the 'agreement' claimed becomes as unintelligible as the why of it. Neither content nor motive can be imagined for it. It is an absolutely meaningless abstraction.*

Surely in this field of truth it is the pragmatists and not the rationalists who are the more genuine defenders of the universe's rationality.

* I am not forgetting that Professor Rickert long ago gave up the whole notion of truth being founded on agreement with reality. Reality according to him, is whatever agrees with truth, and truth is founded solely on our primal duty. This fantastic flight, together with Mr. Joachim's candid confession of failure in his book *The Nature of Truth,* seems to me to mark the bankruptcy of rationalism when dealing with this subject. Rickert deals with part of the pragmastic position under the head of what he calls 'Relativismus.' I can not discuss his text here. Suffice it to say that his argumentation in that chapter is so feeble as to seem almost incredible in so generally able a writer.

The Varieties of Religious Experience

THE PIVOT ROUND WHICH THE RELIGIOUS LIFE, AS WE HAVE TRACED IT, RE-volves, is the interest of the individual in his private personal destiny. Religion, in short, is a monumental chapter in the history of human egotism. The gods believed in—whether by crude savages or by men disciplined intellectually—agree with each other in recognizing personal calls. Religious thought is carried on in terms of personality, this being, in the world of religion, the one fundamental fact. To-day, quite as much as at any previous age, the religious individual tells you that the divine meets him on the basis of his personal concerns.

Science, on the other hand, has ended by utterly repudiating the personal point of view. She catalogues her elements and records her laws indifferent as to what purpose may be shown forth by them, and constructs her theories quite careless of their bearing on human anxieties and fates. Though the scientist may individually nourish a religion, and be a theist in his irresponsible hours, the days are over when it could be said that for Science herself the heavens declare the glory of God and the firmament showeth his handiwork. Our solar system, with its harmonies, is seen now as but one passing case of a certain sort of moving equilibrium in the heavens, realized by a local accident in an appalling wilderness of worlds where no life can exist. In a span of time which as a cosmic interval will count but as an hour, it will have ceased to be. The Darwinian notion of chance production, and subsequent destruction, speedy or deferred, applies to the largest as well as to the smallest facts. It is impossible, in the present temper of the scientific imagination, to find in the driftings of the cosmic atoms, whether they work on the universal or on the particular scale, anything but a kind of aimless weather, doing and undoing, achieving no proper history, and leaving no result. Nature has no one distinguishable ultimate tendency with which it is possible to feel a sympathy. In the vast rhythm of her processes, as the scientific mind now follows them, she appears to cancel herself. The books of natural theology which satisfied the intellects of our grandfathers seem to us quite grotesque, representing, as they did, a God who conformed the largest things of nature to the paltriest of our private wants. The God whom science recognizes must be a God of universal laws exclusively, a God who does a wholesale, not a retail business. He cannot accommodate his processes to the convenience of individuals. The bubbles on the foam which coats a stormy sea are floating episodes, made and unmade by the forces of the wind and water. Our private selves are like those bubbles—epiphenomena, as Clifford, I believe, ingeniously called them; their destinies weigh nothing and determine nothing in the world's irremediable currents of events.

You see how natural it is, from this point of view, to treat religion as a mere survival, for religion does in fact perpetuate the traditions of the most primeval thought. To coerce the spiritual powers, or to square them and get them on our side, was, during enormous tracts of time, the one great object in our dealings with the natural world. For our ancestors, dreams, hallucinations, revelations, and cock-and-bull stories were inextricably mixed with facts. Up to a comparatively recent date such distinctions as those between what has been verified and what is only conjectured, between the impersonal and the personal aspects of existence, were hardly suspected or conceived. Whatever you imagined in a lively manner, whatever you thought fit to be true, you affirmed confidently; and whatever you affirmed, your comrades believed. Truth was what had not yet been contradicted, most things were taken into the mind from the point of view of their human suggestiveness, and the attention confined itself exclusively to the æsthetic and dramatic aspects of events.

How indeed could it be otherwise? The extraordinary value, for explanation and prevision, of those mathematical and mechanical modes of conception which science uses was a result that could not possibly have been expected in advance. Weight, movement, velocity, direction, position, what thin, pallid, uninteresting ideas! How could the richer animistic aspects of Nature, the peculiarities and oddities that make phenomena picturesquely striking or expressive, fail to have been first singled out and followed by philosophy as the more promising avenue to the knowledge of Nature's life? Well, it is still in these richer animistic and dramatic aspects that religion delights to dwell. It is the terror and beauty of phenomena, the "promise" of the dawn and of the rainbow, the "voice" of the thunder, the "gentleness" of the summer rain, the "sublimity" of the stars, and not the physical laws which these things follow, by which the religious mind still continues to be most impressed; and just as of yore, the devout man tells you that in the solitude of his room or of the fields he still feels the divine presence, that inflowings of help come in reply to his prayers, and that sacrifices to this unseen reality fill him with security and peace.

Pure anachronism! says the survival-theory;—anachronism for which deanthropomorphization of the imagination is the remedy required. The less we mix the private with the cosmic, the more we dwell in universal and impersonal terms, the truer heirs of Science we become.

In spite of the appeal which this impersonality of the scientific attitude makes to a certain magnanimity of temper, I believe it to be shallow, and

I can now state my reason in comparatively few words. That reason is that, so long as we deal with the cosmic and the general, we deal only with the symbols of reality, but *as soon as we deal with private and personal phenomena as such, we deal with realities in the completest sense of the term.* I think I can easily make clear what I mean by these words.

The world of our experience consists at all times of two parts, an objective and a subjective part, of which the former may be incalculably more extensive than the latter, and yet the latter can never be omitted or suppressed. The objective part is the sum total of whatsoever at any given time we may be thinking of, the subjective part is the inner "state" in which the thinking comes to pass. What we think of may be enormous—the cosmic times and spaces, for example—whereas the inner state may be the most fugitive and paltry activity of mind. Yet the cosmic objects, so far as the experience yields them, are but ideal pictures of something whose existence we do not inwardly possess but only point at outwardly, while the inner state is our very experience itself; its reality and that of our experience are one. A conscious field *plus* its object as felt or thought of *plus* an attitude towards the object *plus* the sense of a self to whom the attitude belongs—such a concrete bit of personal experience may be a small bit, but it is a solid bit as long as it lasts; not hollow, not a mere abstract element of experience, such as the "object" is when taken all alone. It is a *full* fact, even though it be an insignificant fact; it is of the *kind* to which all realities whatsoever must belong; the motor currents of the world run through the like of it; it is on the line connecting real events with real events. That unsharable feeling which each one of us has of the pinch of his individual destiny as he privately feels it rolling out on fortune's wheel may be disparaged for its egotism, may be sneered at as unscientific, but it is the one thing that fills up the measure of our concrete actuality, and any would-be existent that should lack such a feeling, or its analogue, would be a piece of reality only half made up.

If this be true, it is absurd for science to say that the egotistic elements of experience should be suppressed. The axis of reality runs solely through the egotistic places—they are strung upon it like so many beads. To describe the world with all the various feelings of the individual pinch of destiny, all the various spiritual attitudes, left out from the description—they being as describable as anything else—would be something like offering a printed bill of fare as the equivalent for a solid meal. Religion makes no such blunder. The individual's religion may be egotistic, and those private realities which it keeps in touch with may be narrow enough; but at any rate it always remains infinitely less hollow and abstract, as far as it goes, than a science which prides itself on taking no account of anything private at all.

A bill of fare with one real raisin on it instead of the word "raisin," with one real egg instead of the word "egg," might be an inadequate meal, but it would at least be a commencement of reality. The contention of the survival-theory that we ought to stick to non-personal elements exclusively seems like saying that we ought to be satisfied forever with reading the naked bill of fare. I think, therefore, that however particular questions connected with our individual destinies may be answered, it is only by acknowledging them as genuine questions, and living in the sphere of thought which they open up, that we become profound. But to live thus is to be religious; so I unhesitatingly repudiate the survival-theory of religion, as being founded on an egregious mistake. It does not follow, because our ancestors made so many errors of fact and mixed them with their religion, that we should therefore leave off being religious at all. By being religious we establish ourselves in possession of ultimate reality at the only points at which reality is given us to guard. Our responsible concern is with our private destiny, after all.

You see now why I have been so individualistic throughout these lectures, and why I have seemed so bent on rehabilitating the element of feeling in religion and subordinating its intellectual part. Individuality is founded in feeling; and the recesses of feeling, the darker, blinder strata of character, are the only places in the world in which we catch real fact in the making, and directly perceive how events happen, and how work is actually done. Compared with this world of living individualized feelings, the world of generalized objects which the intellect contemplates is without solidity or life. As in stereoscopic or kinetoscopic pictures seen outside the instrument, the third dimension, the movement, the vital element, are not there. We get a beautiful picture of an express train supposed to be moving, but where in the picture, as I have heard a friend say, is the energy or the fifty miles an hour?

Let us agree, then, that Religion, occupying herself with personal destinies and keeping thus in contact with the only absolute realities which we know, must necessarily play an eternal part in human history. The next thing to decide is what she reveals about those destinies, or whether indeed she reveals anything distinct enough to be considered a general message to mankind. We have done as you see, with our preliminaries, and our final summing up can now begin.

I am well aware that after all the palpitating documents which I have quoted, and all the perspectives of emotion-inspiring institution and belief that my previous lectures have opened, the dry analysis to which I now advance may appear to many of you like an anti-climax, a tapering-off and flattening out of the subject, instead of a crescendo of interest and result. I said a while ago that the religious attitude of Protestants appears poverty-stricken to the Catholic imagination. Still more poverty-stricken, I fear, may my final summing up of the subject appear at first to some of you. On which account I pray you now to bear this point in mind, that in the present part of it I am expressly trying to reduce religion to its lowest admissible terms, to that minimum, free from individualistic excrescences, which all religions contain as their nucleus, and on which it may be hoped that all religious persons may agree. That established, we should have a result which might be small, but would at least be solid; and on it and round it the ruddier additional beliefs on which the different individuals make their venture might be grafted, and flourish as richly as you please. I shall add my own over-belief (which will be, I confess, of a somewhat pallid kind, as befits a critical philosopher), and you will, I hope, also add your over-beliefs, and we shall soon be in the varied world of concrete religious constructions once more. For the moment, let me dryly pursue the analytic part of the task.

Both thought and feeling are determinants of conduct, and the same conduct may be determined either by feeling or by thought. When we survey the whole field of religion, we find a great variety in the thoughts that have prevailed there; but the feelings on the one hand and the conduct on the other are almost always the same, for Stoic, Christian, and Buddhist saints are practically indistinguishable in their lives. The theories which Religion generates, being thus variable, are secondary; and if you wish to grasp her essence, you must look to the feelings and the conduct as being the more constant elements. It is between these two elements that the short circuit exists on which she carries on her principal business, while the ideas and symbols and other institutions form loop-lines which may be perfections and improvements, and may even some day all be united into one harmonious system, but which are not to be regarded as organs with an indispensable function, necessary at all times for religious life to go on. This seems to me the first conclusion which we are entitled to draw from the phenomena we have passed in review.

The next step is to characterize the feelings. To what psychological order do they belong?

The resultant outcome of them is in any case what Kant calls a "sthenic" affection, an excitement of the cheerful, expansive, "dynamogenic" order which, like any tonic, freshens our vital powers. In almost every lecture, but especially in the lectures on Conversion and on Saintliness, we have seen how this emotion overcomes temperamental melancholy and imparts endurance to the Subject, or a zest, or a meaning, or an enchantment and glory to the common objects of life. The name of "faith-state," by which Professor Leuba designates it, is a good one. It is a biological as well as a psychological condition, and Tolstoy is absolutely accurate in classing faith among the forces *by which men live*. The total absence of it, anhedonia, means collapse.

The faith-state may hold a very minimum of intellectual content. We saw examples of this in those sudden raptures of the divine presence, or in such mystical seizures as Dr. Bucke described. It may be a mere vague enthusiasm, half spiritual, half vital, a courage, and a feeling that great and wondrous things are in the air.

When, however, a positive intellectual content is associated with a faith-state, it gets invincibly stamped in upon belief, and this explains the passionate loyalty of religious persons everywhere to the minutest details of their so widely differing creeds. Taking creeds and faith-state together, as forming "religions," and treating these as purely subjective phenomena, without regard to the question of their "truth," we are obliged, on account of their extraordinary influence upon action and endurance, to class them amongst the most important biological functions of mankind. Their stimulant and anæsthetic effect is so great that Professor Leuba, in a recent article, goes so far as to say that so long as men can *use* their God, they care very little who he is, or even whether he is at all. "The truth of the matter can be put," says Leuba, "in this way: *God is not known, he is not understood; he is used*—sometimes as meat-purveyor, sometimes as moral support, sometimes as friend, sometimes as an object of love. If he proves himself useful, the religious consciousness asks for no more than that. Does God really exist? How does he exist? What is he? are so many irrelevant questions. Not God, but life, more life, a larger, richer, more satisfying life, is, in the last analysis, the end of religion. The love of life, at any and every level of development, is the religious impulse."

At this purely subjective rating, therefore, Religion must be considered vindicated in a certain way from the attacks of her critics. It would seem that she cannot be a mere anachronism and survival, but must exert a permanent function, whether she be with or without intellectual content, and whether, if she have any, it be true or false.

We must next pass beyond the point of view of merely subjective utility, and make inquiry into the intellectual content itself.

First, is there, under all the discrepancies of the creeds, a common nucleus to which they bear their testimony unanimously?

And second, ought we to consider the testimony true?

I will take up the first question first, and answer it immediately in the affirmative. The warring gods and formulas of the various religions do indeed cancel each other, but there is a certain uniform deliverance in which religions all appear to meet. It consists of two parts:—

1. An uneasiness; and
2. Its solution.

1. The uneasiness, reduced to its simplest terms, is a sense that there is *something wrong about us* as we naturally stand.

2. The solution is a sense that *we are saved from the wrongness* by making proper connection with the higher powers.

In those more developed minds which alone we are studying, the wrongness takes a moral character, and the salvation takes a mystical tinge. I think we shall keep well within the limits of what is common to all such minds if we formulate the essence of their religious experience in terms like these:—

The individual, so far as he suffers from his wrongness and criticises it, is to that extent consciously beyond it, and in at least possible touch with something higher, if anything higher exist. Along with the wrong part there is thus a better part of him, even though it may be but a most helpless germ. With which part he should identify his real being is by no means obvious at this stage; but when stage 2 (the stage of solution or salvation) arrives, the man identifies his real being with the germinal higher part of himself; and does so in the following way. *He becomes conscious that this higher part is conterminous and continuous with a* MORE *of the same quality, which is operative in the universe outside of him, and which he can keep in working touch with, and in a fashion get on board of and save himself when all his lower being has gone to pieces in the wreck.*

It seems to me that all the phenomena are accurately describable in these very simple general terms. They allow for the divided self and the struggle; they involve the change of personal centre and the surrender of the lower self; they express the appearance of exteriority of the helping power and yet account for our sense of union with it; and they fully justify our feelings of security and joy. There is probably no autobiographic document, among all those which I have quoted, to which the description will not well apply. One need only add such specific details as will adapt it to various theologies and various personal temperaments, and one will then have the various experiences reconstructed in their individual forms.

So far, however, as this analysis goes, the experiences are only psychological phenomena. They possess, it is true, enormous biological worth. Spiritual strength really increases in the subject when he has them, a new life opens for him, and they seem to him a place of conflux where the forces of two universes meet; and yet this may be nothing but his subjective way of feeling things, a mood of his own fancy, in spite of the effects produced. I now turn to my second question: What is the objective "truth" of their content?

The part of the content concerning which the question of truth most pertinently arises is that "MORE of the same quality" with which our own higher self appears in the experience to come into harmonious working relation. Is such a "more" merely our own notion, or does it really exist? If so, in what shape does it exist? Does it act, as well as exist? And in what form should we conceive of that "union" with it of which religious geniuses are so convinced?

It is in answering these questions that the various theologies perform their theoretic work, and that their divergencies most come to light. They all agree that the "more" really exists; though some of them hold it to exist in the shape of a personal god or gods, while others are satisfied to conceive it as a stream of ideal tendency embedded in the eternal structure of the world. They all agree, moreover, that it acts as well as exists, and that something really is effected for the better when you throw your life into its hands. It is when they treat of the experience of "union" with it that their speculative differences appear most clearly. Over this point pantheism and theism, nature and second birth, works and grace and karma, immortality and reincarnation, rationalism and mysticism, carry on inveterate disputes.

At the end of my lecture on Philosophy I held out the notion that an impartial science of religions might sift out from the midst of their discrepancies a common body of doctrine which she might also formulate in terms to which physical science need not object. This, I said, she might adopt as her own reconciling hypothesis, and recommend it for general belief. I also said that in my last lecture I should have to try my own hand at framing such an hypothesis.

The time has now come for this attempt. Who says "hypothesis" renounces the ambition to be coercive in his arguments. The most I can do is, accordingly, to offer something that may fit the facts so easily that your scientific logic will find no plausible pretext for vetoing your impulse to welcome it as true.

The "more," as we called it, and the meaning of our "union" with it, form the nucleus of our inquiry. Into what definite description can these words be translated, and for what definite facts do they stand? It would never do for us to place ourselves offhand at the position of a particular theology, the Christian theology, for example, and proceed immediately to define the "more" as Jehovah, and the "union" as his imputation to us of the righteousness of Christ. That would be unfair to other religions, and, from our present standpoint at least, would be an over-belief.

We must begin by using less particularized terms; and, since one of the duties of the science of religions is to keep religion in connection with the rest of science, we shall do well to seek first of all a way of describing the "more," which psychologists may also recognize as real. The *subconscious self* is nowadays a well-accredited psychological entity; and I believe that in it we have exactly the mediating term required. Apart from all religious considerations, there is actually and literally more life in our total soul than we are at any time aware of. The exploration of the transmarginal field has hardly yet been seriously undertaken, but what Mr. Myers said in 1892 in his essay on the Subliminal Consciousness is as true as when it was first written: "Each of us is in reality an abiding psychical entity far more extensive than he knows—an individuality which can never express itself completely through any corporeal manifestation. The Self manifests through the organism; but there is always some part of the Self unmanifested; and always, as it seems, some power of organic expression in abeyance or reserve." Much of the content of this larger background against which our conscious being stands out in relief is insignificant. Imperfect memories, silly jingles, inhibitive timidities, "dissolutive" phenomena of various sorts, as Myers calls them, enters into it for a large part. But in it many of the performances of genius seem also to have their origin; and in our study of conversion, of mystical experiences, and of prayer, we have seen how striking a part invasions from this region play in the religious life.

Let me then propose, as an hypothesis, that whatever it may be on its *farther* side, the "more" with which in religious experience we feel ourselves connected is on its *hither* side the subconscious continuation of our conscious life. Starting thus with a recognized psychological fact as our basis, we seem to preserve a contact with "science" which the ordinary theologian lacks. At the same time the theologian's contention that the religious man is moved by an external power is vindicated, for it is one of the peculiarities of invasions from the subconscious region to take on objective appearances, and to suggest to the Subject an external control. In the religious life the control is felt as "higher"; but since on our hypothesis it is primarily the higher faculties of our own hidden mind which are controlling, the sense of union with the power beyond us is a sense of something, not merely apparently, but literally true.

This doorway into the subject seems to me the best one for a science of religions, for it mediates between a number of different points of view. Yet it is only a doorway, and difficulties present themselves as soon as we step through it, and ask how far our transmarginal consciousness carries us if we follow it on its remoter side. Here the over-beliefs begin: here mysticism and the conversion-rapture and Vedantism and transcendental idealism bring in their monistic interpretations and tell us that the finite self rejoins the absolute self, for it was always one with God and identical with the soul of the world. Here the prophets of all the different religions come with their visions, voices, raptures, and other openings, supposed by each to authenticate his own peculiar faith.

Those of us who are not personally favored with such specific revelations must stand outside of them altogether and, for the present at least, decide that, since they corroborate incompatible theological doctrines, they neutralize one another and leave no fixed results. If we follow any one of them, or if we follow philosophical theory and embrace monistic pantheism on non-mystical grounds, we do so in the exercise of our individual freedom, and build out our religion in the way most congruous with our personal susceptibilities. Among these susceptibilities intellectual ones play a decisive part. Although the religious question is primarily a question of life, of living or not living in the higher union which opens itself to us as a gift, yet the spiritual excitement in which the gift appears a real one will often fail to be aroused in an individual until certain particular intellectual beliefs or ideas which, as we say, come home to him, are touched. These ideas will thus be essential to that individual's religion;—which is as much as to say that over-beliefs in various directions are absolutely indispensable, and that we should treat them with tenderness and tolerance so long as they are not intolerant themselves. As I have elsewhere written, the most interesting and valuable things about a man are usually his over-beliefs.

Disregarding the over-beliefs, and confining ourselves to what is common and generic, we have in *the fact that the conscious person is continuous with a wider self through which saving experiences come,* a positive content of religious experience which, it seems to me, *is literally and objectively true as far as it goes.* If I now proceed to state my own hypothesis about the farther limits of this extension of our personality, I shall be offering my own over-belief—though I know it will appear a sorry under-belief to some of you—for which I can only bespeak the same indulgence which in a converse case I should accord to yours.

The further limits of our being plunge, it seems to me, into an altogether other dimension of existence from the sensible and merely "understandable" world. Name it the mystical region, or the supernatural region, whichever you choose. So far as our ideal impulses originate in this region (and most of them do originate in it, for we find them possessing us in a way for which we cannot articulately account), we belong to it in a more intimate sense than that in which we belong to the visible world, for we belong in the most intimate sense wherever our ideals belong. Yet the unseen region in question is not merely ideal, for it produces effects in this world. When we commune with it, work is actually done upon our finite personality, for we are turned into new men, and consequences in the way of conduct follow in the natural world upon our regenerative change. But that which produces effects within another reality must be termed a reality itself, so I feel as if we had no philosophic excuse for calling the unseen or mystical world unreal.

God is the natural appellation, for us Christians at least, for the supreme reality, so I will call this higher part of the universe by the name of God. We and God have business with each other; and in opening ourselves to his influence our deepest destiny is fulfilled. The universe, at those parts of it which our personal being constitutes, takes a turn genuinely for the worse or for the better in proportion as each one of us fulfills or evades God's demands. As far as this goes I probably have you with me, for I only translate into schematic language what I may call the instinctive belief of mankind: God is real since he produces real effects.

The real effects in question, so far as I have as yet admitted them, are exerted on the personal centres of energy of the various subjects, but the spontaneous faith of most of the subjects is that they embrace a wider sphere than this. Most religious men believe (or "know," if they be mystical) that not only they themselves, but the whole universe of beings to whom the God is present, are secure in his parental hands. There is a sense, a dimension, they are sure, in which we are *all* saved, in spite of the gates of hell and all adverse terrestrial appearances. God's existence is the guarantee of an ideal order that shall be permanently preserved. This world may indeed, as science assures us, some day burn up or freeze; but if it is part of his order, the old ideals are sure to be brought elsewhere to fruition, so that where God is, tragedy is only provisional and partial, and shipwreck and dissolution are not the absolutely final things. Only when this farther step of faith concerning God is taken, and remote objective consequences are predicted, does religion, as it seems to me, get wholly free from the first immediate subjective experience, and bring a *real hypothesis* into play. A good hypothesis in science must have other properties than those of the phenomenon it is immediately invoked to explain, otherwise it is not prolific enough. God, meaning only what enters into the religious man's experience of union, falls short of being an hypothesis of this more useful order. He needs to enter into wider cosmic relations in order to justify the subject's absolute confidence and peace.

That the God with whom, starting from the hither side of our own extra-marginal self, we come at its remoter margin into commerce should be the absolute world-ruler, is of course a very considerable over-belief. Over-belief as it is, though, it is an article of almost every one's religion. Most of us pretend in some way to prop it upon our philosophy, but the philosophy itself is really propped upon this faith. What is this but to say that Religion, in her fullest exercise of function, is not a mere illumination of facts already elsewhere given, not a mere passion, like love, which views things in a rosier light. It is indeed that, as we have seen abundantly. But it is something more, namely, a postulator of new *facts* as well. The world interpreted religiously is not the materialistic world over again, with an altered expression; it must have, over and above the altered expression, *a natural constitution* different at some point from that which a materialistic world would have. It must be such that different events can be expected in it, different conduct must be required.

This thoroughly "pragmatic" view of religion has usually been taken as a matter of course by common men. They have interpolated divine miracles into the field of nature, they have built a heaven out beyond the grave. It is only transcendentalist metaphysicians who think that, without adding any concrete details to Nature, or subtracting any, but by simply calling it the expression of absolute spirit, you make it more divine just as it stands. I believe the pragmatic way of taking religion to be the deeper way. It gives it body as well as soul, it makes it claim, as everything real must claim, some characteristic realm of fact as its very own. What the more characteristically divine facts are, apart from the actual inflow of energy in the faith-state and the prayer-state, I know not. But the over-belief on which I am ready to make my personal venture is that they exist. The whole drift of my education goes to persuade me that the world of our present consciousness is only one out of many worlds of consciousness that exist, and that those other worlds must contain experiences which have a meaning for our life also; and that although in the main their experiences and those of this world keep discrete, yet the two become continuous at certain points, and higher energies filter in. By being faithful in my poor measure to this over-belief, I seem to myself to keep more sane and true. I *can,* of course, put myself into the sectarian scientist's attitude, and imagine vividly that the world of sensations and of scientific laws and objects may be all. But whenever I do this, I hear that inward monitor of which W. K. Clifford once wrote, whispering the word "bosh!" Humbug is humbug, even though it bear the scientific name, and the total expression of human experience, as I view it objectively, invincibly urges me beyond the narrow "scientific" bounds. Assuredly, the real world is of a different temperament—more intricately built than physical science allows. So my objective and my subjective conscience both hold me to the over-belief which I express. Who knows whether the faithfulness of individuals here below to their own poor over-beliefs may not actually help God in turn to be more effectively faithful to his own greater tasks?

JOSIAH ROYCE

(1855-1916)

Josiah Royce was born in California in 1855. One of the University of California's first graduates, he subsequently studied in Germany and at Johns Hopkins, and then returned to California to teach literature. With the help and encouragement of William James, however, he returned East after four years to take a position as a teacher of philosophy at Harvard. There he remained until his death in 1916, one of the most honored figures in American intellectual life, and exercizing an influence on students at least as great as that of James himself.

Royce is perhaps as close to the traditional image of the philosopher as any American has come. He was a teacher and critic of literature, an historical scholar and, under the influence of Peirce, an informed and interested student of mathematical logic. He wrote with polish and with just enough flamboyance to give color to his sustained excursions in abstraction. And he combined powerful dialectical skills with an unflagging moral high-mindedness, and a sympathetic understanding of diverse points of view with a desire to make everything fit within his system. Above all, he was in his time the most distinguished and eloquent representative in America of the classic tradition of philosophical idealism.

Royce's contributions to American philosophy, however, go far beyond his influence on those who agreed with him. His conceptions of the self, of the role of moral ideals, and of the nature of freedom—or conceptions much like his—can be detected in the work of pragmatists like George Herbert Mead and John Dewey. These thinkers tried to remove the echoes of the idealist tradition from these ideas and to frame them in straightforward biological and sociological terms. But if we think of pragmatism's social and moral content, it can be defined as the movement that brought Royce's moral idealism and scientific theories of evolution together.

Even more than this, however, Royce was one of the fixed stars from which the philosophers of two generations took their direction. It was probably his version of idealism more than any other which stirred pragmatism and the new realism into active life and gave them the material against which they could test their mettle. In particular, Royce was in-

timately tied to James by the twin bonds of personal affection and intellectual disagreement—"the Absolute himself must get great fun out of being you," James once wrote him. He kept James' intellectual fires going, and the words that James wrote Royce in 1900, while James was in Germany, suggest Royce's place in James' life and in the intellectual history of their generation as well. "Beloved Royce," James wrote, "I need not say, my dear old boy, how touched I am at your expressions of affection, or how it pleases me to hear that you have missed me. I too miss you profoundly. . . . You are still the centre of my gaze, the pole of my mental magnet. When I write, 'tis with one eye on the page, and one on you. When I compose my Gifford lectures mentally, it is with the design exclusively of overthrowing your system, and ruining your peace. . . ."

In the year following James' lectures on pragmatism at the Lowell Institute, Royce was invited to give a similar series of lectures. These were published in 1908 as The Philosophy of Loyalty. *The selections that follow are taken from this book, with the exception of Royce's letter to James, which appears in Ralph Barton Perry's* The Thought and Character of William James.

The Philosophy of Loyalty

NATURE AND NEED OF LOYALTY

WHAT DO WE LIVE FOR? WHAT IS OUR DUTY? WHAT IS THE TRUE IDEAL OF life? What is the true difference between right and wrong? What is the true good which we all need? Whoever begins seriously to consider such questions as these soon observes certain great truths about the moral life which he must take into account if his enterprise is to succeed, that is, if he is ever to answer these questions.

The first truth is this: We all of us first learned about what we ought to do, about what our ideal should be, and in general about the moral law, through some authority external to our own wills. Our teachers, our parents, our playmates, society, custom, or perhaps some church,—these taught us about one or another aspect of right and wrong. The moral law came to us from without. It often seemed to us, in so far, something other than our will, something threatening or socially compelling, or externally restraining. In so far as our moral training is still incomplete, the moral law may at any moment have to assume afresh this air of an external authority merely in order to win our due attention. But if we have learned the moral law, or any part of it, and if we do not ask any longer how we first learned, or how we may still have to learn afresh our duty, but if, on the contrary, we rather ask: "What reason can I now give to myself why a given act is truly right? What reason can I give why my duty is my duty?"—then, indeed, we find that no external authority, viewed merely as external, can give one any reason why an act is truly right or wrong. Only a calm and reasonable view of what it is that I myself really will,—only this can decide such a question. My duty is simply my own will brought to my clear self-consciousness. That which I can rightly view as good for me is simply the object of my own deepest desire set plainly before my insight. For your own will and your own desire, once fully brought to self-consciousness, furnish the only valid reason for you to know what is right and good.

This comment which I now make upon the nature of the moral law is familiar to every serious student of ethics. In one form or another this fact, that the ultimate moral authority for each of us is determined by

230

our own rational will, is admitted even by apparently extreme partisans of authority. Socrates long ago announced the principle in question when he taught that no man is willingly base. Plato and Aristotle employed it in developing their ethical doctrines. When St. Augustine, in a familiar passage in his Confessions, regards God's will as that in which, and in which alone, our wills can find rest and peace, he indeed makes God's will the rule of life; but he also shows that the reason why each of us, if enlightened, recognizes the divine will as right, is that, in Augustine's opinion, God has so made us for himself that our own wills are by nature inwardly restless until they rest in harmony with God's will. Our restlessness, then, so long as we are out of this harmony, gives us the reason why we find it right, if we are enlightened, to surrender our self-will.

If you want to find out, then, what is right and what is good for you, bring your own will to self-consciousness. Your duty is what you yourself will to do in so far as you clearly discover who you are, and what your place in the world is. This is, indeed, a first principle of all ethical inquiry. Kant called it the Principle of the Autonomy or self-direction of the rational will of each moral being.

But now there stands beside this first principle a second principle, equally inevitable and equally important. This principle is, that I can never find out what my own will is by merely brooding over my natural desires, or by following my momentary caprices. For by nature I am a sort of meeting place of countless streams of ancestral tendency. From moment to moment, if you consider me apart from my training, I am a collection of impulses. There is no one desire that is always present to me. Left to myself alone, I can never find out what my will is.

You may interpose here the familiar thesis that there is one desire which I always have, namely, the desire to escape from pain and to get pleasure. But as soon as you try to adjust this thesis to the facts of life, it is a thesis which simplifies nothing, and which at best simply gives me back again, under new names, that chaos of conflicting passions and interests which constitutes, apart from training, my natural life. What we naturally desire is determined for us by our countless instincts and by whatever training they have received. We want to breathe, to eat, to walk, to run, to speak, to see, to hear, to love, to fight, and, amongst other things, we want to be more or less reasonable. Now, if one of these instinctive wants of ours drives us at any moment to action, we normally take pleasure in such action, in so far as it succeeds. For action in accordance with desire means relief from tension; and that is usually accompanied with pleasure. On the other hand, a thwarted activity gives us pain. But only under special circumstances does this resulting pleasure or pain of the successful or of the hindered activity come to constitute a principal object of our desire. We all do like pleasure, and we all do shun pain. But a great deal of what we desire is desired by instinct, apart from the

memory or the expectation of pleasure and pain, and often counter to
the warnings that pleasure and pain have given to us. It is normal to
desire food because one is hungry, rather than because one loves the
pleasures of the table. It is water that the thirsty man in the desert longs
for, rather than pleasure, and rather than even mere relief from pain as
such. For much of the pain appears to his consciousness as largely due to
his longing for water. Pain, then, is indeed an evil, but it is in part secondary to thwarted desire; while, when pain appears as a brute fact of
our feelings, which we indeed hate, such pain is even then only one
amongst the many ills of life, only one of the many undesirable objects.
The burnt child, indeed, dreads the fire; but the climbing child, instinctively loving the ways of his remote arboreal ancestors, is little deterred
by the pain of an occasional fall.

Furthermore, if I even admitted that I always desire pleasure and relief
from pain, and nothing else, I should not learn from such a principle
what it is that, on the whole, I am to will to do, in order to express my
desire for pleasure, and in order to escape from pain. For no art is harder
than the art of pleasure seeking. I can never learn that art alone by
myself. And so I cannot define my own will, and hence cannot define my
duty, merely in terms of pleasure and pain.

So far, then, we have a rather paradoxical situation before us. Yet it is
the moral situation of every one of us. If I am to know my duty, I must
consult my own reasonable will. I alone can show myself why I view this
or this as my duty. But on the other hand, if I merely look within myself
to find what it is that I will, my own private individual nature, apart
from due training, never gives me any answer to the question: What do
I will? By nature I am a victim of my ancestry, a mass of world-old
passions and impulses, desiring and suffering in constantly new ways as
my circumstances change, and as one or another of my natural impulses
comes to the front. By nature, then, apart from a specific training, I have
no personal will of my own. One of the principal tasks of my life is to
learn to have a will of my own. To learn your own will,—yes, to create
your own will, is one of the largest of your human undertakings.

Here, then, is the paradox. I, and only I, whenever I come to my own,
can morally justify to myself my own plan of life. No outer authority can
ever give me the true reason for my duty. Yet I, left to myself, can never
find a plan of life. I have no inborn ideal naturally present within myself.
By nature I simply go on crying out in a sort of chaotic self-will, according as the momentary play of desire determines.

Whence, then, can I learn any plan of life? The moral education of any
civilized person easily reminds you how this question is, in one respect,
very partially, but, so far as ordniary training goes, constantly answered.
One gets one's various plans of life suggested through the models that are
set before each one of us by his fellows. Plans of life first come to us in

connection with our endless imitative activities. These imitative processes begin in our infancy, and run on through our whole life. We learn to play, to speak, to enter into our social realm, to take part in the ways and so in the life of mankind. This imitative social activity is itself due to our instincts as social beings. But in turn the social activities are the ones that first tend to organize all of our instincts, to give unity to our passions and impulses, to transform our natural chaos of desires into some sort of order—usually, indeed, a very imperfect order. It is our social existence, then, as imitative beings,—it is this that suggests to us the sorts of plans of life which we get when we learn a calling, when we find a business in life, when we discover our place in the social world. And so our actual plans of life, namely, our callings, our more or less settled daily activities, come to us from without. We in so far learn what our own will is by first imitating the wills of others.

Yet no,—this, once more, is never the whole truth about our social situation, and is still less the whole truth about our moral situation. By ourselves alone, we have said, we can never discover in our own inner life any one plan of life that expresses our genuine will. So then, we have said, all of our plans get suggested to us by the social order in which we grow up. But on the other hand, our social training gives us a mass of varying plans of life,—plans that are not utterly chaotic, indeed, but imperfectly ordered,—mere routine, not ideal life. Moreover, social training tends not only to teach us the way of other people, but to heighten by contrast our vague natural sense of the importance of having our own way. Social training stimulates the will of the individual self, and also teaches this self customs and devices for self-expression. We never merely imitate. Conformity attracts, but also wearies us. Meanwhile, even by imitation, we often learn how to possess, and then to carry out, our own self-will. For instance, we learn speech first by imitation; but henceforth we love to hear ourselves talk; and our whole plan of life gets affected accordingly. Speech has, indeed, its origin in social conformity. Yet the tongue is an unruly member, and wags rebelliously. Teach men customs, and you equip them with weapons for expressing their own personalities. As you train the social being, you make use of his natural submissiveness. But as a result of your training he forms plans; he interprets these plans with reference to his own personal interests; he becomes aware who he is; and he may end by becoming, if not original, then at least obstreperous. And thus society is constantly engaged in training up children who may, and often do, rebel against their mother. Social conformity gives us social power. Such power brings to us a consciousness of who and what we are. Now, for the first time, we begin to have a real will of our own. And hereupon we may discover this will to be in sharp conflict with the will of society. This is what normally happens to most of us, for a time at least, in youth.

You see, so far, how the whole process upon which man's moral life

depends involves this seemingly endless play of inner and outer. How
shall my duty be defined? Only by my own will, whenever that will is
brought to rational self-consciousness. But what is my will? By nature I
know not; for by birth I am a mere eddy in the turbulent stream of inherited human passion. How, then, shall I get a will of my own? Only
through social training. That indeed gives me plans, for it teaches me the
settled ways of my world. Yet no,—for such training really teaches me
rather the arts whereby I may express myself. It makes me clever, ambitious, often rebellious, and in so far it teaches me how to plan opposition to the social order. The circular process thus briefly indicated goes
on throughout the lives of many of us. It appears in new forms at various
stages of our growth. At any moment we may meet new problems of
right and wrong, relating to our plans of life. We hereupon look within,
at what we call our own conscience, to find out what our duty is. But, as
we do so, we discover, too often, what wayward and blind guides our own
hearts so far are. So we look without, in order to understand better the
ways of the social world. We cannot see the inner light. Let us try the outer
one. These ways of the world appeal to our imitativeness, and so we
learn from the other people how we ourselves are in this case to live. Yet
no,—this very learning often makes us aware of our personal contrast
with other people, and so makes us self-conscious, individualistic, critical,
rebellious; and again we are thrown back on ourselves for guidance.
Seeing the world's way afresh, I see that it is not my way. I revive. I
assert myself. My duty, I say, is my own. And so, perhaps, I go back
again to my own wayward heart.

It is this sort of process which goes on, sometimes in a hopelessly
circular way, when, in some complicated situation, you are morally perplexed, and after much inner brooding give up deciding by yourself and
appeal to friends for advice. The advice at first pleases you, but soon may
arouse your self-will more than before. You may become, as a result,
more wayward and sometimes more perplexed, the longer you continue
this sort of inquiry. We all know what it is to seek advice, just with the
result of finding out what it is that we do not want to do.

Neither within nor without, then, do I find what seems to me a settled
authority,—a settled and harmonious plan of life,—unless, indeed, one
happy sort of union takes place between the inner and the outer, between
my social world and myself, between my natural waywardness and the
ways of my fellows. This happy union is the one that takes place whenever my mere social conformity, my docility as an imitative creature,
turns into exactly that which, in these lectures, I shall call loyalty. Let us
consider what happens in such cases.

Suppose a being whose social conformity has been sufficient to enable
him to learn many skilful social arts,—arts of speech, of prowess in con-

test, of influence over other men. Suppose that these arts have at the same time awakened this man's pride, his self-confidence, his disposition to assert himself. Such a man will have in him a good deal of what you can well call social will. He will be no mere anarchist. He will have been trained into much obedience. He will be no natural enemy of society, unless, indeed, fortune has given him extraordinary opportunities to win his way without scruples. On the other hand, this man must acquire a good deal of self-will. He becomes fond of success, of mastery, of his own demands. To be sure, he can find within himself no one naturally sovereign will. He can so far find only a general determination to define some way of his own, and to have his own way. Hence the conflicts of social will and self-will are inevitable, circular, endless, so long as this is the whole story of the man's life. By merely consulting convention, on the one hand, and his disposition to be somebody, on the other hand, this man can never find any one final and consistent plan of life, nor reach any one definition of his duty.

But now suppose that there appears in this man's life some one of the greater social passions, such as patriotism well exemplifies. Let his country be in danger. Let his elemental passion for conflict hereupon fuse with his brotherly love for his own countrymen into that fascinating and blood-thirsty form of humane but furious ecstasy, which is called the war-spirit. The mood in question may or may not be justified by the passing circumstances. For that I now care not. At its best the war-spirit is no very clear or rational state of anybody's mind. But one reason why men may love this spirit is that when it comes, it seems at once to define a plan of life,—a plan which solves the conflicts of self-will and conformity. This plan has two features: (1) it is through and through a social plan, obedient to the general will of one's country, submissive; (2) it is through and through an exaltation of the self, of the inner man, who now feels glorified through his sacrifice, dignified in his self-surrender, glad to be his country's servant and martyr,—yet sure that through this very readiness for self-destruction he wins the rank of hero.

Well, if the man whose case we are supposing gets possessed by some such passion as this, he wins for the moment the consciousness of what I call loyalty. This loyalty no longer knows anything about the old circular conflicts of self-will and of conformity. The self, at such moments, looks indeed *outwards* for its plan of life. "The country needs me," it says. It looks, meanwhile, *inwards* for the inspiring justification of this plan. "Honor, the hero's crown, the soldier's death, the patriot's devotion— these," it says, "are my will. I am not giving up this will of mine. It is my pride, my glory, my self-assertion, to be ready at my country's call." And now there is no conflict of outer and inner.

How wise or how enduring or how practical such a passion may prove, I do not yet consider. What I point out is that this war-spirit, for the time

at least, makes self-sacrifice seem to be self-expression, makes obedience
to the country's call seem to be the proudest sort of display of one's own
powers. Honor now means submission, and to obey means to have one's
way. Power and service are at one. Conformity is no longer opposed to
having one's own will. One has no will but that of the country.

As a mere fact of human nature, then, there are social passions which
actually tend to do at once two things: (1) to intensify our self-consciousness, to make us more than ever determined to express our own will and
more than ever sure of our own rights, of our own strength, of our dignity,
of our power, of our value; (2) to make obvious to us that this our will
has no purpose but to do the will of some fascinating social power. This
social power is the cause to which we are loyal.

Loyalty, then, fixes our attention upon some one cause, bids us look
without ourselves to see what this unified cause is, shows us thus some
one plan of action, and then says to us, "In this cause is your life, your
will, your opportunity, your fulfilment."

Thus loyalty, viewed merely as a personal attitude, solves the paradox
of our ordinary existence, by showing us outside of ourselves the cause
which is to be served, and inside of ourselves the will which delights to
do this service, and which is not thwarted but enriched and expressed in
such service.

I have used patriotism and the war-spirit merely as a first and familiar
illustration of loyalty. But now, as we shall later see, there is no necessary
connection between loyalty and war; and there are many other forms of
loyalty besides the patriotic forms. Loyalty has its domestic, its religious,
its commercial, its professional forms, and many other forms as well. The
essence of it, whatever forms it may take, is, as I conceive the matter, this:
Since no man can find a plan of life by merely looking within his own
chaotic nature, he has to look without, to the world of social conventions,
deeds, and causes. Now, a loyal man is one who has found, and who sees,
neither mere individual fellow-men to be loved or hated, nor mere conventions, nor customs, nor laws to be obeyed, but some social cause, or
some system of causes, so rich, so well knit, and, to him, so fascinating,
and withal so kindly in its appeal to his natural self-will, that he says to
his cause: "Thy will is mine and mine is thine. In thee I do not lose but
find myself, living intensely in proportion as I live for thee." If one could
find such a cause, and hold it for his lifetime before his mind, clearly
observing it, passionately loving it, and yet calmly understanding it, and
steadily and practically serving it, he would have one plan of life, and
this plan of life would be his own plan, his own will set before him, expressing all that his self-will has ever sought. Yet this plan would also
be a plan of obedience, because it would mean living for the cause.

Now, in all ages of civilized life there have been people who have won
in some form a consciousness of loyalty, and who have held to such a

consciousness through life. Such people may or may not have been right in their choice of a cause. But at least they have exemplified through their loyalty one feature of a rational moral life. They have known what it was to have unity of purpose.

And again, the loyal have known what it was to be free from moral doubts and scruples. Their cause has been their conscience. It has told them what to do. They have listened and obeyed, not because of what they took to be blind convention, not because of a fear of external authority, not even because of what seemed to themselves any purely private and personal intuition, but because, when they have looked first outwards at their cause, and then inwards at themselves, they have found themselves worthless in their own eyes, except when viewed as active, as confidently devoted, as willing instruments of their cause. Their cause has forbidden them to doubt; it has said: "You are mine, you cannot do otherwise." And they have said to the cause: "I am, even of my own will, thine. I have no will except thy will. Take me, use me, control me, and even thereby fulfil me and exalt me." That is again the speech of the devoted patriots, soldiers, mothers, and martyrs of our race. They have had the grace of this willing, this active loyalty.

Now, people loyal in this sense have surely existed in the world, and, as you all know, the loyal still exist amongst us. And I beg you not to object to me, at this point, that such devoted people have often been loyal to very bad causes; or that different people have been loyal to causes which were in deadly war with one another, so that loyal people must often have been falsely guided. I beg you, above all, not to interpose here the objection that our modern doubters concerning moral problems simply cannot at present see to what one cause they ought to be loyal, so that just herein, just in our inability to see a fitting and central object of loyalty, lies the root of our modern moral confusion and distraction. All those possible objections are indeed perfectly fair considerations. I shall deal with them in due time; and I am just as earnestly aware of them as you can be. But just now we are getting our first glimpse of our future philosophy of loyalty. All that you can say of the defects of loyalty leaves still untouched the one great fact that, if you want to find a way of living which surmounts doubts, and centralizes your powers, it must be some such a way as all the loyal in common have trodden, since first loyalty was known amongst men. What form of loyalty is the right one, we are hereafter to see. But unless you can find some sort of loyalty, you cannot find unity and peace in your active living. You must find, then, a cause that is really worthy of the sort of devotion that the soldiers, rushing cheerfully to certain death, have felt for their clan or for their country, and that the martyrs have shown on behalf of their faith. This cause must be indeed rational, worthy, and no object of a false devotion. But once found, it must become your conscience, must tell you the truth about your duty, and must unify, as from without and from above, your motives, your special ideals, and your plans. You ought, I say, to find such a cause, if indeed there be any ought at all. And this is my first hint of our moral code.

But you repeat, perhaps in bewilderment, your question: "Where, in our distracted modern world, in this time when cause wars with cause, and when all old moral standards are remorselessly criticised and doubted, are we to find such a cause—a cause, all-embracing, definite, rationally compelling, supreme, certain, and fit to centralize life? What cause is there that for us would rationally justify a martyr's devotion?" I reply: "A perfectly simple consideration, derived from a study of the very spirit of loyalty itself, as this spirit is manifested by all the loyal, will soon furnish to us the unmistakable answer to this question." For the moment we have won our first distant glimpse of what I mean by the general nature of loyalty, and by our common need of loyalty.

LOYALTY TO LOYALTY

We have deliberately declined, so far, to consider what the causes are to which men ought to be loyal. To turn to this task is the next step in our philosophy of loyalty.

Your first impression may well be that the task in question is endlessly complex. In our opening lecture we defined indeed some general characteristics which a cause must possess in order to be a fitting object of loyalty. A cause, we said, is a possible object of loyalty only in case it is such as to join many persons into the unity of a single life. Such a cause, we said, must therefore be at once personal, and, for one who defines personality from a purely human point of view, superpersonal. Our initial illustrations of possible causes were, first, a friendship which unites several friends into some unity of friendly life; secondly, a family, whose unity binds its members' lives together; and, thirdly, the state, in so far as it is no mere collection of separate citizens, but such an unity as that to which the devoted patriot is loyal. As we saw, such illustrations could be vastly extended. All stable social relations may give rise to causes that may call forth loyalty.

Now, it is obvious that nobody can be equally and directly loyal to all of the countless actual social causes that exist. It is obvious also that many causes which conform to our general definition of a possible cause may appear to any given person to be hateful and evil causes, to which he is justly opposed. A robber band, a family engaged in a murderous feud, a pirate crew, a savage tribe, a Highland robber clan of the old days— these might constitute causes to which somebody has been, or is, profoundly loyal. Men have loved such causes devotedly, have served them for a lifetime. Yet most of us would easily agree in thinking such causes unworthy of anybody's loyalty. Moreover, different loyalties may obviously stand in mutual conflict, whenever their causes are opposed. Family feuds are embittered by the very strength of the loyalty of both sides. My country, if I am the patriot inflamed by the war-spirit, seems an absolutely worthy cause; but my enemy's country usually seems hateful to me just because of my own loyalty; and therefore even my individual enemy may be hated because of the supposed baseness of his cause. War-songs call the individual enemy evil names just because he possesses the very personal quality that, in our own loyal fellow-countrymen, we most admire. "No refuge could save the hireling and slave." Our enemy, as you see, is a slave, because he serves his cause so obediently. Yet just such service we call, in our own country's heroes, the worthiest devotion.

Meanwhile, in the foregoing account of loyalty as a spiritual good to the loyal man, we have insisted that true loyalty, being a willing devotion of the self to its cause, involves some element of autonomous choice. Tradition has usually held that a man ought to be loyal to just that cause which his social station determines for him. Common sense generally says, that if you were born in your country, and still live there, you ought to be loyal to that country, and to that country only, hating the enemies across the border whenever a declaration of war requires you to hate them. But we have declared that true loyalty includes some element of free choice. Hence our own account seems still further to have complicated the theory of loyalty. For in answering in our last lecture the ethical individualists who objected to loyalty, we have ourselves deliberately given to loyalty an individualistic coloring. And if our view be right, and if tradition be wrong, so much the more difficult appears to be the task of defining wherein consists that which makes a cause worthy of loyalty for a given man, since tradition alone is for us an insufficient guide.

To sum up, then, our apparent difficulties, they are these: Loyalty is a good for the loyal man; but it may be michievous for those whom his cause assails. Conflicting loyalties may mean general social disturbances; and the fact that loyalty is good for the loyal does not of itself decide whose cause is right when various causes stand opposed to one another. And if, in accordance with our own argument in the foregoing lecture, we declare that the best form of loyalty, for the loyal individual, is the one that he freely chooses for himself, so much the greater seems to be the complication of the moral world, and so much the more numerous become the chances that the loyalties of various people will conflict with one another.

In order to overcome such difficulties, now that they have arisen in our way, and in order to discover a principle whereby one may be guided in choosing a right object for his loyalty, we must steadfastly bear in mind that, when we declared loyalty to be a supreme good for the loyal man himself, we were not speaking of a good that can come to a few men only—to heroes or to saints of an especially exalted mental type. As we expressly said, the mightiest and the humblest members of any social order can be morally equal in the exemplification of loyalty. Whenever I myself begin to look about my own community to single out those people whom I know to be, in the sense of our definition, especially loyal to their various causes, I always find, amongst the most exemplary cases of loyalty, a few indeed of the most prominent members of the community, whom your minds and mine must at once single out because their public services and their willing sacrifices have made their loyalty to their chosen causes a matter of common report and of easy observation. But my own mind also chooses some of the plainest and obscurest of the people whom I chance to know, the most straightforward and simpleminded of folk, whose loyalty is even all the more sure to me because I can certainly affirm that they, at least, cannot be making any mere display of loyalty in order that they should be seen of men. Nobody knows of their loyalty except those who are in more or less direct touch with them; and these usually appreciate this loyalty too little. You all of you similarly know plain and wholly obscure men and women, of whom the world has never heard, and is not worthy, but who have possessed and who have proved in the presence of you who have chanced to observe them, a loyalty to their chosen causes which was not indeed expressed in martial deeds, but which was quite as genuine a loyalty as that of a Samurai, or as that of Arnold von Winkelried when he rushed upon the Austrian spears. As for the ordinary expressions of loyalty, not at critical moments and in the heroic instants that come to the plainest lives, but in daily business, we are all aware how the letter carrier and the housemaid may live, and often do live, when they choose, as complete a daily life of steadfast loyalty as could any knight or king. Some of us certainly know precisely such truly great personal embodiments of loyalty in those who are, in the world's ill-judging eyes, the little ones of the community.

Now these facts, I insist, show that loyalty is in any case no aristocratic gift of the few. It is, indeed, too rare a possession to-day in our own American social order; but that defect is due to the state of our present moral education. We as a nation, I fear, have been forgetting loyalty. We have been neglecting to cultivate it in our social order. We have been making light of it. We have not been training ourselves for it. Hence we, indeed, often sadly miss it in our social environment. But all sound human beings are made for it and can learn to possess it and to profit by it. And it is an essentially accessible and practical virtue for everybody.

This being true, let us next note that all the complications which we just reported are obviously due, in the main, to the fact that, as loyal men at present are, their various causes, and so their various loyalties, are viewed by them as standing in mutual, sometimes in deadly conflict. In general, as is plain if somebody's loyalty to a given cause, as for instance to a family, or to a state, so expresses itself as to involve a feud with a neighbor's family, or a warlike assault upon a foreign state, the result is obviously an evil; and at least part of the reason why it is an evil is that, by reason of the feud or the war, a certain good, namely, the enemy's loyalty, together with the enemy's opportunity to be loyal, is assailed, is thwarted, is endangered, is, perhaps, altogether destroyed. If the loyalty of A is a good for him, and if the loyalty of B is a good for him, then a feud between A and B, founded upon a mutual conflict between the causes that they serve, obviously involves this evil, namely, that each of the combatants assails, and perhaps may altogether destroy, precisely what we have seen to be the best spiritual possession of the other, namely, his chance to have a cause and to be loyal to a cause. The militant loyalty, indeed, also assails, in such a case, the enemy's physical comfort and well-being, his property, his life; and herein, of course, militant loyalty does evil to the enemy. But if each man's having and serving a cause is his best good, the worst of the evils of a feud is the resulting attack, not upon the enemy's comfort or his health or his property or his life, but upon the most precious of his possessions, his loyalty itself.

If loyalty is a supreme good, the mutually destructive conflict of loyalties is in general a supreme evil. If loyalty is a good for all sorts and conditions of men, the war of man against man has been especially mischievous, not so much because it has hurt, maimed, impoverished, or slain men, as because it has so often robbed the defeated of their causes, of their opportunities to be loyal, and sometimes of their very spirit of loyalty.

If, then, we look over the field of human life to see where good and evil have most clustered, we see that the best in human life is its loyalty; while the worst is whatever has tended to make loyalty impossible, or to destroy it when present, or to rob it of its own while it still survives. And of all things that thus have warred with loyalty, the bitterest woe of humanity has been that so often it is the loyal themselves who have thus blindly and eagerly gone about to wound and to slay the loyalty of their brethren. The spirit of loyalty has been misused to make men commit sin against this very spirit, holy as it is. For such a sin is precisely what any wanton conflict of loyalties means. Where such a conflict occurs, the best, namely, loyalty, is used as an instrument in order to compass the worst, namely, the destruction of loyalty.

It is true, then, that some causes are good, while some are evil. But the test of good and evil in the causes to which men are loyal is now definable in terms which we can greatly simplify in view of the foregoing considerations.

If, namely, I find a cause, and this cause fascinates me, and I give myself over to its service, I in so far attain what, for me, if my loyalty is complete, is a supreme good. But my cause, by our own definition, is a social cause, which binds many into the unity of one service. My cause, therefore, gives me of necessity, fellow-servants, who with me share this loyalty, and to whom this loyalty, if complete, is also a supreme good. So far, then, in being loyal myself, I not only get but give good; for I help to sustain, in each of my fellow-servants, his own loyalty, and so I help him to secure his own supreme good. In so far, then, my loyalty to my cause is also a loyalty to my fellow's loyalty. But now suppose that my cause, like the family in a feud, or like the pirate ship, or like the aggressively warlike nation, lives by the destruction of the loyalty of other families, or of its own community, or of other communities. Then, indeed, I get a good for myself and for my fellow-servants by our common loyalty; but I war against this very spirit of loyalty as it appears in our opponent's loyalty to his own cause.

And so, a cause is good, not only for me, but for mankind, in so far as it is essentially a *loyalty to loyalty,* that is, is an aid and a furtherance of loyalty in my fellows. It is an evil cause in so far as, despite the loyalty that it arouses in me, it is destructive of loyalty in the world of my fellows. My cause is, indeed, always such as to involve some loyalty to loyalty, because, if I am loyal to any cause at all, I have fellow-servants whose loyalty mine supports. But in so far as my cause is a predatory cause, which lives by overthrowing the loyalties of others, it is an evil cause, because it involves disloyalty to the very cause of loyalty itself.

In view of these considerations, we are now able still further to simplify our problem by laying stress upon one more of those very features which seemed, but a moment since, to complicate the matter so hopelessly. Loyalty, as we have defined it, is the willing devotion of a self to a cause. In answering the ethical individualists, we have insisted that all of the higher types of loyalty involve autonomous choice. The cause that is to appeal to me at all must indeed have some elemental fascination for me. It must stir me, arouse me, please me, and in the end possess me. Moreover, it must, indeed, be set before me by my social order as a possible, a practically significant, a living cause, which binds many selves in the unity of one life. But, nevertheless, if I am really awake to the significance of my own moral choices, I must be in the position of accepting this cause, as the Speaker of the House, in the incident that I have narrated, had freely accepted his Speakership. My cause cannot be merely forced upon me. It is I who make it my own. It is I who willingly say: "I have no eyes to see nor tongue to speak save as this cause shall command." However much the cause may seem to be assigned to me by my social station, I must coöperate in the choice of the cause, before the act of loyalty is complete.

Since this is the case, since my loyalty never is my mere fate, but is always also my choice, I can of course determine my loyalty, at least to some extent, by the consideration of the actual good and ill which my proposed cause does to mankind. And since I now have the main criterion of the good and ill of causes before me, I can define a principle of choice which may so guide me that my loyalty shall become a good, not merely to myself, but to mankind.

This principle is now obvious. I may state it thus: In so far as it lies in your power, so choose your cause and so serve it, that, by reason of your choice and of your service, there shall be more loyalty in the world rather than less. And, in fact, so choose and so serve your individual cause as to secure thereby the greatest possible increase of loyalty amongst men. More briefly: *In choosing and in serving the cause to which you are to be loyal, be, in any case, loyal to loyalty.*

This precept, I say, will express how one should guide his choice of a cause, in so far as he considers not merely his own supreme good, but that of mankind. That such autonomous choice is possible, tends, as we now see, not to complicate, but to simplify our moral situation. For if you regard men's loyalty as their fate, if you think that a man must be loyal simply to the cause which tradition sets before him, without any power to direct his own moral attention, then indeed the conflict of loyalties seems an insoluble problem; so that, if men find themselves loyally involved in feuds, there is no way out. But if, indeed, choice plays a part,—a genuine even if limited part, in directing the individual's choice of the cause to which he is to be loyal, then indeed this choice may be so directed that loyalty to the universal loyalty of all mankind shall be furthered by the actual choices which each enlightened loyal person makes when he selects his cause.

At the close of our first discussion we supposed the question to be asked, Where, in all our complex and distracted modern world, in which at present cause wars with cause, shall we find a cause that is certainly worthy of our loyalty? This question, at this very moment, has received in our discussion an answer which you may feel to be so far provisional,— perhaps unpractical,—but which you ought to regard as, at least in principle, somewhat simple and true to human nature. Loyalty is a good, a supreme good. If I myself could but find a worthy cause, and serve it as the Speaker served the House, having neither eyes to see nor tongue to speak save as that cause should command, then my highest human good, in so far as I am indeed an active being, would be mine. But this very good of loyalty is no peculiar privilege of mine; nor is it good only for me. It is an universally human good. For it is simply the finding of a harmony of the self and the world, —such a harmony as alone can content any human being.

In these lectures I do not found my argument upon some remote ideal. I found my case upon taking our poor passionate human nature just as we find it. This "eager anxious being" of ours, as Gray calls it, is a being that we can find only in social ties, and that we, nevertheless, can never fulfil without a vigorous self-assertion. We are by nature proud, untamed, restless, insatiable in our private self-will. We are also imitative, plastic, and in bitter need of ties. We profoundly want both to rule and to be ruled. We must be each of us at the centre of his own active world, and yet each of us longs to be in harmony with the very outermost heavens that encompass, with the lofty orderliness of their movements, all our restless doings. The stars fascinate us, and yet we also want to keep our own feet upon our solid human earth. Our fellows, meanwhile, overwhelm us with the might of their customs, and we in turn are inflamed with the naturally unquenchable longing that they should somehow listen to the cries of our every individual desire.

Now this divided being of ours demands reconciliation with itself; it is one long struggle for unity. Its inner and outer realms are naturally at war. Yet it wills both realms. It wants them to become one. Such unity, however, only loyalty furnishes to us,—loyalty, which finds the inner self intensified and exalted even by the very act of outward looking and of upward looking, of service and obedience,—loyalty, which knows its eyes and its tongue to be never so much and so proudly its own as when it earnestly insists that it can neither see nor speak except as the cause demands,—loyalty, which is most full of life at the instant when it is most ready to become weary, or even to perish in the act of devotion to its own. Such loyalty unites private passion and outward conformity in one life. This is the very essence of loyalty. Now loyalty has these characters in any man who is loyal. Its emotions vary, indeed, endlessly with the temperaments of its adherents; but to them all it brings the active peace of that rest in a painful life,—that rest such as we found the mystic, Meister Eckhart, fully ready to prize.

Loyalty, then, is a good for all men. And it is in any man just as much a true good as my loyalty could be in me. And so, then, if indeed I seek a cause, a worthy cause, what cause could be more worthy than the cause of loyalty to loyalty; that is, the cause of making loyalty prosper amongst men? If I could serve that cause in a sustained and effective life, if some practical work for the furtherance of universal human loyalty could become to me what the House was to the Speaker, then indeed my own life-task would be found; and I could then be assured at every instant of the worth of my cause by virtue of the very good that I personally found in its service.

Here would be for me not only an unity of inner and outer, but an unity with the unity of all human life. What I sought for myself I should then be explicitly seeking for my whole world. All men would be my fellow-servants of my cause. In principle I should be opposed to no man's loyalty. I should be opposed only to men's blindness in their loyalty, I should contend only against that tragic disloyalty to loyalty which the feuds of humanity now exemplify. I should preach to all others, I should strive to practise myself, that active mutual furtherance of universal loyalty which is what humanity obviously most needs, if indeed loyalty, just as the willing devotion of a self to a cause, is a supreme good.

And since all who are human are as capable of loyalty as they are of reason, since the plainest and the humblest can be as true-hearted as the great, I should nowhere miss the human material for my task. I should know, meanwhile, that if indeed loyalty, unlike the "mercy" of Portia's speech, is not always mightiest in the mightiest, it certainly, like mercy, becomes the throned monarch better than his crown. So that I should be sure of this good of loyalty as something worthy to be carried, so far as I could carry it, to everybody, lofty or humble.

Thus surely it would be humane and reasonable for me to define my cause to myself,—if only I could be assured that there is indeed some practical way of making loyalty to loyalty the actual cause of my life. Our question therefore becomes this: Is there a practical way of serving the universal human cause of loyalty to loyalty? And if there is such a way, what is it? Can we see how personally so to act that we bring loyalty on earth to a fuller fruition, to a wider range of efficacy, to a more effective sovereignty over the lives of men? If so, then indeed we can see how to work for the cause of the genuine kingdom of heaven. . . .

Yet herewith we have only begun to indicate how the cause of loyalty to loyalty may be made a cause that one can practically, efficaciously, and constantly serve. Loyalty, namely, is not a matter merely of to-day or of yesterday. The loyal have existed since civilization began. And, even so, loyalty to loyalty is not a novel undertaking. It began to be effective from the time when first people could make and keep a temporary truce during a war, and when first strangers were regarded as protected by the gods, and when first the duties of hospitality were recognized. The way to be loyal to loyalty is therefore laid down in precisely the rational portion of the conventional morality which human experience has worked out.

Herewith we approach a thesis which is central in my whole philosophy of loyalty. I announced that thesis in other words in the opening lecture. My thesis is that *all those duties which we have learned to recognize as the fundamental duties of the civilized man, the duties that every man owes to every man, are to be rightly interpreted as special instances of loyalty to loyalty.* In other words, all the recognized virtues can be defined in terms of our concept of loyalty. And this is why I assert that, when rightly interpreted, loyalty is the whole duty of man.

For consider the best-known facts as to the indirect influence of certain forms of loyal conduct. When I speak the truth, my act is directly an act of loyalty to the personal tie which then and there binds me to the man to whom I consent to speak. My special cause is, in such a case, constituted by this tie. My fellow and I are linked in a certain unity,—the unity of some transaction which involves our speech one to another. To be ready to speak the truth to my fellow is to have, just then, no eye to see and no tongue to speak save as this willingly accepted tie demands. In so far, then, speaking the truth is a special instance of loyalty. But whoever speaks the truth, thereby does what he then can do to help every-body to speak the truth. For he acts so as to further the general confidence of man in man. How far such indirect influence may extend, no man can predict.

Precisely so, in the commercial world, honesty in business is a service, not merely and not mainly to the others who are parties to the single trans-action in which at any one time this faithfulness is shown. The single act of business fidelity is an act of loyalty to that general confidence of man in man upon which the whole fabric of business rests. On the contrary, the unfaithful financier whose disloyalty is the final deed that lets loose the avalanche of a panic, has done far more harm to general public confidence than he could possibly do to those whom his act directly assails. Honesty, then, is owed not merely and not even mainly to those with whom we directly deal when we do honest acts; it is owed to mankind at large, and it benefits the community and the general cause of commercial loyalty.

Such a remark is in itself a commonplace; but it serves to make con-crete my general thesis that every form of dutiful action is a case of loyalty to loyalty. For what holds thus of truthfulness and of commercial honesty holds, I assert, of every form of dutiful action. Each such form is a special means for being, by a concrete deed, loyal to loyalty.

We have sought for the worthy cause; and we have found it. This simp-lest possible of considerations serves to turn the chaotic mass of separate precepts of which our ordinary conventional moral code consists into a system unified by the one spirit of universal loyalty. By your individual deed you indeed cannot save the world, but you can at any moment do what in you lies to further the cause which both for you and for the hu-man world constitutes the supreme good, namely, the cause of universal loyalty. Herein consists your entire duty.

Review in the light of this simple consideration, the usually recognized range of human duties. How easily they group themselves about the one principle: *Be loyal to loyalty*.

Have I, for instance, duties to myself? Yes, precisely in so far as I have the duty to be actively loyal at all. For loyalty needs not only a willing, but also an effective servant. My duty to myself is, then, the duty to pro-vide my cause with one who is strong enough and skilful enough to be effective according to my own natural powers. The care of health, self-cultivation, self-control, spiritual power—these are all to be morally esti-mated with reference to the one principle that, since I have no eyes to see or tongue to speak save as the cause commands, I will be as worthy an instrument of the cause as can be made, by my own efforts, out of the poor material which my scrap of human nature provides. The highest personal cultivation for which I have time is thus required by our prin-ciple. But self-cultivation which is not related to loyalty is worthless.

Have I private and personal rights, which I ought to assert? Yes, pre-cisely in so far as my private powers and possessions are held in trust for the cause, and are, upon occasion, to be defended for the sake of the cause. My rights are morally the outcome of my loyalty. It is my right to protect my service, to maintain my office, and to keep my own merely in order that I may use my own as the cause commands. But rights which are not determined by my loyalty are vain pretence.

As to my duties to my neighbors, these are defined by a well-known tradition in terms of two principles, justice and benevolence. These two principles are mere aspects of our one principle. Justice means, in general, fidelity to human ties in so far as they are ties. Justice thus concerns itself with what may be called the mere forms in which loyalty expresses itself. Justice, therefore, is simply one aspect of loyalty—the more formal and abstract side of loyal life. If you are just, you are decisive in your choice of your personal cause, you are faithful to the loyal decision once made, you keep your promise, you speak the truth, you respect the loyal ties of all other men, and you contend with other men only in so far as the defence of your own cause, in the interest of loyalty to the universal cause of loyalty, makes such contest against aggression unavoidable. All these types of activity, within the limits that loyalty determines, are demanded if you are to be loyal to loyalty. Our principle thus at once requires them, and enables us to define their range of application. But justice, without loyalty, is a vicious formalism.

Benevolence, on the other hand, is that aspect of loyalty which directly concerns itself with your influence upon the inner life of human beings who enjoy, who suffer, and whose private good is to be affected by your deeds. Since no personal good that your fellow can possess is superior to his own loyalty, your own loyalty to loyalty is itself a supremely benevolent type of activity. And since your fellow-man is an instrument for the furtherance of the cause of universal loyalty, his welfare also concerns you, in so far as, if you help him to a more efficient life, you make him better able to be loyal. Thus benevolence is an inevitable attendant of loyalty. And the spirit of loyalty to loyalty enables us to define wherein consists a wise benevolence. Benevolence without loyalty is a dangerous sentimentalism. Thus viewed, then, loyalty to universal loyalty is indeed the fulfilment of the whole law.

LOYALTY, TRUTH, AND REALITY

In closing my last lecture I said that whatever trains us in the arts of loyalty enables us to enter into a world of spiritual truth. These words were intended to indicate that the loyal life has another aspect than the one hitherto most emphasized in these lectures. Our foregoing account has been deliberately one-sided. We have been discussing the moral life as if one could define a plan of conduct without implying more about man's place in the real universe than we have yet made explicit in these lectures. Hence our discussion, so far, is open to obvious objections. . . .

What must be true about the universe if even loyalty itself is a genuine good, and not a merely inevitable human illusion?

Well, loyalty is a service of causes. A cause, if it really is what our definition requires, links various human lives into the unity of one life. Therefore, if loyalty has any basis in truth, human lives can be linked in some genuine spiritual unity. Is such unity a fact, or is our belief in our causes a mere point of view, a pathetic fallacy? Surely, if any man, however loyal, discovers that his cause is a dream, and that men remain as a fact sundered beings, not really linked by genuine spiritual ties, how can that man remain loyal? Perhaps his supreme good indeed lies in believing that such unities are real. But if this belief turns out to be an illusion, and if a man detects the illusion, can he any longer get the good out of loyalty?

And as for even this personal good that is to be got out of loyalty, we have all along seen that such good comes to a loyal man's mind in a very paradoxical way. A loyal man gets good, but since he gets it by believing that his cause has a real existence outside of his private self, and is of itself a good thing, he gets the fascination of loyalty not as a private delight of his own, but as a fulfilment of himself through self-surrender to an externally existing good,—through a willing abandonment of the seeking of his own delight. And so the loyal man's good is essentially an anticipation of a good that he regards as not his own, but as existent in the cause. The cause, however, is itself no one fellow-man, and no mere collection of fellow-men. It is a family, a country, a church, or is such a rational union of many human minds and wills as we have in mind when we speak of a science or an art. Now, can such causes contain any good which is not simply a collection of separate human experiences of pleasure or of satisfaction? Thus, then, both the reality and the good of a loyal man's cause must be objects of the loyal man's belief in order that he should be able to get the experience of loyalty. And if his loyalty is indeed well founded, there must be unities of spiritual life in the universe such that no one man ever, by himself, experiences these unities as facts of his own consciousness. And these higher unities of life must possess a degree and a type of goodness,—a genuine value, such that no one man, and no mere collection of men, can ever exhaustively experience this goodness, or become personally possessed of this value.

How paradoxical a world, then, must the real world be, if the faith of the loyal is indeed well founded! A spiritual unity of life, which transcends the individual experience of any man, must be real. For loyalty, as we have seen, is a service of causes that, from the human point of view, appear superpersonal. Loyalty holds these unities to be good. If loyalty is right, the real goodness of these causes is never completely manifested to any one man, or to any mere collection of men. Such goodness, then, if completely experienced at all, must be experienced upon some higher level of consciousness than any one human being ever reaches. If loyalty is right, social causes, social organizations, friendships, families, countries, yes, humanity, as you see, must have the sort of unity of consciousness which individual human persons fragmentarily get, but must have this unity upon a higher level than that of our ordinary human individuality.

Some such view, I say, must be held if we are to regard loyalty as in the end anything more than a convenient illusion. Loyalty has its metaphysical aspect. It is an effort to conceive human life in an essentially superhuman way, to view our social organizations as actual personal unities of consciousness, unities wherein there exists an actual experience of that good which, in our loyalty, we only partially apprehend. If the loyalty of the lovers is indeed well founded in fact, then they, as separate individuals, do not constitute the whole truth. Their spiritual union also has a personal, a conscious existence, upon a higher than human level. An analogous unity of consciousness, an unity superhuman in grade, but intimately bound up with, and inclusive of, our apparently separate personalities, must exist, if loyalty is well founded, wherever a real cause wins the true devotion of ourselves. Grant such an hypothesis, and then loyalty becomes no pathetic serving of a myth. The good which our causes possess, then, also becomes a concrete fact for an experience of a higher than human level. That union of self-sacrifice with self-assertion which loyalty expresses becomes a consciousness of our genuine relations to a higher social unity of consiousness in which we all have our being. For from this point of view we are, and we have our worth, by virtue of our relation to a consciousness of a type superior to the human type. And meanwhile the good of our loyalty is itself a perfectly concrete good, a good which is present to that higher experience, wherein our cause is viewed in its truth, as a genuine unity of life. And because of this fact we can straightforwardly say: We are loyal not for the sake of the good that we privately get out of loyalty, but for the sake of the good that the cause—this higher unity of experience—gets out of this loyalty. Yet our loyalty gives us what is, after all, our supreme good, for it defines our true position in the world of that social will wherein we live and move and have our being.

I doubt not that such a view of human life,—such an assertion that the social will is a concrete entity, just as real as we are, and of still a higher grade of reality than ourselves,—will seem to many of you mythical enough. Yet thus to view the unity of human life is, after all, a common tendency of the loyal. That fact I have illustrated in every lecture of this course. That such a view need not be mythical, that truth and reality can be conceived only in such terms as these, that our philosophy of loyalty is a rational part of a philosophy which must view the whole world as one unity of consciousness, wherein countless lesser unities are synthesized,—this is a general philosophical thesis which I must next briefly expound to you.

My exposition, as you see, must be, in any case, an attempt to show that the inevitable faith of the loyal—their faith in their causes, and in the real goodness of their causes—has truth, and since I must thus, in any case, discourse of truth, I propose briefly to show you that whoever talks of any sort of truth whatever, be that truth moral or scientific, the truth of common sense or the truth of a philosophy, inevitably implies, in all his assertions about truth, that the world of truth of which he speaks is a world possessing a rational and spiritual unity, is a conscious world of experience, whose type of consciousness is higher in its level than is the type of our human minds, but whose life is such that our life belongs as part to this living whole. This world of truth is the one that you must define, so I insist, if you are to regard any proposition whatever as true, and are then to tell, in a reasonable way, what you mean by the truth of that proposition.

The world of truth is therefore essentially a world such as that in whose reality the loyal believe when they believe their cause to be real. Moreover, this truth world has a goodness about it, essentially like that which the loyal attribute to their causes. Truth seeking and loyalty are therefore essentially the same process of life merely viewed in two different aspects. Whoever is loyal serves what he takes to be a truth, namely, his cause. On the other hand, whoever seeks truth for its own sake fails of his business if he seeks it merely as a barren abstraction, that has no life in it. If a truth seeker knows his business, he is, then, in the sense of our definition, serving a cause which unifies our human life upon some higher level of spiritual being than the present human level. He is therefore essentially loyal. Truth seeking is a moral activity; and on the other hand, morality is wholly inadequate unless the light of eternal truth shines upon it.

This, I say, will be my thesis. Some of you will call it very mystical, or at least a very fantastic thesis. It is not so. It ought to be viewed as a matter of plain sense. It is, I admit, a thesis which many of the most distinguished amongst my colleagues, who are philosophers, nowadays view sometimes with amusement, and sometimes with a notable impatience. This way of regarding the world of truth, which I have just defined as mine, is especially and most vivaciously attacked by my good friends, the pragmatists,—a group of philosophers who have of late been disposed to take truth under their especial protection, as if she were in danger from the tendency of some people who take her too seriously.

When I mention pragmatism, I inevitably bring to your minds the name of one whom we all honor,—the philosopher who last year so persuasively stated, before the audience of this Institute, the pragmatist theory of philosophical method, and of the nature of truth. It is impossible for me to do any justice, within my limits, to the exposition which Professor James gave of his own theory of truth. Yet since the antithesis between his views and those which I have now to indicate to you may be in itself an aid to my own exposition, I beg you to allow me to use, for the moment, some of his assertions about the nature of truth as a means of showing, by contrast, how I find myself obliged to interpret the same problem. . . .

May we venture to ask ourselves, then: Is this pragmatism a fair expression of what we mean by truth?

In reply let me at once point out the extent to which I personally agree with my colleague, and accept his theory of truth. I fully agree with him that whenever a man asserts a truth, his assertion is a deed,—a practical attitude, an active acknowledgment of some fact. I fully agree that the effort to verify this acknowledgment by one's own personal experience, and the attempt to find truth in the form of a practical congruity between our assertions and our attained empirical results, is an effort which in our individual lives inevitably accompanies and sustains our every undertaking in the cause of truth seeking. Modern pragmatism is not indeed as original as it seems to suppose itself to be in emphasizing such views. The whole history of modern idealism is full of such assertions. I myself, as a teacher of philosophy, have for years insisted upon viewing truth in this practical way. I must joyously confess to you that I was first taught to view the nature of truth in this way when I was a young student of philosophy; and I was taught this by several great masters of modern thought. These masters were Kant, Fichte, Hegel, and Professor James himself, whose lectures, as I heard them in my youth at the Johns Hopkins University, and whose beautiful conversations and letters in later years, inspired me with an insight that helped me, rather against his own advice, to read my German idealists aright, and to see what is, after all, the eternal truth beneath all this pragmatism. For Professor James's pragmatism, despite its entertaining expressions of horror of the eternal, actually does state one aspect of eternal truth. It is, namely, eternally true that all search for truth is a practical activity, with an ethical purpose, and that a purely theoretical truth, such as should guide no significant active process, is a barren absurdity. This, however, is so far precisely what Fichte spent his life in teaching. Professor James taught me, as a student, much the same lesson; and I equally prize and honor all of my masters for that lesson; and I have been trying to live up to it ever since I first began to study the nature of truth.

So far, then, I am a pragmatist. And I also fully agree that, if we ever get truth, the attainment of truth means a living and practical success in those active undertakings in terms of which we have been trying to assert and to verify our truth. I doubt not that to say, "This is true," is the same as to say: "The ideas by means of which I define this truth are the practically and genuinely successful ideas, the ideas such that, when I follow them, I really fulfil my deepest needs." All this I not only admit; but I earnestly insist that truth is an ethical concept; and I thank from my heart the great pragmatist who so fascinated his audience last year in this place; I thank him that he taught them what, in my youth, he helped to teach me, namely, that winning the truth means winning the success which we need, and for which the whole practical nature of our common humanity continually groans and travails together in pain until now.

And yet, and yet all this still leaves open one great question. When we seek truth, we indeed seek successful ideas. But what, in Heaven's name, constitutes success? Truth-seeking is indeed a practical endeavor. But what, in the name of all the loyal, is the goal of human endeavor? Truth is a living thing. We want leading and guidance. "Lead, kindly light,"—thus we address the truth. We are lost in the woods of time. We want the way, the truth, and the life. For nothing else does all our science and our common sense strive. But what is it to have genuine abundance of life? For what do we live?

Here our entire philosophy of loyalty, so far as it has yet been developed, comes to our aid. The loyal, as we have said, are the only human beings who can have any reasonable hope of genuine success. If they do not succeed, then nobody succeeds. And of course the loyal do indeed live with a constant, although not with an exclusive, reference to their own personal experience and to that of other individual men. They feel their present fascination for their cause. It thrills through them. Their loyalty has, even for them, in their individual capacity what Professor James calls a cash value. And of course they like to have their friends share such cash values. Yet I ask you: Are the loyal seeking *only* the mere collection of their private experiences of their personal thrills of fascination? If you hear loyal men say: "We are in this business just for what we as individuals —we and our individual fellows—can get out of it," do you regard that way of speech as an adequate expression of their really loyal spirit? When Arnold von Winkelried rushed on the Austrian spears, did he naturally say: "Look you, my friends, I seek, in experiential terms, the cash value of my devotion; see me draw the cash." My colleague would of course retort that the hero in question, according to the legend, said, as he died: "Make way for liberty." He therefore wanted liberty, as one may insist, to get these cash values. Yes, but liberty was no individual man, and no mere heap of individual men. Liberty was a cause, a certain superhuman unity of the ideal life of a free community. It was indeed expedient that one man should die for the people. But the people also was an *unio mystica* of many in one. For that cause the hero died. And no man has ever yet experienced, in his private and individual life, the whole true cash value of that higher unity. Nor will all the individual Swiss patriots, past, present, or future, viewed as a mere collection of creatures of a day, ever draw the cash in question. If the cause exists, the treasure exists, and is indeed a cash value upon a level higher than that of our passing human life. But loyalty does not live by selling its goods for present cash in the temple of its cause. Such pragmatism it drives out of the temple. It serves, and worships, and says to the cause: "Be thine the glory."

Loyalty, then, seeks success and from moment to moment indeed thrills with a purely fragmentary and temporary joy in its love of its service. But the joy depends on a belief in a distinctly superhuman type of unity of life. And so you indeed cannot express the value of your loyalty by pointing at the mere heap of the joyous thrills of the various loyal individuals. The loyal serve a real whole of life, an experiential value too rich for any expression in merely momentary terms.

Now, is it not very much so with our love of any kind of truth? Of course, we mortals seek for whatever verification of our truths we can get in the form of present success. But can you express our human definition of truth in terms of any collection of our human experiences of personal expediency?

Well, as to our concept of truth, let us consider a test case by way of helping ourselves to answer this question. Let us suppose that a witness appears, upon some witness-stand, and objects to taking the ordinary oath, because he has conscientious scruples, due to the fact that he is a recent pragmatist, who has a fine new definition of truth, in terms of which alone he can be sworn. Let us suppose him, hereupon, to be granted entire liberty to express his oath in his own way. Let him accordingly say, using, with technical scrupulosity, my colleague's definition of truth: "I promise to tell whatever is expedient and nothing but what is expedient, so help me future experience." I ask you: Do you think that this witness has expressed, with adequacy, that view of the nature of truth that you really wish a witness to have in mind? Of course, if he were a typical pragmatist, you would indeed be delighted to hear his testimony on the witness-stand or anywhere else. But would you accept his formula?

But let me be more precise as to the topic of this witness's possible testimony. I will use for the purpose Kant's famous case. Somebody, now dead, let us suppose, has actually left with the witness a sum of money as a wholly secret deposit to be some time returned. No written record was made of the transaction. No evidence exists that can in future be used to refute the witness if he denies the transaction and keeps the money. The questions to be asked of the witness relate, amongst other things, to whatever it may be that he believes himself to know about the estate of the deceased. I now ask, not what his duty is, but simply what it is that he rationally means to do in case he really intends to tell the truth about that deposit. Does he take merely the "forward-looking" attitude of my colleague's pragmatism? Does he mean merely to predict, as expedient, certain consequences which he expects to result either to himself or to the heirs of the estate? Of course his testimony will have consequences. But is it these which he is trying to predict? Are they his true object? Or does the truth of his statement mean the same as the expediency, either to himself or to the heirs, of any consequences whatever which may follow from his statement? Does the truth of his statement about the deposit even mean the merely present empirical fact that he now feels a belief in this statement or that he finds it just now congruent with the empirical sequences of his present memories? No, for the witness is not trying merely to tell how he feels. He is trying to tell the truth about the deposit. And the witness's belief is not the truth of his belief. Even his memory is not the truth to which he means to be a witness. And the future consequences of his making a true statement are for the witness irrelevant, since they are for the law and the heirs to determine. Yet one means something perfectly definite by the truth of the testimony of that witness. And that truth is simply inexpressible in such terms as those which my colleague employs. Yet the truth here in question is a simple truth about the witness's own personal past experience.

Now, such a case is only one of countless cases where we are trying to tell the truth about something which we all regard as being, in itself, a matter of genuine and concrete experience, while nevertheless we do not mean, "It is expedient just now for me to think this," nor yet, "I predict such and such consequences for my own personal experience, or for the future experience of some other individual man; and these predicted consequences constitute the truth of my present assertion." I say there are countless such cases where the truth that we mean is empirical indeed, but transcends all such expediencies and personal consequences. The very assertion, "Human experience, taken as a totality of facts, exists," is a momentous example of just such an assertion. We all believe that assertion. If that assertion is not actually true, then our whole frame of natural science, founded as it is on the common experience of many observers, crumbles into dust, our common sense world is nothing, business and society are alike illusions, loyalty to causes is meaningless. Now that assertion, "Human experience, that is, the totality of the experiences of many men, really exists," is an assertion which you and I regard as perfectly true. Yet no individual man ever has verified, or ever will verify, that assertion. For no man, taken as this individual man, experiences the experience of anybody but himself. Yet we all regard that assertion as true.

My colleague, of course, would say, as in fact he has often said, that his assertion is one of the numerous instances of that process of trading on credit which he so freely illustrates. We do not verify this assertion. But we accept it on credit as verifiable. However, the credit simile is a dangerous one here, so long as one conceives that the verification which would pay the cash would be a payment in the form of such human experience as you and I possess. For the assertion, "The experience of many men exists," is an assertion that is essentially unverifiable by any one man. If the "cash value" of the assertion means, then, its verifiability by any man, then the credit in question is one that simply cannot be turned into such cash by any conceivable process, occurring in our individual lives, since the very idea of the real existence of the experience of many men excludes, by its definition, the direct presence of this experience of various men within the experience of any one of these men. The credit value in question would thus be a *mere* fiat value, so long as the only cash values are those of the experiences of individual men, and the truth of our assertion would mean simply that we find it expedient to treat as verifiable what we know cannot be verified. Hereupon, of course, we should simply be trading upon currency that has no cash value. Whoever does verify the fact that the experience of many men exists, if such a verifier there be, is a superhuman being, an union of the empirical lives of many men in the complex of a single experience. And if our credit of the assertion that many men exist is convertible into cash at all, that cash is not laid up where the moth and rust of our private human experience doth from moment to moment corrupt the very data that we see; but is laid up in a realm where our experiences, past, present, future, are the object of a conspectus that is not merely temporal and transient. Now all the natural sciences make use of the persuasion that the experiences of various men exist, and that there is a unity of such experiences. This thesis, then, is no invention of philosophers.

My colleague, in answer, would of course insist that as a fact you and I are now believing that many men exist, and that human experience in its entirety exists, *merely* because, in the long run, we find that this belief is indeed congruous with our current and purely personal experience, and is therefore an expedient idea of ours. But I, in answer, insist that common sense well feels this belief to be indeed from moment to moment expedient, and yet clearly distinguishes between that expediency and the truth which common sense all the while attributes to the belief. The distinction is precisely the one which my fancied illustration of the pragmatist on the witness-stand has suggested. It is a perfectly universal distinction and a commonplace one. Tell me, "This opinion is true," and whatever you are talking about I may agree or disagree or doubt; yet in any case you have stated a momentous issue. But tell me, "I just now find this belief expedient, it feels to me congruous" and you have explicitly given me just a scrap of your personal biography, and have told me no other truth whatever than a truth about the present state of your feelings.

If, however, you emphasize my colleague's wording to the effect that a truth is such because it proves to be an idea that is expedient "in the long run," I once more ask you: *When* does a man experience the whole of the real facts about the "long run"? At the beginning of the long run, when the end is not yet, or at the end, when, perhaps, he forgets, like many older men, what were once the expediencies of his youth? What decides the truth about the long run? My exalted moments, when anything that I like seems true, or my disappointed moments, when I declare that I have always had bad luck? To appeal to the genuinely real "long run" is only to appeal in still another form to a certain ideally fair conspectus of my own whole life,—a conspectus which I, in my private human experience, never get. Whoever gets the conspectus of my whole life, to see what, in the long run, is indeed for me expedient,—whoever, I say, gets that conspectus, if such a being there indeed is,—is essentially superhuman in his type of consciousness. For he sees what I only get in the form of an idea; namely, the true sense and meaning of my life.

In vain, then, does one try adequately to define the whole of what we mean by truth either in terms of our human feelings of expediency or in terms of our instantaneous thrills of joy in success, or in terms of any other verifications that crumble as the instant flies. All such verifications we use, just as we use whatever perishes. Any such object is a fragment, but we want the whole. Truth is itself a cause, and is largely as one must admit, for us mortals, just now, what we called, in our last lecture, a lost cause—else how should these pragmatists be able thus to imagine a vain thing, and call that truth which is but the crumbling expediency of the moment? Our search for truth is indeed a practical process. The attainment of truth means success. Our verifications, so far as we ever get them, are momentary fragments of that success. But the genuine success that we demand is an ethical success, of precisely the type which all the loyal seek, when they rejoice in giving all for their cause.

But you will now all the more eagerly demand in what sense we can ever get any warrant for saying that we know any truth whatever. In seeking truth we do not seek the mere crumbling successes of the passing instants of human life. We seek a city out of sight. What we get of success within our passing experience is rationally as precious to us as it is, just because we believe that attainment to be a fragment of an essentially superhuman success, which is won in the form of a higher experience than ours,—a conspectus wherein our human experiences are unified. But what warrant have we for this belief?

I will tell you how I view the case. We need unity of life. In recognizing that need my own pragmatism consists. Now, we never find unity present to our human experience in more than a fragmentary shape. We get hints of higher unity. But only the fragmentary unity is won at any moment of our lives. We therefore form ideas—very fallible ideas—of some unity of experience, an unity such as our idea of any science or any art or any united people or of any community or of any other cause, any other union of many human experiences in one, defines. Now, if our ideas are in any case indeed true, then such an unity is as a fact successfully experienced upon some higher level than ours, and is experienced in some conspectus of life which wins what we need, which approves our loyalty, which fulfils our rational will, and which has in its wholeness what we seek. And then we ourselves with all our ideas and strivings are in and of this higher unity of life. Our loyalty to truth is a hint of this unity. Our transient successes are fragments of the true success. But suppose our ideas about the structure of this higher unity to be false in any of their details. Suppose, namely, any of our causes to be wrongly viewed by us. Then there is still real that state of facts, whatever it is, which, if just now known to us, would show us this falsity of our various special ideas. Now, only an experience, a consciousness of some system of contents, could show the falsity of any idea. Hence this real state of facts, this constitution of the genuine universe, whatever it is, must again be a reality precisely in so far as it is also a conspectus of facts of experience.

We therefore already possess at least one true idea, precisely in so far as we say: "The facts of the world are what they are; the real universe exposes our errors and makes them errors." And when we say this, we once more appeal to a conspectus of experience in which ours is included. For I am in error only in case my present ideas about the true facts of the whole world of experience are out of concord with the very meaning that I myself actively try to assign to these ideas. My ideas are in any detail false, only if the very experience to which I mean to appeal, contains in its conspectus contents which I just now imperfectly conceive. In any case, then, the truth is possessed by precisely that whole of experience which I never get, but to which my colleague also inevitably appeals when he talks of the "long run," or of the experiences of humanity in general.

Whatever the truth, then, or the falsity of any of my special convictions about this or that fact may be, the real world, which refutes my false present ideas in so far as they clash with its wholeness, and which confirms them just in so far as they succeed in having significant relations to its unity,—this real world, I say, is a conspectus of the whole of experience. And this whole of experience is in the closest real relation to my practical life, precisely in so far as, for me, the purpose of my life is to get into unity with the whole universe, and precisely in so far as the universe itself is just that conspectus of experience that we all mean to define and to serve whatever we do, or whatever we say.

But the real whole conspectus of experience, the real view of the totality of life, the real expression of that will to live in and for the whole, which every assertion of truth and every loyal deed expresses—well, it must be a conspectus that includes whatever facts are indeed facts, be they past, present, or future. I call this whole of experience an eternal truth. I do not thereby mean, as my colleague seems to imagine, that the eternal first exists, and that then our life in time comes and copies that eternal order. I mean simply that the whole of experience includes all temporal happenings, contains within itself all changes, and, since it is the one whole that we all want and need, succeeds in so far as it supplements all failures, accepts all, even the blindest of services, and wins what we seek. Thus winning it is practically good and worthy.

But if one insists, How do you know all this? I reply: I know simply that to try to deny the reality of this whole truth is simply to reaffirm it. Any special idea of mine may be wrong, even as any loyal deed may fail, or as any cause may become, to human vision, a lost cause. But to deny that there is truth, or that there is a real world, is simply to say that the

whole truth is that there is no whole truth, and that the real fact is that
there is no fact real at all. Such assertions are plain self-contradictions.
And on the other hand, by the term "real world," defined as it is for us
by our ideal needs, we mean simply that whole of experience in which
we live, and in unity with which we alone succeed.

Loyalty, then, has its own metaphysic. This metaphysic is expressed in
a view of things which conceives our experience as bound up in a real
unity with all experience,—an unity which is essentially good, and in
which all our ideas possess their real fulfilment and success. Such a view
is true, simply because if you deny its truth you reaffirm that very truth
under a new form.

Truth, meanwhile, means, as pragmatism asserts, the fulfilment of a
need. But we all need the superhuman, the city out of sight, the union
with all life,—the essentially eternal. This need is no invention of the
philosophers. It is the need which all the loyal feel, whether they know it
or not, and whether they call themselves pragmatists or not. To define
this need as pragmatism in its recent forms has done, to reduce truth to
expediency, is to go about crying *cash, cash,* in a realm where there is no
cash of the sort that loyalty demands, that every scientific inquiry presupposes, and that only the unity of the experiences of many in one
furnishes.

If we must, then, conceive recent pragmatism under the figure of a
business enterprise,—a metaphor which my colleague's phraseology so
insistently invites,—I am constrained therefore to sum up its position
thus: First, with a winning clearness, and with a most honorable frankness
it confesses bankruptcy, so far as the actually needed cash payments of
significant truth are concerned. Secondly, it nevertheless declines to go
into the hands of any real receiver, for it is not fond of anything that
appears too absolute. And thirdly, it proposes simply and openly to go on
doing business under the old style and title of the truth. "After all," it says,
"are we not, every one of us, fond of credit values?"

But I cannot conceive the position of the loyal to be, in fact, so hopelessly embarrassed as this. The recent pragmatists themselves are, in fact,
practically considered very loyal lovers of genuine truth. They simply
have mistaken the true state of their accounts. We all know, indeed, little
enough. But the loyal man, I think, whether he imagines himself to be a
recent pragmatist or not, has a rational right to say this: My cause par-
takes of the nature of the only truth and reality that there is. My life is an
effort to manifest such eternal truth, as well as I can, in a series of temporal
deeds. I may serve my cause ill. I may conceive it erroneously. I may lose
it in the thicket of this world of transient experience. My every human
deed may involve a blunder. My mortal life may seem one long series of
failures. But I know that my cause liveth. My true life is hid with the cause
and belongs to the eternal.

Letter to James

Southern Ocean, circ. 600 miles out of Melbourne
Lat. circ. 40° S; Long. circ. 135° E.
May 21, 1888

DEAR JAMES,—

It ought to be a long letter, if it were to undertake to tell the whole story of my life since I last saw Boston Light; but it must be a short one, since I have so many others to write. . . . I don't know, of course, how I shall feel on land, but here in my place of safety I seem to myself to be entirely cured. There was indeed a long period of depression . . . but all this . . . is no longer in order. With the winds and the birds of the southern sea came a new life. My wits had been working all along. In the deepest of my nothingness I read mechanics, and mathematics, and Martineau, and even Casanova, with an impartial insight into the essential nothingness of definite integrals, easily conquered maidens, and divine laws—one and all. But while I mused dispassionately upon the world of passion, my head was clear so far as the mere mechanics of thinking went. And now that passion has come again, and the good Lord seems to have some life in his world of *Sonnen und Milchstrassen,* my wits grow more constructive, and I more and more look upon the voyage as a very highly educating experience. In fine, I have largely straightened out the big metaphysical tangle about continuity, freedom, and the world-formula which, as you remember, I had aboard with me when I started; and I am ready to amuse you with a metaphysical speculation of a very simple, but, as now seems to me, of a very expansive nature, which does more to make the dry bones of my "Universal Thought" live than any prophesying that I have heretofore had the fortune to do. The fields of speculation are very wide and romantic, after all, and great is the fun of bringing down new game.

My companionships aboard the ship have been highly agreeable. The Captain, a Yankee and Cape Cod man, who has read a good deal in the long sea hours of his life, is contemplative. Once in a while I have to explain to him metaphysics, as thus: We sit on deck in the tropics, gazing into the heavens, and talking over Newcomb's *Astronomy,* which Captain has been reading. He grows now more and more meditative over the vast stellar distances, and the rest, and at last observes: "Well, sometimes it seems to me like nothing so much as a dream. Don't it ever occur to you that perhaps the whole thing above there and our life, too, is a dream of ours, and perhaps there ain't anything anyhow, that's real?" I admit having had such thoughts. "Well now, what do you teach your classes at Harvard about all this?" Thus called upon to explain amid the trade-winds, and under the softly flapping canvas, the mysteries of absolute idealism, I put the thing thus: "There was once a countryman," I say, "from Cape Cod, who went to Boston to hear Mark Twain lecture, and to delight his soul with the most mirth-compelling of our humorists. But, as I have heard, when he was in Boston, he was misdirected, so that he heard not Mark Twain, but one of Joseph Cook's Monday Lectures. But he steadfastly believed that he was hearing Mark. So when he went home to Cape Cod, they asked him of Mark Twain's lecture. 'Was it *very* funny?' 'Oh, it was *funny,* yes,—it was *funny,*' replies the countryman cautiously, 'but then, you see, it wasn't so *damned* funny.' Even so, Captain," say I, "I teach at Harvard that the world and the heavens and the stars are all *real,* but not so *damned* real, you see." The Captain has been a devout student of the *Religious Aspect* from time to time ever since, though in lucid intervals he affirms that the whole is consarned nonsense, and thereupon he falls back upon Macaulay's essay on Bacon, which he reads to his wife as a fortification of his commonsense. The rest of the ship's life is very amusing, on the whole. I escaped altogether sea-sickness, at the outset of the voyage, probably because of my abnormal nerves. God be with thine house. . . . Yours very truly,

JOSIAH ROYCE

GEORGE SANTAYANA

(1863-1952)

George Santayana was born in Madrid in 1863 and died in Rome in 1952. *The main facts of his life are related in his "General Confession," which is the first of the selections that follow. Brought to the United States at the age of eight, Santayana grew up in Boston, attended Harvard, and was for more than twenty years the colleague of James and Royce, who admired their former student but who also seem to have been puzzled by him. He wrote extensively in philosophy, composed poems and dialogues, a novel, and superbly polished essays and literary criticism. He was one of the supreme stylists in the history of philosophy, and the author of what may well be the finest work in substantive moral philosophy produced in the twentieth century,* The Life of Reason.

Santayana lived alone, and he stood alone in philosophy. He was indifferent and almost contemptuous of the controversies between different schools, and he pursued his own interests in his own way. His importance as a philosopher, therefore, can easily be overlooked. His approach to philosophy was personal and literary, and he did not pretend to offer radically new solutions to ancient problems. Yet underneath its limpid and elegant style The Life of Reason *was an immensely serious work. Its five volumes present a coherent philosophy of civilization based on the study of the symbols by which men live in their common-sense affairs, and in society, religion, art and science. Its program was the same as Hegel's—to study the progress of the mind through life and time, and to appraise human institutions in the light of rational ideals. Yet it was uncompromisingly naturalistic and biological in its premises, and frankly relativistic in its justification of the moral outlook it presented. The book is noteworthy for unrelenting critical standards combined with an unillusioned acceptance of men as they are, and for its mixture of detached irony with dramatic sympathy for diverse ways of life. It is the book of a man who practiced philosophy unapologetically as an exercize in the arts of discrimination, as an effort to find the lights by which a reasonable man might live.*

Santayana's later work, though he seems to have preferred it to The Life of Reason, *has at once a more argumentative and a less public character. It is more austere; it is also more crabbed in the preferences it expresses, and at times seems to be the work of a man who is merely striking an attitude. The dialectic in Santayana's later books such as* Scepticism and Animal Faith, *however, is more clearly and carefully developed than in* The Life of Reason. *His theory of knowledge, his "materialism" in natural philosophy, and his detached moral æstheticism, all emerge in starker outline, and it is to these books that one must go to find the fundamental principles of Santayana's systematic philosophy. Even in Santayana's early work there is a combination of the pragmatic view of human intelligence with a view of the mind that goes back to earlier British empiricism, and which stresses the passivity of the mind and the role of consciousness as a mere signal of the existence of a world which consciousness never directly apprehends. This view becomes dominant in Santayana's later work.*

Santayana's relation to the American scene has interested both him and his critics. Though he was sometimes sympathetic to what he thought were America's special qualities, he disliked the busyness of American life, criticized its pressures towards conformity, and spent the last forty years of his life in Europe, but while there is much in Santayana's philosophy that is all his own, there is also much that cannot be understood unless we remember that he grew to maturity in America and was reacting to American themes. "It is as an American writer," he wrote, "that I must be counted, if I am counted at all."

"A General Confession" consists of three separate essays. The first appeared in 1930 in Contemporary American Philosophy, *edited by G. P. Adams and William P. Montague; the second is an excerpt from the preface written by Santayana in 1936 to Volume I of the Triton Edition of his collected works; the third is the preface to Volume VII of these works. These essays first appeared together, in the form in which they are reprinted here, in* The Philosophy of George Santayana, *edited by Paul Arthur Schlipp (1940). The first selection from* The Life of Reason *is the introduction to* Reason in Common Sense; *it is followed by selections from* Reason in Religion, Reason in Art, *and* Reason in Science *(1905), and by Santayana's preface to the second edition of* The Life of Reason *(1922). The philosophical dialogue, "Normal Madness," is from* Dialogues in Limbo, *published in 1926. Although it appeared three years later than* Scepticism and Animal Faith, *from which the succeeding selection is taken, it provides a concise introduction to Santayana's later philosophy. The letters which conclude these selections from Santayana's works are all taken from* The Letters of George Santayana, *edited by Daniel Cory (1955).*

A General Confession

HOW CAME A CHILD BORN IN SPAIN OF SPANISH PARENTS TO BE EDUCATED in Boston and to write in the English language? The case of my family was unusual. We were not emigrants; none of us ever changed his country, his class, or his religion. But special circumstances had given us hereditary points of attachment in opposite quarters, moral and geographical; and now that we are almost extinct—I mean those of us who had these mixed associations—I may say that we proved remarkably staunch in our complex allegiances, combining them as well as logic allowed, without at heart ever disowning anything. My philosophy in particular may be regarded as a synthesis of these various traditions, or as an attempt to view them from a level from which their several deliverances may be justly understood. I do not assert that such was actually the origin of my system; in any case its truth would be another question. I propose simply to describe as best I can the influences under which I have lived, and leave it for the reader, if he cares, to consider how far my philosophy may be an expression of them.

In the first place, we must go much farther afield than Boston or Spain, into the tropics, almost to the antipodes. Both my father and my mother's father were officials in the Spanish civil service in the Philippine Islands. This was in the 1840's and 1850's, long before my birth; for my parents were not married until later in life, in Spain, when my mother was a widow. But the tradition of the many years which each of them separately had spent in the East was always alive in our household. Those had been, for both, their more romantic and prosperous days. My father had studied the country and the natives, and had written a little book about the Island of Mindanao; he had been three times round the world in the sailing-ships of the period, and had incidentally visited England and the United States, and been immensely impressed by the energy and order prevalent in those nations. His respect for material greatness was profound, yet not unmixed with a secret irony or even repulsion. He had a seasoned and incredulous mind, trained to see other sorts of excellence also: in his boyhood he had worked in the studio of a professional painter of the school of Goya, and had translated the tragedies of Seneca into Spanish verse. His transmarine experiences, therefore, did not rattle, as so often happens, in an empty head. The sea itself, in those days, was still vast and blue, and the lands beyond it full of lessons and wonders. From childhood I have lived in the imaginative presence of interminable ocean spaces, coconut islands, blameless Malays, and immense continents swarming with Chinamen, polished and industrious, obscene and philosophical. It was habitual with me to think of scenes and customs pleasanter than those about me. My own travels have never carried me far from the frontiers of Christendom or of respectability, and chiefly back and forth across the North Atlantic—thirty-eight fussy voyages; but in mind I have always seen these things on an ironical background enormously empty, or breaking out in spots, like Polynesia, into nests of innocent particoloured humanity.

My mother's figure belonged to the same broad and somewhat exotic landscape; she had spent her youth in the same places; but the moral note resounding in her was somewhat different. Her father, José Borrás, of Reus in Catalonia, had been a disciple of Rousseau, an enthusiast and a wanderer: he taught her to revere pure reason and republican virtue and to abhor the vices of a corrupt world. But her own temper was cool and stoical, rather than ardent, and her disdain of corruption had in it a touch of elegance. At Manila, during the time of her first marriage, she had been rather the grand lady, in a style half Creole, half early Victorian. Virtue, beside those tropical seas, might stoop to be indolent. She had given a silver dollar every morning to her native major-domo, with which to provide for the family and the twelve servants, and keep the change for his wages. Meantime she bathed, arranged the flowers, received visits, and did embroidery. It had been a spacious life; and in our narrower circumstances in later years the sense of it never forsook her.

Her first husband, an American merchant established in Manila, had been the ninth child of Nathaniel Russell Sturgis, of Boston (1779-1856). In Boston, accordingly, her three Sturgis children had numerous relations and a little property, and there she had promised their father to bring them up in case of his death. When this occurred, in 1857, she therefore established herself in Boston; and this fact, by a sort of prenatal or pre-established destiny, was the cause of my connection with the Sturgis family, with Boston, and with America.

It was in Madrid in 1862, where my mother had gone on a visit intended to be temporary, that my father and she were married. He had been an old friend of hers and of her first husband's, and was well aware of her settled plan to educate her children in America, and recognized the propriety of that arrangement. Various projects and combinations were mooted: but the matter eventually ended in a separation, friendly, if not altogether pleasant to either party. My mother returned with her Sturgis children to live in the United States and my father and I remained in Spain. Soon, however, this compromise proved unsatisfactory. The education and prospects which my father, in his modest retirement, could offer me in Spain were far from brilliant; and in 1872 he decided to take me to Boston, where, after remaining for one cold winter, he left me in my mother's care and went back to Spain.

I was then in my ninth year, having been born on December 16, 1863, and I did not know one word of English. Nor was I likely to learn the language at home, where the family always continued to speak a Spanish more or less pure. But by a happy thought I was sent during my first winter in Boston to a Kindergarten, among much younger children, where there were no books, so that I picked up English by ear before knowing how it was written: a circumstance to which I probably owe speaking the language without a marked foreign accent. The Brimmer School, the Boston Latin School, and Harvard College then followed in order: but apart from the taste for English poetry which I first imbibed from our excellent English master, Mr. Byron Groce, the most decisive influences over my mind in boyhood continued to come from my family, where, with my grown-up brother and sisters, I was the only child. I played no games, but sat at home all the afternoon and evening reading or drawing; especially devouring anything I could find that regarded religion, architecture, or geography.

In the summer of 1883, after my Freshman year, I returned for the first time to Spain to see my father. Then, and during many subsequent holidays which I spent in his company, we naturally discussed the various careers that might be open to me. We should both of us have liked the Spanish army or diplomatic service: but for the first I was already too old, and our means and our social relations hardly sufficed for the second. Moreover, by that time I felt like a foreigner in Spain, more acutely so than in America, although for more trivial reasons: my Yankee manners seemed outlandish there, and I could not do myself justice in the language. Nor was I inclined to overcome this handicap, as perhaps I might have done with a little effort: nothing in Spanish life or literature at that time particularly attracted me. English had become my only possible instrument, and I deliberately put away everything that might confuse me in that medium. English, and the whole Anglo-Saxon tradition in literature and philosophy, have always been a medium to me rather than a source. My natural affinities were elsewhere. Moreover, scholarship and learning of any sort seemed to me a means, not an end. I always hated to be a professor. Latin and Greek, French, Italian, and German, although I can read them, were languages which I never learned well. It seemed an accident to me if the matters which interested me came clothed in the rhetoric of one or another of these nations: I was not without a certain temperamental rhetoric of my own in which to recast what I adopted. Thus in renouncing everything else for the sake of English letters I might be said to have been guilty, quite unintentionally, of a little stratagem, as if I had set out to say plausibly in English as many un-English things as possible.

This brings me to religion, which is the head and front of everything. Like my parents, I have always set myself down officially as a Catholic: but this is a matter of sympathy and traditional allegiance, not of philosophy. In my adolescence, religion on its doctrinal and emotional side occupied me much more than it does now. I was more unhappy and unsettled; but I have never had any unquestioning faith in any dogma, and have never been what is called a practising Catholic. Indeed, it would hardly have been possible. My mother, like her father before her, was a Deist: she was sure there was a God, for who else could have made the world? But God was too great to take special thought for man: sacrifices, prayers, churches, and tales of immortality were invented by rascally priests in order to dominate the foolish. My father, except for the Deism, was emphatically of the same opinion. Thus, although I learned my prayers and catechism by rote, as was then inevitable in Spain, I knew that my parents regarded all religion as a work of human imagination: and I agreed, and still agree, with them there. But this carried an implication in their minds against which every instinct in me rebelled, namely that the works of human imagination are bad. No, said I to myself even as a boy: they are good, they alone are good; and the rest—the whole real world—is ashes in the mouth. My sympathies were entirely with those other members of my family who were devout believers. I loved the Christian epic, and all those doctrines and observances which bring it down into daily life: I thought how glorious it would have been to be a Dominican friar, preaching that epic eloquently, and solving afresh all the knottiest and sublimest mysteries of theology. I was delighted with anything, like Mallock's *Is Life Worth Living?*, which seemed to rebuke the fatuity of that age. For my own part, I was quite sure that life was not worth living; for if religion was false everything was worthless, and almost everything, if religion was true. In this youthful pessimism I was hardly more foolish than so many amateur mediævalists and religious æsthetes of my generation. I saw the same alternative between Catholicism and complete disillusion: but I was never afraid of disillusion, and I have chosen it.

Since those early years my feeling on this subject have become less strident. Does not modern philosophy teach that our idea of the so-called real world is also a work of imagination? A religion—for there are other religions than the Christian—simply offers a system of faith different from the vulgar one, or extending beyond it. The question is which imaginative system you will trust. My matured conclusion has been that no system is to be trusted, not even that of science in any literal or pictorial sense; but all systems may be used and, up to a certain point, trusted as symbols. Science expresses in human terms our dynamic relation to surrounding reality. Philosophies and religions, where they do not misrepresent these same dynamic relations and do not contradict science, express destiny in moral dimensions, in obviously mythical and poetical images: but how else should these moral truths be expressed at all in a traditional or popular fashion? Religions are the great fairy-tales of the conscience.

When I began the formal study of philosophy as an undergraduate at Harvard, I was already alive to the fundamental questions, and even had a certain dialectical nimbleness, due to familiarity with the fine points of theology: the arguments for and against free will and the proofs of the existence of God were warm and clear in my mind. I accordingly heard James and Royce with more wonder than serious agreement: my scholastic logic would have wished to reduce James at once to a materialist and Royce to a solipsist, and it seemed strangely irrational in them to resist such simplification. I had heard many Unitarian sermons (being taken to hear them lest I should become too Catholic), and had been interested in them so far as they were rationalistic and informative, or even amusingly irreligious, as I often thought them to be: but neither in those discourses nor in Harvard philosophy was it easy for me to understand the Protestant combination of earnestness with waywardness. I was used to see water flowing from fountains, architectural and above ground: it puzzled me to see it drawn painfully in bucketfuls from the subjective well, muddied, and half spilt over.

There was one lesson, however, which I was readier to learn, not only at Harvard from Professor Palmer and afterwards at Berlin from Paulsen, but from the general temper of that age well represented for me by the *Revue Des Deux Mondes* (which I habitually read from cover to cover) and by the works of Taine and of Matthew Arnold—I refer to the historical spirit of the nineteenth century, and to that splendid panorama of nations and religions, literatures and arts, which it unrolled before the imagination. These picturesque vistas into the past came to fill in circumstantially that geographical and moral vastness to which my imagination was already accustomed. Professor Palmer was especially skilful in bending the mind to a suave and sympathetic participation in the views of all philosophers in turn: were they not all great men, and must not the aspects of things which seemed persuasive to them be really persuasive? Yet even this form of romanticism, amiable as it is, could not altogether put to sleep my scholastic dogmatism. The historian of philosophy may be as sympathetic and as self-effacing as he likes: the philosopher in him must still ask whether any of those successive views were true, or whether the later ones were necessarily truer than the earlier: he cannot, unless he is a shameless sophist, rest content with a truth *pro tem*. In reality the sympathetic reconstruction of history is a literary art, and it depends for its plausibility as well as for its materials on a conventional belief in the natural world. Without this belief no history and no science would be anything but a poetic fiction, like a classification of the angelic choirs. The necessity of naturalism as a foundation for all further serious opinions was clear to me from the beginning. Naturalism might indeed be criticized —and I was myself intellectually and emotionally predisposed to criticize it, and to oscillate between supernaturalism and solipsism—but if naturalism was condemned, supernaturalism itself could have no point of application in the world of fact; and the whole edifice of human knowledge would crumble, since no perception would then be a report and no judgment would have a transcendent object. Hence historical reconstruction seemed to me more honestly and solidly practised by Taine, who was a professed naturalist, than by Hegel and his school, whose naturalism, though presupposed at every stage, was disguised and distorted by a dialectic imposed on it by the historian and useful at best only in simplifying his dramatic perspectives and lending them a false absoluteness and moralistic veneer.

The influence of Royce over me, though less important in the end than that of James, was at first much more active. Royce was the better dialectician, and traversed subjects in which I was naturally more interested. The point that particularly exercised me was Royce's Theodicy or justification for the existence of evil. It would be hard to exaggerate the ire which his arguments on this subject aroused in my youthful breast. Why that emotion? Romantic sentiment that could find happiness only in tears and virtue only in heroic agonies was something familiar to me and not unsympathetic: a poetic play of mine, called *Lucifer,* conceived in those days, is a clear proof of it. I knew Leopardi and Musset largely by heart; Schopenhauer was soon to become, for a brief period, one of my favourite authors. I carried Lucretius in my pocket: and although the spirit of the poet in that case was not romantic, the picture of human existence which he drew glorified the same vanity. Spinoza, too, whom I was reading under Royce himself, filled me with joy and enthusiasm: I gathered at once from him a doctrine which has remained axiomatic with me ever since, namely that good and evil are relative to the natures of animals, irreversible in that relation, but indifferent to the march of cosmic events, since the force of the universe infinitely exceeds the force of any one of its parts. Had I found, then, in Royce only a romantic view of life, or only pessimism, or only stoical courage and pantheistic piety, I should have taken no offence, but readily recognized the poetic truth or the moral legitimacy of those positions. Conformity with fate, as I afterwards came to see, belongs to post-rational morality, which is a normal though optional development of human sentiment: Spinoza's "intellectual love of God" was a shining instance of it.

But in Royce these attitudes, in themselves so honest and noble, seemed to be somehow embroiled and rendered sophistical: nor was he alone in this, for the same moral equivocation seemed to pervade Hegel, Browning, and Nietzsche. That which repelled me in all these men was the survival of a sort of forced optimism and pulpit unction, by which a cruel and nasty world, painted by them in the most lurid colours, was nevertheless set up as the model and standard of what ought to be. The duty of an honest moralist would have been rather to distinguish, in this bad or mixed reality, the part, however small, that could be loved and chosen from the remainder, however large, which was to be rejected and renounced. Certainly the universe was in flux and dynamically single: but this fatal flux could very well take care of itself; and it was not so fluid that no islands of a relative permanence and beauty might not be formed in it. Ascetic conformity was itself one of these islands: a scarcely inhabitable peak from which almost all human passions and activities were excluded. And the Greeks, whose deliberate ethics was rational, never denied the vague early Gods and the environing chaos, which perhaps would return in the end: but meantime they built their cities bravely on the hill-tops, as we all carry on pleasantly our temporal affairs, although we know that to-morrow we die. Life itself exists only by a modicum of organization, achieved and transmitted through a world of change: the momentum of such organization first creates a difference between good and evil, or gives them a meaning at all. Thus the core of life is always hereditary, steadfast, and classical; the margin of barbarism and blind adventure round it may be as wide as you will, and in some wild hearts the love of this fluid margin may be keen, as might be any other loose passion. But to *preach* barbarism as the only good, in ignorance or hatred of the possible perfection of every natural thing, was a scandal: a belated Calvinism that remained fanatical after ceasing to be Christian. And there was a further circumstance which made this attitude particularly odious to me. This romantic love of evil was not thoroughgoing: wilfulness and disorder were to reign only in spiritual matters; in government and industry, even in natural science, all was to be order and mechanical progress. Thus the absence of a positive religion and of a legislation, like that of the ancients, intended to be rational and final, was very far from liberating the spirit for higher flights: on the contrary, it opened the door to the pervasive tyranny of the world over the soul. And no wonder: a soul rebellious to its moral heritage is too weak to reach any firm definition of its inner life. It will feel lost and empty unless it summons the random labours of the contemporary world to fill and to enslave it. It must let mechanical and civic achievements reconcile it to its own moral confusion and triviality.

It was in this state of mind that I went to Germany to continue the study of philosophy—interested in all religious or metaphysical systems, but sceptical about them and scornful of any romantic worship or idealization of the real world. The life of a wandering student, like those of the Middle Ages, had an immense natural attraction for me—so great, that I have never willingly led any other. When I had to choose a profession, the prospect of a quiet academic existence seemed the least of evils. I was fond of reading and observation, and I liked young men; but I have never been a diligent student either of science or art, nor at all ambitious to be learned. I have been willing to let cosmological problems and technical questions solve themselves as they would or as the authorities agreed for the moment that they should be solved. My pleasure was rather in expression, in reflection, in irony: my spirit was content to intervene, in whatever world it might seem to find itself, in order to disentangle the intimate moral and intellectual echoes audible to it in that world. My naturalism or materialism is no academic opinion: it is not a survival of the alleged materialism of the nineteenth century, when all the professors of philosophy were idealists: it is an everyday conviction which came to me, as it came to my father, from experience and observation of the world at large, and especially of my own feelings and passions. It seems to me that those who are not materialists cannot be good observers of themselves: they may hear themselves thinking, but they cannot have watched themselves acting and feeling; for feeling and action are evidently accidents of matter. If a Democritus or Lucretius or Spinoza or Darwin works within the lines of nature, and clarifies some part of that familiar object, that fact is the ground of my attachment to them: they have the savour of truth; but what the savour of truth is, I know very well without their help. Consequently there is no opposition in my mind between materialism and a Platonic or even Indian discipline of the spirit. The recognition of the material world and of the conditions of existence in it merely enlightens the spirit concerning the source of its troubles and the means to its happiness or deliverance: and it was happiness or deliverance, the supervening supreme expression of human will and imagination, that alone really concerned me. This alone was genuine philosophy: this alone was the life of reason.

Had the life of reason ever been cultivated in the world by people with a sane imagination? Yes, once, by the Greeks. Of the Greeks, however, I knew very little: the philosophical and political departments at Harvard had not yet discovered Plato and Aristotle. It was with the greater pleasure that I heard Paulsen in Berlin expounding Greek ethics with a sweet reasonableness altogether worthy of the subject: here at last was a vindication of order and beauty in the institutions of men and in their ideas. Here, through the pleasant medium of transparent myths or of summary scientific images, like the water of Thales, nature was essentially understood and honestly described; and here, for that very reason, the free mind could disentangle its true good, and could express it in art, in manners, and even in the most refined or the most austere spiritual discipline. Yet, although I knew henceforth that in the Greeks I should find the natural support and point of attachment for my own philosophy, I was not then collected or mature enough to pursue the matter; not until ten years later, in 1896-1897, did I take the opportunity of a year's leave of absence to go to

England and begin a systematic reading of Plato and Aristotle under Dr. Henry Jackson of Trinity College, Cambridge. I am not conscious of any change of opinion supervening, nor of any having occurred earlier; but by that study and change of scene my mind was greatly enriched; and the composition of *The Life of Reason* was the consequence.

This book was intended to be a summary history of the human imagination, expressly distinguishing those phases of it which showed what Herbert Spencer called an adjustment of inner to outer relations; in other words, an adaptation of fancy and habit to material facts and opportunities. On the one hand, then, my subject being the imagination, I was never called on to step beyond the subjective sphere. I set out to describe, not nature or God, but the ideas of God or nature bred in the human mind. On the other hand, I was not concerned with these ideas for their own sake, as in a work of pure poetry or erudition, but I meant to consider them in their natural genesis and significance; for I assumed throughout that the whole life of reason was generated and controlled by the animal life of man in the bosom of nature. Human ideas had, accordingly, a symptomatic, expressive, and symbolic value: they were the inner notes sounded by man's passions and by his arts: and they became rational partly by their vital and inward harmony—for reason is a harmony of the passions—and partly by their adjustment to external facts and possibilities—for reason is a harmony of the inner life with truth and with fate. I was accordingly concerned to discover what wisdom is possible to an animal whose mind, from beginning to end, is poetical: and I found that this could not lie in discarding poetry in favour of a science supposed to be clairvoyant and literally true. Wisdom lay rather in taking everything good-humouredly, with a grain of salt. In science there was an element of poetry, pervasive, inevitable, and variable: it was strictly scientific and true only in so far as it involved a close and prosperous adjustment to the surrounding world, at first by its origin in observation and at last by its application in action. Science was the mental accompaniment of art.

Here was a sort of pragmatism: the same which I have again expressed, I hope more clearly, in one of the *Dialogues in Limbo* entitled "Normal Madness." The human mind is a faculty of dreaming awake, and its dreams are kept relevant to its environment and to its fate only by the external control exercised over them by Punishment, when the accompanying conduct brings ruin, or by Agreement, when it brings prosperity. In the latter case it is possible to establish correspondences between one part of a dream and another, or between the dreams of separate minds, and so create the world of literature, or the life of reason. I am not sure whether this notion, that thought is a controlled and consistent madness, appears among the thirteen pragmatisms which have been distinguished, but I have reason to think that I came to it under the influence of William James; nevertheless, when his book on *Pragmatism* appeared, about the same time

as my *Life of Reason,* it gave me a rude shock. I could not stomach that
way of speaking about truth; and the continual substitution of human psychology—normal madness, in my view—for the universe, in which man
is but one distracted and befuddled animal, seemed to me a confused
remnant of idealism, and not serious.

The William James who had been my master was not this William
James of the later years, whose pragmatism and pure empiricism and romantic metaphysics have made such a stir in the world. It was rather the
puzzled but brilliant doctor, impatient of metaphysics, whom I had known
in my undergraduate days, one of whose maxims was that to study the
abnormal was the best way of understanding the normal; or it was the
genial author of *The Principles of Psychology,* chapters of which he read
from the manuscript and discussed with a small class of us in 1889. Even
then what I learned from him was perhaps chiefly things which explicitly
he never taught, but which I imbibed from the spirit and background of
his teaching. Chief of these, I should say, was a sense for the immediate:
for the unadulterated, unexplained, instant fact of experience. Actual experience, for William James, however varied or rich its assault might be,
was always and altogether of the nature of a sensation: it possessed a vital,
leaping, globular unity which made the only fact, the flying fact, of our
being. Whatever continuities of quality might be traced in it, its existence
was always momentary and self-warranted. A man's life or soul borrowed
its reality and imputed wholeness from the intrinsic actuality of its successive parts; existence was a perpetual rebirth, a travelling light to which
the past was lost and the future uncertain. The element of indetermination
which James felt so strongly in this flood of existence was precisely the
pulse of fresh unpredictable sensation, summoning attention hither and
thither to unexpected facts. Apprehension in him being impressionistic—
that was the age of impressionism in painting too—and marvellously free
from intellectual assumptions or presumptions, he felt intensely the fact
of contingency, or the contingency of fact. This seemed to me not merely
a peculiarity of temperament in him, but a profound insight into existence,
in its inmost irrational essence. Existence, I learned to see, is intrinsically
dispersed, seated in its distributed moments, and arbitrary not only as a
whole, but in the character and place of each of its parts. Change the bits,
and you change the mosaic: nor can we count or limit the elements, as in
a little closed kaleidoscope, which may be shaken together into the next
picture. Many of them, such as pleasure and pain, or the total picture itself, cannot possibly have pre-existed.

But, said I to myself, were these novelties for that reason unconditioned?
Was not sensation, by continually surprising us, a continual warning to
us of fatal conjunctions occurring outside? And would not the same conjunctions, but for memory and habit, always produce the same surprises?
Experience of indetermination was no proof of indeterminism; and when

James proceeded to turn immediate experience into ultimate physics, his thought seemed to me to lose itself in words or in confused superstitions. Free will, a deep moral power contrary to a romantic indetermination in being, he endeavoured to pack into the bias of attention—the most temperamental of accidents. He insisted passionately on the efficacy of consciousness, and invoked Darwinian arguments for its utility—arguments which assumed that consciousness was a material engine absorbing and transmitting energy: so that it was no wonder that presently he doubted whether consciousness existed at all. He suggested a new physics or metaphysics in which the essences given in immediate experience should be deployed and hypostatized into the constituents of nature: but this pictorial cosmology had the disadvantage of abolishing the human imagination, with all the pathos and poetry of its animal status. James thus renounced that gift for literary psychology, that romantic insight, in which alone he excelled; and indeed his followers are without it. I pride myself on remaining a disciple of his earlier unsophisticated self, when he was an agnostic about the universe, but in his diagnosis of the heart an impulsive poet: a master in the art of recording or divining the lyric quality of experience as it actually came to him or to me.

Lyric experience and literary psychology, as I have learned to conceive them, are chapters in the life of one race of animals, in one corner of the natural world. But before relegating them to that modest station (which takes nothing away from their spiritual prerogatives) I was compelled to face the terrible problem which arises when, as in modern philosophy, literary psychology and lyric experience are made the fulcrum or the stuff of the universe. Has this experience any external conditions? If it has, are they knowable? And if it has not, on what principle are its qualities generated or its episodes distributed? Nay, how can literary psychology or universal experience have any seat save the present fancy of the psychologist or the historian? Although James had been bothered and confused by these questions, and Royce had enthroned his philosophy upon them, neither of these my principal teachers seemed to have come to clearness on the subject: it was only afterwards, when I read Fichte and Schopenhauer, that I began to see my way to a solution. We must oscillate between a radical transcendentalism, frankly reduced to a solipsism of the living moment, and a materialism posited as a presupposition of conventional sanity. There was no contradiction in joining together a scepticism which was not a dogmatic negation of anything and an animal faith which avowedly was a mere assumption in action and description. Yet such oscillation, if it was to be justified and rendered coherent, still demanded some understanding of two further points: what, starting from immediate experience, was the *causa cognoscendi* of the natural world; and what, starting from the natural world, was the *causa fiendi* of immediate experience?

On this second point (in spite of the speculations of my friend Strong) I have not seen much new light. I am constrained merely to register as a brute fact the emergence of consciousness in animal bodies. A psyche, or nucleus of hereditary organization, gathers and governs these bodies, and at the same time breeds within them a dreaming, suffering, and watching mind. Such investigations as those of Fraser and of Freud have shown how rich and how mad a thing the mind is fundamentally, how pervasively it plays about animal life, and how remote its first and deepest intuitions are from any understanding of their true occasions. An interesting and consistent complement to these discoveries is furnished by behaviourism, which I heartily accept on its positive biological side: the hereditary life of the body, modified by accident or training, forms a closed cycle of habits and actions. Of this the mind is a concomitant spiritual expression, invisible, imponderable, and epiphenomenal, or, as I prefer to say, hypostatic: for in it the moving unities and tensions of animal life are synthesized on quite another plane of being, into actual intuitions and feelings. This spiritual fertility in living bodies is the most natural of things. It is unintelligible only as all existence, change, or genesis is unintelligible; but it might be better understood, that is, better assimilated to other natural miracles, if we understood better the life of matter everywhere, and that of its different aggregates.

On the other point raised by my naturalism, namely on the grounds of faith in the natural world, I have reached more positive conclusions. Criticism, I think, must first be invited to do its worst: nothing is more dangerous here than timidity or convention. A pure and radical transcendentalism will disclaim all knowledge of fact. Nature, history, the self become ghostly presences, mere notions of such things; and the being of these images becomes purely internal to them; they exist in no environing space or time; they possess no substance or hidden parts, but are all surface, all appearance. Such a being, or quality of being, I call an essence; and to the consideration of essences, composing of themselves an eternal and infinite realm, I have lately devoted much attention. To that sphere I transpose the familiar pictures painted by the senses, or by traditional science and religion. Taken as essences, all ideas are compatible and supplementary to one another, like the various arts of expression; it is possible to perceive, up to a certain point, the symbolic burden of each of them, and to profit by the spiritual criticism of experience which it may embody. In particular, I recognize this spiritual truth in the Neo-Platonic and Indian systems, without admitting their fabulous side: after all, it is an old maxim with me that many ideas may be convergent as poetry which would be divergent as dogmas. This applies, in quite another quarter, to that revolution in physics which is now loudly announced, sometimes as the bankruptcy of science, sometimes as the breakdown of materialism. This revolution becomes, in my view, simply a change in notation. Matter may be called gravity or an electric charge or a tension in an ether; mathematics may readjust its equations to more accurate observations; any fresh description of nature which may result will still be a product of human wit, like the Ptolemaic and the Newtonian systems, and nothing but an intellectual symbol for man's contacts with matter, in so far as they have gone or as he has become distinctly sensitive to them. The real matter, within him and without, will meantime continue to rejoice in its ancient ways, or to adopt new ones, and incidentally to create these successive notions of it in his head.

When all the data of immediate experience and all the constructions of thought have thus been purified and reduced to what they are intrinsically, that is, to eternal essences, by a sort of counterblast the sense of existence, of action, of ambushed reality everywhere about us, becomes all the clearer and more imperious. This assurance of the not-given is involved in action, in expectation, in fear, hope, or want: I call it animal faith. The object of this faith is the substantial energetic thing encountered in action, whatever this thing may be in itself; by moving, devouring, or transforming this thing I assure myself of its existence; and at the same time my respect for it becomes enlightened and proportionate to its definite powers. But throughout, for the description of it in fancy, I have only the essences which my senses or thought may evoke in its presence; these are my inevitable signs and names for that object. Thus the whole sensuous and intellectual furniture of the mind becomes a store whence I may fetch terms for the description of nature, and may compose the silly home-poetry in which I talk to myself about everything. All is a tale told, if not by an idiot, at least by a dreamer; but it is far from signifying nothing. Sensations are rapid dreams: perceptions are dreams sustained and developed at will; sciences are dreams abstracted, controlled, measured, and rendered scrupulously proportional to their occasions. Knowledge accordingly always remains a part of imagination in its terms and in its seat; yet by virtue of its origin and intent it becomes a memorial and a guide to the fortunes of man in nature.

In the foregoing I have said nothing about my sentiments concerning æsthetics or the fine arts; yet I have devoted two volumes to those subjects, and I believe that to some people my whole philosophy seems to be little but rhetoric or prose poetry. I must frankly confess that I have written some verses; and at one time I had thoughts of becoming an architect or even a painter. The decorative and poetic aspects of art and nature have always fascinated me and held my attention above everything else. But in philosophy I recognize no separable thing called æsthetics; and what has gone by the name of the philosophy of art, like the so-called philosophy of history, seems to me sheer verbiage. There is in art nothing but manual knack and professional tradition on the practical side, and on the contemplative side pure intuition of essence, with the inevitable intellectual or luxurious pleasure which pure intuition involves. I can draw no distinction—save for academic programmes—between moral and æsthetic values: beauty, being a good, is a moral good; and the practice and enjoyment of art, like all practice and all enjoyment, fall within the sphere of morals—at least if by morals we understand moral economy and not moral superstition. On the other hand, the good, when actually realized and not merely pursued from afar, is a joy in the immediate; it is possessed with wonder and is in that sense æsthetic. Such pure joy when blind is called pleasure, when centred in some sensible image is called beauty, and when diffused over the thought of ulterior propitious things is called happiness, love, or religious rapture. But where all is manifest, as it is in intuition, classifications are pedantic. Harmony, which might be called an æsthetic principle, is also the principle of health, of justice, and of happiness. Every impulse, not the æsthetic mood alone, is innocent and irresponsible in its origin and precious in its own eyes; but every impulse or indulgence, including the æsthetic, is evil in its effect, when it renders harmony impossible in the general tenor of life, or produces in the soul division and ruin. There is no lack of folly in the arts; they are full of inertia and affectation and of what must seem ugliness to a cultivated taste; yet there is no need of bringing the catapult of criticism against it: indifference is enough. A society will breed the art which it is capable of, and which it deserves; but even in its own eyes this art will hardly be important or beautiful unless it engages deeply the resources of the soul. The arts may die of triviality, as they were born of enthusiasm. On the other hand, there will always be beauty, or a transport akin to the sense of beauty, in any high contemplative moment. And it is only in contemplative moments that life is truly vital, when routine gives place to intuition, and experience is synthesized and brought before the spirit in its sweep and truth. The intention of my philosophy has certainly been to attain, if possible, such wide intuitions, and to celebrate the emotions with which they fill the mind. If this object be æsthetic and merely poetical, well and good: but it is a poetry or æstheticism which shines by disillusion and is simply intent on the unvarnished truth.

II

The liberal age in which I was born and the liberal circles in which I was educated flowed contentedly towards intellectual dissolution and anarchy. No atmosphere could have been more unfavourable to that solidity and singleness of conviction to which by nature I was addressed. I suffered from a slack education, conflicting traditions, deadening social pressure, academic lumber, and partisan heat about false problems. The pure philosophy to which, in spirit, I was wedded from the beginning, the orthodox human philosophy in which I ought to have been brought up, has never had time to break through and show all its native force, pathos, and simplicity. I ought to have begun where I have ended.

Would it be possible to indicate, in a page or two, what I conceive orthodox human philosophy to be? Perhaps: because the thing is not un-known. The ancients came innocently upon it in various fields. Yet not even Aristotle, much less the moderns, ever conceived it in its entirety, with a just balance of its parts. I seem to recognise three orthodox schools of philosophy, each humanly right in its own sphere, but wrong in ignor-ing or denying the equal human rightness of the other two.

The Indians are orthodox in transcendental reflection. They take sys-tematically the point of view of the spirit. For there is an invisible and inevitable moral witness to everything, not a physical or psychological self, but a higher centre of observation to which this world, or any world, or any God, is an imposed and questionable accident. Being morally in-spired, being the voice of a living soul, this spirit has dramatic relations with the world which it encounters. The encounter may occasionally turn into a passionate embrace in which the spirit and all things seem merged in utterable unity. But that is a dramatic episode like any other: the tragic spirit revives and recovers its solitude. It would not be an actual spirit at all if it were not a personal moral being subject to fortune and needing to be saved. Spiritual philosophy would therefore not be orthodox if it were not ascetic and detached from the world.

The Greeks before Socrates reached orthodoxy in natural philosophy, which was re-established later in Spinoza and in modern science. Natural philosophers quarrel among themselves just because they are engaged in a common task with the issue undetermined. Yet they are all conspiring to trace and conceive the structure and history of this natural world in which everyone finds himself living.

The Greeks after Socrates founded orthodoxy in morals. I have en-deavoured to retrace this theme in *The Life of Reason* and in my entire criticism of literature and religion. The principles of orthodoxy here were most clearly laid down by Plato in the *Philebus* and in the First Book of the *Republic;* but unfortunately, contrary to the modesty of Socrates himself, these principles were turned instinctively into a new mythology, in the effort to lend power and cosmic ascendency to the good: a good which is *good* only because, at each point, life and aspiration are spon-taneously directed upon it. Ethics, as Aristotle said, is a part of politics, the foundation of this art being human nature, and its criterion harmony in living. But how should harmony be achieved in living if the inward spirit is distracted and the outer conditions of existence are unknown? Soundness in natural and in spiritual philosophy therefore seems requisite to soundness in politics.

That is all my message: that morality and religion are expressions of human nature; that human nature is a biological growth; and finally that spirit, fascinated and tortured, is involved in the process, and asks to be saved. What is salvation? Some organic harmony in forms and movements is requisite for life; but physical life is blind and groping and runs up continually against hostile forces, disease and death. It is therefore in the interests of life to become more intelligent and to establish a harmony also with the environment and the future. But life enlightened is spirit: the voice of life, and therefore aspiring to all the perfections to which life aspires, and loving all the beauties that life loves; yet at the same time spirit is the voice of truth and of destiny, bidding life renounce beauty and perfection and life itself, whenever and wherever these are impossible.

III

In *Winds of Doctrine* and my subsequent books, a reader of my earlier writings may notice a certain change of climate. There were natural causes for this change. I was weathering the age of fifty. My nearer relations were dead or dispersed. I had resigned my professorship at Harvard, and no longer crossed and re-crossed the Atlantic. I have explained the effect of these changes in the Preface to the later edition of the *Life of Reason,* and in what has already preceded here. My *Soliloquies in England* contain clear indications that, in spite of the war then raging, fancy in me had taken a new lease of life. I felt myself nearer than ever before to rural nature and to the perennial animal roots of human society. It was not my technical philosophy that was principally affected, but rather the meaning and status of philosophy for my inner man. The humanism characteristic of the *Sense of Beauty* and *Life of Reason* remained standing; but foundations were now supplied for that humanism by a more explicit and vigorous natural philosophy; a natural philosophy which, without being otherwise changed than as the growth of natural science might suggest, was itself destined to be enveloped later by the ontology contained in *Realms of Being.* These additions are buttresses and supports: the ontology justifies materialism, and the materialism justifies rational ethics and an æsthetic view of the mind.

Certainly materialism cannot justify moral ideals *morally.* Morally a sentiment can be confirmed only by another sentiment, for whatever that may be worth. But materialism justifies the life of reason martially, as a fighting organisation, and explains its possible strength and dominance. What from the moral point of view we call the instruments of reason are primarily the ground and cause of reason: and reason can control matter only because reason is matter organised, and assuming a form at once distinctive, plastic, and opportune. Unity of direction is thus imposed on our impulses; the impulses remain and continue to work and to take themselves most seriously; things tempt and hurt us as much as ever. Yet this very synthesis imposed upon the passions has brought steadiness and scope into the mind. The passions seem less absolute than before: we see them in a more tragic or comic light; and we see that even our noble and civilised life of reason is bought at a price. As there were wild animal joys that it has banished, so there may be divine insights that it cannot heed.

I had begun philosophising quite normally, by bleating like any young lamb: agitated by religion, passionately laying down the law for art and politics, and even bubbling over into conventional verses, which I felt to be oracular and irresistible. But my vocation was clear: my earliest speculation was at once intimate and universal, and philosophically religious, as it has always remained; yet not exclusively on the lines of that complete Christian system which first offered itself to my imagination. I was always aware of alternatives; nor did these alternatives seem utterly hostile and terrible. My enthusiasm was largely dramatic; I recited my Lucretius with as much gusto as my Saint Augustine; and gradually Lucretius sank deeper and became more satisfying. What I demanded unconditionally was dramatic wholeness. I wanted to articulate each possible system, to make it consistent, radical, and all-embracing. Hesitation and heresy were odious to me in any quarter; and I cared more for the internal religious force of each faith than for such external reasons as might be urged to prove that faith or to disprove it. What indeed could such external reasons be but corollaries to some different system, itself needing to be believed?

A judicial comparison of various systems of life and morals was therefore not possible for me until I had found a sure foothold for criticism, other than the histrionic convictions between which my youthful sentiment could so easily oscillate. This foothold was supplied to me by human nature, as each man after due Socratic self-questioning might find it in himself, and as Plato and Aristotle express it for mankind at large in their rational ethics. There is nothing unalterably fixed in this moral physiognomy of man, any more than in his bodily structure; but both are sufficiently recognisable and constant for the purposes of medicine and politics. The point of chief speculative interest is that morality, like health, is determined by the existing constitution of our animal nature, and the opportunities or denials that materially confront us; so that we are much deeper and more deeply bound to physical reality than our wayward thoughts and wishes might suggest. The potential, in an organic being developing through time, is necessarily richer and more important than the actual. The actual is superficial, occasional, ephemeral; present will and present consciousness are never the true self. They are phenomena elicited by circumstances from a psyche that remains largely unexpressed. Yet this psyche, this inherited nature or seed, flowers in those manifestations, filling them as they pass with beauty and passion: and nothing will be moral or personal in ideas except what they borrow by a secret circulation from the enduring heart. There, and not in any superstitious precepts, lies the root of duty and the criterion of perfection.

In saying this I am far from wishing to attribute a metaphysical fixity or unity to the psyche, or to claim for my own person an absolute singleness and consistency. Some passive drifting and some fundamental vagueness there must be in every animal mind; and the best-knit psyche still participates in the indefinite flux of matter, is self-forgetful in part, and is mortal. But this only proves that no man can be wholly a philosopher or an artist, or wholly himself. We are moral individuals, we exist as persons, only imperfectly, by grace of certain essences kindly imputed to us by our own thoughts or by the thoughts of others. There is always a moral chaos, though it be a dynamic mathematical order, beneath our rationalised memory or criticism: a chaos which is an indispensable support and continual peril to the spirit, as the sea is to a ship. Yet in our nautical housekeeping we may disregard the background. The deluge keeps our rational ark afloat, and our thoughts follow our treasures.

Yet not necessarily all our thoughts. The need of keeping a look-out may generate a disinterested interest in the winds and tides, and we may end by smiling at the moral reasons which we first assigned for the deluge. In my later writings I speak of something called the spiritual life; of a certain *disintoxication* clarifying those passions which the life of reason endeavours to harmonise. Is spirit then hostile to reason? Is reason hostile to spirit? Neither: but within the life of reason there is incidental rivalry in the types of organisation attempted, in their range, and in the direction in which the inevitable sacrifices are accepted. Spirit and reason, as I use the words, spring from the same root in organic life, namely, from the power of active adaptation possessed by animals, so that the external world and the future are regarded in their action. Being regarded in action, absent things are then regarded in thought; and this is intelligence. But intelligence and reason are often merely potential, as in habit, memory, institutions, and books: they become spirit only when they flower into actual consciousness. Spirit is essentially simpler, less troubled, more lyrical than reason: it is not specifically human. It may exist in animals, perhaps in plants, as it certainly exists in children; and in its outlook, far from being absorbed in tasks and cares, like reason, it is initially universal and addressed to anything and everything that there may happen to be.

Between the spiritual life and the life of reason there is accordingly no contradiction: they are concomitant: yet there is a difference of temper and level, as there is between agriculture and music. The ploughman may sing, and the fiddler at times may dig potatoes; but the vocations pull in different ways. Being ready for everything, and a product of vital harmony, spirit finds an initial delight in art and contrivance, in adventure and discovery, for these are forms of order and enlarged harmony: yet in the midst of business, spirit suspends business, and begins to wonder, to laugh, or to pray. A family quarrel may easily arise between these mental faculties; a philosopher sympathises naturally with speculation; but the ethics of this conflict are the same as in other conflicts: to know oneself, and to impose on oneself or on others only the sacrifices requisite to bring one's chosen life to perfection.

I have always disliked mystics who were not definite in their logic and orthodox in their religion. Spirit is not a power: it comes to fulfil, not to destroy. By understanding the world we may in a certain ideal sense transcend it; but we do not transcend it by misunderstanding it: on the contrary, we remain in that case dupes of our own flesh and our own egotism. Every temperament and every vocation, even the highest, engages us in a special course that imposes sweeping renunciations in other directions. But these renunciations would not be true sacrifices if the things sacrificed were not admittedly good. Marriage and wealth, sport and adventure, dominion and war are not condemned by the spiritual man in being renounced. They are left benevolently or sadly for the natural man, who is generously and inevitably engaged in them. The passions are the elements of life; nevertheless they are deceptive and tragic. They fade from the mind of the old man who can survey their full course; unless indeed he makes himself a shrill and emasculated echo of them, forgetting the dignity of years. Sometimes these passions shock and repel a young soul even at their first assault: and then we have the saint or seer by nature, who can transcend common experience without having tasted it; but this is a rare faculty, abnormal and not to be expected or even desired. Thus there is a certain option and practical incompatibility between spirituality and humanism, between poetry and business, between sheer logic and sound sense; but the conflict is only marginal, the things are concentric, and spirit merely heightens and universalises the synthesis which reason makes partially, as occasion requires, in the service of natural interests. To make this synthesis is itself a natural interest, as the child loves to look and to explore: and spirit, the conscience of nature that sees the truth of nature, is the most natural of things.

My later philosophy, then, on the moral side, merely develops certain ultimate themes of the inner life which had run in my head from the beginning: they had dominated my verse, and had reappeared in my early accounts of poetry and religion, of Platonic love, and post-rational morality. The developments in no way disturb the biological basis assigned to all life; they do not make my naturalistic ethics dogmatic. They are proposed merely as optional. They are confessions of the sentiment with which the spectacle of things and the discipline of experience can fill a reflective mind.

Within the same naturalistic frame my later philosophy has also elaborated the analysis of perception, of belief, and of "ideas" in general; and in this direction I have come to discriminate something which seems strangely to irritate my critics: I mean, what I call essence and the realm of essence. These words, and my whole presentation of this subject, were perhaps unfortunate. I have advanced an emancipating doctrine in traditional terms; the terms excite immediate scorn in modern radical quarters, while the emancipating doctrine horrifies those conservatives to whom the terms might not give offense. I am sorry: but this accident after all is of little consequence, especially as the same doctrine—loaded, no doubt, with other accidental lumber—is being propagated by various influential writers in uglier and more timely terms. The point is to reduce evidence to the actually evident, and to relegate all the rest to hypothesis, presumption, and animal faith. What I call essence is not something alleged to exist or subsist in some higher sphere: it is the last residuum of scepticism and analysis. Whatsoever existing fact we may think we encounter, there will be obvious features distinguishing that alleged fact from any dissimilar fact and from nothing. All such features, discernible in sense, thought, or fancy, are essences; and the realm of essence which they compose is simply the catalogue, infinitely extensible, of all characters logically distinct and ideally possible. Apart from the events they may figure in, these essences have no existence; and since the realm of essence, by definition, is infinitely comprehensive and without bias, it can exercise no control over the existing world, nor determine what features shall occur in events, or in what order.

Indeed, it might seem idle to have mentioned these pure essences at all, which living thought traverses unwittingly, as speech does the words of one's native language; yet the study of grammar is enlightening, and there is a clarifying and satiric force in the discrimination of essences. For the irony of fate will have it that these ghosts are the only realities we ever actually can find: and it is rather the thought-castles of science and the dramatic vistas of history that, for instant experience, are ghostly and merely imagined. What should mind be, if it were not a poetic cry? Mind does not come to repeat the world but to celebrate it. The essences evoked in sensation and thought are naturally original, graphic, and morally coloured. Consciousness was created by the muses; but meantime industrious nature, in our bodily organisation, takes good care to keep our actions moderately sane, in spite of our poetic genius.

Thus as in my younger days in respect to religions, so now in respect to all experience and all science, critical reflection has emancipated me from the horrid claim of ideas to literal truth. And just as religion, when seen to be poetry, ceases to be deceptive and therefore odious, and becomes humanly more significant than it seemed before; so experience and science, when seen to be woven out of essences and wholly symbolic, gain in moral colour and spirituality what they lose in dead weight. The dead weight falls back from sensuous images and intellectual myths to the material fatality that breeds and sustains them.

This fatality itself, in proving wholly arbitrary, seems to oppress us less; it inspires courage and good humour, rather than supplications and fears. Perhaps what the realm of essence, in its mute eternity, chiefly adds to our notion of nature is the proof that nature is contingent. An infinite canvas is spread before us on which any world might have been painted. The actuality of things is sharpened and the possibilities of things are enlarged. We cease to be surprised or distressed at finding existence unstable and transitory. Why should it have been otherwise? Not only must our own lives be insecure, as earthly seasons change, but perhaps all existence is in flux, even down to its first principles. *Dum vivimus vivamus*. Everything, so long as it recognisably endures, is free to deploy its accidental nature; and we may lead the life of reason with a good grace, harmonising as well as possible our various impulses and opportunities, and exploring the realm of essence as our genius may prompt.

The exposition of my philosophy is still incomplete, and in many directions, as for instance in mathematical physics, the development of it is beyond my powers. Yet virtually the whole system was latent in me from the beginning. When in adolescence I oscillated between solipsism and the Catholic faith, that was an accidental dramatic way of doing honour both to rigour and to abundance. But the oscillation was frivolous and the two alternate positions were self-indulgent. A self-indulgent faith sets up its casual myths and rashly clings to them as to literal truths; while a self-indulgent scepticism pretends to escape all dogma, forgetting its own presuppositions. With time it was natural that oscillation should give place to equilibrium; not, let us hope, to a compromise, which of all things is the most unstable and unphilosophical; but to a radical criticism putting each thing where it belongs. Without forgetting or disowning anything, myth might then be corrected by disillusion, and scepticism by sincerity. So transformed, my earliest affections can survive in my latest.

The Life of Reason

REASON IN COMMON SENSE

WHATEVER FORCES MAY GOVERN HUMAN LIFE, IF THEY ARE TO BE RECOG-
nised by man, must betray themselves in human experience. Progress in
science or religion, no less than in morals and art, is a dramatic episode
in man's career, a welcome variation in his habit and state of mind; although this variation may often regard or propitiate things external, adjustment to which may be important for his welfare. The importance of these
external things, as well as their existence, he can establish only by the
function and utility which a recognition of them may have in his life. The
entire history of progress is a moral drama, a tale man might unfold in a
great autobiography, could his myriad heads and countless scintillas of
consciousness conspire, like the seventy Alexandrian sages, in a single
version of the truth committed to each for interpretation. What themes
would prevail in such an examination of heart? In what order and with
what emphasis would they be recounted? In which of its adventures would
the human race, reviewing its whole experience, acknowledge a progress
and a gain? To answer these questions, as they may be answered speculatively and provisionally by an individual, is the purpose of the following
work.

A philosopher could hardly have a higher ambition than to make himself a mouth-piece for the memory and judgment of his race. Yet the most
casual consideration of affairs already involves an attempt to do the same
thing. Reflection is pregnant from the beginning with all the principles of
synthesis and valuation needed in the most comprehensive criticism. So
soon as man ceases to be wholly immersed in sense, he looks before and
after, he regrets and desires: and the moments in which prospect or retrospect takes place constitute the reflective or representative part of his life,
in contrast to the unmitigated flux of sensations in which nothing ulterior
is regarded. Representation, however, can hardly remain idle and merely
speculative. To the ideal function of envisaging the absent, memory and reflection will add (since they exist and constitute a new complication in
being) the practical function of modifying the future. Vital impulse, however, when it is modified by reflection and veers in sympathy with judg-

ments pronounced on the past, is properly called reason. Man's rational life consists in those moments in which reflection not only occurs but proves efficacious. What is absent then works in the present, and values are imputed where they cannot be felt. Such representation is so far from being merely speculative that its presence alone can raise bodily change to the dignity of action. Reflection gathers experiences together and perceives their relative worth; which is as much as to say that it expresses a new attitude of will in the presence of a world better understood and turned to some purpose. The limits of reflection mark those of concerted and rational action; they circumscribe the field of cumulative experience, or, what is the same thing, of profitable living.

Thus if we use the word life in a eulogistic sense to designate the happy maintenance against the world of some definite ideal interest, we may say with Aristotle that life is reason in operation. The *Life of Reason* will then be a name for that part of experience which perceives and pursues ideals— all conduct so controlled and all sense so interpreted as to perfect natural happiness.

Without reason, as without memory, there might still be pleasures and pains in existence. To increase those pleasures and reduce those pains would be to introduce an improvement into the sentient world, as if a devil suddenly died in hell or in heaven a new angel were created. Since the beings, however, in which these values would reside, would, by hypothesis, know nothing of one another, and since the betterment would take place unprayed-for and unnoticed, it could hardly be called a progress; and certainly not a progress in man, since man, without the ideal continuity given by memory and reason, would have no moral being. In human progress, therefore, reason is not a casual instrument, having its sole value in its service to sense; such a betterment in sentience would not be progress unless it were a progress in reason, and the increasing pleasure revealed some object that could please; for without a picture of the situation from which a heightened vitality might flow, the improvement could be neither remembered nor measured nor desired. The Life of Reason is accordingly neither a mere means nor a mere incident in human progress; it is the total and embodied progress itself, in which the pleasures of sense are included in so far as they can be intelligently enjoyed and pursued. To recount man's rational moments would be to take an inventory of all his goods; for he is not himself (as we say with unconscious accuracy) in the others. If he ever appropriates them in recollection or prophecy, it is only on the ground of some physical relation which they may have to his being.

Reason is as old as man and as prevalent as human nature; for we should not recognise an animal to be human unless his instincts were to some degree conscious of their ends and rendered his ideas in that measure relevant to conduct. Many sensations, or even a whole world of dreams, do not amount to intelligence until the images in the mind begin to represent in some way, however symbolic, the forces and realities confronted in action. There may well be intense consciousness in the total absence of rationality. Such consciousness is suggested in dreams, in madness, and may be found, for all we know, in the depths of universal nature. Minds peopled only by desultory visions and lusts would not have the dignity of human souls even if they seemed to pursue certain objects unerringly; for that pursuit would not be illumined by any vision of its goal. Reason and humanity begin with the union of instinct and ideation, when instinct becomes enlightened, establishes values in its objects, and is turned from a process into an art, while at the same time consciousness becomes practical and cognitive, beginning to contain some symbol or record of the co-ordinate realities among which it arises.

Reason accordingly requires the fusion of two types of life, commonly led in the world in well-nigh total separation, one a life of impulse expressed in affairs and social passions, the other a life of reflection expressed in religion, science, and the imitative arts. In the Life of Reason, if it were brought to perfection, intelligence would be at once the universal method of practice and its continual reward. All reflection would then be applicable in action and all action fruitful in happiness. Though this be an ideal, yet everyone gives it from time to time a partial embodiment when he practises useful arts, when his passions happily lead him to enlightenment, or when his fancy breeds visions pertinent to his ultimate good. Everyone leads the Life of Reason in so far as he finds a steady light behind the world's glitter and a clear residuum of joy beneath pleasure or success. No experience not to be repented of falls without its sphere. Every solution to a doubt, in so far as it is not a new error, every practical achievement not neutralised by a second maladjustment consequent upon it, every consolation not the seed of another greater sorrow, may be gathered together and built into this edifice. The Life of Reason is the happy marriage of two elements—impulse and ideation—which if wholly divorced would reduce man to a brute or to a maniac. The rational animal is generated by the union of these two monsters. He is constituted by ideas which have ceased to be visionary and actions which have ceased to be vain.

Thus the Life of Reason is another name for what, in the widest sense of the word, might be called Art. Operations become arts when their purpose is conscious and their method teachable. In perfect art the whole idea is creative and exists only to be embodied, while every part of the product is rational and gives delightful expression to that idea. Like art, again, the Life of Reason is not a power but a result, the spontaneous expression of liberal genius in a favouring environment. Both art and reason have natural sources and meet with natural checks; but when a process is turned successfully into an art, so that its issues have value and the ideas that accompany it become practical and cognitive, reflection, finding little that it cannot in some way justify and understand, begins to boast that it directs and has created the world in which it finds itself so much at home. Thus if art could extend its sphere to include every activity in nature, reason, being everywhere exemplified, might easily think itself omnipotent. This ideal, far as it is from actual realisation, has so dazzled men, that in their religion and mythical philosophy they have often spoken as if it were already actual and efficient. This anticipation amounts, when taken seriously, to a confusion of purposes with facts and of functions with causes, a confusion which in the interests of wisdom and progress it is important to avoid; but these speculative fables, when we take them for what they are—poetic expressions of the ideal—help us to see how deeply rooted this ideal is in man's mind, and afford us a standard by which to measure his approaches to the rational perfection of which he dreams. For the Life of Reason, being the sphere of all human art, is man's imitation of divinity.

To study such an ideal, dimly expressed though it be in human existence, is no prophetic or visionary undertaking. Every genuine ideal has a natural basis; anyone may understand and safely interpret it who is attentive to the life from which it springs. To decipher the Life of Reason nothing is needed but an analytic spirit and a judicious love of man, a love quick to distinguish success from failure in his great and confused experiment of living. The historian of reason should not be a romantic poet, vibrating impotently to every impulse he finds afoot, without a criterion of excellence or a vision of perfection. Ideals are free, but they are neither more numerous nor more variable than the living natures that generate them. Ideals are legitimate, and each initially envisages a genuine and innocent good; but they are not realisable together, nor even singly when they have no deep roots in the world. Neither is the philosopher compelled by his somewhat judicial office to be a satirist or censor, without sympathy for those tentative and ingenuous passions out of which, after all, his own standards must arise. He is the chronicler of human progress, and to measure that progress he should be equally attentive to the impulses that give it direction and to the circumstances amid which it stumbles toward its natural goal.

There is unfortunately no school of modern philosophy to which a critique of human progress can well be attached. Almost every school, indeed, can furnish something useful to the critic, sometimes a physical theory, sometimes a piece of logical analysis. We shall need to borrow from current science and speculation the picture they draw of man's conditions and environment, his history and mental habits. These may furnish a theatre and properties for our dramas; but they offer no hint of its plot and meaning. A great imaginative apathy has fallen on the mind. One-half the learned world is amused in tinkering obsolete armour, as Don Quixote did his helmet; deputing it, after a series of catastrophes, to be at last sound and invulnerable. The other half, the naturalists who have studied psychology and evolution, look at life from the outside, and the processes of Nature make them forget her uses. Bacon indeed had prized science for adding to the comforts of life, a function still commemorated by positivists in their eloquent moments. Habitually, however, when they utter the word progress it is, in their mouths, a synonym for inevitable change, or at best for change in that direction which they conceive to be on the whole predominant. If they combine with physical speculation some elements of morals, these are usually purely formal, to the effect that happiness is to be pursued (probably, alas! because to do so is a psychological law); but what happiness consists in we gather only from casual observations or by putting together their national prejudices and party saws.

The truth is that even this radical school, emancipated as it thinks itself, is suffering from the after-effects of supernaturalism. Like children escaped from school, they find their whole happiness in freedom. They are proud of what they have rejected, as if a great wit were required to do so; but they do not know what they want. If you astonish them by demanding what is their positive ideal, further than that there should be a great many people and that they should be all alike, they will say at first that what ought to be is obvious, and later they will submit the matter to a majority vote. They have discarded the machinery in which their ancestors embodied the ideal; they have not perceived that those symbols stood for the Life of Reason and gave fantastic and embarrassed expression to what, in itself, is pure humanity; and they have thus remained entangled in the colossal error that ideals are something adventitious and unmeaning, not having a soil in mortal life nor a possible fulfilment there.

The profound and pathetic ideas which inspired Christianity were attached in the beginning to ancient myths and soon crystallised into many new ones. The mythical manner pervades Christian philosophy; but myth succeeds in expressing ideal life only by misrepresenting its history and conditions. This method was indeed not original with the Fathers; they borrowed it from Plato, who appealed to parables himself in an open and harmless fashion, yet with disastrous consequences to his school. Nor was he the first; for the instinct to regard poetic fictions as revelations of supernatural facts is as old as the soul's primitive incapacity to distinguish dreams from waking perceptions, sign from thing signified, and inner emotions from external powers. Such confusions, though in a way they obey moral forces, make a rational estimate of things impossible. To misrepresent the conditions and consequences of action is no merely speculative error; it involves a false emphasis in character and an artificial balance and co-ordination among human pursuits. When ideals are hypostasised into powers alleged to provide for their own expression, the Life of Reason cannot be conceived; in theory its field of operation is pre-empted and its function gone, while in practice its inner impulses are turned awry by artificial stimulation and repression.

The Patristic systems, though weak in their foundations, were extraordinarily wise and comprehensive in their working out; and while they inverted life they preserved it. Dogma added to the universe fabulous perspectives; it interpolated also innumerable incidents and powers which gave a new dimension to experience. Yet the old world remained standing in its strange setting, like the Pantheon in modern Rome; and, what is more important, the natural springs of human action were still acknowledged, and if a supernatural discipline was imposed, it was only because experience and faith had disclosed a situation in which the pursuit of earthly happiness seemed hopeless. Nature was not destroyed by its novel appendages, nor did reason die in the cloister: it hibernated there, and could come back to its own in due season, only a little dazed and weakened by its long confinement. Such, at least, is the situation in Catholic regions, where the Patristic philosophy has not appreciably varied. Among Protestants Christian dogma has taken a new and ambiguous direction, which has at once minimised its disturbing effect in practice and isolated its primary illusion. The symptoms have been cured and the disease driven in.

The tenets of Protestant bodies are notoriously varied and on principle subject to change. There is hardly a combination of tradition and spontaneity which has not been tried in some quarter. If we think, however, of broad tendencies and ultimate issues, it appears that in Protestantism myth, without disappearing, has changed its relation to reality: instead of being an extension to the natural world myth has become its substratum. Religion no longer reveals divine personalities, future rewards, and tenderer Elysian consolations; nor does it seriously propose a heaven to be reached by a ladder nor a purgatory to be shortened by prescribed devotions. It merely gives the real world an ideal status and teaches men to accept a natural life on supernatural grounds. The consequence is that the most pious can give an unvarnished description of things. Even immortality and the idea of God are submitted, in liberal circles, to scientific treatment. On the other hand, it would be hard to conceive a more inveterate obsession than that which keeps the attitude of these same minds inappropriate to the objects they envisage. They have accepted natural conditions; they will not accept natural ideals. The Life of Reason has no existence for them, because, although its field is clear, they will not tolerate any human or finite standard of value, and will not suffer extant interests, which can alone guide them in action or judgment, to define the worth of life.

The after-effects of Hebraism are here contrary to its foundations; for the Jews loved the world so much that they brought themselves, in order to win and enjoy it, to an intense concentration of purpose; but this effort and discipline, which had of course been mythically sanctioned, not only failed of its object, but grew far too absolute and sublime to think its object could ever have been earthly; and the supernatural machinery which was to have secured prosperity, while that still enticed, now had to furnish some worthier object for the passion it had artificially fostered. Fanaticism consists in redoubling your effort when you have forgotten your aim.

An earnestness which is out of proportion to any knowledge or love of real things, which is therefore dark and inward and thinks itself deeper than the earth's foundations—such an earnestness, until culture turns it into intelligent interest, will naturally breed a new mythology. It will try to place some world of Afrites and shadowy giants behind the constellations, which it finds too distinct and constant to be its companions or supporters; and it will assign to itself vague and infinite tasks, for which it is doubtless better equipped than for those which the earth now sets before it. Even these, however, since they are parts of an infinite whole, the mystic may (histrionically, perhaps, yet zealously) undertake; but as his eye will be perpetually fixed on something invisible beyond, and nothing will be done for its own sake or enjoyed in its own fugitive presence, there will be little art and little joy in existence. All will be a tossing servitude and illiberal mist, where the parts will have no final values and the whole no pertinent direction.

In Greek philosophy the situation is far more auspicious. The ancients led a rational life and envisaged the various spheres of speculation as men might whose central interests were rational. In physics they leaped at once to the conception of a dynamic unity and general evolution, thus giving that background to human life which shrewd observation would always have descried, and which modern science has laboriously rediscovered. Two great systems offered, in two legitimate directions, what are doubtless the final and radical accounts of physical being. Heraclitus, describing the immediate, found it to be in constant and pervasive change: no substances, no forms, no identities could be arrested there, but as in the human soul, so in nature, all was instability, contradiction, reconstruction, and oblivion. This remains the empirical fact; and we need but to rescind the artificial division which Descartes has taught us to make between nature and life, to feel again the absolute aptness of Heraclitus's expressions. These were thought obscure only because they were so disconcertingly penetrating and direct. The immediate is what nobody sees, because convention and reflection turn existence, as soon as they can, into ideas; a man who discloses the immediate seems profound, yet his depth is nothing but innocence recovered and a sort of intellectual abstention. Mysticism, scepticism, and transcendentalism have all in their various ways tried to fall back on the immediate; but none of them has been ingenuous enough. Each has added some myth, or sophistry, or delusive artifice to its direct observation. Heraclitus remains the honest prophet of immediacy; a mystic without raptures or bad rhetoric, a sceptic who does not rely for his results on conventions unwittingly adopted, a transcendentalist without false pretentions or incongruous dogmas.

The immediate is not, however, a good subject for discourse, and the expounders of Heraclitus were not unnaturally blamed for monotony. All they could do was to iterate their master's maxim, and declare everything to be in flux. In suggesting laws of recurrence and a reason in which what is common to many might be expressed, Heraclitus had opened the door into another region: had he passed through, his philosophy would have been greatly modified, for permanent forms would have forced themselves on his attention no less than shifting materials. Such a Heraclitus would have anticipated Plato; but the time for such a synthesis had not yet arrived.

At the opposite pole from immediacy lies intelligibility. To reduce phenomena to constant elements, as similar and simple as possible, and to conceive their union and separation to obey constant laws, is what a natural philosopher will inevitably do so soon as his interest is not merely to utter experience but to understand it. Democritus brought this scientific ideal to its ultimate expression. By including psychic existence in his atomic system, he indicated a problem which natural science has since practically abandoned but which it may some day be compelled to take up. The atoms of Democritus seem to us gross, even for chemistry, and their quality would have to undergo great transformation if they were to support intelligibly psychic being as well; but that very grossness and false simplicity had its merits, and science must be for ever grateful to the man who at its inception could so clearly formulate its mechanical ideal. That the world is not so intelligible as we could wish is not to be wondered at. In other respects also it fails to respond to our ideals; yet our hope must be to find it more propitious to the intellect as well as to all the arts in proportion as we learn better how to live in it.

The atoms of what we call hydrogen or oxygen may well turn out to be worlds, as the stars are which make atoms for astromomy. Their inner organisation might be negligible on our rude plane of being; did it disclose itself, however, it would be intelligible in its turn only if constant parts and constant laws were discernible within each system. So that while atomism at a given level may not be a final or metaphysical truth, it will describe, on every level, the practical and efficacious structure of the world. We owe to Democritus this ideal of practical intelligibility; and he is accordingly an eternal spokesman of reason. His system, long buried with other glories of the world, has been partly revived; and although it cannot be verified in haste, for it represents an ultimate ideal, every advance in science reconstitutes it in some particular. Mechanism is not one principle of explanation among others. In natural philosophy, where to explain means to discover origins, transmutations, and laws, mechanism is explanation itself.

Heraclitus had the good fortune of having his physics absorbed by Plato. It is a pity that Democritus' physics was not absorbed by Aristotle. For with the flux observed, and mechanism conceived to explain it, the theory of existence is complete; and had a complete physical theory been incorporated into the Socratic philosophy, wisdom would have lacked none of its parts. Democritus, however, appeared too late, when ideal science had overrun the whole field and initiated a verbal and dialectical physics; so that Aristotle, for all his scientific temper and studies, built his natural philosophy on a lamentable misunderstanding, and condemned thought to confusion for two thousand years.

If the happy freedom of the Greeks from religious dogma made them the first natural philosophers, their happy political freedom made them the first moralists. It was no accident that Socrates walked the Athenian agora; it was no petty patriotism that made him shrink from any other scene. His science had its roots there, in the personal independence, intellectual vivacity, and clever dialectic of his countrymen. Ideal science lives in discourse; it consists in the active exercise of reason, in signification, appreciation, intent, and self-expression. Its sum total is to know oneself, not as psychology or anthropology might describe a man, but to know, as the saying is, one's own mind. Nor is he who knows his own mind forbidden to change it; the dialectician has nothing to do with future possibilities or with the opinion of anyone but the man addressed. This kind of truth is but adequate veracity; its only object is its own intent. Having developed in the spirit the consciousness of its meanings and purposes, Socrates rescued logic and ethics for ever from authority. With his friends the Sophists, he made man the measure of all things, after bidding him measure himself, as they neglected to do, by his own ideal. That brave humanity which had first raised its head in Hellas and had endowed so many things in heaven and earth, where everything was hitherto monstrous, with proportion and use, so that man's works might justify themselves to his mind, now found in Socrates its precise definition; and it was naturally where the Life of Reason had been long cultivated that it came finally to be conceived.

Socrates had, however, a plebeian strain in his humanity, and his utilitarianism, at least in its expression, hardly did justice to what gives utility to life. His condemnation for atheism—if we choose to take it symbolically —was not altogether unjust: the gods of Greece were not honoured explicitly enough in his philosophy. Human good appeared there in its principle; you would not set a pilot to mend shoes, because you knew your own purpose; but what purposes a civilised soul might harbour, and in what highest shapes the good might appear was a problem that seems not to have attracted his genius. It was reserved to Plato to bring the Socratic ethics to its sublimest expression and to elicit from the depths of the Greek conscience. Those ancestral ideals which had inspired its legislators and had been embodied in its sacred civic traditions. The owl of Minerva flew, as Hegel says, in the dusk of evening; and it was horror at the abandonment of all creative virtues that brought Plato to conceive them so sharply and to preach them in so sad a tone. It was after all but the love of beauty that made him censure the poets; for like a true Greek and a true lover he wished to see beauty flourish in the real world. It was love of freedom that made him harsh to his ideal citizens, that they might be strong enough to preserve the liberal life. And when he broke away from political preoccupations and turned to the inner life, his interpretations proved the absolute sufficiency of the Socratic method; and he left nothing pertinent unsaid on ideal love and ideal immortality.

Beyond this point no rendering of the Life of Reason has ever been carried. Aristotle improved the detail, and gave breadth and precision to many a part. If Plato possessed greater imaginative splendour and more enthusiasm in austerity, Aristotle had perfect sobriety and adequacy, with greater fidelity to the common sentiments of his race. Plato, by virtue of his scope and plasticity, together with a certain prophetic zeal, outran at times the limits of the Hellenic and the rational; he saw human virtue so surrounded and oppressed by physical dangers that he wished to give it mythical sanctions, and his fondness for transmigration and nether punishments was somewhat more than playful. If as a work of imagination his philosophy holds the first place, Aristotle's has the decisive advantage of being the unalloyed expression of reason. In Aristotle the conception of human nature is perfectly sound; everything ideal has a natural basis and everything natural an ideal development. His ethics, when thoroughly digested and weighed, especially when the meagre outlines are filled in with Plato's more discursive expositions, will seem therefore entirely final. The Life of Reason finds there its classic explication.

As it is improbable that there will soon be another people so free from preoccupations, so gifted, and so fortunate as the Greeks, or capable in consequence of so well exemplifying humanity, so also it is improbable that a philosopher will soon arise with Aristotle's scope, judgment, or authority, one knowing so well how to be both reasonable and exalted. It might seem vain, therefore, to try to do afresh what has been done before with unapproachable success; and instead of writing inferior things at great length about the Life of Reason, it might be simpler to read and to propagate what Aristotle wrote with such immortal justness and masterly brevity. But times change; and though the principles of reason remain the same the facts of human life and of human conscience alter. A new background, a new basis of application, appears for logic, and it may be useful to restate old truths in new words, the better to prove their eternal validity. Aristotle is, in his morals, Greek, concise, and elementary. As a Greek, he mixes with the ideal argument illustrations, appreciations, and conceptions which are not inseparable from its essence. In themselves, no doubt, these accessories are better than what in modern times would be substituted for them, being less sophisticated and of a nobler stamp; but to our eyes they disguise what is profound and universal in natural morality by embodying it in images which do not belong to our life. Our direst struggles and the last sanctions of our morality do not appear in them. The pagan world, because its maturity was simpler than our crudeness, seems childish to us. We do not find there our sins and holiness, our love, charity, and honour.

The Greek too would not find in our world the things he valued most, things to which he surrendered himself, perhaps, with a more constant self-sacrifice—piety, country, friendship, and beauty; and he might add that his ideals were rational and he could attain them, while ours are extravagant and have been missed. Yet even if we acknowledged his greater good fortune, it would be impossible for us to go back and become like him. To make the attempt would show no sense of reality and little sense of humour. We must dress in our own clothes, if we do not wish to substitute a masquerade for practical existence. What we can adopt from Greek morals is only the abstract principle of their development; their foundation in all the extant forces of human nature and their effort toward establishing a perfect harmony among them. These forces themselves have perceptibly changed, at least in their relative power. Thus we are more conscious of wounds to stanch and wrongs to fight against, and less of goods to attain. The movement of conscience has veered; the centre of gravity lies in another part of the character.

Another circumstance that invites a restatement of rational ethics is the impressive illustration of their principle which subsequent history has afforded. Mankind has been making extraordinary experiments of which Aristotle could not dream; and their result is calculated to clarify even his philosophy. For in some respects it needed experiments and clarification. He had been led into a systematic fusion of dialectic with physics, and of this fusion all pretentious modern philosophy is the aggravated extension. Socrates' pupils could not abandon his ideal principles, yet they could not bear to abstain from physics altogether; they therefore made a mock physics in moral terms, out of which theology was afterward developed. Plato, standing nearer to Socrates and being no naturalist by disposition, never carried the fatal experiment beyond the mythical stage. He accordingly remained the purer moralist, much as Aristotle's judgment may be preferred in many particulars. Their relative position may be roughly indicated by saying that Plato had no physics and that Aristotle's physics was false; so that ideal science in the one suffered from want of environment and control, while in the other it suffered from misuse in a sphere where it had no application.

What had happened was briefly this: Plato, having studied many sorts of philosophy and being a bold and universal genius, was not satisfied to leave all physical questions pending, as his master had done. He adopted, accordingly, Heraclitus's doctrine of the immediate, which he now called the realm of phenomena; for what exists at any instant, if you arrest and name it, turns out to have been an embodiment of some logical essence, such as discourse might define; in every fact some idea makes its appearance, and such an apparition of the ideal is a phenomenon. Moreover, another philosophy had made a deep impression on Plato's mind and had helped to develop Socratic definitions: Parmenides had called the concept of pure Being the only reality; and to satisfy the strong dialectic by which this doctrine was supported and at the same time to bridge the infinite chasm between one formless substance and many appearances irrelevant to it, Plato substituted the many Socratic ideas, all of which were relevant to appearance, for the one concept of Parmenides. The ideas thus acquired what is called metaphysical subsistence; for they stood in the place of the Eleatic Absolute, and at the same time were the realities that phenomena manifested.

The technique of this combination is much to be admired; but the feat is technical and adds nothing to the significance of what Plato has to say on any concrete subject. This barren triumph was, however, fruitful in misunderstandings. The characters and values a thing possessed were now conceived to subsist apart from it, and might even have preceded it and caused its existence; a mechanism composed of values and definitions could thus be placed behind phenomena to constitute a substantial physical world. Such a dream could not be taken seriously, until good sense was wholly lost and a bevy of magic spirits could be imagined peopling the infinite and yet carrying on the business of earth. Aristotle rejected the metaphysical subsistence of ideas, but thought they might still be essences operative in nature, if only they were identified with the life or form of particular things. The dream thus lost its frank wildness, but none of its inherent incongruity: for the sense in which characters and values make a thing what it is, is purely dialectical. They give it its status in the ideal world; but the appearance of these characters and values here and now is what needs explanation in physics, an explanation which can be furnished, of course, only by the physical concatenation and distribution of causes.

Aristotle himself did not fail to make this necessary distinction between efficient cause and formal essence; but as his science was only natural history, and mechanism had no plausibility in his eyes, the efficiency of the cause was always due, in his view, to its ideal quality; as in heredity the father's human character, not his physical structure, might seem to warrant the son's humanity. Every ideal, before it could be embodied, had to pre-exist in some other embodiment; but as when the ultimate purpose of the cosmos is considered it seems to lie beyond any given embodiment, the highest ideal must somehow exist disembodied. It must pre-exist, thought Aristotle, in order to supply, by way of magic attraction, a physical cause for perpetual movement in the world.

It must be confessed, in justice to this consummate philosopher, who is not less masterly in the use of knowledge than unhappy in divination, that the transformation of the highest good into a physical power is merely incidental with him, and due to a want of faith (at that time excusable) in mechanism and evolution. Aristotle's deity is always a moral ideal and every detail in its definition is based on discrimination between the better and the worse. No accommodation to the ways of nature is here allowed to cloud the kingdom of heaven; this deity is not condemned to do whatever happens nor to absorb whatever exists. It is mythical only in its physical application; in moral philosophy it remains a legitimate conception.

Truth certainly exists, if existence be not too mean an attribute for that eternal realm which is tenanted by ideals; but truth is repugnant to physical or psychical being. Moreover, truth may very well be identified with an impassible intellect, which should do nothing but possess all truth, with no point of view, no animal warmth, and no transitive process. Such an intellect and truth are expressions having a different metaphorical background and connotation, but, when thought out, an identical import. They both attempt to evoke that ideal standard which human thought proposes to itself. This function is their effective essence. It insures their eternal fixity, and this property surely endows them with a very genuine and sublime reality. What is fantastic is only the dynamic function attributed to them by Aristotle, which obliges them to inhabit some fabulous extension to the physical world. Even this physical efficacy, however, is spiritualised as much as possible, since deity is said to move the cosmos only as an object of love or an object of knowledge may move the mind. Such efficacy is imputed to a hypostasised end, but evidently resides in fact in the functioning and impulsive spirit that conceives and pursues an ideal, endowing it with whatever attraction it may seem to have. The absolute intellect described by Aristotle remains, therefore, as pertinent to the Life of Reason as Plato's idea of the good. Though less comprehensive (for it abstracts from all animal interests, from all passion and mortality), it is more adequate and distinct in the region it dominates. It expresses sublimely the goal of speculative thinking; which is none other than to live as much as may be in the eternal and to absorb and be absorbed in the truth.

The rest of ancient philosophy belongs to the decadence and rests in physics on eclecticism and in morals on despair. That creative breath which had stirred the founders and legislators of Greece no longer inspired their descendants. Helpless to control the course of events, they took refuge in abstention or in conformity, and their ethics became a matter of private economy and sentiment, no longer aspiring to mould the state or give any positive aim to existence. The time was approaching when both speculation and morals were to regard the other world; reason had abdicated the throne, and religion, after that brief interregnum, resumed it for long ages.

Such are the threads which tradition puts into the hands of an observer who at the present time might attempt to knit the Life of Reason ideally together. The problem is to unite a trustworthy conception of the conditions under which man lives with an adequate conception of his interests. Both conceptions, fortunately, lie before us. Heraclitus and Democritus, in systems easily seen to be complementary, gave long ago a picture of nature such as all later observation, down to our own day, has done nothing but fill out and confirm. Psychology and physics still repeat their ideas, often with richer detail, but never with a more radical or prophetic glance. Nor does the transcendental philosophy, in spite of its self-esteem, add anything essential. It was a thing taken for granted in ancient and scholastic philosophy that a being dwelling, like man, in the immediate, whose moments are in flux, needed constructive reason to interpret his experience and paint in his unstable consciousness some symbolic picture of the world. To have reverted to this constructive process and studied its stages is an interesting achievement; but the construction is already made by common-sense and science, and it was visionary insolence in the Germans to propose to make that construction otherwise. Retrospective self-consciousness is dearly bought if it inhibits the intellect and embarrasses the inferences which, in its spontaneous operation, it has known perfectly how to make. In the heat of scientific theorising or dialectical argument it is sometimes salutary to be reminded that we are men thinking; but, after all, it is no news. We know that life is a dream, and how should thinking be more? Yet the thinking must go on, and the only vital question is to what practical or poetic conceptions it is able to lead us.

Similarly the Socratic philosophy affords a noble and genuine account of what goods may be realised by living. Modern theory has not done so much to help us here, however, as it has in physics. It seldom occurs to modern moralists that theirs is the science of all good and the art of its attainment; they think only of some set of categorical precepts or some theory of moral sentiments, abstracting altogether from the ideals reigning in society, in science, and in art. They deal with the secondary question What ought I to do? without having answered the primary question, What ought to be? They attach morals to religion rather than to politics, and this religion unhappily long ago ceased to be wisdom expressed in fancy in order to become superstition overlaid with reasoning. They divide man into compartments and the less they leave in the one labelled "morality" the more sublime they think their morality is; and sometimes pedantry and scholasticism are carried so far that nothing but an abstract sense of duty remains in the broad region which should contain all human goods.

Such trivial sanctimony in morals is doubtless due to artificial views about the conditions of welfare; the basis is laid in authority rather than in human nature, and the goal in salvation rather than in happiness. One great modern philosopher, however, was free from these preconceptions, and might have reconstituted the Life of Reason had he had a sufficient interest in culture. Spinoza brought man back into nature, and made him the nucleus of all moral values, showing how he may recognise his environment and how he may master it. But Spinoza's sympathy with mankind fell short of imagination; any noble political or poetical ideal eluded him. Everything impassioned seemed to him insane, everything human necessarily petty. Man was to be a pious tame animal, with the stars shining above his head. Instead of imagination Spinoza cultivated mysticism, which is indeed an alternative. A prophet in speculation, he remained a levite in sentiment. Little or nothing would need to be changed in his system if the Life of Reason, in its higher ranges, were to be grafted upon it; but such affiliation is not necessary, and it is rendered unnatural by the lack of sweep and generosity in Spinoza's practical ideals.

For moral philosophy we are driven back, then, upon the ancients; but not, of course, for moral inspiration. Industrialism and democracy, the French Revolution, the Renaissance, and even the Catholic system, which in the midst of ancient illusions enshrines so much tenderness and wisdom, still live in the world, though forgotten by philosophers, and point unmistakably toward their several goals. Our task is not to construct but only to interpret ideals, confronting them with one another and with the conditions which, for the most part, they alike ignore. There is no need of refuting anything, for the will which is behind all ideals and behind most dogmas cannot itself be refuted; but it may be enlightened and led to reconsider its intent, when its satisfaction is seen to be either naturally impossible or inconsistent with better things. The age of controversy is past; that of interpretation has succeeded.

Here, then, is the programme of the following work: Starting with the immediate flux, in which all objects and impulses are given, to describe the Life of Reason; that is, to note what facts and purposes seem to be primary, to show how the conception of nature and life gathers around them, and to point to the ideals of thought and action which are approached by this gradual mastering of experience by reason. A great task, which it would be beyond the powers of a writer in this age either to execute or to conceive, had not the Greeks drawn for us the outlines of an ideal culture at a time when life was simpler than at present and individual intelligence more resolute and free.

REASON IN RELIGION

HOW RELIGION MAY BE AN EMBODIMENT OF REASON

Experience has repeatedly confirmed that well-known maxim of Bacon's, that "a little philosophy inclineth man's mind to atheism, but depth in philosophy bringeth men's minds about to religion." In every age the most comprehensive thinkers have found in the religion of their time and country something they could accept, interpreting and illustrating that religion so as to give it depth and universal application. Even the heretics and atheists, if they have had profundity, turn out after a while to be forerunners of some new orthodoxy. What they rebel against is a religion alien to their nature; they are atheists only by accident, and relatively to a convention which inwardly offends them, but they yearn mightily in their own souls after the religious acceptance of a world interpreted in their own fashion. So it appears in the end that their atheism and loud protestation were in fact the hastier part of their thought, since what emboldened them to deny the poor world's faith was that they were too impatient to understand it. Indeed, the enlightenment common to young wits and worm-eaten old satirists, who plume themselves on detecting the scientific ineptitude of religion—something which the blindest half see—is not nearly enlightened enough: it points to notorious facts incompatible with religious tenets literally taken, but it leaves unexplored the habits of thought from which those tenets sprang, their original meaning, and their true function. Such studies would bring the sceptic face to face with the mystery and pathos of mortal existence. They would make him understand why religion is so profoundly moving and in a sense so profoundly just. There must needs be something humane and necessary in an influence that has become the most general sanction of virtue, the chief occasion for art and philosophy, and the source, perhaps, of the best human happiness. If nothing, as Hooker said, is "so malapert as a splenetic religion," a sour irreligion is almost as perverse.

At the same time, when Bacon penned the sage epigram we have quoted he forgot to add that the God to whom depth in philosophy brings back men's minds is far from being the same from whom a little philosophy estranges them. It would be pitiful indeed if mature reflection bred no better conceptions than those which have drifted down the muddy stream of time, where tradition and passion have jumbled everything together. Traditional conceptions, when they are felicitous, may be adopted by the poet, but they must be purified by the moralist and disintegrated by the philosopher. Each religion, so dear to those whose life it sanctifies, and fulfilling so necessary a function in the society that has adopted it, necessarily contradicts every other religion, and probably contradicts itself. What religion a man shall have is a historical accident, quite as much as what language he shall speak. In the rare circumstances where a choice is possible, he may, with some difficulty, make an exchange; but even then he is only adopting a new convention which may be more agreeable to his personal temper but which is essentially as arbitrary as the old.

The attempt to speak without speaking any particular language is not more hopeless than the attempt to have a religion that shall be no religion in particular. A courier's or a dragoman's speech may indeed be often unusual and drawn from disparate sources, not without some mixture of personal originality; but that private jargon will have a meaning only because of its analogy to one or more conventional languages and its obvious derivation from them. So travellers from one religion to another, people who have lost their spiritual nationality, may often retain a neutral and confused residuum of belief, which they may egregiously regard as the essence of all religion, so little may they remember the graciousness and naturalness of that ancestral accent which a perfect religion should have. Yet a moment's probing of the conceptions surviving in such minds will show them to be nothing but vestiges of old beliefs, creases which thought, even if emptied of all dogmatic tenets, has not been able to smooth away at its first unfolding. Later generations, if they have any religion at all, will be found either to revert to ancient authority, or to attach themselves spontaneously to something wholly novel and immensely positive, to some faith promulgated by a fresh genius and passionately embraced by a converted people. Thus every living and healthy religion has a marked idiosyncrasy. Its power consists in its special and surprising message and in the bias which that revelation gives to life. The vistas it opens and the mysteries it propounds are another world to live in; and another world to live in—whether we expect ever to pass wholly into it or no—is what we mean by having a religion.

What relation, then, does this great business of the soul, which we call religion, bear to the Life of Reason? That the relation between the two is close seems clear from several circumstances. The Life of Reason is the seat of all ultimate values. Now the history of mankind will show us that whenever spirits at once lofty and intense have seemed to attain the highest joys, they have envisaged and attained them in religion. Religion would therefore seem to be a vehicle or a factor in rational life, since the ends of rational life are attained by it. Moreover, the Life of Reason is an ideal to which everything in the world should be subordinated; it establishes lines of moral cleavage everywhere and makes right eternally different from wrong. Religion does the same thing. It makes absolute moral decisions. It sanctions, unifies, and transforms ethics. Religion thus exercises a function of the Life of Reason. And a further function which is common to both is that of emancipating man from his personal limitations. In different ways religions promise to transfer the soul to better conditions. A supernaturally favoured kingdom is to be established for posterity upon earth, or for all the faithful in heaven, or the soul is to be freed by repeated purgations from all taint and sorrow, or it is to be lost in the absolute, or it is to become an influence and an object of adoration in the places it once haunted or wherever the activities it once loved may be carried on by future generations of its kindred. Now reason in its way lays before us all these possibilities: it points to common objects, political and intellectual, in which an individual may lose what is mortal and accidental in himself and immortalise what is rational and human; it teaches us how sweet and fortunate death may be to those whose spirit can still live in their country and in their ideas; it reveals the radiating effects of action and the eternal objects of thought.

Yet the difference in tone and language must strike us, so soon as it is philosophy that speaks. That change should remind us that even if the function of religion and that of reason coincide, this function is performed in the two cases by very different organs. Religions are many, reason one.

Religion consists of conscious ideas, hopes, enthusiasms, and objects of worship; it operates by grace and flourishes by prayer. Reason, on the other hand, is a mere principle or potential order, on which, indeed, we may come to reflect, but which exists in us ideally only, without variation or stress of any kind. We conform or do not conform to it: it does not urge or chide us, nor call for any emotions on our part other than those naturally aroused by the various objects which it unfolds in their true nature and proportion. Religion brings some order into life by weighting it with new materials. Reason adds to the natural materials only the perfect order which it introduces into them. Rationality is nothing but a form, an ideal constitution which experience may more or less embody. Religion is a part of experience itself, a mass of sentiments and ideas. The one is an inviolate principle, the other a changing and struggling force. And yet this struggling and changing force of religion seems to direct man toward something eternal. It seems to make for an ultimate harmony within the soul and for an ultimate harmony between the soul and all the soul depends upon. So that religion, in its intent, is a more conscious and direct pursuit of the Life of Reason than is society, science, or art. For these approach and fill out the ideal life tentatively and piecemeal, hardly regarding the goal or caring for the ultimate justification of their instinctive aims. Religion also has an instinctive and blind side, and bubbles up in all manner of chance practices and intuitions; soon, however, it feels its way toward the heart of things, and, from whatever quarter it may come, veers in the direction of the ultimate.

Nevertheless, we must confess that this religious pursuit of the Life of Reason has been singularly abortive. Those within the pale of each religion may prevail upon themselves to express satisfaction with its results, thanks to a fond partiality in reading the past and generous draughts of hope for the future; but any one regarding the various religions at once and comparing their achievements with what reason requires, must feel how terrible is the disappointment which they have one and all prepared for mankind. Their chief anxiety has been to offer imaginary remedies for mortal ills, some of which are incurable essentially, while others might have been really cured by well-directed effort. The Greek oracles, for instance, pretended to heal our natural ignorance, which has its appropriate though difficult cure, while the Christian vision of heaven pretended to be an antidote to our natural death, the inevitable correlate of birth and of a changing and conditioned existence. By methods of this sort little can be done for the real betterment of life. To confuse intelligence and dislocate sentiment by gratuitous fictions is a short-sighted way of pursuing happiness. Nature is soon avenged. An unhealthy exaltation and a one-sided morality have to be followed by regrettable reactions. When these come, the real rewards of life may seem vain to a relaxed vitality, and the very name of virtue may irritate young spirits untrained in any natural excellence. Thus religion too often debauches the morality it comes to sanction, and impedes the science it ought to fulfil.

What is the secret of this ineptitude? Why does religion, so near to rationality in its purpose, fall so far short of it in its texture and in its results? The answer is easy: Religion pursues rationality through the imagination. When it explains events or assigns causes, it is an imaginative substitute for science. When it gives precepts, insinuates ideals, or remoulds aspiration, it is an imaginative substitute for wisdom—I mean for the deliberate and impartial pursuit of all good. The conditions and the aims of life are both represented in religion poetically, but this poetry tends to arrogate to itself literal truth and moral authority, neither of which it possesses. Hence the depth and importance of religion become intelligible no less than its contradictions and practical disasters. Its object is the same as that of reason, but its method is to proceed by intuition and by unchecked poetical conceits. These are repeated and vulgarised in proportion to their original fineness and significance, till they pass for reports of objective truth and come to constitute a world of faith, superposed upon the world of experience and regarded as materially enveloping it, if not in space at least in time and in existence. The only truth of religion comes from its interpretation of life, from its symbolic rendering of that moral experience which it springs out of and which it seeks to elucidate. Its falsehood comes from the insidious misunderstanding which clings to it, to the effect that these poetic conceptions are not merely representations of experience as it is or should be, but are rather information about experience or reality elsewhere—an experience and reality which, strangely enough, supply just the defects betrayed by reality and experience here.

Thus religion has the same original relation to life that poetry has; only poetry, which never pretends to literal validity, adds a pure value to existence, the value of a liberal imaginative exercise. The poetic value of religion would initially be greater than that of poetry itself, because religion deals with higher and more practical themes, with sides of life which are in greater need of some imaginative touch and ideal interpretation than are those pleasant or pompous things which ordinary poetry dwells upon. But this initial advantage is neutralised in part by the abuse to which religion is subject, whenever its symbolic rightness is taken for scientific truth. Like poetry, it improves the world only by imagining it improved, but not content with making this addition to the mind's furniture—an addition which might be useful and ennobling—it thinks to confer a more radical benefit by persuading mankind that, in spite of appearances, the world is really such as that rather arbitrary idealisation has painted it. This spurious satisfaction is naturally the prelude to many a disappointment, and the soul has infinite trouble to emerge again from the artificial problems and sentiments into which it is thus plunged. The value of religion becomes equivocal. Religion remains an imaginative achievement, a symbolic representation of moral reality which may have a most important function in vitalising the mind and in transmitting, by way of parables, the lessons of experience. But it becomes at the same time a continuous incidental deception; and this deception, in proportion as it is strenuously denied to be such, can work indefinite harm in the world and in the conscience.

On the whole, however, religion should not be conceived as having taken the place of anything better, but rather as having come to relieve situations which, but for its presence, would have been infinitely worse. In the thick of active life, or in the monotony of practical slavery, there is more need to stimulate fancy than to control it. Natural instinct is not much disturbed in the human brain by what may happen in that thin superstratum of ideas which commonly overlays it. We must not blame religion for preventing the development of a moral and natural science which at any rate would seldom have appeared; we must rather thank it for the sensibility, the reverence, the speculative insight which it has introduced into the world.

We may therefore proceed to analyse the significance and the function which religion has had at its different stages, and, without disguising or in the least condoning its confusion with literal truth, we may allow ourselves to enter as sympathetically as possible into its various conceptions and emotions. They have made up the inner life of many sages, and of all those who without great genius or learning have lived steadfastly in the spirit. The feeling of reverence should itself be treated with reverence, although not at a sacrifice of truth, with which alone, in the end, reverence is compatible. Nor have we any reason to be intolerant of the partialities and contradictions which religions display. Were we dealing with a science, such contradictions would have to be instantly solved and removed; but when we are concerned with the poetic interpretation of experience, contradiction means only variety, and variety means spontaneity, wealth of resource, and a nearer approach to total adequacy.

If we hope to gain any understanding of these matters we must begin by taking them out of that heated and fanatical atmosphere in which the Hebrew tradition has enveloped them. The Jews had no philosophy, and when their national traditions came to be theoretically explicated and justified, they were made to issue in a puerile scholasticism and a rabid intolerance. The question of monotheism, for instance, was a terrible question to the Jews. Idolatry did not consist in worshipping a god who, not being ideal, might be unworthy of worship, but rather in recognising other gods than the one worshipped in Jerusalem. To the Greeks, on the contrary, whose philosophy was enlightened and ingenuous, monotheism and polytheism seemed perfectly innocent and compatible. To say God or the gods was only to use different expressions for the same influence, now viewed in its abstract unity and correlation with all existence, now viewed in its various manifestations in moral life, in nature, or in history. So that what in Plato, Aristotle, and the Stoics meets us at every step—the combination of monotheism with polytheism—is no contradiction, but merely an intelligent variation of phrase to indicate various aspects or functions in physical and moral things. When religion appears to us in this light its contradictions and controversies lose all their bitterness. Each doctrine will simply represent the moral plane on which they live who have devised or adopted it. Religions will thus be better or worse, never true or false. We shall be able to lend ourselves to each in turn, and seek to draw from it the secret of its inspiration.

REASON IN RELIGION

MYTHOLOGY

Primitive thought has the form of poetry and the function of prose. Being thought, it distinguishes objects from the experience that reveals them and it aspires to know things as they are; but being poetical, it attributes to those objects all the qualities which the experience of them contains, and builds them out imaginatively in all directions, without distinguishing what is constant and efficacious in them. This primitive habit of thought survives in mythology, which is an observation of things encumbered with all they can suggest to a dramatic fancy. It is neither conscious poetry nor valid science, but the common root and raw material of both. Free poetry is a thing which early man is too poor to indulge in; his wide-open eyes are too intently watching this ominous and treacherous world. For pure science he has not enough experience, no adequate power to analyse, remember, and abstract; his soul is too hurried and confused, too thick with phantoms, to follow abstemiously the practical threads through the labyrinth. His view of things is immensely overloaded; what he gives out for description is more than half soliloquy; but his expression of experience is for that very reason adequate and quite sincere. Belief, which we have come to associate with religion, belongs really to science; myths are not believed in, they are conceived and understood. To demand belief for an idea is already to contrast interpretation with knowledge; it it to assert that that idea has scientific truth. Mythology cannot flourish in that dialectical air; it belongs to a deeper and more ingenuous level of thought, when men pored on the world with intense indiscriminate interest, accepting and recording the mind's vegetation no less than that observable in things, and mixing the two developments together in one wayward drama.

A good mythology cannot be produced without much culture and intelligence. Stupidity is not poetical. Nor is mythology essentially a half-way house between animal vagueness in the soul and scientific knowledge. It is conceivable that some race, not so dreamful as ours, should never have been tempted to use psychic and passionate categories in reading nature, but from the first should have kept its observations sensuous and pure,

elaborating them only on their own plane, mathematically and dialectically. Such a race, however, could hardly have had lyric or dramatic genius,
and even in natural science, which requires imagination, they might never
have accomplished anything. The Hebrews, denying themselves a rich
mythology, remained without science and plastic art; the Chinese, who
seem to have attained legality and domestic arts and a tutored sentiment
without passing through such imaginative tempests as have harassed us,
remain at the same time without a serious science or philosophy. The
Greeks, on the contrary, precisely the people with the richest and most
irresponsible myths, first conceived the cosmos scientifically, and first
wrote rational history and philosophy. So true it is that vitality in any
mental function is favourable to vitality in the whole mind. Illusions incident to mythology are not dangerous in the end, because illusion finds
in experience a natural though painful cure. Extravagant error is unstable,
unless it be harmless and confined to a limbo remote from all applications;
if it touches experience it is stimulating and brief, while the equipoise of
dulness may easily render dulness eternal. A developed mythology shows
that man has taken a deep and active interest both in the world and in
himself, and has tried to link the two, and interpret the one by the other.
Myth is therefore a natural prologue to philosophy, since the love of ideas
is the root of both. Both are made up of things admirable to consider.

Nor is the illusion involved in fabulous thinking always so complete
and opaque as convention would represent it. In taking fable for fact,
good sense and practice seldom keep pace with dogma. There is always
a race of pedants whose function it is to materialise everything ideal, but
the great world, half shrewdly, half doggedly, manages to escape their contagion. Language may be entirely permeated with myth, since the affinities
of language have much to do with men gliding into such thoughts; yet
the difference between language itself and what it expresses is not so
easily obliterated. In spite of verbal traditions, people seldom take a myth
in the same sense in which they would take an empirical truth. All the doctrines that have flourished in the world about immortality have hardly
affected men's natural sentiment in the face of death, a sentiment which
those doctrines, if taken seriously, ought wholly to reverse. Men almost
universally have acknowledged a Providence, but that fact has had no
force to destroy natural aversions and fears in the presence of events;
and yet, if Providence had ever been really trusted, those preferences
would all have lapsed, being seen to be blind, rebellious, and blasphemous.
Prayer, among sane people, has never superseded practical efforts to secure
the desired end; a proof that the sphere of expression was never really
confused with that of reality. Indeed, such a confusion, if it had passed
from theory to practice, would have changed mythology into madness.
With rare exceptions this declension has not occurred and myths have been
taken with a grain of salt which not only made them digestible, but heightened their savour.

It is always by its applicability to things known, not by its revelation of things unknown and irrelevant, that a myth at its birth appeals to mankind. When it has lost its symbolic value and sunk to the level of merely false information, only an inert and stupid tradition can keep it above water. Parables justify themselves but dogmas call for an apologist. The genial offspring of prophets and poets then has to be kept alive artificially by professional doctors. A thing born of fancy, moulded to express universal experience and its veritable issues, has to be hedged about by misrepresentation, sophistry, and party spirit. The very apologies and unintelligent proofs offered in its defence in a way confess its unreality, since they all strain to paint in more plausible colours what is felt to be in itself extravagant and incredible.

Yet if the myth was originally accepted it could not be for this falsity plainly written on its face; it was accepted because it was understood, because it was seen to express reality in an eloquent metaphor. Its function was to show up some phase of experience in its totality and moral issue, as in a map we reduce everything geographically in order to overlook it better in its true relations. Had those symbols for a moment descended to the plane of reality they would have lost their meaning and dignity; they would tell us merely that they themselves existed bodily, which would be false, while about the real configuration of life they would no longer tell us anything. Such an error, if carried through to the end, would nullify all experience and arrest all life. Men would be reacting on expressions and meeting with nothing to express. They would all be like word-eating philosophers or children learning the catechism.

The true function of mythical ideas is to present and interpret events in terms relative to spirit. Things have uses in respect to the will which are direct and obvious, while the inner machinery of these same things is intricate and obscure. We therefore conceive things roughly and superficially by their eventual practical functions and assign to them, in our game, some counterpart of the interest they affect in us. This counterpart, to our thinking, constitutes their inward character and soul. So conceived, soul and character are purely mythical, being arrived at by dramatising events according to our own fancy and interest. Such ideas may be adequate in their way if they cover all the uses we may eventually find in the objects they transcribe for us dramatically. But the most adequate mythology is mythology still; it does not, like science, set things before us in the very terms they will wear when they are gradually revealed to experience. Myth is expression, it is not prophecy. For this reason myth is something on which the mind rests; it is an ideal interpretation in which the phenomena are digested and transmuted into human energy, into imaginative tissue. Scientific formulas, on the contrary, cry aloud for retranslation into perceptual terms; they are like tight-ropes, on which a man may walk but on which he cannot stand still. These unstable symbols lead, however, to real facts and define their experimental relations; while the mind reposing contentedly in a myth needs to have all observation and experience behind it, for it will not be driven to gather more. The perfect and stable myth would rest on a complete survey and steady focussing of all interests really affecting the one from whose point of view the myth was framed. Then each physical or political unit would be endowed with a character really corresponding to all its influence on the thinker. This symbol would render the diffuse natural existences which it represented in an eloquent figure; and since this figure would not mislead practically it might be called true. But truth, in a myth, means a sterling quality and standard excellence, not a literal or logical truth. It will not, save by a singular accident, represent their proper internal being, as a forthright unselfish intellect would wish to know it. It will translate into the language of a private passion the smiles and frowns which that passion meets with in the world.

There are accordingly two factors in mythology, a moral consciousness and a corresponding poetic conception of things. Both factors are variable, and variations in the first, if more hidden, are no less important than variations in the second. Had fable started with a clear perception of human values, it would have gained immensely in significance, because its pictures, however wrong the external notions they built upon, would have shown what, in the world so conceived, would have been the ideals and prizes of life. Thus Dante's bad cosmography and worse history do not detract from the spiritual penetration of his thought, though they detract from its direct applicability. Had nature and destiny been what Dante imagined, his conception of the values involved would have been perfect, for the moral philosophy he brought into play was Aristotelian and rational. So his poem contains a false instance or imaginary rehearsal of true wisdom. It describes the Life of Reason in a fantastic world. We need only change man's situation to that in which he actually finds himself, and let the soul, fathomed and chastened as Dante left it, ask questions and draw answers from this steadier dream.

Myth travels among the people, and in their hands its poetic factor tends to predominate. It is easier to carry on the dialectic or drama proper to a fable than to confront it again with the facts and give them a fresh and more genial interpretation. The poet makes the fable; the sophist carries it on. Therefore historians and theologians discuss chiefly the various forms which mythical beings have received, and the internal logical or moral implications of those hypostases. They would do better to attend instead to the moral factor. However interesting a fable may be in itself, its religious value lies wholly in its revealing some function which nature has in human life. Not the beauty of the god makes him adorable, but his dispensing benefits and graces. Side by side with Apollo (a god having moral functions and consequently inspiring a fervent cult and tending himself to assume a moral character) there may be a Helios or a

Phaëthon, poetic figures expressing just as well the sun's physical operation, and no less capable, if the theologian took hold of them, of suggesting psychological problems. The moral factor, however, was not found in
these minor deities. Only a verbal and sensuous poetry had been employed
in defining them; the needs and hopes of mankind had been ignored.
Apollo, on the contrary, in personifying the sun, had embodied also the
sun's relations to human welfare. The vitality, the healing, the enlightenment, the lyric joy flowing into man's heart from that highest source of
his physical being are all beautifully represented in the god's figure and
fable. The religion of Apollo is therefore a true religion, as religions may
be true: the mythology which created the god rested on a deep, observant
sense for moral values, and drew a vivid, if partial, picture of the ideal,
attaching it significantly to its natural ground.

The first function of mythology is to justify magic. The weak hope on
which superstition hangs, the gambler's instinct which divines in phenomena a magic solicitude for human fortunes, can scarcely be articulated without seeking to cover and justify itself by some fable. A magic function
is most readily conceived and defined by attributing to the object intentions
hostile or favourable to men, together with human habits of passion and
discourse. For lack of resources and observations, reason is seldom able
to discredit magic altogether. Reasonable men are forced, therefore, in
order to find some satisfaction, to make magic as intelligible as possible
by assimilating it to such laws of human action as may be already mastered
and familiar. Magic is thus reduced to a sort of system, regulated by principles of its own and naturalised, as it were, in the commonwealth of
science.

Such an avowed and defended magic usually takes one of two forms.
When the miracle is interpreted dramatically, by analogy to human life,
we have mythology; when it is interpreted rationalistically, by analogy to
current logic or natural science, we have metaphysics or theosophy. The
metaphysical sort of superstition has never taken deep root in the western
world. Pythagorean mysteries and hypnotisations, although periodically
fashionable, have soon shrivelled in our too salubrious and biting air.
Even such charming exotics as Plato's myths have not been able to flourish without changing their nature and passing into ordinary dramatic
mythology—into a magic system in which all the forces, once terms in
moral experience, became personal angels and demons. Similarly with
the Christian sacraments: these magic rites, had they been established in
India among a people theosophically minded, might have furnished cues
to high transcendental mysteries. Baptism might have been interperted as
a symbol for the purged and abolished will, and Communion as a symbol
for the escape from personality. But European races, though credulous
enough, are naturally positivistic, so that, when they were called upon to
elucidate their ceremonial mysteries, what they lit upon was no meta-

physical symbolism but a material and historical drama. Communion became a sentimental interview between the devout soul and the person of Christ; baptism became the legal execution of a mythical contract once entered into between the first and second persons of the Trinity. Thus, instead of a metaphysical interpretation, the extant magic received its needful justification through myths.

When mythology first appears in western literature it already possesses a highly articulate form. The gods are distinct personalities, with attributes and histories which it is hard to divine the source of and which suggest no obvious rational interpretation. The historian is therefore in the same position as a child who inherits a great religion. The gods and their doings are *prima facie* facts in his world like any other facts, objective beings that convention puts him in the presence of and with which he begins by having social relations. He envisages them with respect and obedience, or with careless defiance, long before he thinks of questioning or proving their existence. The attitude he assumes towards them makes them in the first instance factors in his moral world. Much subsequent scepticism and rationalising philosophy will not avail to efface the vestiges of that early communion with familiar gods. It is hard to reduce to objects of science what are essentially factors in moral intercourse. All thoughts on religion remain accordingly coloured with passion, and are felt to be, above all, a test of loyalty and an index to virtue. The more derivative, unfathomable, and opaque is the prevalent idea of the gods, the harder it is for a rational feeling to establish itself in their regard. Sometimes the most complete historical enlightenment will not suffice to dispel the shadow which their moral externality casts over the mind. In vain do we discard their fable and the thin proofs of their existence when, in spite of ourselves, we still live in their presence.

This pathetic phenomenon is characteristic of religious minds that have outgrown their traditional faith without being able to restate the natural grounds and moral values of that somehow precious system in which they no longer believe. The dead gods, in such cases, leave ghosts behind them, because the moral forces which the gods once expressed, and which, of course, remain, remain inarticulate; and therefore, in their dumbness, these moral forces persistently suggest their only known but now discredited symbols. To regain moral freedom—without which knowledge cannot be put to its rational use in the government of life—we must rediscover the origin of the gods, reduce them analytically to their natural and moral constituents, and then proceed to rearrange those materials, without any quantitative loss, in forms appropriate to a maturer reflection.

Of the innumerable and rather monotonous mythologies that have flourished in the world, only the Græco-Roman and the Christian need concern us here, since they are by far the best known to us and the best defined in themselves, as well as the only two likely to have any continued influence on the western mind. Both these systems presuppose a long prior development. The gods of Greece and of Israel have a full-blown character when we first meet them in literature. In both cases, however, we are fortunate in being able to trace somewhat further back the history of mythology, and do not depend merely on philosophic analysis to reach the elements which we seek.

In the Vedic hymns there survives the record of a religion remarkably like the Greek in spirit, but less dramatic and articulate in form. The gods of the Vedas are unmistakably natural elements. Vulcan is there nothing but fire, Jupiter nothing but the sky. This patriarchal people, fresh from the highlands, had not yet been infected with the manias and diseases of the jungle. It lived simply, rationally, piously, loving all natural joys and delighted with all the instruments of a rude but pure civilisation. It saluted without servility the forces of nature which ministered to its needs. It burst into song in the presence of the magnificent panoramma spread out before it—day-sky and night-sky, dawn and gloaming, clouds, thunder and rain, rivers, cattle and horses, grain, fruit, fire, and wine. Nor were the social sanctities neglected. Commemoration was made of the stages of mortal life, of the bonds of love and kinship, of peace, of battle, and of mourning for the dead. By a very intelligible figure and analogy the winds became shepherds, the clouds flocks, the day a conqueror, the dawn a maid, the night a wise sibyl and mysterious consort of heaven. These personifications were tentative and vague, and the consequent mythology was a system of rhetoric rather than of theology. The various gods had interchangeable attributes, and, by a voluntary confusion, quite in the manner of later Hindu poetry, each became on occasion any or all of the others.

Here the Indian pantheistic vertigo begins to appear. Many dark superstitions, no doubt, bubbled up in the torrent of that plastic reverie; for this people, clean and natural as on the whole it appears, cannot have been without a long and ignoble ancestry. The Greeks themselves, heirs to kindred general traditions, retained some childish and obscene practices in their worship. But such hobgoblins naturally vanish under a clear and beneficent sun and are scattered by healthy mountain breezes. A cheerful people knows how to take them lightly, play with them, laugh at them, and turn them again into figures of speech. Among the early speakers of Sanskrit, even more than among the Greeks, the national religion seems to have been nothing but a poetic naturalism.

Such a mythology, however, is exceedingly plastic and unstable. If the poet is observant and renews his impressions, his myths will become more and more accurate descriptions of the facts, and his hypotheses about phenomena will tend to be expressed more and more in terms of the phenomena themselves; that is, will tend to become scientific. If, on the contrary and as usually happens, the inner suggestions and fertility of his fables absorb his interest, and he neglects to consult his external perceptions any further, or even forgets that any such perceptions originally inspired the myth, he will tend to become a dramatic poet, guided henceforth in his fictions only by his knowledge and love of human life.

When we transport ourselves in fancy to patriarchal epochs and Arcadian scenes, we can well feel the inevitable tendency of the mind to mythologise and give its myths a more and more dramatic character. The phenomena of nature, unintelligible rationally but immensely impressive, must somehow be described and digested. But while they compel attention they do not, after a while, enlarge experience. Husbandmen's lore is profound, practical, poetic, superstitious, but it is singularly stagnant. The cycle of natural changes goes its perpetual round and the ploughman's mind, caught in that narrow vortex, plods and plods after the seasons. Apart from an occasional flood, drought, or pestilence, nothing breaks his laborious torpor. The most cursory inspection of field and sky yields him information enough for his needs. Practical knowledge with him is all instinct and tradition. His mythology can for that very reason ride on nature with a looser rein. If at the same time, however, his circumstances are auspicious and he feels practically secure, he will have much leisure to ripen inwardly and to think. He will hasten to unfold in meditation the abstract potentialities of his mind. His social and ideal passions, his aptitude for art and fancy, will arouse within him a far keener and more varied experience than his outer life can supply. Yet all his fortunes continue to be determined by external circumstances and to have for their theatre this given and uncontrollable world. Some conception of nature and the gods —that is, in his case, some mythology—must therefore remain before him always and stand in his mind for the real forces controlling experience.

His moral powers and interests have meantime notably developed. His sense for social relations has grown clear and full in proportion as his observation of nature has sunk into dull routine. Consequently, the myths by which reality is represented lose, so to speak, their birthright and first nationality. They pass under the empire of abstract cogitation and spontaneous fancy. They become naturalised in the mind. The poet cuts loose from nature and works out instead whatever hints of human character or romantic story the myth already supplies. Analogies drawn from moral and passionate experience replace the further portraiture of outer facts. Human tastes, habits, and dreams enter the fable, expanding it into some little drama, or some mystic anagram of mortal life. While in the beginning the sacred poet had transcribed nothing but joyous perceptions and familiar industrial or martial actions, he now introduces intrigue, ingenious adventures, and heroic passions.

When we turn from the theology of the Vedas to that of Homer we see this revolution already accomplished. The new significance of mythology has obscured the old, and what was a symbol for material facts has become a drama, an apologue, and an ideal. Thus one function of mythology has been nothing less than to carry religion over from superstition into wisdom, from an excuse and apology for magic into an ideal representation of moral goods. In his impotence and sore need a man appeals to magic; this appeal he justifies by imagining a purpose and a god behind the natural agency. But after his accounts when the phenomena are settled by his own labour and patience, he continues to be fascinated by the invisible spirit he has evoked. He cherishes this image; it becomes his companion, his plastic and unaccountable witness and refuge in all the exigencies of life. Dwelling in the mind continually, the deity becomes acclimated there; the worship it receives endows it with whatever powers and ideal faculties are most feared or honourd by its votary. Now the thunder and the pestilence which were once its essence come to be regarded as its disguises and its foils. Faith comes to consist in disregarding what it was once religion to regard, namely, the ways of fortune and the conditions of earthly happiness. Thus the imagination sets up its ideals over against the world that occasioned them, and mythology, instead of cheating men with false and magic aids to action, moralises them by presenting an ideal standard for action and a perfect object for contemplation.

If we consider again, for instance, Apollo's various attributes and the endless myths connected with his name, we shall find him changing his essence and forgetting to be the material sun in order to become the light of a cultivated spirit. At first he is the sky's child, and has the moon for twin sister. His mother is an impersonation of darkness and mystery. He travels yearly from the hyperborean regions toward the south, and daily he traverses the firmament in a chariot. He sleeps in a sea-nymph's bosom or rises from the dawn's couch. In all this we see clearly a scarcely figurative description of the material sun and its motions. A quasi-scientific fancy spins these fables almost inevitably to fill the vacuum not yet occupied by astronomy. Such myths are indeed compacted out of wonders, not indeed to add wonder to them (for the original and greatest marvel persists always in the sky), but to entertain us with pleasant consideration of them and with their assimilation to our own fine feats. This assimilation is unavoidable in a poet ignorant of physics, whom human life must supply with all his vocabulary and similies. Fortunately in this need of introducing romance into the phenomena lies the leaven that is to leaven the lump, the subtle influence that is to moralise religion. For presently Apollo becomes a slayer of monsters (a function no god can perform until he has ceased to be a monster himself), he becomes the lovely and valorous champion of humanity, the giver of prophecy, of music, of lyric song, even the patron of medicine and gymnastics.

What a humane and rational transformation! The spirit of Socrates was older than the man and had long been at work in the Greeks. Interest had been transferred from nature to art, from the sources to the fruits of life. We in these days are accustomed as a matter of course to associate religion with ideal interests. Our piety, unlike our barbarous pantheistic theology, has long lost sight of its rudimentary material object, and habituated us to the worship of human sanctity and human love. We have need all the more to remember how slowly and reluctantly religion has suffered spiritualisation, how imperfectly as yet its superstitious origin has been outgrown. We have need to retrace with the greatest attention the steps by which a moral value has been insinuated into what would otherwise be nothing but a medley of magic rites and poetic physics. It is this submerged idealism which alone, in an age that should have finally learned how to operate in nature and how to conceive her processes, could still win for religion a philosopher's attention or a legislator's mercy.

CONFLICT OF MYTHOLOGY WITH MORAL TRUTH

That magic and mythology have no experimental sanction is clear so soon as experience begins to be gathered together with any care. As magic attempts to do work by incantations, so myth tries to attain knowledge by playing with lies. The attempt is in the first instance inevitable and even innocent, for it takes time to discriminate valid from valueless fancies in a mind in which they spring up together, with no intrinsic mark to distinguish them. The idle notion attracts attention no less than the one destined to prove significant; often it pleases more. Only watchful eyes and that rare thing, conscience applied to memory, can pluck working notions from the gay and lascivious vegetation of the mind, or learn to prefer Cinderella to her impudent sisters. If a myth has some modicum of applicability or significance it takes root all the more firmly side by side with knowledge. There are many subjects of which man is naturally so ignorant that only mythical notions can seem to do them justice; such, for instance, are the minds of other men. Myth remains for this reason a constituent part even of the most rational consciousness, and what can at present be profitably attempted is not so much to abolish myth as to become aware of its mythical character.

The mark of a myth is that it does not interpret a phenomenon in terms capable of being subsumed under the same category with that phenomenon itself, but fills it out instead with images that could never appear side by side with it or complete it on its own plane of existence. Thus if meditating on the moon I conceive her other side or the aspect she would wear if I were travelling on her surface, or the position she would assume in relation to the earth if viewed from some other planet, or the structure she would disclose could she be cut in halves, my thinking, however fanciful, would be on the scientific plane and not mythical, for it would forecast possible perceptions, complementary to those I am trying to enlarge. If, on the other hand, I say the moon is the sun's sister, that she carries a silver bow, that she is a virgin and once looked lovingly on the sleeping Endymion, only the fool never knew it—my lucubration is mythical; for I do not pretend that this embroidery on the aspects which the moon actually wears in my feeling and in the intersticcs of my thoughts could ever be translated into perceptions making one system with the present image. By going closer to that disc I should not see the silver bow, nor by retreating in time should I come to the moment when the sun and moon were actually born at Latona. The elements are incongruous and do not form one existence but two, the first sensible, the other only to be enacted dramatically, and having at best to the first the relation of an experience to its symbol. These fancies are not foretastes of possible perceptions, but are free interpretations or translations of the perceptions I have actually had.

Mythical thinking has its roots in reality, but, like a plant, touches the ground only at one end. It stands unmoved and flowers wantonly into the air, transmuting into unexpected and richer forms the substances its sucks from the soil. It is therefore a fruit of experience, an ornament, a proof of animal vitality; but it is no *vehicle* for experience; it cannot serve the purposes of transitive thought or action. Science, on the other hand, is constituted by those fancies which, arising like myths out of perception, retain a sensuous language and point to further perceptions of the same kind; so that the suggestions drawn from one object perceived are only ideas of other objects similarly perceptible. A scientific hypothesis is one which represent something continuous with the observed facts and conceivably existent in the same medium. Science is a bridge touching experience at both ends, over which practical thought may travel from act to act, from perception to perception.

To separate fable from knowledge nothing is therefore requisite except close scrutiny and the principle of parsimony. Were mythology merely a poetic substitute for natural science the advance of science would sufficiently dispose of it. What remained over would, like the myths in Plato, be at least better than total silence on a subject that interests us and makes us think, although we have no means of testing our thoughts in its regard. But the chief source of perplexity and confusion in mythology is its confusion with moral truth. The myth which originally was but a symbol substituted for empirical descriptions becomes in the sequel an idol substituted for ideal values. . . .

Nothing could be clearer than the grounds on which pious men in the beginning recognise divine agencies. We see, they say, the hand of God in our lives. He has saved us from dangers, he has comforted us in sorrow. He has blessed us with the treasures of life, of intelligence, of affection. He has set around us a beautiful world, and one still more beautiful within us. Pondering all these blessings, we are convinced that he is mighty in the world and will know how to make all things good to those who trust in him. In other words, pious men discern God in the excellence of things.

If all were well, as they hope it may some day be, God would henceforth be present in everything. While good is mixed with evil, he is active in the good alone. The pleasantness of life, the preciousness of human possessions, the beauty and promise of the world, are proof of God's power; so is the stilling of tempests and the forgiveness of sins. But the sin itself and the tempest, which optimistic theology has to attribute just as much to God's purposes, are not attributed to him at all by pious feeling, but rather to his enemies. In spite of centuries wasted in preaching God's omnipotence, his omnipotence is contradicted by every Christian judgment and every Christian prayer. If the most pious of nations is engaged in war, and suffers a great accidental disaster, such as it might expect to be safe from, *Te deums* are sung for those that were saved and *Requiems* for those that perished. God's office, in both cases, is to save only. No one seriously imagines that Providence does more than *govern*—that is, watch over and incidentally modify the natural course of affairs—not even in the other world, if fortunes are still changeable there.

The criterion of divine activity could not be placed more squarely and unequivocally in the good. Plato and Aristotle are not in this respect better moralists than is an unsophisticated piety. God is the ideal, and what manifests the ideal manifests God. Are you confident of the permanence and triumph of the things you prize? Then you trust in God, you live in the consciousness of his presence. The proof and measure of rationality in the world, and of God's power over it, is the extent of human satisfactions. In hell, good people would disbelieve in God, and it is impious of the trembling devils to believe in him there. The existence of any evil—and if evil is felt it exists, for experience is its locus—is a proof that some accident has intruded into God's works. If that loyalty to the good, which is the prerequisite of rationality, is to remain standing, we must admit into the world, while it contains anything practically evil, a principle, however minimised, which is not rational. This irrational principle may be inertia in matter, accidental perversity in the will, or ultimate conflict of interests. Somehow an element of resistance to the rational order must be introduced somewhere. And immediately, in order to distinguish the part furnished by reason from its irrational alloy, we must find some practical test; for if we are to show that there is a great and triumphant rationality in the world, in spite of irrational accidents and brute opposition, we must frame an idea of rationality different from that of being. It will no longer do to say, with the optimists, the rational is the real, the real is the rational. For we wish to make a distinction, in order to maintain our loyalty to the good, and not to eviscerate the idea of reason by emptying it of its essential meaning, which is action addressed to the good and thought envisaging the ideal. To pious feeling, the free-will of creatures, their power, active or passive, of independent origination, is the explanation of all defects; and everything which is not helpful to men's purposes must be assigned to their own irrationality as its cause. Herein lies the explanation of that paradox in religious feeling which attributes sin to the free will, but repentance and every good work to divine grace. Physically considered—as theology must consider the matter—both acts and both volitions are equally necessary and involved in the universal order; but practical religion calls divine only what makes for the good. Whence it follows at once that, both within and without us, what is done well is God's doing, and what is done ill is not.

Thus what we may call the practical or Hebrew theory of cosmic rationality betrays in plainest possible manner that reason is primarily a function of human nature. Reason dwells in the world in so far as the world is good, and the world is good in so far as it supports the wills it generates—the excellence of each creature, the value of its life, and the satisfaction of its ultimate desires. Thus Hebrew optimism could be moral because, although it asserted in a sense the morality of the universe, it asserted this only by virtue of a belief that the universe supported human ideals. Undoubtedly much insistence on the greatness of that power which made for righteousness was in danger of passing over into idolatry of greatness and power, for whatever they may make. Yet these relapses into Nature-worship are the more rare in that the Jews were not a speculative people, and had in the end to endow even Job with his worldly goods in order to rationalise his constancy. It was only by a scandalous heresy that Spinoza could so change the idea of God as to make him indifferent to his creatures; and this transformation, in spite of the mystic and stoical piety of its author, passed very justly for atheism; for that divine government and policy had been denied by which alone God was made manifest to the Hebrews.

If Job's reward seems to us unworthy, we must remember that we have since passed through the discipline of an extreme moral idealism, through a religion of sacrifice and sorrow. We should not confuse the principle that virtue must somehow secure the highest good (for what should not secure it would not be virtue) with the gross symbols by which the highest good might be expressed at Jerusalem. That Job should recover a thousand she-asses may seem to us a poor sop for his long anguish of mind and body, and we may hardly agree with him in finding his new set of children just as good as the old. Yet if fidelity had led to no good end, if it had not somehow brought happiness to somebody, that fidelity would have been folly. There is a noble folly which consists in pushing a principle usually beneficent to such lengths as to render it pernicious; and the pertinacity of Job would have been a case of such noble folly if we were not somehow assured of its ultimate fruits. In Christianity we have the same principle, save that the fruits of virtue are more spiritually conceived; they are inward peace, the silence of the passions, the possession of truth, and the love of God and of our fellows. This is a different conception of happiness, incomplete, perhaps, in a different direction. But were even this attenuated happiness impossible to realise, all rationality would vanish not merely from Christian charity and discipline, but from the whole Christian theory of creation, redemption, and judgment. Without some window open to heaven, religion would be more fantastic than worldliness without being less irrational and vain.

Revelation has intervened to bring about a conception of the highest good which never could have been derived from an impartial synthesis of human interests. The influence of great personalities and the fanaticism of peculiar times and races have joined in imposing such variations from the natural ideal. The rationality of the world, as Christianity conceived it, is due to the plan of salvation; and the satisfaction of human nature, however purified and developed, is what salvation means. If an ascetic ideal could for a moment seem acceptable, it was because the decadence and sophistication of the world had produced a great despair in all noble minds; and they thought it better that an eye or a hand which had offended should perish, and that they should enter blind and maimed into the kingdom of heaven, than that, whole and seeing, they should remain for ever in hell-fire. Supernatural, then, as the ideal might seem, and imposed on human nature from above, it was yet accepted only because nothing else, in that state of conscience and imagination, could revive hope; nothing else seemed to offer an escape from the heart's corruption and weariness into a new existence.

REASON IN ART

JUSTIFICATION OF ART

It is no longer the fashion among philosophers to decry art. Either its influence seems to them too slight to excite alarm, or their systems are too lax to subject anything to censure which has the least glamour or ideality about it. Tired, perhaps, of daily resolving the conflict between science and religion, they prefer to assume silently a harmony between morals and art. Moral harmonies, however, are not given; they have to be made. The curse of superstition is that it justifies and protracts their absence by proclaiming their invisible presence. Of course a rational religion could not conflict with a rational science; and similarly an art that was wholly admirable would necessarily play into the hands of progress. But as the real difficulty in the former case lies in saying what religion and what science would be truly rational, so here the problem is how far extant art is a benefit to mankind, and how far, perhaps, a vice or a burden.

That art is *prima facie* and in itself a good cannot be doubted. It is a spontaneous activity, and that settles the question. Yet the function of ethics is precisely to revise *prima facie* judgments of this kind and to fix the ultimate resultant of all given interests, in so far as they can be combined. In the actual disarray of human life and desire, wisdom consists in knowing what goods to sacrifice and what simples to pour into the supreme

mixture. The extent to which æsthetic values are allowed to colour the
resultant or highest good is a point of great theoretic importance, not only
for art but for general philosophy. If art is excluded altogether or given
only a trivial rôle, perhaps as a neccssary relaxation, we feel at once that
a philosophy so judging human arts is ascetic or post-rational. It pretends
to guide life from above and from without; it has discredited human nature
and mortal interests, and has thereby undermined itelf, since it is at best
but a partial expression of that humanity which it strives to transcend. If,
on the contrary, art is prized as something supreme and irresponsible, if
the poetic and mystic glow which it may bring seems its own complete
justification, then philosophy is evidently still prerational or, rather, non-
existent; for the beasts that listened to Orpheus belong to this school.

To be bewitched is not to be saved, though all the magicians and
æsthetes in the world should pronounce it to be so. Intoxication is a sad
business, at least for a philosopher; for you must either drown yourself
altogether, or else when sober again you will feel somewhat fooled by
yesterday's joys and somewhat lost in to-day's vacancy. The man who
would emancipate art from discipline and reason is trying to elude rationality, not merely in art, but in all existence. He is vexed at conditions of
excellence that make him conscious of his own incompetence and failure.
Rather than consider his function, he proclaims his self-sufficiency. A way
foolishness has of revenging itself is to excommunicate the world.

It is in the world, however, that art must find its level. It must vindicate
its function in the human commonwealth. What direct acceptable contribution does it make to the highest good? What sacrifices, if any, does it
impose? What indirect influence does it exert on other activities? Our
answer to these questions will be our apology for art, our proof that art
belongs to the Life of Reason.

When moralists deprecate passion and contrast it with reason, they do
so, if they are themselves rational, only because passion is so often
"guilty," because it works havoc so often in the surrounding world and
leaves, among other ruins, "a heart high-sorrowful and cloyed." Were
there no danger of such after-effects within and without the sufferer, no
passion would be reprehensible. Nature is innocent, and so are all her
impulses and moods when taken in isolation; it is only on meeting that
they blush. If it be true that matter is sinful, the logic of this truth is far
from being what the fanatics imagine who commonly propound it. Matter
is sinful only because it is insufficient, or is wastefully distributed. There
is not enough of it to go round among the legion of hungry ideas. To
embody or enact an idea is the only way of making it actual; but its embodiment may mutilate it, if the material or the situation is not propitious.
So an infant may be maimed at birth, when what injures him is not being
brought forth, but being brought forth in the wrong manner. Matter has
a double function in respect to existence; essentially it enables the spirit
to be, yet chokes it incidentally. Men sadly misbegotten, or those who are

thwarted at every step by the times' penury, may fall to thinking of matter only by its defect, ignoring the material ground of their own aspirations. All flesh will seem to them weak, except that forgotten piece of it which makes their own spiritual strength. Every impulse, however, had initially the same authority as this censorious one, by which the others are now judged and condemned.

If a practice can point to its innocence, if it can absolve itself from concern for a world with which it does not interfere, it has justified itself to those who love it, though it may not yet have recommended itself to those who do not. Now *art,* more than any other considerable pursuit, more even than speculation, is abstract and inconsequential. Born of suspended attention, it ends in itself. It encourages sensuous abstraction, and nothing concerns it less than to influence the world. Nor does it really do so in a notable degree. Social changes do not reach artistic expression until after their momentum is acquired and their other collateral effects are fully predetermined. Scarcely is a school of art established, giving expression to prevailing sentiment, when this sentiment changes and makes that style seem empty and ridiculous. The expression has little or no power to maintain the movement it registers, as a waterfall has little or no power to bring more water down. Currents may indeed cut deep channels, but they cannot feed their own springs—at least not until the whole revolution of nature is taken into account.

In the individual, also, art registers passions without stimulating them; on the contrary, in stopping to depict them it steals away their life; and whatever interest and delight it transfers to their expression it subtracts from their vital energy. This appears unmistakably in erotic and in religious art. Though the artist's avowed purpose here be to arouse a practical impulse, he fails in so far as he is an artist in truth; for he then will seek to move the given passions only through beauty, but beauty is a rival object of passion in itself. Lascivious and pious works, when beauty has touched them, cease to give out what is wilful and disquieting in their subject and become altogether intellectual and sublime. There is a high breathlessness about beauty that cancels lust and superstition. The artist, in taking the latter for his theme, renders them innocent and interesting, because he looks at them from above, composes their attitudes and surroundings harmoniously, and makes them food for the mind. Accordingly it is only in a refined and secondary stage that active passions like to amuse themselves with their æsthetic expression. Unmitigated lustiness and raw fanaticism will snarl at pictures. Representations begin to interest when crude passions recede, and feel the need of conciliating liberal interests and adding some intellectual charm to their dumb attractions. Thus art, while by its subject it may betray the preoccupations among which it springs up, embodies a new and quite innocent interest.

This interest is more than innocent, it is liberal. Not being concerned with material reality so much as with the ideal, it knows neither ulterior motives nor quantitative limits; the more beauty there is the more there can be, and the higher one artist's imagination soars the better the whole flock flies. In æsthetic activity we have accordingly one side of rational life; sensuous experience is dominated there as mechanical or social realities ought to be dominated in science and politics. Such dominion comes of having faculties suited to their conditions and consequently finding an inherent satisfaction in their operation. The justification of life must be ultimately intrinsic; and wherever such self-justifying experience is attained, the ideal has been in so far embodied. To have realised it in a measure helps us to realise it further; for there is a cumulative fecundity in those goods which come not by increase of force or matter, but by a better organisation and form.

Art has met, on the whole, with more success than science or morals. Beauty gives men the best hint of ultimate good which their experience as yet can offer; and the most lauded geniuses have been poets, as if people felt that those seers, rather than men of action or thought, had lived ideally and known what was worth knowing. That such should be the case, if the fact be admitted, would indeed prove the rudimentary state of human civilisation. The truly comprehensive life should be the statesman's, for whom perception and theory might be expressed and rewarded in action. The ideal dignity of art is therefore merely symbolic and vicarious. As some people study character in novels, and travel by reading tales of adventure, because real life is not yet so interesting to them as fiction, or because they find it cheaper to make their experiments in their dreams, so art in general is a rehearsal of rational living, and recasts in idea a world which we have no present means of recasting in reality. Yet this rehearsal reveals the glories of a possible performance better than do the miserable experiments until now executed on the reality.

When we consider the present distracted state of government and religion, there is much relief in turning from them to almost any art, where what is good is altogether and finally good, and what is bad is at least not treacherous. When we consider further the senseless rivalries, the vanities, the ignominy that reign in the "practical" world, how doubly blessed it becomes to find a sphere where limitation is an excellence, where diversity is a beauty, and where every man's ambition is consistent with every other man's and even favourable to it! It is indeed so in art; for we must not import into its blameless labours the bickerings and jealousies of criticism. Critics quarrel with other critics, and that is a part of philosophy. With an artist no sane man quarrels, any more than with the colour of a child's eyes. As nature, being full of seeds, rises into all sorts of crystallisations, each having its own ideal and potential life, each a nucleus of order and a habitation for the absolute self, so art, though in a medium poorer than pregnant matter, and incapable of intrinsic life, generates a semblance of all conceivable beings. What nature does with existence, art does with appearance; and while the achievement leaves us, unhappily, much where we were before in all our efficacious relations, it entirely renews our vision and breeds a fresh world in fancy, where all form has the same inner justification that all life has in the real world. As no insect is without its rights and every cripple has his dream of happiness, so no artistic fact, no child of imagination, is without its small birthright of beauty. In this freer element, competition does not exist and everything is Olympian. Hungry generations do not tread down the ideal but only its spokesmen or embodiments, that have cast in their lot with other material things. Art supplies constantly to contemplation what nature seldom affords in concrete experience—the union of life and peace.

The ideal, however, would not come down from the empyrean and be conceived unless somebody's thought were absorbed in the conception. Art actually segregates classes of men and masses of matter to serve its special interests. This involves expense; it impedes some possible activities and imposes others. On this ground, from the earliest times until our own, art has been occasionally attacked by moralists, who have felt that it fostered idolatry or luxury or irresponsible dreams. Of these attacks the most interesting is Plato's because he was an artist by temperament, bred in the very focus of artistic life and discussion, and at the same time a consummate moral philosopher. His æsthetic sensibility was indeed so great that it led him, perhaps, into a relative error, in that he overestimated the influence which art can have on character and affairs. Homer's stories about the gods can hardly have demoralised the youths who recited them. No religion has ever given a picture of deity which men could have imitated without the grossest immorality. Yet these shocking representations have not had a bad effect on believers. The deity was opposed to their own vices; those it might itself be credited with offered no contagious example. In spite of the theologians, we know by instinct that in speaking of the gods we are dealing in myths and symbols. Some aspect of nature or some law of life, expressed in an attribute of deity, is what we really regard, and to regard such things, however sinister they may be, cannot but chasten and moralise us. The personal character that such a function would involve, if it were exercised willingly by a responsible being, is something that never enters our thoughts. No such painful image comes to perplex the plain sense of instinctive, poetic religion. To give moral importance to myths, as Plato tended to do, is to take them far too seriously and to belittle what they stand for. Left to themselves they float in an ineffectual stratum of the brain. They are understood and grow current precisely by not being pressed, like an idiom or a metaphor. The same æsthetic sterility appears at the other end of the scale, where fancy is anything but sacred. A Frenchman once saw in "Punch and Judy" a shocking proof of British brutality, destined further to demoralise the nation; and yet the scandal may pass. That black tragedy reflects not very pretty manners, but puppets exercise no suasion over men.

To his supersensitive censure of myths Plato added strictures upon music and the drama: to excite passions idly was to enervate the soul. Only martial or religious strains should be heard in the ideal republic. Furthermore, art put before us a mere phantom of the good. True excellence was the function things had in use; the horseman knew the bridle's value and essence better than the artisan did who put it together; but a painted bridle would lack even this relation to utility. It would rein in no horse, and was an impertinent sensuous reduplication of what, even when it had material being, was only an instrument and a means.

This reasoning has been little uderstood, because Platonists so soon lost sight of their master's Socratic habit and moral intent. They turned the good into an existence, making it thereby unmeaning. Plato's dialectic, if we do not thus abolish the force of its terms, is perfectly cogent: representative art has indeed no utility, and, if the good has been identified with efficiency in a military state, it can have no justification. Plato's Republic was avowedly a fallen state, a church militant, coming sadly short of perfection; and the joy which Plato as much as any one could feel in sensuous art he postponed, as a man in mourning might, until life should be redeemed from baseness.

Never have art and beauty received a more glowing eulogy than is implied in Plato's censure. To him nothing was beautiful that was not beautiful to the core, and he would have thought to insult art—the remodelling of nature by reason—if he had given it a narrower field than all practice. As an architect who had fondly designed something impossible, or which might not please in execution, would at once erase it from the plan and abandon it for the love of perfect beauty and perfect art, so Plato wished to erase from pleasing appearance all that, when its operation was completed, would bring discord into the world. This was done in the ultimate interest of art and beauty, which in a cultivated mind are inseparable from the vitally good. It is mere barbarism to feel that a thing is æsthetically good but morally evil, or morally good but hateful to perception. Things partially evil or partially ugly may have to be chosen under stress of unfavourable circumstances, lest some worse thing come; but if a thing were ugly it would *thereby* not be wholly good, and if it were *altogether* good it would perforce be beautiful.

To criticise art on moral grounds is to pay it a high compliment by assuming that it aims to be adequate, and is addressed to a comprehensive mind. The only way in which art could disallow such criticism would be to protest its irresponsible infancy, and admit that it was a more or less amiable blatancy in individuals, and not *art* at all. Young animals often gambol in a delightful fashion, and men also may, though hardly when they intend to do so. Sportive self-expression can be prized because human nature contains a certain elasticity and margin for experiment, in which waste activity is inevitable and may be precious: for this license may lead, amid a thousand failures, to some real discovery and advance. Art, like life, should be free, since both are experimental. But it is one thing to make room for genius and to respect the sudden madness of poets through which, possibly, some god may speak, and it is quite another not to judge the result by rational standards. The earth's bowels are full of all sorts of rumblings; which of the oracles drawn thence is true can be judged only by the light of day. If an artist's inspiration has been happy, it has been so because his work can sweeten or ennoble the mind and because its total effect will be beneficent. Art being a part of life, the criticism of art is a part of morals.

Maladjustments in human society are still so scandalous, they touch matters so much more pressing than fine art, that maladjustments in the latter are passed over with a smile, as if art were at any rate an irresponsible miraculous parasite that the legislator had better not meddle with. The day may come, however, if the state is ever reduced to a tolerable order, when questions of art will be the most urgent questions of morals, when genius at last will feel responsible, and the twist given to imagination will seem the most crucial thing in life. Under a thin disguise, the momentous character of imaginative choices has already been fully recognised by mankind. Men have passionately loved their special religions, languages, and manners, and preferred death to a life flowering in any other fashion. In justifying this attachment forensically, with arguments on the low level of men's named and consecrated interests, people have indeed said, and perhaps come to believe, that their imaginative interests were material interests at bottom, thinking thus to give them more weight and legitimacy; whereas in truth material life itself would be nothing worth, were it not, in its essence and its issue, ideal.

It was stupidly asserted, however, that if a man omitted the prescribed ceremonies or had unauthorised dreams about the gods, he would lose his battles in this world and go to hell in the other. He who runs can see that these expectations are not founded on any evidence, on any observation of what actually occurs; they are obviously a *mirage* arising from a direct ideal passion, that tries to justify itself by indirection and by falsehoods, as it has no need to do. We all read facts in the way most congruous with our intellectual habit, and when this habit drives us to effulgent creations, absorbing and expressing the whole current of our being, it not merely biasses our reading of this world but carries us into another world altogether, which we posit instead of the real one, or beside it.

Grotesque as the blunder may seem by which we thus introduce our poetic tropes into the sequence of external events or existences, the blunder is intellectual only; morally, zeal for our special rhetoric may not be irrational. The lovely Phœbus is no fact for astronomy, nor does he stand behind the material sun, in some higher heaven, physically superintending its movements; but Phœbus is a fact in his own region, a token of man's joyful piety in the presence of the forces that really condition his welfare. In the region of symbols, in the world of poetry, Phœbus has his inalienable rights. Forms of poetry are forms of human life. Languages express national character and enshrine particular ways of seeing and valuing events. To make substitutions and extensions in expression is to give the soul, in her inmost substance, a somewhat new constitution. A method of apperception is a spontaneous variation in mind, perhaps the origin of a new moral species.

The value apperceptive methods have is of course largely representative, in that they serve more or less aptly to dominate the order of events and to guide action; but quite apart from this practical value, expressions possess a character of their own, a sort of vegetative life, as languages possess euphony. Two reports of the same fact may be equally trustworthy, equally useful as information, yet they may embody two types of mental rhetoric, and this diversity in genius may be of more intrinsic importance than the raw fact it works upon. The non-representative side of human perception may thus be the most momentous side of it, because it represents, or even constitutes, the man. After all, the chief interest we have in things lies in what we can make of them or what they can make of us. There is consequently nothing fitted to colour human happiness more pervasively than art does, nor to express more deeply the mind's internal habit. In educating the imagination art crowns all moral endeavour, which from the beginning is a species of art, and which becomes a fine art more completely as it works in a freer medium.

How great a portion of human energies should be spent on art and its appreciation is a question to be answered variously by various persons and nations. There is no ideal *à priori;* an ideal can but express, if it is genuine, the balance of impulses and potentialities in a given soul. A mind at once sensuous and mobile will find its appropriate perfection in studying and reconstructing objects of sense. Its rationality will appear chiefly on the plane of perception, to render the circle of visions which makes up its life as delightful as possible. For such a man art will be the most satisfying, the most significant activity, and to load him with material riches or speculative truths or profound social loyalties will be to impede and depress him. The irrational is what does not justify itself in the end; and the born artist, repelled by the soberer and bitterer passions of the world, may justly call them irrational. They would not justify themselves in his experience; they make grievous demands and yield nothing in the end which is intelligible to him. His picture of them, if he be a dramatist, will hardly fail to be satirical; fate, frailty, illusion will be his constant themes. If his temperament could find political expression, he would minimise the machinery of life and deprecate any calculated prudence. He would trust the heart, enjoy nature, and not frown too angrily on inclination. Such a Bohemia he would regard as an ideal world in which humanity might flourish congenially.

A puritan moralist, before condemning such an infantile paradise, should remember that a commonwealth of butterflies actually exists. It is not any inherent wrongness in such an ideal that makes it unacceptable, but only the fact that human butterflies are not wholly mercurial and that even imperfect geniuses are but an extreme type in a society whose guiding ideal is based upon a broader humanity than the artist represents. Men of science or business will accuse the poet of folly, on the very grounds on which he accuses them of the same. Each will seem to the other to be obeying a barren obsession. The statesman or philosopher who should aspire to adjust their quarrel could do so only by force of intelligent sympathy with both sides, and in view of the common conditions in which they find themselves. What ought to be done is that which, when done, will most nearly justify itself to all concerned. Practical problems of morals are judicial and political problems. Justice can never be pronounced without hearing the parties and weighing the interests at stake.

A circumstance that complicates such a calculation is this: æsthetic and other interests are not separable units, to be compared externally; they are rather strands interwoven in the texture of everything. Æsthetic sensibility colours every thought, qualifies every allegiance, and modifies every product of human labour. Consequently the love of beauty has to justify itself not merely intrinsically, or as a constituent part of life more or less to be insisted upon; it has to justify itself also as an influence. A hostile influence is the most odious of things. The enemy himself, the alien creature, lies in his own camp, and in a speculative moment we may put ourselves in his place and learn to think of him charitably; but his spirit in our own souls is like a private tempter, a treasonable voice weakening our allegiance to our own duty. A zealot might allow his neighbours to be damned in peace, did not a certain heretical odour emitted by them infect the sanctuary and disturb his own dogmatic calm. In the same way practical people might leave the artist alone in his oasis, and even grant him a pittance on which to live, as they feed the animals in a zoological garden, did he not intrude into their inmost conclave and vitiate the abstract cogency of their designs. It is not so much art in its own field that men of science look askance upon, as the love of glitter and rhetoric and false finality trespassing upon scientific ground; while men of affairs may well deprecate a rooted habit of sensuous absorption and of sudden transit to imaginary worlds, a habit which must work havoc in their own sphere. In other words, there is an element of poetry inherent in thought, in conduct, in affection; and we must ask ourselves how far this ingredient is an obstacle to their proper development.

The fabled dove who complained, in flying, of the resistance of the air, was as wise as the philosopher who should lament the presence and influence of sense. Sense is the native element and substance of experience; all its refinements are still part of it existentially; and whatever excellence belongs specifically to sense is a preliminary excellence, a value antecedent to any which thought or action can achieve. Science and morals have but representative authority; they are principles of ideal synthesis and safe transition; they are bridges from moment to moment of sentience. Their function is indeed universal and their value overwhelming, yet their office remains derivative or secondary, and what they serve to put in order has previously its intrinsic worth. An æsthetic bias is native to sense, being indeed nothing but its form and potency; and the influence which æsthetic habits exercise on thought and action should not be regarded as an intrusion to be resented, but rather as an original interest to be built upon and developed. Sensibility contains the distinctions which reason afterward carries out and applies; it is sensibility that involves and supports primitive diversities, such as those between good and bad, here and there, fast and slow, light and darkness. There are complications and harmonies inherent in these oppositions, harmonies which æsthetic faculty proceeds to note; and from these we may then construct others, not immediately presentable, which we distinguish by attributing them to reason. Reason may well outflank and transform æsthetic judgments, but can never undermine them. Its own materials are the perceptions which if full and perfect are called beauties. Its function is to endow the parts of sentience with a consciousness of the system in which they lie, so that they may attain a mutual relevance and ideally support one another. But what could relevance or support be worth if the things to be buttressed were themselves worthless? It is not to organise pain, ugliness, and boredom that reason can be called into the world.

When a practical or scientific man boasts that he has laid aside æsthetic prejudices and is following truth and utility with a single eye, he can mean, if he is judicious, only that he has not yielded to æsthetic preference after his problem was fixed, nor in an arbitrary and vexatious fashion. He has not consulted taste when it would have been in bad taste to do so. If he meant that he had rendered himself altogether insensible to æsthetic values, and that he had proceeded to organise conduct or thought in complete indifference to the beautiful, he would be simply proclaiming his inhumanity and incompetence. A right observance of æsthetic demands does not obstruct utility nor logic; for utility and logic are themselves beautiful, while a sensuous beauty that ran counter to reason could never be, in the end, pleasing to an exquisite sense. Æsthetic vice is not favourable to æsthetic faculty: it is an impediment to the greatest æsthetic satisfactions. And so when by yielding to a blind passion for beauty we derange theory and practice, we cut ourselves off from those beauties which alone could have satisfied our passion. What we drag in so obstinately will bring but a cheap and unstable pleasure, while a double beauty will thereby be lost or obscured—first, the unlooked-for beauty which a genuine and stable system of things could not but betray, and secondly the coveted beauty itself, which, being imported here into the wrong context, will be rendered meretricious and offensive to good taste. If a jewel worn on the wrong finger sends a shiver through the flesh, how disgusting must not rhetoric be in diplomacy or unction in metaphysics!

The poetic element inherent in thought, affection, and conduct is prior to their prosaic development and altogether legitimate. Clear, well-digested perception and rational choices follow upon those primary creative impulses, and carry out their purpose systematically. At every stage in this development new and appropriate materials are offered for æsthetic contemplation. Straightness, for instance, symmetry, and rhythm are at first sensuously defined; they are characters arrested by æsthetic instinct; but they are the materials of mathematics. And long after these initial forms have disowned their sensuous values, and suffered a wholly dialectical expansion or analysis, mathematical objects again fall under the æsthetic eye, and surprise the senses by their emotional power. A mechanical system, such as astronomy in one region has already unveiled, is an inexhaustible field for æsthetic wonder. Similarly, in another sphere, sensuous affinity leads to friendship and love, and makes us huddle up to our fellows and feel their heart-beats; but when human society has thereupon established a legal and moral edifice, this new spectacle yields new imaginative transports, tragic, lyric, and religious. Æsthetic values everywhere precede and accompany rational activity, and life is, in one aspect, always a fine art; not by introducing inaptly æsthetic vetoes or æsthetic flourishes, but by giving to everything a form which, implying a structure, implies also an ideal and a possible perfection. This perfection, being felt, is also a beauty, since any process, though it may have become intellectual or practical, remains for all that a vital and sentient operation, with its inherent sensuous values. Whatever is to be representative in import must first be immediate in existence; whatever is transitive in operation must be at the same time actual in being. So that an æsthetic sanction sweetens all successful living; animal efficiency cannot be without grace, nor moral achievement without a sensible glory.

These vital harmonies are natural; they are neither perfect nor preordained. We often come upon beauties that need to be sacrificed, as we come upon events and practical necessities without number that are truly regrettable. There are a myriad conflicts in practice and in thought, conflicts between rival possibilities, knocking inopportunely and in vain at the door of existence. Owing to the initial disorganisation of things, some demands continually prove to be incompatible with others arising no less naturally. Reason in such cases imposes real and irreparable sacrifices, but it brings a stable consolation if its discipline is accepted. Decay, for instance, is a moral and æsthetic evil; but being a natural necessity it can become the basis for pathetic and magnificent harmonies, when once imagination is adjusted to it. The hatred of change and death is ineradicable while life lasts, since it expresses that self-sustaining organisation in a creature which we call its soul; yet this hatred of change and death is not so deeply seated in the nature of things as are death and change themselves, for the flux is deeper than the ideal. Discipline may attune our higher and more adaptable part to the harsh conditions of being, and the resulting sentiment, being the only one which can be maintained successfully, will express the greatest satisfactions which can be reached, though not the greatest that might be conceived or desired. To be interested in the changing seasons is, in this middling zone, a happier state of mind than to be hopelessly in love with spring. Wisdom discovers these possible accommodations, as circumstances impose them; and education ought to prepare men to accept them.

It is for want of education and discipline that a man so often insists petulantly on his random tastes, instead of cultivating those which might find some satisfaction in the world and might produce in him some pertinent culture. Untutored self-assertion may even lead him to deny some fact that should have been patent, and plunge him into needless calamity. His Utopias cheat him in the end, if indeed the barbarous taste he has indulged in clinging to them does not itself lapse before the dream is half formed. So men have feverishly conceived a heaven only to find it insipid, and a hell to find it ridiculous. Theodicies that were to demonstrate an absolute cosmic harmony have turned the universe into a tyrannous nightmare, from which we are glad to awake again in this unintentional and somewhat tractable world. Thus the fancies of effeminate poets in violating science are false to the highest art, and the products of sheer confusion, instigated by the love of beauty, turn out to be hideous. A rational severity in respect to art simply weeds the garden; it expresses a mature æsthetic choice and opens the way to supreme artistic achievements. To keep beauty in its place is to make all things beautiful.

REASON IN SCIENCE

THE VALIDITY OF SCIENCE

The same despair or confusion which, when it overtakes human purposes, seeks relief in arbitrary schemes of salvation, when it overtakes human knowledge, may breed arbitrary substitutes for science. There are post-rational systems of nature as well as of duty. Most of these are myths hardly worth separating from the post-rational moralities they adorn, and have been sufficiently noticed in the last chapter; but a few aspire to be critical revisions of science, themselves scientific. It may be well, in bringing this book to a close, to review these proposed revisions. The validity of science is at stake, and with it the validity of that whole Life of Reason which science crowns, and justifies to reflection.

There are many degrees and kinds of this critical retractation. Science

may be accepted bodily, while its present results are modified by suggesting speculatively what its ultimate results might be. This is natural philosophy or legitimate metaphysics. Or science may be accepted in part,
and in part subjected to control by some other alleged vehicle of knowledge. This is traditional or intuitive theology. Or science may be retracted
and withdrawn altogether, on the ground that it is but methodological
fiction, its facts appearances merely, and its principles tendencies to feign.
This is transcendentalism; whereupon a dilemma presents itself. We may
be invited to abstain from all hypostasis or hearty belief in anything, and
to dwell only on the consciousness of imaginative activity in a vacuum—
which is radical idealism. Or we may be assured that, science being a
dream, we may awake from it into another cosmos, built upon principles
quite alien to those illustrated in nature or applicable in practice—which
is idealism of the mythical sort. Finally it may occur to us that the criticism of science is an integral part of science itself, and that a transcendental method of survey, which marshals all things in the order of their
discovery, far from invalidating knowledge can only serve to separate it
from incidental errors and to disclose the relative importance of truths.
Science would then be rehabilitated by criticism. The primary movement
of the intellect would not be condemned by that subsequent reflection
which it makes possible, and which collates its results. Science, purged
of all needless realism and seen in its relation to human life, would continue to offer the only conception of reality which is pertinent or possible
to the practical mind.

We may now proceed to discuss these various attitudes in turn.

A first and quite blameless way of criticising science is to point out
that science is incomplete. That it grows fast is indeed its commonest
boast; and no man of science is so pessimistic as to suppose that its
growth is over. To wish to supplement science and to regard its conclusions as largely provisional is therefore more than legitimate. It is actually
to share the spirit of inquiry and to feel the impulse toward investigation.
When new truths come into view, old truths are thereby reinterpreted
and put in a new light; so that the acquisitions of science not only admit
of revision but loudly call for it, not wishing for any other authority or
vindication than that which they might find in the context of universal
truth.

To revise science in this spirit would be merely to extend it. No new
method, no transverse philosophy, would be requisite or fitted for the task.
Knowledge would be transformed by more similar knowledge, not by
some verbal manipulation. Yet while waiting for experience to grow and
accumulate its lessons, a man of genius, who had drunk deep of experience
himself, might imagine some ultimate synthesis. He might venture to
carry out the suggestions of science and anticipate the conclusions it
would reach when completed. The game is certainly dangerous, especially

if the prophecy is uttered with any air of authority; yet with good luck and a fine instinct, such speculation may actually open the way to discovery and may diffuse in advance that virtual knowledge of physics which is enough for moral and poetic purposes. Verification in detail is needed, not so much for its own sake as to check speculative errors; but when speculation is by chance well directed and hits upon the substantial truth, it does all that a completed science would do for mankind; since science, if ever completed, would immediately have to be summed up again and reduced to generalities. Under the circumstances of human life, ultimate truth must forego detailed verification and must remain speculative. The curse of modern philosophy is only that it has not drawn its inspiration from science; as the misfortune of science is that it has not yet saturated the mind of philosophers and recast the moral world. The Greek physicists, puerile as was their notion of natural mechanism, had a more integral view of things. They understood nature's uses and man's conditions in an honest and noble way. If no single phenomenon had been explained correctly by any philosopher from Thales to Lucretius, yet by their frank and studious contemplation of nature they would have liberated the human soul.

Unfortunately the supplements to science which most philosophers supply in our day are not conceived in a scientific spirit. Instead of anticipating the physics of the future they cling to the physics of the past. They do not stimulate us by a picture, however fanciful, of what the analogies of nature and politics actually point to; they seek rather to patch and dislocate current physics with some ancient myth, once the best physics obtainable, from which they have not learned to extricate their affections.

Sometimes these survivals are intended to modify scientific conceptions but slightly, and merely to soften a little the outlines of a cosmic picture to which religion and literature are not yet accustomed. There is a school of political conservatives who, with no specific interest in metaphysics cannot or dare not break with traditional modes of expression, with the customs of their nation, or with the clerical classes. They accordingly append to current knowledge certain sentimental postulates, alleging that what is established by tradition and what appeals to the heart must somehow correspond to something which is needful and true. But their conventional attachment to a religion which in its original essence was perhaps mystical and revolutionary, scarcely modifies, in their eyes, the sum of practical assurances or the aim of human life. As language exercises some functions which science can hardly assume (as, for instance, in poetry and communication) so theology and metaphysics, which to such men are nothing but languages, might provide for inarticulate interests, and unite us to much that lies in the dim penumbra of our workaday world. Ancient revelations and mysteries, however incredible if taken literally, might therefore be suffered to flourish undisturbed, so long as they did not clash with any clear fact or natural duty. They might continue to decorate with a mystical aureole the too prosaic kernel of known truth.

Mythology and ritual, with the sundry divinations of poets, might in fact be kept suspended with advantage over human passion and ignorance, to furnish them with decent expression. But once indulged, divination is apt to grow arrogant and dogmatic. When its oracles have become traditional they are almost inevitably mistaken for sober truths. Hence the second kind of supplement offered to science, so that revelations with which moral life has been intertwined may find a place beside or beyond science. The effort is honest, but extraordinarily short-sighted. Whatever value those revelations may have they draw from actual experience or inevitable ideals. When the ground of that experience and those ideals is disclosed by science, nothing of any value is lost; it only remains to accustom ourselves to a new vocabulary and to shift somewhat the associations of those values which life contains or pursues. Revelations are necessarily mythical and subrational; they express natural forces and human interests in a groping way, before the advent of science. To stick in them, when something more honest and explicit is available, is inconsistent with caring for attainable welfare or understanding the situation. It is to be stubborn and negligent under the cloak of religion. These prejudices are a drag on progress, moral no less than material; and the sensitive conservatism that fears they may be indispensable is entangled in a pathetic delusion. It is conservatism in a shipwreck. It has not the insight to embrace the fertile principles of life, which are always ready to renew life after no matter what natural catastrophe. The good laggards have no courage to strip for the race. Rather than live otherwise, and live better, they prefer to nurse the memories of youth and to die with a retrospective smile upon their countenance.

Far graver than the criticism which shows science to be incomplete is that which shows it to be relative. The fact is undeniable, though the inferences made from it are often rash and gratuitous. We have seen that science is nothing but developed perception, interpreted intent, common-sense rounded out and minutely articulated. It is therefore as much an instinctive product, as much a stepping forth of human courage in the dark, as is any inevitable dream or impulsive action. Like life itself, like any form of determinate existence, it is altogether autonomous and unjustifiable from the outside. It must lean on its own vitality; to sanction reason there is only reason, and to corroborate sense there is nothing but sense. Inferential thought is a venture not to be approved of, save by a thought no less venturesome and inferential. This is once for all the fate of a living being—it is the very essence of spirit—to be ever on the wing, borne by inner forces toward goals of its own imagining, confined to a passing apprehension of a represented world. Mind, which calls itself the organ of truth, is a permanent possibility of error. The encouragement and corroboration which science is alleged to receive from moment to moment may, for aught it knows, be simply a more ingenious self-deception, a form of that cumulative illusion by which madness can confirm itself, creating a whole world, with an endless series of martyrs, to bear witness to its sanity.

To insist on this situation may seem idle, since no positive doctrine can gain thereby in plausibility, and no particular line of action in reasonableness. Yet this transcendental exercise, this reversion to the immediate, may be recommended by way of a cathartic, to free the mind from ancient obstructions and make it hungrier and more agile in its rational faith. Scepticism is harmless when it is honest and universal; it clears the air and is a means of reorganising belief on its natural foundations. Belief is an inevitable accompaniment of practice and intent, both of which it will cling to all the more closely after a thorough criticism. When all beliefs are challenged together, the just and necessary ones have a chance to step forward and to re-establish themselves alone. The doubt cast on science, when it is an ingenuous and impartial doubt, will accordingly serve to show what sort of thing science is, and to establish it on a sure foundation. Science will then be seen to be tentative, genial, practical, and humane, full of ideality and pathos, like every great human undertaking.

Unfortunately a searching disintegration of dogma, a conscientious reversion to the immediate, is seldom practised for its own sake. So violent a disturbance of mental habits needs some great social upheaval or some revolutionary ambition to bring it about. The transcendental philosophy might never have been put forward at all, had its authors valued it for what it can really accomplish. The effort would have seemed too great and the result too nugatory. Their criticism of knowledge was not freely undertaken, with the pure speculative motive of understanding and purifying human science. They were driven on by the malicious psychology of their predecessors, by the perplexities of a sophistical scepticism, and by the imminent collapse of traditional metaphysics. They were enticed at the same time by the hope of finding a new basis for the religious myths associated with that metaphysics. In consequence their transcendentalism was not a rehearsal of the Life of Reason, a retrospect criticising and justifying the phases of human progress. It was rather a post-rational system of theology, the dangerous cure to a harmless disease, inducing a panic to introduce a fable. The panic came from the assumption (a wholly gratuitous one) that a spontaneous constructive intellect cannot be a trustworthy instrument, that appearances cannot be the properties of reality, and that things cannot be what science finds that they are. We were forbidden to believe in anything we might discover or to trust in anything we could see. The artificial vacuum thus produced in the mind ached to be filled with something, and of course a flood of rhetorical commonplaces was at hand, which might rush in to fill it.

The most heroic transcendentalists were but men, and having imagined that logic obliged them to abstain from every sort of hypostasis, they could not long remain true to their logic. For a time, being of a buoyant disposition, they might feel that nothing could be more exhilarating than to swim in the void, altogether free from settled conditions, altogether the ignorant creators of each moment's vision. Such a career evidently affords all sorts of possibilities, except perhaps the possibility of being a career. But when a man has strained every nerve to maintain an absolute fluidity and a painful fidelity to the immediate, he can hardly be blamed if he lapses at last into some flattering myth, and if having satisfied himself that all science is fiction he proclaims some fairy-tale to be the truth. The episodes of experience, not being due to any conceivable machinery beneath, might come of mere willing, or at the waving of a dialectical wand. Yet apart from this ulterior inconsistency and backsliding into credulity, transcendentalism would hear nothing of causes or grounds. All phenomena existed for it on one flat level. We were released from all dogma and reinstated in the primordial assurance that we were all there was, but without understanding what we were, and without any means of controlling our destiny, though cheered by the magnificent feeling that that destiny was great.

It is intelligible that a pure transcendentalism of this sort should not be either stable or popular. It may be admired for its analytic depth and its persistency in tracing all supposed existences back to the experience that vouches for them. Yet a spirit that finds its only exercise in gloating on the consciousness that it is a spirit, one that has so little skill in expression that it feels all its embodiments to be betrayals and all its symbols to be misrepresentations, is a spirit evidently impotent and confused. It is self-inhibited, and cannot fulfil its essential vocation by reaching an embodiment at once definitive and ideal, philosophical and true. We may excuse a school that has done one original task so thoroughly as transcendentalism has done its examination of the cognitive conscience, if it has failed to do something else to which it did not distinctly address itself and for which it had no aptitude—namely, to discover what is really true. But it becomes necessary to note this limitation, especially when it is virtually disallowed, and when science is systematically disparaged in favour of a method that is merely disintegrating and incapable of establishing a single positive truth.

The legitimacy of the transcendental method is so obvious that it is baffling when unfamiliar and trifling when understood. It is somewhat like the scientific discovery that man is an animal; for in spite of its pompous language and unction, transcendentalism, when not transcended, is a stopping short at the vegetative and digestive stage of consciousness, where nothing seems to be anything but a play of variations in the immediate. That is what science has risen from; it is the primordial slime. But to stop there and make life consist in hearing the mind work is illiberal and childish. Maturity lies in taking reason at its word and learning to believe and to do what it bids us. Inexperience, pedantry, and mysticism—three obstacles to wisdom—were not absent from those academic geniuses by whom transcendentalism was first brought forth. They became consequently entangled in their profundity, and never were masters of their purposes or of their tools.

The dethronement of empirical knowledge which these philosophers announced was occasioned by the discovery that empirical knowledge was ideal and hypothetical; that its terms, like all terms in thought, were thrown out during the fission or crystallisation of a growing experience. Science accordingly was merely a set of ideas; its subject-matter seemed to be sucked in and absorbed by the theory that presented it, so that when the history of science was written the whole substance and meaning of science was exhausted. This damaging implication, that what is ideal is imaginary and that what is inferred exists only in the fooled mind that infers it, would, if it were allowed, make short work of all philosophy. Theology would fare no better than science, and it is hard to see how transcendental idealism itself could stand, if it pretended to constitute an articulate theory of reality. All faith would be invalidated, since it would be proved to be faith only, having no real object. But then history itself is a science; and to represent a series of events or related phenomena in time would be to pretend to impossible knowledge. It would become necessary to retract and withdraw the alleged evolution of thought itself, in which science was to figure as an imaginative device and a passing episode. History and experience would be nothing but the idea of them; and the Absolute Ego or Absolute Life also, in so far as anything could be said of it, would be simply an integral term in the discourse that described it. And this discourse, this sad residuum of reality, would remain an absolute datum without a ground, without a subject-matter, without a past, and without a future.

It suffices, therefore, to take the supposed negative implication in transcendentalism a little seriously to see that it leaves nothing standing but negation and imbecility; so that we may safely conclude that such a negative implication is gratuitous, and also that in taking the transcendental method for an instrument of reconstruction its professors were radically false to it. They took the starting-point of experience, on which they had fallen back, for its ultimate deliverance, and in reverting to protoplasm they thought they were rising to God. The transcendental method is merely retrospective; its use is to recover more systematically conceptions already extant and inevitable. It invalidates nothing in science; much less does it carry with it any rival doctrine of its own. Every philosophy, even materialism, may find a transcendental justification, if experience as it develops will yield no other terms. What has reason to tremble at a demand for its credentials is surely not natural science; it is rather those mystical theologies or romantic philosophies of history which aspire to take its place. Such lucubrations, even if reputed certain, can scarcely be really credited or regarded in practice; while scientific tenets are necessarily respected, even when they are declared to be fictions. This nemesis is inevitable; for the mind must be inhabited, and the ideas with which science peoples it are simply its involuntary perceptions somewhat more clearly arranged.

That the relativity of science—its being an emanation of human life—is nothing against its truth appears best, perhaps, in the case of dialectic. Dialectic is valid by virtue of an intended meaning and felt congruity in its terms; but these terms, which intent fixes, are external and independent in their ideal nature, and the congruity between them is not created by being felt but, whether incidentally felt or not, is inherent in their essence. Mathematical thinking is the closest and most intimate of mental operations, nothing external being called in to aid; yet mathematical truth is as remote as possible from being personal or psychic. It is absolutely self-justified and is necessary before it is discovered to be so. Here, then, is a conspicuous region of truth, disclosed to the human intellect by its own internal exercise, which is nevertheless altogether independent, being eternal and indefeasible, while the thought that utters it is ephemeral.

The validity of material science, not being warranted by pure insight, cannot be so quickly made out; nevertheless it cannot be denied systematically, and the misunderstood transcendentalism which belittles physics contradicts its own basis. For how are we supposed to know that what we call facts are mere appearances and what we call objects mere creations of thought? We know this by physics. It is physiology, a part of physics, that assures us that our senses and brains are conditions of our experience. Were it not for what we know of the outer world and of our place in it, we should be incapable of attaching any meaning to subjectivity. The flux of things would then go on in their own medium, not in our minds; and no suspicion of illusion or of qualification by mind would attach to any event in nature. So it is in a dream; and it is our knowledge of physics, our reliance on the world's material coherence, that marks our awakening, and that constitutes our discovery that we exist as minds and are subject to dreaming. It is quite true that the flux, as it exists in men, is largely psychic; but only because the events it contains are effects of material causes and the images in it are flying shadows cast by solid external things. This is the meaning of psychic existence, and its differentia. Mind is an expression, weighted with emotion, of mechanical relations among bodies. Suppose the bodies all removed: at once the images formerly contrasted with those bodies would resume their inherent characteristics and mutual relation; they would become existences in their own category, large, moving, coloured, distributed to right and left; that is, save for their values, they would become material things.

Physics is accordingly a science which, though hypothetical and only verifiable by experiment, is involved in history and psychology and therefore in any criticism of knowledge. The contradiction would be curious if a man should declare that his ideas were worthless, being due to his organs of sense, and that therefore these organs (since he had an idea of them) did not exist. Yet on this grave argument idealism chiefly rests. It asserts that bodies are mere ideas, because it is through our bodies that we perceive them. When physics has discovered the conditions under which knowledge of physics has arisen, physics is supposed to be spirited away; whereas, of course, it has only closed its circle and justified its sovereignty. Were all science retracted and reduced to symbolic calculation nothing would remain for this calculation to symbolise. The whole force of calling a theory merely a vehicle or method of thought, leading us to something different from itself, lies in having a literal knowledge of this other thing. But such literal knowledge is the first stage of science, which the other stages merely extend. So that when, under special circumstances, we really appeal to algebraic methods of expression and think in symbols, we do so in the hope of transcribing our terms, when the reckoning is over, into the language of familiar facts. Were these facts not forthcoming, the symbolic machinery would itself become the genuine reality—since it is really given—and we should have to rest in it, as in the ultimate truth. This is what happens in mythology, when the natural phenomena expressed by it are forgotten. But natural phenomena themselves are symbols of nothing, because they are primary data. They are the constitutive elements of the reality they disclose.

The validity of science in general is accordingly established merely by establishing the truth of its particular propositions, in dialectic on the authority of intent and in physics on that of experiment. It is impossible to base science on a deeper foundation or to override it by a higher knowledge. What is called metaphysics, if not anticipation of natural science, is a confusion of it with dialectic or a mixture of it with myths. If we have the faculty of being utterly sincere and if disintegrating the conventions of language and religion, we must confess that knowledge is only a claim we put forth, a part of that unfathomable compulsion by force of which we live and hold our painted world together for a moment. If we have any insight into mind, or any eye for human history, we must confess at the same time that the oracular substitutes for knowledge to which, in our perplexities, we might be tempted to fly, are pathetic popular fables, having no other sanctity than that which they borrow from the natural impulses they play upon. To live by science requires intelligence and faith, but not to live by it is folly.

If science thus contains the sum total of our rational convictions and gives us the only picture of reality on which we should care to dwell, we have but to consult the sciences in detail to ascertain, as far as that is possible, what sort of a universe we live in. The result is as yet far from satisfactory. The sciences have not joined hands and made their results coherent, showing nature to be, as it doubtless is, all of one piece. The moral sciences especially are a mass of confusion. Negative, I think, must be the attitude of reason, in the present state of science, upon any hypothesis far outrunning the recorded history and the visible habitat of the human race. Yet exactly the same habits and principles that have secured our present knowledge are still active within us, and promise further discoveries. It is more desirable to clarify our knowledge within these bounds than to extend it beyond them. For while the reward of action is contemplation or, in more modern phrase, experience and consciousness, there is nothing stable or interesting to contemplate except objects relevant to action—the natural world and the mind's ideals.

Both the conditions and the standards of action lie well within the territory which science, after a fashion, already dominates. But there remain unexplored jungles and monster-breeding lairs without our nominal jurisdiction which it is the immediate task of science to clear. The darkest spots are in man himself, in his fitful, irrational disposition. Could a better system prevail in our lives a better order would establish itself in our thinking. It has not been for want of keen senses, or personal genius, or a constant order in the outer world, that mankind have fallen back repeatedly into barbarism and superstition. It has been for want of good character, good example, and good government. There is a pathetic capacity in men to live nobly, if only they would give one another the chance. The ideal of political perfection, vague and remote as it yet seems, is certainly approachable, for it is as definite and constant as human nature. The knowledge of all relevant truth would be involved in that ideal, and no intellectual dissatisfaction would be felt with a system of ideas that should express and illumine a perfect life.

REASON IN COMMON SENSE

PREFACE TO THE SECOND EDITION

Twenty years separate me from the man I was when I wrote this book—years enlivened for me by many changes of scene and branded by a great war. There is hardly a page that would not need to be rewritten, if it was perfectly to express my present feelings.

> *Mais quand l'homme change sans cesse,*
> *au passé pourquoi rien changer?*

Some readers would perhaps prefer the original to my revised version, and if I lived another twenty years I might myself prefer it. The written letter, then, may as well stand; especially as nothing hinders me from setting forth my matured views in fresh works, leaving it for others to decide whether I have changed for the better. After all, there has been no change in my deliberate doctrine; only some changes of mental habit. I now dwell by preference on other perspectives, in which the same objects appear with their relative bulks reversed, and inversely hiding one another; what lay before in the background—nature—has come forward, and the life of reason, which then held the centre of the stage, has receded. The vicissitudes of human belief absorb me less; the life of reason has become in my eyes a decidedly episodical thing, polyglot, interrupted, insecure. I cannot take every phase of art or religion or philosophy seriously, simply because it takes itself so. These things seem to me less tragic than they did, and more comic; and I am less eager to choose and to judge among them, as if only one form could be right. When our architecture is too pretentious, before we have set the cross on the spire, the foundations are apt to give way.

I am consequently far less inclined to take a transcendental point of view, as if the spirit at every point were absolute, and its objects its creations. Spirit is absolute enough, so to speak, relatively, and in its own eyes, since willy-nilly it must soliloquize; but any puppet in the hands of a ventriloquist seems to soliloquize, if we have no notion whence its voice comes. The self that speaks in us is deeper than we suppose, and less ours; but that is nothing against it. Spirit is always worth listening to, and worth understanding sympathetically; the ventriloquist, if not the manikin, deserves admiration. It is spirit, too, that listens and understands, and grows thereby riper and more secure. Yet the oracles of spirit all have to be discounted; they are uttered in a cave.

It was this murmur of nature, wayward and narcotic as it is, that I called reason in this book, and tried to catch and interpret nobly. I could hardly have undertaken or carried out such a task if I had not been accustomed to slip into the subjective, recovering at each step as far as I might the innocence of intellectual illusion, and painting things as they would seem from that angle, not as they are. From childhood up I had lived in imagination, being fond of religion and poetry, and driven by circumstances to lead my inner life alone; and the philosophy that prevailed about me, though not one which I ever personally trusted, could not help encouraging me in this subjective habit, representing it as deeper, more critical, and more philosophical than any dogmatism. Nevertheless, subjectivity in me was never more than a method, a habit of poetic sympathy with the dreaming mind, whatever it might dream. It was a method appropriate to a book like this, a presumptive biography of the human intellect, which instead of the Life of Reason might have been called the Romance of Wisdom. Moreover, the thoughts I was endeavouring to evoke and to analyse were not all dead thoughts. Many of them survived in my own perplexities or in the various idealisms of those about me. One consequence was that I was often betrayed into expressions which, if not taken dramatically, would contradict my naturalism; that vulgar belief in material things about us which not only underlay the whole life of reason as I conceived it, but was also its explicit final deliverance. Another consequence was that, when I knew or feared that my reader might harbour the very illusion I was rehearsing, I was tempted to analyse it destructively, or argue against it: something really alien to the essential character of my task. It was only when the thoughts considered were unmistakably dead—as was Greek mythology or (to my probable reader) Catholic piety—that I could warm freely to my work, without fear of confusing myself or other people. On the other hand, when the idea considered was a living and indispensable one (no better description of the envisaged reality being as yet at hand) it was hard to relegate this idea to its native subjective sphere, where all ideas, of course, belong, without seeming to assert that its object also was a figment of human thought—a simply bottomless fallacy.

Let a single instance suffice as a hint to the critic, and as an apology for all the equivocations of this kind of which I may have been guilty. I find myself saying . . . that "nature is drawn like a sponge, heavy and dripping from the waters of sentience." Obviously the "nature" in question is the *idea* of nature, vague at first and overloaded with myth, then growing distinct, constant, articulate. Existing nature could not be drawn either soaking or dry from the waters of sentience: for existing nature is a system of bodies long antedating sentience and making sentience appropriate and significant: or else (on the hypothesis of idealism) existing nature is the flood of sentience itself, from which nothing can ever emerge. That which on its first appearance comes drenched out of its watery element, is the dramatic notion of nature created by mythology. And matching this primitive notion of nature, and growing slowly distinguishable over against it, is another primitive notion which I mention in the same passage, the ghostly notion of mind. This, I say, is composed of the "parings of experience, when the material world has been cut out of the whole cloth." "Mind," too, is here a personage in the play of reason; it is the *category* of mind. Evidently the origin of existing mind could not lie in a discrimination which mind itself is making; but the discovery of mind may well come in that way. Shall I be blamed for giving the same name to the idea of nature and to existing nature, to the category of mind and to existing mind? I admit that, if the words are pressed, they become confusing; and yet at the play I might innocently say to a friend: "There is Hamlet coming on the stage. What a get-up! He looks more like Bunthorne." Clearly the phenomenon I should then be calling Hamlet would not be the real Hamlet, neither the Danish prince nor the presumable ideal in the mind of Shakespeare. This Hamlet is only the absurd actor playing Hamlet for the time being. Why should the verbal ambiguity be more annoying if in reviewing the life of reason I confidentially turn to the friendly reader, whom I suppose to be watching the same drama, and say: "See mind and nature coming on the scene. What a travesty the green-room of fancy has made of them! Here is nature tricked out in will and purpose like a moral being, and mind tumbling about in motley and gibbering!"

This drama, as I conceived it, was far from being a mere comedy of errors, to be treated satirically; it was a chequered experience from which wisdom might be gleaned. The story might be romantic, but the moral of it was classical. Error, under the influence of the existing object which it attempts to describe, suffers correction: and those first mythical notions of nature and of mind may be gradually clarified, until nature is seen to be a mechanism, and mind to be pure intelligence. The life of reason will mark a real progress whenever it gives fuller expression to the interests that prompt its gropings, and reaches the truth about such facts as, for its own purposes, it is concerned to discover. I was not studying history or psychology for their own sake: my retrospect was to be frankly selective and critical, guided by a desire to discriminate the better from the worse.

But by what standard could I distinguish them? The first suggestion for such a work had come to me in my student days, on reading Hegel's *Phaenomenologie des Geistes*. It had seemed to me that myth and sophistry there spoilt a very fine subject. The subject was the history of human ideas: the sophistry was imposed on Hegel by his ambition to show that the episodes he happened to review formed a dialectical chain: and the myth sprang from the constant suggestion that this history of human ideas made up the whole of cosmic evolution, and that those episodes were the scattered syllables of a single eternal oracle. It occurred to me that a more honest criticism of progress might be based on tracing the distracted efforts of man to satisfy his natural impulses in his natural environment. Yet if these impulses were infinitely wayward and variable, and if the environment itself was inconstant or undiscoverable, what criterion of progress could it be possible to set up? As for me, I was utterly without the learning and the romantic imagination that might have enabled some emancipated rival of Hegel, some systematic Nietzsche or some dialectical Walt Whitman, to write a history of the Will to Be Everything and Anything. An omnivorous spirit was no spirit for me, and I could not write the life of reason without distinguishing it from madness.

The suggestion of such a work accordingly lay dormant in my mind for years, until maturity, aided by Platonic studies, supplied me with a fresh point of departure, and enabled me to conceive the whole subject in a way that seemed to rescue it at once from pretension and from futility. All that was needed was to know oneself. No unnatural constancy need be imposed on human nature at large: it sufficed that the critic himself should have a determinate character and a sane capacity for happiness. He was not likely to be so original that, if he was sincere, nobody else would be found to share and approve his judgments. No conceited postulates need be made about the universe, commanding it to be exceptionally friendly, or to preserve us or those like us forever, or to "conserve values," as if the duration or the multiplication of instances had anything to do with excellence. The wisdom of Socrates was enough for living and judging rightly in any world, the most magical or the most mechanical, the best or the worst. I had no need to adopt the cosmology of Plato—a mythical and metaphysical creation, more or less playful and desperate, designed to buttress his moral philosophy. I was old enough, when I came under his influence, to discount this sort of priestcraft in thought, so familiar in Christian apologists. Experience, knowledge of my own heart, attachment to Spinoza, even the science of the day, protected me against those voluntary illusions. Indeed, to undermine them gently, by showing how unnecessary and treacherous they are in the healthy life of the spirit, was a chief part of my undertaking. In order to discern this healthy life, for the soul no less than for the body, not much learning is required; only a little experience, a little reflection, and a little candour.

Moral philosophy is not a science. It moves exclusively in the realm of familiar discourse. The units it distinguishes are dramatic units, like those of literary psychology and historical fiction: ideas, persons, passions, destinies such as imagination presents to me when I survey my own past, or conceive the adventures of another. This limitation is far from involving the assumption that nothing but human discourse can exist, or that nature must be composed of rhetorical unities of that description. On the contrary, it is important for sanity and for art that human discourse should acknowledge the far deeper embosoming realms of matter and of essence, to which physics and dialectic are respectively addressed; otherwise moral philosophy would threaten to become myth and discourse mere ravings. Nevertheless, the uses of science remain human, in that it employs the mind nobly, chastens the feelings, or increases the safety and comfort of life. To investigate nature or refine dialectic beyond those uses, out of mere curiosity, may be an innocent automatic impulse in men of science, but it is vain. Physics and dialectic accordingly enter the life of reason only as developments of human discourse, coloured by human passions and serving them: the moralist accepts their reports, as he does those of memory and history, that they may enlighten him about the conditions and the possible forms of happiness. His own art, to which this book is essentially dedicated, is to express his reasoned preferences amongst all the forms of experience which his imagination can propose. To imagination the reader must appeal in turn if he would understand the argument; and if he would correct the conclusion, he must make sure that he is speaking for his heart, for his most secret dream of happiness.

May, 1922.

Dialogues in Limbo

NORMAL MADNESS

Democritus. YOU REAPPEAR IN SEASON, INQUISITIVE PILGRIM, AND TO-
day you must take a seat beside me. These young men are compelling my
hoary philosophy to disclose the cause of all the follies that they per-
petrated when alive. They still wear, as you see, their youthful and lusty
aspect; for when we enter these gates Minos and Rhadamanthus restore
to each of us the semblance of that age at which his spirit on earth had
been most vivid and masterful and least bent by tyrant circumstance out
of its natural straightness. Therefore Alcibiades and Dionysius and Aristippus walk here in the flower of their youth, and I sit crowned with all
the snows and wisdom of extreme old age; because their souls, though
essentially noble, grew daily more distracted in the press of the world
and more polluted, but mine by understanding the world grew daily purer
and stronger. They are still ready for every folly, though luckily they lack
the means; and the chronicle of vanity remains full of interest for them,
because they are confident of shining in it. Yet the person whom this subject most nearly touches is you, since you are still living, and life is at once
the quintessence and the sum of madness. Here our spirits can be mad only
vicariously and at the second remove, as the verses in which Sophocles
expresses the ravings of Ajax are themselves sanely composed, and a calm
image of horror. But your thoughts, in the confusion and welter of existence, are still rebellious to metre; you cannot yet rehearse your allotted
part, as we do here, with the pause and pomp of a posthumous self-knowl-
edge. My discourse on madness, therefore, will not only celebrate your
actions, but may open your eyes; and I assign to you on this occasion the
place of honour, as nearest of kin to the goddess Mania, who to-day pre-
sides over our games.

There is little philosophy not contained in the distinction between
things as they exist in nature, and things as they appear to opinion; yet
both the substance and its appearance often bear the same name, to the
confusion of discourse. So it is with the word madness, which sometimes
designates a habit of action, sometimes an illusion of the mind, and sometimes only the opprobrium which a censorious bystander may wish to cast
upon either.

Moralists and ignorant philosophers like Socrates—of whom women and young men often think so highly—do not distinguish nature from convention, and because madness is inconvenient to society they call it contrary to nature. But nothing can be contrary to nature; and that a man should shriek or see wild visions or talk to the air, or to a guardian genius at his elbow, or should kill his children and himself, when the thing actually occurs, is not contrary to nature, but only to the habit of the majority. The diseases which destroy a man are no less natural than the instincts which preserve him. Nature has no difficulty in doing what she does, however wonderful or horrible it may seem to a fancy furnished only with a few loose images and incapable of tracing the currents of substance; and she has no hostility to what she leaves undone and no longing to do it. You will find her in a thousand ways unmaking what she makes, trying again where failure is certain, and neglecting the fine feats which she once easily accomplished, as if she had forgotten their secret. How simple it was once to be a Greek and ingenuously human; yet nature suffered that honest humanity to exist only for a few doubtful years. It peeped once into being, like a weed amid the crevices of those Aegean mountains, and all the revolving aeons will not bring it back. Nature is not love-sick; she will move on; and if to the eye of passion her works seem full of conflict, vanity, and horror, these are not horrors, vanities, or conflicts to her. She is no less willing that we should be mad than that we should be sane. The fly that prefers sweetness to a long life may drown in honey; nor is an agony of sweetness forbidden by nature to those inclined to sing or to love.

Moral terms are caresses or insults and describe nothing; but they have a meaning to the heart, and are not forbidden. You may, therefore, without scientific error, praise madness or deride it. Your own disposition and habit will dictate these judgements.. A weak and delicate animal like man could have arisen only in an equable climate, in which at all seasons he might hunt and play, and run naked or gaily clad accordiing to his pleasure: he therefore at first regards the Hyperborean regions, where summer and winter are sharply contrasted, as cruel and uninhabitable; yet if by accident or necessity he becomes hardened to those changes, he begins to think his native forests pestiferous and fit only for snakes and monkeys. So it is also with the climates of the mind. Every nation thinks its own madness normal and requisite; more passion and more fancy it calls folly, less it calls imbecility. Of course, according to nature, to possess no fancy and no passion is not to possess too little, and a stone is no imbecile; while to have limitless passion and fancy is not to have too much, and a drone among bees or a poet among men is not a fool for being all raptures. In the moralist aspiration is free to look either way. If some gymnosophist sincerely declares that to move or to breathe or to think is vanity, and that to become insensible is the highest good, in that it abolishes illusion and all other evils, to him I object nothing; if starkness is his treasure, let him preserve it. If on the other hand Orpheus or Pythagoras or Plato, having a noble contempt for the body, aspire to soar in a perpetual ecstasy, and if with their eyes fixed on heaven they welcome any accidental fall from a throne or from a housetop as a precious liberation of their spirits, fluttering to be free, again I oppose nothing to their satisfaction: let them hug Icarian madness to their bosoms, as being the acme of bliss and glory.

What, Aristippus and Dionysius, are you so soon asleep? I confidently expected you at this point to applaud my oration. But sleep on, if you prefer dreams to an understanding of dreams.

Perhaps you others, whose wits are awake, may ask me how, if in nature there be nothing but atoms in motion, madness comes to exist at all. I will not reply that motion and division are themselves insanity, although wise men have said so; for if division and motion are the deepest nature of things, insanity would be rather the vain wish to impose upon them unity and rest. For by sanity I understand assurance and peace in being what one is, and in becoming what one must become; so that the void and the atoms, unruffled and ever ready, are eminently sane. Not so, however, those closed systems which the atoms often form by their cyclical motion: these systems are automatic; they complete and repeat themselves by an inward virtue whenever circumstances permit; yet even when circumstances do not permit, they madly endeavour to do so. This mad endeavour, when only partially defeated, may restore and propagate itself with but slight variations, and it is then called life. Of life madness is an inseparable and sometimes a predominant part: every living body is mad in so far as it is inwardly disposed to permanence when things about it are unstable, or is inwardly disposed to change when, the circumstances being stable, there is no occasion for changing. That which is virtue in season is madness out of season, as when an old man makes love; and Prometheus or Alexander attempting incredible feats is a miracle of sanity, if he attempts them at the right moment.

So much for madness in action, inevitable whenever the impulses of bodies run counter to opportunity. But life, both in its virtue and in its folly, is also expressed in fancy, creating the world of appearance. In the eye of nature all appearance is vain and a mere dream, since it adds something to substance which substance is not; and it is no less idle to think what is true than to think what is false. If ever appearance should become ashamed of being so gratuitous and like an old gossip should seek to excuse its garrulity by alleging its truth, neither the void nor the atoms would heed that excuse or accept it. Are they, forsooth, insecure that they should call upon that sleepy witness to give testimony to their being? Their being is indomitable substance and motion and action, and to add thought, impalpable and ghostly, is to add madness. Indeed fancy as if aware of its vanity, makes holiday as long as it can; its joy is in fiction, and it would soon fade and grow weary if it had to tell the truth. The heroes in the *Iliad*, instead of doing a man's work in silence, like honest atoms, love to recite their past exploits and to threaten fresh deeds of blood: had they respected reality they would have been content to act, but they must prate and promise, because they live by imagination. If their boasts are lies, as is probable, they are all the more elated. These fools might almost have perceived their own idiocy, if they had merely described their true actions, saying, "I am standing on two legs; I am hurling a spear, I am running away, I am lying flat and dead on the ground." The truth, my friends, is not eloquent, except unspoken; its vast shadow lends eloquence to our sparks of thought as they die into it. After all there was some sense in that nonsense of Socrates about the sun and moon being governed by reason, for they go their rounds soberly, without talking or thinking.

That the intoxication of life is the first cause of appearance you have all observed and experienced when you have danced in a chorus, or performed your military exercises, stamping on the ground in unison and striking your swords together; ordered motion being naturally fertile in sound, in flashing light, and in gladness. Such appearances, in the safe and liberal life of a god, would not be deceptive, since a god need not be concerned about his own existence, which is secure, or that of other things, which is indifferent, and he is not tempted to assert falsely, as men do, that sound and splendour and gladness are the substance of those things or of himself. In him the intoxication of life in creating appearance would not create illusion, but only an innocent and divine joy. Accordingly, when the voice of a god traverses the air, the burden of it is neither true nor false; only the priest or the people, anxiously interpreting that oracle according to their fears and necessities, render false or true by their presumption such scraps of it as they may hear. The god, however, was not mindful of them but was singing to himself his own song. This divine simplicity of nature is ill understood by mortals, who address everything to their mean uses and vain advantage; whereby in the struggle to lengthen their days a little they fill them with distraction.

This is a third and most virulent form of madness, in which the dreams of the vegetative soul are turned into animal error and animal fury. For animals cannot wait for the slow ministrations of earth and air, but as you see in birds and kittens and young children, must be in a fidget to move; prying in all directions and touching and gobbling everything within reach. This is their only entertainment, for they have lost all fine inner sensibility, and their feelings and fancies arise only when their whole soul is addressed to external things of which they are necessarily ignorant—for what can a simpleton know of the streams of atoms actually coursing about him? His mind is furnished only with feelings and images generated within, but being distracted by the urgency of his lusts and fears, he takes those images and feelings for pleasant lures or fantastic and stalking enemies. Thus whereas locomotion by itself would be unconscious and fancy by itself would be innocent and free from error, fancy married with locomotion, as it must be in the strife of animals, begets false opinion and wraps the naked atoms in a veil of dreams.

Such is the origin of opinion; and as the chief endeavour of the animal body is to defend and propagate itself at all costs, so the chief and most lasting illusion of the mind is the illusion of its own importance. What madness to assert that one collocation of atoms or one conjunction of feelings is right or is better, and another is wrong or is worse! Yet this baseless opinion every living organism emits in its madness, contradicting the equal madness of all its rivals. They say the stars laugh at us for this, but what is their own case? The sun and the planets may seem to gaping observation to lead a sane life, having found paths of safety; yet to the sharp eye of science the ambush is visible into which they glide. If they think themselves immortal gods, and feast and laugh together as they revolve complacently, they are mad, because a sudden surprise awaits them, and the common doom. Had they been wise, like philosophers who know themselves mortal, they should have consented and made ready to die, seeing that they are not pure atoms or the pure void, and that in forming them nature was not in earnest but playing. They would have done well to laugh, if they had laughed at themselves; for those who will not laugh with nature in her mockery and playfulness, turn her sport first into delusion and then into anguish.

Such being the nature and causes of madness, is there no remedy for it? In answering this question I broach the second and kindlier part of my discourse, when having described the disease I bring hope of health and prescribe the cure. A radical cure, though it exists, I will not propose to you, for you are young and inquisitive and not ready to renounce all life and all knowledge. Only some great and heroic sage can begin by disowning madness altogether and felling the tree of opinion at the root; nor would he, by leaping into total salvation, attain to any understanding of his former distress. In abolishing illusion he would have forgotten its existence and virtually denied it; so that for the blatant errors of his lusty years he would have substituted one great mute and perpetual error: the total ignorance which besets the atoms regarding the patterns and the dreams which in fact they generate. Suddenly to renounce all madness is accordingly to miss the truth about madness, together with the whole comic rout of this world, which is marvellously fertile in comedy.

My physic accordingly will be more gentle; I will not prescribe instant death as the only medicine. Wisdom is an evanescent madness, when the dream still continues but no longer deceives. In all illusions there is some truth, since being products of nature they all have some relation to nature, and a prudent mind by lifting their masks may discover their true occasions. Doubtless the number and swiftness of the atoms, even in a little space, must always elude human discernment; but the more foolish images of sense may be disallowed in favour of others more faithful to the true rhythms and divisions of nature. Thus to the innocent eye the six stout spokes of a chariot-wheel revolving rapidly are merged and blurred in one whirling disc; but the philosopher, though no less subject than other men to this illusion, on seeing the disc will remember the spokes, and in all his fevers and griefs will be mindful of the atoms; his forced illusions will not deceive him altogether, since he knows their cause, and it is in his power, if the worst befall, by a draught of atoms artfully mingled, to dispel all his griefs and fevers for ever. Meantime, in the interest of human life, without inquiring into its ultimate vanity, a conventional distinction may be drawn between madness and sanity. Belief in the imaginary and desire for the impossible will justly be called madness; but those habits and ideas will be conventionally called sane which are sanctioned by tradition and which, when followed, do not lead directly to the destruction of oneself or of one's country. Such conventional sanity is a normal madness like that of images in sense, love in youth, and religion among nations.

Two protecting deities, indeed, like two sober friends supporting a drunkard, flank human folly and keep it within bounds. One of these deities is Punishment, and the other Agreement. The very mad man chokes, starves, runs into the sea, or having committed some fearful rape or murder is sentenced to death by the magistrate. Even if harmless, he is tied with a chain, and dies like a dog in his kennel. Punishment thus daily removes the maddest from the midst of mankind. The remnant, though their thoughts be in their homely way still dull or fantastic, then plod on in relative safety, while the unhappy souls whom Punishment has overtaken rest from their troubles. For no sooner has the system of atoms forming an animal body lost its equilibrium and been dispersed in death, than no pain or fancy or haggard hope subsists in that system any longer, and the peace of indifference and justice returns to the world; and if here or in the memory of men some echo of that life reverberates, it rings without anguish, the note once sounded repeating itself perpetually, pure and undisturbed. This is the good work which Punishment does daily, healing and harmonizing the worst of follies.

Yet before dying in the arms of Punishment madness may be mitigated and tamed by Agreement, like a young colt broken in and trained to gallop in harness. The automatism of life, which is necessarily spontaneous and blind, may by adjustment with its occasions become a principle of health and genius, the parent of noble actions and beautiful works. Fancy, too, in creating images which have no originals in nature—since in nature there is nothing but atoms and the void—may by union with the times and order of natural events become the mother of names, pleasant and familiar, by which those events are called in the language of sense. Thus the most diverse imaginations in various species of animals may be rendered compatible with sagacity and with a prosperous life. Migratory fowl do not record their voyages in books, like human geographers, yet they have appointed dreams and secret sensations which warn them of the season for flight, and they are well informed about Egypt without consulting Herodotus. If omens were observed scientifically and not superstitiously interpreted, augury might be a true art of substitution, like language. There are many false tales told both by Greeks and barbarians which at times are useful to the state, because by an artful disposition of signs and sounds they dispose the inner parts of men favourably for breasting labour or war. Thus the most deed-dyed illusion, if it be interwoven with good habits, may flourish in long amity with things, naming and saluting them, as we do the stars, or gods, without understanding their nature.

Such amity can the god Agreement establish even between aliens, but between brothers he weaves a subtler and a sweeter bond. For when kindred bodies have the same habitat and the same arts they also have the same illusions; and their common madness gives to each a perfect knowledge of the other's mind. Whereas the images in the eye or the thoughts of the heart can agree but loosely and, as it were, politically with material things, they may agree exactly with the images in another eye, and the thoughts of another heart. This free unanimity was called friendship by the Greeks, who alone of all nations have understood the nature of friendship. Barbarians of course may fight faithfully in bands, and may live in tribes and in cities, hugging their wives and children to their bosom; but such instinctive love, which all animals manifest, is not friendship. It moves in the realm of nature, and concerns only action and fate, whereas friendship is agreement in madness, when the same free thoughts and the same fraternal joys visit two kindred spirits. It was not for fighting loyally side by side that the Spartan phalanx or the Theban band were incomparable in the annals of war, but for fighting side by side for the sake of the beautiful, and in order that the liberal madness of their friendship might not end, unless it ended in death. All the glories of Greece are the fruits of this friendship and belong to the realm of madness tempered by Agreement; for out of the very fountain of madness Apollo and the Muses drew that intoxication which they taught to flow in the paths of health and of harmony. The Greeks in the intervals between their wars, instead of sinking into luxury and sloth, or into a vain industry, instituted games, in which peace was made keen and glorious by a beautiful image of war. Actual war is a conflict of matter with matter, as blind as it is inevitable; but the images which it breeds survive in peace, as we survive in these removed spaces after the battle of existence. So even the wisest when alive play with images and interests, and the glitter of many rival opinions hides the deep harmony with nature by which these opinions live. There is sweetness and quaint reason in these frail thoughts of our after-life, as in the wisdom of children. What could be madder than a ghost? Yet by the harmony which each of us has long since attained with himself, and by the freedom and peace which we gladly grant to one another, we immortalize the life of friendship and share it with the gods.

Let such, then, be my discourse upon madness. Philosophers are unjust to the madness of the vulgar, and the vulgar to that of madmen and philosophers, not seeing how plausible a substitute it is for their own, because everybody thinks himself sane; wherein precisely shines his blinding illusion. I have wished in a manner to remove the mystery and the odium from this universal predicament of mortals, and to show it to be no anomaly. Madness is natural and, like all things natural, it loves itself, and often, by its innocence or by its signification, it lives in harmony with the rest of nature; otherwise, by the action it comports, it finds its quietus in punishment and death.

Alcibiades. Your discourse, indomitable Sage, has filled us all with wonder, and left us without the wish to speak. The Stranger, if he had dared, should have broken this silence rather than I, for you tell us that madness comes of being alive, and very likely he thinks that such an opinion comes of being dead.

Democritus. Very likely, but let him speak for himself.

The Stranger. I should not hesitate to do so if I had anything to object to so persuasive a discourse, but words on my part are superfluous, since I recognize the truth of every part of it. To show you, however, that the living are not always unwilling to confess their plight, I will repeat an old story of the sort which we compose for children. It seems curiously to confirm all that the noble Democritus has taught us.

Once upon a time, so the story runs, the whole world was a garden in which a tender fair-haired child, whose name was Autologos, played and babbled alone. There was, indeed, an old woman who tended the garden, a goddess in disguise; but she lived in a cave and came out only at night when the child was asleep, for like the bat and the astronomer she could see better in the dark. She had a sharp pruning-hook on a very long pole, with which she silently pruned every tree and shrub in the garden, even the highest branches, cutting off the dead twigs and shaking down the yellow leaves in showers; and often, muttering surly words to herself which were not intelligible, she would cut off some flower or some bud as well, so that when the child awoke he missed them and could not imagine what had become of them. Now the child in his play gave names to everything that he liked or disliked; and the rose he called Beauty, and the jasmin Pleasure, and the hyacinth Sweetness, and the violet Sadness, and the thistle Pain, and the olive Merit, and the laurel Triumph, and the vine Inspiration. He was highly pleased with all these names, and they made those flowers and plants so much more interesting to him, that he thought those names were their souls. But one day, having pricked himself with the thorns of a rose, he changed her name to Love; and this caused him to wonder why he had given those particular names to everything rather than quite different names; and the child began to feel older. As he sat brooding on this question, for he had stopped playing, a man in a black gown came into the garden who was a botanist, and said: "It matters little what names you give to flowers because they already have scientific names which indicate their true genera and species; the rose is only a rose, and is neither Beauty nor Love; and so with all the other flowers. They are flowers and plants merely, and they have no souls." Hearing this the child began to cry, very much to the botanist's annoyance, for being a busy man he disliked emotion. "After all," he added, "those names of yours will do no harm, and you may go on using them if you please; for they are prettier than those which truly describe the flowers, and much shorter; and if the word soul is particularly precious to you, you may even say that plants and flowers have souls: only, if you wish to be a man and not always a child, you must understand that the soul of each flower is only a name for its way of life, indicating how it spreads its petals in the morning and perhaps closes them at night, as you do your eyes. You must never suppose, because the flower has a soul, that this soul does anything but what you find the flower actually doing." But the child was not comforted, and when the wind had dried his tears, he answered: "If I cannot give beautiful names to the plants and flowers which shall be really their souls, and if I cannot tell myself true tales about them, I will not play in the garden any more. You may have it all to yourself and botanize in it, but I hate you." And the child went to sleep that night quite flushed and angry. Then, as silently as the creeping moonlight, the old woman came out of her cave and went directly to the place where the child was sleeping, and with a great stroke of her pruning-knife cut off his head; and she took him into her cave and buried him under the leaves which had fallen on that same night, which were many. When the botanist returned in the morning and found the child gone he was much perplexed. "To whom," said he to himself, "shall I now teach botany? There is nobody now to care for flowers, for I am only a professor, and if I can't teach anybody the right names for flowers, of what use are flowers to me?" This thought oppressed the poor man so much that he entirely collapsed, and as he was rather wizened to begin with, he was soon reduced to a few stiff tendons and bones, like the ribs of a dry leaf; and even these shreds soon crumbled, and he evaporated altogether. Only his black gown remained to delight the rag-picker. But the goddess in guise of that old woman went on pruning the garden, and it seemed to make no difference in her habits that the child and the botanist were dead.

I think we may surmise that the true name of this goddess must have been Dikè, the same that the wise Democritus was calling Punishment;

and the botanist's name must have been Nomos, whom he was calling Agreement; and of course the child Autologos was that innocent illusion which was the theme of his whole discourse.

Aristippus. If this be the nature of madness, I propose that we immediately raise an altar to that deity, and worship him hereafter as the only beneficent god; and in order to avoid the protests of the vulgar, who think madness an evil, we will disguise our deity under the name of Autologos, borrowed from the Stranger's tale; and we will not identify him with the Furies or Harpies, but with Pan, Apollo, Orpheus, and Dionysus.

Dionysius. Agreed: and since my name is derived from that of Dionysus, who must have been my ancestor, I proclaim myself high priest of the new temple.

Democritus. You pay my speech a great tribute. I have celebrated the mad god so fitly that I have filled his votaries with a new frenzy of worship.

Alcibiades. Aristippus and Dionysius are enemies of science, and you, Democritus, are a believer in it. Being no judge in the matter, I will not pronounce between you, but I can conceive that a man who has spent his whole long life distilling herbs and grinding stones into powder should believe that he knows something of their substance. Nevertheless, intense study, too, is hypnotic, and might not the lucid theory of nature which you think partly awakens you out of the dream of life, be but a dream within a dream and the deepest of your illusions? My whole career seems a myth to me now in memory; yet when I interpret it in terms of your philosophy and imagine instead nothing but clouds of atoms drifting through a black sky, I seem to be descending into an even deeper cavern of reverie. Suppose I was dreaming of a chariot-race, hearing the shouting crowds, blushing to be myself the victor, and reining in my quivering steeds to receive the crown, and suppose that suddenly my dream was transformed, and Olympia and the sunshine and myself and my horses and my joy and the praises of the Athenians turned to atoms fatally combined—I am afraid that, like the child in the Stranger's tale, I should burst into tears at that change of dreams.

Democritus. Do you think I should blame you? Is the sublimity of truth impatient of error? I know well the shock that comes to innocence on discovering that the beautiful is unsubstantial. The soul, too, has her virginity and must bleed a little before bearing fruit. You misconceive my philosophy if you suppose that I deny the beautiful or would madly forbid it to appear. Has not my whole discourse been an apology for illusion and a proof of its necessity? When I discover that the substance of the beautiful is a certain rhythm and harmony in motion, as the atoms dance in circles through the void (and what else should the substance of the beautiful be if it has a substance at all?) far from destroying the beautiful in the realm of appearance my discovery raises its presence there to a double dignity; for its witchery, being a magic birth, is witchery indeed; and in it its parent nature, whose joy it is, proves her fertility. I deny nothing. Your Olympian victory and your trembling steeds, spattered with foam, and your strong lithe hand detaining them before the altar of Apollo, while you receive the crown—how should science delete these verses from the book of experience or prove that they were never sung? But where is their music now? What was it when passing? A waking dream. Yes, and grief also is a dream, which if it leaves a trace leaves not one of its own quality, but a transmuted and serene image of sorrow in this realm of memory and truth. As the grief of Priam in Homer and the grief of Achilles, springing from the dreadful madness of love and pride in their two bosoms, united in the divine ecstasy of the poet, so all the joys and griefs of illusion unite and become a strange ecstasy in a sane mind. What would you ask of philosophy? To feed you on sweets and lull you in your errors in the hope that death may overtake you before you understand anything? Ah, wisdom is sharper than death and only the brave can love her. When in the thick of passion the veil suddenly falls, it leaves us bereft of all we thought ours, smitten and consecrated to an unearthly revelation, walking dead among the living, not knowing what we seem to know, not loving what we seem to love, but already translated into an invisible paradise where none of these things are, but one only companion, smiling and silent, who by day and night stands beside us and shakes his head gently, bidding us say Nay, nay, to all our madness. Did you think, because I would not spare you, that I never felt the cold steel? Has not my own heart been pierced? Shed your tears, my son, shed your tears. The young man who has not wept is a savage, and the old man who will not laugh is a fool.

Scepticism and Animal Faith

PREFACE

HERE IS ONE MORE SYSTEM OF PHILOSOPHY. IF THE READER IS TEMPTED to smile, I can assure him that I smile with him, and that my system—to which this volume is a critical introduction—differs widely in spirit and pretensions from what usually goes by that name. In the first place, *my system is not mine, nor new*. I am merely attempting to express for the reader the principles to which he appeals when he smiles. There are convictions in the depths of his soul, beneath all his overt parrot beliefs, on which I would build our friendship. I have a great respect for orthodoxy; not for those orthodoxies which prevail in particular schools or nations, and which vary from age to age, but for a certain shrewd orthodoxy which the sentiment and practice of laymen maintain everywhere. I think that common sense, in a rough dogged way, is technically sounder than the special schools of philosophy, each of which squints and overlooks half the facts and half the difficulties in its eagerness to find in some detail the key to the whole. I am animated by distrust of all high guesses, and by sympathy with the old prejudices and workaday opinions of mankind: they are ill expressed, but they are well grounded. What novelty my version of things may possess is meant simply to obviate occasions for sophistry by giving to everyday beliefs a more accurate and circumspect form. I do not pretend to place myself at the heart of the universe nor at its origin, nor to draw its periphery. I would lay siege to the truth only as animal exploration and fancy may do so, first from one quarter and then from another, expecting the reality to be not simpler than my experience of it, but far more extensive and complex. I stand in philosophy exactly where I stand in daily life; I should not be honest otherwise. I accept the same miscellaneous witnesses, bow to the same obvious facts, make conjectures no less instinctively, and admit the same encircling ignorance.

My system, accordingly, is *no system of the universe*. The Realms of Being of which I speak are not parts of a cosmos, nor one great cosmos together: they are only kinds of categories of things which I find conspicuously different and worth distinguishing, at least in my own thoughts. I do not know how many things in the universe at large may fall under each of

354

these classes, nor what other Realms of Being may not exist, to which I have no approach or which I have not happened to distinguish in my personal observation of the world. Logic, like language, is partly a free construction and partly a means of symbolising and harnessing in expression the existing diversities of things; and whilst some languages, given a man's constitution and habits, may seem more beautiful and convenient to him than others, it is a foolish heat in a patriot to insist that only his native language is intelligible or right. No language or logic is right in the sense of being identical with the facts it is used to express, but each may be right by being faithful to these facts, as a translation may be faithful. My endeavour is to think straight in such terms as are offered to me, to clear my mind of cant and free it from the cramp of artificial traditions; but I do not ask any one to think in my terms if he prefers others. Let him clean better, if he can, the windows of his soul, that the variety and beauty of the prospect may spread more brightly before him.

Moreover, my system, save in the mocking literary sense of the word, is *not metaphysical*. It contains much criticism of metaphysics, and some refinements in speculation, like the doctrine of essence, which are not familiar to the public; and I do not disclaim being metaphysical because I at all dislike dialectic or disdain immaterial things: indeed, it is of immaterial things, essence, truth, and spirit that I speak chiefly. But logic and mathematics and literary psychology (when frankly literary) are not metaphysical, although their subject-matter is immaterial, and their application to existing things is often questionable. Metaphysics, in the proper sense of the word, is dialectical physics, or an attempt to determine matters of fact by means of logical or moral or rhetorical constructions. It arises by a confusion of those Realms of Being which it is my special care to distinguish. It is neither physical speculation nor pure logic nor honest literature, but (as in the treatise of Aristotle first called by that name) a hybrid of the three, materialising ideal entities, turning harmonies into forces, and dissolving natural things into terms of discourse. Speculations about the natural world, such as those of the Ionian philosophers, are not metaphysics, but simply cosmology or natural philosophy. Now in natural philosophy I am a decided materialist—apparently the only one living; and I am well aware that idealists are fond of calling materialism, too, metaphysics, in rather an angry tone, so as to cast discredit upon it by assimilating it to their own systems. But my materialism, for all that, is not metaphysical. I do not profess to know what matter is in itself, and feel no confidence in the divination of those *esprits forts* who, leading a life of vice, thought the universe must be composed of nothing but dice and billiard-balls. I wait for the men of science to tell me what matter is, in so far as they can discover it, and am not at all surprised or troubled at the abstractness and vagueness of their ultimate conceptions: how should our notions of things so remote from the scale and scope of our senses be anything but schematic? But whatever matter may be, I call it matter boldly, as I call my acquaintances Smith and Jones without knowing their secrets: whatever it may be, it must present the aspects and undergo the motions of the gross objects that fill the world: and if belief in the existence of hidden parts and movements in nature be metaphysics, then the kitchen-maid is a metaphysician whenever she peels a potato.

My system, finally, though, of course, formed under the fire of contemporary discussions, is *no phase of any current movement*. I cannot take at all seriously the present flutter of the image-lovers against intelligence. I love images as much as they do, but images must be discounted in our waking life, when we come to business. I also appreciate the other reforms and rebellions that have made up the history of philosophy. I prize their sharp criticism of one another and their several discoveries; the trouble is that each in turn has denied or forgotten a much more important truth than it has asserted. The first philosophers, the original observers of life and nature, were the best; and I think only the Indians and the Greek naturalists, together with Spinoza, have been right on the chief issue, the relation of man and of his spirit to the universe. It is not unwillingness to be a disciple that prompts me to look beyond the modern scramble of philosophies: I should gladly learn of them all, if they had learned more of one another. Even as it is, I endeavour to retain the positive insight of each, reducing it to the scale of nature and keeping it in its place; thus I am a Platonist in logic and morals, and a transcendentalist in romantic soliloquy, when I choose to indulge in it. Nor is it necessary, in being teachable by any master, to become eclectic. All these vistas give glimpses of the same wood, and a fair and true map of it must be drawn to a single scale, by one method of projection, and in one style of calligraphy. All known truth can be rendered in any language, although the accent and poetry of each may be incommunicable; and as I am content to write in English, although it was not my mother-tongue, and although in speculative matters I have not much sympathy with the English mind, so I am content to follow the European tradition in philosophy, little as I respect its rhetorical metaphysics, its humanism, and its worldliness.

There is one point, indeed, in which I am truly sorry not to be able to profit by the guidance of my contemporaries. There is now a great ferment in natural and mathematical philosophy and the times seem ripe for a new system of nature, at once ingenuous and comprehensive, such as has not appeared since the earlier days of Greece. We may soon be all believing in an honest cosmology, comparable with that of Heraclitus, Pythagoras, or Democritus. I wish such scientific systems joy, and if I were competent to follow or to forecast their procedure, I should gladly avail myself of their results, which are bound to be no less picturesque than instructive. But what exists to-day is so tentative, obscure, and confused by bad philosophy, that there is no knowing what parts may be sound and what parts merely personal and scatter-brained. If I were a mathematician I should no doubt regale myself, if not the reader, with an electric or logistic system of the universe expressed in algebraic symbols. For good or ill, I am an ignorant man, almost a poet, and I can only spread a feast of what everybody knows. Fortunately exact science and the books of the learned are not necessary to establish my essential doctrine, nor can any of them claim a higher warrant than it has in itself: for it rests on public experience. It needs, to prove it, only the stars, the seasons, the swarm of animals, the spectacle of birth and death, of cities and wars. My philosophy is justified, and has been justified in all ages and countries, by the facts before every man's eyes; and no great wit is requisite to discover it, only (what is rarer than wit) candour and courage. Learning does not liberate men from superstition when their souls are cowed or perplexed; and, without learning, clear eyes and honest reflection can discern the hang of the world, and distinguish the edge of truth from the might of imagination. In the past or in the future, my language and my borrowed knowledge would have been different, but under whatever sky I had been born, since it is the same sky, I should have had the same philosophy.

ULTIMATE SCEPTICISM

Why should the mystic, in proportion as he dismisses the miscellany of experience as so much illusion, feel that he becomes one with reality and attains to absolute existence? I think that the same survival of vulgar presumptions which leads the romantic solipsist to retain his belief in his personal history and destiny, leads the mystic to retain, and fondly to embrace, the feeling of existence. His speculation is indeed inspired by the love of security: his grand objection to the natural world, and to mortal life, is that they are deceptive, that they cheat the soul that loves them, and prove to be illusions: the assumption apparently being that reality must be permanent, and that he who has hold on reality is safe for ever. In this the mystic, who so hates illusions, is the victim of an illusion himself: for the reality he has hold of is but the burden of a single moment, which in its solipsism thinks itself absolute. What is reality? As I should like to use the term, reality is being of any sort. If it means character or essence, illusions have it as much as substance, and more richly. If it means substance, then sceptical concentration upon inner experience, or ecstatic abstraction, seems to me the last place in which we should look for it. The immediate and the visionary are at the opposite pole from substance; they are on the surface or, if you like, at the top; whereas substance if it is anywhere is at the bottom. The realm of immediate illusion is as real as any other, and very attractive; many would wish it to be the only reality, and hate substance; but if substance exists (which I am not yet ready to assert) they have no reason to hate it, since it is the basis of those immediate feelings which fill them with satisfaction. Finally, if reality means existence, certainly the mystic and his meditation may exist, but not more truly than any other natural fact; and what would exist in them would be a pulse of animal being, kindling that momentary ecstasy, as animal life at certain intensities is wont to do. The theme of that meditation, its visionary object, need not exist at all; it may be incapable of existing if it is essentially timeless and dialectical. The animal mind treats its data as facts, or as signs of facts, but the animal mind is full of the rashest presumptions, positing time, change, a particular station in the midst of events yielding a particular perspective of those events, and the flux of all nature precipitating that experience at that place. None of these posited objects is a datum in which a sceptic could rest. Indeed, existence or fact, in the sense which I give to these words, cannot be a datum at all, because existence involves external relations and actual (not merely specious) flux: whereas, however complex a datum may be, with no matter what perspectives opening within it, it must be embraced in a single stroke of apperception, and nothing outside it can belong to it at all. The datum is a pure image; it is essentially illusory and unsubstantial, however thunderous its sound or keen its edge, or however normal and significant its presence may be. When the mystic asserts enthusiastically the existence of his immediate, ideal, unutterable object, Absolute Being, he is peculiarly unfortunate in his faith: it would be impossible to choose an image less relevant to the agencies that actually bring that image before him. The burden and glow of existence which he is conscious of come entirely from himself; his object is eminently empty, impotent, non-existent; but the heat and labour of his own soul suffuse that emptiness with light, and the very hum of change within him, accelerated almost beyond endurance and quite beyond discrimination, sounds that piercing note.

The last step in scepticism is now before me. It will lead me to deny existence to any datum, whatever it may be; and as the datum, by hypothesis, is the whole of what solicits my attention at any moment, I shall deny the existence of everything, and abolish that category of thought altogether. If I could not do this, I should be a tyro in scepticism. Belief in the existence of anything, including myself, is something radically incapable of proof, and resting, like all belief, on some irrational persuasion or prompting of life. Certainly, as a matter of fact, when I deny existence I exist; but doubtless many of the other facts I have been denying, because I found no evidence for them, were true also. To bring me evidence of their existence is no duty imposed on facts, nor a habit of theirs: I must employ private detectives. The point is, in this task of criticism, to discard every belief that is a belief merely; and the belief in existence, in the nature of the case, can be a belief only. The datum is an idea, a description; I may contemplate it without belief; but when I assert that such a thing exists I am hypostatising this datum, placing it in presumptive relations which are not internal to it, and worshipping it as an idol or thing. Neither its existence nor mine nor that of my belief can be given in any datum. These things are incidents involved in that order of nature which I have thrown over; they are no part of what remains before me.

Assurance of existence expresses animal watchfulness: it posits, within me and round me, hidden and imminent events. The sceptic can easily cast a doubt on the remoter objects of this belief; and nothing but a certain obduracy and want of agility prevents him from doubting present existence itself. For what could present existence mean, if the imminent events for which animal sense is watching failed altogether, failed at the very roots, so to speak, of the tree of intuition, and left nothing but its branches flowering *in vacuo?* Expectation is admittedly the most hazardous of beliefs: yet what is watchfulness but expectation? Memory is notoriously full of illusion; yet what would experience of the present be if the veracity of primary memory were denied, and if I no longer believed that anything had just happened, or that I had ever been in the state from which I suppose myself to have passed into this my present condition?

It will not do for the sceptic to take refuge in the confused notion that expectation *possesses* the future, or memory the past. As a matter of fact, expectation is like hunger; it opens its mouth, and something probably drops into it, more or less, very often, the sort of thing it expected; but sometimes a surprise comes, and sometimes nothing. Life involves expectation, but does not prevent death: and expectation is never so thoroughly stultified as when it is not undeceived, but cancelled. The open mouth does not then so much as close upon nothing. It is buried open. Nor is memory in a better case. As the whole world might collapse and cease at any moment, nullifying all expectation, so it might at any moment have sprung out of nothing: for it is thoroughly contingent, and might have begun to-day, with this degree of complexity and illusive memory, as well as long ago, with whatever energy or momentum it was first endowed with. The backward perspective of time is perhaps really an inverted expectation; but for the momentum of life forward, we might not be able to space the elements active in the present so as to assign to them a longer or a shorter history; for we should not attempt to discriminate amongst these elements such as we could still count on in the immediate future, and such as we might safely ignore: so that our conception of the past implies, perhaps, a distinction between the living and the dead. This distinction is itself practical, and looks to the future. In the absolute present all is specious; and to pure intuition the living are as ghostly as the dead, and the dead as present as the living.

In the sense of existence there is accordingly something more than the obvious character of that which is alleged to exist. What is this complement? It cannot be a feature in the datum, since the datum by definition is the whole of what is found. Nor can it be, in my sense at least of the word existence, the intrinsic constitution or specific being of this object, since existence comports external relations, variable, contingent, and not discoverable in a given being when taken alone: for there is nothing that may not lose its existence, or the existence of which might not be conceivably denied. The complement added to the datum when it is alleged to exist seems, then, to be added by *me;* it is the finding, the occurrence, the assault, the impact of that being here and now; it is the experience of it. But what can experience be, if I take away from it the whole of what is experienced? And what meaning can I give to such words as impact, assault, occurrence, or finding, when I have banished and denied my body, my past, my residual present being, and everything except the datum which I find? The sense of existence evidently belongs to the intoxication, to the *Rausch,* of existence itself; it is the strain of life within me, prior to all intuition, that in its precipitation and terror, passing as it continually must from one untenable condition to another, stretches my attention absurdly over what is not given, over the lost and the unattained, the before and after which are wrapped in darkness, and confuses my breathless apprehension of the clear presence of all I can ever truly behold.

Indeed, so much am I a creature of movement, and of the ceaseless metabolism of matter, that I should never catch even these glimpses of the light, if there were not rhythms, pauses, repetitions, and nodes in my physical progress, to absorb and reflect it here and there: as the traveller, hurried in a cloud of smoke and dust through tunnel after tunnel in the Italian Riviera, catches and loses momentary visions of blue sea and sky, which he would like to arrest, but cannot; yet if he had not been rushed and whistled along these particular tunnels, even those snatches, in the form in which they come to him, would have been denied him. So it is the rush of life that, at its open moments, floods me with intuitions, partial and confused, but still revelations; the landscape is wrapped in the smoke of my little engine, and turned into a tantalising incident of my hot journey. What appears (which is an ideal object and not an event) is thus confused with the event of its appearance; the picture is identified with the kindling or distraction of my attention falling by chance upon it; and the strain of my material existence, battling with material accidents, turns the ideal object too into a temporal fact, and makes it seem substantial. But this fugitive existence which I egotistically attach to it, as if its fate was that of my glimpses of it, is no part of its true being, as even my intuition discerns it; it is a practical dignity or potency attributed to it by the irrelevant momentum of my animal life. Animals, being by nature hounded and hungry creatures, spy out and take alarm at any datum of sense or fancy, supposing that there is something substantial there, something that will count and work in the world. The notion of a moving world is brought implicitly with them; they fetch it out of the depths of their vegetating psyche, which is a small dark cosmos, silently revolving within. By being noticed, and treated as a signal for I know not what material opportunity or danger, the given image is taken up into the business world, and puts on the garment of existence. Remove this frame, strip off all suggestion of a time when this image was not yet present, or a time when it shall be past, and the very notion of existence is removed. The datum ceases to be an appearance, in the proper and pregnant sense of this word, since it ceases to imply any substance that appears or any mind to which it appears. It is an appearance only in the sense that its nature is wholly manifest, that it is a specific being, which may be mentioned, thought of, seen, or defined, if any one has the wit to do so. But its own nature says nothing of any hidden circumstances that shall bring it to light, or any adventitious mind that shall discover it. It lies simply in its own category. If a colour, it is just this colour; if a pain, just this pain. Its appearance is not an event: its presence is not an experience; for there is no surrounding world in which it can arise, and no watchful spirit to appropriate it. The sceptic has here withdrawn into the intuition of a surface form, without roots, without origin or environment, without a seat or a locus; a little universe, an immaterial absolute theme, rejoicing merely in its own quality. This theme, being out of all adventitious relations and not in the least threatened with not being the theme it is, has not the contingency nor the fortunes proper to an existence; it is simply that which it inherently, logically, and unchangeably is.

Existence, then, not being included in any immediate datum, is a fact always open to doubt. I call it a fact notwithstanding, because in talking about the sceptic I am positing his existence. If he has any intuition, however little the theme of that intuition may have to do with any actual world, certainly I who think of his intuition, or he himself thinking of it afterwards, see that this intuition of his must have been an event, and his existence at that time a fact; but like all facts and events, this one can be known only by an affirmation which posits it, which may be suspended or reversed, and which is subject to error. Hence all this business of intuition may perfectly well be doubted by the sceptic: the existence of his own doubt (however confidently I may assert it for him) is not given to him then: all that is given is some ambiguity or contradiction in images; and if afterwards he is sure that he has doubted, the sole cogent evidence which that fact can claim lies in the psychological impossibility that, so long as he believes he has doubted, he should not believe it. But he may be wrong in harbouring this belief, and he may rescind it. For all an ultimate scepticism can see, therefore, there may be no facts at all, and perhaps nothing has ever existed.

Scepticism may thus be carried to the point of denying change and memory, and the reality of all facts. Such a sceptical dogma would certainly be false, because this dogma itself would have to be entertained, and that event would be a fact and an existence: and the sceptic in framing that

dogma discourses, vacillates, and lives in the act of contrasting one assertion with another—all of which is to exist with a vengeance. Yet this false
dogma that nothing exists is tenable intuitively and, while it prevails, is
irrefutable. There are certain motives (to be discussed later) which render
ultimate scepticism precious to a spiritual mind, as a sanctuary from grosser
illusions. For the wayward sceptic, who regards it as no truer than any
other view, it also has some utility: it accustoms him to discard the dogma
which an introspective critic might be tempted to think self-evident, namely,
that he himself lives and thinks. That he does so is true; but to establish
that truth he must appeal to animal faith. If he is too proud for that, and
simply stares at the datum, the last thing he will see is himself.

THE DISCOVERY OF ESSENCE

The loss of faith, as I have already observed, has no tendency to banish
ideas; on the contrary, since doubt arises on reflection, it tends to keep
the imagination on the stretch, and lends to the whole spectacle of things
a certain immediacy, suavity, and humour. All that is sordid or tragic falls
away, and everything acquires a lyric purity, as if the die had not yet been
cast and the ominous choice of creation had not been made. Often the
richest philosophies are the most sceptical; the mind is not then tethered
in its home paddock, but ranges at will over the wilderness of being. The
Indians, who deny the existence of the world, have a keen sense for its
infinity and its variegated colours; they play with the monstrous and miraculous in the grand manner, as in the *Arabian Nights*. No critic has had a
sharper eye for the outlines of ideas than Hume, who found it impossible
seriously to believe that they revealed anything. In the critic, as in the
painter, suspension of belief and of practical understanding is favourable
to vision; the arrested eye renders every image limpid and unequivocal.
And this is not merely an effect of physiological compensation, in that perhaps the nervous energy withdrawn from preparations for action is allowed
to intensify the process of mere sensation. There ensues a logical clarification as well; because so long as belief, interpretation, and significance entered in, the object in hand was ambiguous; in seeking the fact the mind
overlooked or confused the datum. Yet each element in this eager investigation—including its very eagerness—is precisely what it is; and if I renounce
for the moment all transitive intelligence, and give to each of these elements
its due definition, I shall have a much richer as well as clearer collection
of terms and relations before me, than when I was clumsily attempting to
make up my mind. Living beings dwell in their expectations rather than
in their senses. If they are ever to *see* what they see, they must first in a
manner stop living; they must suspend the will, as Schopenhauer put it;
they must photograph the idea that is flying past, veiled in its very swiftness.
This swiftness is not its own fault, but that of my haste and inattention; my
hold is loose on it, as in a dream; or else perhaps those veils and that swift-

ness are the truth of the picture; and it is they that the true artist should be concerned to catch and to eternalise, restoring to all that the practical intellect calls vague its own specious definition. Nothing is vague in itself, or other than just what it is. Symbols are vague only in respect to their signification, when this remains ambiguous.

It is accordingly an inapt criticism often passed upon Berkeley and Hume that they overlooked vagueness in ideas, although almost every human idea is scandalously vague. No, their intuition of ideas, at least initially, was quite direct and honest. The ambiguity they overlooked lay in the relation of ideas to physical things, which they wished to reduce to groups or series of these pellucid ideas—a chimerical physics. Had they abstained altogether from identifying ideas with objects of natural knowledge (which are events and facts), and from trying to construct material things out of optical and tactile images, they might have much enriched the philosophy of specious reality, and discerned the innocent realm of ideas as directly as Plato did, but more accurately. In this they need not have confused or undermined faith in natural things. Perception *is* faith; more perception may extend this faith or reform it, but can never recant it except by sophistry. These virgin philosophers were like the cubists or futurists in the painting of to-day. They might have brought to light curious and neglected forms of direct intuition. They could not justly have been charged with absurdity for seeing what they actually saw. But they lapse into absurdity, and that irremediably, if they pretend to be the first and only masters of anatomy and topography.

Far from being vague or abstract the obvious ideas remaining to a complete sceptic may prove too absorbing, too multitudinous, or too sweet. A moral reprobation of them is no less intelligible than is the scientific criticism which rejects them as illusions and as no constituents of the existing world. Conscience no less than business may blame the sceptic for a sort of luxurious idleness; he may call himself a lotus-eater, may heave a sigh of fatigue at doing nothing, and may even feel a touch of the vertigo and wish to close the eyes on all these images that entertain him to no purpose. But scepticism is an exercise, not a life; it is a discipline fit to purify the mind of prejudice and render it all the more apt, when the time comes, to believe and to act wisely; and meantime the pure sceptic need take no offence at the multiplicity of images that crowd upon him, if he is scrupulous not to trust them and to assert nothing at their prompting. Scepticism is the chastity of the intellect, and it is shameful to surrender it too soon or to the first comer: there is nobility in preserving it coolly and proudly through a long youth, until at last, in the ripeness of instinct and discretion, it can be safely exchanged for fidelity and happiness. But the philosopher, when he is speculative only, is a sort of perpetual celibate; he is bent on not being betrayed, rather than on being annexed or inspired; and although if he is at all wise he must see that the true marriage of the mind is with nature and science and the practical arts, yet in his special theoretic vocation, it will be a boon to him to view all experience simply, in the precision and distinctness which all its parts acquire when not referred to any substance which they might present confusedly, nor to any hypothesis or action which they might suggest.

The sceptic, then, as a consequence of carrying his scepticism to the greatest lengths, finds himself in the presence of more luminous and less equivocal objects than does the working and believing mind; only these objects are without meaning, they are only what they are obviously, all surface. They show him everything thinkable with the greatest clearness and force; but he can no longer imagine that he sees in these objects anything save their instant presence and their face-value. Scepticism therefore suspends all knowledge worthy of the name, all that transitive and presumptive knowledge of facts which is a form of belief; and instead it bestows intuition of ideas, contemplative, æsthetic, dialectical, arbitrary. But whereas transitive knowledge, though important if true, may always be challenged, intuition, on the contrary, which neither has nor professes to have any ulterior object or truth, runs no risks of error, because it claims no jurisdiction over anything alien or eventual.

In this lucidity and calmness of intuition there is something preternatural. Imagine a child accustomed to see clothes only on living persons and hardly distinguishing them from the magical strong bodies that agitate them, and suddenly carry this child into a costumer's shop, where he will see all sorts of garments hung in rows upon manikins, with hollow breasts all of visible wire, and little wooden nobs instead of heads: he might be seriously shocked or even frightened. How should it be possible for clothes standing up like this not to be people? Such abstractions, he might say to himself, are metaphysically impossible. Either these figures must be secretly alive and ready, when he least expects it, to begin to dance, or else they are not real at all, and he can only fancy that he sees them. Just as the spectacle of all these gaunt clothes without bodies might make the child cry, so later might the whole spectacle of nature, if ever he became a sceptic. The little word *is* has its tragedies; it marries and identifies different things with the greatest innocence; and yet no two are ever identical, and if therein lies the charm of wedding them and calling them one, therein too lies the danger. Whenever I use the word *is,* except in sheer tautology, I deeply misuse it; and when I discover my error, the world seems to fall asunder and the members of my family no longer know one another. Existence is the strong body and familiar motion which the young mind expects to find in every dummy. The oldest of us are sometimes no less recalcitrant to the spectacle of the garments of existence—which is all we ever saw of it—when the existence is taken away. Yet it is to these actual and familiar, but now disembowelled objects, that scepticism introduces us, as if to a strange world; a vast costumer's gallery of ideas where all sorts of patterns and models are on exhibition, without bodies to wear them, and where no human habits of motion distract the eye from the curious cut and precise embroideries of every article. This display, so complete in its spectacular reality, not a button nor a feather wanting or unobserved, is not the living crowd that it ought to be, but a mockery of it, like the palace of the Sleeping Beauty. To my conventional mind, clothes without bodies are no less improper than bodies without clothes; yet the conjunction of these things is but human. All nature runs about naked, and quite happy; and I am not so remote from nature as not to revert on occasion to that nakedness—which is unconsciousness—with profound relief. But ideas without things and apparel without wearers seem to me a stranger condition; I think the garments were made to fit the limbs, and should collapse without them. Yet, like the fig leaves of Eden, they are not garments essentially. They become such by accident, when one or another of them is appropriated by the providential buyer—not necessarily human—whose instinct may choose it; or else it is perfectly content to miss its chance, and to lie stacked for ever among its motley neighbours in this great store of neglected finery.

It was the fear of illusion that originally disquieted the honest mind, congenitally dogmatic, and drove it in the direction of scepticism; and it may find three ways, not equally satisfying to its honesty, in which that fear of illusion may be dispelled. One is death, in which illusion vanishes and is forgotten; but although anxiety about error, and even positive error, are thus destroyed, no solution is offered to the previous doubt: no explanation of what could have called forth that illusion or what could have dissipated it. Another way out is by correcting the error, and substituting a new belief for it: but while in animal life this is the satisfying solution, and the old habit of dogmatism may be resumed in consequence without practical inconvenience, speculatively the case is not at all advanced; because no criterion of truth is afforded except custom, comfort, and the accidental absence of doubt; and what is absent by chance may return at any time unbidden. The third way, at which I have now arrived, is to entertain the illusion without succumbing to it, accepting it openly as an illusion, and forbidding it to claim any sort of being but that which it obviously has; and then, whether it profits me or not, it will not deceive me. What will remain of this non-deceptive illusion will then be a truth, and a truth the being of which requires no explanation, since it is utterly impossible that it should have been otherwise. Of course I may still ask why the identity of this particular thing with itself should have occurred to *me;* a question which could only be answered by plunging into a realm of existence and natural history every part and principle of which would be just as contingent, just as uncalled-for, and just as inexplicable as this accident of my being; but that this particular thing, or any other which might have occurred to me instead, should be constituted as it is raises no problem; for how could *it* have been constituted otherwise? Nor is there any moral offence any longer in the contingency of my view of it, since my view of it involves no error. The error came from a wild belief about it; and the possibility of error came from a wild propensity to belief. Relieve now the pressure of that animal haste and that hungry presumption; the error is washed out of the illusion; it is no illusion now, but an idea. Just as food would cease to be food, and poison poison, if you removed the stomach and the blood that they might nourish or infect; and just as beautiful things would cease to be beautiful if you removed the wonder and the welcome of living souls, so if you eliminate your anxiety, deceit itself becomes entertainment, and every illusion but so much added acquaintance with the realm of form. For the unintelligible accident of existence will cease to appear to lurk in this manifest being, weighting and crowding it, and threatening it with being swallowed up by nondescript neighbours. It will appear dwelling in its own world, and shining by its own light, however brief may be my glimpse of it: for no date will be written on it, no frame of full or of empty time will shut it in; nothing in it will be addressed to me, nor suggestive of any spectator. It will seem an event in no world, an incident in no experience. The quality of it will have ceased to exist: it will be merely the quality which it inherently, logically, and inalienably is. It will be an ESSENCE.

Retrenchment has its rewards. When by a difficult suspension of judgement I have deprived a given image of all adventitious significance, when it is taken neither for the manifestation of a substance nor for an idea in a mind nor for an event in a world, but simply if a colour for that colour and if music for that music, and if a face for that face, then an immense cognitive certitude comes to compensate me for so much cognitive abstention. My scepticism at last has touched bottom, and my doubt has found honourable rest in the absolutely indubitable. Whatever essence I find and note, that essence and no other is established before me. I cannot be mistaken about it, since I now have no object of intent other than the object of intuition. If for some private reason I am dissatisfied, and wish to change my entertainment, nothing prevents; but the change leaves the thing I first saw possessed of all its quality, for the sake of which I perhaps disliked or disowned it. That, while one essence is before me, some one else may be talking of another, which he calls by the same name, is nothing to the purpose; and if I myself change and correct myself, choosing a new essence in place of the old, my life indeed may have shifted its visions and its interests, but the characters they had when I harboured them are theirs without change. Indeed, only because each essence is the essence defined by instant apprehension can I truly be said to have changed my mind; for I can have discarded any one of them only by substituting something different. This new essence could not be different from the former one, if each were not unchangeably itself.

There is, then, a sort of play with the non-existent, or game of thought, which intervenes in all alleged knowledge of matters of fact, and survives that knowledge, if this is ever questioned or disproved. To this mirage of the non-existent, or intuition of essence, the pure sceptic is confined; and confined is hardly the word; because though without faith and risk he can never leave that thin and bodiless plane of being, this plane in its tenuity is infinite; and there is nothing possible elsewhere that, as a shadow and a pattern, is not prefigured there. To consider an essence is, from a spiritual point of view, to enlarge acquaintance with true being; but it is not even to broach knowledge of fact; and the ideal object so defined may have no natural significance, though it has æsthetic immediacy and logical definition. The modest scope of this speculative acquaintance with essence renders it infallible, whilst the logical and æsthetic ideality of its object renders that object eternal. Thus the most radical sceptic may be consoled, without being rebuked or refuted; he may leap at one bound over the whole human tangle of beliefs and dogmatic claims, elude human incapacity and bias, and take hold of the quite sufficient assurance that any essence or ideal quality of being which he may be intuiting has just the characters he is finding in it, and has them eternally.

This is no idle assurance. After all, the only thing that can ultimately interest me in other men's experience or, apart from animal egotism, in my own, is just this character of the essences which at any time have swum into our ken; not at all the length of time through which we may have beheld them, nor the circumstances that produced that vision; unless these circumstances in turn, when considered, place before the mind the essences which it delights to entertain. Of course, the choice and the interest of essences come entirely from the bent of the animal that elicits the vision of them from his own soul and its adventures; and nothing but affinity with my animal life lends the essences I am able to discern their moral colour, so that to my mind they are beautiful, horrible, trivial, or vulgar. The good essences are such as accompany and express a good life. In them, whether good or bad, that life has its eternity. Certainly when I cease to exist and to think, I shall lose hold on this assurance; but the theme in which for a moment I found the fulfilment of my expressive impulses will remain, as it always was, a theme fit for consideration, even if no one else should consider it, and I should never consider it again.

Nor is this all. Not only is the character of each essence inalienable, and, so long as it is open to intuition, indubitable, but the realm of essences is infinite. Since any essence I happen to have hit upon is independent of me and would possess its precise character if I had never been born, or had never been led by the circumstances of my life and temperament to apprehend that particular essence, evidently all other essences, which I have not been led to think of, rejoice in the same sort of impalpable being—impalpable, yet the only sort of being that the most rugged experience can ever actually find. Thus a mind enlightened by scepticism and cured of noisy dogma, a mind discounting all reports, and free from all tormenting anxiety about its own fortunes or existence, finds in the wilderness of essence a very sweet and marvellous solitude. The ultimate reaches of doubt and renunciation open out for it, by an easy transition, into fields of endless variety and peace, as if through the gorges of death it had passed into a paradise where all things are crystallised into the image of themselves, and have lost their urgency and their venom.

THE WATERSHED OF CRITICISM

I have now reached the culminating point of my survey of evidence, and the entanglements I have left behind me and the habitable regions I am looking for lie spread out before me like opposite valleys. On the one hand I see now a sweeping reason for scepticism, over and above all particular contradictions or fancifulness of dogma. Nothing is ever present to me except some essence; so that nothing that I possess in intuition, or actually see, is ever *there;* it can never exist bodily, nor lie in that place or exert that power which belongs to the objects encountered in action. Therefore, if I regard my intuitions as knowledge of facts, all my experience is illusion, and life is a dream. At the same time I am now able to give a clearer meaning to this old adage; for life would not be a dream, and all experience would not be illusion, if I abstained from believing in them. The evidence of data is only obviousness; they give no evidence of anything else; they are not witnesses. If I am content to recognise them for pure essences, they cannot deceive me; they will be like works of literary fiction, more or less coherent, but without any claim to exist on their own account. If I hypostatise an essence into a fact, instinctively placing it in relations which are not given within it, I am putting my trust in animal faith, not in any evidence or implication of my actual experience. I turn to an assumed world about me, because I have organs for turning, just as I expect a future to reel itself out without interruption because I am wound up to go on myself. To such ulterior things no manifest essence can bear any testimony. They must justify themselves. If the ulterior fact is some intuition elsewhere, its existence, if it happens to exist, will justify that belief; but the fulfilment of my prophecy, in taking my present dream for testimony to that ulterior experience, will be found only in the realm of truth—a realm which is itself an object of belief, never by any possibility of intuition, human or divine. So too when the supposed fact is thought of as a substance, its existence, if it is found in the realm of nature, will justify that supposition; but the realm of nature is of course only another object of belief, more remote if possible from intuition than even the realm of truth. Intuition of essence, to which positive experience and certitude are confined, is therefore always illusion, if we allow our hypostatising impulse to take it for evidence of anything else.

In adopting this conclusion of so many great philosophers, that all is illusion, I do so, however, with two qualifications. One is emotional and moral only, in that I do not mourn over this fatality, but on the contrary rather prefer speculation in the realm of essence—if it can be indulged without practical inconvenience—to alleged information about hard facts. It does not seem to me ignominious to be a poet, if nature has made one a poet unexpectedly. Unexpectedly nature lent us existence, and if she has made it a condition that we should be poets, she has not forbidden us to enjoy that art, or even to be proud of it. The other qualification is more austere: it consists in not allowing exceptions. I cannot admit that some particular essence—water, fire, being, atoms, or Brahma—is the intrinsic essence of all things, so that if I narrow my imagination to that one intuition I shall have intuited the heart and the whole of existence. Of course I do not deny that there is water and that there is being, the former in most things on earth, and the latter in everything anywhere; but these images or words of mine are not the things they designate, but only names for them. Desultory and partial propriety these names may have, but no metaphysical privilege. No more has the expedient of some modern critics who would take illusion as a whole and call it the universe; for in the first place they are probably reverting to belief in discourse, as conventionally conceived, so that their scepticism is halting; and in the second place, even if human experience could be admitted as known and vouched for, there would be an incredible arrogance in positing it as the whole of being, or as itself confined to the forms and limits which the critic assigns to it. The life of reason as I conceive it is a mere romance, and the life of nature a mere fable; such pictures have no metaphysical value, even if as sympathetic fictions they had some psychological truth.

The doctrine of essence thus renders my scepticism invincible and complete, while reconciling me with it emotionally.

If now I turn my face in the other direction and consider the prospect open to animal faith, I see that all this insecurity and inadequacy of alleged knowledge are almost irrelevant to the natural effort of the mind to describe natural things. The discouragement we may feel in science does not come from failure; it comes from a false conception of what would be success. Our worst difficulties arise from the assumption that knowledge of existences ought to be literal, whereas knowledge of existences has no need, no propensity, and no fitness to be literal. It is symbolic initially, when a sound, a smell, an indescribable feeling are signals to the animal of his dangers or chances; and it fulfils its function perfectly—I mean its moral function of enlightening us about our natural good—if it remains symbolic to the end. Can anything be more evident than that religion, language, patriotism, love, science itself speak in symbols? Given essences unify for intuition, in entirely adventitious human terms, the diffuse processes of nature; the æsthetic image—the sound, the colour, the expanse of space, the scent, taste, and sweet or cruel pressure of bodies—wears an aspect altogether unlike the mechanisms it stands for. Sensation and thought (between which there is no essential difference) work in a conventional medium, as do literature and music. The experience of essence is direct; the expression of natural facts through that medium is indirect. But this indirection is no obstacle to expression, rather its condition; and this vehicular manifestation of things may be knowledge of them, which intuition of essence is not. The theatre, for all its artifices, depicts life in a sense more truly than history, because the medium has a kindred movement to that of real life, though an artificial setting and form; and much in the same way the human medium of knowledge can perform its pertinent synthesis and make its pertinent report all the better when it frankly abandons the plane of its object and expresses in symbols what we need to know of it. The arts of expression would be impossible if they were not extensions of normal human perception. The Greeks recognised that astronomy and history were presided over by Muses, sisters of those of tragic and comic poetry; had they been as psychological as modern reflection has become, they might have had Muses of sight, hearing, and speech. I think they honoured, if they did not express, this complementary fact also, that all the Muses, even the most playful, are witnesses to the nature of things. The arts are evidences of wisdom, and sources of it; they include science. No Muse would be a humane influence, nor worthy of honour, if she did not studiously express the truth of nature with the liberty and grace appropriate to her special genius.

Philosophers would not have overlooked the fact that knowledge is, and ought to be, symbolical, if intuition did not exist also, giving them a taste of something which perhaps they think higher and more satisfying. Intuition, when it is placid and masterful enough to stand alone, free from anxiety or delusion about matters of fact, is a delightful exercise, like play; it employs our imaginative faculty without warping it, and lets us live without responsibility. The playful and godlike mind of philosophers has always been fascinated by intuition; philosophers—I mean the great ones—are the infant prodigies of reflection. They often take intuition of essence for their single ideal, and wish to impose it on the workaday thoughts of men; they make a play-world for themselves which it is glorious to dominate, much as other men of genius, prolonging the masterfulness of childhood, continue to play at this or at that in their politics and their religion. But knowledge of existence has an entirely different method and an entirely different ideal. It is playful too, because its terms are intuitive and its grammar or logic often very subjective. Perception, theory, hypothesis are rapid, pregnant, often humorous; they seize a fact by its skirts from some unexpected quarter, and give it a nickname which it might be surprised to hear, such as the rainbow or the Great Bear. Yet in the investigation of facts all this play of mind is merely instrumental and indicative: the intent is practical, the watchfulness earnest, the spirit humble. The mind here knows that it is at school; and even its fancies are docile. Its nicknames for things and for their odd ways of behaving are like those which country people give to flowers; they often pointedly describe how things look or what they do to us. The ideas we have of things are not fair portraits; they are political caricatures made in the human interest; but in their partial way they may be masterpieces of characterisation and insight. Above all, they are obtained by labour, by investigating what is not given, and by correcting one impression by another, drawn from the same object—a thing impossible in the intuition of essences. They therefore conduce to wisdom, and in their perpetual tentativeness have a cumulative truth.

Consider the reason why, instead of cultivating congenial intuitions, a man may be drawn to the study of nature at all. It is because things, by their impact, startle him into attention and a new thought. Such external objects interest him for what they do, not for what they are; and knowledge of them is significant, not for the essence it displays to intuition (beautiful as this may be) but for the events it expresses or foreshadows. It matters little therefore to the pertinent knowledge of nature that the substance of things should remain recondite or unintelligible, if their movement and operation can be rightly determined on the plane of human perception. It matters little if their very existence is vouched for only by animal faith and presumption, so long as this faith posits existence where existence is, and this presumption expresses a prophetic preadaptation of animal instincts to the forces of the environment. The function of perception and natural science is, not to flatter the sense of omniscience in an absolute mind, but to dignify animal life by harmonising it, in action and in thought, with its conditions. It matters little if the news these methods can bring us of the world is fragmentary and is expressed rhetorically; what matters is that science should be integrated with art, and that the arts should substitute the dominion of man over circumstances, as far as this is possible, for the dominion of chance. In this there is no sacrifice of truth to utility; there is rather a wise direction of curiosity upon things on the human scale, and within the range of art. Speculation beyond those limits cannot be controlled, and is irresponsible; and the symbolic terms in which it must be carried on, even at close quarters, are the best possible indications for the facts in question. All these inadequacies and imperfections are proper to perfect signs, which should be brief and sharply distinguished.

Complete scepticism is accordingly not inconsistent with animal faith; the admission that nothing given exists is not incompatible with belief in things not given. I may yield to the suasion of instinct, and practise the arts with a humble confidence, without in the least disavowing the most rigorous criticism of knowledge or hypostatising any of the data of sense or fancy. And I need not do this with a bad conscience, as Parmenides and Plato and the Indians seem to have done, when they admitted illusion or opinion as an epilogue to their tight metaphysics, on the ground that otherwise they would miss their way home. It is precisely by *not* yielding to opinion and illusion, and by *not* delegating any favourite essences to be the substance of things, that I aspire to keep my cognitive conscience pure and my practical judgement sane; because in order to find my way home I am by no means compelled to yield ignominiously to any animal illusion; what guides me there is not illusion but habit; and the intuitions which accompany habit are normal signs for the circle of objects and forces by which that habit is sustained. The images of sense and science will not delude me if instead of hypostatising them, as those philosophers did the terms of their dialectic, I regard them as graphic symbols for home and for the way there. That such external things exist, that I exist myself, and live more or less prosperously in the midst of them, is a faith not founded on reason but precipitated in action, and in that intent, which is virtual action, involved in perception. This faith, which it would be dishonest not to confess that I share, does no violence to a sceptical analysis of experience; on the contrary, it takes advantage of that analysis to interpret this volatile experience as all animals do and must, as a set of symbols for existences that cannot enter experience, and which, since they are not elements in knowledge, no analysis of knowledge can touch—they are in another realm of being.

I propose now to consider what objects animal faith requires me to posit, and in what order; without for a moment forgetting that my assurance of their existence is only instinctive, and my description of their nature only symbolic. I may know them by intent, based on bodily reaction; I know them initially as whatever confronts me, whatever it may turn out to be, just as I know the future initially as whatever is coming, without knowing what will come. That something confronts me here, now, and from a specific quarter, is in itself a momentous discovery. The aspect this thing wears, as it first attracts my attention, though it may deceive me in some particulars, can hardly fail to be, in some respects, a telling indication of its nature in its relation to me. Signs identify their objects for discourse, and show us where to look for their undiscovered qualities. Further signs, catching other aspects of the same object, may help me to lay siege to it from all sides; but signs will never lead me into the citadel, and if its inner chambers are ever opened to me, it must be through sympathetic imagination. I might, by some happy unison between my imagination and its generative principles, intuit the essence which is actually the essence of that thing. In that case (which may often occur when the object is a sympathetic mind) knowledge of existence, without ceasing to be instinctive faith, will be as complete and adequate as knowledge can possibly be. The given essence will be the essence of the object meant; but knowledge will remain a claim, since the intuition is not satisfied to observe the given essence passively as a disembodied essence, but instinctively affirms it to be the essence of an existence confronting me, and beyond the range of my possible apprehension. Therefore the most perfect knowledge of fact is perfect only pictorially, not evidentially, and remains subject to the end to the insecurity inseparable from animal faith, and from life itself.

Animal faith being a sort of expectation and open-mouthedness, is earlier than intuition; intuitions come to help it out and lend it something to posit. It is more than ready to swallow any suggestion of sense or fancy; and perhaps primitive credulity, as in a dream, makes no bones of any contradiction or incongruity in successive convictions, but yields its whole soul to every image. Faith then hangs like a pendulum at rest; but when perplexity has caused that pendulum to swing more and more madly, it may for a moment stop quivering at a point of unstable equilibrium at the top; and this vertical station may be likened to universal scepticism. It is a more wonderful and a more promising equilibrium than the other, because it cannot be maintained; but before declining from the zenith and desisting from pointing vertically at zero, the pendulum of faith may hesitate for an instant which way to fall, if at that uncomfortable height it has really lost all animal momentum and all ancient prejudice. Before giving my reasons—which are but prejudices and human—for believing in events, in substances, and in the variegated truths which they involve, it may be well to have halted for breath at the apex of scepticism, and felt all the negative privileges of that position. The mere possibility of it in its purity is full of instruction; and although I have, for my own part, dwelt upon it only ironically, by a scruple of method, and intending presently to abandon it for common sense, many a greater philosopher has sought to maintain himself acrobatically at that altitude. They have not succeeded; but an impossible dwelling-place may afford, like a mountain-top, a good point of view in clear weather from which to map the land and choose a habitation.

Letters

To WILLIAM JAMES

AVILA, AUGUST 7, 1888

Dear Prof. James—

Many thanks for your letter, and for your expressions of interest. I have not seen anywhere that residents can't hold the Walker Fellowship, but if such be the case or even if it be thought that non-residents have a better claim to it, of course I am quite ready to resign. The doubt you express about my "fulfilling the purposes, etc." was a reason in my mind for returning to Harvard. I fancy that if I were there I should run less danger of being considered an unprofitable servant. Being a foreigner and coming from a rather different intellectual and moral milieu, I have a lighter and less-conscience-stricken way of taking things, which produces the impression of idleness and frivolity in the absence of ocular proof that after all I do as much work as other people. You interpret my disillusions in the matter of philosophy rather too seriously. There is nothing tragic about them. I was drawn to philosophy in the beginning by curiosity and a natural taste for ingenious thinking, and my attachment to philosophy remains as firm as ever, as I said in my previous letters. These things never came to me as a personal problem, as a question of what was necessary for salvation. I was simply interested in seeing what pictures of the world and of human nature men had succeeded in sketching: on better acquaintance I see reason to think that they are conventional and hieroglyphic in the extreme. But the interest in these delineations is no more destroyed for me by not trusting their result or their method than the charm of a play is destroyed if it is not historical. Philosophy does not cease to be a field of human activity and as such to have its significance and worth, and I cannot see why one so inclined by temperament cannot make good use of his time in that study, as in the study of art or comparative religion. Renan has said that no one can be a good historian of religion who has

374

not been a believer and who is not a sceptic: the same may be true of philosophy. I therefore do not think that my present attitude unfits me to study philosophy or to teach it, although I can easily imagine that others may not be of my opinion in this respect. I will therefore not throw up the fellowship on the ground that I have had a moral and mental collapse, a conversion to the devil, as it were, that unfits me, as insanity might, to hold any official position. I have had nothing of the sort. My notions about the possibilities of human thought and knowledge have gradually changed, and I have become convinced that most of our scheme of doctrine is built on false or arbitrary axioms. But this has been no personal crisis, no inner transformation. There have been moments when I have tired of certain authors, or certain problems, and in this mood I may have said something likely to be misunderstood. But the good authors, the sharp and radical thinkers, are still my delight and even my chief amusement, and I can imagine no more congenial task than to talk them over with other students. I have known all along that there was little chance of my being trusted anywhere with a professorship of philosophy; but I have taken this opportunity of study for its own sake and for mine, thinking that I could always live by teaching one thing or another, while I have not enough to live on without work.

This is frankly the way I feel about the matter. If it seems to you that under the circumstances it would be better to give up the fellowship, I am ready to do so. At any rate I intend to return to America, as it is a better country than this to get a living in, and for the present I can live with my mother. I shall probably arrive about Sept. 15, when I hope to have the pleasure of seeing you.

Yours ever

To WILLIAM JAMES

60 BRATTLE STREET
[CAMBRIDGE, MASS.]
EASTER, 1900

Dear James

Palmer* has just sent me your delightful letter by which I see with

* [Professor George Herbert Palmer.]

joy that you are full of life again in this season of resurrection. May the revival be perennial for you and full of fruits! You must have thought me very unfeeling not to write and make personal inquiries during all these months; it has not been for lack of concern but merely from perplexity in finding the right moment and the right words, as well as from the knowledge of how little my platonic sympathies would count in the midst of the affection of your many friends. But I am as glad as any of them can be at the change for the better, and full of confidence that you underestimate the amount of energy that you will find again in yourself ere long.

I see that you have discovered me in the *Poetry & Religion** more than in my verses or the *Sense of Beauty,* although I fancy there is no less of me in those other books. But there is more to come, and although I daresay you won't like the *Life of Reason* much better than you like my attitude hitherto, I think you will find that, apart from temperament, I am nearer to you than you now believe. What you say, for instance, about the value of the good lying in its *existence,* and about the continuity of the world of values with that of fact, is not different from what I should admit. Ideals would be irrelevant if they were not natural entelechies, if they were not called for by something that exists and if consequently their realization would not be a present and actual good. And the point in insisting that all the eggs at breakfast are rotten is nothing at all except the consequent possibility and endeavour to find good eggs for the morrow. The only thing I object to and absolutely abhor is the assertion that all the eggs indiscriminately are good because the hen has laid them.

You tax me several times with impertinence and superior airs. I wonder if you realize the years of suppressed irritation which I have past in the midst of an unintelligible sanctimonious and often disingenuous Protestantism, which is throughly alien and repulsive to me, and the need I have of joining hands with something far away from it and far above it. My Catholic sympathies didn't justify me in speaking out because I felt them to be merely sympathies and not to have a rational and human backing: but the study of Plato and Aristotle has given me confidence and, backed by such an authority as they and all who have accepted them represent, I have the right to be sincere, to be absolutely objective and unapologetic, because it is not I that speak but human reason that speaks in me. Truly the Babel in which we live has nothing in it so respectable as to put on the defensive the highest traditions of the human mind. No doubt, as you say, Latinity is moribund, as Greece itself was when it transmitted to the rest of the world the seeds of its own rationalism; and for that reason there is the more need of transplanting and propagating straight thinking among the peoples who hope to be masters of the world in the immediate future.

* [*Interpretations of Poetry and Religion* (1900).]

Otherwise they will be its physical masters only, and the Muses will fly over them to alight among some future race that may understand the Gods better. . . .

Always sincerely yours

To WILLIAM JAMES

HÔTEL FOYOT
PARIS, DEC. 6, 1905

Dear Mr James

I forgot yesterday to answer one of your questions, which I remember may be of importance to you. The lectures are at five o'clock in the afternoon on Tuesdays and Saturdays. I have no doubt they would change the hour for you if you wished. To everything they say "comme vous voudrez", and things here, as in England, seem to go by prerogative. You could also give as many or as few lectures as you chose—the great Hyde consenting.

Another omission. Blood's poem,* after about six readings, has become intelligible to me, and I like the thought very much, also the diction, but the *composition* is deplorable. Why can't people begin and end, and give one some indication of what they are talking about? As to the Tychism of it, it seems to me a good surface philosophy, a good expression of consciousness and the look of the flux. Of course what must be, if it must be, would never be known beforehand; and the machinery that may actually support our feelings doesn't deprive them of their dramatic novelty and interest, any more than the printed *dénouement* of a novel, extant in the last chapter, takes away from the dreamful excitement of perusing it and of wondering what will come next.

Now that I am launched I will say a word about some of the criticisms in your letter. You are very generous; I feel that you want to give me credit for everything good that can possibly be found in my book.* But you don't yet see my philosophy, nor my temper from the inside; your praise, like your blame, touches only the periphery, accidental aspects presented to this or that preconceived and disparate interest. The style is good, the tone is supercilious, here is a shrewd passage, etc., etc. And

* [*Reveries of One,* by B. P. Blood.]
* [*The Life of Reason.*]

you say I am less hospitable than Emerson. Of course. Emerson might pipe
his woodnotes and chirp at the universe most blandly; his genius might be
tender and profound and Hamlet-like, and that is all beyond my range and
contrary to my purpose. I am a Latin, and nothing seems serious to me except politics, except the sort of men that your ideas will involve and the
sort of happiness they will be capable of. The rest is exquisite moonshine.
Religion in particular was *found out* more than 100 years ago, and it seems
to me intolerable that we should still be condemned to ignore the fact and
to give the parsons and the "idealists" a monopoly of indignation and of
contemptuous dogmatism. It is they, not we, that are the pest; and while
I wish to be just and to understand people's feelings, wherever they are
at all significant, I am deliberately minded to be contemptuous toward
what seems to me contemptible, and not to have any share in the conspiracy of mock respect by which intellectual ignominy and moral stagnation are kept up in our society. What did Emerson know or care about
the passionate insanities and political disasters which religion, for instance,
has so often been another name for? He could give that name to his last
personal intuition, and ignore what it stands for and what it expresses in
the world. It is the latter that absorbs me; and I care too much about mortal
happiness to be interested in the charming vegetation of cancer-microbes in
the system—except with the idea of suppressing it.

A more technical point. You say "activity" can be spiritual only. Is
your activity, or sense of activity, not rather an ἐνέργεια [actuality] than
a δύναμις [potentiality]? Of course I should be the first to agree that activity, in the sense of actuality and conscious stress, belongs only to consciousness or even to the rational and reflective energy of thought. But
efficiency, in the sense of regular predictable contiguity with other specific
events, belongs only to δύναμις, to the potential (=the potent.) In a
dream there is the sense of activity, there is commotion and actualization,
ἐνέργεια; but there is no δύναμις, no material efficacy, save through
the underlying metabolism in the brain; the story in the dream stops short;
its purposes evaporate. This may be contrary to common sense, meaning
ordinary ways of expressing oneself; but it seems to me quite of a piece
with common sense of a progressive sort, with science. It might be contrary to common sense to say that the sun is larger than the earth, but
not to the common sense applied to the full situation. So this doctrine
seems to me reasonable in its method and result, though as yet paradoxical
in its language.

I have read practically no reviews of my book so that I don't know if
any one has felt in it something which, I am sure, is there: I mean the
tears. "Sunt lachrimae rerum, et mentem mortalia tangunt" ["E'en here
the tear of pity springs/And hearts are touched by human things." Con-
ington]. Not that I care to moan over the gods of Greece, turned into the
law of gravity, or over the stained-glass of cathedrals broken to let in the
sunlight and the air. It is not the past that seems to me affecting, entranc-

ing, or pitiful to lose. It is the ideal. It is that vision of perfection that we just catch, or for a moment embody in some work of art, or in some idealised reality: it is the concomitant inspiration of life, always various, always beautiful, hardly ever expressible in its fulness. And it is my adoration of this real and familiar good, this love often embraced but always elusive, that makes me detest the Absolutes and the dragooned myths by which people try to cancel the passing ideal, or to denaturalise it. That is an inhumanity, an impiety, that I can't bear. And much of the irritation which I may betray and which, I assure you is much greater than I let it seem, comes of affection. It comes of exasperation at seeing the only things that are beautiful or worth having treated as if they were of no account.

I seldom write to any one so frankly as I have here. But I know *you* are human, and tolerant to anything, however alien, that smells of blood.

Always sincerely yours,

TO GEORGE LAWTON

ROME, MARCH 29, 1922.

Dear Mr. Lawton,

It is always pleasant to be urged to do something on the ground that one can do it well; and I have some sympathy with your cry: No more metaphysics.* I am nevertheless at work on a book of philosophy (which I do not like to call metaphysics); it will take a year or two; after that I promise you to renounce the subject—except as an ingredient in pleasanter things. The "Three Proofs of Realism" is only a short paper, and has already appeared. But now I come to the part of your advice which I don't mean to follow at all. Criticism is something purely incidental—talk about talk—and to my mind has no serious value except perhaps as an expression of *Philosophy* in the critic. When I have been led to write criticism it has never been for any other reason; and you don't know me at all if you suppose me capable of *reading up* Meredith or Thomas Hardy or any one else who hasn't come in my way, in order to describe them to other people. If you like that sort of vicarious literary nourishment, read Croce, or any other competent person who sets out to express the impression which literature has made upon him. But I should advise you to read the originals instead, and be satisfied with the impression they make upon you.

* [When a student of philosophy at Columbia, Dr. Lawton had written to Santayana and urged him to give up metaphysics and devote all his time to literary criticism.]

You know Plato's contempt for the image of an image; but as a man's view of things is an image in the first place, and his work is an image of that, and the critic's feelings are an image of that work, and his writings an image of his feelings, and your idea of what the critic means only an image of his writings,—please consider that you are steeping your poor original tea-leaves in their fifth wash of hot water, and are drinking slops. May not the remarkable sloppiness and feebleness of the cultivated American mind be due to this habit of drinking life in its fifth dilution only? What you need is not more criticism of current authors, but more *philosophy:* more courage and sincerity in facing nature directly, and in criticising books or institutions only with a view to choosing among them whatever is most harmonious with the life you want to lead. For as Dryden (or is it Pope?) says, "If you think the world worth winning, think, oh think it worth enjoying." I accordingly intend to devote such years as may remain to me exclusively to philosophy; although I hope the form in which it will be expressed will not lead you to call it metaphysics.

Yours very truly,

TO MATTHEW HOEHN, O.S.B.

CORTINA D'AMPEZZO
AUGUST 10, 1939

Dear Father Hoehn,

I was christened in the Church and profess no other religion, so that from the point of view of the census-taker I am unmistakably a Catholic. My Protestant and Jewish critics also discover a good deal of Catholicism in my writings; but I have never been a practising Catholic, and my views in philosophy and history are incompatible with belief in any revelation. It would therefore be wholly misleading to classify me among "Catholic Authors".

This is a sufficient answer to your inquiry, for the purpose of your book of biographies, in which I ought not to be included. Yet I may add, in case you are at all interested in my real relation to the Faith, that a well-grounded Catholic student might find my philosophy useful (like that of some of the ancients) in defending the moral, political and mystical doctrines of the Church. I think that all religious ideas are merely symbolical; but I think the same of the ideas of science and even of the senses: so that the way is cleared for faith, in deciding which set of symbols one will trust.

Sincerely yours

JOHN DEWEY

(1859-1952)

Probably no American philosopher is more strongly attacked today or more staunchly defended than John Dewey. He was throughout his life equable and generous in temper, but he was also indefatigable, honest, and courageous, for more than a generation his name has been the major symbol in the United States for progressive education, liberal social philosophy, and an uncompromising secular outlook. Dewey was not perhaps the equal of Peirce in logical acumen and he did not have James' quick and pungent brilliance. But he was full of rich insights that pulled disparate issues together or helped philosophers to see old problems in a new light, and of all the pragmatists he was the most actively interested in concrete issues in politics and education. He went further than any of his predecessors in reinterpreting philosophy in social terms and spelling out the social and educational implications of the pragmatic method.

Dewey was born in Burlington, Vermont in 1859. He was one of the first graduate students at The Johns Hopkins University, and after receiving his doctorate he went on to teach philosophy and psychology at Minnesota, Michigan and the University of Chicago. At Johns Hopkins Dewey came under the influence of German philosophy and he was for some years a convinced Hegelian. His point of view gradually shifted, however, in good part through his study of James' Psychology, *and in the eighteen-nineties he began to develop an "experimental logic" which culminated in the publication in 1903 of the important* Studies in Logical Theory. *This book, which Dewey produced with a group of his colleagues at Chicago, gave a new and independent statement of pragmatism, and marked the emergence of what came to be known as the "Chicago school" of pragmatism or "instrumentalism."*

Dewey's pragmatism, however, was also strongly influenced by his practical activities, particularly in the field of education. While at Chicago he established an experimental school which attracted widespread attention in the United States, and after 1904, when he came to Columbia University, he continued to teach in both philosophy and education and to be actively associated with experimental schools and a wide variety of civic activities. In 1930 he retired from active teaching at Columbia, but from nothing else. In the Thirties he produced a number of important books in logic, aesthetics, and social philosophy, and continued to participate energetically in the life of his times. Perhaps the most notable of his practical ventures was his journey to Mexico in 1937 as chairman of the unofficial commission that found Leon Trotsky innocent of the charges made against him by Stalin's courts. Dewey died in 1952.

Dewey began as an Hegelian, and while he devoted a good part of his philosophy to an attack on philosophic idealism, the heart of his thought lies in his Hegelian dislike of "dualisms." He was suspicious of all "dualisms"—all sharp and rigid distinctions between "theory" and "practice," "facts" and "values," "subject" and "object." Dewey's polemical powers were great but he did not always state his own position unambiguously. In his anxiety to avoid separating things that go together he sometimes seems unwilling even to make an intellectual distinction between them. Yet Dewey's attack on dualisms was motivated by a fresh and liberating insight into the conditions of worthwhile human experience. He opposed dualisms because he opposed discontinuities in experience—insulated routines that robbed education of significance and pleasure, snob values that put art into museums, distinctions between "means" and "ends" that condemned practical life to brutality and turned morality into a genteel retreat from practical affairs. When human experience is rightly organized, Dewey believed, there is no event that is merely a means and no event that is merely an end. Theory is firmest when it is tested in practice; practice is most interesting when it is illuminated by theory. Work is best when it has the intrinsic delights of play; play is best when it grows out of things done in the past and is a preparation for things to be done in the future.

Despite the exaggerated claims that are made by Dewey's critics (and perhaps by some of his defenders) concerning the extent of his influence, Dewey's educational philosophy and his critique of American industrial society can hardly be said as yet to have achieved the purposes for which Dewey designed them. But it cannot be doubted that they have changed the context in which educational and social issues are discussed. It is now difficult—although, as recent discussions suggest, it is not impossible—to discuss the conduct of education while ignoring psychological facts or social conditions. And in the discussion of the problems of democracy it is now much harder than it was a century ago to take refuge in abstract ideals or to forget that democracy's existence and rewards depend on the concrete institutions that form men's intimate habits and give their everyday experience the quality that it has. Dewey thought that the function of philosophy was essentially imaginative—to release a vision of the possibilities of an age so that men might move more intelligently to desired goals. In the last half-century no American philosopher has better fulfilled this function than this apparently homely and prosaic thinker.

The first of the selections that follow, "From Absolutism to Experimentalism," presents Dewey's reminiscent reflections on his philosophical development. It appeared initially in Contemporary American Philosophy, *edited by G. P. Adams and W. P. Montague (1930). The selections from* Reconstruction in Philosophy *(1920) and* The Quest for Certainty *(1929) exemplify Dewey's conception of philosophy and his critique of the so-called "classic tradition." The first of these books was based on lectures Dewey delivered in Japan after World War I, and the second on his Gifford Lectures in Scotland. The next selection is from* Democracy and Education, *the book Dewey himself believed to contain the fullest exposition of his philosophy, and which shows the application of his philosophy to the problems of education. The final selection is from* Freedom and Culture, *published in 1939, in the early days of World War II.*

From Absolutism to Experimentalism

IN THE LATE 'SEVENTIES, WHEN I WAS AN UNDERGRADUATE, "ELECTIVES" were still unknown in the smaller New England colleges. But in the one I attended, the University of Vermont, the tradition of a "senior-year course" still subsisted. This course was regarded as a kind of intellectual coping to the structure erected in earlier years, or, at least, as an insertion of the key-stone of the arch. It included courses in political economy, international law, history of civilization (Guizot), psychology, ethics, philosophy of religion (Butler's *Analogy*), logic, etc., not history of philosophy, save incidentally. The enumeration of these titles may not serve the purpose for which it is made; but the idea was that after three years of somewhat specialized study in languages and sciences, the last year was reserved for an introduction into serious intellectual topics of wide and deep significance—an introduction into the world of ideas. I doubt if in many cases it served its alleged end; however, it fell in with my own inclinations, and I have always been grateful for that year of my schooling. There was, however, one course in the previous year that had excited a taste that in retrospect may be called philosophical. That was a rather short course, without laboratory work, in Physiology, a book of Huxley's being the text. It is difficult to speak with exactitude about what happened to me intellectually so many years ago, but I have an impression that there was derived from that study a sense of interdependence and interrelated unity that gave form to intellectual stirrings that had been previously inchoate, and created a kind of type or model of a view of things to which material in any field ought to conform. Subconsciously, at least, I was led to desire a world and a life that would have the same properties as had the human organism in the picture of it derived from study of Huxley's treatment. At all events, I got great stimulation from the study, more than from anything I had had contact with before; and as no desire was awakened in me to continue that particular branch of learning, I date from this time the awakening of a distinctive philosophic interest.

The University of Vermont rather prided itself upon its tradition in philosophy. One of its earlier teachers, Dr. Marsh, was almost the first person in the United States to venture upon the speculative and dubiously orthodox seas of German thinking—that of Kant, Schelling, and Hegel.

The venture, to be sure, was made largely by way of Coleridge; Marsh edited an American edition of Coleridge's *Aids to Reflection*. Even this degree of speculative generalization, in its somewhat obvious tendency to rationalize the body of Christian theological doctrines, created a flutter in ecclesiastical dovecots. In particular, a controversy was carried on between the Germanizing rationalizers and the orthodox representatives of the Scottish school of thought through the representatives of the latter at Princeton. I imagine—although it is a very long time since I have had any contact with this material—that the controversy still provides data for a section, if not a chapter, in the history of thought in this country.

Although the University retained pride in its pioneer work, and its atmosphere was for those days theologically "liberal"—of the Congregational type—the teaching of philosophy had become more restained in tone, more influenced by the still dominant Scotch school. Its professor, Mr. H. A. P. Torrey, was a man of genuinely sensitive and cultivated mind, with marked esthetic interest and taste, which, in a more congenial atmosphere than that of northern New England in those days, would have achieved something significant. He was, however, constitutionally timid, and never really let his mind go. I recall that, in a conversation I had with him a few years after graduation, he said: "Undoubtedly pantheism is the most satisfactory form of metaphysics intellectually, but it goes counter to religious faith." I fancy that remark told of an inner conflict that prevented his native capacity from coming to full fruition. His interest in philosophy, however, was genuine, not perfunctory; he was an excellent teacher, and I owe to him a double debt, that of turning my thoughts definitely to the study of philosophy as a life-pursuit, and of a generous gift of time to me during a year devoted privately under his direction to a reading of classics in the history of philosophy and learning to read philosophic German. In our walks and talks during this year, after three years on my part of high-school teaching, he let his mind go much more freely than in the classroom, and revealed potentialities that might have placed him among the leaders in the development of a freer American philosophy—but the time for the latter had not yet come.

Teachers of philosophy were at that time, almost to a man, clergymen; the supposed requirements of religion, or theology, dominated the teaching of philosophy in most colleges. Just how and why Scotch philosophy lent itself so well to the exigencies of religion I cannot say; probably the causes were more extrinsic than intrinsic; but at all events there was a firm alliance established between religion and the cause of "intuition". It is probably impossible to recover at this date the almost sacrosanct air that enveloped the idea of intuitions; but somehow the cause of all holy and valuable things was supposed to stand or fall with the validity of intuitionalism; the only vital issue was that between intuitionalism and a sensational empiricism that explained away the reality of all higher objects. The story of this almost forgotten debate, once so urgent, is probably a factor in developing in me a certain scepticism about the depth and range of purely contemporary issues; it is likely that many of those which seem highly important to-day will also in a generation have receded to the status of the local and provincial. It also aided in generating a sense of the value of the history of philosophy; some of the claims made for this as a sole avenue of approach to the study of philosophic problems seem to me misdirected and injurious. But its value in giving perspective and a sense of proportion in relation to immediate contemporary issues can hardly be over-estimated.

I do not mention this theological and intuitional phase because it had any lasting influence upon my own development, except negatively. I learned the terminology of an intuitional philosophy, but it did not go deep, and in no way did it satisfy what I was dimly reaching for. I was brought up in a conventionally evangelical atmosphere of the more "liberal" sort; and the struggles that later arose between acceptance of that faith and the discarding of traditional and institutional creeds came from personal experiences and not from the effects of philosophical teaching. It was not, in other words, in this respect that philosophy either appealed to me or influenced me—though I am not sure that Butler's *Analogy,* with its cold logic and acute analysis, was not, in a reversed way, a factor in developing "scepticism".

During the year of private study, of which mention has been made, I decided to make philosophy my life-study, and accordingly went to Johns Hopkins the next year (1884) to enter upon that new thing, "graduate work". It was something of a risk; the work offered there was almost the only indication that there were likely to be any self-supporting jobs in the field of philosophy for others than clergymen. Aside from the effect of my study with Professor Torrey, another influence moved me to undertake the risk. During the years after graduation I had kept up philosophical readings and I had even written a few articles which I sent to Dr. W. T. Harris, the well-known Hegelian, and the editor of the *Journal of Speculative Philosophy,* the only philosophic journal in the country at that time, as he and his group formed almost the only group of laymen devoted to philosophy for non-theological reasons. In sending an article I asked Dr. Harris for advice as to the possibility of my successfully prosecuting philosophic studies. His reply was so encouraging that it was a distinct factor in deciding me to try philosophy as a professional career.

The articles sent were, as I recall them, highly schematic and formal; they were couched in the language of intuitionalism; [of Hegel I was then ignorant.] My deeper interests had not as yet been met, and in the absence of subject-matter that would correspond to them, the only topics at my command were such as were capable of a merely formal treatment. I imagine that my development has been controlled largely by a struggle between a native inclination toward the schematic and formally logical, and those incidents of personal experience that compelled me to take account of actual material. Probably there is in the consciously articulated ideas of every thinker an over-weighting of just those things that are contrary to his natural tendencies, an emphasis upon those things that are contrary to his intrinsic bent, and which, therefore, he has to struggle to bring to expression, while the native bent, on the other hand, can take care of itself. Anyway, a case might be made out for the proposition that the emphasis upon the concrete, empirical, and "practical" in my later writings is partly due to considerations of this nature. It was a reaction against what was more natural, and it served as a protest and protection against something in myself which, in the pressure of the weight of actual experiences, I knew to be a weakness. It is, I suppose, becoming a commonplace that when anyone is unduly concerned with controversy, the remarks that seem to be directed against others are really concerned with a struggle that is going on inside himself. The marks, the stigmata, of the struggle to weld together the characteristics of a formal, theoretic interest and the material of a maturing experience of contacts with realities also showed themselves, naturally, in style of writing and manner of presentation. During the time when the schematic interest predominated, writing was comparatively easy; there were even compliments upon the clearness of my style. Since then thinking and writing have been hard work. It is easy to give way to the dialectic development of a theme; the pressure of concrete experiences was, however, sufficiently heavy, so that a sense of intellectual honesty prevented a surrender to that course. But, on the other hand, the formal interest persisted, so that there was an inner demand for an intellectual technique that would be consistent and yet capable of flexible adaptation to the concrete diversity of experienced things. It is hardly necessary to say that I have not been among those to whom the union of abilities to satisfy these two opposed requirements, the formal and the material, came easily. For that very reason I have been acutely aware, too much so, doubtless, of a tendency of other thinkers and writers to achieve a specious lucidity and simplicity by the mere process of ignoring considerations which a greater respect for concrete materials of experience would have forced upon them.

It is a commonplace of educational history that the opening of Johns Hopkins University marked a new epoch in higher education in the United States. We are probably not in a condition as yet to estimate the extent to which its foundation and the development of graduate schools in other universities, following its example, mark a turn in our American culture. The 'eighties and 'nineties seem to mark the definitive close of our pioneer period, and the turn from the civil war era into the new industrialized and commercial age. In philosophy, at least, the influence of Johns Hopkins was not due to the size of the provision that was made. There was a half-year of lecturing and seminar work given by Professor George Sylvester

Morris, of the University of Michigan; belief in the "demonstrated" (a favourite word of his) truth of the substance of German idealism, and of belief in its competency to give direction to a life of aspiring thought, emotion, and action. I have never known a more single-hearted and whole-souled man—a man of a single piece all the way through; while I long since deviated from his philosophic faith, I should be happy to believe that the influence of the spirit of his teaching has been an enduring influence.

While it was impossible that a young and impressionable student, unacquainted with any system of thought that satisfied his head and heart, should not have been deeply affected, to the point of at least a temporary conversion, by the enthusiastic and scholarly devotion of Mr. Morris, this effect was far from being the only source of my own "Hegelianism". The 'eighties and 'nineties were a time of new ferment in English thought; the reaction against atomic individualism and sensationalistic empiricism was in full swing. It was the time of Thomas Hill Green, of the two Cairds, of Wallace, of the appearance of the *Essays in Philosophical Criticism,* co-operatively produced by a younger group under the leadership of the late Lord Haldane. This movement was at the time the vital and constructive one in philosophy. Naturally its influence fell in with and reinforced that of Professor Morris. There was but one marked difference, and that, I think, was in favour of Mr. Morris. He came to Kant through Hegel instead of to Hegel by way of Kant, so that his attitude toward Kant was the critical one expressed by Hegel himself. Moreover, he retained something of his early Scotch philosophical training in a common-sense belief in the existence of the external world. He used to make merry over those who thought the *existence* of this world and of matter were things to be proved by philosophy. To him the only philosophical question was as to the *meaning* of this existence; his idealism was wholly of the objective type. Like his contemporary, Professor John Watson, of Kingston, he combined a logical and idealistic metaphysics with a realistic epistemology. Through his teacher at Berlin, Trendelenburg, he had acquired a great reverence for Aristotle, and he had no difficulty in uniting Aristoteleanism with Hegelianism.

There were, however, also "subjective" reasons for the appeal that Hegel's thought made to me; it supplied a demand for unification that was doubtless an intense emotional craving, and yet was a hunger that only an intellectualized subject-matter could satisfy. It is more than difficult, it is impossible, to recover that early mood. But the sense of divisions and separations that were, I suppose, borne in upon me as a consequence of a heritage of New England culture, divisions by way of isolation of self from the world, of soul from body, of nature from God, brought a painful oppression—or, rather, they were an inward laceration. My earlier philosophic study had been an intellectual gymnastic. Hegel's synthesis of subject and object, matter and spirit, the divine and the human, was, however, no mere intellectual formula; it operated as an immense release, a liberation. Hegel's treatment of human culture, of institutions and the arts, involved the same dissolution of hard-and-fast dividing walls, and had a special attraction for me.

As I have already intimated, while the conflict of traditional religious beliefs with opinions that I could myself honestly entertain was the source of a trying personal crisis, it did not at any time constitute a leading philosophical problem. This might look as if the two things were kept apart; in reality it was due to a feeling that any genuinely sound religious experience could and should adapt itself to whatever beliefs one found oneself intellectually entitled to hold—a half unconscious sense at first, but one which ensuing years have deepened into a fundamental conviction. In consequence, while I have, I hope, a due degree of personal sympathy with individuals who are undergoing the throes of a personal change of attitude, I have not been able to attach much importance to religion as a philosophic problem; for the effect of that attachment seems to be in the end a subornation of candid philosophic thinking to the alleged but factitious needs of some special set of convictions. I have enough faith in the depth of the religious tendencies of men to believe that they will adapt themselves to any required intellectual change, and that it is futile (and likely to be dishonest) to forecast prematurely just what forms the religious interest will take as a final consequence of the great intellectual transformation that is going on. As I have been frequently criticized for undue reticence about the problems of religion, I insert this explanation: it seems to me that the great solicitude of many persons, professing belief in the universality of the need for religion, about the present and future of religion proves that in fact they are moved more by partisan interest in a particular religion than by interest in religious experience.

The chief reason, however, for inserting these remarks at this point is to bring out a contrast effect. Social interests and problems from an early period had to me the intellectual appeal and provided the intellectual sustenance that many seem to have found primarily in religious questions. In undergraduate days I had run across, in the college library, Harriet Martineau's exposition of Comte. I cannot remember that his law of "the three stages" affected me particularly; but his idea of the disorganized character of Western modern culture, due to a disintegrative "individualism", and his idea of a synthesis of science that should be a regulative method of an organized social life, impressed me deeply. I found, as I thought, the same criticisms combined with a deeper and more far-reaching integration in Hegel. I did not, in those days when I read Francis Bacon, detect the origin of the Comtean idea in him, and I had not made acquaintance with Condorcet, the connecting link.

I drifted away from Hegelianism in the next fifteen years; the word "drifting" expresses the slow and, for a long time, imperceptible character of the movement, though it does not convey the impression that there was an adequate cause for the change. Nevertheless I should never think of ignoring, much less denying, what an astute critic occasionally refers to as a novel discovery—that acquaintance with Hegel has left a permanent deposit in my thinking. The form, the schematism, of his system now seems to me artificial to the last degree. But in the content of his ideas there is often an extraordinary depth; in many of his analyses, taken out of their mechanical dialectical setting, an extraordinary acuteness. Were it possible for me to be a devotee of any system, I still should believe that there is greater richness and greater variety of insight in Hegel than in any other single systematic philosopher—though when I say this I exclude Plato, who still provides my favorite philosophic reading. For I am unable to find in him that all-comprehensive and overriding system which later interpretation has, as it seems to me, conferred upon him as a dubious boon. The ancient sceptics overworked another aspect of Plato's thought when they treated him as their spiritual father, but they were nearer the truth, I think, than those who force him into the frame of a rigidly systematized doctrine. Although I have not the aversion to system as such that is sometimes attributed to me, I am dubious of my own ability to reach inclusive systematic unity, and in consequence, perhaps, of that fact also dubious about my contemporaries. Nothing could be more helpful to present philosophizing than a "Back to Plato" movement; but it would have to be back to the dramatic, restless, co-operatively inquiring Plato of the Dialogues, trying one mode of attack after another to see what it might yield; back to the Plato whose highest flight of metaphysics always terminated with a social and practical turn, and not to the artificial Plato constructed by unimaginative commentators who treat him as the original university professor.

The rest of the story of my intellectual development I am unable to record without more faking than I care to indulge in. What I have so far related is so far removed in time that I can talk about myself as another person; and much has faded, so that a few points stand out without my having to force them into the foreground. The philosopher, if I may apply that word to myself, that I became as I moved away from German idealism, is too much the self that I still am and is still too much in process of change to lend itself to record. I envy, up to a certain point, those who can write their intellectual biography in a unified pattern, woven out of a few distinctly discernible strands of interest and influence. By contrast, I seem to be unstable, chameleon-like, yielding one after another to many diverse and even incompatible influences; struggling to assimilate something from each and yet striving to carry it forward in a way that is logically consistent with what has been learned from its predecessors. Upon the whole, the forces that have influenced me have come from persons and from situations more than from books—not that I have not, I hope, learned a great deal from philosophical writings, but that what I have learned from them has been technical in comparison with what I have been forced to think upon and about because of some experience in which I found myself entangled. It is for this reason that I cannot say with candour that I envy completely, or envy beyond a certain point, those to whom I have referred. I like to think, though it may be a defence reaction, that with all the inconveniences of the road I have been forced to travel, it has the compensatory advantage of not inducing an immunity of thought to experiences—which perhaps, after all, should not be treated even by a philosopher as the germ of a disease to which he needs to develop resistance.

While I cannot write an account of intellectual development without giving it the semblance of a continuity that it does not in fact own, there are four special points that seem to stand out. One is the importance that the practice and theory of education have had for me: especially the education of the young, for I have never been able to feel much optimism regarding the possibilites of "higher" education when it is built upon warped and weak foundations. This interest fused with and brought together what might otherwise have been separate interests—that in psychology and that in social institutions and social life. I can recall but one critic who has suggested that my thinking has been too much permeated by interest in education. Although a book called *Democracy and Education* was for many years that in which my philosophy, such as it is, was most fully expounded, I do not know that philosophic critics, as distinct from teachers, have ever had recourse to it. I have wondered whether such facts signified that philosophers in general, although they are themselves usually teachers, have not taken education with sufficient seriousness for it to occur to them that any rational person could actually think it possible that philosophizing should focus about education as the supreme human interest in which, moreover, other problems, cosmological, moral, logical, come to a head. At all events, this handle is offered to any subsequent critic who may wish to lay hold of it.

A second point is that as my study and thinking progressed, I became more and more troubled by the intellectual scandal that seemed to me involved in the current (and traditional) dualism in logical standpoint and method between something called "science" on the one hand and something called "morals" on the other. I have long felt that the construction of a logic, that is, a method of effective inquiry, which would apply without abrupt breach of continuity to the fields designated by both of these words, is at once our needed theoretical solvent and the supply of our greatest practical want. This belief has had much more to do with the development of what I termed, for lack of a better word, "instrumentalism", than have most of the reasons that have been assigned.

The third point forms the great exception to what was said about no very fundamental vital influence issuing from books; it concerns the influence of William James. As far as I can discover one specifiable philosophic factor which entered into my thinking so as to give it a new direction and quality, it is this one. To say that it proceeded from his *Psychology* rather than from the essays collected in the volume called *Will to Believe,* his *Pluralistic Universe,* or *Pragmatism,* is to say something that needs explanation. For there are, I think, two unreconciled strains in the *Psychology*. One is found in the adoption of the subjective tenor of prior psychological tradition; even when the special tenets of that tradition are radically criticized, an underlying subjectivism is retained, at least in vocabulary—and the difficulty in finding a vocabulary which will intelligibly convey a genuinely new idea is perhaps the obstacle that most retards the easy progress of philosophy. I may cite as an illustration the substitution of the "stream of consciousness" for discrete elementary states: the advance made was enormous. Nevertheless the point of view remained that of a realm of consciousness set off by itself. The other strain is objective, having its roots in a return to the earlier biological conception of the *psyche,* but a return possessed of a new force and value due to the immense progress made by biology since the time of Aristotle. I doubt if we have as yet begun to realize all that is due to William James for the introduction and use of this idea; as I have already intimated, I do not think that he fully and consistently realized it himself. Anyway, it worked its way more and more into all my ideas and acted as a ferment to transform old beliefs.

If this biological conception and mode of approach had been prematurely hardened by James, its effect might have been merely to substitute one schematism for another. But it is not tautology to say that James's sense of life was itself vital. He had a profound sense, in origin artistic and moral, perhaps, rather than "scientific", of the difference between the categories of the living and of the mechanical; some time, I think, someone may write an essay that will show how the most distinctive factors in his general philosophic view, pluralism, novelty, freedom, individuality, are all connected with his feeling for the qualities and traits of that which lives. Many philosophers have had much to say about the idea of organism; but they have taken it structurally and hence statically. It was reserved for James to think of life in terms of life in action. This point, and that about the objective biological factor in James's conception of thought (discrimination, abstraction, conception, generalization), is fundamental when the rôle of psychology in philosophy comes under consideration. It is true that the effect of its introduction into philosophy has often, usually, been to dilute and distort the latter. But that is because the psychology was bad psychology.

I do not mean that I think that in the end the connection of psychology with philosophy is, in the abstract, closer than is that of other branches of science. Logically it stands on the same plane with them. But historically and at the present juncture the revolution introduced by James had, and still has, a peculiar significance. On the negative side it is important, for it is indispensable as a purge of the heavy charge of bad psychology that is so embedded in the philosophical tradition that is not generally recognized to be psychology at all. As an example, I would say that the problem of "sense data", which occupies such a great bulk in recent British thinking, has to my mind no significance other than as a survival of an old and outworn psychological doctrine—although those who deal with the problem are for the most part among those who stoutly assert the complete irrelevance of psychology to philosophy. On the positive side we have the obverse of this situation. The newer objective psychology supplies the easiest way, pedagogically if not in the abstract, by which to reach a fruitful conception of thought and its work, and thus to better our logical theories—provided thought and logic have anything to do with one another. And in the present state of men's minds the linking of philosophy to the significant issues of actual experience is facilitated by constant interaction with the methods and conclusions of psychology. The more abstract sciences, mathematics and physics, for example, have left their impress deep upon traditional philosophy. The former, in connection with an exaggerated anxiety about formal certainty, has more than once operated to divorce philosophic thinking from connection with questions that have a source in existence. The remoteness of psychology from such abstractions, its nearness to what is distinctively human, gives it an emphatic claim for a sympathetic hearing at the present time.

In connection with an increasing recognition of this human aspect, there developed the influence which forms the fourth heading of this recital. The objective biological approach of the Jamesian psychology led straight to the perception of the importance of distinctive social categories, especially communication and participation. It is my conviction that a great deal of our philosophizing needs to be done over again from this point of view, and that there will ultimately result an integrated synthesis in a philosophy congruous with modern science and related to actual needs in education, morals, and religion. One has to take a broad survey in detachment from immediate prepossessions to realize the extent to which the characteristic traits of the science of to-day are connected with the development of social subjects—anthropology, history, politics, economics, language and literature, social and abnormal psychology, and so on. The movement is both so new, in an intellectual sense, and we are so much of it and it so much of us, that it escapes definite notice. Technically the influence of mathematics upon philosophy is more obvious; the great change that has taken place in recent years in the ruling ideas and methods of the physical sciences attracts attention much more easily than does the growth of the social subjects, just because it is farther away from impact upon us. Intellectual prophecy is dangerous; but if I read the cultural signs of the times aright, the next synthetic movement in philosophy will emerge when the significance of the social sciences and arts has become an object of reflective attention in the same way that mathematical and physical sciences have been made the objects of thought in the past, and when their full import is grasped. If I read these signs wrongly, nevertheless the statement may stand as a token of a factor significant in my own intellectual development.

In any case, I think it shows a deplorable deadness of imagination to suppose that philosophy will indefinitely revolve within the scope of the problems and systems that two thousand years of European history have bequeathed to us. Seen in the long perspective of the future, the whole of western European history is a provincial episode. I do not expect to see in my day a genuine as distinct from a forced and artificial, integration of thought. But a mind that is not too egotistically impatient can have faith that this unification will issue in its season. Meantime a chief task of those who call themselves philosophers is to help get rid of the useless lumber that blocks our highways of thought, and strive to make straight and open the paths that lead to the future. Forty years spent in wandering in a wilderness like that of the present is not a sad fate—unless one attempts to make himself believe that the wilderness is after all itself the promised land.

Reconstruction in Philosophy

CHANGING CONCEPTIONS OF PHILOSOPHY

MAN DIFFERS FROM THE LOWER ANIMALS BECAUSE HE PRESERVES HIS past experiences. What happened in the past is lived again in memory. About what goes on today hangs a cloud of thoughts concerning similar things undergone in bygone days. With the animals, an experience perishes as it happens, and each new doing or suffering stands alone. But man lives in a world where each occurrence is charged with echoes and reminiscences of what has gone before, where each event is a reminder of other things. Hence he lives not, like the beasts of the field, in a world of merely physical things but in a world of signs and symbols. A stone is not merely hard, a thing into which one bumps; but it is a monument of a deceased ancestor. A flame is not merely something which warms or burns, but is a symbol of the enduring life of the household, of the abiding source of cheer, nourishment and shelter to which man returns from his casual wanderings. Instead of being a quick fork of fire which may sting and hurt, it is the hearth at which one worships and for which one fights. And all this which marks the difference between bestiality and humanity, between culture and merely physical nature, is because man remembers, preserving and recording his experiences.

The revivals of memory are, however, rarely literal. We naturally remember what interests us and because it interests us. The past is recalled not because of itself but because of what it adds to the present. Thus the primary life of memory is emotional rather than intellectual and practical. Savage man recalled yesterday's struggle with an animal not in order to study in a scientific way the qualities of the animal or for the sake of calculating how better to fight tomorrow, but to escape from the tedium of today by regaining the thrill of yesterday. The memory has all the excitement of the combat without its danger and anxiety. To revive it and revel in it is to enhance the present moment with a new meaning, a meaning different from that which actually belongs either to it or to the past. Memory is vicarious experience in which there is all the emotional values of actual experience without its strains, vicissitudes and troubles. The triumph of battle is even more poignant in the memorial war dance than at the moment of victory; the conscious and truly human experience of the chase comes when it is talked over and re-enacted by the camp fire.

396

At the time, attention is taken up with practical details and with the strain of uncertainty. Only later do the details compose into a story and fuse into a whole of meaning. At the time of practical experience man exists from moment to moment, preoccupied with the task of the moment. As he re-surveys all the moments in thought, a drama emerges with a beginning, a middle and a movement toward the climax of achievement or defeat.

Since man revives his past experience because of the interest added to what would otherwise be the emptiness of present leisure, the primitive life of memory is one of fancy and imagination, rather than of accurate recollection. After all, it is the story, the drama, which counts. Only those incidents are selected which have a present emotional value, to intensify the present tale as it is rehearsed in imagination or told to an admiring listener. What does not add to the thrill of combat or contribute to the goal of success or failure is dropped. Incidents are rearranged till they fit into the temper of the tale. Thus early man when left to himself, when not actually engaged in the struggle for existence, lived in a world of memories which was a world of suggestions. A suggestion differs from a recollection in that no attempt is made to test its correctness. Its correctness is a matter of relative indifference. The cloud suggests a camel or a man's face. It could not suggest these things unless some time there had been an actual, literal experience of camel and face. But the real likeness is of no account. The main thing is the emotional interest in tracing the camel or following the fortunes of the face as it forms and dissolves.

Students of the primitive history of mankind tell of the enormous part played by animal tales, myths and cults. Sometimes a mystery is made out of this historical fact, as if it indicated that primitive man was moved by a different psychology from that which now animates humanity. But the explanation is, I think, simple. Until agriculture and the higher industrial arts were developed, long periods of empty leisure alternated with comparatively short periods of energy put forth to secure food or safety from attack. Because of our own habits, we tend to think of people as busy or occupied, if not with doing at least with thinking and planning. But then men were busy only when engaged in the hunt or fishing or fighting expedition. Yet the mind when awake must have some filling; it cannot remain literally vacant because the body is idle. And what thoughts should crowd into the human mind except experiences with animals, experiences transformed under the influence of dramatic interest to make more vivid and coherent the events typical of the chase? As men in fancy dramatically re-lived the interesting parts of their actual lives, animals inevitably became themselves dramatized.

They were true *dramatis personæ* and as such assumed the traits of persons. They too had desires, hopes and fears, a life of affections, loves and hates, triumphs and defeats. Moreover, since they were essential to the support of the community, their activities and sufferings made them, in the imagination which dramatically revived the past, true sharers in the life of the community. Although they were hunted, yet they permitted themselves after all to be caught, and hence they were friends and allies. They devoted themselves, quite literally, to the sustenance and well-being of the community group to which they belonged. Thus were produced not merely the multitude of tales and legends dwelling affectionately upon the activities and features of animals, but also those elaborate rites and cults which made animals ancestors, heroes, tribal figure-heads and divinities.

I hope that I do not seem to you to have gone too far afield from my topic, the origin of philosophies. For it seems to me that the historic source of philosophies cannot be understood except as we dwell, at even greater length and in more detail, upon such considerations as these. We need to recognize that the ordinary consciousness of the ordinary man left to himself is a creature of desires rather than of intellectual study, inquiry or speculation. Man ceases to be primarily actuated by hopes and fears, loves and hates, only when he is subjected to a discipline which is foreign to human nature, which is, from the standpoint of natural man, artificial. Naturally our books, our scientific and philosophical books, are written by men who have subjected themselves in a superior degree to intellectual discipline and culture. Their thoughts are habitually reasonable. They have learned to check their fancies by facts, and to organize their ideas logically rather than emotionally and dramatically. When they do indulge in reverie and day-dreaming—which is probably more of the time than is conventionally acknowledged—they are aware of what they are doing. They label these excursions, and do not confuse their results with objective experiences. We tend to judge others by ourselves, and because scientific and philosophic books are composed by men in whom the reasonable, logical and objective habit of mind predominates, a similar rationality has been attributed by them to the average and ordinary man. It is then overlooked that both rationality and irrationality are largely irrelevant and episodical in undisciplined human nature; that men are governed by memory rather than by thought, and that memory is not a remembering of actual facts, but is association, suggestion, dramatic fancy. The standard used to measure the value of the suggestions that spring up in the mind is not congruity with fact but emotional congeniality. Do they stimulate and reinforce feeling, and fit into the dramatic tale? Are they consonant with the prevailing mood, and can they be rendered into the traditional hopes and fears of the community? If we are willing to take the word dreams with a certain liberality, it is hardly too much to say that man, save in his occasional times of actual work and struggle, lives in a world of dreams, rather than of facts, and a world of dreams that is organized about desires whose success and frustration form its stuff.

To treat the early beliefs and traditions of mankind as if they were attempts at scientific explanation of the world, only erroneous and absurd attempts, is thus to be guilty of a great mistake. The material out of which philosophy finally emerges is irrelevant to science and to explanation. It is figurative, symbolic of fears and hopes, made of imaginations and suggestions, not significant of a world of objective fact intellectually confronted. It is poetry and drama, rather than science, and is apart from scientific truth and falsity, rationality or absurdity of fact in the same way in which poetry is independent of these things.

This original material has, however, to pass through at least two stages before it becomes philosophy proper. One is the stage in which stories and legends and their accompanying dramatizations are consolidated. At first the emotionalized records of experiences are largely casual and transitory. Events that excite the emotions of an individual are seized upon and lived over in tale and pantomime. But some experiences are so frequent and recurrent that they concern the group as a whole. They are socially generalized. The piecemeal adventure of the single individual is built out till it becomes representative and typical of the emotional life of the tribe. Certain incidents affect the weal and woe of the group in its entirety and thereby get an exceptional emphasis and elevation. A certain texture of tradition is built up; the story becomes a social heritage and possession; the pantomime develops into the stated rite. Tradition thus formed becomes a kind of norm to which individual fancy and suggestion conform. An abiding framework of imagination is constructed. A communal way of conceiving life grows up into which individuals are inducted by education. Both unconsciously and by definite social requirement individual memories are assimilated to group memory or tradition, and individual fancies are accommodated to the body of beliefs characteristic of a community. Poetry becomes fixated and systematized. The story becomes a social norm. The original drama which re-enacts an emotionally important experience is institutionalized into a cult. Suggestions previously free are hardened into doctrines.

The systematic and obligatory nature of such doctrines is hastened and confirmed through conquests and political consolidation. As the area of a government is extended, there is a definite motive for systematizing and unifying beliefs once free and floating. Aside from natural accommodation and assimilation springing from the fact of intercourse and the needs of common understanding, there is often political necessity which leads the ruler to centralize traditions and beliefs in order to extend and strengthen his prestige and authority. Judea, Greece, Rome, and I presume all other countries having a long history, present records of a continual working over of earlier local rites and doctrines in the interests of a wider social unity and a more extensive political power. I shall ask you to assume with me that in this way the larger cosmogonies and cosmologies of the race as well as the larger ethical traditions have arisen. Whether this is literally so or not, it is not necessary to inquire, much less to demonstrate. It is enough for our purposes that under social influences there took place a fixing and organizing of doctrines and cults which gave general traits to the imagination and general rules to conduct, and that such a consolidation was a necessary antecedent to the formation of any philosophy as we understand that term.

Although a necessary antecedent, this organization and generalization of ideas and principles of belief is not the sole and sufficient generator of philosophy. There is still lacking the motive for logical system and intellectual proof. This we may suppose to be furnished by the need of reconciling the moral rules and ideals embodied in the traditional code with the matter of fact positivistic knowledge which gradually grows up. For man can never be wholly the creature of suggestion and fancy. The requirements of continued existence make indispensable some attention to the actual facts of the world. Although it is surprising how little check the environment actually puts upon the formation of ideas, since no notions are too absurd not to have been accepted by some people, yet the environment does enforce a certain minimum of correctness under penalty of extinction. That certain things are foods, that they are to be found in certain places, that water drowns, fire burns, that sharp points penetrate and cut, that heavy things fall unless supported, that there is a certain regularity in the changes of day and night and the alternation of hot and cold, wet and dry:—such prosaic facts force themselves upon even primitive attention. Some of them are so obvious and so important that they have next to no fanciful context. Auguste Comte says somewhere that he knows of no savage people who had a God of weight although every other natural quality or force may have been deified. Gradually there grows up a body of homely generalizations preserving and transmitting the wisdom of the race about the observed facts and sequences of nature. This knowledge is especially connected with industries, arts and crafts where observation of materials and processes is required for successful action, and where action is so continuous and regular that spasmodic magic will not suffice. Extravagantly fantastic notions are eliminated because they are brought into juxtaposition with what actually happens.

The sailor is more likely to be given to what we now term superstitions than say the weaver, because his activity is more at the mercy of sudden change and unforeseen occurrence. But even the sailor while he may regard the wind as the uncontrollable expression of the caprice of a great spirit, will still have to become acquainted with some purely mechanical principles of adjustment of boat, sails and oar to the wind. Fire may be conceived as a supernatural dragon because some time or other a swift, bright and devouring flame called before the mind's eye the quick-moving and dangerous serpent. But the housewife who tends the fire and the pots wherein food cooks will still be compelled to observe certain mechanical facts of draft and replenishment, and passage from wood to ash. Still more will the worker in metals accumulate verifiable details about the conditions and consequences of the operation of heat. He may retain for special and ceremonial occasions traditional beliefs, but everyday familiar use will expel these conceptions for the greater part of the time, when fire will be to him of uniform and prosaic behavior, controllable by practical relations of cause and effect. As the arts and crafts develop and become more elaborate, the body of positive and tested knowledge enlarges, and the sequences observed become more complex and of greater scope. Technologies of this kind give that common-sense knowledge of nature out of which science takes its origin. They provide not merely a collection of positive facts, but they give expertness in dealing with materials and tools, and promote the development of the experimental habit of mind, as soon as an art can be taken away from the rule of sheer custom.

For a long time the imaginative body of beliefs closely connected with the moral habits of a community group and with its emotional indulgences and consolations persists side by side with the growing body of matter of fact knowledge. Wherever possible they are interlaced. At other points, their inconsistencies forbid their interweaving, but the two things are kept apart as if in different compartments. Since one is merely superimposed upon the other their incompatibility is not felt, and there is no need of reconciliation. In most cases, the two kinds of mental products are kept apart because they become the possession of separate social classes. The religious and poetic beliefs having acquired a definite social and political value and function are in the keeping of a higher class directly associated with the ruling elements in the society. The workers and craftsmen who possess the prosaic matter of fact knowledge are likely to occupy a low social status, and their kind of knowledge is affected by the social disesteem entertained for the manual worker who engages in activities useful to the body. It doubtless was this fact in Greece which in spite of the keenness of observation, the extraordinary power of logical reasoning and the great freedom of speculation attained by the Athenian, postponed the general and systematic employment of the experimental method. Since the industrial craftsman was only just above the slave in social rank, his type of knowledge and the method upon which it depended lacked prestige and authority.

Nevertheless, the time came when matter of fact knowledge increased to such bulk and scope that it came into conflict with not merely the detail but with the spirit and temper of traditional and imaginative beliefs. Without going into the vexed question of how and why, there is no doubt that this is just what happened in what we term the sophistic movement in Greece, within which originated philosophy proper in the sense in which the western world understands that term. The fact that the sophists had a bad name given them by Plato and Aristotle, a name they have never been able to shake off, is evidence that with the sophists the strife between the two types of belief was the emphatic thing, and that the conflict had a disconcerting effect upon the traditional system of religious beliefs and the moral code of conduct bound up with it. Although Socrates was doubtless sincerely interested in the reconciliation of the two sides, yet the fact that he approached the matter from the side of matter of fact method, giving its canons and criteria primacy, was enough to bring him to the condemnation of death as a contemner of the gods and a corrupter of youth.

The fate of Socrates and the ill-fame of the sophists may be used to suggest some of the striking contrasts between traditional emotionalized belief on one hand and prosaic matter of fact knowledge on the other:— the purpose of the comparison being to bring out the point that while all the advantages of what we call science were on the side of the latter, the advantages of social esteem and authority, and of intimate contact with what gives life its deeper lying values were on the side of traditional belief. To all appearances, the specific and verified knowledge of the environment had only a limited and technical scope. It had to do with the arts, and the purpose and good of the artisan after all did not extend very far. They were subordinate and almost servile. Who would put the art of the shoemaker on the same plane as the art of ruling the state? Who would put even the higher art of the physician in healing the body, upon the level of the art of the priest in healing the soul? Thus Plato constantly draws the contrast in his dialogues. The shoemaker is a judge of a good pair of shoes, but he is no judge at all of the more important question whether and when it is good to wear shoes; the physician is a good judge of health, but whether it is a good thing or not to be well or better to die, he knows not. While the artisan is expert as long as purely limited technical questions arise, he is helpless when it comes to the only really important questions, the moral questions as to values. Consequently, his type of knowledge is inherently inferior and needs to be controlled by a higher kind of knowledge which will reveal ultimate ends and purposes, and thus put and keep technical and mechanical knowledge in its proper place. Moreover, in Plato's pages we find, because of Plato's adequate dramatic sense, a lively depicting of the impact in particular men of the conflict between tradition and the new claims of purely intellectual knowledge. The conservative is shocked beyond measure at the idea of teaching the military art by abstract rules, by science. One does not just fight, one fights for one's country. Abstract science cannot convey love and loyalty, nor can it be a substitute, even upon the more technical side, for those ways and means of fighting in which devotion to the country has been traditionally embodied.

The way to learn the fighting art is through association with those who have themselves learned to defend the country, by becoming saturated with its ideals and customs; by becoming in short a practical adept in the Greek tradition as to fighting. To attempt to derive abstract rules from a comparison of native ways of fighting with the enemies' ways is to begin to go over to the enemies' traditions and gods: it is to begin to be false to one's own country.

Such a point of view vividly realized enables us to appreciate the antagonism aroused by the positivistic point of view when it came into conflict with the traditional. The latter was deeply rooted in social habits and loyalties; it was surcharged with the moral aims for which men lived and the moral rules by which they lived. Hence it was as basic and as comprehensive as life itself, and palpitated with the warm glowing colors of the community life in which men realized their own being. In contrast, the positivistic knowledge was concerned with merely physical utilities, and lacked the ardent associations of belief hallowed by sacrifices of ancestors and worship of contemporaries. Because of its limited and concrete character it was dry, hard, cold.

Yet the more acute and active minds, like that of Plato himself, could no longer be content to accept, along with the conservative citizen of the time, the old beliefs in the old way. The growth of positive knowledge and of the critical, inquiring spirit undermined these in their old form. The advantages in definiteness, in accuracy, in verifiability were all on the side of the new knowledge. Tradition was noble in aim and scope, but uncertain in foundation. The unquestioned life, said Socrates, was not one fit to be lived by man, who is a questioning being because he is a rational being. Hence he must search out the reason of things, and not accept them from custom and political authority. What was to be done? Develop a method of rational investigation and proof which should place the essential elements of traditional belief upon an unshakable basis; develop a method of thought and knowledge which while purifying tradition should preserve its moral and social values unimpaired; nay, by purifying them, add to their power and authority. To put it in a word, that which had rested upon custom was to be restored, resting no longer upon the habits of the past, but upon the very metaphysics of Being and the Universe. Metaphysics is a substitute for custom as the source and guarantor of higher moral and social values—that is the leading theme of the classic philosophy of Europe, as evolved by Plato and Aristotle—a philosophy, let us always recall, renewed and restated by the Christian philosophy of Medieval Europe.

Out of this situation emerged, if I mistake not, the entire tradition regarding the function and office of philosophy which till very recently has controlled the systematic and constructive philosophies of the western world. If I am right in my main thesis that the origin of philosophy lay in an attempt to reconcile the two different types of mental product, then the key is in our hands as to the main traits of subsequent philosophy so far as that was not of a negative and heterodox kind. In the first place, philosophy did not develop in an unbiased way from an open and unprejudiced origin. It had its task cut out for it from the start. It had a mission to perform, and it was sworn in advance to that mission. It had to extract the essential moral kernel out of the threatened traditional beliefs of the past. So far so good; the work was critical and in the interests of the only true conservatism—that which will conserve and not waste the values wrought out by humanity. But it was also pre-committed to extracting this moral essence in a spirit congenial to the spirit of past beliefs. The association with imagination and with social authority was too intimate to be deeply disturbed. It was not possible to conceive of the content of social institutions in any form radically differ-ent from that in which they had existed in the past. It became the work of philosophy to justify on rational grounds the spirit, though not the form, of accepted beliefs and traditional customs.

The resulting philosophy seemed radical enough and even dangerous to the average Athenian because of the difference of form and method. In the sense of pruning away excrescences and eliminating factors which to the average citizen were all one with the basic beliefs, it was radical. But looked at in the perspective of history and in contrast with different types of thought which developed later in different social environments, it is now easy to see how profoundly, after all, Plato and Aristotle reflected the meaning of Greek tradition and habit, so that their writings remain, with the writings of the great dramatists, the best introduction of a student into the innermost ideals and aspirations of distinctively Greek life. With-out Greek religion, Greek art, Greek civic life, their philosophy would have been impossible; while the effect of that science upon which the philosophers most prided themselves turns out to have been superficial and negligible. This apologetic spirit of philosophy is even more apparent when Medieval Christianity about the twelfth century sought for a sys-tematic rational presentation of itself and made use of classic philosophy, especially that of Aristotle, to justify itself to reason. A not unsimilar occurrence characterizes the chief philosophic systems of Germany in the early nineteenth century, when Hegel assumed the task of justifying in the name of rational idealism the doctrines and institutions which were menaced by the new spirit of science and popular government. The result has been that the great systems have not been free from party spirit exer-cised in behalf of preconceived beliefs. Since they have at the same time professed complete intellectual independence and rationality, the result has been too often to impart to philosophy an element of insincerity, all the more insidious because wholly unconscious on the part of those who sustained philosophy.

And this brings us to a second trait of philosophy springing from its origin. Since it aimed at a rational justification of things that had been previously accepted because of their emotional congeniality and social prestige, it had to make much of the apparatus of reason and proof. Because of the lack of intrinsic rationality in the matters with which it dealt, it leaned over backward, so to speak, in parade of logical form. In dealing with matters of fact, simpler and rougher ways of demonstration may be resorted to. It is enough, so to say, to produce the fact in question and point to it—the fundamental form of all demonstration. But when it comes to convincing men of the truth of doctrines which are no longer to be accepted upon the say-so of custom and social authority, but which also are not capable of empirical verification, there is no recourse save to magnify the signs of rigorous thought and rigid demonstration. Thus arises that appearance of abstract definition and ultra-scientific argumentation which repels so many from philosophy but which has been one of its chief attractions to its devotees.

At the worst, this has reduced philosophy to a show of elaborate terminology, a hair-splitting logic, and a fictitious devotion to the mere external forms of comprehensive and minute demonstration. Even at the best, it has tended to produce an overdeveloped attachment to system for its own sake, and an over-pretentious claim to certainty. Bishop Butler declared that probability is the guide of life; but few philosophers have been courageous enough to avow that philosophy can be satisfied with anything that is merely probable. The customs dictated by tradition and desire had claimed finality and immutability. They had claimed to give certain and unvarying laws of conduct. Very early in its history philosophy made pretension to a similar conclusiveness, and something of this temper has clung to classic philosophies ever since. They have insisted that they were more scientific than the sciences—that, indeed, philosophy was necessary because after all the special sciences fail in attaining final and complete truth. There have been a few dissenters who have ventured to assert, as did William James, that "philosophy is vision" and that its chief function is to free men's minds from bias and prejudice and to enlarge their perceptions of the world about them. But in the main philosophy has set up much more ambitious pretensions. To say frankly that philosophy can proffer nothing but hypotheses, and that these hypotheses are of value only as they render men's minds more sensitive to life about them, would seem like a negation of philosophy itself.

In the third place, the body of beliefs dictated by desire and imagination and developed under the influence of communal authority into an authoritative tradition, was pervasive and comprehensive. It was, so to speak, omnipresent in all the details of the group life. Its pressure was unremitting and its influence universal. It was then probably inevitable that the rival principle, reflective thought, should aim at a similar universality and comprehensiveness. It would be as inclusive and far-reaching metaphysically as tradition had been socially. Now there was just one way in which this pretension could be accomplished in conjunction with a claim of complete logical system and certainty.

All philosophies of the classic type have made a fixed and fundamental distinction between two realms of existence. One of these corresponds to the religious and supernatural world of popular tradition, which in its metaphysical rendering became the world of highest and ultimate reality. Since the final source and sanction of all important truths and rules of conduct in community life had been found in superior and unquestioned religious beliefs, so the absolute and supreme reality of philosophy afforded the only sure guaranty of truth about empirical matters, and the sole rational guide to proper social institutions and individual behavior. Over against this absolute and noumenal reality which could be apprehended only by the systematic discipline of philosophy itself stood the ordinary empirical, relatively real, phenomenal world of everyday experience. It was with this world that the practical affairs and utilities of men were connected. It was to this imperfect and perishing world that matter of fact, positivistic science referred.

This is the trait which, in my opinion, has affected most deeply the classic notion about the nature of philosophy. Philosophy has arrogated to itself the office of demonstrating the existence of a transcendent, absolute or inner reality and of revealing to man the nature and features of this ultimate and higher reality. It has therefore claimed that it was in possession of a higher organ of knowledge than is employed by positive science and ordinary practical experience, and that it is marked by a superior dignity and importance—a claim which is undeniable *if* philosophy leads man to proof and intuition of a Reality beyond that open to day-by-day life and the special sciences.

This claim has, of course, been denied by various philosophers from time to time. But for the most part these denials have been agnostic and sceptical. They have contented themselves with asserting that absolute and ultimate reality is beyond human ken. But they have not ventured to deny that such Reality would be the appropriate sphere for the exercise of philosophic knowledge provided only it were within the reach of human intelligence. Only comparatively recently has another conception of the proper office of philosophy arisen. This course of lectures will be devoted to setting forth this different conception of philosophy in some of its main contrasts to what this lecture has termed the classic conception. At this point, it can be referred to only by anticipation and in cursory fashion. It is implied in the account which has been given of the origin of philosophy out of the background of an authoritative tradition; a tradition originally dictated by man's imagination working under the influence of love and hate and in the interest of emotional excitement and satisfaction. Common frankness requires that it be stated that this account of the origin of philosophies claiming to deal with absolute Being in a systematic way has been given with malice prepense. It seems to me that this genetic method of approach is a more effective way of undermining this type of philosophic theorizing than any attempt at logical refutation could be.

If this lecture succeeds in leaving in your minds as a reasonable hypothesis the idea that philosophy originated not out of intellectual material, but out of social and emotional material, it will also succeed in leaving with you a changed attitude toward traditional philosophies. They will be viewed from a new angle and placed in a new light. New questions about them will be aroused and new standards for judging them will be suggested.

If any one will commence without mental reservations to study the history of philosophy not as an isolated thing but as a chapter in the development of civilization and culture; if one will connect the story of philosophy with a study of anthropology, primitive life, the history of religion, literature and social institutions, it is confidently asserted that he will reach his own independent judgment as to the worth of the account which has been presented today. Considered in this way, the history of philosophy will take on a new significance. What is lost from the standpoint of would-be science is regained from the standpoint of humanity. Instead of the disputes of rivals about the nature of reality, we have the scene of human clash of social purpose and aspirations. Instead of impossible attempts to transcend experience, we have the significant record of the efforts of men to formulate the things of experience to which they are most deeply and passionately attached. Instead of impersonal and purely speculative endeavors to contemplate as remote beholders the nature of absolute things-in-themselves, we have a living picture of the choice of thoughtful men about what they would have life to be, and to what ends they would have men shape their intelligent activities.

Any one of you who arrives at such a view of past philosophy will of necessity be led to entertain a quite definite conception of the scope and aim of future philosophizing. He will inevitably be committed to the notion that what philosophy has been unconsciously, without knowing or intending it, and, so to speak, under cover, it must henceforth be openly and deliberately. When it is acknowledged that under disguise of dealing with ultimate reality, philosophy has been occupied with the precious values embedded in social traditions, that it has sprung from a clash of social ends and from a conflict of inherited institutions with incompatible contemporary tendencies, it will be seen that the task of future philosophy is to clarify men's ideas as to the social and moral strifes of their own day. Its aim is to become so far as is humanly possible an organ for dealing with these conflicts. That which may be pretentiously unreal when it is formulated in metaphysical distinctions becomes intensely significant when connected with the drama of the struggle of social beliefs and ideals. Philosophy which surrenders its somewhat barren monopoly of dealings with Ultimate and Absolute Reality will find a compensation in enlightening the moral forces which move mankind and in contributing to the aspirations of men to attain to a more ordered and intelligent happiness.

The Quest for Certainty

THE ART OF ACCEPTANCE AND THE ART OF CONTROL

THERE WAS A TIME WHEN "ART" AND "SCIENCE" WERE VIRTUALLY equivalent terms. There is a reminiscence of this period in university organization in the phrase "faculty of arts and sciences." A distinction was drawn between the "mechanical" and the "liberal" arts. In part, this distinction was between industrial arts and social arts, those concerned with things and those concerned directly with persons. Grammar and rhetoric, for example, in dealing with speech, the interpretation of literature and the arts of persuasion, were higher than blacksmithing and carpentry. The mechanical arts dealt with things which were merely means; the liberal arts dealt with affairs that were ends, things having a final and intrinsic worth. The obviousness of the distinction was reënforced by social causes. Mechanics were concerned with mechanical arts; they were lower in the social scale. The school in which their arts were learned was the school of practice: apprenticeship to those who had already mastered the craft and mystery. Apprentices literally "learned by doing," and "doing" was routine repetition and imitation of the acts of others, until personal skill was acquired. The liberal arts were studied by those who were to be in some position of authority, occupied with some exercise of social rule. Such persons had the material means that afforded leisure, and were to engage in callings that had especial honor and prestige. Moreover, they learned not by mechanical repetition and bodily practice in manipulation of materials and tools, but "intellectually," through a kind of study which involved mind, not body.

The situation is not recalled as if it had a merely historical significance. It describes in large measure a state of affairs that exists to-day. The distinction between "learned professions" and the occupations of the shop and factory, with corresponding differences of social status, of educational preparation, of concern chiefly with material things or with persons and social relations, is too familiar to call for recourse to past history. The chief difference in the present situation is due to the rise of technological industry and of a pecuniary economy, at the expense of the inherited status of the "gentleman," the owner of large estates in land. So our

408

allusion is pertinent not to history, but to still existing conditions that are influential in creating and maintaining the division between theory and practice, mind and body, ends and instrumentalities.

In addition to this distinction between higher and lower arts, there always hovered in the background a distinction between all arts and "science" in the true and ultimate sense of the words. The liberal arts involved much more of knowledge and of theoretical study, of use of "mind," than did the mechanical. But in their ultimate import they were still connected with art, with doing, although with a mode of practice held in higher esteem. They remained within the limits of experience, although of an experience having a kind of value not found in the baser arts. The philosophic tradition, as for example it is formulated by Aristotle, ranked social arts lower than pure intellectual inquiry, than knowledge as something not to be put to any use, even a social and moral one. It is conceivable that historically this point of view might have remained a mere laudation of its own calling on the part of a small intellectual class. But, as we have already noted, in the expansion of the Church as a dominant power in Europe, religion affiliated this philosophic conception to itself. Theology was regarded as "science" in a peculiar, a unique, sense, for it alone was knowledge of supreme and ultimate Being. And the Church had a direct influence over the hearts and conduct, the beliefs and judgments, of men that a secluded intellectual class could never win. As the guardians and dispensers of the truths and sacraments that determined the eternal destiny, the eternal happiness or misery of the soul, they effected the embodiment of ideas originating in philosophy in the culture of Christendom.

In consequence, differences and distinctions characteristic of actual social life received the sanction not merely of the rational formulation of a few philosophic thinkers but of that power which had the highest authority and influence in the lives of men. For this reason, the survey that has been made of the classic philosophic statement of the dualism between theory and practice, between mind and body, between reason and experience (always thought of in terms of sense and the body) is much more than a piece of historic information. For in spite of enormous extension of secular interests and of natural science, of expansion of practical arts and occupations, of the almost frantic domination of present life by concern for definite material interests and the organization of society by forces fundamentally economic, there is no widely held philosophy of life which replaces the traditional classic one as that was absorbed and modified by the Christian faith.

Traditional philosophy thus has a treble advantage. It has behind it the multitude of imaginative and emotional associations and appeals that cluster about any tradition which has for long centuries been embodied in a dominant institution; they continue to influence, unconsciously, the minds of those who no longer give intellectual assent to the tenets on which the tradition intellectually rests. It has, secondly, the backing of the persistence of the social conditions out of which the formulation of the dualism between theory and practice originally grew—the familiar grading of activities from the servile and mechanical to the liberal, the free and socially esteemed. In addition, there is the enforced recognition of the peril and frustration in the actual world of meanings and goods most prized, a matter which makes men ready to listen to the story of a higher realm in which these values are eternally safe.

In the third place, and finally, there is the negative counterpart of these positive facts. Conditions and forces that dominate in actual fact the modern world have not attained any coherent intellectual expression of themselves. We live, as is so often remarked, in a state of divided allegiance. In outward activities and current enjoyments, we are frenetically absorbed in mundane affairs in ways which, if they were formulated for intellectual acceptance, would be repudiated as low and unworthy. We give our emotional and theoretical assent to principles and creeds which are no longer actively operative in life. We have retained enough of the older tradition to recognize that a philosophy which formulated what, on the whole and in the mass, we are most concerned with, would be intolerably materialistic in character. On the other hand, we are not prepared, either intellectually or morally, to frame such a philosophy of the interests and activities that actually dominate our lives as would elevate *them* to a plane of truly liberal and humane significance. We are unable to show that the ideals, values and meanings which the philosophy we nominally hold places in another world, are capable of characterizing in a concrete form, with some measure of security, the world in which we live, that of our actual experience.

On this account any sincere empirical philosophy that holds to the possibility of the latter alternative must be prophetic rather than descriptive. It can offer hypotheses rather than report of facts adequately in existence. It must support these hypotheses by argument, rather than by appeal to matters clearly within the range of easy observation. It is speculative in that it deals with "futures." Candor demands that these considerations be frankly set forth. But there is also another side to the matter. There is a distinction between hypotheses generated in that seclusion from observable fact which renders them fantasies, and hypotheses that are projections of the possibilities of facts already in existence and capable of report. There is a difference between the imaginative speculations that recognize no law except their own dialectic consistency, and those which rest on an observable movement of events, and which foresee these events carried to a limit by the force of their own movement. There is a difference between support by argument from arbitrarily assumed premises, and an argument which sets forth the implications of propositions resting upon facts already vitally significant.

The groundwork of fact that is selected for especial examination and description in the hypothesis which is to be set forth is the procedure of present scientific inquiry, in those matters that are most fully subject to intellectual control—namely, the physical sciences. The state of inquiry in them is an observable fact, not a speculation nor a matter of opinion and argument. The selection of this field of fact rather than some other as that from which to project a hypothesis regarding a future possible experience in which experience will itself provide the values, meanings and standards now sought in some transcendent world, has both theoretical and practical justification. From the point of view of technical philosophy, the nature of knowledge has always been the foundation and point of departure for philosophies that have separated knowing from doing and making, and that in consequence have elevated the objects of knowledge, as measures of genuine reality, above experiences of objects had by the way of affection and practical action. If, accordingly, it can be shown that the actual procedures by which the most authentic and dependable knowledge is attained have completely surrendered the separation of knowing and doing; if it can be shown that overtly executed operations of interaction are requisite to obtain the knowledge called scientific, the chief fortress of the classic philosophical tradition crumbles into dust. With this destruction disappears also the reason for which some objects, as fixed in themselves, out of and above the course of human experience and its consequences, have been set in opposition to the temporal and concrete world in which we live.

The *practical* reason for selecting such a technical matter as the method of physical science is the fact that the application of natural science, through the medium of inventions and technologies, is the finally controlling and characteristic fact of modern life. That western civilization is increasingly industrial in character is a commonplace; it should be an equally familiar fact that this industrialization is the direct fruit of the growth of the experimental method of knowing. The effects of this industrialization in politics, social arrangements, communication and intercourse, in work and play, in the determination of the locus of influence, power and prestige, are characteristic marks of present experience in the concrete. They are the ultimate source of that waning of the effective influence of older beliefs that has been alluded to. They also provide the reason why a philosophy which merely reflected and reported the chief features of the existing situation as if they were final, without regard to what they may become, would be so repulsively materialistic. Both the positive fact that our actual life is more and more determined by the results of physical science, and the negative fact that these results are so largely an obstacle to framing a philosophy consonant with present experience—so influential in inducing men to hold on to elements of the older tradition—are reasons for selecting the procedure of natural science as the main theme of our examination.

There will be little time and opportunity for discussion of the problem in its immediately practical form—the potential significance of that industrial society which has emerged in consequence of the conclusions and methods of physical knowledge. But it may be pointed out that, in principle, it signifies simply that the results of intelligence, instead of remaining aloof and secluded from practice, are embodied in influential ways in the activities and experience which actually obtains. Say what we please in derogation of "applied science," in principle this is what the latter signifies. And there are few persons, I imagine, who would wittingly proclaim that incarnation of knowledge and understanding in the concrete experiences of life is anything but a good. Derogation on principle of application of knowledge is, in itself, merely an expression of the old tradition of the inherent superiority of knowledge to practice, of reason to experience.

There is a genuine and extremely serious problem in connection with the application of science in life. But it is a practical, not theoretical, one. That is to say, it concerns the economic and legal organization of society in consequence of which the knowledge which regulates activity is so much the monopoly of the few, and is used by them in behalf of private and class interests and not for general and shared use. The problem concerns the possible transformation of social conditions with respect to their economic and pecuniary basis. This problem time and space will not permit me to consider. But the pecuniarily economic phase of society is something radically different from industrialization, and from the inherent consequences of technology in current life. To identify the two affairs breeds only confusion. It must also be noted that this is a question which has of itself nothing to do with the matter of the relations of theory and practice, of knowledge and its application in doing and making. The practical and social problem is one of effecting a more general equitable distribution of the elements of understanding and knowledge in connection with work done, activities undertaken, and a consequent freer and more generously shared participation in their results.

Before engaging in consideration of the significance of the method of science for formation of the theory of knowledge and of mind, we shall take up some general points. These are all connected, at bottom, with the contrast between the idea of experience framed when arts were mainly routine, skills acquired by *mere* exercise and practice, and the idea of experience appropriate when arts have become experimental: or, put briefly, between experience as *empirical* and as *experimental*. "Experience" once meant the results accumulated in memory of a variety of past doings and undergoings that were had without control by insight, when the net accumulation was found to be practically available in dealing with present situations. Both the original perceptions and uses and the application of their outcome in present doings were accidental—that is, neither was determined by an understanding of the relations of cause and effect, of means and consequences, involved. In that sense they were non-rational, non-scientific. A typical illustration is a bridge builder who constructs simply on the basis of what has been done and what happened in the past, without reference to knowledge of strains and stresses, or in general of physical relationships actually involved; or the art of medicine, as far as it rests simply upon the accidents of remedial measures used in the past without knowledge of *why* some worked and others did not. A measure of skill results, but it is the fruit of cut and dried methods, of trial and error—in short it is "empirical."

The disparaging notion of experience framed under such conditions is an honest report of actual conditions; philosophers in setting experience down as inherently inferior to rational science were truthful. What they added was another matter. It was a statement that this inferiority was inherently connected with the body, with the senses, with material things, with the uncertainly changing as over against the certain because immutable. Unfortunately their theories in explanation of the defects of experience persisted and became classic after experience itself, in some of its forms, had become experimental in the sense of being directed by understanding of conditions and their consequences. Two points are especially significant with reference to the split thus produced between the traditional theory of experience and that which results from noting its experimental character.

In the traditional theory, which still is the prevailing one, there were alleged to exist inherent defects in perception and observation as means of knowledge, in reference to the subject-matter they furnish. This material, in the older notion, is inherently so particular, so contingent and variable, that by no possible means can it contribute to *knowledge;* it can result only in opinion, mere belief. But in modern science, there are only *practical* defects in the senses, certain limitations of vision, for example, that have to be corrected and supplemented by various devices, such as the use of the lens. Every insufficiency of observation is an instigation to invent some new instrument which will make good the defect, or it is a stimulus to devising indirect means, such as mathematical calculations, by which the limitations of sense will be circumvented. The counterpart of this change is one in the conception of thought and its relation to knowing. It was earlier assumed that higher knowledge must be supplied by pure thought; pure because apart from experience, since the latter involves the senses. Now, it is taken for granted that thought, while indispensable to knowledge of natural existence, can never in itself provide that knowledge. Observation is indispensable both to provide authentic materials to work upon and to test and verify the conclusions reached by theoretical considerations. A specified kind of experience is indispensable to science instead of all experience setting a limit to the possibility of true science.

There is an objective counterpart of this shift. In the older theory, sense and experience were barriers to true science because they are implicated in natural change. Their appropriate and inevitable subject-matter was variable and changing things. Knowledge in its full and valid sense is possible only of the immutable, the fixed; that alone answers the quest for certainty. With regard to changing things, only surmise and opinion are possible, just as practically these are the source of peril. To a scientific man, in terms of what he does in inquiry, the notion of a natural science which should turn its back upon the changes of things, upon events, is simply incomprehensible. What he is interested in knowing, in understanding, are precisely the changes that go on; they set his problems, and problems are solved when changes are interconnected with one another. Constants and relative invariants figure, but they are relations between changes, not the constituents of a higher realm of Being. With this modification with respect to the object comes one in the structure and content of "experience." Instead of there being a fixed difference between it and something higher—rational thought—there is a difference between two kinds of experience; one which is occupied with uncontrolled change and one concerned with directed and regulated change. And this difference, while fundamentally important, does not mark a fixed division. Changes of the first type are something *to be brought under control* by means of action directed by understanding of relationships.

In the old scheme, knowledge, as science, signified precisely and exclusively turning away from change to the changeless. In the new experimental science, knowledge is obtained in exactly the opposite way, namely, through deliberate institution of a definite and specified course of change. *The* method of physical inquiry is to introduce some change in order to see what other change ensues; the correlation between these changes, when measured by a series of operations, constitutes the definite and desired object of knowledge. There are two degrees of control of change which differ practically but are alike in principle. In astronomy, for example, we cannot introduce variation into remote heavenly bodies. But we can deliberately alter the conditions under which we observe them, which is the same thing in principle of logical procedure. By special instruments, the use of lens and prism, by telescopes, spectroscopes, interferometers, etc., we modify observed data. Observations are taken from widely different points in space and at successive times. By such means interconnected variations are observed. In physical and chemical matters closer at hand and capable of more direct manipulation, changes introduced affect the things under inquiry. Appliances and re-agents for bringing about variations in the things studied are employed. The progress of inquiry is identical with advance in the invention and construction of physical instrumentalities for producing, registering and measuring changes.

Moreover, there is no difference in logical principle between the method of science and the method pursued in technologies. The difference is practical; in the scale of operations conducted; in the lesser degree of control through isolation of conditions operative, and especially in the purpose for the sake of which regulated control of modifications of natural existences and energies is undertaken; especially, since the dominant motive of large scale regulation of the course of change is material comfort or pecuniary gain. But the technique of modern industry, in commerce, communication, transportation and all the appliances of light, heat and electricity, is the fruit of the modern application of science. And this so-called "application" signifies that the same kind of intentional introduction and management of changes which takes place in the laboratory is induced in the factory, the railway and the power house.

The central and outstanding fact is that the change in the method of knowing, due to the scientific revolution begun in the sixteenth and seventeenth centuries, has been accompanied by a revolution in the attitude of man toward natural occurrences and their interactions. This transformation means, as was intimated earlier, a complete reversal in the traditional relationship of knowledge and action. Science advances by adopting the instruments and doings of directed practice, and the knowledge thus gained becomes a means of the development of arts which bring nature still further into actual and potential service of human purposes and valuations. The astonishing thing is that in the face of this change wrought in civilization, there still persist the notions about mind and its organs of knowing, together with the inferiority of practice to intellect, which developed in antiquity as the report of a totally different situation.

The hold which older conceptions have gained over the minds of thinkers, the sway of inertia in habits of philosophic thought, can be most readily judged by turning to books on epistemology and to discussions of problems connected with the theory of knowledge published in the philosophical periodicals. Articles on logical method will be found which reflect the procedures of actual knowing, that is of the practice of scientific inquiry. But logic is then usually treated as "mere" methodology, having little (probably nothing would be nearer the mark) to do with the theory of knowledge. The latter is discussed in terms of conceptions about mind and its organs; these conceptions are supposed to be capable of adequate formation apart from observation of what goes on when men engage in successful inquiry. Of late, the main problem in such discussions is to frame a theory of "consciousness" which shall explain knowing, as if consciousness were either a fact whose meaning is self-evident, or something less obscure in content and more observable than are the objective and public procedures of scientific investigation. This type of discussion persists; it is, in current conception, *the* theory of knowledge, the natural and inevitable way in which to discuss its basic problems! Volumes could not say more for the persistence of traditional ideas. The import of even a rudimentary discussion of actual experimental method can hardly be gathered, then, without bearing in mind its significance as a contrast effect.

While the traits of experimental inquiry are familiar, so little use has been made of them in formulating a theory of knowledge and of mind in relation to nature that a somewhat explicit statement of well known facts is excusable. They exhibit three outstanding characteristics. The first is the obvious one that all experimentation involves *overt* doing, the making of definite changes in the environment or in our relation to it. The second is that experiment is not a random activity but is directed by ideas which have to meet the conditions set by the need of the problem inducing the active inquiry. The third and concluding feature, in which the other two receive their full measure of meaning, is that the outcome of the directed activity is the construction of a new empirical situation in which objects are differently related to one another, and such that the *consequences* of directed operations form the objects that have the property of being *known*.

The rudimentary prototype of experimental doing for the sake of knowing is found in ordinary procedures. When we are trying to make out the nature of a confused and unfamiliar object, we perform various acts with a view to establishing a new relationship to it, such as will bring to light qualities which will aid in understanding it. We turn it over, bring it into a better light, rattle and shake it, thump, push and press it, and so on. The object as it is experienced prior to the introduction of these changes baffles us; the intent of these acts is to make changes which will elicit some previously unperceived qualities, and by varying conditions of perception shake loose some property which as it stands blinds or misleads us.

While such experimentations, together with a kind of experimental playing with things just to see what will happen, are the chief source of the everyday non-scientific store of information about things around us, forming the bulk of "common-sense" knowledge, the limitations of the mode of procedure are so evident as to require no exposition. The important thing in the history of modern knowing is the reinforcement of these active doings by means of instruments, appliances and apparatus devised for the purposes of disclosing relations not otherwise apparent, together with, as far as overt action is concerned, the development of elaborate techniques for the introduction of a much greater range of variations—that is, a systematic variation of conditions so as to produce a corresponding series of changes in the thing under investigation. Among these operations should be included, of course, those which give a permanent register of what is observed and the instrumentalities of exact measurement by means of which changes are correlated with one another.

These matters are so familiar that their full import for the theory of knowing readily escapes notice. Hence the need of comparing this kind of knowledge of natural existences with that obtaining before the rise of the experimental method. The striking difference is, of course, the dependence placed upon doing, doing of a physical and overt sort. Ancient science, that is, what passed as science, would have thought it a kind of treason to reason as the organ of knowing to subordinate it to bodily activity on material things, helped out with tools which are also material. It would have seemed like admitting the superiority of matter to rational mind, an admission which from its standpoint was contradictory to the possibility of knowledge.

With this fundamental change goes another, that in the attitude taken toward the material of direct sense-perception. No notion could be further away from the fact than the somewhat sedulously cultivated idea that the difference between ancient and modern science is that the former had no respect for perception and relied exclusively upon speculation. In fact, the Greeks were keenly sensitive to natural objects and were keen observers. The trouble lay not in substitution of theorizing from the outset for the material of perception, but in that they took the latter "as is"; they made no attempt to modify it radically before undertaking thinking and theorizing about it. As far as observation unaided by artificial appliances and means for deliberate variation of observed material went, the Greeks went far.

Their disrespect for sensibly observed material concerned only its form. For it had to be brought under logical forms supplied by rational thought. The fact that the material was not exclusively logical, or such as to satisfy the requirements of rational form, made the resulting knowledge less scientific than that of pure mathematics, logic and metaphysics occupied with eternal Being. But as far as science extended, it dealt with the material of sense-perception as it directly offered itself to a keen and alert observer. In consequence, the material of Greek natural science is much closer to "common sense" material than are the results of contemporary science. One can read the surviving statements of it without any more technical preparation than say a knowledge of Euclidean geometry, while no one can follow understandingly the reports of most modern investigations in physics without a highly technical preparatory education. One reason the atomic theory propounded in antiquity made so little headway is that it did not agree with the results of ordinary observation. For this presented objects clothed with rich qualities and falling into kinds or species that were themselves marked by qualitative, rather than by merely quantitative and spatial, differences. In antiquity it was the atomic theory which was purely speculative and "deductive" in character.

These statements would be misunderstood if they were taken to imply an allegation that in ancient science sense gives knowledge, while modern science excludes the material of sense; such an idea inverts the facts. But ancient science accepted the *material* of sense-material on its face, and then organized it, as it naturally and originally stood, by operations of logical definition, classification into species and syllogistic subsumption. Men either had no instruments and appliances for modifying the ordinary objects of observation, for analyzing them into their elements and giving them new forms and arrangements, or they failed to use those which they had. Thus in *content,* or subject-matter, the conclusions of Greek science (which persisted till the scientific revolution of the seventeenth century), were much closer to the objects of everyday experience than are the objects of present scientific thought. It is not meant that the Greeks had more respect for the *function* of perception through the senses than has modern science, but that, judged from present practice, they had altogether too much respect for the *material* of direct, unanalyzed sense-perception.

They were aware of its defects from the standpoint of knowledge. But they supposed that they could correct these defects and supplement their lack by purely logical or "rational" means. They supposed that thought could take the material supplied by ordinary perception, eliminate varying and hence contingent qualities, and thus finally reach the fixed and immutable form which makes particulars have the character they have; define this form as the essence or true reality of the particular things in question, and then gather a group of perceived objects into a species which is as eternal as its particular exemplifications are perishable. The passage from ordinary perception to scientific knowledge did not therefore demand the introduction of actual, overt and observed changes into the *material* of sense perception. Modern science, with its changes in the subject-matter of direct perception effected by the use of apparatus, gets away not from observed material as such, but from the qualitative characteristics of things as they are originally and "naturally" observed.

It may thus be fairly asserted that the "categories" of Greek description and explanation of natural phenomena were esthetic in character; for perception of the esthetic sort is interested in things in their immediate qualitative traits. The logical features they depended upon to confer scientific form upon the material of observation were harmony, proportion or measure, symmetry: these constitute the "logos" that renders phenomena capable of report in rational discourse. In virtue of these properties, superimposed upon phenomena but thought to be elicited from them, natural objects are knowable. Thus the Greeks employed thinking not as a means of changing given objects of observation so as to get at the conditions and effects of their occurrence, but to impose upon them certain static properties not found in them in their changeable occurrence. The essence of the static properties conferred upon them was harmony of form and pattern. Craftsmen, architects, sculptors, gymnasts, poets had taken raw material and converted it into finished forms marked by symmetry and proportion; they accomplished this task without the prior disintegrative reduction which characterizes modern making in the factory. Greek thinkers performed a like task for nature as a whole. Instead, however, of employing the material tools of the crafts, they depended upon thought alone. They borrowed the *form* provided them in Greek art in abstraction from its material appliances. They aimed at constructing out of nature, as observed, an artistic whole for the eye of the soul to behold. Thus for science nature was a cosmos. It was composed, but it was not a composite of elements. That is, it was a qualitative whole, a whole as is a drama, a statue or a temple, in virtue of a pervading and dominant qualitative unity; it was not an aggregate of homogenous units externally arranged in different modes. Design was the form and pattern intrinsically characteristic of things in their fixed kinds, not something first formed in a designing mind and then imposed from without.

In his *Creative Evolution,* Bergson remarks that to the Greek mind that reality which is the object of the truest knowledge is found in some privileged moment when a process of change attains its climactic apogee. The Ideas of Plato and the Forms of Aristotle, as he says, may be compared in their relation to particular things to the horses of the Parthenon frieze in relation to the casual movements of horses. The essential movement which gives and defines the character of the horse is summed up in the eternal moment of a static position and form. To see, to grasp, that culminating and defining form, and by grasping to possess and enjoy it, is to know.

This *aperçu* of Bergson illustrates the conception of the essentially artistic character possessed for Greek science by the object of knowledge. It is borne out by the details of Greek science. I know of no one thing more significant for an understanding of Greek science than Aristotle's treatment of quantity as an accident, that is, as something which can vary within limits (set by the inherent essence and measure, *logos*) of a thing without affecting its nature. When we think of the Cartesian definition of quantity as the essence of matter, we appreciate that an intellectual revolution has taken place: a radical change in point of view and not just the product of more, and more accurately stated, information, but a change involving surrender of the esthetic character of the object. Contrast the place occupied in modern science by relations with the Aristotelian illustrations of their nature—namely, distinctions of more and less, greater and smaller, etc. For the point of Aristotle's treatment is that relations, like quantity, are indifferent to the essence or nature of the object, and hence are of no final account for scientific knowledge. This conception is thoroughly appropriate to an esthetic point of view, wherein that which is internally complete and self-sufficing is the all-important consideration.

The addiction of Pythagorean-Platonism to number and geometry might seem to contradict what has been said. But it is one of the exceptions that proves the rule. For geometry and number in this scheme were means of ordering natural phenomena as they are directly observed. They were principles of measure, symmetry and allotment that satisfied canons essentially esthetic. Science had to wait almost two thousand years for mathematics to become an instrument of analysis, of resolution into elements for the sake of recomposition, through equations and other functions.

I pass by the evidence of the qualitative character of Greek science afforded by the central position of kinds or species in Peripatetic science. The instance is too obvious. More instructive is the purely qualitative treatment of movements, especially as this is the matter that gives the clue to the revolution wrought by Galileo. Movement was a term covering all sorts of qualitative alterations, such as warm things becoming cold, growth from embryo to adult form, etc. It was never conceived of as merely motion, i.e., change of position in a homogeneous space. When we speak of a musical movement, or a political movement, we come close to the sense attached to the idea in ancient science: a series of changes tending to complete or perfect a qualitative whole and fulfill an end.

Movement instead of continuing indefinitely spent itself; it tended inherently toward its own cessation, toward rest. The problem was not what external forces bring the arrow to a state of relative rest but what external forces, currents of air, etc., keep it moving and prevent its speedier attainment of its own natural goal, rest. Cessation of movement is either exhaustion, a kind of fatigue, or it marks the culmination of intrinsic proper being or essence. The heavenly bodies, just because they are heavenly, and therefore quasi-divine, are unwearied, never tiring, and so keep up their ceaseless round. For rest when it meant fulfillment was not dead quiescence but complete and therefore *unchanging* movement. Only thought is completely possessed of this perfect self-activity; but the constant round of heavenly bodies is the nearest physical manifestation of the self-enclosed changeless activity of thought, which discovers nothing, learns nothing, effects nothing, but eternally revolves upon itself.

The treatment of place—or rather places—is the counterpart of this qualitative diversification of movements. There is movement up from the earth, in the measure of their lightness, of those things which belong in the upper spaces; a downward movement to the earth of those things which because of their grossness attain their end and arrive at their home only in the gross and relatively cold earth. To the intermediate regions is appropriate neither upward nor downward movement but the back and forth and wavering movement characteristic of winds and the (apparent) motions of the planets. As the cold and heavy moves down, the light and fiery, the finest material moves upward. The stars of the firmament being the most nearly divine, the most purged of the irregular and merely potential, pursue that undeviating circular course which is the nearest approach in nature to the eternal self-activity of thought, which is at once beyond nature and its culmination or "final cause."

These details are mentioned to make clear the completely qualitative character of antique science. There was no conflict with ideas about values, because the qualities belonging to objects of science *are* values; they are the things we enjoy and prize. Throughout nature as a qualitative whole there is a hierarchy of forms from those of lower value to those of higher. The revolution in science effectively initiated by Galileo consisted precisely in the abolition of qualities as traits of scientific objects *as such*. From this elimination proceeded just that conflict and need of reconciliation between the scientific properties of the real and those which give moral authority. Therefore to apprehend what the new astronomy and physics did for human beliefs, we have to place it in its contrast with the older natural science in which the qualities possessed by objects of scientific knowledge were precisely the same as those possessed by works of art, the properties which are one with beauty and with all that is admirable.

The work of Galileo was not a development, but a revolution. It marked a change from the qualitative to the quantitative or metric; from the heterogeneous to the homogeneous; from intrinsic forms to relations; from esthetic harmonies to mathematical formulæ; from contemplative enjoyment to active manipulation and control; from rest to change; from eternal objects to temporal sequence. The idea of a two-realm scheme persisted for moral and religious purposes; it vanished for purposes of natural science. The higher realm which had been the object of true science became the exclusive habitat of objects connected with values that in their relation to man furnish the norm and end of human destiny. The lower realm of change which had been the subject of opinion and practice became the sole and only object of natural science. The realm in which opinion held sway was no longer a genuine although inferior portion of objective being. It was a strictly human product, due to ignorance and error. Such was the philosophy which, because of the new science, replaced the old metaphysics. But—and this "but" is of fundamental importance— in spite of the revolution, the old conceptions of knowledge as related to an antecedent reality and of moral regulation as derived from properties of this reality, persisted.

Neither the scientific nor the philosophic change came at once, even after experimental inquiry was initiated. In fact as we shall see later, philosophy proceeded conservatively by compromise and accommodation, and was read into the new science, so that not till our own generation did science free itself from some basic factors of the older conception of nature. Much of the scientific revolution was implicit, however, in the conclusions which Galileo drew from his two most famous experiments. The one with falling bodies at the tower of Pisa destroyed the old distinction of intrinsic qualitative differences of gravity and levity, and thus gave an enormous shock to the qualitative explanatory principles of science. It thus tended to undermine the description and explanation of natural phenomena in terms of heterogeneous qualities. For it showed that the immanent motion of bodies was connected with a common homogeneous property, one measured by their resistance to being set in motion and to having their motion arrested or deflected when once set in operation. This property, called inertia, was finally identified by Newton with mass, so that mass or inertia became the scientific definition or stable co-efficient of matter, in complete indifference to the qualitative differentiations of wet-dry, hot-cold, which were henceforth things to be explained by means of mass and motion, not fundamental explanatory principles.

Taken in isolation, it is conceivable that this result would have been only a shock, or at most a ferment. Not so, however, when it was connected with his experiment of balls rolling down a smooth inclined plane (of which his experiment with the pendulum was a variation), the nearest approximation he could make to observation of freely falling bodies. His purpose was to determine the relation of the measured time of falling to the measured space passed through. Observed results confirmed the hypothesis he had previously formed, namely, that the space traversed is proportional to the square of the elapsed time. If we forget the background of Peripatetic science against which this conclusion was projected, it appears as a mathematical determination of acceleration, and in connection with the concept of mass, as affording a new and accurate definition of force. This result is highly important. But apart from the classic background of beliefs about nature, it would have been of the same type as important discoveries in physics to-day. In its opposition to the basic ideas of Peripatetic science, it ushered in the scientific revolution. Galileo's conclusions were absolutely fatal to the traditional conception that all bodies in motion come naturally to rest because of their own intrinsic tendency to fulfill an inherent nature. The ingenious mind of Galileo used his results to show that if a body moving on a horizontal plane, not subjected to the independent force of uniform gravity, were substituted for the body on an inclined plane, it would when once set in motion continue in motion indefinitely—the idea later formulated in Newton's first law of motion.

The revolution opened the way to description and explanation of natural phenomena on the basis of homogeneous space, time, mass and motion. Our discussion is not an account of the historic development, and details are passed over. But some of the generic results which followed must be summarily mentioned. Galileo's conclusion did not at first affect the tradition that bodies at rest remained at rest. But his logic and the further use of his methods revealed that when a gross body is brought to rest, motion is transferred to its own particles and to those of the body which checked its movement. Thus heat became subject to mechanical treatment, and in the end the conversion of mechanical motion, heat, light, electricity into one another without loss of energy was established. Then it was shown by Newton, following Copernicus and Huygens, that the movements of the planets obey the same mechanical laws of mass and acceleration as mundane bodies. Heavenly bodies and movements were brought under the same laws as are found in terrestrial phenomena. The idea of the difference in kind between phenomena in different parts of space was abolished. All that counted for science became mechanical properties formulated in mathematical terms:—the significance of mathematical formulation marking the possibility of complete equivalence or homogeneity of translation of different phenomena into one another's terms.

From the standpoint of the doctrine that the purpose of knowledge is to grasp reality and that the object of cognition and real objects are synonymous terms, there was but one conclusion possible. This, in the words of a recent writer, was that "the Newtonian astronomy revealed the whole heavenly realm as a dark and limitless emptiness wherein dead matter moved under the impulse of insensate forces, and thus finally destroyed the poetic dream of ages."*

The conclusion holds good, however, only under condition that the premise be held to. If and as far as the qualitative world was taken to be an object of knowledge, and not of experience in some other form than knowing, and as far as knowing was held to be the standard or sole valid mode of experiencing, the substitution of Newtonian for Greek science (the latter being but a rationalized arrangement of the qualitatively enjoyed world of direct experience) signified that the properties that render the world one of delight, admiration and esteem, have been done away with. There is, however, another interpretation possible. A philosophy which holds that we experience things as they really are apart from knowing, and that knowledge is a mode of experiencing things which facilitates control of objects for purposes of non-cognitive experiences, will come to another conclusion. . . .

THE NATURALIZATION OF INTELLIGENCE

. . . Probably everyone has heard of the child who expressed surprise at the fact that rivers or bodies of water are always located conveniently near great cities. Suppose every one had had engrained in his mind the notion that cities, like rivers, are works of nature. Suppose it was then suddenly ascertained that cities were man-made and were located near bodies of water in order that the activities of men in industry and commerce might be better carried on and human purposes and needs be better served. We can imagine that the discovery would bring with it a shock. It would be upsetting because it would seem unnatural; for the ordinary measure of the natural is psychological; it is what we have become accustomed to. But in time the new idea in becoming familiar would also become "natural." If men had always previously conceived of the connection

* Barry, *The Scientific Habit of Mind* (New York, 1927) p. 249. I owe much more to this volume than this particular quotation.

between cities and rivers as one which was intrinsic and fixed by nature, instead of being a product of human art, it is moreover probable that in time a liberation would be experienced by discovery that the contrary was the case. Men would be led to take fuller advantage of the facilities afforded by natural conditions. These would be used in new and more diversified ways when it was realized that cities were near them because of and for the sake of the uses they provide.

The analogy suggested seems to me close. From the standpoint of traditional notions, it appears that nature, intrinsically, is *irrational*. But the quality of irrationality is imputed only because of conflict with a prior definition of rationality. Abandon completely the notion that nature *ought* to conform to a certain definition, and nature intrinsically is neither rational nor irrational. Apart from the use made of it in knowing, it exists in a dimension irrelevant to either attribution, just as rivers inherently are neither located near cities nor are opposed to such location. Nature is intelli*gible* and understand*able*. There are operations by means of which it *becomes* an object of knowledge, and is turned to human purposes, just as rivers provide conditions which *may* be utilized to promote human activities and to satisfy human need.

Moreover, just as commerce, carried on by natural bodies of water, signifies interactions within nature, by which changes are affected in natural conditions—the building of docks and harbors, erection of warehouses and factories, construction of steamships and also in invention of new modes of interaction—so with knowing and knowledge. The organs, instrumentalities and operations of knowing are inside nature, not outside. Hence they are changes of what previously existed: the object of knowledge is a constructed, existentially produced, object. The shock to the traditional notion that knowledge is perfect in the degree in which it grasps or beholds without change some thing previously complete in itself is tremendous. But in effect it only makes us aware of what we have always done, as far as ever we have actually succeeded in knowing: it clears away superfluous and irrelevant accompaniments and it concentrates attention upon the agencies which are actually effective in obtaining knowledge, eliminating waste and making actual knowing more controllable. It installs man, thinking man, within nature.

The doctrine that nature is inherently rational was a costly one. It entailed the idea that reason in man is an outside spectator of a rationality already complete in itself. It deprived reason in man of an active and creative office; its business was simply to copy, to re-present symbolically, to view a given rational structure. Ability to make a transcript of this structure in mathematical formulæ gives great delight to those who have the required ability. But it *does* nothing; it makes no difference in nature. In effect, it limits thought in man to retraversing in cognition a pattern fixed and complete in itself. The doctrine was both an effect of the traditional separation between knowledge and action and a factor in perpetuating it. It relegated practical making and doing to a secondary and relatively irrational realm.

Its paralyzing effect on human action is seen in the part it played in the eighteenth and nineteenth century in the theory of "natural laws" in human affairs, in social matters. These natural laws were supposed to be inherently fixed; a science of social phenomena and relations was equivalent to discovery of them. Once discovered, nothing remained for man but to conform to them; they were to rule his conduct as physical laws govern physical phenomena. They were the sole standard of conduct in economic affairs; the laws of economics are the "natural" laws of all political action; other so-called laws are artificial, man-made contrivances in contrast with the normative regulations of nature itself.

Laissez-faire was the logical conclusion. For organized society to attempt to regulate the course of economic affairs, to bring them into service of humanly conceived ends, was a harmful interference.

This doctrine is demonstratively the offspring of that conception of universal laws that phenomena must observe which was a heritage of the Newtonian philosophy. But if man in knowing is a participator in the natural scene, a factor in generating things known, the fact that man participates as a factor in social affairs is no barrier to knowledge of them. On the contrary, a certain method of directed participation is a precondition of his having any genuine understanding. Human intervention for the sake of effecting ends is no interference, and it is a means of knowledge.

There is thus involved more than a verbal shift if we say that the new scientific development effects an exchange of reason for intelligence. In saying this, "reason" has the technical meaning given to it in classic philosophic tradition, the *nous* of the Greeks, the *intellectus* of the scholastics. In this meaning, it designates both an inherent immutable order of nature, superempirical in character, and the organ of mind by which this universal order is grasped. In both respects, reason is with respect to changing things the ultimate fixed standard—the law physical phenomena obey, the norm human action should obey. For the marks of "reason" in its traditional sense are necessity, universality, superiority to change, domination of the occurrence and the understanding of change.

Intelligence on the other hand is associated with *judgment;* that is, with selection and arrangement of means to effect consequences and with choice of what we take as our ends. A man is intelligent not in virtue of having reason which grasps first and indemonstrable truths about fixed principles, in order to reason deductively from them to the particulars which they govern, but in virtue of his capacity to estimate the possibilties of a situation and to act in accordance with his estimate. In the large sense of the term, intelligence is as practical as reason is theoretical. Wherever intelligence operates, things are judged in their capacity of signs of other things. If scientific knowledge enables us to estimate more accurately the worth of things as signs, we can afford to exchange a loss of theoretical certitude for a gain in practical judgment. For if we can judge events as indications of other events, we can prepare in all cases for the coming of what is anticipated. In some cases, we can forestall a happening; desiring one event to happen rather than another, we can intentionally set about institution of those changes which our best knowledge tells us to be connected with that which we are after.

What has been lost in the theoretical possibility of exact knowledge and exact prediction is more than compensated for by the fact that the knowing which occurs within nature involves possibility of direction of change. This conclusion gives intelligence a foothold and a function within nature which "reason" never possessed. That which acts outside of nature and is a mere spectator of it is, by definition, not a participator in its changes. Therefore it is debarred from taking part in directing them. Action may follow but it is only an external attachment to knowing, not an inherent factor in it. As a mechanical addendum, it is inferior to knowledge. Moreover, it must either issue automatically from knowledge or else there must be some intervening act of "will" to produce it. In any case, because of its externality it adds nothing to intelligence or knowledge. It can only increase personal shrewdness in prudential manipulation of conditions.

We may, indeed, engage during knowing in experimentation. But according to the classic logic the effect was not to reorganize prior conditions, but merely to bring about a change in our own subjective or mental attitude. The act no more entered into the constitution of the known object than traveling to Athens to see the Parthenon had any effect on architecture. It makes a change in our own personal attitude and posture so that we can see better what was there all the time. It is a practical concession to the weakness of our powers of apprehension. The whole scheme hangs together with the traditional depreciation of practical activity on the part of the intellectual class. In reality, it also condemns intelligence to a position of impotency. Its exercise is an enjoyable use of leisure. The doctrine of its supreme value is largely a compensation for the impotency that attached to it in contrast with the force of executive acts.

The realization that the observation necessary to knowledge enters into the natural object known cancels this separation of knowing and doing. It makes possible and it demands a theory in which knowing and doing are intimately connected with each other. Hence, as we have said, it domesticates the exercise of intelligence within nature. This is part and parcel of nature's own continuing interactions. Interactions go on anyway and produce changes. Apart from intelligence, these changes are not directed. They are effects but not consequences, for consequences imply means deliberately employed. When an interaction intervenes which directs the course of change, the scene of natural interaction has a new quality and dimension. This added type of interaction *is* intelligence. The intelligent activity of man is not something brought to bear upon nature from without; it is nature realizing its own potentialities in behalf of a fuller and richer issue of events. Intelligence within nature means liberation and expansion, as reason outside of nature means fixation and restriction.

The change does not mean that nature has lost intelligibility. It rather signifies that we are in position to realize that the term intellig*ible* is to be understood literally. It expresses a potentiality rather than an actuality. Nature is capable of being understood. But the possibility is realized not by a mind thinking about it from without but by operations conducted from within, operations which give it new relations summed up in production of a new individual object. Nature *has* intelligible order as its possession in the degree in which we by our own overt operations realize potentialities contained in it. The change from intrinsic rationality in the traditional sense to an intelligibility to be realized by human action places responsibility upon human beings. The devotion we show to the ideal of intelligence determines the extent in which the actual order of nature is congenial to mind. . . .

Democracy and Education

EDUCATION AS GROWTH

The Conditions of Growth.—IN DIRECTING THE ACTIVITIES OF THE young, society determines its own future in determing that of the young. Since the young at a given time will at some later date compose the society of that period, the latter's nature will largely turn upon the direction children's activities were given at an earlier period. This cumulative movement of action toward a later result is what is meant by growth. . . .

Habits as Expressions of Growth.—Education is not infrequently defined as consisting in the acquisition of those habits that effect an adjustment of an individual and his environment. The definition expresses an essential phase of growth. But it is essential that adjustment be understood in its active sense of *control* of means for achieving ends. If we think of a habit simply as a change wrought in the organism, ignoring the fact that this change consists in ability to effect subsequent changes in the environment, we shall be led to think of 'adjustment' as a conformity to environment as wax conforms to the seal which impresses it. The environment is thought of as something fixed, providing in its fixity the end and standard of changes taking place in the organism; adjustment is just fitting ourselves to this fixity of external conditions.* Habit as *habituation* is indeed something *relatively* passive; we get used to our surroundings—to our clothing, our shoes, and gloves; to the atmosphere as long as it is fairly equable; to our daily associates, etc. Conformity to the environment, a change wrought in the organism without reference to ability to modify surroundings, is a marked trait of such habituations. Aside from the fact that we are not entitled to carry over the traits of such adjustments (which might well be called *accommodations,* to mark them off from active adjustments) into habits of active use of our surroundings, two features of habituations are worth notice. In the first place, we get used to things by *first* using them.

Consider getting used to a strange city. At first, there is excessive stimu-

---

* This conception is, of course, a logical correlate of the conceptions of the external relation of stimulus and response, considered in the last chapter, and of the negative conceptions of immaturity and plasticity noted in this chapter.

lation and excessive and ill-adapted response. Gradually certain stimuli are selected because of their relevancy, and others are degraded. We can say either that we do not respond to them any longer, or more truly that we have effected a persistent response to them—an equilibrium of adjustment. This means, in the second place, that this enduring adjustment supplies the background upon which are made specific adjustments, as occasion arises. We are never interested in changing the *whole* environment; there is much that we take for granted and accept just as it already is. Upon this background our activities focus at certain points in an endeavor to introduce needed changes. Habituation is thus our adjustment to an environment which at the time we are not concerned with modifying, and which supplies a leverage to our active habits.

Adaptation, in fine, is quite as much adaptation *of* the environment to our own activities as of our activities *to* the environment. A savage tribe manages to live on a desert plain. It adapts itself. But its adaptation involves a maximum of accepting, tolerating, putting up with things as they are, a maximum of passive acquiescence, and a minimum of active control, of subjection to use. A civilized people enters upon the scene. It also adapts itself. It introduces irrigation; it searches the world for plants and animals that will flourish under such conditions; it improves, by careful selection, those which are growing there. As a consequence, the wilderness blossoms as a rose. The savage is merely habituated; the civilized man has habits which transform the environment.

The significance of habit is not exhausted, however, in its executive and motor phase. It means formation of intellectual and emotional disposition as well as an increase in ease, economy, and efficiency of action. Any habit marks an *inclination*—an active preference and choice for the conditions involved in its exercise. A habit does not wait, Micawber-like, for a stimulus to turn up so that it may get busy; it actively seeks for occasions to pass into full operation. If its expression is unduly blocked, inclination shows itself in uneasiness and intense craving. A habit also marks an intellectual disposition. Where there is a habit, there is acquaintance with the materials and equipment to which action is applied. There is a definite way of understanding the situations in which the habit operates. Modes of thought, of observation and reflection, enter as forms of skill and of desire into the habits that make a man an engineer, an architect, a physician, or a merchant. In unskilled forms of labor, the intellectual factors are at minimum precisely because the habits involved are not of a high grade. But there are habits of judging and reasoning as truly as of handling a tool, painting a picture, or conducting an experiment.

Such statements are, however, understatements. The habits of mind involved in habits of the eye and hand supply the latter with their significance. Above all, the intellectual element in a habit fixes the relation of the habit to varied and elastic use, and hence to continued growth. We speak of *fixed* habits. Well, the phrase may mean powers so well established that their possessor always has them as resources when needed. But the phrase is also used to mean ruts, routine ways, with loss of freshness, openmindedness, and originality. Fixity of habit may mean that something has a fixed hold upon us, instead of our having a free hold upon things. This fact explains two points in a common notion about habits: their identification with mechanical and external modes of action to the neglect of mental and moral attitudes, and the tendency to give them a bad meaning, an identification with "bad habits." Many a person would feel surprised to have his aptitude in his chosen profession called a habit, and would naturally think of his use of tobacco, liquor, or profane language as typical of the meaning of habit. A habit is to him something which has a hold on him, something not easily thrown off even though judgment condemn it.

Habits reduce themselves to routine ways of acting, or degenerate into ways of action to which we are enslaved just in the degree in which intelligence is disconnected from them. Routine habits are unthinking habits; "bad" habits are habits so severed from reason that they are opposed to the conclusions of conscious deliberation and decision. As we have seen, the acquiring of habits is due to an original plasticity of our natures: to our ability to vary responses till we find an appropriate and efficient way of acting. Routine habits, and habits that possess us instead of our possessing them, are habits which put an end to plasticity. They mark the close of power to vary. There can be no doubt of the tendency of organic plasticity, of the physiological basis, to lessen with growing years. The instinctively mobile and eagerly varying action of childhood, the love of new stimuli and new developments, too easily passes into a "settling down," which means aversion to change and a resting on past achievements. Only an environment which secures the full use of intelligence in the process of forming habits can counteract this tendency. Of course, the same hardening of the organic conditions affects the physiological structures which are involved in thinking. But this fact only indicates the need of persistent care to see to it that the function of intelligence is invoked to its maximum possibility. The short-sighted method which falls back on mechanical routine and repetition to secure external efficiency of habit, motor skill without accompanying thought, marks a deliberate closing in of surroundings upon growth.

The Educational Bearings of the Conception of Development.—We have had so far but little to say in this chapter about education. We have been occupied with the conditions and implications of growth. If our conclusions are justified, they carry with them, however, definite educational consequences. When it is said that education is development, everything depends upon *how* development is conceived. Our net conclusion is that life is development, and that developing, growing, is life. Translated into its educational equivalents, this means *(i)* that the educational process has no cnd beyond itself; it is its own end; and that *(ii)* the educational process is one of continual reorganizing, reconstructing, transforming.

1. Development when it is interpreted in *comparative* terms, that is, with respect to the special traits of child and adult life, means the direction of power into special channels: the formation of habits involving executive skill, definiteness of interest, and specific objects of observation and thought. But the comparative view is not final. The child has specific powers; to ignore that fact is to stunt or distort the organs upon which his growth depends. The adult uses his powers to transform his environment, thereby occasioning new stimuli which redirect his powers and keep them developing. Ignoring this fact means arrested development, a passive accommodation. Normal child and normal adult alike, in other words, are engaged in growing. The difference between them is not the difference between growth and no growth, but between the modes of growth appropriate to different conditions. With respect to the development of powers devoted to coping with specific scientific and economic problems we may say the child should be growing in manhood. With respect to sympathetic curiosity, unbiased responsiveness, and openness of mind, we may say that the adult should be growing in childlikeness. One statement is as true as the other.

Three ideas which have been criticized, namely, the merely privative nature of immaturity, static adjustment to a fixed environment, and rigidity of habit, are all connected with a false idea of growth or development,—that it is a movement toward a fixed goal. Growth is regarded as *having* an end, instead of *being* an end. The educational counterparts of the three fallacious ideas are first, failure to take account of the instinctive or native powers of the young; secondly, failure to develop initiative in coping with novel situations; thirdly, an undue emphasis upon drill and other devices which secure automatic skill at the expense of personal perception. In all cases, the adult environment is accepted as a standard for the child. He is to be brought up *to* it.

Natural instincts are either disregarded or treated as nuisances—as obnoxious traits to be suppressed, or at all events to be brought into conformity with external standards. Since conformity is the aim, what is distinctively individual in a young person is brushed aside, or regarded as a source of mischief or anarchy. Conformity is made equivalent to uniformity. Consequently, there are induced lack of interest in the novel, aversion to progress, and dread of the uncertain and the unknown. Since the end of growth is outside of and beyond the process of growing, external agents have to be resorted to to induce movement towards it. Whenever a method of education is stigmatized as mechanical, we may be sure that external pressure is brought to bear to reach an external end.

2. Since in reality there is nothing to which growth is relative save more growth, there is nothing to which education is subordinate save more

education. It is a commonplace to say that education should not cease when one leaves school. The point of this commonplace is that the purpose of school education is to insure the continuance of education by organizing the powers that insure growth. The inclination to learn from life itself and to make the conditions of life such that all will learn in the process of living is the finest product of schooling.

When we abandon the attempt to define immaturity by means of fixed comparison with adult accomplishments, we are compelled to give up thinking of it as denoting lack of desired traits. Abandoning this notion, we are also forced to surrender our habit of thinking of instruction as a method of supplying this lack by pouring knowledge into a mental and moral hole which awaits filling. Since life means growth, a living creature lives as truly and positively at one stage as at another, with the same intrinsic fullness and the same absolute claims. Hence education means the enterprise of supplying the conditions which insure growth, or adequacy of life, irrespective of age. We first look with impatience upon immaturity, regarding it as something to be got over as rapidly as possible. Then the adult formed by such educative methods looks back with impatient regret upon childhood and youth as a scene of lost opportunities and wasted powers. This ironical situation will endure till it is recognized that living has its own intrinsic quality and that the business of education is with that quality.

Realization that life is growth protects us from that so-called idealizing of childhood which in effect is nothing but lazy indulgence. Life is not to be identified with every superficial act and interest. Even though it is not always easy to tell whether what appears to be mere surface fooling is a sign of some nascent as yet untrained power, we must remember that manifestations are not to be accepted as ends in themselves. They are signs of possible growth. They are to be turned into means of development, of carrying power forward, not indulged or cultivated for their own sake. Excessive attention to surface phenomena (even in the way of rebuke as well as of encouragement) may lead to their fixation and thus to arrested development. What impulses are moving toward, not what they have been, is the important thing for parent and teacher. The true principle of respect for immaturity cannot be better put than in the words of Emerson: "Respect the child. Be not too much his parent. Trespass not on his solitude. But I hear the outcry which replies to this suggestion: Would you verily throw up the reins of public and private discipline; would you leave the young child to the mad career of his own passions and whimsies, and call this anarchy a respect for the child's nature? I answer,—Respect the child, respect him to the end, but also respect yourself. . . . The two points in a boy's training are, to keep his *naturel* and train off all but that; to keep his *naturel,* but stop off his uproar, fooling, and horseplay; keep his nature *and arm it with knowledge in the very direction in which it points.*" And as Emerson goes on to show this reverence for childhood and youth instead of opening up an easy and easy-going path to the instructors, "involves at once, immense claims on the time, the thought, on the life of the teacher. It requires time, use, insight, event, all the great lessons and assistances of God; and only to think of using it implies character and profoundness. . . ."

THE DEMOCRATIC CONCEPTION IN EDUCATION

We have now to make explicit the differences in the spirit, material, and method of education as it operates in different types of community life. To say that education is a social function, securing direction and development in the immature through their participation in the life of the group to which they belong, is to say in effect that education will vary with the quality of life which prevails in a group. Particularly is it true that a society which not only changes but which has the ideal of such change as will improve it, will have different standards and methods of education from one which aims simply at the perpetuation of its own customs. To make the general ideas set forth applicable to our own educational practice, it is, therefore, necessary to come to closer quarters with the nature of present social life.

The Implications of Human Association.—Society is one word, but many things. Men associate together in all kinds of ways and for all kinds of purposes. One man is concerned in a multitude of diverse groups, in which his associates may be quite different. It often seems as if they had nothing in common except that they are modes of associated life. Within every larger social organization there are numerous minor groups: not only political subdivisions, but industrial, scientific, religious, associations. There are political parties with differing aims, social sets, cliques, gangs, corporations, partnerships, groups bound closely together by ties of blood, and so in endless variety. In many modern states, and in some ancient, there is great diversity of populations, of varying languages, religions, moral codes, and traditions. From this standpoint, many a minor political unit, one of our large cities, for example, is a congeries of loosely associated societies, rather than an inclusive and permeating community of action and thought.

The terms society, community, are thus ambiguous. They have both a eulogistic or normative sense, and a descriptive sense; a meaning *de jure* and a meaning *de facto*. In social philosophy, the former connotation is almost always uppermost. Society is conceived as one by its very nature. The qualities which accompany this unity, praiseworthy community of purpose and welfare, loyalty to public ends, mutuality of sympathy, are emphasized. But when we look at the facts which the term *denotes* instead of confining our attention to its intrinsic *connotation*, we find not unity, but a plurality of societies, good and bad. Men banded together in a criminal conspiracy, business aggregations that prey upon the public while serving it, political machines held together by the interest of plunder, are included. If it is said that such organizations are not societies because they do not meet the ideal requirements of the notion of society, the answer, in part, is that the conception of society is then made so "ideal" as to be of no use, having no reference to facts; and in part, that each of these organizations, no matter how opposed to the interests of other groups, has something of the praiseworthy qualities of "Society" which hold it together. There is honor among thieves, and a band of robbers has a common interest as respects its members. Gangs are marked by fraternal feeling, and narrow cliques by intense loyalty to their own codes. Family life may be marked by exclusiveness, suspicion, and jealousy as to those without, and yet be a model of amity and mutual aid within. Any education given by a group tends to socialize its members, but the quality and value of socialization depends upon the habits and aims of the group.

Hence, once more, the need of a measure for the worth of any given mode of social life. In seeking this measure, we have to avoid two extremes. We cannot set up, out of our heads, something we regard as an ideal society. We must base our conception upon societies which actually exist, in order to have any assurance that our ideal is a practicable one. But, as we have just seen, the ideal cannot simply repeat the traits which are actually found. The problem is to extract the desirable traits of forms of community life which actually exist, and employ them to criticize undesirable features and suggest improvement. Now in any social group whatever, even in a gang of thieves, we find some interest held in common, and we find a certain amount of interaction and coöperative intercourse with other groups. From these two traits we derive our standard. How numerous and varied are the interests which are consciously shared? How full and free is the interplay with other forms of association? If we apply these considerations to, say, a criminal band, we find that the ties which consciously hold the members together are few in number, reducible almost to a common interest in plunder; and that they are of such a nature as to isolate the group from other groups with respect to give and take of the values of life. Hence, the education such a society gives is partial and distorted. If we take, on the other hand, the kind of family life which illustrates the standard, we find that there are material, intellectual, æsthetic interests in which all participate and that the progress of one member has worth for the experience of other members—it is readily communicable—and that the family is not an isolated whole, but enters intimately into relationships with business groups, with schools, with all the agencies of culture, as well as with other similar groups, and that it plays a due part in the political organization and in return receives support from it. In short, there are many interests consciously communicated and shared; and there are varied and free points of contact with other modes of association. . . .

The Democratic Ideal.—The two elements in our criterion both point to democracy. The first signifies not only more numerous and more varied points of shared common interest, but greater reliance upon the recognition of mutual interests as a factor in social control. The second means not only freer interaction between social groups (once isolated so far as intention could keep up a separation) but change in social habit—its continuous readjustment through meeting the new situations produced by varied intercourse. And these two traits are precisely what characterize the democratically constituted society.

Upon the educational side, we note first that the realization of a form of social life in which interests are mutually interpenetrating, and where progress, or readjustment, is an important consideration, makes a democratic community more interested than other communities have cause to be in deliberate and systematic education. The devotion of democracy to education is a familiar fact. The superficial explanation is that a government resting upon popular suffrage cannot be successful unless those who elect and who obey their governors are educated. Since a democratic society repudiates the principle of external authority, it must find a substitute in voluntary disposition and interest; these can be created only by education. But there is a deeper explanation. A democracy is more than a form of government; it is primarily a mode of associated living, of conjoint communicated experience. The extension in space of the number of individuals who participate in an interest so that each has to refer his own action to that of others, and to consider the action of others to give point and direction to his own, is equivalent to the breaking down of those barriers of class, race, and national territory which kept men from perceiving the full import of their activity. These more numerous and more varied points of contact denote a greater diversity of stimuli to which an individual has to respond; they consequently put a premium on variation in his action. They secure a liberation of powers which remain suppressed as long as the incitations to action are partial, as they must be in a group which in its exclusiveness shuts out many interests.

The widening of the area of shared concerns, and the liberation of a greater diversity of personal capacities which characterize a democracy, are not of course the product of deliberation and conscious effort. On the contrary, they were caused by the development of modes of manufacture and commerce, travel, migration, and intercommunication which flowed from the command of science over natural energy. But after greater individualization on one hand, and a broader community of interest on the other have come into existence, it is a matter of deliberate effort to sustain and extend them. Obviously a society to which stratification into separate classes would be fatal, must see to it that intellectual oppor-

tunities are accessible to all on equable and easy terms. A society marked
off into classes need be specially attentive only to the education of its
ruling elements. A society which is mobile, which is full of channels for
the distribution of a change occurring anywhere, must see to it that its
members are educated to personal initiative and adaptability. Otherwise,
they will be overwhelmed by the changes in which they are caught and
whose significance or connections they do not perceive. The result will
be a confusion in which a few will appropiate to themselves the results of
the blind and externally directed activities of others. . . .

Freedom and Culture

DEMOCRACY AND AMERICA

I MAKE NO APOLOGY FOR LINKING WHAT IS SAID IN THIS CHAPTER WITH the name of Thomas Jefferson. For he was the first modern to state in human terms the principles of democracy. Were I to make an apology, it would be that in the past I have concerned myself unduly, if a comparison has to be made, with the English writers who have attempted to state the ideals of self-governing communities and the methods appropiate to their realization. If I now prefer to refer to Jefferson it is not, I hope, because of American provincialism, even though I believe that only one who was attached to American soil and who took a consciously alert part in the struggles of the country to attain its independence, could possibly have stated as thoroughly and intimately as did Jefferson the aims embodied in the American tradition: "the definitions and axioms of a free government," as Lincoln called them. Nor is the chief reason for going to him, rather than to Locke or Bentham or Mill, his greater sobriety of judgment due to that constant tempering of theory with practical experience which also kept his democratic doctrine within human bounds.

The chief reason is that Jefferson's formulation is moral through and through: in its foundations, its methods, its ends. The heart of his faith is expressed in his words "Nothing is unchangeable but inherent and inalienable rights of man." The words in which he stated the moral basis of free institutions have gone out of vogue. We repeat the opening words of the Declaration of Independence, but unless we translate them they are couched in a language that, even when it comes readily to our tongue, does not penetrate today to the brain. He wrote: "These truths are self-evident: that all men are created equal; that they are endowed by their Creator with inherent and unalienable rights; that among these are life, liberty and the pursuit of happiness." Today we are wary of anything purporting to be self-evident truths; we are not given to associating politics with the plans of the Creator; the doctrine of natural rights which governed his style of expression has been weakened by historic and by philosophic criticism.

To put ourselves in touch with Jefferson's position we have therefore to translate the word "natural" into *moral*. Jefferson was under the influence of the Deism of his time. Nature and the plans of a benevolent and wise Creator were never far apart in his reflections. But his fundamental beliefs remain unchanged in substance if we forget all special associations with the word *Nature* and speak instead of ideal aims and values to be realized—aims which, although ideal, are not located in the clouds but are backed by something deep and indestructible in the needs and demands of humankind.

Were I to try to connect in any detail what I have to say with the details of Jefferson's speeches and letters—he wrote no theoretical treatises—I should probably seem to be engaged in a partisan undertaking; I should at times be compelled to indulge in verbal exegesis so as to attribute to him ideas not present in his mind. Nevertheless, there are three points contained in what has to be said about American democracy that I shall here explicitly connect with his name. In the first place, in the quotation made, it was the *ends* of democracy, the rights of *man*—not of men in the plural—which are unchangeable. It was not the forms and mechanisms through which inherent moral claims are realized that are to persist without change. Professed Jeffersonians have often not even followed the words of the one whose disciples they say they are, much less his spirit. For he said: "I know that laws and institutions must go hand in hand with the progress of the human mind. . . . As new discoveries are made, new truths disclosed, and manners and opinions change with the change of circumstances, institutions must change also and keep pace with the times. We might as well require a man to wear the coat which fitted him when a boy, as civilized society to remain ever under the regime of their barbarous ancestors."

Because of the last sentence his idea might be interpreted to be a justification of the particular change in government he was championing against earlier institutions. But he goes on to say: "Each generation has a right to choose for itself the form of government it believes the most promotive of its own happiness." Hence he also said: "The idea that institutions established for the use of a nation cannot be touched or modified, even to make them answer their end . . . may perhaps be a salutary provision against the abuses of a monarch, but is most absurd against the nation itself." "A generation holds all the rights and powers their predecessors once held and may change their laws and institutions to suit themselves." He engaged in certain calculations based on Buffon, more ingenious than convincing, to settle upon a period of eighteen years and eight months that fixed the natural span of the life of a generation; thereby indicating the frequency with which it is desirable to overhaul "laws and institutions" to bring them into accord with "new discoveries, new truths, change of manners and opinions." The word *culture* is not used; Jefferson's statement would have been weakened by its use. But it is not only professed followers of Jefferson who have failed to act upon his teaching. It is true of all of us so far as we have set undue store by established mechanisms. The most flagrantly obvious violation of Jefferson's democratic point of view is found in the idolatry of the Constitution as it stands that has been sedulously cultivated. But it goes beyond this instance. As believers in democracy we have not only the right but the duty to question existing mechanisms of, say, suffrage and to inquire whether some functional organization would not serve to formulate and manifest public opinion better than the existing methods. It is not irrelevant to the point that a score of passages could be cited in which Jefferson refers to the American Government as an *experiment*.

The second point of which I would speak is closely bound up with an issue which has become controversial and partisan, namely, states rights versus federal power. There is no question of where Jefferson stood on that issue, nor as to his fear in general of governmental encroachment on liberty—inevitable in his case, since it was the cause of the Rebellion against British domination and was also the ground of his struggle against Hamiltonianism. But any one who stops with this particular aspect of Jefferson's doctrine misses an underlying principle of utmost importance. For while he stood for state action as a barrier against excessive power at Washington, and while on the *practical side* his concern with it was most direct, in his theoretical writings chief importance is attached to local self-governing units on something like the New England town-meeting plan. His project for general political organization on the basis of small units, small enough so that all its members could have direct communication with one another and take care of all community affairs was never acted upon. It never received much attention in the press of immediate practical problems.

But without forcing the significance of this plan, we may find in it an indication of one of the most serious of present problems regarding democracy. I spoke earlier of the way in which individuals at present find themselves in the grip of immense forces whose workings and consequences they have no power of affecting. The situation calls emphatic attention to the need for face-to-face associations, whose interactions with one another may offset if not control the dread impersonality of the sweep of present forces. There is a difference between a society, in the sense of an association, and a community. Electrons, atoms and molecules are in association with one another. Nothing exists in isolation anywhere throughout nature. Natural associations are conditions for the existence of a community, but a community adds the function of communication in which emotions and ideas are shared as well as joint undertakings engaged in. Economic forces have immensely widened the scope of associational activities. But it has done so largely at the expense of the intimacy and directness of communal group interests and activities. The American habit of "joining" is a tribute to the reality of the problem but has not gone far in solving it. The power of the rabblerouser, especially in the totalitarian direction, is mainly due to his power to create a factitious sense of direct union and communal solidarity—if only by arousing the emotion of common intolerance and hate.

I venture to quote words written some years ago: "Evils which are uncritically and indiscriminately laid at the door of industrialism and democracy might, with greater intelligence, be referred to the dislocation and unsettlement of local communities. Vital and thorough attachments are bred only in the intimacy of an intercourse which is of necessity restricted in range. . . . Is it possible to restore the reality of the less communal organizations and to penetrate and saturate their members with a sense of local community life? . . . Democracy must begin at home, and its home is the neighborly community."* On account of the vast extension of the field of association, produced by elimination of distance and lengthening of temporal spans, it is obvious that social agencies, political and non-political, cannot be confined to localities. But the problem of harmonious adjustment between extensive activities, precluding direct contacts, and the intensive activities of community intercourse is a pressing one for democracy. It involves even more than apprenticeship in the practical processes of self-government, important as that is, which Jefferson had in mind. It involves development of local agencies of communication and cooperation, creating stable loyal attachments, to militate against the centrifugal forces of present culture, while at the same time they are of a kind to respond flexibly to the demands of the larger unseen and indefinite public. To a very considerable extent, groups having a functional basis will probably have to replace those based on physical contiguity. In the family both factors combine.

The third point of which I would make express mention as to Jefferson and democracy has to do with his ideas about property. It would be absurd to hold that his personal views were "radical" beyond fear of concentrated wealth and a positive desire for general distribution of wealth without great extremes in either direction. However, it is sometimes suggested that his phrase "pursuit of happiness" stood for economic activity, so that life, liberty, and property were the rights he thought organized society should maintain. But just here is where he broke most completely with Locke. In connection with property, especially property in land, he makes his most positive statements about the inability of any generation to bind its successors. Jefferson held that property rights are created by the "social pact" instead of representing inherent individual moral claims which government is morally bound to maintain.

The right to pursue happiness stood with Jefferson for nothing less than the claim of every human being to choose his own career and to act

* *The Public and its Problems* (1927), pp. 212-13.

upon his own choice and judgment free from restraints and constraints imposed by the arbitrary will of other human beings—whether these others are officials of government, of whom Jefferson was especially afraid, or are persons whose command of capital and control of the opportunities for engaging in useful work limits the ability of others to "pursue happiness." The Jeffersonian principle of equality of rights without special favor to any one justifies giving supremacy to personal rights when they come into conflict with property rights. While his views are properly enough cited against ill-considered attacks upon the economic relations that exist at a given time, it is sheer perversion to hold that there is anything in Jeffersonian democracy that forbids political action to bring about equalization of economic conditions in order that the equal right of all to free choice and free action be maintained.

I have referred with some particularity to Jefferson's ideas upon special points because of the proof they afford that the source of the American democratic tradition is moral—not technical, abstract, narrowly political nor materially utilitarian. It is moral because based on faith in the ability of human nature to achieve freedom for individuals accompanied with respect and regard for other persons and with social stability built on cohesion instead of coercion. Since the tradition is a moral one, attacks upon it, however they are made, wherever they come from, from within or from without, involve moral issues and can be settled only upon moral grounds. In as far as the democratic ideal has undergone eclipse among us, the obscuration is moral in source and effect. The dimming is both a product and a manisfestation of the confusion that accompanies transition from an old order to a new one for the arrival of the latter was heralded only as conditions plunged it into an economic regime so novel that there was no adequate preparation for it and which dislocated the established relations of persons with one another.

Nothing is gained by attempts to minimize the novelty of the democratic order, nor the scope of the change it requires in old and long cherished traditions. We have not even as yet a common and accepted vocabulary in which to set forth the order of moral values involved in realization of democracy. The language of Natural Law was once all but universal in educated Christendom. The conditions which gave it force disappeared. Then there was an appeal to natural rights, supposed by some to center in isolated individuals—although not in the original American formulation. At present, appeal to the individual is dulled by our inability to locate the individual with any assurance. While we are compelled to note that his freedom can be maintained only through the working together toward a single end of a large number of different and complex factors, we do not know how to coordinate them on the basis of voluntary purpose.

The intimate association that was held to exist between individualism and business activity for private profit gave, on one side, a distorted meaning to individualism. Then the weakening, even among persons who nominally retain older theological beliefs, of the imaginative ideas and emotions connected with the sanctity of the individual, disturbed democratic individualism on the positive moral side. The moving energy once associated with things called spiritual has lessened; we use the word *ideal* reluctantly, and have difficulty in giving the word *moral* much force beyond, say, a limited field of mutually kindly relations among individuals. That such a syllogism as the following once had a vital meaning to a man of affairs like Jefferson today seems almost incredible: "Man was created for social intercourse, but social intercourse cannot be maintained without a sense of justice; then man must have been created with a sense of justice."

Even if we have an abiding faith in democracy, we are not likely to express it as Jefferson expressed his faith: "I have no fear but that the result of our experiment will be that men may be trusted to govern themselves without a master. Could the contrary of this be proved, I should conclude either there is no God or that he is a malevolent being." The belief of Jefferson that the sole legitimate object of government among men "is to secure the greatest degree of happiness possible to the general mass of those associated under it" was connected with his belief that Nature—or God—benevolent in intent, had created men for happiness on condition they attained knowledge of natural order and observed the demands of that knowledge in their actions. The obsolescence of the language for many persons makes it the more imperative for all who would maintain and advance the ideals of democracy to face the issue of the moral ground of political institutions and the moral principles by which men acting together may attain freedom of individuals which will amount to fraternal associations with one another. The weaker our faith in Nature, in its laws and rights and its benevolent intentions for human welfare, the more urgent is the need for a faith based on ideas that are now intellectually credible and that are consonant with present economic conditions, which will inspire and direct action with something of the ardor once attached to things religious.

Human power over the physical energies of nature has immensely increased. In moral ideal, power of man over physical nature should be employed to reduce, to elminate progressively, the power of man over man. By what means shall we prevent its use to effect new, more subtle, more powerful agencies of subjection of men to other men? Both the issue of war or peace between nations, and the future of economic relations for years and generations to come in contribution either to human freedom or human subjection are involved. An increase of power undreamed of a century ago, one to whose further increase no limits can be put as long as scientific inquiry goes on, is an established fact. The thing still uncertain is what we are going to do with it. That it is power signifies of itself it is electrical, thermic, chemical. What will be done with it is a moral issue.

Physical interdependence has increased beyond anything that could have been foreseen. Division of labor in industry was anticipated and was looked forward to with satisfaction. But it is relatively the least weighty phase of the present situation. The career of individuals, their lives and security as well as prosperity is now affected by events on the other side of the world. The forces back of these events he cannot touch or influence—save perhaps by joining in a war of nations against nations. For we seem to live in a world in which nations try to deal with the problems created by the new situation by drawing more and more into themselves, by more and more extreme assertions of independent nationalist sovereignty, while everything they do in the direction of autarchy leads to ever closer mixture with other nations—but in war.

War under existing conditions compels nations, even those professedly the most democratic, to turn authoritarian and totalitarian as the World War of 1914-18 resulted in Fascist totalitarianism in non-democratic Italy and Germany and in Bolshevist totalitarianism in non-democratic Russia, and promoted political, economic and intellectual reaction in this country. The necessity of transforming physical interdependence into moral—into human—interdependence is part of the democratic problem: and yet war is said even now to be the path of salvation for democratic countries!

Individuals can find the security and protection that are prerequisites for freedom only in association with others—and then the organization these associations take on, as a measure of securing their efficiency, limits the freedom of those who have entered into them. The importance of organization has increased so much in the last hundred years that the word is now quite commonly used as a synonym for association and society. Since at the very best organization is but the mechanism through which association operates, the identification is evidence of the extent in which a servant has become a master; in which means have usurped the place of the end for which they are called into existence. The predicament is that individuality demands association to develop and sustain it and association requires arrangement and coordination of its elements, or organization—since otherwise it is formless and void of power. But we have now a kind of molluscan organization, soft individuals within and a hard constrictive shell without. Individuals voluntarily enter associations which have become practically nothing but organizations; and then conditions under which they act take control of what they do whether they want it or not.

Persons acutely aware of the dangers of regimentation when it is imposed by government remain oblivious of the millions of persons whose behavior is regimented by an economic system through whose intervention alone they obtain a livelihood. The contradiction is the more striking because the new organizations were for the most part created in the name of freedom, and, at least at the outset, by exercise of voluntary choice. But the kind of working-together which has resulted is too much like that of the parts of a machine to represent a co-operation which expresses freedom and also contributes to it. No small part of the democratic problem is to achieve associations whose ordering of parts provides the strength that comes from stability, while they promote flexibility of response to change.

Lastly, in this brief survey, there is the problem of the relation of human nature and physical nature. The ancient world solved the problem, in abstract philosophical theory, by endowing all nature, in its cosmic scope, with the moral qualities of the highest and most ideal worth in humanity. The theology and rites of the Church gave this abstract theory direct significance in the lives of the peoples of the western world. For it provided practical agencies by means of which the operation of the power creating and maintaining the universe were supposed to come to the support of individuals in this world and the next. The rise of physical science rendered an ever increasing number of men skeptical of the intellectual foundation provided by the old theory. The unsettlement, going by the name of the conflict of science and religion, proves the existence of the division in the foundations upon which our culture rests, between ideas in the form of knowledge and ideas that are emotional and imaginative and that directly actuate conduct.

This disturbance on the moral side has been enormously aggravated by those who are remote from the unsettlement due to intellectual causes. It comes home to everyone by the effects of the practical application of the new physical science. For all the physical features of the present regime of production and distribution of goods and services are products of the new physical science, while the distinctively *human* consequences of science are still determined by habits and beliefs established before its origin. That democracy should not as yet have succeeded in healing the breach is no cause for discouragement: provided there is effected a union of human possibilities and ideals with the spirit and methods of science on one side and with the workings of the economic system on the other side. For a considerable period laissez-faire individualism prevented the problem from being even seen. It treated the new economic movement as if it were simply an expression of forces that were fundamental in the human constitution but were only recently released for free operation. It failed to see that the great expansion which was occurring was in fact due to release of *physical* energies; that as far as human action and human freedom is concerned, a problem, not a solution, was thereby instituted: the problem, namely, of management and direction of the new physical energies so they would contribute to realization of human possibilities.

The reaction that was created by the inevitable collapse of a movement that failed so disastrously in grasp of the problem has had diverse results, the diversity of which is part of the present confused state of our lives. Production of the material means of a secure and free life has been indefinitely increased and at an accelerated rate. It is not surprising that there is a large group which attributes the gains which have accrued, actually and potentially, to the economic regime under which they have occurred—instead of to the scientific knowledge which is the source of physical control of natural energies. The group is large. It is composed not only of the immediate beneficiaries of the system but also of the much larger number who hope that they, or at least their children, are to have full share in its benefits. Because of the opportunities furnished by free land, large unused natural resources and the absence of fixed class differences (which survive in European countries in spite of legal abolition of feudalism), this group is particularly large in this country. It is represented by those who point to the higher standard of living in this country and by those who have responded to the greater opportunities for advancement this country has afforded to them. In short, this group, in both categories of its constituents, is impressed by actual gains that have come about. They have a kind of blind and touching faith that improvement is going to continue in some more or less automatic way until it includes them and their offspring.

Then there is a much smaller group who are as sensitive, perhaps more so, to the immense possibilities represented by the physical means now potentially at our command, but who are acutely aware of our failure to realize them; who see instead the miseries, cruelties, oppressions and frustrations which exist. The weakness of this group has been that it has also failed to realize the involvement of the new scientific method in producing the existing state of affairs, and the need for its further extensive and unremitting application to determine analytically—in detail—the causes of present ills, and to project means for their elimination. In social affairs, the wholesale mental attitude that has been referred to persists with little change. It leads to formation of ambitious and sweeping beliefs and policies. The human *ideal* is indeed comprehensive. As a standpoint from which to view existing conditions and judge the direction change should take, it cannot be too inclusive. But the problem of production of change is one of infinite attention to means; and means can be determined only by definite analysis of the conditions of each problem as it presents itself. Health is a comprehensive, a "sweeping" ideal. But progress toward it has been made in the degree in which recourse to panaceas has been abandoned and inquiry has been directed to determinate disturbances and means for dealing with them. The group is represented at its extreme by those who believe there is a necessary historical law which governs the course of events so that all that is needed is deliberate acting in accord with it. The law by which class conflict produces by its own dialectic its complete opposite becomes then the supreme and sole regulator for determining policies and methods of action.

That more adequate knowledge of human nature is demanded if the release of physical powers is to serve human ends is undeniable. But it is a mistake to suppose that this knowledge of itself enables us to control human energies as physical science has enabled us to control physical energies. It suffers from the fallacy into which those have fallen who have supposed that physical energies put at our disposal by science are sure to produce human progress and prosperity. A more adequate science of human nature might conceivably only multiply the agencies by which some human beings manipulate other human beings for their own advantage. Failure to take account of the moral phase of the problem, the question of values and ends, marks, although from the opposite pole, a relapse into the fallacy of the theorists of a century ago who assumed that "free" —that is to say, politically unrestrained—manifestation of human wants and impulses would tend to bring about social prosperity, progress, and harmony. It is a counterpart fallacy to the Marxist notion that there is an economic or "materialistic," dialectic of history by which a certain desirable (and in that sense moral) end will be brought about with no intervention of choice of values and efforts to realize them. As I wrote some years ago, "the assimilation of human science to physical science represents only another form of absolutistic logic, a kind of physical absolutism."

Social events will continue, in any case, to be products of interaction of human nature with cultural conditions. Hence the primary and fundamental question will always be what sort of social results we supremely want. Improved science of human nature would put at our disposal means, now lacking, for defining the problem and working effectively for its solution. But save as it should reinforce respect for the morale of science, and thereby extend and deepen the incorporation of the attitudes which form the method of science into the disposition of individuals, it might add a complication similar to that introduced by improved physical science. Anything that obscures the fundamentally moral nature of the social problem is harmful, no matter whether it proceeds from the side of physical or of psychological theory. Any doctrine that eliminates or even obscures the function of choice of values and enlistment of desires and emotions in behalf of those chosen weakens personal responsibility for judgment and for action. It thus helps create the attitudes that welcome and support the totalitarian state.

I have stated in bare outline some of the outstanding phases of the problem of culture in the service of democratic freedom. Difficulties and obstacles have been emphasized. This emphasis is a result of the fact that a *problem* is presented. Emphasis upon the problem is due to belief that many weaknesses which events have disclosed are connected with failure to see the immensity of the task involved in setting mankind upon the democratic road. That with a background of millennia of non-democratic societies behind them, the earlier advocates of democracy tremendously simplified the issue is natural. For a time the simplification was an undoubted asset. Too long continued it became a liability.

Recognition of the scope and depth of the problem is neither depressing nor discouraging when the democratic movement is placed in historic perspective. The ideas by which it formulated itself have a long history behind them. We can trace their source in Hellenic humanism and in Christian beliefs; and we can also find recurrent efforts to realize this or that special aspect of these ideas in some special struggle against a particular form of oppression. By proper selection and arrangement, we can even make out a case for the idea that all past history has been a movement, at first unconscious and then conscious, to attain freedom. A more sober view of history discloses that it took a very fortunate conjunction of events to bring about the rapid spread and seemingly complete victory of democracy during the nineteenth century. The conclusion to be drawn is not the depressing one that it is now in danger of destruction because of an unfavorable conjunction of events. The conclusion is that what was won in a more or less external and accidental manner must now be achieved and sustained by deliberate and intelligent endeavor.

The contrast thus suggested calls attention to the fact that underlying persistent attitudes of human beings were formed by traditions, customs, institutions, which existed when there was no democracy—when in fact democratic ideas and aspirations tended to be strangled at birth. Persistence of these basic dispositions accounts, on one side, for the sudden attack upon democracy; it is a reversion to old emotional and intellectual habits; or rather it is not so much a reversion as it is a manifestation of attitudes that have been there all the time but have been more or less covered up. Their persistence also explains the depth and range of the present problem. The struggle for democracy has to be maintained on as many fronts as culture has aspects: political, economic, international, educational, scientific and artistic, religious. The fact that we now have to accomplish of set purpose what in an earlier period was more or less a gift of grace renders the problem a moral one to be worked out on moral grounds.

Part of the fortunate conjunction of circumstances with respect to us who live here in the United States consists, as has been indicated, of the fact that our forefathers found themselves in a new land. The shock of physical dislocation effected a very considerable modification of old attitudes. Habits of thought and feeling which were the products of long centuries of acculturation were loosened. Less entrenched dispositions dropped off. The task of forming new institutions was thereby rendered immensely easier. The readjustment thus effected has been a chief factor in creating a general attitude of adaptability that has enabled us, save for the Civil War, to meet change with a minimum of external conflict and, in spite of an heritage of violence, with good nature. It is because of such consequences that the geographical New World may become a New World in a human sense. But, all the more on this account, the situation is such that most of the things about which we have been complacent and self-congratulatory now have to be won by thought and effort, instead of being results of evolution of a manifest destiny.

In the present state of affairs, a conflict of the moral Old and New Worlds is the essence of the struggle for democracy. It is not a question for us of isolationism, although the physical factors which make possible physical isolation from the warring ambitions of Europe are a factor to be cherished in an emergency. The conflict is not one waged with arms, although the question whether we again take up arms on European battle-fields for ends that are foreign to the ends to which this country is dedicated will have weight in deciding whether we win or lose our own battle on our own ground. It is possible to stay out for reasons that have nothing to do with the maintenance of democracy, and a good deal to do with pecuniary profit, just as it is possible to be deluded into participation in the name of fighting for democracy.

The conflict as it concerns the democracy to which our history commits us is *within* our own institutions and attitudes. It can be won only by ex-tending the application of democratic methods, methods of consultation, persuasion, negotiation, communication, co-operative intelligence, in the task of making our own politics, industry, education, our culture generally, a servant and an evolving manifestation of democratic ideas. Resort to military force is a first sure sign that we are giving up the struggle for the democratic way of life, and that the Old World has conquered morally as well as geographically—succeeding in imposing upon us its ideals and methods.

If there is one conclusion to which human experience unmistakably points it is that democratic ends demand democratic methods for their realization. Authoritarian methods now offer themselves to us in new guises. They come to us claiming to serve the ultimate ends of freedom and equity in a classless society. Or they recommend adoption of a totalitarian regime in order to fight totalitarianism. In whatever form they offer them-selves, they owe their seductive power to their claim to serve ideal ends. Our first defense is to realize that democracy can be served only by the slow day by day adoption and contagious diffusion in every phase of our common life of methods that are identical with the ends to be reached and that recourse to monistic, wholesale, absolutist procedures is a betrayal of human freedom no matter in what guise it presents itself. An American democracy can serve the world only as it demonstrates in the conduct of its own life the efficacy of plural, partial, and experimental methods in securing and maintaining an ever-increasing release of the powers of human nature, in service of a freedom which is co-operative and a co-operation which is voluntary.

We have no right to appeal to time to justify complacency about the ultimate result. We have every right to point to the long non-democratic and anti-democratic course of human history and to the recentness of democracy in order to enforce the immensity of the task confronting us. The very novelty of the experiment explains the impossibility of restricting the problem to any one element, aspect, or phase of our common everyday life. We have every right to appeal to the long and slow process of time to protect ourselves from the pessimism that comes from taking a short-span temporal view of events—under one condition. We must know that the dependence of ends upon means is such that the only *ultimate* result is the result that is attained today, tomorrow, the next day, and day after day, in the succession of years and generations. Only thus can we be sure that we face our problems in detail one by one as they arise, with all the resources provided by collective intelligence operating in co-operative action. At the end as at the beginning the democratic method is as fundamentally simple and as immensely difficult as is the energetic, unflagging, unceasing creation of an ever-present new road upon which we can walk together.

RALPH BARTON PERRY

(1876-1957)

Ralph Barton Perry was born in 1876 and died in 1957. For most of his life he was a member of the Department of Philosophy at Harvard. Perry was a versatile man and his contributions to philosophy were various. He was the author of a remarkable philosophical biography, The Thought and Character of William James *(1935), and of a penetrating historical and philosophical account of American ideals,* Puritanism and Democracy *(1944). In addition to his interest in the history of American thought and in movements of thought in the contemporary world, he was particularly interested in the philosophy of ethics. His* General Theory of Value *(1926) was, until World War II, the largest systematic exposition of a naturalistic theory of ethical judgment that had been produced in the United States. Throughout his life Perry made the effort to use philosophy to comment actively and practically on issues in the world at large. He was a courageous champion of civil liberty and intellectual freedom, and in both World War I and World War II he wrote philosophical expositions of the issues at stake.*

Over and above these activities, however, Perry was a major figure in the emergence of an important and distinctive philosophical movement in the United States—the "new realism." In 1910 there appeared in the Journal of Philosophy *a short article entitled "The Program and First Platform of Six Realists." It was followed in 1912 by a larger cooperative volume,* The New Realism, *by the same six authors—Perry, Edwin B. Holt, Walter T. Marvin, William Pepperrell Montague, Walter B. Pitkin and Edward Gleason Spaulding. The "new realism" which these men defined set loose developments in American philosophy whose influence can be seen in the characteristics of American philosophic discussion today.*

The new realism proposed an alternative to both idealism and pragmatism. It reaffirmed, though with critical refinements, the ordinary "realistic" belief of common sense that the structure which human beings find in the world is not a creation of the human mind. But the new realism proposed something else besides—a change in the methods and standards of philosophic discussion. It condemned the "disposition in philosophy" to employ terms in an unlimited sense, and to make unlimited assertions as "the principal reason why philosophy at the present time possesses no common body of theory," and indeed does not even have "any common plan of work to be done." The new realists called for a reform in philosophy that would begin by taking words seriously, defining them clearly, and using them scrupulously in accordance with definite rules. They argued that logical analysis is the fundamental method in philosophy, and that philosophers should try to settle specific, limited questions first before they go on to the construction of large systems. And they urged that philosophers make the effort to work together, to address themselves to a common group of problems, and to define their agreements explicitly. In short, the new realism proposed to treat philosophy as a cooperative scientific discipline.

Although there are some significant differences between the pragmatists and the new realists, there are some significant similarities as well. Both groups took a naturalistic view of ethics and both were humanistic in their interests. Both groups, furthermore, believed that philosophy must accept and use the results of the sciences, and that, in general, the sciences provide man with his most reliable knowledge of the world. Like Wright, Peirce and Dewey, the new realists regarded it as one of the historical scandals in philosophy that its devotees should claim the right to overturn the results of the special sciences in the name of a higher truth which only philosophy could achieve.

The essay by Perry that follows represents this important movement in American philosophy. It first appeared in Contemporary American Philosophy, *edited by G. P. Adams and W. P. Montague (1930).*

Realism in Retrospect

I. THE CAMPAIGN AGAINST IDEALISM

I UNDERSTAND THAT THE PURPOSE OF THE PRESENT BOOK IS TO DELIVER its authors from the bonds of reticence, or from that canon of literary taste which limits the use of the first person. I therefore begin with the pronoun "I," and shall use it with reckless frequency. I shall also speak out the faith that is in me, allowing my beliefs to override my critical conscience. To begin with, let me confess that when, for the purpose of recovering the past, I re-read my earliest writings, they impress me as extremely convincing, affording an unexpected confirmation of my present philosophical bias. Myself of twenty-five years ago committed blunders, no doubt, but his faults were the faults of youth and inexperience. His heart was in the right place.

Such philosophical nourishment as I received in early youth was derived from Emerson and Carlyle. From them I caught no hint of transcendental metaphysics, but only a desire to be heroic. This influence, together with an intense adolescent religious experience, brought me to the threshold of manhood with a vague eagerness "to do good," or to contribute something to the triumph of that cause of righteousness which I identified with Christianity. My pre-natal philosophical experience was obtained at Princeton, where an emeritus McCosh still walked the campus, and where "Jeremy" Ormond, ponderous, high-minded, and unintelligible, accustomed the ear and the pen to a polysyllabic vocabulary. Migrating from Princeton to Harvard in the middle 'nineties was for me a perilous spiritual adventure, an abrupt transition from faith to criticism. Here, for the first time, something happened to my *mind,* and the vocation of the ministry was gradually transformed, without reaction or bitterness, into that of the teacher and scholar. Creeds and dogmas having become impossible, I thought that I had found a way in which I might think freely and still "do good." It is that naïve hope that has sustained me ever since.

At Harvard in the late 'nineties it was, for most of us, a choice between James and Royce. Palmer taught us ethics, and by his example taught us how to teach. Santayana was historical and critical, Münsterberg schematic, and Everett learned. These were important elements in the configuration,

454

and they generated both heat and light. But as regards fundamentals, whether of doctrine, method, or temper of mind, there was the way of Royce and the way of James. Royce was the battleship, heavily armoured, both for defence and offence. James combined the attributes of the light cruiser, the submarine, and the bombing aeroplane. It was natural to suppose that Royce was impregnable and irresistible. To surrender to him was as easy and as unexciting as to be a fundamentalist in Arkansas. James provided the rallying-point for those in whom the youthful spirit of revolt was stronger than tradition and prestige. Royce was the latest and nearest of a mighty race. His philosophy was powerfully reinforced by the texts of Bradley and Green, and by the great cult of Kant. His was the party of law and order, of piety and decency. This was not Royce's fault, nor did it at all adequately express his personal traits; but he suffered, none the less, from the taint of established things. So when James, overcoming his earlier fears, had the audacity to make jokes about the Absolute, there were Athenian youths who laughed with him. Many of us have, since that time, become sadder, and, I hope, wiser. But the spell of absolute idealism was irreparably broken. There arose a generation of younger philosophers who were, as Creighton expressed it (speaking more in sorrow than in anger), "flippant, like James."

James's right to flippancy was well earned. In the year 1896-97 he conducted a group of us through the text of Kant, and when, after months of intense effort and profound discouragement, he told me that I might sometimes attribute my difficulty to the author's obscurity or pedantry, rather than to my own feebleness, he conferred on me the title to a canine bark of my own even when Sir Oracle had spoken. James's example did not suggest an ignorance of philosophical literature, but it did beget in all of his students the habit of checking every text, no matter how authoritative, by their own experience. The question "What does the text say?" was incidental to the ulterior questions, "What does the author mean?" and "Is it so?" I was not surprised, therefore, that upon receiving a copy of my maiden effort on "The Abstract Freedom of Kant,"* James should have written me expressing the hope that I might now feel justified in casting off the Kantian "ball and chain" which had for many years hampered the movements of philosophy.

To specify my indebtedness to James is as impossible as it would be to enumerate the traits which I have inherited from my parents. In view of contemporary developments in philosophy, I should like, however, to record the most vivid of the doctrinal impressions which he left upon me in the early days. I can remember even the stage-setting—the interior of the room in Sever Hall, the desk with which the lecturer took so many liberties, and the gestures with which James animatedly conveyed to us

* *Philosophical Review,* 1900.

the intuition of common-sense realism. From that day I confess that I
have never wavered in the belief that our perceptual experience disclosed a
common world, inhabited by our perceiving bodies and our neighbours,
and qualified by the evidence of our senses.*

It was the controversial atmosphere of my early studies that led to my
preoccupation with the shortcomings of idealism, and to my sustained interest in the classification of contemporary philosophical tendencies.* European and American Philosophy, as I saw it at the close of the nineteenth
century, was a dispute between the extravagant claims of the party of
science (naturalism) and the equally extravagant claims of that post-
Kantian idealistic philosophy, which, invigorated by its transplantation
from Germany to a foreign soil, had become the bulwark of English-speaking Protestant piety.

It is unprofitable to quarrel over the diverse meanings of the term
"idealism." That idealism which I went out to slay was born of the marriage of subjectivism and universalism. Its proof seemed to me then, as
it seems to me still, to consist in an unseaworthy subjectivism rescued
from the shipwreck of solipsism by the miraculous intervention of absolutism. The first premise is subjectivism, the doctrine, namely, that to be
= to be perceived or thought. The second premise is universalism, the doctrine, namely, that being cannot be a product of human perception or
thought, because man is a part of nature, and because the truth is a
standard by which human perception and thought are themselves to be
judged and corrected. The conclusion is absolute idealism, the doctrine,
namely, that to be = to be perceived or thought (or willed, or felt, or
otherwise manifested) by a transfinite, all-containing and infallible mind,
commonly called *"the* Absolute."

The argument is dialectical and a priori, and its force depends on the
truth of both premises. The critics of this reigning doctrine are readily
divisible into two groups: those commonly called "realists," who have attacked the first premise; and those variously called "pragmatists," "instru-
mentalists," and "humanists," who have attacked the second premise. The
former group being united by their rejection of subjectivism, are divided
among themselves on the question of universalism; the latter, being united
by their rejection of universalism, are divided on the issue of subjectivism.
Both groups reject absolute idealism, but while one rejects this doctrine on
the score of its idealism, the other rejects it on the score of its absolutism.

For the realist, then, the Absolute, construed as an individual mind or
spirit, in which the imperfections of humanity are overcome and its pre-

* The substance of this teaching was afterwards embodied in the article entitled
"How Two Minds Can Know One Thing," which James published in the *Journal
of Philosophy, Psychology, and Scientific Methods,* 1905.
* "Professor Royce's Refutation of Realism and Pluralism," *Monist,* 1902; *The
Approach to Philosophy,* 1905; *Present Philosophical Tendencies,* 1912; *Present Con-
flict of Ideals,* 1918; *Philosophy of the Recent Past,* 1926.

rogatives maximated—construed, in other words, as a being qualified to serve at one and the same time as the metaphysical reality, the moral stand-ard and the object of worship—is the offspring of subjectivism. Such a be-ing is not merely absolute: it is mind conceived as absolute. "I perceive," or "I judge," or "I will," or some similar act of conscious mind, is first supposed to be the inescapable form of reality; and since to identify this "I" with you or me or any or all finite creatures is palpably absurd, it is then inferred that there must be an "I" which is no creature at all, but the Creator. And, as Bradley has put it, what must be, is. Hence in so far as the realist refutes subjectivism he at the same time destroys the meaning and the ground of the Absolute in this idealistic sense.

An idealist of the post-Kantian school resents being called a "subjec-tivist," but this is because he takes the term to imply that the "subject" in question is the natural or phychological subject. If "subjectivism" be used to mean that all being is the dependent creation of *some* subject, or self, or mind, whether finite or absolute, then, I think, the term can be applied to the idealist without offence. In accordance with this usage absolute idealism is that species of subjectivism in which the unconditioned and all-condition-ing subject has, over and above such properties as make it a subject, those other properties of infinity, perfection, and systematic unity, which the term "Absolute" is intended to convey. With this understanding I shall hereinafter use the terms "subjectivism" and "idealism" interchangeably.

The wide prevalence of subjectivism has always seemed to me to be due, in the first place, to excessive insistence on a relation which the reflective habits of the philosopher dispose him to magnify. Subjectivism exploits the relation, namely, which the world indubitably has to the human sub-ject whenever he perceives it, or thinks about it, or otherwise concerns himself with it. He exploits this him-ward aspect of things *metaphysically*—that is, he construes it as fundamental, or takes it as affording the deepest insight. The realist, on the other hand, calls attention to the fact that this emphasis, natural as it is, may be misleading. Thus when Pistol says, "Why, then the world's mine oyster," we recognize that he is taking liberties with the world. It is true that the world is, among other things, Pistol's oyster, and Pistol is excusable for having mentioned the fact. But if, as a philosopher, one were interested in making the most significant possible statement about the world, it would scarcely be pertinent to remark that the world is that which is opened by Pistol's sword. This is not one of those central and pregnant characteristics of the world of which the metaphysi-cian is in search. In the course of its career the world does meet Pistol, but this conjunction does not determine its orbit or destiny, nor does the bivalvular aspect which it presents to Pistol's sword afford the best clue to its essential structure.

In a sense that is at least superficially similar to Pistol's oyster, nature is Berkeley's percept and Kant's thought, or the idea of any philosopher who applies his mind to it. And it is not strange that sooner or later some philosopher should have taken this fact as the key to metaphysics. But the realist is one who is disposed, until more decisive evidence is advanced, to construe this indubitable relationship of the world to the mind that deals with it, as an accidental or subordinate aspect of the world. He refuses to assume* that knowing the world implies proprietorship. It is still open to him to suppose, with common sense, that the world *lends* itself to being known without surrendering itself wholly to that use. Such a view has its support in experiences that are no less authentic than Pistol's sense of ownership. If the idealist is justified in saying with Margaret Fuller, "I accept the universe," the realist is equally justified in remarking with Carlyle, "By gad, she'd better."

The question of the place of knowing mind in the universe, whether central or peripheral, is complicated by what I have called the "ego-centric predicament."* This was a successful bit of phrase-making, if one is to judge by the frequency with which it has been misunderstood. My purpose in introducing the phrase was to call attention to the fact that idealists have used as an argument what is, in fact, only a difficulty. The difficulty or predicament consists in the fact that the extent to which knowledge conditions any situation in which it is present cannot be discovered by the simple and conclusive method of direct elimination. I cannot see what things look like when my eyes are shut, or judge the effect of extinguishing my thought. If I cognize *a* in any way, shape, or manner, I am not cognizing *a* in the absence of that way, shape, or manner of cognition. This is, of course, a truism, and in itself of no significance whatever. It does, however, bring to light the fact that the question which subjectivism raises is unique. In order that the question shall be *answered* at all, it is necessary to introduce the very factor, namely, the answering mind, which in examining this question it would be convenient to exclude. It follows that either the question must remain unanswered or that it must be attacked in some more indirect and perhaps less conclusive manner. If, for example, one can find out what the cognizing mind is and what it does, one can then discount its presence, or learn how much of the situation to ascribe to it.

Idealism has been guilty, historically, of arguing from what is only a methodological difficulty. It has created the appearance of a significant affirmation by concealing a redundancy. No one would think it worth while to say, "It is impossible for me to discover anything which is, when I discover it, undiscovered by me," or, "It is impossible that anything should

---

* Arbitrarily to assign the leading rôle to a predicate merely because it happens to come first in the order of discovery or of discourse, has been called the "Fallacy of Initial Predication" (*The New Realism*, 1912, p. 15).

* "The Ego-Centric Predicament," *Journal of Philosophy, Psychology, and Scientific Method*, 1910.

remain totally unknown after it has become known;" but to say, "It is impossible to discover anything that is not thought," or, "It is impossible to find anything that is not known," has seemed to many idealists to be the beginning of philosophical wisdom—in spite of the fact that the self-evidence of the last two propositions consists entirely in the fact that "discover" and "thought," "find" and "known," are taken as meaning the same thing.

My contention has been, then, that the "ego-centric predicament" creates not the slightest presumption either for idealism or for realism. It is equally compatible with either alternative, although it has been, and still is, very generally supposed to nourish idealism and to stick in the crop of realism.

So far idealism is seen to rest on bias or ambiguity. The other arguments which have been advanced in its behalf are deserving of more respectful consideration, since they appeal to material facts for which any alternative theory must provide.

The oldest of the idealistic arguments are those which idealism shares with scepticism. Idealism has been held sometimes to *be* scepticism, sometimes to furnish the only authentic *escape* from it. Arguments of this general class may be summarily treated under the heads of "physiological relativism" and "psychological relativism."

Physiological relativism rests on the fact that sensation is doubly conditioned: externally, by a physical stimulus; and internally by the position, properties, and state of the organism. Sensation is then construed as the joint product or appearance created by these factors. At this point of the argument three alternatives diverge. The confirmed sceptic will hold that sensation, untrustworthy as it is, affords the only knowledge we possess, since thought is only its paler reflection. This is idealism of a sort, but a bankrupt, insolvent idealism—patently self-contradictory. The two remaining alternatives are realistic. The physico-chemical realist credits scientific thought as a way of escape from the subjective relativities of sensation. The agnostic realist, holding with the sceptic that physico-chemical concepts are only reproductions of sense-experience, and equally subjective, still credits the residual reflection that sense-experience is produced by the action *of* something he knows not how *upon* something he knows not what. It is clear that, whatever their validity, arguments from physiological relativism afford small comfort to the idealist.

Psychological relativism is a scepticism of thought rather than of sense; indeed, it is often used as an argument in support of sense. The argument rests on the fact of prejudice. Thought is held to be an effect of emotion, will, habit, imitation, historical development, or social *milieu;* and reality, as man thinks it, to be a mere projection of human bias. Here, again, three paths diverge. If, in the first place, one appeals from thought to sense on the ground that sense is externally controlled, one moves in the direction of the scepticisms and realisms already considered. The second alternative is to rest in the relativity of thought, or to accept psychological scepticism as the last word. This view, that the world is what man thinks it, and that man's thinking of it varies from individual to individual and from time to time, is a widespread doctrine in modern philosophy; but it is not that idealism with which I am here concerned. The third alternative, the absolute idealism which modern realism seeks to slay, is an idealism which has already slain and devoured scepticism, and which rests its claim to acceptance largely upon that conquest. Psychological relativism is held to be intolerable, because it gives equal credit to contradictory human assertions, and because, since it places nature inside of a mind which is itself inside of nature, it is viciously circular. Realism and absolute idealism here take the same ground, and both attribute to thought a power to recognize and transcend its own relativities. The difference lies in the nature of this corrective thought. For realism its nature lies in its more perfect fidelity to fact, or in its more dispassionate and colourless objectivity. For idealism its nature lies in its profounder and more authoritative subjectivity. For realism thinking truly is a conformity of mind to the given reality, while for idealism thinking truly is a conformity of the finite mind to a universal mind.*

This resort to absolute idealism as the way of escape from psychological relativism involves two steps, both of which the realist refuses to take. The first step is to discredit sense-perception. The relative passivity of this mode of experience, instead of being construed as a mark of cognitive superiority because it suggests a deference of the knowing mind to its objects, is construed as a mark of inferiority because the genius of the mind itself is too imperfectly manifested. Sense becomes a virtual, incipient, or degraded form of thought. The absolute idealist can usually be recognized by his insistence that pure sensation is a myth, but pure or impure he can hardly deny it, and it still remains as one of his most serious stumbling-blocks.

The second step is to construe thought as essentially creative. There is a widespread disposition (a disposition connected, no doubt, with the common-sense dogma that if things are not physical they must be mental) to suppose that the objects of thought, such as laws, mathematical quantities and forms, principles, categories, concepts, universals, necessities, possibilities, relations, and systematic unities, are the *creatures* of thought. Since the orderly structure of nature, as exhibited in the sciences, would

* Since this universal mind may be itself governed by will or emotion, as well as by cold logic, absolute idealism does not necessarily imply the rejection of moral, æsthetic, or religious experiences as sources of metaphysical insight. Any idealizing activity of mind, in which man recognizes the gap between aspiration and present attainment, may be taken as a revelation of that standard spiritual being whose self-realization furnishes the motive force of creation.

fall to pieces without such connective tissue, this supposition is of decisive consequence, and is chiefly responsible for the hold of modern idealism upon those "tougher" minds which are not affected by its sentimental appeal.

Hence the rejection of a subjectivistic logic, and mathematics is one of the major arguments in the realistic polemic. Claiming the support of Socrates and Plato, and alliance with the whole stream of philosophical doctrine down through the Scholastics and Cartesians, modern realism distinguishes between the imaginative play of speculative thought, on the one hand, and, on the other hand, those moments of insight, acceptance, or contemplation in which the mind is confronted by a being not of its own making. Thought has moments in which its own caprice is superseded by specificities, connections, and consequences as intrusive and inexorable as the resistance of material bodies. One may think what one will, but having thought one finds oneself involved in natures and relations which have a way of their own, a way which must now be loyally followed if one is to think truly. The realms of mathematics and logic are not governed by psychological laws, but by laws intrinsic to themselves. Idealists recognize this autonomy, and thereupon extend and exalt the meaning of mind to embrace the larger domain. But to confer the term "mind" upon the intelligible features of the world, whether viewed abstractedly in hierarchies of categories, or concretely in the systematic unity of nature, can serve no useful purpose. It adds nothing to our understanding of that specific mode of natural existence associated with animal bodies from which the term "mind" derives its original meaning, while at the same time it invests the intelligible features of the world with an aspect of complaisance to man, and thus flatters hopes that it does not really justify.

No summary of idealistic arguments would be complete without mention of that argument which idealism shares with spiritualism. The distinctive mark of modern idealism is, I believe, its annexation of the object to the act or state or mode of knowledge, whether in the Berkeleyan or in the Kantian manner. But modern idealism also absorbs and continues a strain of metaphysical speculation which is much older. According to this older or spiritualistic view, the metaphysical demand for a substantial being and an originating cause can be met only by self-consciousness, which, as intuitively apprehended, dissolves the dialectical difficulties which beset the time-worn topics of the "one and the many," "the thing and its qualities," "identity and difference," "freedom and necessity," and "infinity." Mind, so it is alleged, is superlatively and exclusively qualified for reality. This view rests, however, on the assumption that the nature of mind is self-evident. Modern realists, for the most part, reject this alleged revelation in the name of patient observation and rigorous analysis. They regard the nature of mind, not as the primal insight, but as a highly complicated and

baffling problem which possesses in an eminent degree whatever difficulties beset the problem of reality in general.* The first personal pronoun
is felt to resemble a question-mark more than an exclamation point.

To these counter-arguments, by which realism has disputed the claims
of idealism, I should like to add the difference of philosophical method
and attitude which has often divided these opposing schools. It was not an
accident that realists should have formulated a platform and attempted
collaboration. Anglo-American idealism, impregnated as it is with the
romantic tradition, has encouraged the individual to regard himself as an
authoritative organ of truth, or a fountain of lyric self-expression. To members of such a cult every attempt to define terms or to organize research
must necessarily be abhorrent. Realists, on the other hand, cling to the
naïve view that in the presence of common objects two philosophical minds
should be able to find some area of agreement, or at least to localize and
formulate their disagreement. The realist is baffled and annoyed by what
seems to him the arrogant obscurity of idealism, which appears to claim
the licence of poetry without assuming its artistic responsibilities. For the
same reasons the realist is attracted by the use of the mathematical method,
as a possible means of rendering philosophical discourse genuinely com-
municative, and philosophical discussion profitable and conclusive.

There is another incompatibility of temper which has divided idealists
and realists. Idealistic metaphysics is essentially an a priori doctrine. Its
central reality is inferred and not experienced. Indeed, the whole realm
of human experience is disparaged as appearance. There is a tendency to
solve problems in principle rather than in detail, or merely to read them by
title. Since truth consists in the light shed by the whole on the part, since the
Absolute is thus by definition the supreme solver of problems, and since all
other minds are tainted with finitude, there is a temptation to rest cheerfully in the midst of unconquered difficulties, even when they are difficulties
of the philosopher's own making. But pious resignation is not fruitful in
philosophy. Whatever be the reasons, it seems to me in any case to be a
fact that the idealist has contributed nothing to our understanding of infinity and continuity comparable with the contributions of the mathematical
logician; and nothing to our understanding of the nature of consciousness,
perception, matter, causality, or the relation of mind and body, comparable
with the contributions made by their contemporaries of the pragmatist and
realist schools. Idealists have been system-builders and have staked all on
the monumental perfection of the whole. James, Bergson, Russell, and

* I have argued that the idealist's position rests here upon a confusion between
the apparent simplicity of the familiar or the innocence of the eye, and the objective
simplicity which survives the effort to distinguish an internal multiplicity. I have
termed this error 'the fallacy of pseudo-simplicity." Cf. "Realism as a Polemic and
Programme of Reform," *Journal of Philosophy,* vol. vii (1910), p. 371.

Whitehead, on the other hand, pay as they go. You do not have to be converted to their gospel in order to profit by them. They abound in suggestive hypothesis, shrewd observation, and delicate analysis which you can detach and build into your own thinking. The newer philosophy which has grown up in opposition to idealism, and which has set a fashion which even idealism is now adopting, has something of the fruitfulness of empirical science. It is achieving results which, because of their factual basis, may survive the decline of the systematic theories in which they are presently embodied.

Such, in brief, is the train of argument by which I have justified my own dissent from idealism, and in which for the most part I have been in agreement with those of my American colleagues who in 1910 formulated a "Programme and First Platform,"* and in 1912 wrote in collaboration the volume entitled *The New Realism*. The defence against the idealistic argument is only a part of the realistic polemic, but it is the most indispensable part—the declaration of independence, by which a new philosophy has sought to gain diplomatic recognition. This war of liberation has, it is true, been supported by an invasion of the enemy's territory. But here the chief weapon employed has been that charge of solipsism which is as familiar to idealists as to their opponents. Realism has, furthermore, been compelled in turn to consolidate and defend its own position. But the historic significance of the American movement at the opening of the present century will, I think, lie in its having revived and modernized a way of thinking which, in spite of its antiquity and its agreement both with science and with common sense, had at the close of the previous century been consigned to the obituary columns of the most authoritative philosophical organs.

Absolute idealism, at the very moment of its seeming triumph over naturalism, was attacked on both flanks: on the one by pragmatism, and on the other by the new realism. The former attack came first and had already lowered the morale of the idealistic forces when the realistic onslaught occurred. The issue of the battle is decisive only in the sense that the supremacy of idealism is destroyed. The hopes of naturalism, as well as of medieval scholasticism, have revived owing to assistance received from unexpected quarters. The idealists, though checked, have rallied. Pragmatists and realists have fallen afoul of one another at the point of their convergent attack. Former enemies are fraternizing. Ranks are broken and regimental colours are abandoned on the field. What have realists to contribute to the reconstruction that now promises to follow after war?

The answer to this question is too long and too recent a story to find a place in this brief retrospect. Furthermore, it does not belong, in any exclusive sense, to an account of realism. Still less does it belong to my own

---

* *Journal of Philosophy*, vol. vii (1910), p. 393.

personal philosophical autobiography. Indeed, that which is most characteristic of the present moment in philosophy, as I understand it, is a con-
fluence of currents which have hitherto run in separate channels. We are
(and I am glad, as well as convinced, that it is so) less inclined than formerly to pride ourselves on partisan loyalties and polemical victories. A
contemplative observer of the times would have great difficulty in describing its characteristic philosophical activity in terms of the doctrinal cleav-
ages that were so well marked at the opening of the century. Its most
conspicuous feature is, I think, an avoidance of the dualisms and disjunc-
tions with which the influence of Descartes is associated. This attitude is
due in part to recent changes in science, in part to a revival of interest in
ancient and medieval philosophy, and in part to a growing sense of the
inadequacy of any of the sharply antithetical alternatives which divided the
thought of the last century. Conceptions such as "pattern," "aspect," "pure
experience," "essence," "emergence," "event" owe their present vogue to
the hope of healing the breach between mind and matter, soul and body,
religion and science, teleology and mechanism, or substance and attribute.
Viewed in the light of this conjunctive or reconciling motive, there is a
recognizable strain of similarity in the thought of James, Bergson, Husserl,
Alexander, Bosanquet, McTaggart, Stout, Whitehead, Russell, Broad,
Dewey, Santayana, Strong, Montague, and Holt. It would be pretentious
and unwarranted for realism to claim the credit for this tendency, but it
would be blind to deny that the Anglo-American realism of the first decade
of the century helped notably to prepare the way.*

II. A PRACTICAL CREED AND THE REASONS WHY

That element in my composition which inclined me in earlier years to
the Christian ministry is accountable, no doubt, for my sustained interest
in moral philosophy,* an interest which in recent years had broadened to
embrace the whole realm of "value." The passing of years, the habit of
philosophizing, and, perhaps, the changed atmosphere of the times, have
combined to give this interest more of reflective detachment and less of
that reforming zeal which once burned within me.

At the foundation of my moral philosophy lies a temper of mind which
I take to be the same as that which has led me to the rejection of idealism
in other fields. Knowledge I regard as essentially a facing of facts, the con-
forming of a belief to that which, relatively to the belief, is antecedent and
fixed. As between knowing and the object-to-be-known, it is the latter
which, under the rules of this particular game, makes the first cast of the
die. It is a case of "I match you," or, to use a better analogy, the lock is
prior to the key. If the cogitans-key does not fit and unlock the cogitan-

* Cf. my article entitled, "Peace without Victory in Philosophy," *Journal of Philosophical Studies*, vol. iii. (1928), p. 300.
    * Cf. *The Moral Economy* (1909.)

dum-lock, then it is the key and not the lock which has failed, and for which a better must be found. One who identifies himself fundamentally with this view of the rôle of cognitive mind, finds himself committed to a certain fundamental attitude in practical philosophy. He will endeavour, in taking account of his cosmic fortunes, to purge himself of preconceptions and of emotional bias. He will not ignore the human tendency to fashion reality after the human heart, or in accordance with human ways of thinking; on the contrary, he will be peculiarly alive to these disturbing factors in order, if possible, to correct the findings of his compass. Nor will he, merely because he does not wish to be blinded by the emotions, be in the least inclined to disparage them. The love of a fellow-creature may be the most sacred and the most powerful thing in a man's life, and yet, like a good physician, he may most scrupulously refuse to allow his hopes and fears to colour his judgment of the facts. He may realize that if his knowledge is to serve his passion, it must first be dispassionate. To the realist it is not even necessary that belief should be limited to evident facts. The man who can best afford to indulge in "over-beliefs," or in a faith supported by love and hope, is the man who is aware of the difference between cash and credit or between science and poetry. It is confusion, and not feeling, imagination, or conviction, which the knowing mind has most to fear.

In this context there is one specific doctrine that I should like to single out for special emphasis. It is essential to realism that a fact should not be construed as the creation of that act of mind which we designate as the knowing of it. But this does not at all imply that the fact in question should be non-mental. It would, of course, be palpably absurd for a realist, as for any other philosopher, to deny that there are mental facts. That which at any given moment I undertake to know may even be an act of my own cognition. In such a case there are two acts of cognition—the act-of-cognition-to-be-known, and the superadded act-of-knowing-it, both acts falling within that complex unity which the first personal pronoun is used to designate. What is true of cognition is *a fortiori* true of emotion. While emotion must not deflect knowledge, or substitute its own fond imagining for the intended object, an emotion is itself a kind of fact. Hence it is in no wise inconsistent with a fundamental realism to suppose that good and evil are emotionally conditioned.

Let me restate as simply as possible a view for which I have elsewhere argued at length.* The value of any object, in the most inclusive sense, as distinguished from its indifference, consists of that object's *moving* quality. Positive value (good) embraces the various modes of *attractiveness,* such as "desired," "loved," "joyous," "charming," "alluring," "auspicious"; negative value (bad) embraces the various modes of *repulsiveness,* such as "odious," "alarming," "portentous," "distasteful." In taking this

* *General Theory of Value* (1926).

view, I dissent from those who hold that the positive value of an object consists in its colour, shape, unity, harmony, or universality—its negative value in the absence of these characters, or in their opposites; and I dissent from those who hold that "good" and "bad" are terms for which there are no equivalents, referring to unique qualities other than such as are mentioned above. I do not, of course, mean to deny that unified, harmonious, or universal objects are good, but only that if this be so it means that unity, harmony, and universality are attractive.

In the next place, attractiveness consists in attracting, and repulsiveness consists in repelling. In taking this view I dissent from those who hold that the various modes of attractiveness and repulsiveness can inhere in objects unrelated to minds. Attractiveness and repulsiveness are not those elements in an object *by virtue* of which it evokes feeling or will, they *are* the evoking of will and feeling and mean nothing apart from motor-affective response.

Finally, in order that a given individual may know that an object possesses the moving quality which constitutes value, it is not necessary that *he* should be moved by it; any more than, in order to know that an object is destructive, it is necessary that he should be destroyed by it. In the knowing of value the knower's own will and feeling is no more involved than in his knowing of anything else. It is true that in so far as I am conscious of being attracted or repelled by an object I know that that object is good or evil, but such evidence is no more authentic than the consciousness that somebody else is attracted or repelled by it. In taking this view I dissent from those idealists who hold that the knowledge of an object's value is inseparably one with the emotional response which makes it valuable. According to idealism, there can be no such thing as the discovery or recognition of a value already there, nor can a value possess that character of independence which facts are assumed to possess when they are cited in proof or disproof of judgments made about them.

Idealism seems to me, here again, to reduce to the same untenable alternatives solipsism, relativism, absolutism. The solipsist says, "Only what I approve is good, only what I disapprove is evil." Idealistically he cannot be argued from his position, because it has been conceded to him in advance that he can know values only in the approving or disapproving act of making them. Relativism is the illegitimate generalization of this position—doubly illegitimate: first, because the generalization itself claims to be true about values, despite the fact that it is neither an approval nor a disapproval; second, because solipsists contradict one another. One solipsist is justified in saying: "This, since it attracts me, is good"; another, in saying: "Since it does not attract *me,* it is not good." Thereupon idealism enters and redeems a situation for which it is itself responsible. The prerogative of creating values in the act of knowing them is now reserved for a universal Approver and Disapprover, alleged to be the *real* will and feeling of all finite individuals, or their will and feeling when they will and feel as they ought. An original idealistic sin is atoned by a tardy idealistic repentance. The remedy is gratuitous, since the disease was avoidable; and it is ineffectual, since the resulting problem of the relation between the Absolute and finite man is only a new name for the old problems with which the whole inquiry began.

The issue is central to ethics and the social sciences, since it touches the question of the logic of moral reasoning. Realism transcends moral egoism from the outset, judgments of right and wrong being attested, not by the will and feeling of the judge, but by wills and feelings generally. Similarly, authority, whether of conscience, State, or God proceeds from the greater goods which these powers represent. If the judgment of conscience is authoritative over the judgment of appetite, it is because conscience affirms truly that the integral good is better than any of its parts, which the appetite blindly denies. If the State, speaking for the nation, is authoritative over the individual, speaking for himself, it is because the good of all members of a nation *is* better than that of one of its individual members, all being greater than one. The authority of God has to be justified in the same way as the judgment which correctly sets the claims of a universe above those of either individual or nation. Authority, in other words, attaches to a true judgment as to what is best—true, namely, as agreeing with the nature of what *is* best.

Idealism, on the other hand, must hold that as nothing can be known to be good save in the very act of feeling it or willing it, so nothing can be known to be better or best save in the act of *preferring* it. You cannot, by this logic, argue with the egoist except in terms of his existing bias. There is no fulcrum of fact by which you can dislodge him. You may seek to arouse his "higher self," or to appeal to his "collective will," or to quicken his "divine spark." If, as unfortunately happens, you find none of these things in him, the matter ends there; for you have conceded in advance that so far as *his* judgment is concerned *his* preference shall be final. You cannot even argue that a unified self, or a social will, or a divine Love *would* be better than his present disposition, for on your idealistic premises he can have no evidence of their being better until he already possesses them.

Such a philosophy tends to a confused psychology as well as to an impotent logic. Clinging to the common belief that personality, sociality, and humanity *are* objectively better, or that their betterness possesses a validity that is binding on all individual judges, the idealist imputes to all individual judges a disposition to prefer them. In default of observable facts, he appeals to latencies and virtualities. Logically, the result is to destroy the force of moral reasoning. An obligation cannot be said to be binding until it is acknowledged, but then the time for its argument is past. If there is any virtue in moral reasoning, it must lie in its power to prove the claims of the ideal upon one to whom the ideal as yet makes no appeal: the claims of conscience upon the creature of passion, the claims of society upon the selfish individual, the claims of the State upon the lawless rebel, of international accord upon the chauvinist, or of piety upon the worldling. There is but one method by which this can be done, by assuming, namely, that a certain projected course of action is intrinsically superior, because of the greater value which it embraces or promotes; that it would be superior, though no man should adopt it; that it is really superior, though no man deems it so, or actively prefers it. Only in this way is it possible to legitimate the title of an authority when it is refused allegiance.

I have emphasized this question of the logic of the moral sciences, not only because it furnishes the link between these fields of inquiry and a man's general philosophical position, and distinguishes, as I believe, between the way of the realist and the way of the idealist; but also because it deeply underlies the practical creed with which I should like to conclude this personal confession. I suspect egoism, opportunism, dictatorship, militarism, theocracy, and mysticism (strange bed-fellows) of being the practical sequel to a theory which finds the ground of authority in the will or feeling of the judge rather than in the correctness of his judgment. I myself am one of those lonely beings who used to be called "liberals," and who are now viewed with suspicion both from the left and from the right. I have always held, and do still hold, to that view of life which I have always supposed, and do still suppose, to be Christian and democratic. The best way, I think, is the way that provides for the happiness of mankind, severally and in the aggregate. All individuals without exception are "equally" entitled to so much happiness as their multiplicity and differences, their inherent capacities, their common environmental resources, permit. The major problem of life is to promote sentiments and devise modes of organization by which human suffering may be mitigated, and by which every unnecessary thwarting of human desire may be eliminated.

If I am asked *why* I define the goal of endeavour in these terms, my answer is simply that if happiness be good, then the happiness of all is better than the happiness of one, and an innocent or radiant and fruitful happiness is better than a happiness which is produced at the cost of unhappiness. The pre-eminent good of the general happiness of sentient beings I hold to be a fact which is independent of judgment or sentiment, in the same sense as is the fact that a pair is greater than one of its members, or that a century of history embraces a greater span than one of its included decades. This greatest good may meet with neglect or cold indifference, without being in the least invalidated thereby. It is *there*, to be pointed out for the illumination or edification of mankind. From this stubborn objectivity the faculties, sentiments, maxims, and institutions of men derive such legitimate authority as they possess; legitimate, not in the sense of any law formulated and enforced by God or men, but in the sense which the philosophers of the seventeenth and eighteenth centuries obscurely intended when they spoke of "natural law" or the "law of reason."

It is this first principle, with its irrevocable force and its indifference to human ignorance or weakness, which justifies to me the major tenets of the Occidental and American tradition. Evil is as stubborn a fact as good, and there is no metaphysical sleight of hand by which the worse may be *made* the better course, however much it may *appear* to be. Hence the final truth of moral dualism. The greater good is not the mere outcropping of the deeper natural propensity, but can be attained only by the procrustean fitting of plastic materials to a mould defined by reason. Hence the profound truth of moral rigorism. Convinced as I am of the indefeasible, though partial, truth of dualism and rigorism, the contemptuous dismissal of Puritanism strikes me as atavistic or sophomoric rather than as evidence of philosophic emancipation.

This same criterion of the universal happiness of individuals justifies the Christian doctrine of love, not merely as poetry, but as science. Judged by the same criterion, the ideal polity must be that in which the happiness of citizens is the end, and their enlightened consent the seat, of sovereignty; or that form of society in which men rule themselves by discussion, persuasion, and agreement, for the sake of their common and maximum happiness. Hence democracy strikes me as Utopian only in the sense in which the best is always beyond the reach of present attainment; and the sceptics of democracy appear to me, not as shrewd political discoverers (for the failures of democracy are as old as human history), but as shallow opportunists, or victims of circumstance, or blind fanatics, or rhetorical adventurers, who are unconsciously retracing more primitive stages of political development.

By this same principle, I judge some general concord among the nations of the earth to lie ahead on the upward path by which men have painfully ascended from the condition of beasts who prey upon their own kind. I can understand those who believe that such a concord lies upon a remote, or even an inaccessible, summit. I can understand its discouraged or even its desparing devotees. But in the cynical or gleeful enemies of international peace, in those who refuse even their homage to such a cause, I can see only a recrudescence of original sin.

Finally, it is by the same principle that I find myself compelled to judge of religion. I would not belittle the comforts and compensations yielded by religion, but a *true* religion must be that which confirms man's humanity to man; or which, like Christianity, conceives the object of worship as compassionate and beneficent. The Father who pities his children is the superlatively appropiate symbol of God, not because the worshipper, being one of the children, may hope to profit by paternal indulgence, but because all-reaching and infinitely patient love is the one thing supremely worshipful. Nietzsche's rejection of Christianity strikes me, therefore, as intelligently and absolutely false; while the little Nietzscheans assume in my eyes the rôle of bad boys who have happily found an adult to justify their incorrigible naughtiness.

It is evident, then, that in practical matters I am old-fashioned—that is to say, Christian and democratic in the historic senses of these terms. Much of what is now taken to be prophetic appear in my eyes as a tedious revival of old errors, not infrequently prompted by juvenile delinquency. Or, since Christianity and democracy were once revolutionary, and are still regarded with suspicion by the friends of tyranny and established privilege, I might describe myself as one who is revolutionary enough to remain loyal to the great revolutions of the past.

CLARENCE IRVING LEWIS

(1883—)

Born in 1883, C. I. Lewis belongs to the second generation of pragmatists. His philosophy offers a sophisticated restatement of pragmatism in the light of thirty years of discussion and controversy in America and abroad. Of all the pragmatists after Peirce, Lewis is the best informed and most original in the field of mathematical logic, and he is also the man most concerned to face the American realists, or English philosophers like Russell and G. E. Moore, on their own ground and to use the methods of philosophical argument which they prefer. Lewis' Mind and the World Order *(1929), from which the following selection has been taken, therefore offers the opportunity to take the measure of pragmatism as a mature and corrected intellectual tradition.*

During a large part of his career Lewis has devoted considerable attention to the examination of subtle questions in modern logic such as the notion of "material implication" and the development of what is known as a "modal logic". Since World War II and his retirement from active teaching at Harvard, he has also continued his effort to restate fundamental ideas of pragmatism in the face of new philosophical tendencies like "logical empiricism" and "analytic philosophy." He has paid particular attention to questions of ethics, and to the reaffirmation of the pragmatic view that ethical judgments can be objectively defended. His lengthy Analysis of Knowledge and Valuation *(1946) is the most elaborate reply by a pragmatist to recent positions in Anglo-American philosophy which hold (or seem to hold) that ethical judgments are merely "emotive." Here as elsewhere Lewis has made it plain that pragmatism, though it is severely critical of traditional notions of the nature of reason, stands foursquare for the consistent use of rational methods in all domains.*

Mind and the World Order

THE NATURE OF THE A PRIORI, AND
THE PRAGMATIC ELEMENT IN KNOWLEDGE

IN EXPERIENCE, MIND IS CONFRONTED WITH THE CHAOS OF THE GIVEN. IN the interest of adaptation and control, it seeks to discover within or impose upon this chaos some kind of stable order, through which distinguishable items may become the signs of future possibilities. Those patterns of distinction and relationship which we thus seek to establish are our concepts. These must be determined in advance of the particular experience to which they apply in order that what is given may have meaning. Until the criteria of our interpretation have been fixed, no experience could be the sign of anything or even answer any question. Concepts thus represent what mind brings to experience. That truth which is a priori rises from the concept itself. This happens in two ways. In the first place, there is that kind of truth, exemplified most clearly by pure mathematics, which represents the elaboration of concepts in the abstract, without reference to any particular application to experience. Second, the concept in its application to the given exhibits the predetermined principles of interpretation, the criteria of our distinguishing and relating, of classification, and hence the criteria of reality of any sort. This is most clearly evident in the case of those basic concepts, determining major classes of the real, which may be called the categories, though in less important ways it holds true of concepts in general.

For both these ways in which the truth is fixed, independently of experience or in advance of it, it represents the explication or elaboration of the concept itself. *The a priori is not a material truth, delimiting or delineating the content of experience as such, but is definitive or analytic in its nature.*

The a priori as thus definitive or explicative, representing principles of order and criteria of the real, meets all the requirements which emerge from the discussion of the preceding chapter. Since it is a truth about our own interpretative attitude, it imposes no limitation upon the future possibilities of experience; that is a priori which we can maintain in the face of all experience, come what will. And although it represents the contribution

473

of the mind itself to knowledge, it does not require that this mind be universal, absolute, or a reality of a higher order than the object of its knowledge. The a priori does not need to be conceived as the inscrutable legislation of a transcendent mind, the objects of which, being limited by its forms of intuition, are phenomenal only. Hence the distinction of the legislative mind as ultimate reality from its object which is not thus ultimate, falls away, and with it the difficulty of knowing the mind and of recognizing what is a priori as that which is determined by our own active attitude. The a priori is knowable simply through the reflective and critical formulation of our own principles of classification and interpretation. Such legislation can be recognized as our own act because the a priori principle which is definitive, and not a material truth of the content of experience, *has alternatives*. It can be recognized as due to the mind itself by the ordinary criteria of responsibility in general—that a different mode of acting is possible and makes a discoverable difference. Where there is no possibility of refraining from our actor acting otherwise, there can be no discoverable activity—indeed, there is no act. As has been pointed out, if what is a priori sprang from a transcendent mind, acting in unalterable ways, it never could be known to be our own creation or distinguished from those facts of life which are due to the nature of the independent real. What can be known to be a priori must meet the apparently contradictory requirements that it may be known in advance to hold good for all experience and that it have alternatives. The principle of classification or interpretation meets these requirements, because the alternative to a definition or a rule is not its falsity but merely its abandonment in favor of some other. Thus the determination of the a priori is in some sense like free choice and deliberate action.

This meets also another difficulty which will already have presented itself to the reader. If the a priori is something made by mind, mind may also alter it. There will be no assurance that what is a priori will remain fixed and absolute throughout the history of the race or for the developing individual. From the point of view here presented, this is no difficulty at all but the explanation of an interesting historical fact. The rationalist prejudice of an absolute human reason, universal to all men and to all time, has created an artificially exalted and impossible conception of the categories as fixed and unalterable modes of mind. One result has been to limit the usefulness of the conception, so that what we could call, in ordinary parlance, "the categories of physics" or "the categories of biology" would not serve as examples of "the categories" because it is obvious that the fundamental principles and concepts of any natural science change progressively with its development. This, in turn, has served to obscure the large and important part played in science by that element of categorial order which cannot be determined by merely empirical fact but must be provided by the scientist himself in his setting of the problem and fixing the criteria by which the meaning of experimental findings is to be interpreted. Thus the most impressive examples of human knowledge have been too little drawn upon in discussions of epistemology.

The assumption that our categories are fixed for all time by an original human endowment, is a superstition comparable to the belief of primitive peoples that the general features of their life and culture are immemorial and of supernatural origin. The grand divisions of our thought-world differ from those of our early ancestors as our modern machines differ from their primitive artifacts and our geographical and astronomical outlook from their world bounded by a distant mountain range or the pillars of Hercules and shut up under the bowl of the sky. Certain fundamental categories are doubtless very ancient and permanent: thing and property, cause and effect, mind and body, and the relations of valid inference, doubtless have their counterparts wherever and whenever the human mind has existed. But even here, the supposition of complete identity and continuity is at variance with facts which should be obvious.

For all primitive peoples, for example, and for some who distinctly are not primitive, the properties of a thing are not localized in time and space, as for us. Almost anything may be a talisman or fetish, whose action takes place (without intermediaries) at a distance and in a time posterior to its destruction by fire or by being eaten. Things also have doubles, inscrutably operating in that other-world whose influence mysteriously interpenetrates the realm which we call "nature." Furthermore, the long-persistent problem in physics of action at a distance increasingly comes back to haunt us and to unite with new problems of physical interpretation which threaten to drive us once more to dissipate the "material thing" throughout all time and space; to find its manifestation and even its very being in a spatio-temporal spread of events indefinitely extended.

That the present distinction of mind and body corresponds only roughly with that division in ancient thought; that body of inert matter and mind which does not occupy space are no older than the advent of that esoteric doctrine which dawned in Europe with the Greek mysteries and Christianity —this can hardly escape us. This mode of distinction contrasts with the tripartite division into body, mind, and spirit, and with the five-fold and *n*-fold divisions of more easterly cultures. It is also obvious that the pressure of modern science in the field of biology and our present uneasiness about this twofold nature of the individual, augur some departure from the clarity of Cartesian dualism.

The *names* of our categories may be very old and stable, but the *concepts,* the modes of classifying and interpreting which they represent, undergo progressive alteration with the advance of thought.

Probably those modes of thought embodied in logic and in the forms of language are more fundamental than others. And very likely what we recognize as explicit categories are always superficial as compared with more deep-lying forms which only the persistent and imaginative student can catch, in some vague and fleeting insight, because they are so nearly the marrow of our being and so all-pervasive that they can hardly be phrased in significant expression. These go back to the point where mind is continuous with the objective and indistinguishable from it. For we can know our own nature only in so far as we comprehend or vaguely imagine what it would mean to be other than we are. We can recognize the presence of mind only where mind makes a discoverable difference. If we should think of mind as what the rationalists suppose—superimposing on reality a rigid mask of form outside which mind itself could never catch a glimpse—then this altogether universal and un-get-overable form could never become self-conscious. It would remain—in Fichte's phrase—the "Great Thought which no man has ever thought." It would be not of mind but of the objective reality; it would be the Absolute which forever conditions but never can be known. But the idealistic rationalist can not eat his cake and have it too; the mind which can be recognized as such is *ipso facto* finite and limited by discoverable bounds. That mind is thus continuous with the finally mysterious—the is-ness of what is—we must of course grant; in the contemplation of mind we contemplate one aspect of the Great Fact in the presence of which all explicit thought is silenced. But the categories are not the form of that which, having no alternative and no bounds, is formless. They are the explicit bounds of that which, if it transcend them, must—fall into some other category. They are divisions within the comprehensible in general, but not the shape of comprehensibility itself.

It will be well to make clear that the conception here presented does not imply that because the a priori is something made by mind and capable of alteration, it is therefore arbitrary in the sense of being capriciously determined. That it is not, and cannot be, determined by the given, does not imply that it answers to no criteria whatever. That type of a priori truth which pure mathematics illustrates—that is, the elaboration of concepts in abstraction from all questions of particular applications—answers only to the criteria of self-consistency. Just to the extent that the development of such a purely analytic system is withdrawn from every consideration of useful application, its truth is simply truth to the original meanings embodied in its basic concepts. But when concepts are intended to be applied in experience, and a priori principles are to determine modes of classification and interpretation, the case is different. Here mind is still uncompelled by any possible content of experience. But knowledge has a practical business to perform, the interests of action which it seeks to serve. The mode of the mind's activity answers to our need to understand, in the face of an experience always more or less baffling, and of our need to control. There is also another factor which helps to determine what modes of attempted comprehension will be most easily and most widely useful. While that absolute human reason which the rationalist supposes to be completely and universally possessed by every human is a myth, nevertheless man, being a species of animal, has characteristics which mark him as such, and some of these at least are reflected in the bent of human thought. Some modes of thought are simpler and come more naturally to us than others which still are possible and which might, indeed, be called upon if an enlarged experience should sufficiently alter our problems—just as some modes of bodily translation are more easy and natural, though these may be somewhat altered when the environment includes a sufficient number of automobiles and airplanes. Moreover, the fundamental likeness in our modes of thought, which represents whatever community of nature marks our original mental endowment, is continually enhanced by the fact that the needs of individual humans are mostly served by coöperation with others. "The human mind" is distinctly a social product, and our categories will reflect that fact.

In brief, while the a priori is dictated neither by what is presented in experience nor by any transcendent and eternal factor of human nature, it still answers to criteria of the general type which may be termed pragmatic. The human animal with his needs and interests confronts an experience in which these must be satisfied, if at all. Both the general character of the experience and the nature of the animal will be reflected in the mode of behavior which marks this attempt to realize his ends. This will be true of the categories of his thinking as in other things. And here, as elsewhere, the result will be reached by a process in which attitudes tentatively assumed, disappointment in the ends to be realized, and consequent alteration of behavior will play their part.

Confirmation of this conception of the a priori could only come from comprehensive and detailed examination of at least the major categories of thought and the underlying principles of common-sense and scientific explanation. Such a task cannot be undertaken here; at most only a few illustrations can be offered with the hope that they are typical.

The paradigm of the a priori in general is the definition. It has always been clear that the simplest and most obvious case of truth which can be known in advance of experience is the explicative proposition and those consequences of definition which can be derived by purely logical analysis. These are necessarily true, true under all possible circumstances, because definition is legislative. Not only is the meaning assigned to words more or less a matter of choice—that consideration is relatively trivial—but the manner in which the precise classifications which definition embodies shall be affected, is something not dictated by experience. If experience were other than it is, the definition and its corresponding classification might be inconvenient, useless, or fantastic, but it could not be false. Mind makes classifications and determines meanings; in so doing, it creates that truth without which there could be no other truth.

Traditionally propositions which have been recognized as analytic have often not been classed with the a priori; they have been regarded as too unimportant; sometimes they have even been repudiated as not truth at

all but merely verbal statements. The main reasons for this cava-
lier attitude have been two; in the first place, it has been overlooked that
the real itself is a matter of definition and that the dichotomy of real and
unreal is that first and basic classification which the mind confronted with
experience must make. And second, the powerful sweep and consequence
of purely logical analysis has not been understood.

The clearest example of this power of analysis is to be found, of course,
in mathematics. The historical importance of mathematics as a paradigm
of a priori truth needs no emphasis. Almost one may say that traditional
conceptions of the a priori are the historical shadow of Euclidean geometry. But in mathematics much water has gone under the bridge since
the time of Kant, and in the light of the changes which have come about,
these traditional conceptions are proved totally impossible. The course of
this development will be familiar to the reader; only the outstanding features of it need be mentioned.

Though there are anticipations of current mathematical conceptions as
far back as Plato, the movement which led to their present acceptance dates
principally from the discovery of the non-Euclidean geometries. In developing these systems, it was obviously impossible to depend on intuitions of
space, either pure or empirical. If Euclid is true of our space, then no one of
these geometries can be; if Euclid is not true and certain, then the main
ground of the supposition that we can rely on intuitions of the spatial is
discredited. Hence in developing the non-Euclidean systems, all constructions such as helping-lines, and any step in proof which should depend not
upon pure logic but upon the character of space must be dispensed with.
If a step in proof cannot be taken by rigorous logic alone, it cannot be taken
at all. When it was found thus possible to develop the non-Euclidean systems without appeal to any extra-logical aids, a similar revision of Euclid
was carried out, eliminating all explicit or implicit reliance upon constructions, superpositions or other appeal to spatial intuition. This new method,
together with certain indicated generalizations, constituted the so-called
"modern geometry."

Next it was demonstrated that not only geometry but other branches as
well can be developed by the deductive method, from a relatively few assumptions, and likewise without reliance upon empirical data. As a result
all pure mathematics is found to be abstract, in the sense of being independent of any particular application. Because if all the theorems follow logically from the definitions and postulates, then we can alter at will what we
let the terms, such as "point" and "line," denote without in the least disturbing any step in the proofs. *Whatever* "point" and "line" may mean,
given these assumptions about them, these consequences—the rest of the
system—must also hold of them, since the theorems follow from the
assumptions by rigorous and purely logical deduction.

The question of the truth of the mathematical system *in application* was
thus completely separated from its mathematical or logical integrity. Still

further changes went along with this. The "truth" of initial assumptions lost all meaning in any other sense than their exhibition of certain patterns of logical relationship to be adhered to throughout. The distinguishing assumptions of a non-Euclidean geometry, for example, so far from being self-evident, were supposedly mere arbitrary falsehoods with respect to their most obvious empirical denotation. The term "axiom" was replaced by "postulate" or "primitive proposition." In the interest of logical simplicity alternative sets of assumptions which would give the same system of propositions were investigated. What should be initially assumed and what proved became a question merely of such logical simplicity. It became customary to speak of the truth of mathematics as hypothetical or to say that what mathematics asserts is only the relation of implication between postulates and theorems. It is truth about certain patterns of logical relationship established by initial definition or postulate.

Further, it became clear that the distinction between those assumptions of the form called "definitions" and those termed "postulates" was relatively arbitrary and unimportant. Logically it makes little difference except for simplicity of procedure, how far the order of a system is set up by propositions in which "is" means logical equivalence and how far by those in which it means only the one-way implication of concepts or subsumption of classes. Since the content of the concepts of pure mathematics is simply that order to which they give rise, that manner of development in which essential relationships are exhibited as the definitive meaning of the concepts is truest to the nature of the subject.

The completion of this last refinement of mathematical method was made by Whitehead and Russell in "Principia Mathematica." It was here proved that the initial assumptions of mathematics can all be dispensed with, except the definitions. The truths of mathematics follow merely from definitions which exhibit the meaning of its concepts, by purely logical deduction. Judgment of such mathematical truth is, thus, completely and exclusively analytic; no synthetic judgment, a priori or otherwise, is requisite to knowledge of pure mathematics. The content of the subject consists entirely of the rigorous logical analysis of abstract concepts, in entire independence of all data of sense or modes of intuition. The definitions which embody these concepts are not required to be true in any other sense than that they should be precise and clear; the formulation of them represents an act of mind which is legislative or creative and in some sense arbitrary; it answers to no criteria save self-consistency and adequacy to whatever purposes the elaboration of the system itself may be supposed to satisfy. It may still be true that "concepts without precepts are empty," but it must be granted that there is a kind of knowledge of "empty" concepts. Or at least such admission can be avoided only by a restriction of the term "knowledge" to exclude pure mathematics and logic. The importance of such a priori analytic knowledge is witnessed by the basic character of these subjects for all other sciences.

Pure mathematics stands between logic on the one side and the empirical application of mathematics on the other. Logic is in some respects the illustration *par excellence* of the a priori, since its laws are the most completely general of any. The laws of logic cannot be proved unless they should first be taken for granted as the principles of their own demonstration. They make explicit the basic principles of all interpretation and of our general modes of classification. And they impose no limitation upon the content of experience. Sometimes we are asked to tremble before the specter of the "alogical" in order that we may thereafter rejoice that we are saved from this by the dependence of reality upon mind. But the "alogical" is pure bogey, a word without a meaning. What kind of experience could defy the principle that everything must either be or not be, that nothing can both be and not be, or that if X is Y and Y is Z, then X is Z? If anything imaginable or unimaginable could violate such laws, then the ever-present fact of change would do it every day. The laws of logic are purely formal; they forbid nothing but what concerns the use of terms and the corresponding modes of classification and analysis. The law of contradiction tells us that nothing can be both white and not white, but it does not and can not tell us whether black is not white or soft or square is not white. To discover what contradicts what we must turn to more particular considerations. Similarly the law of the excluded middle formulates our decision that whatever is not designated by a certain term shall be designated by its negative. It declares our purpose to make, for every name, a complete dichotomy of experience, instead—as we might choose—of classifying on the basis of a tripartite division into opposites and a middle ground between the two. Our rejection of such tripartite division represents only our penchant for simplicity and similar considerations.

Further laws of logic are of like significance. They are principles of procedure, the parliamentary rules of intelligent thought and action. Such laws are independent of the given because they impose no limitations whatever upon it. They are legislative because they are addressed to ourselves—because definition, classification, and inference represent no operation in the world of things, but only our categorial attitudes of mind.

Furthermore, the ultimate criteria of the laws of logic are pragmatic. Indeed, how could they be anything else? The truth of logic is not material truth but a truth about the modes of self-consistency. Since this is so, logic must be the test of its *own* consistency, and hence of its own truth, as well as the test of the consistency of everything else. But if logic tests its own truth, then what can be the test of truth in a genuine issue of logic, which is not a question of mere inadvertence on one side or the other? Those who suppose that there is *a* logic which everyone would agree to if he understood it and understood himself, are more optimistic than those versed in the history of logical discussion have a right to be. The fact is that, as was pointed out in the preceding chapter, there are several logics, markedly different, each self-consistent *in its own terms* and such that whoever, using it, avoids false premises, will never reach a false conclusion. Mr. Russell, for example, bases *his* logic on an implication relation such that if twenty sentences be cut from a newspaper and put in a hat, and then two of these be drawn at random, one of them will certainly imply the other, and it is an even chance that the implication will be mutual. Yet upon a foundation so remote from ordinary modes of inference the whole structure of "Principia Mathematica" is built. This logic is utterly self-consistent and valid in its own terms. There are others even more strange of which the same may be said. Genuine issues of logic are those which stand above such questions of the merely self-critical integrity of the logical system. There are such issues, and these cannot be determined—nay, cannot even be argued—except on pragmatic grounds of human bent and intellectual convenience. That we have been blind to this fact, and that much good paper and ink has been wasted by logicians who have tried to argue on some other grounds what are only questions of convenience or of value, itself reflects traditional errors in the conception of the a priori.

Pure mathematics and logic exemplify that type of the a priori which have the highest degree of abstraction from experience—whose concepts are so general that we may call them "empty." Concerning these, there may be a question whether there will not be issues of an entirely different sort when we attempt to apply them in experience. One may say, for example, that when geometry becomes abstract and freed from all necessary reference to our intuitions of the spatial, the question of the *truth about space* becomes an entirely separate one, and one with respect to which there must be reference to forms of intuition or something of the sort, or there will be nothing which is determinable a priori at all. Similarly one may say that if arithmetic as a purely abstract deductive system has no necessary reference to the character of countable objects, then its a priori truth is of no value for the anticipation of the behavior of concrete things. This will be true, of course, and of importance. If there should be a priori truth *only* with respect to concepts in utter abstraction from experience, and if this a priori character were to vanish when these concepts are given a concrete denotation, then the significance of the a priori for the natural sciences and for common practice would be largely, if not completely, lost.

But there *is* an a priori truth of concepts which have concrete denotation. Let us consider the example of arithmetic. Arithmetic depends *in toto* upon the operation of counting or correlating, a procedure which can be carried out in any world containing identifiable things, regardless of the further characters of experience. Mill challenged this a priori character of arithmetic. He asked us to suppose a demon sufficiently powerful and maleficent so that every time two things were brought together with two other things, this demon should always introduce a fifth. The conclusion which he supposed to follow is that under such circumstances $2+2=5$ would be a universal law of arithmetic. But Mill was quite mistaken. In such a world we should be obliged to become a little clearer than usual about the distinction between arithmetic and physics, that is all. If two black marbles were put in the same box with two white ones, the demon could take his choice of colors, but it would be evident that there were more black marbles or more white ones than were put in. The same would be true of all objects in any wise identifiable. We should simply find ourselves in the presence of an extraordinary physical law, which we should recognize as universal in our world, that whenever two things were brought into proximity with two others, an additional and similar thing was always created by the process. Mill's world would be physically most extraordinary. The world's work would be enormously facilitated if hats or locomotives or tons of coal could be thus multiplied by anyone possessed originally of two pairs. But the laws of mathematics would not be affected. It is because this is true that arithmetic is a priori. Its laws prevent *nothing;* they are compatible with anything which happens or could conceivably happen in nature. They are true in any possible world. Mathematical addition is not a physical transformation. The only bringing together it implies is in the mind; if translation in general affected numerical alteration, we should always count things *in situ,* but we should count and add as usual. Physical changes which result in an increase or decrease of the countable things involved are matters of everyday occurrence. Such physical processes present us with phenomena in which the purely mathematical has to be separated out by analysis. It is because we shall always separate out that part of the phenomenon not in conformity with arithmetic and designate it by some other category—physical change, chemical reaction, optical illusion—that arithmetic is a priori. *Its laws constitute criteria of our categorial classification and interpretation.* As this example serves to illustrate, such categorial interpretation of the concrete and empirical throws out of court whatever would otherwise violate the a priori principles which embody the category, but it does not thereby legislate anything phenomenal out of existence.

Perhaps, however, we have gone too far. Mill's illustration is of an alteration of experience in general which is too simple and too poorly carried out to make it plausible that our categorial interpretation would be different in such a world. But if translation in general affected numerical alteration then an entirely different mode of categorial interpretation might better serve the purposes. Our present categories would not—*could not*—be prohibited but other modes might more simply reduce the phenomenal to order and facilitate control. Or in such a world, arithmetic might be confined to mental phenomena—since these would be exempt from the effects of change of place—and numerical principles would be laws of psychology. If we were jelly-fish in a liquid world, we should probably not add at all, because the useful purposes served by such conceptions would be so slight. Still if some super-jelly-fish should invent arithmetic by a *jeu d'esprit* (as Hamilton invented quaternions) he would find nothing in any possible experience to controvert it, and he might with some profit apply it to his own distinct ideas.

The ideal illustration of the a priori in applied geometry would be a consideration of physical relativity, showing how geometrical truth may turn upon the place where the dividing line is drawn between the properties of *space* and those of *matter*. Applied geometrical principles are a priori true of all space-filling things. But this a priori truth has its pragmatic aspect since there are these alternatives about the manner in which the category of "the spatial" shall be bounded. But to carry out this illustration in detail would be beyond my competence.

Incidentally it may be pointed out that the ideas which have gained currency through relativity-theory make clear the nature of Kant's mistakes in the supposition of a limited form of spatial intuition. For Kant, the spatial or geometrical has to do with relations of the simultaneous; the shape of a triangle, for example, is something instantaneously imaginable. But for celestial triangles, such instantaneous intuition has no meaning; what exists or happens at a distance is not directly verifiable here and now; a passage of something through time, as well as space, is inextricably bound up with the determination of the distant fact. Hence the imagination of a "curved-space" need not mean something like flattening out a hemisphere without disturbing the relations of great circles on its surface. It means only imagining *certain uniform sequences* to characterize our experience of the spatial under certain conditions. The "unimaginable" character of curved-space in the sense that we cannot visualize a non-Euclidean triangle on the blackboard, has nothing to do with the matter. Triangles on different scales have different "shapes" in non-Euclidean space, and triangles big enough to "verify" the nature of space are too big to "imagine." Our ancestors who believed the earth was flat could certainly "imagine" a non-Euclidean space, in the only sense which is required, since the geometry of the earth's surface is (in an obvious sense) Riemannian.

The a priori element in natural sciences goes much deeper than might be supposed. All order of sufficient importance to be worthy of the name of law depends eventually upon some ordering by mind. Without initial principles by which we guide our attack upon the welter of experience, it would remain forever chaotic and refractory. In every science there are fundamental laws which are a priori because they formulate just such definitive concepts or categorial tests by which alone investigation becomes possible.

A good example of this is to be found in Einstein's little book "Relativity." The question under discussion is the criteria of simultaneity for events at a distance. Suppose the lightning strikes a railroad track at two places, *A* and *B*. How shall we tell whether these events happen at the same time? "We . . . require a definition of simultaneity such that this definition supplies us with a method by which . . . we can decide whether or not the lightning strokes occurred simultaneously. As long as this requirement is not satisfied, I allow myself to be deceived as a physicist (and of course the same applies if I am not a physicist) when I imagine that I am able to attach a meaning to the statement of simultaneity. . . .

"After thinking the matter over for some time you then offer the following suggestion with which to test simultaneity. By measuring along the rails, the connecting line *A B* should be measured up and an observer placed at the mid-point *M* of the distance *A B*. This observer should be supplied with an arrangement (*e. g.,* two mirrors inclined at 90°) which allows him visually to observe both places *A* and *B* at the same time. If the observer perceives the two flashes at the same time, they are simultaneous.

"I am very pleased with this suggestion, but for all that I cannot regard the matter as quite settled, because I feel constrained to raise the following objection: 'Your definition would certainly be right, if I only knew that the light by means of which the observer at *M* perceives the lighting flashes travels along the length *A-M* with the same velocity as along the length *B-M*. But an examination of this supposition would only be possible if we already had at our disposal the means of measuring time. It would thus appear as though we were moving here in a logical circle.'

"After further consideration you cast a somewhat disdainful glance at me—and rightly so—and you declare: 'I maintain my previous definition nevertheless because in reality it assumes nothing whatever about light. There is only *one* demand to be made of the definition of simultaneity, namely, that in every real case it must supply us with an empirical decision as to whether or not the conception which has to be defined is fulfilled. That light requires the same time to traverse the path *A-M* as for the path *B-M* is in reality *neither a supposition nor a hypothesis* about the physical nature of light, but a *stipulation* which I can make of my own free-will in order to arrive at a definition of simultaneity.' . . . We are thus led to a definition of 'time' in physics."

As this example well illustrates, we cannot even ask the questions which discovered law would answer until we have first by a priori stipulation formulated definitive criteria. Such concepts are not verbal definitions nor classifications merely; they are themselves laws which prescribe a certain behavior to whatever is thus named. Such definitive laws are a priori; only so can we enter upon the investigation by which further laws are sought. Yet it should also be pointed out that such a priori laws are subject to abandonment if the structure which is built upon them does not succeed in simplifying our interpretation of phenomena. If, in the illustration given, the relation "simultaneous with," as defined, should not prove transitive—if event *A* should prove simultaneous with *B* and *B* with *C,* but not *A* with *C*—this definition would certainly be rejected.

Indeed *all* definitions and *all* concepts exercise this function of prescribing fundamental law to whatever they denote, because everything which has a name is to be identified with certainty only over some stretch of time. The definition provides criteria of the thing defined which, in application, become necessary or essential laws of its behavior. This is especially evident in the case of scientific definitions because the "things" of science are of a deep-lying sort, representing uniformities of behavior of a high order. If definition is unsuccessful, as early scientific definitions mostly have been, it is because the classification thus set up corresponds with no natural cleavage and does not correlate with sufficiently important uniformities of behavior. Early attempts to reduce phenomena to law are based upon the "things" of common-sense which represent classification according to properties which are relatively easy of direct observation and impressive to the senses. When such attempts fail, it is largely because of this superficiality of initial classification. The alchemist's definitions of the elements, for example, are the clue to his indifferent success; the definitive properties pick out amorphous groups which have little significance of further uniformity. Not until such crucial properties as combining weights become the basis of classification is it possible to arrive at satisfactory laws of chemistry. The earlier definitions can not be said to have been false; they were merely useless, or insufficient to the purposes in hand. A large part of the scientific search is, thus, for *things worth naming*.

We have reached a point today where we understand that the typical procedure of science is neither deduction from what is self-evident or relatively certain nor direct generalization from experience. If any one method is more characteristic of science than another it is that of hypothesis and verification. But we seem still to overlook the fact that the *terms* in which hypothesis and law are framed themselves represent a scientific achievement. We still suffer from the delusion that fixed and eternal categories of human thought on the one side are confronted with equally fixed and given "things" on the other. Is it not obvious, to dispassionate observation, that scientific categories and classifications are subject to progressive modification or even abrupt alteration, and that these have a directive and controlling influence upon the other phases of scientific research? And here too, as in hypothesis and verification, the development takes place, not by logical derivation from antecedent principles nor by direct formulation of empirical content, but by the hazarding of something by the mind and its retention or repudiation according to the success or non-success of what is based upon it. The test of success here is not, however, simple conformity with experience, as in the testing of hypothesis, but is the achievement of intelligible order amongst the phenomena in question, and responds also to such criteria as intellectual simplicity, economy, and comprehensiveness of principle.

The reader will perhaps feel that, in so far as this is true, what is here represented as a priori is nothing of the sort but is merely something that we learn from experience. But if so, I hope that he will reread the illustration from Einstein, with due regard for the logic of it. However much the give and take between the purposes of science and discovered fact may contribute to alter the procedure by which those aims are sought, and may induce new basic principles and categories, still the naming, classifying, defining activity is at each step prior to the investigation. We cannot even interrogate experience without a network of categories and definitive concepts. Until our meanings are definite and our classifications are fixed, experience cannot conceivably determine anything. We must first be in possession of criteria which tell us what experience would answer what questions, and how, before observation or experiment could tell us anything.

The uniformities which science seeks are of a high order and represent a further reach of those same purposes exhibited on a humbler scale by the uniformities of common sense comprehension. The categorizing and classifying activity of thought is, thus, more deliberate and self-conscious in the case of science and, by comparison, easier to observe than in the case of common sense. Because scientific categories are in some part built upon more basic distinction, the functioning of them as criteria of the real is less frequent and perhaps less important. It is, nevertheless, sometimes to be observed in the interplay between new principles of scientific interpretation and residual phenomena which are unexplained or reports of observation which are regarded as possibly involving error. If Röntgen had been unable to repeat the experience in which he first saw the bones of his hand, that perception would have been discredited. Because no one but their discoverer could see the "N-rays" with any assurance, and it was found that he saw them when the refracting prism was removed as well as with it, they were discarded as illusory. The phenomena of hypnotism remained for a long time in the limbo of the dubious, and even today offer a difficult problem of separation of veridical phenomenon from illusion, self-deception and the like. The phenomena of "dual personality" would challenge a very fundamental category if only there were not so much doubt about what it is that is "dual" and whether it is genuinely dual. To choose a different sort of example, when the eclipse-photographs which figured in the discussion of relativity were examined, the question was raised whether the star-displacements as measured on them represented simply the bending of light-rays or were due in part to halation of the sensitive film. Thus, for a moment at least, so fundamental a problem as that of abandoning the categories of independent space and time was intertwined with the question whether the position of dots on a photographic plate represented authentic star-photographs or was due to something which took place inside the camera.

What needs to be observed here is at once the continuity of scientific problems of a high order with the apparently simple and fundamental criteria of the real, and the fact that such decisions of reality or unreality are themselves interpretations involving principles of the same order as scientific law. They are such as forbid, for example, the non-biological transformations and non-physical successions which occur in dreams. A mouse which disappears where there is no hole, is no real mouse; a landscape which recedes as we approach, is but illusion. The reality of an object of a particular sort is determined by a certain uniformity of its behavior in experience. The formulation of this uniformity is of the type of natural law. So far, such laws are a priori—for this particular sort of thing; the experience which fails to conform to the law is repudiated as non-veridical.

This situation is most paradoxical; principles of the order of natural law are reached by some generalization from experience—that is, from *veridical* experience; there are no generalizations whatever to be had from the unsorted experience of real and unreal both. But what experience is *veridical,* is determined by the criterion of law. Which is first, then; does the content of experience validate the law or does the law validate the experience in attesting its veridical character? The answer is that the law is first precisely so long as and so far as we are prepared to maintain it as criterion of the real. But the "reality" which is in question is likely to be of a highly specific sort. The authentic photograph of stars and the picture affected by halation, for example, are both real, both physically real, both photographs even, in a certain sense. What is an "authentic photograph" has to be very precisely defined in the case in point and is so defined as to exclude the effect of light reflection from the back of the glass of the photographic plate. The manner of this definition or classification obviously will require a correlation of photograph and thing photographed of the type set forth in certain physical laws. In the particular case, failure to exhibit such lawful relationship condemns the phenomenon as not authentic or not real—that is, not really this very specific sort of thing.

Thus all concepts, and not simply those we should call "categories," function as criteria of reality. Every criterion of classification is criterion of reality of some particular sort. There is no such thing as reality in general; to be real, a thing must be a particular sort of real. Furthermore, what is a priori criterion of reality in one connection may be merely empirical law in some other—for example, the law correlating photograph and thing photographed, or the law of the behavior of solid bodies in translation which condemns the mouse that disappears without a hole, or the laws of perspective which exclude a landscape which recedes as we approach it. *The determination of reality, the classification of phenomena, and the discovery of law, all grow up together.* I will not repeat what has already been said so often about the logical priority of criteria; but it should be observed that this is entirely compatible with the shift of categories and classifications with the widening of human experience. If the criteria of the real are a priori, that is not to say that no conceivable character of experience would lead to alteration of them.

For example, spirits cannot be photographed. But if photographs of spiritistic phenomena, taken under properly guarded conditions, should become sufficiently frequent, this a priori dictum would be called in question. What we should do would be to redefine our terms. Whether "spook" was spirit or matter, whether the definition of "spirit" or of "matter" should be changed; all this would constitute one interrelated problem.

What would prove to you that the relative motion of a body effected a foreshortening of it and altered its mass? If the answer is "no conceivable experience" and you are able to formulate a definition of "mass," a conception of motion, and of ideally exact measurement in terms that do not conflict with one another and with your other physical conceptions, there is no possible ground on which you could be proven wrong. To a mind sufficiently resolute for an independent space and time, no possible experience could prove the principles of relativity. The question, "How long shall we persist in holding to our previous categories, when confronted with star-photographs and the displacement of spectrum-lines (or with spiritistic phenomena or evidence of telepathy)?" is one which has no general answer. A stubborn conservatism can be proved unreasonable only on the pragmatic ground that another method of categorial analysis more successfully reduces all experience of the type in question to order and law. Confronting such a problem, we should reopen together the question of definition or classification, of criteria for this sort of real, and of natural law. And the solution of one of these would probably mean the solution of all. Nothing could *force* a redefinition of "spirit" or of "matter." A sufficiently fundamental relation to human bent or to human interests would guarantee continuance unaltered even in the face of unintelligible and baffling experience. And no equipment of categories and concepts which the mind is likely to achieve will enable us to understand experience completely and in every respect. In such problems, the mind finds itself uncompelled save by its own purposes and needs. What is fixed datum and must be conformed to, is only that welter of the given in which not even the distinction of real and unreal is yet made. The rest is completely and exclusively our problem of interpretation. I *may* categorize experience as I will; but what categorial distinctions will best serve my interests and objectify my own intelligence? What the mixed and troubled experience will be—that is beyond me. But what I shall do with it—that is my own question, when the character of experience is before me. I am coerced only by my own need to understand.

It would indeed be inappropriate to characterize as a priori a law which we are prepared to alter in the light of further experience even though in an isolated case we should discard as non-veridical any experience which failed to conform. But the crux of the matter lies in this; beyond such principles as those of logic and pure mathematics whose permanent stability seems attested, there must be further and more particular criteria of the real prior to any investigation of nature. Such definitions, fundamental principles and criteria the mind itself must supply before experience can even begin to be intelligible. These represent more or less deep-lying attitudes, which the human mind has taken in the light of its total experience up to date. But a newer and wider experience may bring about some alteration of these attitudes even though by themselves they dictate nothing as to the content of experience, and no experience can conceivably prove them invalid.

It is the a priori element in knowledge which is thus pragmatic, not the empirical. The pragmatists generally have neglected to make the separation of concept and immediacy, with the result that they seem to put all truth at once at the mercy of experience and within the power of human decision or in a relation of dependence upon the human mind. But this would be an attempt to have it both ways. The sense in which facts are brute and given cannot be the sense in which the truth about them is made by mind or alterable to human needs. To be sure, this a priori element in knowledge runs very deep; it is present whenever there is classification, interpretation, or the distinction of real from unreal—which means that it is present in all knowledge. So I suppose it must be admitted, in the last analysis, that there can be no more fundamental ground than the pragmatic for a truth of any sort. Nothing—not even direct perception —can force the abandonment of an interpretive attitude, nor indeed *should* move us to such abandonment (since illusion or mistake is always possible) except some demand or purpose of the mind itself. But certain important ends, such as intellectual consistency and economy, completeness of comprehension, and simplicity of interpretation, occupy a place so much higher, for the long-run satisfaction of our needs in general, that they rightfully take precedence over any purpose which is merely personal or transitory. In the popular mind especially, pragmatism too often seems to connote the validity of rather superficial and capricious attitudes—for instance, the justification of belief from no deeper ground than personal desire. It is this insufficient regard for intellectual integrity, this tendency to trench upon high-plane purposes from low-plane motives which marks the kind of "pragmatism" which is to be eschewed. We must all be pragmatists, but pragmatists in the end, not in the beginning.

In another respect also, there is a connotation of "pragmatism" which more or less prevails, which is inapplicable to the theory here presented. Concepts and principles of interpretation are subject to historical alteration and in terms of them there may be "new truth." But the situation in which this happens needs analysis. It does not mean the possibility of new truth in any sense in which new truth can genuinely contradict old truth. This may not at first be clear. New ranges of experience such as those due to the invention of the telescope and miscroscope have actually led to alteration of our categories in historic time. The same thing may happen through more penetrating or adequate analysis of old types of experience —witness Virchow's redefinition of disease. What was previously regarded as real—*e. g.,* disease entities—may come to be looked upon as unreal, and what was previously taken to be unreal—*e. g.,* curved space—may be admitted to reality. But when this happens *the truth remains unaltered and new truth and old truth do not contradict.* Categories and concepts do not literally change; they are simply given up and replaced by new ones. When disease entities give place to mere adjectival states of the organism induced by changed conditions such as bacteria, the old description of the phenomena of disease does not become false in any sense in which it was not always false. All objects are abstractions of one sort or another; a disease entity is found to be a relatively poor kind of abstraction for the understanding and control of the phenomena in question. But in terms of this abstraction any interpretation of experience which ever was correctly made will still remain true. Any contradiction between the old truth and the new is *verbal only,* because the old word "disease" has a new meaning. The old word is retained but the old concept is discarded as a poor intellectual instrument and replaced by a better one. Categories and precise concepts are logical structures, Platonic ideas; the implications of them are eternal and the empirical truth about anything given, expressed in terms of them, is likewise through all time unalterable.

In the typical case in which old methods of interpretation are discarded in favor of new ones, it requires new empirical data, which offer some difficulty of interpretation in the old terms, to bring about the change. Any set of basic concepts has vested interests in the whole body of truth expressed in terms of them, and the social practices based upon them. The advantage of the change must be considerable and fairly clear in order to overcome human inertia and the prestige of old habits of thought. Such new and recalcitrant data, which bring about the change, complicate the problem of comparing the "new truth" with the old. The factors which need to be considered are: (1) the two sets of concepts, old and new, (2) the expanding bounds of experience in which what is novel has come to light, (3) the conditions of the application of the concepts to this new body of total relevant experience.

In the case of the Copernican revolution, for example, it was the invention of the telescope and the increasing accuracy of observation which mainly provided the impetus to reinterpretation. But these new data were decisive only in the pragmatic sense. Those who argued the issue supposed that they were discussing a question of empirical fact. But since there is no absolute motion, the question what moves and what is motionless in the heavens is one which cannot be settled by experience alone. The fixed stars prove to be a highly convenient frame of reference, resulting in relatively simple generalizations for the celestial motions, and enabling celestial and sublunary phenomena to be reduced to the same equations, while almost insurmountable complexity and difficulty attend the choice of axes through the earth. Theoretically, however, if any system of motions is describable with respect to one set of axes, it is also describable in terms of any other set which moves with reference to the first according to any general rule. Let us imagine for a moment that this theoretically possible description of astronomical and physical phenomena in terms of a motionless earth had been worked out for all the data now at hand. In terms of which set of concepts, old or new, should we have the truth? Obviously in both. The one would be comprehension and simple truth; the other so complex as to be almost or quite unworkable. But they would no more contradict each other than a measurement in pounds and feet contradicts one in grams and meters.

This situation is not altered by any thought that newly discovered fact may play another than the pragmatic rôle and be decisive of truth in a deeper sense. Nobody has ever supposed that what were only hypotheses or empirical generalization of a high degree of probability were incapable of being disproven by new facts. To the extent that newly discovered empirical evidence may render old principles theoretically impossible, the old truth never was anything but hypothesis and is now proved flatly false. It is not, I hope, the point of the pragmatic theory of knowledge to reduce all truth thus to hypothesis. That would be nothing but a cheerful form of skepticism.

Rather the point of the pragmatic theory is, I take it, the responsiveness of truth to human bent or need, and the fact that in some sense it is made by mind. From the point of view here presented, this is valid, because the interpretation of experience must always be in terms of categories and concepts which the mind itself determines. There may be alternative conceptual systems, giving rise to alternative descriptions of experience, which are equally objective and equally valid, if there be not some purely logical defect in these categorial conceptions. When this is so, choice will be determined, consciously or unconsciously, on pragmatic grounds. New facts may cause a shifting of such grounds. When historically such change of interpretation takes place we shall genuinely have new truth, whose newness represents the creative power of human thought and the ruling consideration of human purpose.

The separation of the factors, however, reveals the fact that the pragmatic element in knowledge concerns the choice in application of conceptual modes of interpretation. On the one side, we have the abstract concepts themselves, with their purely logical implications. The truth about these is absolute, in the fashion in which pure mathematics offers the typical illustration. Such purely abstract a priori truth answers only to the criteria of consistency and adequacy. It is absolute and eternal. On the other side, there is the absolute brute-fact of given experience. Though in one sense ineffable, yet the given is its own fashion determinate; once the categorial system, in terms of which it is to be interpreted, is fixed, and concepts have been assigned a denotation in terms of sensation and imagery, it is this given experience which determines the truths of nature. It is between these two, in the choice of conceptual system for application and in the assigning of sensuous denotation to the abstract concept, that there is a pragmatic element in truth and knowledge. In this middle ground of trial and error, of expanding experience and the continual shift and modification of conception in our effort to cope with it, the drama of human interpretation and the control of nature is forever being played. That the issues here are pragmatic; that they do not touch that truth which still is absolute and eternal—this is the only thing that would save those who appreciate the continually changing character of this spectacle from skepticism.

MORRIS
RAPHAEL COHEN

(1880-1947)

Morris Cohen was born in Russia in 1880 and died in New York in 1947. He attended the City College of New York, received his doctorate from Harvard, and returned to City College where he taught until his retirement. His fame as a teacher of philosophy was very great, and his irony, his unusual erudition, and his redoubtable dialectical skills made him in his time one of the most respected American philosophers in the United States and abroad. He was a student of law and history as well as of the natural sciences, and like the other major figures of the "golden age" he used philosophy to comment on primary subject-matters outside philosophy itself. His contributions to the philosophy of law are particularly noteworthy.

It is not easy to place Cohen in any contemporary philosophical movement. With the pragmatists he stressed the active and constructive role of ideas, but he leaned towards realism in his conception of the nature of truth. His moral outlook was similar to that of Santayana in The Life of Reason—*a book which he much admired—but he was an active and unembarrassed liberal. He was first and foremost, probably, simply a believer in the methods of careful logical analysis both as an antidote to illusion and obscurantism and as a first step toward the construction of a positive philosophy. In this respect, Cohen, though he did not believe that the nature of the universe could be discovered without an appeal to experience, is perhaps the most typical representative in American philosophy of the classic tradition of intellectual rationalism.*

The first of the selections from Cohen's work has been taken from Reason and Nature *(1931). The second selection is one of Cohen's most important essays in legal philosophy and is a rather typical example of his philosophical method. It was published first in the* Cornell Law Review *(1927) and subsequently reprinted in Cohen's* Law and the Social Order *(1933).*

Reason and Nature

PREFACE

THE DISTINCTIVE INTELLECTUAL TRAITS OF WESTERN CIVILIZATION, OR of what is sometimes called the modern mind, have been largely moulded by the appeal to nature against conventional taboos and by the appeal to reason against arbitrary authority. That nature and reason, like warmth and light, may be intimately joined was made evident in the Hellenic ideal of science as a free inquiry into nature and of ethics as concerned with a rational plan for attaining the natural goods of life. Unfortunately for the career of liberal civilization, however, various circumstances have brought about a mutual hostility between these two appeals to what are popularly called the heart and the mind. The appeal to nature is frequently a form of sentimental irrationalism, and the appeal to reason is often a call to suppress nature in the interest of conventional supernaturalism. To understand fully the grounds, causes, and effects of this conflict would involve a thorough survey of contemporary civilization and carry us far into the complexity of the human mind. One of the elements, however, in such a survey is a right understanding of the general bearing or meaning of scientific method, i.e., of the principles of procedure according to which scientific results are obtained and according to which these results are being constantly revised. In developed natural science, reason and nature are happily united.

Such a study of the principles of science I began some twenty years ago. Untoward circumstances have prevented the continuous toil necessary for such a task. Different parts of this work have been written at widely different times and in somewhat different keys. But the favourable reception accorded to those portions of it which have been published from time to time, and the insistence of friends whose judgment compels respect, induce me somewhat reluctantly to publish the present essay rather than wait any longer for the completion of a more satisfactory systematic treatise. I am induced to do this not only by a sense of the inherent importance of the issues I have faced but also by my conviction that the present state of philosophy is especially in need of the method of approach here represented.

There are many indications of a widespread dissatisfaction with the arid state of present-day technical philosophy. Seldom before has the general craving for philosophic light seemed so vast and the offerings of professed philosophers so scant and unsubstantial. Some there are who attribute this poverty to the preoccupation of professional philosophers with the technical problems of epistemology, e.g. how the mind can know a supposedly external world. It has been justly urged that this baffling and strangely fascinating problem has in fact never thrown much light on the nature of any of the great objects of our vital interests, though subjectivist solutions of it have often been used to support traditional views and evaluations. We may grant this without denying that the concentration on the technical problems of epistemology arose out of a well-justified dissatisfaction with the older romantic fashion according to which every philosopher was expected to spin a new view of the universe out of his inner consciousness, or else confirm in a new and strange manner the old familiar views. The critical question, "How do we know?" is a much-needed challenge to those who complacently claim to have solved all the enigmas of existence. Yet the main motive for epistemology is professional. As teachers of philosophy see their colleagues gaining prestige through contributions in special technical fields, they are tempted to take the position: "We too are specialists. We too have a definite technical field of our own, to wit: the nature of knowledge as such." But alas! The ideal of technical competency is not without its snares. A good deal of the unsubstantiality of later scholasticism was no doubt due to the fact that having elaborated a very subtle technical vocabulary, men felt themselves to be distinguished scholars by the mere mastery of such a vocabulary. The change from Latin to the vernacular revealed this emptiness and compelled a greater attention to substantial content. But this gain is now largely frittered away in philosophy and in the related fields of psychology and sociology, in which exercises in technical vocabulary frequently hide the paucity of substantial insight.

Meanwhile, the ancient need of a more or less integrated view of the general panorama of life and existence has shown itself to be too deep to be permanently neglected. New voices have arisen urging philosophy to become again constructive and to cease to lose itself in historical, philologic, and other technical minutiae. There can be little doubt that the philosophic writers of recent days who have most stirred men's imaginations and found the greatest popular response have been of this character, witness James, Bergson, Croce, and Spengler.

Can those who have a sober knowledge of the many failures of previous romantically "constructive" philosophies entertain a naïve and unquestioning hope in these new efforts? This is especially difficult for those who know something about physical science and who cannot agree to banish its solid theoretic achievements as merely practical devices devoid of philosophic value. Doubtless philosophy will long continue to represent interests wider than those of rigidly demonstrative science. Philosophy is primarily a vision and all great philosophers have something in common with the poets and prophets. But while vision, intuition, or wisdom is the substance of any philosophy that is worth while, serious philosophy must also be something more than a poetic image or prophecy. It must, like science, be also vitally concerned with reasoned or logically demonstrable truth. Granted that great truths begin as poetic or prophetic insights, it still remains true that the views of poets and prophets have in fact often proved narrowly one-sided, conflicting, incoherent, and illusory. To introduce order and consistency into our vision, to remove pleasing but illusory plausibilities by contrasting various views with their possible alternatives, and to judge critically all pretended proofs in the light of the most rigorously logical rules of evidence, is the indispensable task of any serious philosophy. The seed which ripens into vision may be a gift of the gods but the labour of cultivating it so that it may bear nourishing fruit is the indispensable function of arduous scientific technique.

If these considerations are in any way sound, philosophy can hope to be genuinely fruitful only by being more scientifically critical or cautious than the recent romantic efforts, and at the same time more daring and substantial than those miscroscopic philosophies which lose sight of the macrocosm. This can be brought about only by intimately confronting the great classical views of the world at the heart of the great humanistic tradition with the painfully critical methods by which the natural sciences have built up their great cosmic vistas.

In turning to the sciences I emphasize their method rather than their results. For, in an age of scientific expansion, not only are the methods the more permanent features of the sciences, but the supposed results are often merely popularized conventions, utterly misleading to all those who do not know the processes by which they are obtained. The life of science is in exploration and in the weighing of evidence. Dead or detached results lend themselves to the mythology of popular science, and ignorance of method leads to the view of science as a new set of dogmas to be accepted on the authority of a new set of priests called scientists. It is doubtless impossible for any single individual to be a trained investigator in all the different fields upon which philosophy touches. It may also be urged that too great devotion to rigorous scientific evidence may narrow our sympathies and prevent us from dealing justly with those vital interests which science has not yet been able to organize. But the difficulty and the dangers of our task cannot prevent it from being indispensable in any case. All that is absolutely worth while has something of the unattainable about it. No faith can live today in anything but a fool's paradise unless it ventures out into the high and open but biting air of critical reason as natural science does.

Greater regard for the rational methods of natural science must be joined with a more serious concern with the great historic traditions in philosophy. Sound logic and the history of science unite to show that an adequately critical appreciation of the reported facts in any realm depends on a knowledge of the hitherto prevailing views which condition what we shall regard as facts.

Moreover to take adequate cognizance of those views which have in fact proved influential is a powerful protection against the temptation to triumphantly exploit one's own views in a narrowly partial and one-sided manner. The notion that we can dismiss the views of all previous thinkers surely leaves no basis for the hope that our own work will prove of any value to others.

The philosopher whose primary interest is to attain as much truth as possible must put aside as a snare the effort at originality. Indeed, it seems to me that the modern penchant for novelty in philosophy is symptomatic of restlessness or low intellectual vitality. At the same time I should not make this book public if I did not hope that thoughtful readers will find its ideas timely, worthy of consideration, and capable of extension. Particular attention is directed to the principle of polarity, the principle that opposite categories like identity and difference, rest and motion, individuality and universality, etc., must always be kept together though never identified. Whatever the inadequacies of my formulation and application of this principle, I am sure that by a more persistent use of it many of the traditional controversies of philosophy can be eliminated, or at least shown to be inadequately stated. The principle of polarity calls attention to the fact that the traditional dilemmas, on which people have for a long time taken opposite stands, generally rest on difficulties rather than real contradictions, and that positive gains in philosophy can be made not by simply trying to prove that one side or the other is the truth, but by trying to get at the difficulty and determining in what respect and to what extent each side is justified. This may deprive our results of sweep and popular glamour, but will achieve the more permanent satisfaction of truth.

While speculations about the future of civilization and philosophy must in the nature of the case be very uncertain, all evidence seems to indicate that in the rhythmic alternation of periods of expansion and consolidation which characterize the life of civilization, different sets of categories are emphasized. Thus the mediaeval mind was dominated by the demand for order in our thought as well as in the world at large. Faced with the centrifugal tendencies due to the pressure of population against the bounds of a fixed land economy, and faced with the doubts as to the traditional theology that resulted from contact with Saracen civilization, the mediaeval mind found in the scholastic method of drawing distinctions a way of introducing order and reconciling conflicting views. It did so by trying to assign to everything its just realm. This method of scholasticism, originated by Abelard in his *Sic et Non,* independently embodied in Gratian's great work on Canon Law, and perfected by St. Thomas in his Summa, rests ultimately on the axiom of Aristotelian logic that opposites cannot be identical, illustrated in Kipling's maxim, "East is East and West is West." The wise or good man, on this view, will draw and respect the proper boundaries between them.

Modern thought, i.e. the thought since the middle of the fifteenth century, has been operating in what has in the main been an expanding economy. The opening of new lands and new methods of production have made the idea of movement or growth the dominant one in the internal as well as in the external world. But the idea of change involves some continuity between opposites. The first modern man who saw this both in mathematics and philosophy was the great Cardinal Cusa, whose doctrine of the coincidence of opposites marks the beginning of modern kinetic views of the world which terminate in nineteenth century Hegelianism and evolutionism. Modern thought emphasizes mobility and the principle that everything changes to something else and must indeed become something other than it was in order to exhibit its true character. The nature of things unfolds itself in time.

There are, however, signs that this period of expansion is about to close. Despite the steady progress of science, Europe seems already to have reached the maximum population that it can support, and the opportunities of exploiting other parts of the world by migration or conquest seem steadily decreasing. Within measurable time, then, the whole earth will become fully explored and the limits of its food and other resources may be definitely attained. The dominant values of life must then become somewhat similar to those of mediaeval and Chinese society—greater stress on order than on expansion. Indeed, already the popular demand is for the organization of knowledge rather than for its expansion. But whatever the future may bring, it is clear that any attempt to see the limitation of the characteristically modern emphasis on the "dynamic," the "evolutionary," and the "progressive" must pay greater attention to the principle of polarity as the union of the values of order and stability with the values of change and progress. Because of these considerations I am confident that no matter how inadequate the results of the studies here published, no just criticism, not even the withering refutation of time, will prove the effort itself to be in the wrong direction.

To readers who have a predilection for conventional labels, I offer the following:

I am a rationalist in believing that reason is a genuine and significant phase of nature; but I am an irrationalist in insisting that nature contains more than reason. I am a mystic in holding that all words point to a realm of being deeper and wider than the words themselves. But I reject as

vicious obscurantism all efforts to describe the indescribable. I reject
the euthanasia or suicide of thought involved in all monisms which identify
the whole totality of things with matter, mind, or any other element in it.
But I also reject the common dualism which conceives *the* mind and *the*
external world as confronting each other like two mutually exclusive
spatial bodies. I believe in the Aristotelian distinction between matter and
form. But I am willing to be called a materialist if that means one who
disbelieves in disembodied spirits; and I should refer to spiritists who localize disembodied spirits in space as crypto-materialists. However, I should
also call myself an idealist, not in the perverse modern sense which applies that term to nominalists like Berkeley who reject real ideas, but in
the Platonic sense according to which ideas, ideals, or abstract universals
are the conditions of real existence, and not mere fictions of the human
mind.

To those who labour under the necessity of passing judgment on this
book in terms of current values, I suggest the following:

The author seems out of touch with everything modern and useful, and
yet makes no whole-hearted plea for the old. He believes in chance and
spontaneity in physics and law and mechanism in life. He has no respect
for *experience, induction, the dynamic, evolution, progress, behaviourism*
and *psychoanalysis,* and does not line up with either the orthodox or
revolutionary party in politics, morals, or religion, though he writes on
these themes. He offers no practical message to the man engaged in the
affairs of life, and seems to be satisfied with purely contemplative surveys
of existence.

But to the thoughtful reader I can offer as a preliminary only the expression of my profound faith in philosophy itself. The task of philosophy
is too complicated to be solved by simple magical formulae. The age
of panaceas, nostrums, and philosopher's stones belongs to the adolescence
of philosophy. In its maturer period, it must, like science and rational industry, depend upon more modest and workmanlike efforts, though it can
never abandon the search for comprehensive vision. We cannot by reasoning achieve absolute certainties as to matters of fact. But we may clarify
our minds as to the rational strength of the evidence for our convictions.
We shall never overcome the infinite sea of ignorance, and we should remember that if ignorance were bliss, this would be a much happier world
than it is. Let not philosophy, therefore, deal in false comforts or gratify
those who crave from it confirmation of established prejudices. It has a
far higher function,—to give men strength to envisage the truth. Vision is
itself a good greater than the perpetual motion without any definite direction which modernists regard as the blessed life. Cosmic vision ennobles
the pathetic futility of our daily crucifixions. But all philosophy is blasphemous if it denies to the gods a sense of humour or the gift of laughter.

One who ranges over as wide a field as that involved in the present
volume cannot hope to escape detectable errors. I should, however, add

that where my views differ from those of well-known authorities it is not always because of my ignorance as to what these authorities maintain. I have taken pains to familiarize myself directly with the views of the great classical philosophers and with the scientific researches on which my generalizations as to scientific methods are based, but I have not tried to escape responsibility for my own judgment.

I have not been at all impressed by the religious and philosophic lessons drawn from science by men like Millikan, Eddington, Coulter, A. H. Compton, E. G. Conklin, and the like. I respect, as every one must, the great achievements of these distinguished workers in their special fields. But scientists do not always carry scientific method into their views of manners, morals, or politics, of justice between nations or social classes, of the reliability of mediums, etc. Neither are they scientific when they make their professional work a springboard from which to jump off into amateurish speculative flights in the fields of religion and philosophy.

I have in the substance and manner of this book tried to reach thoughtful readers irrespective of their previous philosophic studies and have therefore avoided technical terms as far as was consistent with substantial accuracy. Indeed I have used some technical terms of logic in their popular sense, trusting the context to make my meaning clear. It is difficult to know how much of the factual content of science to take for granted. No two readers are exactly alike in this respect, but I have addressed myself to the generally educated public that is not afraid of close and sustained reflection. Some of the chapters, notably the third of Book I, require more effort in that direction than others. But the reader may skip some chapters or change the order of reading them. Though they are all parts of an integral thesis, they were written at different times and have a certain relative independence of each other.

RATIONALISM, NATURALISM AND SUPERNATURALISM

It is frequently asserted that the principle of scientific method cannot rule out in advance the possibility of any fact, no matter how strange or miraculous. This is true to the extent that science as a method of extending our knowledge must not let accepted views prevent us from discovering new facts that may seem to contradict our previous views. Actually, however, certain types of explanation cannot be admitted within the body of scientific knowledge. Any attempt, for instance, to explain physical phenomenon as directly due to Providence or disembodied spirits, is incompatible with the principle of rational determinism. For the nature of these entities is not sufficiently determinate to enable us to deduce definite experimental consequences from them. The Will of Providence, for instance, will explain everything whether it happens one way or another. Hence, no experiment can possibly overthrow it. An hypothesis, however, which we cannot possibly refute cannot possibly be experimentally verified.

In thus ruling out ghostly, magical, and other supernatural influences, it would seem that scientific method impoverishes our view of the world. It is well, however, to remember that a world where no possibility is excluded is a world of chaos, about which no definite assertion can be made. Any world containing some order necessarily involves the elimination of certain abstract or ungrounded possibilities such as fill the minds of the insane.

From this point of view, what may be called the postulate of scientific materialism, viz. that all natural phenomena depend on material conditions, is not merely a well-supported generalization but the requirement of an orderly world, of a cosmos that is not a chaotic phantasmagoria.

As materialism has served as a sort of "bogey-man" to scare immature metaphysicians, it is well to make more explicit its relation to rational scientific method. If materialism means the denial of emotions, imaginings, thoughts, and other mental happenings, it is clearly not something worthy of serious consideration. It is contrary to facts of experience and clearly self-refuting. But this in no way disposes of the materialism of men like Democritus, Lucretius, Hobbes, or Spinoza, or of the assumption that every natural event must have a bodily or material basis.

The truth of the latter proposition is obscured by the popular confused concept of mental efficiency. Even technical discussion of the relation of mind and body is often vitiated by an inadequate analysis of the principle of rational determinism and a consequent misapprehension of the force of principles such as the conservation of energy. If, as it was contended before, scientific causality applies only to certain abstract aspects of entities, there is no reason why entities that determine each other in one way in a certain system may not be bound together in another way in another system. The presence of causal relation does not involve the denial of teleologic relations, while the assertion of the latter presupposes the former.

The principle of conservation of energy, for instance, leaves a wide realm of indetermination that other relations can make determinate. For the assertion that amidst all the transformations of a system the total amount of energy remains constant, is an assertion that clearly does not determine the character of the transformations other than in the one trait explicitly mentioned. The second law of thermodynamics does endeavour to indicate a general direction of phenomena, viz. towards a maximum of entropy. But this is largely problematic in certain regions, and in any case it often leaves room for all sorts of indetermination. Whether energy shall remain potential or be transformed into energy of motion is not completely determined by either principle, since either principle remains fulfilled whether the transformation takes place or not. Teleologic determinations are therefore not ruled out by the laws of energy.

Now the ordinary conception of mental efficiency combines elements of teleologic with strictly causal determination. We achieve certain purposes by taking advantage of natural mechanism. But this is in no way inconsistent with the proposition that every material change is correlated with a previous material condition in accordance with certain laws. What is inconsistent with scientific procedure is the argument that the existence of a mental motive makes the coexistence of a physical cause unnecessary.

Besides the objection from the existence of mental efficiency there is another line of arguments against materialism, viz. that matter is purely passive and cannot explain the activity of the world. Now it is doubtless true that the close connection between the notion of matter and that of mass or inertia, leads to the view that matter by itself cannot explain the active processes of nature, and this leads to the introduction of forces which are the ghosts of spirits or of the volitions often connected with our own bodily movements. This argument, however, is based on a logical fallacy, taking the nature of matter to consist solely in its exclusive and passive aspect. But there is no valid reason against supposing that a purely material system without external influence can contain motion within it; and there is no conclusive argument against the view that under certain conditions material systems such as those which constitute the human body are capable of organic processes, feeling, etc.

The one serious objection to materialism from the point of view of the requisites of scientific method comes into play when materialism allies itself with sensationalistic empiricism and belittles the importance of relations and logical connection between things. The identification of empiricism with the scientific attitude is just a bit of natural complacency. The excessive worship of facts too often hides a disinclination to enter into a genuine inquiry as to whether they are so. A rationalism that is naturalistic must, of course, agree with empiricism in maintaining the factual or immediate aspect of existence. But scientific rationalism is incompatible with the complacent assumption that in sensations or in self-sufficient "facts" we have the only primary existences.

We do not have pure particulars any more than pure universals, to begin with. We begin with vague complexes which raise difficulties when we wish to give a rational or coherent account of them. It is scientific procedure itself which enables us to pass from vague impressions to definite propositions. Definite individuals are, therefore, the goals or limits rather than the data of scientific method. When we attain knowledge of particulars we see that their nature depends upon the universal connections which make them what they are.

To realize that the substance or nature of the individual consists of universals we must get rid of the Lockian confusion between matter and substance, and return to the Aristotelian distinction of ὕλη and ὀυσία. Ὕλη or matter is a relative concept. Bricks are ὕλη for a building but are formed substances for one who makes them out of clay. Absolute primary ὕλη or matter is a limiting concept, not a starting point. The intelligible substance of things, however, is not pure formlessness or empty possibility, but the actual universals which, though arrived at as a result of inquiry, are conditions of what exists. Indeed, inquiry like all other forms of human effort must begin with the partial and can attain the whole or universal—if at all—only by seeing how the parts are conditioned.

The view that identifies the genuine substance of things with those relations or structures which are the objects of rational science is so opposed to the nominalistic tendency of our time, that a host of objections to it is naturally to be expected.

The most serious objection is one that cannot be answered—it is the habit which associates substance with reality and reality with the sensuously or psychologically vivid. But, however decisive the appeal to the subjectively vivid may be in practice, it is after all no evidence as to the objective constitution of the natural world.* More specific objections to our identification of the order of scientific ideas with the intrinsic order of things are the following: (a) Rational scientific method is devised for practical purposes only. Its fictional devices cannot give us truth. (b) The abstractions which science employs have no correspondence with or real existence in the natural world. (c) Reasoning supplies us only ground for belief not ground for existence.

(A) FICTIONALISM

Philosophers as diverse as Bradley, Mach, and Bergson rely heavily on the so-called fictions of science, e.g. corpuscles of light, the ether, etc., which have proved useful, though not literally true. With regard to this we may observe that many of these so-called fictions, e.g. atoms, have turned out to be very much like other empirical entities. We count them, we weigh them and study their behaviour—philosophers to the contrary notwithstanding. I have elsewhere tried to show that contrary to the contention of Vaihinger, none of the so-called fictions of science involve any contradictions.* If they did so, they could not be useful, since no consistent inferences could be drawn from them. Even when not completely true, they are analogies which offer useful suggestions just to the extent that they are true. To the extent that they fail they are subject to the process of correction.

(B) CONCEPTUALISM

The form of reasoning to which science always seeks to attain is mathematics. But do the steps of a mathematical process correspond to anything in the objective world—even when the initial premises and final

* "If reality," argues Bradley, "consists in actual sequence of sensuous phenomena then our reasonings are all false because none of them are sensuous." To which we reply that if reality consists of sensuous material arranged in certain form or order then all the reasoning which is faithful to that form or order is true.
* See "The Logic of Fictions," *Journal of Philosophy*, Vol. XX (1923), p. 477.

conclusions do? Mathematical physicists like Duhem and Mach categorically deny this. What have our equations, differentiations, and integrations to do with natural objects? If the result of a mathematical calculation gives us a true account of objective nature, may not the mathematical process correspond to the sharpening of tools or to the mixing of colours, processes which surely do not correspond to the features which the artist wishes to represent? We must not however allow analogies to lead us away from the facts. Mathematical propositions do relate to the properties of all possible objects. Valid mathematical reasoning therefore deals with processes to which the objects before us are as subject as any others. It is often difficult to recognize these universal aspects in the particular, just as it may be difficult to recognize that an enemy is also a human being, yet truth requires the recognition of just such obvious general or universal aspects. Mathematical reasoning may indeed be too general for a specific situation (if we lack the proper data) but if true it always has objective meaning.

(C) IRRATIONALISM

Bradley has argued that while reasoning determines the ground of our belief, it does not even pretend to determine the ground of existence. In our reasoning, he claims, some datum suffers alteration. Why assume that reality transforms itself in unison? This objection is largely based on the false suggestion of the word *transformation*. Logical reasoning does not produce any temporal change in the object reasoned about. The latter remains the same when we make progress in the recognition of its nature. But the ground of a true belief differs after all from the ground of a false belief precisely in this—that the former *is* connected (though not directly identical) with the ground of existence. For this purpose the most favourable example, for Bradley's objection, would be the case where I conclude that my idea of a given object is false. But even here the ground of existence and the ground of true belief are not independent. I begin in fact with an hypothesis as to the nature of the object. I consider what consequences it (with other things) has if it is true. I find the consequences are impossible because in conflict with actual existence, and I conclude that my original hypothesis is false. If my reasoning is valid it is because it has come into contact with actual facts and the transformations of the entities reasoned about do correspond to reality.

We conclude, then, that if the abstract is unreal, reality is of little moment. For what that is humanly interesting is not abstract? Mr. Bradley has gone through the whole gamut from qualities, relations, and things to our precious selves, and shown with a logic that is more readily ignored than refuted, that all these things are but abstract or detached parts of the absolute totality. But the conclusion that everything short of the absolute totality is appearance and not reality is a logical consequence of an arbitrary view of reality, which identifies it with purely immediate feeling or experience. But though the craving of the flesh for strong sensations and feelings is an important element of life, it is certainly not conclusive even as to the guidance of life. Even the hedonistic ideal cannot be realized except by organizing life on the basis of an intellectual recognition of our possibilities and the rational evaluation of the different factors which determine our happiness.

The contention that abstractions or logical relations form the very substance of things does not, according to the foregoing account, involve panlogism. Rationality does not exhaust existence. The relational form or pattern points to a non-rational or alogical element without which the former has no genuine meaning. For to deny the existence of any irrational elements is to make rationality itself a brute, contingent, alogical fact. The fact that we can rationally use terms like *irrational, alogical, inexpressible,* and the like has given rise to interesting paradoxes. These paradoxes, however, disappear if we recognize that a word may point to something which is not a word at all, and though the pointing is rationalized fact the thing pointed to may not be so. Rational distinctions and relations and all expression hold in the field of being which is thus presupposed but never fully described—just as the various lines on a blackboard may indicate the various objects represented on it but do not fully represent the blackboard itself which conditions them. If this doctrine that our universe thus contains something fundamental to which we may point but which we cannot fully describe be called mysticism, then mysticism is essential to all intellectual sanity. Language ceases to be significant if it cannot indicate something beyond language. But if we use the word *mysticism* to denote this faith in a universe that has ineffable and alogical elements, we cannot too sharply distinguish it from obscurantism. For the former denies our power to know the whole of reality, while the latter holds reality to be definitely revealed to us by non-rational processes. Rationalism does not deny that clear thoughts may begin as vague or obscure premonitions. But the essential difference between rationalism and obscurantism depends upon whether our guesses or obscure visions do or do not submit to the processes of critical examination and logical clarification. Our reason may be a pitiful candle light in the dark and boundless seas of being. But we have nothing better and woe to those who wilfully try to put it out.

EPILOGUE: IN DISPRAISE OF LIFE, EXPERIENCE, AND REALITY

In speaking of the new philosophic movement which began with the present century, William James remarked: "It lacks logical rigour, but it has the tang of life." It is strikingly significant of the temper of our age that this was intended and has generally been taken as praise of the new philosophy. To any of the classical philosophers, to whom not life, but the good life was the object of rational effort, James's dictum would have sounded as a condemnation. For life devoid of logic is confused, unenlightened, and often brutish. Indeed the new philosophy itself maintains that it is precisely because unreflective life is so unsatisfactory that it gives rise to logic. Why then should the word *life* itself be a term of praise except to those who prefer the primitive and dislike intellectual effort?

I can imagine that a classical philosopher living long enough amongst us to penetrate some of our bewildering ways might conclude that our worship of mere life, rather than the good or rational life, reflects the temper of an acquisitive society, feverishly intent on mere accumulation, and mortally afraid to stop to discriminate between what is worth while and what is not. The same preference for terms of promiscuous all-inclusiveness, rather than for those that involve the discrimination essential to philosophic clarity, shows itself also in the use of the terms *experience* and *reality*. It is of course true that surface clarity can readily be obtained by ignoring fundamental difficulties, and that we cannot dispense with terms indicating the unlimited immensities of which our little formulated systems are but infinitesimal selections. But if the world contains many things and therefore distinctions between them, ignoring these distinctions is not the same as profundity. The honorific use of non-discriminating terms can only serve to darken counsel. That this has actually been the case in ethics and in theories of knowledge, in religion and in art, is the burden of this brief epilogue.

That the continuance of mere physical life is an absolute moral good seems to be axiomatic in current ethics. It serves as a basis for the unqualified moral condemnation of all forms of suicide and euthanasia. Now I do not wish to question the biologic proposition that there are forces which make the organism continue to function after we have lost all specifically human goods, such as honour and reason. What I do wish to point out is that this setting up of mere life as an absolute moral good, apart from all its social conditions, is inconsistent with the moral approval of the hero or the martyr who throws away life for the sake of honour or conscience. It would be pathetically absurd to praise the abandoning of life by John Huss or Giordano Bruno on the ground that it increased or prolonged the total amount of life. Indiscriminate increase of population beyond any definite limit is of very doubtful moral value—despite the arguments of those who oppose all forms of birth control. We must not lose sight of the fact that life always carries with it not only the seeds of disease and inevitable death, but also the roots of all that is vicious and hideous in human conduct. We cannot, therefore, dispense with the classical problem of defining the good and discriminating it from the evil of life—a difficult and baffling problem, to be sure; but those who find it profitless are under no obligation to pursue moral philosophy.

The confusion of moral theory by the eulogistic use of the word *life* can

be readily seen in the Nietzschean ethics—all the more instructive
because Nietzsche himself starts from the classical perception of the inadequacy of ordinary utilitarianism in face of the moral values of heroism.
The good life involves the sacrifice of ease and comfort, the receiving as
well as the giving of hard blows. But just because Nietzsche is impatient of
definition he falls into the easy error of sharply opposing the pursuit of
life to the pursuit of knowledge—witness his essay on History. But the
pursuit of knowledge is itself a form of life. This fact cannot be obscured
be rhetorical contrasts between the life of the closet philosopher and the
open-air or what is euphemistically called *real* life. To the eye of philosophic reflection the scholar or persistent thinker shows as much life or
vitality as those who have to cover their naked restlessness by a gospel of
strenuous but aimless perpetual motion—in no particular direction. This
is not the occasion to sing the praises of the intellect and what it has
done to humanize life. We may grant that the distaste for arduous intellectual tasks is natural, blameless, and in some cases even providential.
But when such distaste sets itself up as a philosophy of life it is only
ridiculous.

This brings us to our second point, the vitalistic theory of knowledge
—or perhaps we should refer to it as the theory of a vitalistic intuition
superior to knowledge—I mean the widespread notion that by mere living
we get an insight superior to that of the intellect operative in mathematical and natural science. To prevent misunderstandings, let me say that I am
not referring here to genuine mysticism which asserts that all intellection
and language move in the mist of appearances and cannot reach the ineffable reality. Genuine mysticism always holds fast to the idea that the
substance of reality is altogether beyond the power of language, and hence
it does not use language to describe this reality. It holds that language can
at best only indicate its own shortcomings and thus point the way beyond
itself. When, however, as in the Bergsonian theory, the claim of the scientific intellect is set aside for an instinctive intuition, and when this is held
to provide a superior explanation of empirical phenomena like the formation of the eye of the scallop, it seems to me that philosophy is then not
far removed from glorified quackery where the philosopher's stone is expected to remove the effects of the evil eye or cure toothaches and other
empirical ailments. We may grant that biology as a natural science does
not carry us very far into the mystery of life. But it does not follow that
our ignorance can be cured in any other way. The fallibility of scientific
reasoning is best corrected only by definite experiments and the critical
reasoning of science itself. When men despair of solving theoretic problems and appeal to undefined words like *life* they show themselves devoid
of intellectual stamina. It is doubtless true that in the process of living our
ideas develop, mature, and receive a solid amplitude through an enriched
content. Time tests our judgments and eliminates clever, plausible sophis-

tries. But it is also true that the older a lamb grows the more sheepish he gets. Nothing seems so solidly established by anthropology and history as that men will not learn from what has actually happened to them unless they have developed the power of reflection. The idea that experience alone will teach everybody is a thin optimistic illusion.

The use of the word *experience* without any ascertainable meaning is perhaps the outstanding scandal of recent philosophy. In its original sense, which it still retains in ordinary, intelligible discourse, and from which we cannot altogether liberate ourselves in philosophy, experience denotes conscious feeling or something which happens to us personally. Thus I make my meaning clear when I say, "I did not experience any pain during an operation," or, "I have never experienced what it is to be struck by lightning." I may also speak of not having experienced the panic of 1872 or the other side of the moon. The absence of such experience need not, however, prevent me from knowing a good deal about the operation, the lightning, the panic of 1872, and the other side of the moon—more indeed than about many of my own experiences. For experience in this personal and ordinary sense is but an infinitesimal portion of what is going on in the world of time and space, and even a small part of the world of ordinary human affairs. To identify the substance of the world with the fact of our experience of some part of it is to set up an anthropocentric universe, compared to which the mediaeval one is sane and respectable. For the mediaeval one rebuked the silly and arrogant pretensions of humanity by setting against it the great glory of God.

The absurdity of identifying the whole realm of nature with our little human experience of it is obscured in two ways—to wit, (1) by confusing the nature of possible experience, and (2) by stretching the word *experience* until it *excludes* nothing and therefore includes no definite meaning.

That things known are all objects of a conceivable possible experience to some possible being more or less like us need not be denied. But the object of a possible experience is a matter of intellectual consideration, not the object of actual personal experience. If, on the other hand, we stretch the meaning of the word *experience* and make it include everything that we can think about, e.g. the state of the earth before the advent of life, then there remains no difference between an object considered and an object experienced, and the proposition that knowledge rests on experience ceases to have significance. It is vain to define words so as to deny the fact that we know many things to be beyond our experience. In general, the term *experience* either means something personal and therefore limited, or it becomes so promiscuously all-inclusive that it ceases to have any intelligible negative. Without an alternative term to denote what is not experience it cannot have any pragmatic meaning. With charateristic sensitiveness to the difficulties of his own account, Professor Dewey has realized something of this dilemma in which the use of the term *experience* involves him. He has tried to defend it by the analogy of the use of the terms *zero* and *infinity*. But zero and infinity indicate at least definite directions. They indicate which of two definite terms is to the left or right of the other in a series. The term *experience,* however, in Professor Dewey's thought is equally applicable to everything that is an object of consideration. I cannot therefore see that it serves any definite intellectual function beyond carrying the faint aroma of praise.

In general, when familiar words are stretched and put to new uses, confusion is bound to result. For the meaning we attach to words is based on habits which arbitrary resolutions cannot readily change, and we invariably drag the old meaning into the new context.

An instructive instance of the confusing use of the term *experience* is the current phrase *religious experience,* used by those who regard it as a substitute for rational theology. Here again, I have no quarrel with any one who claims to have had the beatific vision of God or a special revelation of the truths of religion. One who makes such a claim puts himself beyond argument except when he asks others to believe what he believes. Then the doubt which Tennyson applied to his own vision certainly becomes relevant. Nor is my quarrel with those who assume the truths of their religion on the authority of an historic church or revelation fortified by the necessary truths of reason. The current fashion which talks about religious experience distrusts the great streams of historic tradition as it does the claims of systematic theology—witness James's *Varieties of Religious Experience,* in which none of the great historic religions receives any attention. He thinks he can establish "piecemeal supernaturalism" by the methods of natural science and the rules of empirical evidence. An elementary consideration, however, of the logic of induction shows the impossibility of proving the existence of miraculous or supernatural interventions on the basis of the postulate of the uniformity of nature involved in induction. Indeed, the naturalist can well maintain that as instances of mystic experiences have their parallel in the effects of drugs, starvation, etc., the naturalistic explanation of them is the only one that is scientifically worth investigating. In any case, the spiritualistic hypothesis does not lend itself to the crucial test of affording us verifiable predictions. Not only a scientist but even a court of law would be derelict if it accepted as proved anything which rests on no better evidence than that offered by abnormal psychology for a finite, personal God and the immortality of the individual soul.

It is of course true that most people do not hold these beliefs as scientific hypotheses at all. Indeed, most people regard the cold, logical analysis of their religion with a horror like that which would be evoked by a funeral orator who proceeded to give a scientific examination of the character of the deceased. We come to mourn and praise our friend, not to hear him psychoanalyzed. But all this is irrelevant in moments of reflection or when our beliefs are challenged by the contrary beliefs of others. One may say: I hold these truths and the faith in them strengthens my life. But such assertions cannot keep out the lurking doubt that it is the psychologic attitude rather than the truth of what is assumed that produces the practical effects. The pragmatic glorification of belief contains the deep poison of scepticism as to what really exists, and this like a Nessus shirt will destroy any religious belief that puts it on. Religion may begin in ritual conduct, but it inevitably goes on to reflective belief that must submit to the canons of logic. The popular and superficial contrast between religion and theology ignores the fact that where a diversity of religion exists it is impossible to stop a process of reflection as to which of two conflicting claims is true. In such a society, religious creed or theology (including the possibility of a negative or atheistic theory) becomes inescapable. Hazy talk about religious experience will not adequately meet the difficulties.

If terms that have no genuine negatives are to be condemned as devoid of significance, the word *reality* should head the list. I am not unmindful of the many attempts to define the unreal. But the question is: What corresponds to these definitions? The Hindoo mystic is deeply irritated when the wise Chinese suggests that the realm of Maya or illusion does not really exists, or that it is not worth while worrying about it. The reality of illusion is the emphatic centre of the Hindoo's philosophy, and similarly, of all those who sharply contrast reality and appearance. The difficulty here is classic. What I am more especially concerned about, however, is to call attention to the fact that the word *reality* maintains itself as a term of praise rather than of description. To be "in touch with reality" is our way of expressing what our less sophisticated brothers and sisters do by the phrase "in tune with the infinite." It is an expression which carries an agreeable afflatus without dependence on any definite meaning. Such edification is pleasing and would be harmless if it did not also cause intellectual confusion. This the eulogistic use of the word *reality* certainly does in the theory of art, especially in its realistic and expressionistic form.

Professor Neilson defined the realistic motive, in poetry and art generally, as the sense of fact. But whatever else art may involve, the process of selection is certainly essential to it in all its forms, useful as well as ornamental. Hence, the honourific use of a non-discriminating term like *reality* undoubtedly tends to justify the introduction of the inept and the ugly, which certainly cannot be denied to have real existence. But it is not only realism that is thus encouraged to escape or confuse the fundamental problem of what is relevant, fitting, or beautiful in representation and ornament. Expressionistic theories glorify the same lack of discrimination between the beautiful and the ugly. For expressionism is but a subjective realism. This becomes clear when we reflect that the real denotes, first, human affairs, then physical things, and now vivid impres-

sions or emotions, so that abstractions are not real to us. The praise of
reality, therefore, now has as its core the glorification of vivid impressions
or violent expressions, regardless of fitness or coherence. This shows
itself in an indiscriminate admiration for the breaking of all hitherto
accepted rules of art—as if all rules were necessarily hindrances. But rules
of art like the so-called rules of nature are at bottom only statements of
what is relevant and what irrelevant to any given case. Hence it is doubtless true that new situations in art cannot always be profitably decided by
old rules. But this again is a question of specific fitness, not to be disposed
of by the violent assertion that the expression of inner reality is inconsistent
with all rules.

It is doubtful, for instance, whether such a convention as the rules of
the sonnet ever hindered a great poet from expressing himself, though it
doubtless has aided many minor ones, perhaps unduly so.

To conclude, we cannot praise life without including in our praise moral
and physical evil, corruption and death. As experience certainly includes
error and illusion, we cannot praise it indiscriminately as a support of
truth. Finally, as reality undoubtedly includes the useless and the ugly,
its praise cannot but confuse the arts.

Instead of life we want the good life. Instead of accepting experience
science discriminates between the experience of truth and the experience
of illusion. Not all reality, but only a reality free from ugliness and confusing incoherence is the aim of art. Conduct, science, and art thus depend
on rational discrimination. Rational philosophy tries to meet this need by
defining the good, the true, and the beautiful. The essence of the romantic
use of the terms *life, experience,* and *reality* is that it avoids this necessary
task, and is therefore flattering to those to whom the use of reason is
irksome. But the way to serenity and happiness through wisdom is more
arduous and requires a purified vision into our hearts as well as courage to
face the abysmal mystery of existence.

Law and the Social Order

PROPERTY AND SOVEREIGNTY

PROPERTY AND SOVEREIGNTY, AS EVERY STUDENT KNOWS, BELONG TO entirely different branches of the law. Sovereignty is a concept of political or public law and property belongs to civil or private law. This distinction between public and private law is a fixed feature of our law-school curriculum. It was expressed with characteristic eighteenth-century neatness and clarity by Montesquieu, when he said that by political laws we acquire liberty and by civil law property, and that we must not apply the principles of one to the other. Montesquieu's view that political laws must in no way retrench on private property, because no public good is greater than the maintenance of private property, was echoed by Blackstone and became the basis of legal thought in America. Though Austin, with his usual prolix and near-sighted sincerity, managed to throw some serious doubts on this classical distinction, it has continued to be regarded as one of the fixed divisions of the jural field. In the second volume of his *Genossenschaftsrecht* the learned Gierke treated us to some very interesting speculations as to how the Teutons became the founders of public law just as the Romans were the founders of private law. But in later years he somewhat softened this sharp distinction; and common-law lawyers are inclined rather to regard the Roman system as giving more weight to public than to private law.

The distinction between property and sovereignty is generally identified with the Roman discrimination between *dominium,* the rule over things by the individual, and *imperium,* the rule over all individuals by the prince. Like other Roman distinctions, this has been regarded as absolutely fixed in the nature of things. But early Teutonic law—the law of the Anglo-Saxons, Franks, Visigoths, Lombards, and other tribes—makes no such distinction; and the state long continued to be the prince's estate, so that even in the eighteenth century the Prince of Hesse could sell his subjects as soldiers to the King of England. The essence of feudal law—a system not confined to medieval Europe—is the inseparable connection between land tenure and personal homage involving often rather menial services on the part of the tenant and always genuine sovereignty over the tenant by the landlord.

The feudal baron had, for instance, the right to determine the marriage of the ward, as well as the right to nominate the priest; and the great importance of the former as a real property right is amply attested in Magna Carta and in the Statute Quia Emptores. Likewise was the administration of justice in the baron's court an incident of landownership; and if, unlike the French up to the Revolution, the English did not regard the office of judge as a revenue-producing incident of seigniorage to be sold in the open market (as army commissions were up to the time of Gladstone), the local squire did in fact continue to act as justice of the peace. Ownership of the land and local political sovereignty were inseparable.

Can we dismiss all this with the simple exclamation that all this is medieval and we have long outgrown it?

Well, right before our eyes the Law of Property Act of 1925 is sweeping away substantial remains of the complicated feudal land laws of England, by abolishing the difference between the descent of real and that of personal property, and by abolishing all legal (though not equitable) estates intermediate between leaseholds and fees simple absolute. These remains of feudalism have not been mere vestiges. They have played an important part in the national life of England. Their absurdities and indefensible abuses were pilloried with characteristic wit and learning by the peerless Maitland. The same thing had been done most judiciously by Joshua Williams, the teacher of several generations of English lawyers brought up on the seventeen editions of his great text-book on real property law. Yet these and similar efforts made no impression on the actual law. What these great men did not see with sufficient clearness was that back of the complicated law of settlement, fee-tail, copyhold estates, of the heir-at-law, of the postponement of women, and other feudal incidents, there was a great and well-founded fear that by simplifying and modernizing the real property law of England the land might become more marketable. Once land becomes fully marketable it can no longer be counted on to remain in the hands of the landed aristocratic families; and this means the passing of their political power and the end of their control over the destinies of the British Empire. For if American experience has demonstrated anything, it is that the continued leadership by great families cannot be as well founded on a money as on a land economy. The same kind of talent that enables Jay Gould to acquire dominion over certain railroads enables Mr. Harriman to take it away from his sons. From the point of view of an established land economy, a money economy thus seems a state of perpetual war instead of a social order where son succeeds father. The motto that a career should be open to talent thus seems a justification of anarchy, just as the election of rulers (kings or priests) seems an anarchy procedure to those used to the regular succession of father by son.

That which was hidden from Maitland, Joshua Williams, and the other great ones, was revealed to a Welsh solicitor who in the budget of 1910 proposed to tax the land so as to force it on the market. The radically revolutionary character of this proposal was at once recognized in England. It was bitterly fought by all those who treasured what had remained of the old English aristocratic rule. When this budget finally passed, the basis of the old real property law and the effective power of the House of Lords was gone. The legislation of 1925-26 was thus a final completion in the realm of private law of the revolution that was fought in 1910 in the forum of public law, i.e., in the field of taxation and the power of the House of Lords.

As the terms "medievalism" and "feudalism" have become with us terms of opprobrium, we are apt to think that only unenlightened selfishness has until recently prevented English land law from cutting its medieval moorings and embarking on the sea of purely money or commercial economy. This light-hearted judgment, however, may be somewhat sobered by reflection on a second recent event—the Supreme Court decision on the Minimum Wage Law. Without passing judgment at this point on the soundness of the reasoning whereby the majority reached its decision, the result may still fairly be characterized as a high-water mark of law in a purely money or commercial economy. For by that decision private monetary interests receive precedence over the sovereign duty of the state to maintain decent standards of living.

The state, which has an undisputed right to prohibit contracts against public morals or public policy, is here declared to have no right to prohibit contracts under which many receive wages less than the minimum of subsistence, so that if they are not the objects of humiliating public or private charity, they become centres of the physical and moral evils that result from systematic underfeeding and degraded standards of life. Now I do not wish here to argue the merits or demerits of the minimum wage decision. Much less am I concerned with any quixotic attempt to urge England to go back to medievalism. But the two events together show in strong relief how recent and in the main exceptional is the extreme position of the laissez faire doctrine, which, according to the insinuation of Justice Holmes, has led the Supreme Court to read Herbert Spencer's extreme individualism into the Fourteenth Amendment, and according to others, has enacted Cain's motto, "Am I my brother's keeper?" as the supreme law of industry. Dean Pound has shown that in making a property right out of the freedom to contract, the Supreme Court has stretched the meaning of the term "property" to include what it has never before signified in the law or jurisprudence of any civilized country. But whether this extension is justified or not, it certainly means the passing of a certain domain of sovereignty from the state to the private employer of labour, who now has the absolute right to discharge and threaten to discharge any employee who wants to join a trade-union, and the absolute right to pay a wage that is injurious to a basic social interest.

It may be that economic forces will themselves correct the abuse which the Supreme Court does not allow the state to remove directly, that economic forces will eliminate parasitic industries which do not pay the minimum of subsistence, because such industries are not as economically efficient and profitable as those which pay higher wages. It was similarly argued that slavery was bound to disappear on account of its economic inefficiency. Meanwhile, however, the sovereignty of the state is limited by the manner in which the courts interpret the term "property" in the Fifth and Fourteenth Amendments to the Federal Constitution and in the bills of rights in our state constitutions. This makes it imperative for us to consider the nature of private property with reference to the sovereign power of the state to look after the general welfare. A dispassionate scientific study of this requires an examination of the nature of property, its justification, and the ultimate meaning of the policies based on it.

1. PROPERTY AS POWER

Any one who frees himself from the crudest materialism readily recognizes that as a legal term "property" denotes not material things but certain rights. In the world of nature apart from more or less organized society, there are things but clearly no property rights.

Further reflection shows that a property right is not to be identified with the fact of physical possession. Whatever technical definition of property we may prefer, we must recognize that a property right is a relation not between an owner and a thing, but between the owner and other individuals in reference to things. A right is always against one or more individuals. This becomes unmistakably clear if we take specifically modern forms of property such as franchises, patents, goodwill, etc., which constitute such a large part of the capitalized assets of our industrial and commercial enterprises.

The classical view of property as a right over things resolves it into component rights such as the *jus utendi, jus disponendi,* etc. But the essence of private property is always the right to exclude others. The law does not guarantee me the physical or social ability of actually using what it calls mine. By public regulations it may indirectly aid me by removing certain general hindrances to the enjoyment of property. But the law of property helps me directly only to exclude others from using the things that it assigns to me. If, then, somebody else wants to use the food, the house, the land, or the plough that the law calls mine, he has to get my consent. To the extent that these things are necessary to the life of my neighbour, the law thus confers on me a power, limited but real, to make him do what I want. If Laban has the sole disposal of his daughters and his cattle, Jacob must serve him if he desires to possess them. In a régime where land is the principal source of obtaining a livelihood, he who has the legal right over the land receives homage and service from those who wish to live on it.

The character of property as sovereign power compelling service and obedience may be obscured for us in a commerical economy by the fiction of the so-called labour contract as a free bargain and by the frequency with which service is rendered indirectly through a money payment. But not only is there actually little freedom to bargain on the part of the steel-worker or miner who needs a job, but in some cases the medieval subject had as much power to bargain when he accepted the sovereignty of his lord. Today I do not directly serve my landlord if I wish to live in the city with a roof over my head, but I must work for others to pay him rent with which he obtains the personal services of others. The money needed for purchasing things must for the vast majority be acquired by hard labour and disagreeable service to those to whom the law has accorded dominion over the things necessary for subsistence.

To a philosopher this is of course not at all an argument against private property. It may well be that compulsion in the economic as well as the political realm is necessary for civilized life. But we must not overlook the actual fact that dominion over things is also *imperium* over our fellow human beings.

The extent of the power over the life of others which the legal order confers on those called owners is not fully appreciated by those who think of the law as merely protecting men in their possession. Property law does more. It determines what men shall acquire. Thus, protecting the property rights of a landlord means giving him the right to collect rent, protecting the property of a railroad or a public-service corporation means giving it the right to make certain charges. Hence the ownership of land and machinery, with the rights of drawing rent, interest, etc., determines the future distribution of the goods that will come into being —determines what share of such goods various individuals shall acquire. The average life of goods that are either consumable or used for production of other goods is very short. Hence a law that merely protected men in their possessions and did not also regulate the acquisition of new goods would be of little use.

From this point of view it can readily be seen that when a court rules that a gas company is entitled to a return of 6 per cent on its investment, it is not merely protecting property already possessed, it is also determining that a portion of the future social produce shall under certain conditions go to that company. Thus not only medieval landlords but the owners of all revenue-producing property are in fact granted by the law certain powers to tax the future social product. When to this power of taxation there is added the power to command the services of large numbers who are not economically independent, we have the essence of what historically has constituted political sovereignty.

Though the sovereign power possessed by the modern large property owners assumes a somewhat different form from that formerly possessed by the lord of the land, they are not less real and no less extensive. Thus the ancient lord had a limited power to control the modes of expenditure of his subjects by direct sumptuary legislation. The modern captain of industry and of finance has no such direct power himself, though his direct or indirect influence with the legislature may in that respect be considerable. But those who have the power to standardize and advertise certain products do determine what we may buy and use. We cannot well wear clothes except within lines decreed by their manufacturers, and our food is becoming more and more restricted to the kinds that are branded and standardized.

This power of the modern owner of capital to make us feel the necessity of buying more and more of his material goods (that may be more profitable to produce than economical to use) is a phenomenon of the utmost significance to the moral philosopher. The moral philosopher must also note that the modern captain of industry or finance exercises great influence in setting the fashion of expenditure by his personal example. Between a landed aristocracy and the tenantry, the difference is sharp and fixed, so that imitation of the former's mode of life by the latter is regarded as absurd and even immoral. In a money or commercial economy differences of income and mode of life are more gradual and readily hidden, so that there is great pressure to engage in lavish expenditure in order to appear in a higher class than one's income really allows. Such expenditure may even advance one's business credit. This puts pressure not merely on ever greater expenditure but more specifically on expenditure for ostentation rather than for comfort. Though a landed aristocracy may be wasteful in keeping large tracts of land for hunting purposes, the need for discipline to keep in power compels the cultivation of a certain hardihood that the modern wealthy man can ignore. An aristocracy assured of its recognized superiority need not engage in the race of lavish expenditure regardless of enjoyment.

In addition to these indirect ways in which the wealthy few determine the mode of life of the many, there is the somewhat more direct mode that bankers and financiers exercise when they determine the flow of investment, e.g., when they influence building operations by the amount that they will lend on mortgages. This power becomes explicit and obvious when a needy country has to borrow foreign capital to develop its resources.

I have already mentioned that the recognition of private property as a form of sovereignty is not itself an argument against it. Some form of government we must always have. For the most part men prefer to obey and let others take the trouble to think out rules, regulations, and orders. That is why we are always setting up authorities; and when we cannot find any we write to the newspaper as the final arbiter. But although government is a necessity, not all forms of it are of equal value. At any rate it is necessary to apply to the law of property all those considerations of social ethics and enlightened public policy which ought to be brought to the discussion of any just form of government.

To do this, let us begin with a consideration of the usual justifications of private property.

II. THE JUSTIFICATION OF PROPERTY

I. *The Occupation Theory*

The oldest and until recently the most influential defence of private property was based on the assumed right of the original discoverer and occupant to dispose of that which thus became his. This view dominated the thought of Roman jurists and of modern philosophers—from Grotius to Kant—so much so that the right of the labourer to the produce of his work was sometimes defended on the ground that the labourer "occupied" the material that he fashioned into the finished product.

It is rather easy to find fatal flaws in this view. Few accumulations of great wealth were ever simply found. Rather were they acquired by the labour of many, by conquest, by business manipulation, and by other means. It is obvious that today at any rate few economic goods can be acquired by discovery and first occupancy. Even in the few cases when they are, as in fishing and trapping, we are apt rather to think of the labour involved as the proper basis of the property acquired. Indeed, there seems nothing ethically self-evident in the motto "Findings is keepings." There seems nothing wrong in a law that a treasure trove shall belong to the king or the state rather than to the finder. Shall the finder of a river be entitled to all the water in it?

Moreover, even if we were to grant that the original finder or occupier should have possession as against any one else, it by no means follows that he may use it arbitrarily or that his rule shall prevail indefinitely after his death. The right of others to acquire the property from him, by bargain, by inheritance, or by testamentary disposition, is not determined by the principle of occupation.

Despite all these objections, however, there is a kernel of positive value in this principle. Protecting the discoverer or first occupant is really part of the more general principle that possession as such should be protected. There is real human economy in doing so until somebody shows a better claim than the possessor. It makes for certainty and security of transaction as well as for public peace—provided the law is ready to set aside possession acquired in ways that are inimical to public order. Various principles of justice may determine the distribution of goods and the retribution to be made for acts of injustice. But the law must not ignore the principle of inertia in human affairs. Continued possession creates expectations in the possessor and in others, and only a very poor morality would ignore the hardship of frustrating these expectations and rendering human relations insecure, even to correct some old flaws in the orginial acquisition. Suppose some remote ancestor of yours did acquire your property by fraud, robbery, or conquest, e.g., in the days of William of Normandy. Would it be just to take it away from you and your dependents who have held it in good faith? Reflection on the general insecurity that would result from such procedure leads us to see that as habit is the basis of individual life, continued practice must be the basis of social procedure. Any form of property that exists has therefore a claim to continue until it can be shown that the effort to change it is worth while. Continual changes in property laws would certainly discourage enterprise.

Nevertheless, it would be as absurd to argue that the distribution of property must never be modified by law as it would be to argue that the distribution of political power must never be changed. No less a philosopher than Aristotle argued against changing even bad laws, lest the habit of obedience be thereby impaired. There is something to be said for this, but only so long as we are in the realm of merely mechanical obedience. When we introduce the notion of free or rational obedience, Aristotle's argument loses its force in the political realm; and similar considerations apply to any property system that can claim the respect of rational beings.

2. The Labour Theory

That every one is entitled to the full produce of his labour is assumed as self-evident both by socialists and by conservatives who believe that capital is the result of the savings of labour. However, as economic goods are never the result of any one man's unaided labour, our maxim is altogether inapplicable. How shall we determine what part of the value of a table should belong to the carpenter, to the lumberman, to the transport worker, to the policeman who guarded the peace while the work was being done, and to the indefinitely large numbers of others whose coöperation was necessary? Moreover, even if we could tell what any one individual has produced—let us imagine a Robinson Crusoe growing up all alone on an island and in no way indebted to any community—it would still be highly questionable whether he has a right to keep the full produce of his labour when some shipwrecked mariner needs his surplus food to keep from starving.

In actual society no one ever thinks it unjust that a wealthy old bachelor should have part of his presumably just earnings taken away in the form of a tax for the benefit of other people's children, or that one immune to certain diseases should be taxed to support hospitals, etc. We do not think there is any injustice involved in such cases because social interdependence is so intimate that no man can justly say: "This wealth is entirely and absolutely mine as the result of my own unaided effort."

The degree of social solidarity varies, of course; and it is easy to conceive of a sparsely settled community, such as Missouri at the beginning of the nineteenth century, where a family of hunters or isolated cultivators of the soil might regard everything that it acquired as the product of its own labour. Generally, however, human beings start with a stock of tools or information acquired from others and they are more or less dependent upon some government for protection against foreign aggression, etc.

Yet despite these and other criticisms, the labour theory contains too much substantial truth to be brushed aside. The essential truth is that labour has to be encouraged and that property must be distributed in such a way as to encourage ever greater efforts at productivity.

As not all things produced are ultimately good, as even good things may be produced at an unjustified expense in human life and worth, it is obvious that other principles besides that of labour or productivity are needed for an adequate basis or justification of any system of property law. We can only say dialectically that all other things being equal, property should be distributed with due regard to the productive needs of the community. We must, however, recognize that a good deal of property accrues to those who are not productive, and a good deal of productivity does not and perhaps should not receive its reward in property. Nor should we leave this theme without recalling the Hebrew-Christian view—and for that matter, the spe-cifically religious view—that the first claim on property is by the man who needs it rather than the man who has created it. Indeed, the only way of justifying the principle of distribution of property according to labour is to show that it serves the larger social need.

The occupation theory has shown us the necessity for security of posses-sion, and the labour theory the need for encouraging enterprise. These two needs are mutually dependent. Anything that discourages enterprise makes our possessions less valuable, and it is obvious that it is not worth while en-gaging in economic enterprise if there is no prospect of securely possessing the fruit of it. Yet there is also a conflict between these two needs. The owners of land, wishing to secure the continued possession by the family, oppose laws that make it subject to free financial transactions or make it possible that land should be taken away from one's heirs by a judgment creditor for personal debts. In an agricultural economy security of posses-sion demands that the owner of a horse should be able to reclaim it no matter into whose hands it has fallen. But in order that markets should be possible, it becomes necessary that the innocent purchaser should have a good title. This conflict between static and dynamic security has been treated most suggestively by Demogue.

3. *Property and Personality*

Hegel, Ahrens, Lorimer, and other idealists have tried to deduce the right of property from the individual's right to act as a free personality. To be free one must have a sphere of self-assertion in the external world. One's private property provides such an opportunity.

Waiving all traditional difficulties in applying the metaphysical idea of freedom to empirical legal acts, we may still object that the notion of personality is too vague to enable us to deduce definite legal consequences by means of it. How, for example, can the principle of personality help us to decide to what extent there shall be private rather than public property in railroads, mines, gas-works, and other public necessities?

Not the extremest communist would deny that in the interest of privacy certain personal belongings such as are typified by the toothbrush must be under the dominion of the individual owner, to the absolute exclusion of every one else. This, however, will not carry us far if we recall that the major effect of property in land, in the machinery of production, in capital goods, etc., is to enable the owner to exclude others from *their necessities,* and thus to compel them to serve him. Ahrens, one of the chief expounders of the personality theory, argues: "It is undoubtedly contrary to the right of personality to have persons dependent on others on account of material goods." But if this is so, the primary effect of property on a large scale is to limit freedom, since the one thing that private property law does not do is to guarantee a minimum of subsistence or the necessary tools of freedom to every one. So far as a régime of private property fails to do the latter it rather compels people to part with their freedom.

It may well be argued in reply that just as restraining traffic rules in the end give us greater freedom of motion, so, by giving control over things to individual property owners, greater economic freedom is in the end assured to all. This is a strong argument, as can be seen by comparing the different degrees of economic freedom that prevail in lawless and in law-abiding communities. It is, however, an argument for legal order rather than for any particular form of government or private property. It argues for a régime where every one has a definite sphere of rights and duties, but it does not tell us where these lines should be drawn. The principle of freedom of personality certainly cannot justify a legal order wherein a few can, by virtue of their legal monopoly over necessities, compel others to work under degrading and brutalizing conditions. A government that limits the right of large landholders limits the rights of property, and yet may promote real freedom. Property owners, like other individuals, are members of a community and must subordinate their ambition to the larger whole of which they are a part. They may find their compensation in spiritually identifying their good with that of the larger life.

4. *The Economic Theory*

The economic justification of private property is that by means of it a maximum of productivity is promoted. The classical economic argument may be put thus: The successful business man, the one who makes the greatest profit, is the one who has the greatest power to foresee effective demand. If he has not that power his enterprise fails. He is therefore, in fact, the best director of economic activities.

There can be little doubt that if we take the whole history of agriculture and industry, or compare the economic output in Russia under the *mir* system with that in the United States, there is a strong *prima facie* case for the contention that more intensive cultivation of the soil and greater productiveness of industry prevail under individual ownership. Many *a priori* psychologic and economic reasons can also be brought to explain why this must be so, why the individual cultivator will take greater care not to exhaust the soil, etc. All this, however, is so familiar that we may take it for granted and look at the other side of the case, at the considerations which show that there is a difference between socially desirable productivity and the desire for individual profits.

In the first place, let us note that of many things the supply is not increased by making them private property. This is obviously true of land in cities and of other monopoly or limited goods. Private ownership of land does not increase the amount of rainfall, and irrigation works to make the land more fruitful have been carried through by governments more than by private initiative. Nor was the productivity of French or Irish lands reduced when the property of their landlords in rent charges and other incidents of seigniorage was reduced or even abolished. In our own days, we frequently see tobacco, cotton, or wheat farmers in distress because they have succeeded in raising too plentiful crops; and manufacturers who are well informed know when greater profit is to be made by a decreased output. Patents for processes that would cheapen the product are often bought up by manufacturers and never used. Durable goods that are more economic to the consumer are very frequently crowded out of the market by shoddier goods which are more profitable to produce because of the larger turnover. Advertising campaigns often persuade people to buy the less economical goods and to pay the cost of the uneconomic advice.

In the second place, there are inherent sources of waste in a régime of private enterprise and free competition. If the biologic analogy of the struggle for existence were taken seriously, we should see that the natural survival of the economically fittest is attended, as in the biologic field, with frightful wastefulness. The elimination of the unsuccessful competitor may be a gain to the survivor, but all business failures are losses to the community.

Finally, a régime of private ownership in industry is too apt to sacrifice social interests to immediate monetary profits. This shows itself in speeding up industry to such a pitch that men are exhausted in a relatively few years, whereas a slower expenditure of their energy would prolong their useful years. It shows itself in the way in which private enterprise has wasted a good deal of the natural resources of the United States to obtain immediate profits. Even when the directors of a modern industrial enterprise see the uneconomic consequences of immediate profits, the demand of shareholders for immediate dividends, and the ease with which men can desert a business and leave it to others to stand the coming losses, tend to encourage ultimately wasteful and uneconomic activity. Possibly the best illustration of this is child labour, which by lowering wages increases immediate profits, but in the end is really wasteful of the most precious wealth of the country, its future manhood and womanhood.

Surveying our arguments thus far: We have seen the roots of property in custom, in the need for economic productivity, and in individual needs of privacy. But we have also noted that property, being only one among other human interests, cannot be pursued absolutely without detriment to human life. Hence we can no longer maintain Montesquieu's view that private property is sacrosanct and that the general government must in no way interfere with or retrench its domain. The issue before thoughtful people is therefore not the maintenance or abolition of private property, but the determination of the precise lines along which private enterprise must be given free scope and where it must be restricted in the interests of the common good.

III. LIMITATIONS OF PROPERTY RIGHTS

The traditional theory of rights, and the one that still prevails in this country, was moulded by the struggle in the seventeenth and eighteenth centuries against restrictions on individual enterprise. These restrictions in the interest of special privilege were fortified by the divine (and therefore absolute) rights of kings. As is natural in all revolts, absolute claims on one side were met with absolute denials on the other. Hence the theory of the natural rights of the individual took not only an absolute but a negative form: men have *in*alienable rights, the state must never interfere with private property, etc. The state, however, must interfere in order that individual rights should become effective and not degenerate into public nuisances. To permit any one to do absolutely what he likes with his property in creating noise, smells, or danger of fire, would be to make property in general valueless. To be really effective, therefore, the right of property must be supported by restrictions or positive duties on the part of owners, enforced by the state, as much as by the right to exclude others that is the essence of property. Unfortunately, however, whether because of the general decline of juristic philosophy after Hegel or because law has become more interested in defending property against attacks by socialists, the doctrine of natural rights has remained in the negative state and has never developed into a doctrine of the positive contents of rights based upon an adequate notion of the function of these rights in society.

Lawyers occupied with civil or private law have in any case continued the absolutistic conception of property; and in doing this, they are faithful to the language of the great eighteenth century codes, the French, Prussian, and Austrian, and even of nineteenth century codes like the Italian and German, which also begin with a definition of property as absolute or unlimited, though they subsequently introduce qualifying or limiting provisions.

As, however, no individual rights can in fact be exercised in a community except under public regulation, it has been left mainly to publicists, to writers on politics and constitutional and administrative law, to consider the limitations of private property necessary for public safety, peace, health, and morals, as well as for those enterprises like housing, education, the preservation of natural resources, etc., which the community finds it necessary to entrust to the state rather than to private hands. The fact, however, that in the United States the last word on law comes from judges, who, like other lawyers, are for the most part trained in private rather than in public law, is one of the reasons why with us traditional conceptions of property prevail over obvious national interests such as the freedom of labourers to organize, the necessity of preserving certain standards of living, of preventing the future manhood and womanhood of the country from being sacrificed to individual profits, and the like. Our students of property law need, therefore, to be reminded that not only has the whole law since the industrial revolution shown a steady growth in ever new restrictions upon the use of private property, but that the ideal of absolute laissez faire has never in fact been completely operative.

(1) Living in a free land economy we have lost the sense of how exceptional in the history of mankind is the absolutely free power of directing what shall be done with our property after our death. In the history of the common law, wills as to land begin only in the reign of Henry VIII. On the Continent it is still restrained by the system of the reserve. In England no formal restriction has been necessary because of the system of entails or strict settlement. Even in the United States we have kept such rules as that against perpetuities, which is certainly a restraint on absolute freedom of testamentary disposition.

Even as to the general power of alienating the land *inter vivos* history shows that some restrictions are always present. The persistence of dower rights in our own individualistic economy is a case in point. Land and family interest have been too closely connected to sacrifice the former completely to pure individualism. Though the interests of free exchange of goods and services have never been as powerful as in the last century, governments have not abandoned the right to regulate the rate of interest to be charged for the use of money, or to fix the price of certain other services of general public importance, e.g., railway rates, grain-elevator and warehouse charges, etc. The excuse that this applies only to business affected with a public interest, is a very thin one. What large business is there in which the public has not a real interest? Is coal less a public affair than gas, or electricity? Courts and conservative lawyers sometimes speak as if the regulation of wages by the state were a wild innovation that would upset all economic order as well as our legal tradition. Yet the direct regulation of wages has been a normal activity of English law; and we in fact regulate it indirectly by limiting hours of work, prohibiting payment in truck, enforcing certain periodic payments, etc.; and under the compensation acts the law compels an employer to pay his labourer when the latter cannot work at all on account of some accident.

(2) More important than the foregoing limitations upon the transfer of property are limitations on the use of property. Looking at the matter realistically, few will question the wisdom of Holdsworth's remarks, that "at no time can the state be wholly indifferent to the use which the owners make of their property." There must be restrictions on the use of property not only in the interests of other property owners but also in the interests of the health, safety, religion, morals, and general welfare of the whole community. No community can view with indifference the exploitation of the needy by commercial greed. As under the conditions of crowded life the reckless or unconscionable use of one's property is becoming more and more dangerous, enlightened jurists find new doctrines to limit the abuse of ancient rights. The French doctrine of *abus de droit,* the prohibition of chicanery in the German Civil Code, and the rather vague use of "malice" in the common law are all efforts in that direction.

(3) Of greatest significance is the fact that in all civilized legal systems there is a great deal of just expropriation or confiscation without any direct compensation. This may sound shocking to those who think that for the state to take away the property of the citizen is not only theft or robbery but even worse, an act of treachery, since the state avowedly exists to protect people in those very rights.

As a believer in natural rights, I believe that the state can, and unfortunately often does, enact unjust laws. But I think it is a sheer fallacy based on verbal illusion to think that the rights of the community against an individual owner are no better than the rights of a neighbour. Indeed, no one has in fact had the courage of this confusion to argue that the state has no right to deprive an individual of property to which he is so attached that he refuses any money for it. Though no neighbour has such a right, the public interest often justly demands that a proprietor shall part with his ancestral home, to which he may be attached by all the roots of his being.

When taking away a man's property, is the state always bound to pay a direct compensation? I submit that while this is generally advisable in order not to disturb the general feeling of security, no absolute principle of justice requires it. I have already suggested that there is no injustice in taxing an old bachelor to educate the children of others, or taxing one immune to typhoid for the construction of sewers or other sanitary measures. We may go further and say that the whole business of the state depends upon its rightful power to take away the property of some (in the form of taxation) and use it to support others, such as the needy, those invalided in the service of the state in war or peace, and those who are not yet able to produce but in whom the hope of humanity is embodied. Doubtless, taxation and confiscation may be actuated by malice and may impose needless and cruel hardship on some individuals or classes. But this is not to deny that taxation and confiscation are within the just powers of the state. A number of examples may make this clearer.

(a) Slavery. When slavery is abolished by law, the owners have their property taken away. Is the state ethically bound to pay them the full market value of their slaves? It is doubtless a grievous shock to a community to have a large number of slave-owners, whose wealth often makes them leaders of culture, suddenly deprived of their income. It may also be conceded that it is not always desirable for the slave himself to be suddenly taken away from his master and cut adrift on the sea of freedom. But when one reads of the horrible ways in which some of those slaves were violently torn from their homes in Africa and shamelessly deprived of their human right, one is inclined to agree with Emerson that compensation should first be paid to the slaves. This compensation need not be in the form of a direct bounty to them. It may be more effectively paid in the form of rehabilitation and education for freedom; and such a charge may take precedence over the claims of the former owners. After all, the latter claims are no greater than those of a protected industry when the tariff is removed. If the state should decide that certain import duties, e.g., those on scientific instruments or hospital supplies, are unjustified and proceed to abolish them, many manufacturers may suffer. Are they entitled to compensation by the state?

It is undoubtedly for the general good to obviate as much as possible the effect of economic shock to a large number of people. The routine of life prospers on security. But when that security contains a large element of injustice the shock of an economic operation by law may be necessary and ethically justified.

This will enable us to deal with other types of confiscation:

(b) Financial loss through abolition of public office. It is only in very recent times that we have come to forget that public office is and always has been regarded as a source of revenue like any other occupation. When, therefore, certain public offices are abolished for the sake of good government, a number of people are deprived of their expected income. In the older law and often in popular judgment today this does not seem fair. But reflection shows that the state is not obligated to pay any one when it finds that particular services of his are unnecessary. At best, it should help him to find a new occupation.

Part of the prerogative of the English or Scotch landlord was the right to nominate the priest for the parish on his land. To abolish this right of advowson is undoubtedly a confiscation of a definite property right. But while I cannot agree with my friend Mr. Laski that the courts were wrong to refuse to disobey the law that subordinated the religious scruples of a church to the property rights of an individual, I do not see that there could have been any sound ethical objection to the legislature's changing the law without compensating the landlord.

(c) In our own day, we have seen the confiscation of many millions of dollars' worth of property through prohibition. Were the distillers and brewers entitled to compensation for their losses? We have seen that property on a large scale is power, and the loss of it, while evil to those who are accustomed to exercise it, may not be an evil to the community. In point of fact, the shock to the distillers and brewers was not as serious as to others, e.g., saloon-keepers and bartenders, who did not lose any legal property since they were only employees, but who found it difficult late in life to enter new employments.

History is full of examples of valuable property privileges abolished without any compensation, e.g., the immunity of nobles from taxation, their rights to hunt over other persons' lands, etc. It would be absurd to claim that all such legislation was unjust.

These and other examples of justifiable confiscation without compensation are inconsistent with the absolute theory of private property. An adequate theory of private property, however, should enable us to draw the line between justifiable and unjustifiable cases of confiscation. Such a theory I cannot here undertake to elaborate, though the doctrine of security of possession and avoidance of unnecessary shock seem to me suggestive. I wish, however, to urge that if the large property owner is viewed, as he ought to be, as a wielder of power over the lives of his fellow citizens, the law should not hesitate to develop a doctrine as to his positive duties in the public interest. The owner of a tenement house in a modern city is in fact a public official and has all sorts of positive duties. He must keep the halls lighted, he must see that the roof does not leak, that there are fire-escape facilities; he must remove tenants guilty of certain public immoralities, etc.; and he is compensated by the fees of his tenants, which the law is beginning to regulate. Similar is the case of a factory owner. He must install all sorts of safety appliances, hygienic conveniences; see that the workmen are provided with a certain amount of light, air, etc.

In general, there is no reason for the law's insisting that people should make the most economic use of their property. They have a motive in doing so themselves and the cost of the enforcing machinery may be a mischievous waste. Yet there may be times, such as occurred during the late war, when the state may insist that man shall cultivate the soil intensively and be otherwise engaged in socially productive work.

With considerations such as these in mind, it becomes clear that there is no unjustifiable taking away of property when railroads are prohibited from posting notices that they will discharge their employees if the latter join trade unions, and that there is no property taken away without due or just process of law when an industry is compelled to pay its labourers a minimum of subsistence instead of having subsistence provided for them by private or public charity or else systematically starving its workers.

IV. POLITICAL VS. ECONOMIC SOVEREIGNTY

If the discussion of property by those interested in private law has suffered from a lack of realism and from too great a reliance on vague *a priori* plausibilities, much the same can be said about political discussion as to the proper limits of state action in regard to property and economic enterprise. Utterly unreal is all talk of men's being robbed of their power of initiative because the state undertakes some service, e.g., the building of a bridge across a river. Men are not deprived of opportunities for real self-reliance if the state lights their streets at night, fills up holes in the pavements, and removes other dangers to life and limb, or provides opportunities for education to all. The conditions of modern life are complex and distracting enough so that if we can ease the strain by simplifying some things through state action we are all the gainers by it. Certain things have to be done in a community and the question whether they should be left to private enterprise dominated by the profit motive, or to the government dominated by political considerations, is not a question of man versus the state, but simply a question of which organization and motive can best do the work. Both private and government enterprise are initiated and carried through by individual human beings. A realistic attitude would not begin with the assumption that all men in the government service are less or more intelligent or efficient than all those in private business. It would rather inquire what sort of people are drawn into government service and what attitudes their organization develops in contrast with that of private business. This is a matter for specific factual inquiry, unfortunately most sadly neglected. In the absence of such definite knowledge I can only venture a few guesses.

Government officials seem likely to be chosen more for their oratorical ability, popularly likable manners, and political availability, and less for their competence and knowledge of the problems with which they have to deal. The inheritance of wealth, however, may bring incompetent people for a while into control of private business. More serious is the fact that political officials have less incentive to initiate new ventures. Political leaders in touch with public sentiment are apt to be too conservative and prefer to avoid trouble by letting things alone. Their bureaucratic underlings, on whom they are more dependent than business executives are on theirs, are apt to overemphasize the value of red tape, i.e., to care more for uniformity of governmental procedure than for the diverse special needs to which they ought to minister. All business administration, however, also loses in efficiency as its volume increases. On the other hand, experience has shown all civilized peoples the indispensable need for communal control to prevent the abuse of private enterprise. Only a political or general government is competent to deal with a problem like city congestion, because only the general government can coördinate a number of activities some of which have no financial motive. Private business may be more efficient in saving money. It does so largely by paying smaller wages to the many and higher remuneration to those on top. From a social point of view this is not necessarily a good in itself. It is well to note that men of great ability and devotion frequently prefer to work for the government at a lower pay than they can obtain in private employment. There is something more than money in daily employment. Humanity prefers—not altogether unwisely—to follow the lead of those who are sensitive rather than those who are efficient. Business efficiency mars the beauty of our countryside with hideous advertising signs and would, if allowed, ruin the scenic grandeur of Niagara.

The subordination of everything to the single aim of monetary profit leads industrial government to take the form of absolute monarchy. Monarchy has a certain simplicity and convenience; but in the long run it is seldom the best for all concerned. Sooner or later it leads to insurrections. It is short-sighted to assume that an employer cannot possibly run his business without the absolute right to hire and fire his employees whenever he feels like doing so. It is interesting to note that even a modern army is run without giving the general the absolute right to hire and fire. The Shah of Persia was shocked when a British ambassador, Sir John Malcolm, informed him that the King of England could not at his pleasure behead any of his courtiers. But Sir John Malcolm was equally shocked to observe the elaborate precautions that the Shah had to take against assassination. May not democratic or limited constitutional government in industry have some human advantages over unlimited monarchy?

The main difficulty, however, with industrial and financial government is that the governors are released from all responsibility for the actual human effects of their policies. Formerly, the employer could observe and had an interest in the health and morals of his apprentice. Now, the owners or stockholders have lost all personal touch with all but few of those who work for them. The human element is thus completely subordinated to the profit motive. In some cases this even makes for industrial inefficiency, as when railroads or other businesses are run by financiers in the interest of stock manipulation. Very often our captains of finance exercise power by controlling other people's funds. This was strikingly shown when several millions of dollars were paid for some shares that promised little or no direct return but which enabled the purchaser to control the assets of a great life insurance company. Professor Ripley has recently thrown Wall Street into a turmoil by pointing out the extent to which promoters and financiers can with little investment of their own control great industrial undertakings.

There can be no doubt that our property laws do confer sovereign power on our captains of industry and even more so on our captains of finance.

Now it would be unworthy of a philosopher to shy at government by captains of industry and finance. Humanity has been ruled by priests, soldiers, hereditary landlords, and even antiquarian scholars. The results are not such as to make us view with alarm a new type of ruler. But if we are entering a new era involving a new set of rulers, it is well to recognize it and reflect on what is involved.

For the first time in the history of mankind the producer of things is in the saddle—not of course the actual physical producer, but the master mind that directs the currents of production. If this is contrary to the tradition of philosophy from Plato down, we may well be told that our philosophy needs revision. Great captains of industry and finance like the late James J. Hill deal with problems in many respects bigger than those which faced Cæsar and Augustus in building the Roman Empire.

Still the fear may well be expressed that as modern life is becoming more and more complex it is dangerous to give too much sovereignty to those who are after all dealing with the rather simpler aspects of life involved in economic relations.

It may, of course, rightly be contended that the modern captain of industry is not merely concerned with the creation of things, that his success is largely determined by his judgment and ability to manage the large numbers of human beings that form part of his organization. Against this, however, there is the obvious retort that the only ability taken account of in the industrial and financial world, the ability to make money, is a very specialized one; and when business men get into public office they are not notably successful. Too often they forget that while saving the money of the taxpayer may be an admirable incident, it is not the sole or even the principal end of communal life and government. The wise expenditure of money is a more complicated problem than the mere saving it, and a no less indispensable task to those who face the question of how to promote a better communal life. To do this effectively we need a certain liberal insight into the more intangible desires of the human heart. Preoccupation with the management of property has not in fact advanced this kind of insight.

Many things are produced to the great detriment of the health and morals of the consumers as well as the producers. This refers not only to things that are inherently deleterious or enervating to those who create them and those who use them. It includes also many of the things of which people buy more than they need and more than is consistent with the peace and leisure of mind that is the essence of culture.

It is certainly a shallow philosophy that would make human welfare synonymous with the indiscriminate production and consumption of material goods. If there is one iota of wisdom in all the religions or philosophies that have supported the human race in the past it is that man cannot live by economic goods alone but needs vision and wisdom to determine what things are worth while and what things it would be better to do without. This profound human need of controlling and moderating our consumptive demands cannot be left to those whose dominant interest is to stimulate such demands.

It is characteristic of the low state of our philosophy that the merits of capitalism have been argued by both individualists and socialists exclusively from the point of view of the production and distribution of goods. To the more profound question as to what goods are ultimately worth producing from the point of view of the social effects on the producers and consumers almost no attention is paid. Yet surely this is a matter which requires the guidance of collective wisdom, not one to be left to chance or anarchy.

For Further Reading

In addition to the complete texts of the books from which selections have been taken, the following books and articles may be of interest.

CHAUNCEY WRIGHT

Chauncey Wright, *Philosophical Discussions,* edited by C. E. Norton (1877).
  (See especially "The Evolution of Self-Consciousness").
Letters of Chauncey Wright, edited by J. B. Thayer (1878).
William James, "Chauncey Wright," in *Collected Essays and Reviews* (1920).

CHARLES S. PEIRCE

Charles S. Peirce, *Chance, Love, and Logic, edited* with an introduction by Morris R. Cohen (1923).
The Philosophy of Charles Peirce, edited by Justus Buchler (1940). This book also appears in a Dover paperback edition (1955) under the title *Philosophical Writings of Peirce.*
Justus Buchler, *Charles Peirce's Empiricism* (1939).
W. B. Gallie, *Peirce and Pragmatism* (1952).

WILLIAM JAMES

William James, *A Pluralistic Universe* (1908).
            The Meaning of Truth (1909).
            Essays in Radical Empiricism (1912).
            Letters, edited by Henry James (1920).
Ralph Barton Perry, *The Thought and Character of William James* (1935).

JOSIAH ROYCE

Josiah Royce, *The Spirit of Modern Philosophy* (1892).
          The World and the Individual (1900-01).
          Race Questions, Provincialism, and Other American Problems (1908).
          The Problem of Christianity (1913).

George Santayana, Chapter IV in *Character and Opinion in the United States* (1920).
Ralph Barton Perry's *The Thought and Character of William James* contains frequent references to Royce and his relations to James. It also contains the lively and revealing discussion between James and Royce on the Absolute in Appendices V and VI.

GEORGE SANTAYANA

George Santayana, *The Sense of Beauty* (1896).
     Soliloquies in England (1922).
     Platonism and the Spiritual Life (1927).
     Three Philosophical Poets (1927).
     The Last Puritan: A Memoir in the Form of a Novel (1935).
     Realms of Being (1942).
The Philosophy of George Santayana, edited by Irwin Edman (1953).
The Philosophy of George Santayana, edited by Paul Arthur Schilpp (1940).
Santayana wrote a three-volume autobiography, *Persons and Places* (1944-53).

JOHN DEWEY

John Dewey, *The School and Society* (1900).
    Human Nature and Conduct (1922).
    Experience and Nature (1925).
    Art as Experience (1934).
    Logic: The Theory of Inquiry (1938).
John Dewey and J. A. Tufts, *Ethics* (1908).
The Philosopher of the Common Man (1940), a volume of essays in honor
  of Dewey, contains one of Dewey's best statements of his social views,
  "Creative Democracy—The Task Before Us."
Sidney Hook, *John Dewey: An Intellectual Portrait* (1939).
The Philosophy of John Dewey, edited by Paul Arthur Schilpp (1939).

RALPH BARTON PERRY

Ralph Barton Perry, *The Moral Economy* (1909).
     Present Philosophical Tendencies (1916).
     General Theory of Value (1926).
     The Thought and Character of Williams James (1935).
     Puritanism and Democracy (1944).
     Realms of Value (1954).
Ralph Barton Perry *et al, The New Realism: Cooperative Studies in Philosophy*
  (1912).

C. I. LEWIS

C. I. Lewis, *An Analysis of Knowledge and Valuation* (1946).
    A Survey of Symbolic Logic (1918).

MORRIS R. COHEN

Morris R. Cohen, *A Preface to Logic* (1944).
    The Faith of a Liberal (1946).
    The Meaning of Human History (1947).
    A Dreamer's Journey (1949).

Editor's Note

The editor of an anthology has an opportunity to share some of his enthusiasms with others, which is agreeable. But he is also forced by the necessities of space and organization to omit what he would much like to include, which is disagreeable. I cannot know, of course, quite what my sins are when I have excluded material of obvious worth and relevance through prejudice or myopia. But I am aware that there are philosophers who are not represented in this book whom I would have liked to include. Their absence does not imply that I believe their contributions to American thought to be less significant than those of the men who appear here. And I regret equally that I have been unable to find room for certain essays and chapters from the work of the men whose writing is sampled in these pages—for example, Peirce's essay, "The Doctrine of Necessity Examined," the chapter from James' *Psychology* on "The Stream of Thought," Santayana's chapter on "Rational Ethics" in *Reason in Science,* Dewey's early essay on "The Logic of Practical Judgment," and passages from *Experience and Education,* his retrospective and highly interesting critique of progressive education. I hope that this anthology will encourage its readers to find out for themselves what it does not contain.

George Braziller and Edwin Seaver originally suggested this book to me, and I am grateful to them for editorial assistance. My wife read my own contribution to this book in manuscript, and though she had to re-read it several times she never yielded in taste or broke in patience. Only I can know the favors she has done the reader.